Late 12th Century to early/mid 13th Century
HADEWIJCH

c. 1225–1274
AQUINAS

1588–1679
THOMAS HOBBES

1596–1650
RENÉ DESCARTES

1618–1680
ELISABETH OF BOHEMIA

1711–1776
DAVID HUME

1724–1804
IMMANUEL KANT

RUSSELL

1889–1951
LUDWIG WITTGENSTEIN

1898–1979
HERBERT MARCUSE

1931–
RICHARD RORTY

b. 1947
MARTHA NUSSBAUM

b. 1956
JUDITH BUTLER

00 CE | 1050 CE | 1100 CE | 1150 CE | 1200 CE | 1450 CE | 1500 CE | 1550 CE | 1600 CE | 1650 CE | 1700 CE | 1750 CE | 1800 CE | 1850 CE | 1900 CE | 1950 CE | 2000 C

1206?–1280
ALBERTUS MAGNUS

1632–1677
BARUCH SPINOZA

1685–1753
GEORGE BERKELEY

1926–1984
MICHEL FOUCAULT

1925–1961
FRANTZ FANON

1921–2002
JOHN RAWLS

1908–1961
MAURICE MERLEAU-PONTY

1908–1986
SIMONE DE BEAUVOIR

1908–2000
WILLARD VAN ORMAN QUINE

1905–1980
JEAN-PAUL SARTRE

1859–1938
EDMOND HUSSERL

1848–1925
GOTLOB FREGE

1844–1900
FRIEDRICH NIETZSCHE

1820–1895
FRIEDRICH ENGELS

1818–1883
KARL MARX

1813–1855
SØREN KIERKEGAARD

1770–1831
G.W.F. HEGEL

1759–1797
MARY WOLLSTONECRAFT

1712–1778
JEAN-JACQUES ROUSSEAU

ABOUT PHILOSOPHY

NINTH EDITION

Robert Paul Wolff
**Professor of Afro-American
Studies and Philosophy
University of Massachusetts, Amherst**

with the assistance of

R. Eugene Bales
**Emeritus Professor of Philosophy
Menlo College, Atherton, California**

PEARSON

Prentice
Hall

Upper Saddle River,
New Jersey 07458

Library of Congress Cataloging-in-Publication Data

Wolff, Robert Paul.
    About philosophy/Robert Paul Wolff.— 9th ed.
      p. cm.
    Includes index.
    ISBN 0-13-191606-8
    1. Philosophy—Introductions. I. Title.
  BD21. W64 2006
  100—dc22

                              2004025602

Editorial Director: Charlyce Jones-Owen
Assistant Editor: Wendy Yurash
Editorial Assistant: Carla Worner
Senior Media Editor: Deborah O'Connell
Marketing Manager: Kara Kindstrom
Marketing Assistant: Jennifer Lang
Managing Editor: Joanne Riker
Production Liaison: Louise Rothman
Assistant Manufacturing Manager: Mary Ann Gloriande
Manufacturing Buyer: Christina Helder
Cover Design: Bruce Kenselaar
Cover Illustration: Giorgio de Chirico *The Philosopher's Trouble,* 1926. Alinari
    Archives/Corbis. © 2004 Artists Rights Society (ARS), New York, SIAE, Rome.
Image Permission Coordinator: Carolyn Gauntt
Interior Design, Composition and Full-Service Project Management: Pine Tree
    Composition, Inc.
Printer/Binder: Courier Companies, Inc.
Cover Printer: Phoenix Color Corporation

Credits and acknowledgments borrowed from other sources and reproduced, with
permission, in this textbook appear on appropriate page within text and on pages
489–490.

Pearson Education LTD
Pearson Education Singapore, Pte. Ltd
Pearson Education, Canada, Ltd
Pearson Education—Japan
Pearson Education Australia PTY,
    Limited

Pearson Education North Asia Ltd
Pearson Educación de Mexico,
    S.A. de C.V.
Pearson Education Malaysia, Pte.
    Ltd

PEARSON
Prentice
Hall

    10   9 8 7 6 5 4 3 2 1

ISBN 0-13-191606-8

To Susie,

whose courage in the face of adversity

is the manifestation of a true

philosophic spirit.

C o n t e n t s

Preface

It is now fully thirty years since *About Philosophy* first made its appearance. Over the years, a great many young men and women have encountered philosophy for the first time in its pages. Indeed, it is just possible that several of you are the children of students who used this text back in the late 1970's. My own father was the author of a high school biology text from which, in time, I studied. As a boy, I watched it go through a number of editions.

My father was fortunate to have a co-author with whom he shared the burdens and responsibilities of doing justice to biology as it grew and changed. Until now, I have made the periodic revisions and changes in *About Philosophy* myself, always guided by the suggestions of those students and Professors who actually use the text in their classes. For this edition, however, I have called on the assistance of a distinguished Professor of Philosophy, R. Eugene Bales, who has been teaching almost as long as I have. Gene made his career in California, on the West Coast, as I have made mine in the East. Between us, we bridge the nation, and perhaps the field of philosophy as well.

Gene has contributed a number of valuable new sections to this edition, including, among other things, discussions of new directions in the theory of knowledge and the philosophy of science, new (and, dare I say, better?) materials on feminist philosophy, and a fuller discussion of the problem of evil in the philosophy of religion. Both he and I are especially eager to hear from you about these revisions and additions, for the success of *About Philosophy* is due principally to the willingness of its readers to tell us what they like, what they don't like, and what they would like us to add.

Textbooks have changed a good deal since I started teaching, most notably in the use of a wide variety of supplementary materials from many media. We continue, with this edition, the practice of providing ABCNEWS videos of televised discussions of contemporary issues through which it is possible to explore the immediate importance of timeless philosophical issues. There are also study guides and a website to help you in mastering the philosophical themes and arguments of the text. For this edition, we have introduced an entirely new feature—a series of examples drawn from popular culture to illustrate and deepen your understanding of philosophy. You may not have realized it, but there is a great deal to think about in *The Matrix* or *The Simpsons*.

Teaching and Learning Resources

The print and media supplements that accompany *About Philosophy* provide instructors and students with resources that combine sound scholarship, engaging content, and a variety of pedagogical tools to enrich the classroom experience and students' understanding of philosophy.

Instructor's Manual with Tests   The Instructor's Manual with Tests provides summaries, outlines, learning objectives, lecture and discussion topics, and audio/visual resources for each chapter. Test materials include multiple choice, essay, and short-answer questions.

Prentice Hall Test Generator   This commercial-quality, computerized test management program, available for Windows and Macintosh environments, allows instructors to select from testing material in the Instructor's Manual with Tests and design their own exams.

Study Guide   This student study aid reviews key points and concepts, and provides chapter tests for student practice.

Common Philosophical Terms   A glossary of the most common terms to assist students in their study and mastery of philosophy. Available free when packaged with *About Philosophy,* the glossary contains 431 terms students are likely to encournter in their reading of primary and secondary texts. Contact your local Prentice Hall representative for details.

Prentice Hall and Penguin Bundle Program   Prentice Hall and Penguin are pleased to provide adopters of *About Philosophy* with an opportunity to receive significant discounts when orders for *About Philosophy* are bundled together with Penguin titles in philosophy. Contact your local Prentice Hall representative for details.

Media Resources

ABCNEWS   Prentice Hall and ABCNEWS have worked together to bring you the best and most comprehensive video ancillaries available in the college market. Through its wide variety of award-winning programs—*Nightline, Business World, On Business, This Week, World News Tonight,* and *The Health Show*—ABC offers a resource for feature and documentary-style videos related to text concepts and applications. The programs have extremely high production quality, present substantial content, and are hosted by well-versed, well-known anchors. The ABCNEWS/PH Video Library for *About Philosophy* offers video material for almost every chapter in the text. A video guide included in the Instructor's Manual provides suggestions for integrating the videos in the classroom.

The Primary Source: Philosophical Readings with Commentary CDROM   This unique media resource includes 115 original texts with instructive commentary on each reading, key terms, and provocative questions. A list of the relevant readings contained on the CDROM are included at the end of each chapter of the text. The CDROM is bound into every new copy of *About Philosophy.*

Companion Website™ *The Companion Website (www.prenhall.com/wolff)* works with the text to provide students with additional study materials—including quizzes and primary source essay questions—and directs them to appropriate sources in philosophy available on the Internet.

Prentice Hall's *OneSearch with Research Navigator*™ This brief guide introduces students to tools for finding, evaluating and using resources on the internet. It includes a section of avoiding plagiarism and using sources effectively, tips for finding information related to philosophy on the internet and for documenting electronic sources, and an access code to the *Research Navigator*™ website. The *OneSearch* guide with access code is available for free when packaged with *About Philosophy.* Contact your local Prentice Hall representative for details.

Research Navigator™ This unique online resource helps students make the most of their research time. From finding the right articles and journals, to citing sources, drafting and writing effective papers, and completing research assignments, **Research Navigator**™ simplifies and streamlines the entire process. Access to the **Research Navigator**™ website is available with every copy of the *OneSearch* guide. Contact your local Prentice Hall representative for more details or take a tour at *www.researchnavigator.com.*

Acknowledgments

Over the years, a number of men and women have served as Philosophy Editors at Prentice Hall, the publisher of this book. The former editor, Ross Miller, played a larger than usual role in developing ideas for the ninth edition, and both Gene Bales and I are very grateful to him for his thoughtful assistance. Our thanks also to Carla Worner, editorial assistant, who has been endlessly available and responsive to our sometimes incoherent requests.

The authors would like to thank the reviewers of the ninth edition of *About Philosophy:* Hugh J. Matlack, County College of Morris; Charles Cassini, Barry University; Robert Ferrell, University of Texas, El Paso; William H. Bruening, Indiana University, Purdue University Fort Wayne; Ronald L. Massanara, Alma College; Vincent Luizzi, Southwest Texas State University; Jeffrey P. Fry, Ball State University; and Jose Lopez-Gonzalez, Towson University.

One final word of a purely personal nature. In an earlier edition, I used an ABCNEWS video of my older son, Patrick, playing chess (Patrick twice won the United States chess championship). In this edition, I am delighted to be able to use a video of my younger son, Tobias, who is a law professor, debating the issue of same-sex marriage. In the immortal words of Jackie Gleason from a television show popular many years ago, "How sweet it is!"

Robert Paul Wolff
Pelham, Massachusetts

Robert Paul Wolff was born in New York City in 1933. He was educated at Harvard University, where he was awarded a doctorate in Philosophy in 1957. He has taught at Harvard, the University of Chicago, and Columbia University, and, since 1971, at the University of Massachusetts, Amherst. Wolff is the author or editor of twenty books on the philosophy of Immanuel Kant, social and political philosophy, the philosophy of education, the philosophy of law, the philosophy of David Hume, and the economic theories of Karl Marx. He has taught political science at Chicago, Boston University, and Yale, and microeconomics at the University of Massachusetts. Wolff's books have been translated into more than a dozen languages, and have sold more than three-quarters of a million copies. They have been assigned as required reading for the Moral Tripos at Cambridge University, and have been read by students in Soweto, South Africa.

In 1990, Wolff founded University Scholarships for South African Students, Inc. (USSAS), which he runs as a volunteer charitable organization. USSAS currently supports 110 black students at universities in South Africa.

In 1992, Wolff was invited to join the W. E. B. DuBois Department of Afro-American Studies at the University of Massachusetts. He is currently professor of Afro-American Studies and Philosophy, and serves as Director of Graduate Studies in the doctoral program in Afro-American Studies.

Robert Paul Wolff is married to his childhood sweetheart, Susan, and has two sons, Patrick, 32, and Tobias, 30. Asked to describe himself succinctly, he said, "In religion, I am an atheist; in politics, I am an anarchist; in economics, I am a Marxist." A former editor, Ted Bolen, suggested that he not go around saying things like that.

ABOUT PHILOSOPHY

Socrates

Socrates (469?–399 B.C.) was tried by the Athenians on charges of "impiety" and "corrupting the young of Athens," but it seems clear that his real offense was opposition to, or even lack of sufficient support for, the leaders of the newly restored democratic regime.

Socrates had associated with the aristocratic families who overthrew the first democracy, and his disciple, Plato, was a member of one of the powerful families who ruled Athens for a while before the restoration. Since an amnesty had been declared, it was legally impossible for the rulers to prosecute Socrates for political offenses, so they trumped up the religious accusations and enlisted a religious fanatic, Meletus, to bring charges against the seventy-year-old philosopher.

Socrates could have fled from Athens before the trial, during which a conviction could carry the death sentence. Even after his conviction, he could have proposed banishment as an alternative to death, and the Athenian jury of 501 citizens would almost certainly have accepted such a compromise. But Socrates was convinced that he had done Athens no harm by his philosophical questioning. Indeed, he insisted that he had, by his activities, been a benefactor of his native city, and so, as an alternative to the death penalty demanded by the prosecution, he proposed that Athens pension him off as a respected citizen.

The Athenian rulers, trapped by Socrates' uncompromising integrity, were forced to carry out the sentence of death, though they would probably have been all too happy to allow their prisoner to escape before the execution. One month after the trial, following a long night of philosophical discussion with his friends, Socrates drank the poison hemlock prepared for him by his jailers and died.

What is Philosophy?

What Do Philosophers Do?
The Study of Human Nature

When I was a student, one of my professors told us about the conversations he would strike up in the club car on the train from Boston to New York. A group of men would gather around the bar, and each in turn would introduce himself, saying a few words about the line of work he was in. One would announce himself as a lawyer, a second as a traveling salesman, a third as an engineer. When it was my professor's turn, he would say, "I am a philosopher." That, he told us, would always bring the conversation to a dead halt. No one knew quite what to say to a man who described himself as a philosopher. The others were too polite to ask, "What does a philosopher do?" But the announcement always cast a pall over the gathering. Eventually, he took to saying, "I am a teacher." That went over all right, and as long as no one asked what he taught, they could get on to more congenial topics, such as the prospects for the Red Sox, or the weather.

What *do* philosophers do? Oddly enough, that is a question philosophers have been asking for as long as there has been a discipline called **philosophy.** Indeed, "What do philosophers do?" is probably the most common philosophical question! But all of this sounds like double talk, which is just what makes people nervous about philosophy in the first place. You all know what a doctor does; you know what physicists, historians, composers, and sanitation engineers do. Most of you probably even have some sort of idea about what microbiologists do. But philosophers are something else again. Philosophers ask questions—odd questions, such as, "What right does the government—any government—have to tell me what to do?"

The best way to find out what philosophers do is to take a look at one of them, and on anyone's list, the natural first choice must be the most famous philosopher of all times, *Socrates.* Socrates was born in 469 B.C. to a stonemason and a midwife in the Greek city-state of Athens. As far as we know, he spent his entire life in and about Athens, serving his time in the army at one point, taking his turn in the government at another. He was a rather homely man in a society that prized manly beauty, and though he was hardly poor, he seems to have managed on much less money than his friends and disciples had. Athens itself was a city of 130,000, busy and prosperous by the standards of the time but small enough so that everyone who was anyone knew everyone else. In his youth, Socrates studied the scientific theories a number of original thinkers had developed in the preceding several centuries, but he soon became convinced that the most important and puzzling subject was the human condition itself. He developed the practice of going into the public squares and meeting places of Athens to cajole, goad, or draw his fellow townsmen into discussions about how men ought to live their lives. (In the Athens of Socrates' day, it was taken for granted that women would play no role in these discussions, or indeed in any other public business.) Socrates was quick-witted, clever, and tenacious. He had a knack for asking hard or embarrassing questions that forced others to think a good deal more than they really wanted to. Because some of the people he quizzed were important politicians and famous teachers, it was fun to watch him trip them up—as long as you weren't one of those made to look foolish. So a number of wealthy young men gathered around Socrates as a band of disciples and as a sort of permanent audience. Sometimes he talked with them, quizzing them in the same way and forcing them to examine their own lives; sometimes they watched as he took on a local bigwig or visiting personage.

If this practice of asking questions were all there was to Socrates' life, we would never have heard of him 2,400 years later, and we certainly wouldn't think of him as a great philosopher. But three things transformed Socrates from a local curiosity and general pain in the neck into the patron saint of philosophy and one of the great figures of Western civilization.

The first thing was an accident. Among those who followed Socrates was a brilliantly gifted, wealthy young man named Plato. Plato was only twenty-eight years old when his teacher died, but he was deeply, permanently affected by his relationship with the aging Socrates, and many years later he began to write Dialogues, playlets in which the style and personality of Socrates were captured, transformed, and elevated into works of great art. Most of what we believe about Socrates comes to us from these Dialogues, in-cluding, most importantly, our conception of Socrates' techniques of ques-tioning. Scholars still debate how much in the Dialogues is Plato's artistic invention and how much is accurate historical portrayal, but there can be no question that the essential style belonged to Socrates himself.

The second thing that happened was not really an accident, though it may seem so at first glance. The rulers of Athens decided that Socrates was more than an annoyance; he was becoming a threat to their political security. So they trumped up some charges against him and put him on trial. Socrates could have plea-bargained, in effect, and gotten off with a punishment of exile, which would have put him safely out of Athens without making him a martyr. However, he chose instead to defend himself and his life without ex-cuses or apologies. He had done nothing wrong, he insisted, and now that he was seventy, Athens should be thinking of giving him a pension rather than threatening to put him to death. In the end, Socrates forced the government's hand, and a sentence of death was handed down. Even then, he probably could have escaped from jail with the help of his friends, but he stayed and took the poison his jailers gave him. And so he became the first martyr of phi-losophy. It is easy to second-guess the Athenian rulers and conclude that they could have spared themselves a lot of trouble by handling the case a bit more skillfully. But Socrates' persistent questioning of established doctrines and re-ceived opinions really was a threat, not only to the government, but also to

The school, or Academy, of Athens, founded c. 387 B.C. by Plato as a center of philosophical, mathematical, and scientific research. The Academy continued to operate
uninterrupted for 900 years, until it was closed by the Roman Emperor Justinian in 529
A.D. There is an Academy in Athens today that claims to be the descendant of Plato's
school. *(Source:* North Wind Picture Archives.*)*

the lifestyle of the families who ruled Athens. In a way, the accident is not that
Socrates was put to death at the age of seventy, but rather that he had been
permitted to go on for so long before those in power landed on him.

The third and most important reason for Socrates' immortality is no accident at all, but the very essence of his life and calling. Witty though he was,
irreverent though he could be, annoying though he certainly became, Socrates
was deadly serious about his questioning. His death only confirmed what his
life had already proved—that for him, the relentless examination of every
human action and belief was more important than survival itself. As Socrates
said at his trial, "The unexamined life is not worth living," and by drinking the
poison, he showed that he would rather die honorably in the cause of that
principle than flee in dishonor to some foreign refuge.

Philosophy   Literally, love of wisdom, philosophy is the systematic,
critical examination of the way in which we judge, evaluate, and act,
with the aim of making ourselves wiser, more self-reflective, and therefore better men and women.

Each of us makes countless decisions that affect our lives and the lives of those around us to some degree. Many of the decisions are of very little importance, such as whether to go to the movies, where to have dinner, or what to wear. A few of the decisions are truly momentous—whom to marry, what career to pursue; and for some of us, caught up in a war or facing personal tragedy, our decisions may literally determine life and death. Socrates believed in his own time (and I think he would still believe if he were alive today) that these decisions must be questioned, examined, and criticized if we are to live truly good and happy lives. Most of us make even the most important decisions without really asking ourselves what principles we are basing our choices on, and whether those principles are worthy of our respect and commitment. When war comes, young men and women go off to fight and die with hardly more than a passing thought about whether it is morally right to kill another person. A student spends ten years of his or her life working to become a doctor, simply because mom and dad have always wanted it. A man and a woman drift into marriage, have children, buy a house, and settle down, and only twenty years later does one of them ask, "What am I doing here?"

Socrates had a theory about how each of us ought to examine his or her life, subjecting it to critical analysis and questioning. He never set this theory down anywhere, of course (he never set *anything* down, actually), but from what Plato has reported, we can reconstruct what Socrates had in mind. This theory, on which he based the special style of teaching and philosophizing that has come to bear his name, rested on four basic principles:

1. The unexamined life is not worth living. In other words, it is undignified, not really honorable, simply to live from day to day without ever asking oneself, "What am I doing here? Why am I living as I am?" To be truly and completely human, Socrates thought, each man and woman must subject his or her life and convictions to the test of critical self-examination. What is more, by means of this process of self-examination, one can achieve genuine happiness.

2. There really are valid principles of thought and action that must be followed if we are to live good lives—if we are to be, at the same time, genuinely happy and genuinely good. These principles are objective—they are true for all men and women, whenever and wherever they may live. Some people are unjust, self-indulgent, obsessed with worthless goals, estranged from their fellow men and women, confused and blind about what is truly important. These people do not know that certain things are beneath notice, unimportant. They are terrified of shadows, incapable of living or dying with grace. Such people need to find the truth and live in accordance with it.

3. The truth lies within each of us, not in the stars, or in tradition, or in religious books, or in the opinions of the masses. Each of us has within,

however hidden, the true principles of right thinking and acting. In the end, therefore, no one can teach anyone else the truth about life. If that truth were not within you, you would never find it; but it is within you, and only relentless critical self-examination will reveal it to you.

4. Although no one can teach anyone else about the fundamental principles of right action and clear thinking, some people—call them teachers, philosophers, gadflies—can ask questions that prod men and women to begin the task of self-examination. These teachers may also be able to guide the process, at least in its early stages, because they have been over the same ground themselves and know where the pitfalls are.

From these four principles, it follows that philosophy consists of a process of question and answer, a **dialogue** between two people, one of whom is seeking rational insight and understanding, the other of whom has already achieved some measure of self-knowledge and wishes to help the novice. The dialogue begins with whatever beliefs the student brings to the quest. If she thoughtlessly repeats the traditional moral sayings of her society, then the philosopher will try to force her to question those sayings; if she takes up the position that everything is relative, that nothing is true or valid for all persons (a stance many students adopt at about the time they leave home or cut loose from their parents), then the philosopher will try a different line of questioning. The end point of the journey is always the same: wisdom, rational insight into the principles of thought and action, and thus a happier, more integrated, more worthwhile life. But the starting points are as many as the students who make the journey.

Socrates discovered that each journey to wisdom has an enormous obstacle blocking the road. Modern psychoanalysts call the roadblock "resistance," but a simpler way of putting it is that no one wants to admit that he or she needs to learn. Certainly the politicians and public figures with whom Socrates talked did not think of themselves as in need of further wisdom. They were quite convinced that they already knew how to run the state and how to order their own lives. Socrates had to discover a trick for getting inside their defenses so that he could make them see—really see—that they were not yet truly wise. What he did was to invent a verbal form of judo. The basic trick of judo is to let your opponent's force and momentum work for you. Instead of launching a frontal attack, you let him swing or grab, and then you roll with his motion so that, in effect, he throws himself on the mat. Socrates achieved the same effect in his debates by means of a literary device called "irony." Although this is a book about philosophy, not literature, it might be worth taking a few moments to explain how irony works, so that we can see what Socrates was trying to accomplish.

Irony is a kind of speech or communication that assumes a *double audience*. When a speaker makes an ironic statement, she seems to be directing it at one group of people. This group is called the first, or superficial, audience. But in reality, she is directing her remarks at a second audience, called the real audience. Her statement has a double meaning, and the trick of the irony is that while the first audience understands only the superficial or apparent meaning, the second audience understands *both* meanings. This second audience knows that the first audience has misunderstood, so the irony becomes a private joke between the speaker and the second audience—a joke at the expense of the first audience, which never suspects a thing.

For example, suppose a stranger drives up to the general store in a small town to ask directions. "You there!" he says to a farmer seated on the front porch of the store. "Can you tell me the fastest way to get to the state capital? Be quick about it! I have a very important meeting with the governor." "Yes," replies the farmer, with just the slightest wink to his friends on the porch. "I *can* tell you the fastest way." He then proceeds to give the stranger totally wrong directions that will take him hours out of his way.

The farmer is speaking ironically. The stranger is the superficial audience, and the other people on the porch are the real audience. The apparent meaning, as understood by the stranger, is that this country bumpkin, who has been properly impressed with the stranger's importance, can tell him the fastest way and has done so. The real, secret, ironic meaning is, of course, that the farmer can tell this pompous ass the fastest way but has no intention of doing so because he has been so rude. The reply is a private joke between the farmer and his friends at the stranger's expense.

When Socrates strikes up a conversation with a self-important, self-confident, but really rather ignorant man, he does not try a frontal attack, arguing directly against his opponent's false beliefs. That would simply lead to an impasse, in which each participant would be asserting his own convictions and neither would engage in critical self-examination. Instead, Socrates says, with a deceptively modest air, "Of course, I don't know anything at all, and you seem to be very wise indeed, so perhaps you would be so good as to enlighten me." His opponent, thinking Socrates means literally what he says, gets all puffed up with his own importance and pontificates on goodness or justice or truth or beauty or piety. Then Socrates goes to work on him, pretending to be puzzled, asking politely for clarification, poking away at just those places in his opponent's position that are most vulnerable. After a while, the poor man is thoroughly deflated. Embarrassed by his inability to give coherent, defensible answers to Socrates' apparently humble questions, he finally reaches the rather painful conclusion that he does not know what he thought he knew. Now, and only now, can Socrates help him set out on the path to wisdom, for as Socrates so often insists, the first act of true wisdom is to admit that you are ignorant.

When Socrates says that he himself is ignorant, he is speaking ironically. In fact, he is uttering what students of literature call a "double irony." In the first place, he is having a private joke with his followers, at the expense of the man with whom he is debating. His opponent thinks Socrates is really being deferential, that Socrates actually wants to sit at the great man's feet and learn great truths. But of course Socrates means that he is "ignorant" of those great "truths" just because they are false, confused, and not worth knowing. We have all met someone who thinks he is an expert on some subject when in fact he does not know beans about it. "Tell me more!" we say, and sure enough, he does, not realizing that we are kidding him.

At a deeper level, which Socrates' own followers sometimes do not really understand, Socrates genuinely means that he is ignorant, in the sense that *he* does not have a truth to teach any more than his puffed up opponent does. The disciples think that Socrates knows what truth, beauty, justice, goodness, and wisdom really are, and they expect that just as soon as he has deflated his opponent, he will teach them. But Socrates believes that every man must find the truth for himself, and so his followers cannot shortcut their journey by learning the truth from Socrates any more than they could by observing the mistakes and confusions of Socrates' opponents. In this deeper double irony, we, the readers of Plato's Dialogue, are the real audience, and both Socrates' opponents *and* his disciples are superficial or apparent audiences.

General Store. The farmer is speaking ironically. (*Source:* Drawn for Robert Paul Wolff by Prentice Hall.)

The process of questions and answers, by which we gradually, step by step, reach a deeper and deeper insight into the principles of truth and goodness, has come to be called the **Socratic Method.** It is a very powerful technique of argument, of course, and Socrates clearly used it because it gave him an edge on those with whom he argued. But it also serves an independent theoretical purpose—a philosophical purpose, we might say. This next point is a bit tricky, but it is worth paying attention to, because it gives us a real insight into what Plato (or Socrates) is doing.

According to Socrates, things are not always what they seem. We all know that there may be a difference between the way things look on the surface, or at first, and how they really are. A stick half in water and half out looks bent, even though it is straight. The sun looks larger when it is low on the horizon than when it is high in the sky, although it has not changed its size. The magician looks as though she is pulling that coin out of your ear, but really it is coming out of her hand, and so forth.

Socrates took this old, familiar distinction between the way things seem to be and the way they really are and ran with it. He extended the distinction into areas where we might not be so used to encountering it. He pointed out that sometimes an experience *seems* bad for us, but is really good (the dentist is a familiar example). Frequently, the opinions of our friends, our family, or our society *seem* correct, but are really wrong, and so forth.

Socrates thought that in every part of our lives, we must try as hard as we can to get behind the misleading surface appearances and grasp the true, underlying reality. Indeed, a large part of Socrates' wisdom consisted precisely in being able to tell appearance from reality, whether in politics, in ethics, or in daily life.

Now the superficial meaning of an ironic statement is like the surface appearance, behind which the reality lies. Just as the world of the senses is merely an appearance of the true reality grasped by reason, so too the superficial meaning of an ironic statement is the apparent meaning that hides the deeper, real meaning intended for the real audience. Thus, the structure of language mirrors the structure of reality.

This idea—that there is a parallel between language and the world—comes up again and again in philosophy. It is a very important notion, and for 2,500 years philosophers have been turning it this way and that, extracting interesting conclusions from it. Socrates is the philosopher who first developed the idea and used it in his own philosophy.

We have talked enough about Socrates and his debating tricks. It is time to see him in action. The following passage comes from the most famous of Plato's Dialogues, the *Republic.* Socrates and some friends have been having a discussion about the nature of *justice,* by which they mean the fundamental principles of right and wrong. Several suggestions have been made, which Socrates has disposed of without much trouble, and now a young, very excitable, and very bright member of the party named Thrasymachus jumps into the debate. He has been listening to the others impatiently, barely able to control himself.

> What is the matter with you two, Socrates? Why do you go on in this imbecile way, politely deferring to each other's nonsense? If you really want to know what justice means, stop asking questions and scoring off the answers you get. You know very well it is easier to ask questions than to answer them. Answer yourself, and tell us what you think justice means. I won't have you telling us it is the same as what is obligatory or useful or advantageous or profitable or expedient; I want a clear and precise statement; I won't put up with that sort of verbiage.

This is a shrewd attack on Thrasymachus' part, for if he can get Socrates to advance a definition, then perhaps he can turn the tables on the master. But his own uncontrolled impetuosity gets the better of him. When Socrates turns aside the attack with a few mock-humble words, Thrasymachus cannot resist the temptation to teach the teacher. And that, as we shall see, is his downfall. Thrasymachus is no pushover for Socrates, and in a sense their debate ends in a deadlock. In this passage, however, we can see how Socrates used Thrasymachus' own self-confidence to trip him up, just like a judo master who allows his opponent to rush at him headlong and then with a flip of the hip tosses him on his back. Notice the ironic modesty with which Socrates turns aside Thrasymachus' blunt attacks, each time gently showing him that he has not yet thought clearly or deeply enough. The contrast between Socrates' inner quiet and Thrasymachus' tempestuousness is also intended by Plato to teach us a lesson, for he, like Socrates, believed that the truly wise possess a tranquility that the ignorant cannot achieve.

PLATO,
Republic

> *The Nature of Justice*
> Listen then, Thrasymachus began. What I say is that "just" or "right" means nothing but what is to the interest of the stronger party. Well, where is your applause? You don't mean to give it to me.
> I will, as soon as I understand, I said. [This is Socrates talking.] I don't see yet what you mean by right being the interest of the

> **Socratic Method**   A technique of probing questions, developed by Socrates, for the purpose of prodding, pushing, and provoking unreflective persons into realizing their lack of rational understanding of their own principles of thought and action, so that they can set out on the path to philosophical wisdom. As used by Socrates, this method was a powerful weapon for deflating inflated egos.

stronger party. For instance, Polydamas, the athlete, is stronger than we are, and it is to his interest to eat beef for the sake of his muscles; but surely you don't mean that the same diet would be good for weaker men and therefore be right for us?

You are trying to be funny, Socrates. It's a low trick to take my words in the sense you think will be most damaging.

No, no, I protested; but you must explain.

Don't you know, then, that a state may be ruled by a despot, or a democracy, or an aristocracy?

Of course.

And that the ruling element is always the strongest?

Yes.

Well, then, in every case the laws are made by the ruling party in its own interest; a democracy makes democratic laws; a despot, autocratic ones; and so on. By making these laws they define as "right" for their subjects whatever is for their own interest, and they call anyone who breaks them a "wrongdoer" and punish him accordingly. That is what I mean; in all states alike "right" has the same meaning, namely what is for the interest of the party established in power, and that is the strongest. So the sound conclusion is that what is "right" is the same everywhere: the interest of the stronger party.

Now I see what you mean, said I; whether it is true or not, I must try to make out. When you define right in terms of interest, you are yourself giving one of those answers you forbade to me; though, to be sure, you add "to the stronger party."

An insignificant addition, perhaps!

Its importance is not clear yet; what is clear is that we must find out whether your definition is true. I agree myself that right is in a sense a matter of interest; but when you add "to the stronger party," I don't know about that. I must consider.

Go ahead, then.

I will. Tell me this. No doubt you also think it is right to obey the men in power?

I do.

Are they infallible in every type of state, or can they sometimes make a mistake?

Of course they can make a mistake.

In framing laws, then, they may do their work well or badly?

No doubt.

Well, that is to say, when the laws they make are to their own interest; badly, when they are not?

Yes.

But the subjects are to obey any law they lay down, and they will then be doing right?

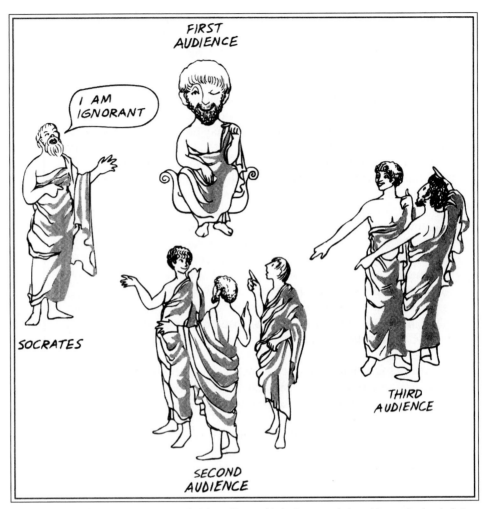

First audience. First, or superficial, audience thinks Socrates is humbly confessing inferiority to him. Second audience (Socrates' followers), realizing Socrates is making fun of first audience, laughs at first audience. Third audience (the reader) laughs at first audience, smiles at second. Third audience realizes **both** that Socrates is making fun of first audience **and** that Socrates' own followers do not realize the true meaning of his statement. *(Source:* Drawn for Robert Paul Wolff by Prentice Hall.*)*

Of course.

If so, by your account, it will be right to do what is not to the interest of the stronger party, as well as what is so.

What's that you are saying?

Just what you said, I believe; but let us look again. Haven't you admitted that the rulers, when they enjoin certain acts on their subjects, sometimes mistake their own best interest, and at the same time that it is right for the subjects to obey, whatever they may enjoin?

Yes, I suppose so.

Well, that amounts to admitting that it is right to do what is not to the interest of the rulers or the stronger party. They may unwittingly enjoin what is to their own disadvantage; and you say it is right for the others to do as they are told. In that case, their duty must be the opposite of what you said, because the weaker will have been ordered to do what is against the interest of the stronger. You with your intelligence must see how that follows. . . . Now, Thrasymachus, tell me, was that what you intended to say—that right means what the stronger thinks is to his interest, whether it really is so or not?

Most certainly not, he replied. Do you suppose I should speak of a man as "stronger" or "superior" at the very moment when he is making a mistake?

I did think you said as much when you admitted that rulers are not always infallible.

That is because you are a quibbler, Socrates. Would you say a man deserves to be called a physician at the moment when he makes a mistake in treating his patient and just in respect of that mistake; or a mathematician, when he does a sum wrong and just insofar as he gets a wrong result? Of course we do commonly speak of a physician or a mathematician or a scholar having made a mistake; but really none of these, I should say, is ever mistaken, insofar as he is worthy of the name we give him. So strictly speaking—and you are all for being precise—no one who practices a craft makes mistakes. A man is mistaken when his knowledge fails him; and at the moment he is no craftsman. And what is true of craftsmanship or any sort of skill is true of the ruler: he is never mistaken so long as he is acting as a ruler; though anyone might speak of a ruler making a mistake, just as he might of a physician. You must understand that I was talking in that loose way when I answered your question just now; but the precise statement is this. The ruler, insofar as he is acting as a ruler, makes no mistakes and consequently enjoins what is best for himself; and that is what the subject is to do. So, as I said at first, "right" means doing what is to the interest of the stronger.

Very well, Thrasymachus, said I. So you think I am quibbling?

I am sure you are.

You believe my questions were maliciously designed to damage your position?

I know it. But you will gain nothing by that. You cannot outwit me by cunning, and you are not the man to crush me in the open.

Bless your soul, I answered, I should not think of trying. But, to prevent any more misunderstanding, when you speak of that ruler or stronger party whose interest the weaker ought to serve, please make it clear whether you are using the words in the ordinary way or in that strict sense you have just defined.

I mean a ruler in the strictest possible sense. Now quibble away and be as malicious as you can. I want no mercy. But you are no match for me.

Do you think me mad enough to beard a lion or try to outwit a Thrasymachus?

You did try just now, he retorted, but it wasn't a success.

Plato, *The Republic*

Although it may not be obvious on first reading, the crucial turning point in this exchange is the point at which Socrates gets Thrasymachus to admit that the people should obey their superior rulers *only* when the rulers are issuing commands that really are in their own interest. If the strong, through ignorance or error, accidentally issue commands that work to the benefit of the weak, then the weak are not to obey!

This may not look like much of an admission, but it is actually fatal to Thrasymachus' position. The reason is that it introduces into the discussion the idea that rulers have a right to be obeyed only when they are, in some way or other, using their intellectual abilities to rule well. At this point, of course, "ruling well" simply means "ruling in such a way as to advance their own interests," but once Thrasymachus has agreed that standards are to be applied to the performance of the rulers, he has started down a slippery slope. Now Socrates has an opening in which to start talking about good and bad rulers, and that permits him to raise all sorts of issues that Thrasymachus has no desire to let into the debate.

Needless to say, Socrates foresees all of this when he asks the first innocent-looking question, just as a chess master foresees the next ten moves when he makes his first simple move. That is part of the skill of philosophical argument.

What Do Philosophers Do?
The Study of the Universe

I told you that Socrates spent some time when he was young studying the theories about the nature of the universe that had been developed by other Greek thinkers during the 200 years before his own time. The Greek word for world or universe is *kosmos,* so we call the study of the nature of the world **cosmology.** The study of the human condition and the study of the cosmos are the two great branches of philosophy, and there is no division more fundamental in philosophy than that between philosophers who study the human experience and philosophers who speculate about the order of the entire universe. (Later on, we shall see that some philosophers have tried to unite the two in a single theoretical framework, but that is getting ahead of our story.)

The Greeks, like all people, had their religious myths about the creation of the world and the origins of their civilization, but some time, roughly 600 years before the birth of Christ, a number of men began to search for a more rational, more factually well-grounded theory of the composition, order, and origin of the world. Some of these early scientists—for that is what they were—flourished in a city-state named Miletus on the coast of what is now Turkey, in the eastern Mediterranean. They are known as Milesians, after their hometown, and they appear to have been the very first philosophers in what we are calling the cosmological tradition. For various reasons, only bits and pieces of what they wrote still survive, and most of what we know about them must be learned indirectly from what other ancient writers say about them. They are little more than names to us today, but perhaps it is worth telling you their names, for we owe them an intellectual debt almost too great to calculate. There was *Thales,* usually spoken of as the very first philosopher of all. Thales was what we today would call an astronomer; the story is told that while walking one evening with his eyes turned to the stars, he fell into a well and thereby created the myth of the absentminded professor. But it also is said of him that by using his superior knowledge of the weather, acquired by his astronomical studies, he managed to corner the market in olive oil and make a fortune. Following Thales were the Milesians *Anaximander* and *Anaximenes,* who expanded and developed speculative theories about the basic components of nature and their order. Their names are strange, and we have long since lost almost all of what they wrote and said, but as you study your physics, chemistry, or astronomy, or watch a rocket lift off for yet another space probe, you might just give them a thought, for they started Western civilization on its scientific journey.

The theories of the ancient cosmologists seem odd to modern readers. When we look behind the surface detail, however, we can see some surprisingly modern ideas. The fundamental problem of the Milesians was to determine the basic stuff or component matter from which all the variety of things in the world were composed. The four categories into which they divided all things were earth, water, air, and fire. Thales claimed that at base everything in the universe was water; earth, air, and fire were simply forms of water, or water in other guises. Anaximenes, by contrast, said that everything was air. Now all of this sounds quaint and very peculiar, but

Cosmology   Literally, the study of the order of the world. Now used to refer to the branch of astronomy that investigates the organization and structure of the entire physical universe, including its origins. In philosophy, cosmology is a part of the subfield called metaphysics, or the study of first principles.

suppose that we say solid instead of earth, liquid instead of water, gas instead of air, and energy instead of fire. Then we have the theory that everything in the universe is solid, liquid, gaseous, or some form of energy, and that isn't a bad guess at all! What is more, the search for some underlying element that simply *appears* in one or another of these forms has a distinctly modern ring to it. The nineteenth-century theory of the atom, for example, told us that ninety and more elements found in nature could really be reduced to differing arrangements of three basic building blocks: neutrons, protons, and electrons. The theory of subatomic particles has become much more complicated since that simple model of the atom was proposed, but the Milesian search goes on today for the building blocks of the universe.

The second great theme of the Milesians and their successors was that natural events were to be understood by appeal to natural forces, not by appeal to the actions of the gods or the interventions of some non-natural forces. The keynote of these early philosopher-scientists was that nature is natural, and in their speculations and observations, they showed remarkable shrewdness and good sense. For example, water seems to turn to ice (a solid) when it is very cold, and into steam (a gas) when it is very hot. Solid things (such as iron) which are very solid indeed actually melt when made hot enough. All of this suggests that there is some underlying stuff which takes on different forms under different conditions.

Here is a short passage from a philosopher who lived very much later in the ancient world, but whose attention to the evidence of his senses is typical of the cosmological frame of mind. Lucretius was a Roman philosopher and poet who lived in the first century before Christ, nearly five centuries after the Milesians. He defended a cosmological theory called atomism, according to which everything in the universe, including even the human soul, is composed of little bits of matter called atoms, which are so small that they cannot be seen by the naked eye (another surprisingly modern doctrine). As you can see, Lucretius uses a variety of familiar observations to prove that, despite appearances to the contrary, all things are composed of tiny, indestructible atoms that themselves have no parts and are absolutely solid.

LUCRETIUS,
On the Nature of Things

Now mark me: since I have taught that things cannot be born from nothing, cannot when begotten be brought back to nothing, that you may not haply yet begin in any shape to mistrust my words, because the first-beginnings of things cannot be seen by the eyes, take moreover this list of bodies which you must yourself admit are in the number of things and cannot be seen. First of all the force of the wind when aroused beats on the harbours and whelms huge ships and scatters clouds; sometimes in swift whirling eddy it scours the plains

Map of spheres according to Ptolomaeus, with the earth in the center of a globe of the world. There are seven heavenly bodies orbiting about the earth: the sun, the moon, Mercury, Venus, Mars, Jupiter, and Saturn. Note that the representation on the earth of Africa and the Orient is quite accurate. (*Sources:* Dutch Atlas by Gerard Valck, 17th century; Corbis/Bettmann.)

and strews them with large trees and scourges the mountain summits with forest-rending blasts: so fiercely does the wind rave with a shrill howling and rage with threatening roar. Winds therefore sure enough are unseen bodies which sweep the seas, the lands, ay and the clouds of heaven, tormenting them and catching them up in sudden whirls. . . . Then again we perceive the different smells of things, yet never see them coming to our nostrils; nor do we behold heats nor can we observe cold with the eyes nor are we used to see voices. Yet all these things must consist of a bodily nature, since they are able to move the senses; for nothing but body can touch and be touched. Again clothes hung up on a shore which waves break upon become moist, and then get dry if spread out in the sun. Yet it has not been seen in

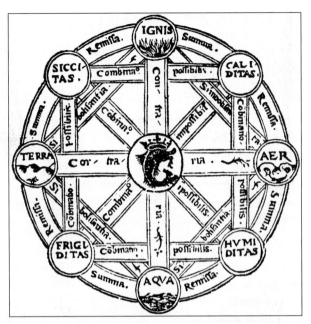

In this schematic representation of the elements, fire is at
the top, air on the right, water at the bottom, and earth to
the left. The fifth substance, or "quintessence," is in the center. Fire is a mixture of dryness and heat, air is a mixture of
heat and humidity, water is a mixture of humidity and coldness, and earth is a mixture of coldness and dryness. *(Source:
Library of Congress.)*

what way the moisture of water has sunk into them nor again in
what way this has been dispelled by heat. The moisture therefore is
dispersed into small particles which the eyes are quite unable to see.
Again after the revolution of many of the sun's years a ring on the finger is thinned on the under side by wearing, the dripping from the
eaves hollows a stone, the bent ploughshare of iron imperceptibly decreases in the fields, and we behold the stone-paved streets worn
down by the feet of the multitude; the brass statues too at the gates
show their right hands to be wasted by the touch of the numerous
passers by who greet them. These things then we see are lessened,
since they have been thus worn down; but what bodies depart at any
given time the nature of vision has jealously shut out our seeing. . . .
Nature therefore works by unseen bodies.

Lucretius, *On
the Nature of Things*

Cosmological speculation goes on today, as it did 2,500 years ago. From
the earliest times, philosophers have been actively involved in the experimental and theoretical advances of what today we call science. Indeed, it is difficult to say just where hard science leaves off and speculative, philosophical

cosmology begins. Thales himself, for example, was said to have discovered a method for measuring the height of the Egyptian pyramids by waiting until the precise hour of the day when a body's shadow was equal to its height. Anaximander devised an instrument known as a gnomon, a rod whose shadow permits us to calculate the direction and height of the sun. The great fourth-century B.C. philosopher Aristotle, pupil and follower of Plato, virtually invented the science of formal logic and made significant contributions to what we would today call taxonomy. Plato's school of followers, the Academy, did important work in the branch of mathematics known as solid geometry. Two thousand years later, René Descartes, the French philosopher and scientist, invented analytic geometry (which we still study in school today) as a tool for analyzing and giving expression to his theory of the nature of the material universe. His successor, Gottfried Leibniz, invented a version of the differential calculus as part of his dispute with Descartes about the nature of matter. In the twentieth century, the logicians and philosophers Bertrand Russell and Alfred North Whitehead established the modern discipline of mathematical logic with their monumental *Principia Mathematica*. Throughout the entire course of Western civilization, philosophical speculation, scientific experiment, and pure logical and mathematical theorizing have advanced together, often in the writings of the same thinkers, sometimes in the very same works. The philosophical enterprise begun by the ancient Milesians has borne splendid fruit, both in an expanded scientific understanding of nature and in a refined conceptual sophistication about those original questions of the nature and order of the cosmos.

One final point before we move on. Thales, Anaximander, and the rest are called "philosophers" in the dictionaries of biography or histories of Western thought. But the people who investigate these questions today are usually classified as "scientists," not as "philosophers." Why is it that cosmological questions are investigated by scientists today, although they were investigated by the philosophers 2,500 years ago? Is this just what labor unions call a "jurisdictional dispute," or has some important theoretical change taken place here?

The most common answer to this question is that "philosophy" used to include just about everything that men and women did by way of systematic, reasoned investigation of the heavens, the earth, or the human condition. In the writings of Plato, Aristotle, and the other ancients, we find discussions that today would be labeled physics, mathematics, astronomy, biology, psychology, economics, political science, sociology, anthropology, theology, and even engineering. Over the past two millennia, one after another of these branches of human knowledge has pulled itself together, broken off from "philosophy," and established itself as an independent discipline with its own rules of inquiry, objects of investigation, and theoretical framework. Philosophy today, according to this way of looking at things, is what remains after all of the intellectual children have left home. Roughly speaking, that reduces philosophy to conceptual analysis, plus some armchair speculation on what-ever the other sciences have not laid claim to yet.

There is another view, however, which seems to me to be a good deal closer to the truth. Philosophy, it holds, is the systematic reflection of the mind on the criteria of right thought and right action, which it employs in all of its activities. On this view, there is a "philosophical" component to virtually everything we do. Political scientists (and politicians too), scientists, artists, economists, and astronomers all need to reflect on the nature of their enter-prises, and the people officially called philosophers are simply those among us who concentrate their attention on this self-critical or reflective side of our intellectual undertakings.

What Do Philosophers Do?
Human Nature and the Universe

Although the study of the human condition and the study of the cosmos are the two great themes of Western philosophy, it must not be supposed that they developed in an unconnected way. Philosophers are, above all else, seek-ers after unity. Where human experience presents a manyness, they seek the underlying oneness. In the long history of Western thought, philosophers have tried two basically different strategies for bringing the two branches of philos-ophy into some interconnected whole.

The first strategy was tried by some of the earliest philosophers, among whom were a group known as *Stoics*. The Stoics claimed that the natural world exhibits a rational order that can be explained by appeal to the existence and operations of a power of reason, which they called *logos*. (We get our word logic from this term, and also the word ending -ology, meaning "study of.") In the cosmos, this logos was often identified with what we today would call God, but it also could be identified with the power of reason in each human being. Therein lies the principle that bridges the gap between the study of human nature and the study of physical nature, for the very same fundamental logos or rational order that makes itself known in the order of the planets, the succession of the seasons, and the regular behavior of natural bodies in space and time also exhibits itself in our capacity for logical reasoning, in our ability to control our passions by the power of our understanding, and in the proper order and arrangement of men and women in a stable, just, and rationally ordered society. Our power of reason was said to be a "spark" or fragment of the divine Logos that informs and governs the universe. Eventually this ancient Greek doc-trine was taken up into the theology of the Christian, Jewish, and Muslim re-ligions and became the basis for much of the religious theology that flourished in the Middle Ages.

After studying cosmology as a youth, Socrates turned away from it, convinced that the proper study for us is our own nature. But if the Stoics were correct, then a philosopher could study human nature and physical nature together, for the same principles that explained the arrangement of the heavenly bodies would, properly understood, also explain how we should live our lives within a well-ordered set of social arrangements.

The unifying doctrine of the Stoics gave rise to one of the most important philosophical ideas in Western thought—the idea of *natural law.* God, or the power of Reason, created the universe in accordance with a rational idea of the proper form and order of its organization. On the cosmic level, this conception determines the existence, nature, and relative positions of the stars, the sun, the moon, and the earth. At the social level, this same idea determines the appropriate hierarchy of classes and statuses from the king or emperor down to the lowliest serf. Within each individual human being, the same idea determines the relative order and importance of the rational, passional, and appetitive elements of the soul. Human beings are unique in the natural order by virtue of their possession of a spark of that logos or reason, for it permits them at one and the same time to understand the grand plan and also to live their own lives freely and responsibly in conformity with it.

Among the greatest of the ancient Stoics was a Roman emperor who ruled from A.D. 161 to 180. Marcus Aurelius combined great skill as a general and ruler with a contemplative nature. His reflections on the universe and our brief stay in it have come down to us in the form of a series of meditations. Following are a few selections that convey the themes and something of the flavor of his thought.

Constantly regard the universe as one living being, having one substance and one soul; and observe how all things have reference to one perception, the perception of this one living being; and how all things act with one movement; and how all things are the co-operating causes of all things which exist; observe too the continuous spinning of the thread and the contexture of the web.

The intelligence of the universe is social. Accordingly it has made the inferior things for the sake of the superior, and it has fitted the superior to one another. Thou seest how it has subordinated, co-ordinated and assigned to everything its proper portion, and has brought together into concord with one another the things which are the best.

All things are implicated with one another, and the bond is holy; and there is hardly anything unconnected with any other thing. For things have been co-ordinated, and they combine to form the same universe (order). For there is one universe made up of all things, and one God who pervades all things, and one substance, and one law, one common reason in all intelligent animals, and one truth; indeed

MARCUS AURELIUS,
Meditations

Fifteenth-century French illuminated manuscript de-
picting the sack of Rome by Alaric and the Goths in
A.D. 410. In the upper left corner of the painting, St.
Augustine is shown offering his book *The City of God*
to the Pope. It was the sack of Rome by the Goths
that prompted Augustine to write this famous
work. *(Source:* Bibliotheque Nationale de France.*)*

Marcus
Aurelius, *Meditations*

there is also one perfection for all animals which are the same stock
and participated in the same reason.

To the rational animal the same act is according to nature and
according to reason.

So the first strategy devised by philosophers for uniting the study of
human nature with the study of physical nature was the Stoic doctrine of natural law. The second strategy was worked out 2,200 years later by a brilliant
group of seventeenth- and eighteenth-century philosophers in the British Isles
and on the continent of Europe. We shall be taking a close look at some of
their theories in Chapter 2 when we talk about the branch of philosophy
known as the "theory of knowledge." In this introductory look at the nature of
philosophy in general, we ought nevertheless to try to form some preliminary

idea of what they were doing, for their ideas and writings have been among the most influential in the entire literature of Western thought.

The key to the new strategy is a very simple, very powerful idea: the universe is vast, and 10,000 generations would be too short a time to say everything that can be learned about it; but every single fact, every theory, every insight, guess, hypothesis, or deduction is *an idea in the human mind.* So instead of turning our eyes outward to the universe, let us turn our eyes inward to the nature of the human mind itself. Let us study *the way in which* we know, rather than *what* we know. The universe may be infinite, but the mind is finite. What is more (these philosophers thought), though the universe is infinitely varied, the human mind is everywhere and always exactly the same. Instead of writing many books on cosmology, physics, psychology, politics, morals, and religion, we need to write just one book on the powers, capacities, forms, and limits of the human mind. So during the seventeenth and eighteenth centuries, we find titles like the following cropping up in the philosophical literature: *An Essay Concerning Human Understanding,* by the Englishman John Locke; *Principles of Human Knowledge,* by the Irishman George Berkeley; *A Treatise of Human Nature,* by the Scotsman David Hume; and the greatest of them all, *Critique of Pure Reason,* by the Prussian Immanuel Kant.

Now it might look at first glance as though these philosophers had simply taken Socrates' advice to forget about the study of physical nature and seek instead a knowledge of human nature. But that would be a mistake, for the British empiricists (as Locke, Berkeley, Hume, and their lesser compatriots are called) and the Continental rationalists (Descartes, Leibniz, Kant, and their fellow philosophers) had gotten their hands on a wholly different way of doing philosophy. Socrates never imagined that we could learn something about the natural sciences by studying ourselves. He simply thought that the search for the just and happy life was more important than speculation about the elements of the universe or the origin of the order of the heavenly bodies. The British empiricists and Continental rationalists, by contrast, thought that they had found a device for combining the study of human nature and the study of the universe in one single philosophical enterprise. If they could learn *how* we know—whether by looking with our eyes, touching with our hands, and listening with our ears; or whether by reasoning with our minds and ignoring the evidence of our senses; or perhaps whether by some combination of what the senses tell us with what reason tells us—if philosophy could study the process of knowledge rather than getting all tangled up in the details of particular bits of knowledge of this and that, then maybe philosophy could give us some very general answers to such questions as: Can we know anything at all? How much can we know? Can we know about things that happened before we were born, or somewhere else in space? Can we know that things *must* happen the way they do, or can we simply say, "This happens, and then this . . ." and let it go at that? Can we know about things we cannot see or feel, like atoms, or the unconscious, or even God? Can one person

MARCUS AURELIUS

Marcus Aurelius (A.D. 121–180) was one of the most remarkable men to hold the exalted position of Roman emperor. For almost five centuries, Rome ruled a vast empire stretching from Great Britain through what is now Western Europe, entirely around the shores of the Mediterranean Sea, and deep into northern Africa and the Middle East. Marcus was both a gifted and successful general, winning many battles against the barbarian tribes that repeatedly attacked Rome's border provinces; and also a wise and thoughtful philosopher, learned in the writings of the Greeks and his Roman predecessors, without illusions about the fleetingness of the power and glory that were his as emperor. During the second century after the birth of Christ, the Empire persecuted the followers of that Eastern prophet, and Marcus, despite (or perhaps even because of) his commitment to Stoicism, carried forward these persecutions. It was not until more than a century later, with the conversion of the Emperor Constantine, that Christianity ceased to be the object of official attack and became instead the established religion of the Roman Empire.

know for sure that there are other persons in the world, and not just bodies that look like persons? Can I, myself, be sure that the whole world is not simply my dream? All these questions, and many more besides, might be answered by a systematic study of the human mind itself. In this way, the study of physical nature would be combined with the study of human nature, not through a theory of universal logos or intelligence, as the Stoics thought, but through a theory of how we know.

One of the best statements of the new strategy is found in the introduction to David Hume's great work, *A Treatise of Human Nature.* Hume was a Scotsman, born in 1711. The *Treatise,* in three volumes, was published in 1739 and 1740, when Hume was not yet thirty years old! There are three important points to notice in the following passage from Hume's *Treatise.* First, as we have already remarked, the basic idea of Hume's strategy is to turn the multiplicity of sciences and fields of study into a unified examination of human nature and the mind's power of knowing. Second, Hume thinks that he shall have to study "the nature of the ideas we employ," for it is from those ideas that we form whatever judgments we wish to make in physics, religion, politics, or morals. And finally, Hume says, he shall have to examine "the operations we perform in our reasonings." In Chapter 2, we shall see that this distinction between the nature of our ideas, on the one hand, and the nature of our reasonings with our ideas, on the other, is an important weapon in the strategy of the new theorists of knowledge. We shall see that there are competing theories of the nature and origin of our knowledge: **empiricism and rationalism.**

Reading selections from the works of the great philosophers is a bit like watching videotaped replays of the moves of great football stars. Since we know who made it to stardom, it is easy for us to spot their greatness from the very first. But let us have a little pity on the poor book reviewer who was handed an anonymous work entitled *A Treatise of Human Nature* and told to write a brief review of it in a few weeks. Here is what one nameless unfortunate had to say about Hume's *Treatise,* in a literary journal rather imposingly called *A History of the Works of the Learned.*

> . . . A Man, who has never had the pleasure of reading Mr. Locke's incomparable Essay, will peruse our author with much less Disgust, than those can who have been used to the irresistible Reasoning and wonderful Perspicuity of that admirable Writer.

Poor Hume was so upset by the negative reviews of the *Treatise* that later in life he disowned it, saying it was merely a first effort of his youth. How many of us, I wonder, would recognize the greatness of a new book of philosophy within months of its publication? Here is a passage from the introduction to the *Treatise.*

> It is evident, that all the sciences have a relation, greater or less, to human nature; and that, however wide any of them may seem to run from it, they still return back by one passage or another. Even *Mathematics, Natural Philosophy,* and *Natural Religion* are in some measure dependent on the science of MAN; since they lie under the cognisance of men, and are judged of by their powers and faculties. It is impossible to tell what changes and improvements we might make

DAVID HUME,
A Treatise of Human Nature

Empiricism and Rationalism Empiricism and rationalism are the two leading epistemological theories of the past four centuries. *Empiricism* is the theory that all human knowledge comes from the evidence of our five senses, and therefore that we can never know more, or know with greater certainty, than our senses will allow. *Rationalism* is the theory that at least some human knowledge comes from reason, unaided by the senses, and therefore that we can know about things that the senses do not reveal to us, and can know with greater certainty than the senses will allow.

DAVID HUME

David Hume (1711–1776) was one of those precocious philosophers whose greatest work was done early in life. Born and reared near Edinburgh in Scotland, Hume attended Edinburgh University, where he studied the new physics of Isaac Newton and the new philosophy of John Locke. When still a teenager, Hume conceived the idea of developing a full-scale theory of human nature along the lines of Newton's revolutionary theory of physical nature. After what seems to have been some sort of mental breakdown, Hume went to France to rest and recover, and while there he wrote his first and greatest book, the monumental *A Treatise of Human Nature.*

Hume went on to become an extremely popular and successful essayist and man of letters. His six-volume *History of England* established his reputation as the first major modern historian. Nevertheless, his skeptical doubts about religion and his attacks on the metaphysical doctrines of his Continental and British predecessors earned him many enemies. One of his most brilliant works, twelve *Dialogues Concerning Natural Religion,* was published only after his death. His friends, including the economist Adam Smith, persuaded him that the book was too controversial and might permanently damage his reputation.

As you can see from the portrait of Hume, the lightness and quickness of his mind was entirely hidden by the lumpishness of his appearance. Nature often plays such tricks on us!

in these sciences were we thoroughly acquainted with the extent and force of human understanding, and could explain the nature of the ideas we employ, and of the operations we perform in our reasonings. And these improvements are the more to be hoped for in natural religion, as it is not content with instructing us in the nature of superior powers, but carries its views further, to their disposition towards us, and our duties towards them; and consequently, we ourselves are not only the beings that reason, but also one of the objects concerning which we reason.

If, therefore, the sciences of mathematics, natural philosophy, and natural religion have such a dependence on the knowledge of man, what may be expected in the other sciences, whose connection with human nature is more close and intimate? The sole end of logic is to explain the principles and operations of our reasoning faculty, and the nature of our ideas; morals and criticism regard our tastes

Fig. 264.—Model Head.

Model head illustrating phrenology. The British and Continental philosophy of the seventeenth and eighteenth centuries sought to determine the limits of human knowledge by a study of the powers and capacities of the mind itself. *(Source:* Corbis/Bettmann.)

and sentiments; and politics consider men as united in society, and dependent on each other. In these four sciences of *Logic, Morals, Criticism,* and *Politics* is comprehended almost everything which it can anyway import us to be acquainted with, or which can tend either to the improvement or ornament of the human mind.

Here then is the only expedient, from which we can hope for success in our philosophical researches, to leave the tedious lingering method, which we have hitherto followed, and, instead of taking now and then a castle or village on the frontier, to march up directly to the capital or center of these sciences, to human nature itself; which being once master of, we may everywhere else hope for an easy victory. From this station we may extend our conquests over all those sciences, which more intimately concern human life, and may afterwards proceed at leisure, to discover more fully those which are the objects of pure curiosity. There is no question of importance, whose decision is not comprised in the science of man; and there is none, which can be decided with any certainty, before we become acquainted with that science. In pretending, therefore, to explain the

David Hume,
Treatise on Human Nature

principles of human nature, we in effect propose a complete system of the sciences, built on a foundation almost entirely new, and the only one upon which they can stand with any security.

The new study of the mind's capacity for knowing came to be called **epistemology,** from the Greek for the study or science (-ology) of knowledge (*episteme*). It was not to be merely descriptive, like psychology, however. Its purpose was to settle some ancient philosophical disputes by finding out what we can legitimately claim to know, and what we cannot claim to know because our claims carry us beyond the limits of the powers of the mind. This *critical* dimension of the new strategy extended across the entire spectrum of philosophical investigations, as the passage from Hume's *Treatise* indicates. In a brief excerpt from Immanuel Kant's *Critique of Pure Reason,* you can get some sense of what a dramatic challenge the new critical epistemology was to the established ways of thinking.

IMMANUEL KANT,
Critique of Pure Reason

Immanuel
Kant, *Critique of Pure Reason*

We often hear complaints of shallowness of thought in our age and of the consequent decline of sound science. But I do not see that the sciences which rest upon a secure foundation, such as mathematics, physics, etc., in the least deserve this reproach. On the contrary, they merit their old reputation for solidity, and, in the case of physics, even surpass it. The same spirit would have become active in other kinds of knowledge, if only attention had first been directed to the determination of their principles. Till this is done, indifference, doubt, and, in the final issue, severe criticism, are themselves proof of a profound habit of thought. Our age is, in especial degree, the age of criticism, and to criticism everything must submit. Religion through its sanctity, and law-giving through its majesty, may seek to exempt themselves from it. But they then awaken just suspicion, and cannot claim the sincere respect which reason accords only to that which has been able to sustain the test of free and open examination.

Epistemology   Literally, the study of knowledge. Epistemology is the study of how we come to know things, what the limits are of our knowledge, and what sort of certainty or uncertainty attaches to our knowledge. Psychology also studies how we come to know, but epistemology is concerned less with the mechanics of knowing than with the possibility of defending, proving, or justifying what we think we know. Since the early seventeenth century, epistemology has been the most important branch of philosophy.

Rationality, Universality, Objectivity

If we cast our eye over the entire 2,500-year history of Western philosophy, we find, over and over again, an emphasis on *three* characteristics that philosophical truths or insights are said to share: rationality, universality, and objectivity. Not all philosophers agree that good philosophy is rational, objective, and universal. Indeed, there really is not anything that *all* philosophers agree on, as you will find. But the overwhelming majority have thought, at least until recently, that philosophy ought to be rational, universal, and objective.

What do these three words mean?

By rationality, philosophers mean the mind's ability to present reasons, evidence, and arguments in support of our beliefs. They mean our ability to deduce conclusions from premises, our willingness to set aside prejudice, passion, and self-interest and use our intelligence to understand the world and ourselves. A *rational* person is a person who thinks instead of simply reacting, who recognizes hard truths even when they are unpleasant, who tries to make logical connections among his or her beliefs, and to test those beliefs against the facts. *Rationality,* as philosophers understand it, is contrasted with irrationality, emotionalism, passion, bias, and unthinking or merely habitual action.

By universality, philosophers mean *applying everywhere and always,* being true for everyone and not just for me, or for my fellow Americans, or for those of a particular gender, race, or economic class. A statement, to qualify as true, philosophers say, must be true for everyone if it is true for anyone. That is why we continue to read the writings of ancient Greeks, medieval Arabs, seventeenth-century Frenchmen, or nineteenth-century Germans. If Plato succeeded in discovering some truth about the human condition, then it must be as true today as it was in Athens in the fifth century before the birth of Christ. *Universality,* as philosophers understand it, is contrasted with particularity, parochialism, and insularity. That is why philosophers so often seem citizens of the world, or even of the universe, rather than of any particular country.

By *objectivity,* philosophers mean being true to the way the world really is, not merely reflecting the inner nature of an individual subject. The word "objectivity" is obviously connected with the word "object." When I describe an object correctly, I list its properties in a way that is independent of me as the observer or speaker. Hence, what I am describing is what is real in the object, not merely apparent in the subject.

Now, if you think about it, there is a connection among these three characteristics—rationality, universality, and objectivity—or at least that is what most philosophers have claimed. The connection goes like this:

- If a truth is *rational,* then it will be true for everyone, because what we all have in common is our reason. It is our passion, our self-interest, our emotion that makes us different from one another, hence, *rationality* implies *universality.* Furthermore, if a truth is *rational,* then it will be *objective*—it will be true *of the object,* not of the subject who is stating the truth. This point is not quite so obvious, but recall what we said earlier in this chapter about the Stoics. The Stoics argued that Reason organizes the universe, and also organizes our thought about the universe. So, insofar as we are rational, our thought is objective, about the object. Even Kant, who denied that we can ever have knowledge of independent reality, ended up claiming that it is our rational power that gives us the knowledge of appearances that we call science and mathematics.

• We get the same result if we start with *universality* instead of *rationality.* If a truth is universal, then it must derive from our reason, because it is reason that we all share, and that is therefore universal. What is more, *universality* implies *objectivity,* since what is true for everyone cannot be based on our subjective and variable nature.

• Finally, *objectivity* implies *rationality* and *universality,* since what is objective is knowable by reason and the same for everyone.

In short, the overwhelming majority of Western philosophers claim that each of these features—rationality, universality, objectivity—implies the other two, and all three of them are the defining marks of genuine philosophical knowledge.

There have always been a few philosophers who dissented from this majority view, and in recent decades their numbers seem to have grown. A number of thinkers have called into question the universality, objectivity, and rationality of philosophical insights, as we shall see in the next chapter. I began my philosophical career very deeply committed to the traditional view. Indeed, what got me interested in philosophy as a teenager was my doubts about ethical questions and my search for some moral certainties that would be true everywhere and for everyone (universal), not merely an expression of my personal feelings or preferences (objective), and defensible by arguments (rational).

But over the years—in fact, during the time that this textbook has been going through successive editions—I have begun to alter my conviction that rationality, universality, and objectivity are necessarily the defining characteristics of good philosophy.

I am still absolutely convinced that all of us, philosophers or not, must be prepared to advance good arguments in support of our moral, political, and scientific beliefs. In short, I am as devoted to *rationality* as I was when I began my philosophical career, and I remain committed to discovering the way the world is, not just to giving expression to my feelings, prejudices, or inner concerns. So I remain committed to *objectivity,* but I now have very serious doubts about *universality*—the third of the three traditional hallmarks of philosophical truth.

My philosophical doubts grow out of my personal experiences in the troubled country of South Africa. For the past ten years, I have been engaged in an effort to raise scholarship funds for needy black South Africans attending universities in South Africa. As a result, I have become more and more deeply committed to the effort by millions of black and white South Africans to put an end to the system of official oppression and discrimination called "apartheid" and to establish a genuinely democratic political system.

Early in my many visits to South Africa, I had a number of long conversations with white defenders of the apartheid ("apartness," or segregation) system, including several who are professors of philosophy at South African universities (this was before the end of the apartheid regime in 1994). The defenders of the segregationist system were, by any reasonable measure, intelligent, rational, and objective. The philosophers among them had read the same philosophical texts I had read, and they could draw conclusions from premises pretty much as well as I could. I think I am being fair when I say that they were not simply trying dishonestly to cling to an unjust system that gave them every advantage and forced black South Africans to live in poverty and unfreedom.

But these defenders of apartheid simply could not imagine what the great African-American scholar, W. E. B. Du Bois, would have called the "double consciousness" of black South Africans. Consequently, the way in which they understood the world, down to the very categories of time, space, causality, and personhood they employed, were incompatible with those that I use, or that are used by my black and white comrades in South Africa.

In the end, I have come to believe, the most basic philosophical concepts with which one interprets the world are shaped and determined by the human commitments one has made to fellow men and women with whom one makes a common cause and a common life.

Within the world of those commitments, I still use my *reason* to distinguish truth from falsehood, the sensible from the senseless, the prudent from the imprudent, and the right from the wrong. I try as hard as ever I did to be *objective,* to distinguish the way the world really is from the way it merely appears to me to be. But I have given up my belief that if I am just *rational* and *objective* enough, I will be able to bring everyone else along with me in *universal* agreement.

What then of *universality?* Although I have given it up as a test of philosophical truth, it remains for me a goal, in somewhat altered form, for I continue to seek ways to widen the circle of those with whom I am able to form a human bond and make a moral commitment. Perhaps I shall never achieve that comradeship with the South African defenders of apartheid, but there is no limit to the circle of men and women with whom I can work for a better and more just world.

The Limitations of the Western Philosophical Tradition

Thus far, we have been sketching in very broad strokes the major themes and authors of an intellectual tradition that we usually call "Western Philosophy." As we have seen, the tradition has its beginning in the eastern Mediterranean in the sixth century B.C., in the cosmological speculations of a number of thoughtful and observant residents of what are now Greece and Turkey. Although commonly associated with Western Europe, the tradition actually draws heavily on the religious and scientific thought of Egyptian culture. During its 2,500-year history, the tradition has encompassed the religious doctrines of the Near East (Judaism and Christianity), the metaphysical speculations of the Arabic philosophers of North Africa, Arabia, and the Middle East, and in recent times, the writings of thinkers in North America, Australia, New Zealand, and South Africa.

Nevertheless, this ancient and very broad tradition of thought and literature is strikingly limited in certain ways. Despite the fact that it is largely the product of "dead white males"—to use a phrase that has achieved a certain popularity lately—this tradition presents itself as the philosophical tradition of Western civilization. And yet, in this tradition, the voices of women and persons of color are scarcely ever heard. What is more, the major thinkers in the tradition present their doctrines as universally true—true for all human beings, or even, in the case of Kant, for example, true for all rational beings, whether human or not.

There is a great deal to be learned from the Western philosophical tradition, as I hope I shall convince you in the pages of this book. But as we proceed to study this tradition, we must ask, in the familiar words of Shakespeare's character Hamlet, whether "there are more things in heaven and earth than are dreamt of in [this] philosophy." In particular, we as Americans must ask whether the experiences, insights, and self-understandings of the substantial groups in our population who are not white males require us to amend, or even to call into question, the received truths of the established tradition of philosophy.

We could begin, of course, by canvassing the writings of the major figures we shall encounter in this book. Since they are among the most profound, thoughtful, and rigorous thinkers ever to put pen to paper—or stylus to tablet—we might expect them to have something helpful to say about the experiences and insights of persons different from themselves. However, were we to follow this suggestion, we would come across some rather surprising and troubling passages.

Consider, for example, several of the major thinkers associated with what we call the Enlightenment—that period during the eighteenth and early nineteenth centuries when the orthodoxies of religion, science, and politics were called into question and the authority of tradition was replaced by the claims of reason. Because these writers speak so movingly about the virtues of reason and the dangers of superstition, we might hope to find a clear-eyed recognition of the variety and richness of the human experience in their writings.

In some of them, no doubt, we do, but all too often we are disappointed. Here, as just one example, is David Hume, in an essay entitled *Of National Characters.* Speaking of the effect of climate on human cultural and intellectual achievements (a favorite topic for eighteenth-century writers), he remarks that "there is some reason to think, that all the nations which live beyond the polar circles or between the tropics, are inferior to the rest of the species, and are incapable of all the higher attainments of the human mind." Then, in a footnote that has become justly infamous, he continues:

> I am apt to suspect the Negroes to be naturally inferior to the Whites. There scarcely ever was a civilized nation of that complexion, nor even any individual eminent either in action or speculation. No ingenious manufactures amongst them, no arts, no sciences. On the other hand, the most rude and barbarous of the Whites, such as the ancient Germans, the present Tartars, have still something eminent about them, in their valour, form of government, or some other particular. Such a uniform and constant difference could not happen, in so many countries and ages, if nature had not made an original distinction between these breeds of men. Not to mention our colonies, there are Negro slaves dispersed all over Europe, of whom none ever discovered any symptoms of ingenuity; though low people, without education, will start up amongst us, and distinguish themselves in every profession. In Jamaica, indeed, they talk of one Negro as a man of parts and learning; but it is likely he is admired for slender accomplishments, like a parrot who speaks a few words plainly.

DAVID HUME,
Of National Characters

Hume's contemptuous view of Africans was challenged by James Beattie, another British philosopher. Beattie wrote a book called *Essay on the Nature and Immutability of the Truth,* in which he mounted a vigorous attack on Hume's most famous book, *A Treatise of Human Nature.* In the course of his attack, Beattie took on Hume's views about people of color. He pointed out that Hume's sweeping condemnations were completely unsupported by observation or evidence. That was a telling blow to Hume, who made so much of the importance of observation elsewhere in his writings.

Immanuel Kant had read Hume's remarks and cited them approvingly in his important early essay, *Observations on the Feeling of the Beautiful and Sublime.* He also had read Beattie, by the way, but he does not seem to have been much impressed by Beattie's arguments.

Kant actually added a story of his own, in an attempt to reinforce Hume's dismissive views of Africans. Kant cited a story by a Dominican missionary, Father Labat, concerning a Negro carpenter. Labat criticized the carpenter for his haughty treatment of his wives, Kant tells us. The carpenter replied with what certainly sounds like a rather shrewd dig: "You whites are indeed fools, for first you make great concessions to your wives, and afterward you complain when they drive you mad."

Kant then adds a comment that I personally consider the single most appalling sentence ever written by a great thinker: "And it might be that there were something in this which perhaps deserved to be considered; but in short, this fellow was quite black from head to foot, a clear proof that what he said was stupid." Even the great Kant could not trust himself to evaluate the merits of a statement when it came from the mouth of a black man, but instead judged its truth by the color of the skin of its author.

These casually dismissive remarks about persons of color, turning up in the pages of even the greatest thinkers of the eighteenth century, were given a world-historical justification by the most important figure of nineteenth-century thought, the German philosopher Georg Hegel. In his most influential book, *Lectures on the Philosophy of History,* Hegel attempted nothing less than a systematic survey of all of human experience and history. He devoted seven or eight pages in his lengthy Introduction to the continent of Africa, describing the inhabitants of that vast continent as childlike creatures whose minds had not developed sufficiently to permit anything interesting to be said about them.

After repeating, as though they were true, a number of fantastic tales about cannibal tribes with gory practices, Hegel draws the comforting conclusion that for these savages, slavery is actually a step *up* the scale of human development from their previous existence, and hence should be removed only very gradually. Hegel concludes grandly in this fashion: "At this point, we leave Africa, not to mention it again. For it is no historical part of the world. . . . What we properly understand by Africa, is the Unhistorical, Undeveloped Spirit, still involved in the conditions of mere nature, and which had to be presented here only as on the threshold of the World's History."

Not all of the great minds of the Western philosophical tradition view persons of color, whether in Europe, in Africa, or in the Americas, as beneath contempt and devoid of any intellectual capacities. Nor do they all justify the institution of slavery, by any means. But by now it should be obvious to us that if we want to know what philosophical insights we can gain from persons of color, we should stop rummaging about in the writings of Hume or Kant or Hegel, and instead look at what persons of color have themselves written.

Once we have made this decision, we can turn either to the philosophical literature now being written by philosophers living in Africa, or to the writings of those of African descent, whose parents or grandparents were brought as slaves to other parts of the world. Let me begin with the writings of one of the most interesting philosophers of any color ever to live and write in this country: William Edward Burghardt Du Bois.

Du Bois was born in 1868, just five years after Abraham Lincoln signed the Emancipation Proclamation freeing some of the American men and women who were held in slavery. Brought up in western Massachusetts in the town of Great Barrington, Du Bois attended Fisk University in Nashville, Tennessee, and then took a doctorate at Harvard University—the first African American to do so.

Du Bois spent the first part of his long life studying the condition of black people in both the North and the South. In addition to scholarly research, he engaged all during his life in political activity aimed at securing some measure of political and economic equality for former slaves and their descendants. He published ground-breaking books on the period of Reconstruction following the end of the Civil War, and on the large black community in Philadelphia. During the same period, from the late 1800s to the early 1900s, he played a central role in founding the National Association for the Advancement of Colored People—the NAACP—and for many years edited its magazine, *The Crisis*.

Du Bois traveled throughout the world, studying in Germany and participating in the first Pan-African Congresses ever organized. For more than half a century, he was the strongest progressive voice in the United States for the interests and aspirations of black people. In 1961, Du Bois gave up his American citizenship and emigrated to Ghana in West Africa, where he died two years later.

W. E. B. Du Bois lived to be ninety-five, his life spanning the century from the end of the Civil War to the beginning of the modern civil rights movement. Three decades after his death, he remains the dominant figure in Afro-American studies. His name graces many organizations, academic chairs, and departments, including the W. E. B. Du Bois Department of Afro-American Studies at the University of Massachusetts, of which I am now a member.

These are the opening words of the *Forethought* to Du Bois' masterpiece, *The Souls of Black Folk,* published in 1903:

> Herein lie buried many things which if read with patience may show the strange meanings of being black here at the dawning of the Twentieth Century; for the problem of the Twentieth Century is the problem of the color line.

The problem of the twentieth century is the problem of the color line

The founder of psychoanalysis, Sigmund Freud, once remarked that if there was any subject, however trivial, that a patient would not allow to be discussed in the course of a psychoanalytic therapy, sooner or later the entire therapy would come to be about that subject. In a way, America's unwilling-ness to confront openly and honestly the problem of the color line, the line separating blacks from whites, has resulted in the public discourse of this country being everywhere and always a concealed debate about race. As we enter the twenty-first century, it appears that Du Bois' diagnosis will apply as well to the next 100 years.

Du Bois, who was himself descended both from former slaves and from Dutch and French immigrants, thought deeply about the experience of being "black" in a country that consigned nonwhites to second-class citizenship. In a famous passage at the beginning of the first chapter of *Souls,* he invoked two biblical images to describe the experience: the image of a veil shutting him off from the white world, and the image of a double consciousness, born of the fact that he saw himself both as he was to himself, inwardly, and also as he was perceived to be by the white world that looked at him from the out-side. Here is the way he describes this distinctive self-awareness:

DU BOIS,
The Souls of Black Folk

Between me and the other world there is ever an unasked question: unasked by some through feelings of delicacy; by others through the difficulty of rightly framing it. All, nevertheless, flutter round it. They approach me in a half-hesitant sort of way, eye me curiously or compassionately, and then, instead of saying directly, How does it feel to be a problem? they say, I know an excellent colored man in my town; or, I fought at Mechanicsville; or, Do not these South-ern outrages make your blood boil? At these I smile, or am inter-ested, or reduce the boiling to a simmer, as the occasion may require. To the real question, How does it feel to be a problem? I an-swer seldom a word.

And yet, being a problem is a strange experience—peculiar even for one who has never been anything else, save perhaps in babyhood and in Europe. It is in the early days of rollicking boy-hood that the revelation first bursts upon one, all in a day, as it were. I remember well when the shadow swept across me. I was a little thing, away up in the hills of New England, where the dark Housatonic winds between Hoosac and Taghkanic to the sea. In a wee wooden schoolhouse, something put it into the boys' and girls' heads to buy gorgeous visiting-cards—ten cents a package—and exchange. The exchange was merry, till one girl, a tall newcomer, refused my card—refused it peremptorily, with a glance. Then it dawned upon me with a certain suddenness that I was differ-ent from the others; or like, mayhap, in heart and life and longing, but shut out from their world by a vast veil. I had thereafter no desire to tear down that veil, to creep through; I held all beyond it in common contempt, and lived above it in a region of blue sky and great wandering shadows. That sky was bluest when I could beat my mates at examination-time, or beat them at a foot-race, or even beat their stringy heads. Alas, with the years all this fine contempt began to fade; for the worlds I longed for, and all their dazzling opportunities, were theirs, not mine. But they should not keep these prizes, I said, some, all, I would wrest from them. Just how I would do it I could never decide: by reading law, by healing the sick, by telling the wonderful tales that swam in my head—some way. With other black boys the strife was not so fiercely sunny: their youth shrunk into tasteless sycophancy, or into silent hatred of the pale world about them and mocking distrust of everything white; or wasted itself in a bitter cry, Why did God make me an outcast and a stranger in mine own house? The shades of the prison-house closed round about us all: walls strait and stubborn to the whitest, but relentlessly narrow, tall, and unscalable to sons of night who must plod darkly on in resignation, or beat unavailing palms against the stone, or steadily, half hopelessly, watch the streak of blue above.

After the Egyptian and Indian, the Greek and Roman, the Teuton and Mongolian, the Negro is a sort of seventh son, born with a veil, and gifted with second-sight in this American world—a world which yields him no true self-consciousness, but only lets him see himself through the revelation of the other world. It is a peculiar sensation, this double-consciousness, this sense of always looking at one's self through the eyes of others, of measuring one's soul by the tape of a world that looks on in amused contempt and pity. One ever feels his twoness—an American, a Negro; two souls, two thoughts, two unreconciled strivings; two warring ideals in one dark body, whose dogged strength alone keeps it from being torn asunder.

W. E. B. Du Bois, *The Souls of Black Folk*

There is a great deal in this brief passage. Let us begin with the theme of double consciousness. To be black in this country, Du Bois is telling us, is always to be de-centered, to be both inside oneself, as all persons are, but also outside oneself, seeing oneself as others see one—experiencing oneself in stereotypical ways, not as W. E. B. Du Bois, but as *a black man*. Those of you reading this book who are black or Latin American or Asian American will understand immediately what Du Bois means. Those of you who are white must try, by an act of imagination, to understand what it is like to be divided in this way.

This de-centering, thrust upon people of color by a dominant white society, has intellectual consequences that reach far beyond the psyches and personal lives of those immediately affected. As African-American thinkers like

Du Bois have reflected on this curious condition, struggling to understand it and thereby to make sense of their lives, they have been led to a much broader critque of the history, politics, social customs, culture, religion, and public myths of white American society. Indeed, it is not too much to say that the reflective self-understandings of black intellectuals constitute the most sustained critique of American society ever attempted.

Is there such a thing as an *African-American philosophy?* What would such a philosophy be? Well, there are now a number of African Americans writing philosophy, most of them teaching in colleges and universities. But a collection of their writings would not constitute an authentic African-American philosophy, any more than a collection of the writings of female professors of philosophy would constitute a feminist philosophy.

There also is a growing literature devoted to the question of the possibility of an authentic African philosophy, most but not all of it written by professors at sub-Saharan African universities, but that also does not constitute a distinctively African-American philosophy.

I should like, rather tentatively, to suggest that a true African-American philosophy must be a literature devoted to an exploration of the philosophical implications of the African-American experience. That exploration, I believe, must focus on what Du Bois labels the "second sight" into the American world yielded by the "double consciousness" thrust upon African Americans by the "color line." Such a literature already exists, as the brief passages from Du Bois' work show. But there is much more to be done, for the double consciousness produced by the color line shifts our perception of every aspect of American life and society.

Consider something as simple as the story of immigration to the American colonies and then to the United States. As that story is told, in school books and scholarly historical treatises, it is a story of English, Scots, Irish, Polish, German, Italian, and Scandinavian immigrants. But in fact, for the first 200 years of the history of immigration, many more men and women arrived (as slaves) from Africa than came from Europe. Not until the middle of the nineteenth century, after the slave trade was ended, did the flow of white immigrants exceed the flow of black immigrants.

Even the most fundamental philosophical categories such as time and space can come to have racial meanings encoded in them. When I was young, students in American schools learned to think of Africa as "the dark continent." This phrase, which some of you have probably heard, echoes Hegel's description of Africa as a "land of childhood . . . enveloped in the dark mantle of night." Now I have been to Africa many times, and I can report that it is not dark at all! To many Europeans and Americans, Africa may be mysterious, dark, unknown, a blank space on the world map. But to the millions of men and women who live in Africa, it is home—as familiar, natural, and sunlit as Kansas or Michigan or Florida.

Nor is Africa "lost in time." Popular writers often talk about Africa as a world in which the prehistoric past lives today. They talk as though when Americans travel to Africa, they are going "back in time" to an earlier period of human development. But the men and women who live in Africa today live at the dawn of the twenty-first century, as do the men and women who live in Europe, North America, or Asia. African communities have histories that reach as far into the past as communities elsewhere in the world.

When you read books or see television programs in which Africa is portrayed as a dark continent, somehow outside the time and space of the modern world, your philosophical understanding is being fundamentally distorted and warped by the racial encoding attached to people of color. All of this, and more, is what Du Bois is trying to show us when he talks of the "double consciousness" created by the *color line.*

What would it be like, philosophically, to overcome this double consciousness? How must we change the way we think about ourselves and the world if we are to erase the color line? If you are black, the first step, I believe, is to reflect on your own understanding of the world, in order to identify ways in which you have developed a double consciousness. Then *use* that double consciousness, that reflective self-awareness, as a tool with which to criticize the way the majority white society talks about themselves and about you. If you are white, then you must develop the imagination to put yourselves in the shoes of a person of color, and try to understand, from the inside, what it would be like to grow up with a double consciousness.

The result of this process, whether you are a person of color or not, will be a much more complicated understanding of American society. The statements of politicians, teachers, business leaders, religious leaders, and your own friends and acquaintances will take on a new meaning. Then you may be able to achieve what W. E. B. Du Bois calls "second sight." You may be able to penetrate the "veil" and see the world as it truly is. That, as Socrates would certainly agree, is the beginning of wisdom.

Now that you are launched into the study of philosophy, it might help you to know what is coming up in the chapters ahead. You will start with a group of three chapters dealing, in one way or another, with our knowledge of ourselves and the cosmos, and our knowledge of knowledge itself, starting with epistemology, on the theory of knowledge (Chapter 2), and going on to metaphysics and the philosophy of mind (Chapter 3). We conclude this opening trio with a look at the philosophy of science (Chapter 4). We then launch into a series of chapters devoted to philosophical investigations of various aspects of the human condition, including theoretical and applied ethics (Chapter 5), social and political philosophy (Chapter 6), the philosophy of art (Chapter 7), and the philosophy of religion (Chapter 8). That is more than

The Watermelon Man: Questions
About Race

If Jeff Gerber isn't an out-and-out cross-burner, he sure is one insensitive guy. He jokes about blacks in the back of the bus, about race riots and looting, and about hijacking an elevator and having the black elevator operator take it to Harlem.

But one morning, Mr. Gerber's perspective changes—along with his skin color. He wakes up to discover that he is no longer white; instead, he is black. Along with the change in skin color come changes in the way that people respond to him. When he was white, he could race his bus for exercise and save on bus fare as well. Now that he is black, white people assume he stole something and is running away so as not to be caught. Before, he was a bigot; now, he is the target of bigotry.

Questions To Consider

If you are white, imagine that you wake up one morning and you are black. Or, if you are not white, imagine that you wake up one morning and you are now white. How would your life and attitudes change? In addition, if you are male, imagine that you wake up one morning as a female, or conversely. How would your life and attitudes change?

enough for one semester or quarter and should give you a pretty good idea of what my old professor meant when he told his traveling companions that he was a "philosopher."

At the end of each chapter, a special section contains a modern discussion of some immediate practical problem to which the philosophy of the chapter can contribute. In this way, you will learn how today's thinkers—both philosophers and nonphilosophers—try to bring the wisdom of philosophy to bear on our current concerns. Perhaps by the time you have finished reading this book, you will find new ways to make philosophy relevant to modern life.

The Main Points in Chapter One

1. The first great philosopher, Socrates, thought of philosophy as a process of critical self-examination, the purpose of which is to arrive at correct principles of judging, choosing, and acting.

2. The Socratic Method of question-and-answer uses *irony* to penetrate the defenses of those who do not wish to face the fact that they are ignorant or confused.

3. The two major traditions of philosophy are (1) the study of human nature and (2) the study of nature. The ancient philosophers who studied nature came up with very modern-sounding theories of atoms and their combinations.

4. In the seventeenth and eighteenth centuries, philosophers combined the two traditions of philosophy in order to discover the limits of our knowledge of nature. This new technique began with Descartes and was brought to its height by Kant.

5. For most philosophers in the Western tradition, the three marks or tests or characteristics of truth are *rationality, universality,* and *necessity.* Each of these characteristics, they believed, entails the other two.

6. Through the experience of African Americans and other peoples who have suffered systematic oppression, we can learn to see the world in a new way and understand things about our society that may have been hidden from those of us who are white.

Questions for Discussion and Review

1. These days, astronomers study the stars, physicists study subatomic particles, psychiatrists study the nature of the healthy personality, and neurophysiological psychologists study the relation between the physical

and psychological aspects of personality. What is left for philosophers to do? Is philosophy an activity that has, over the past several centuries, put itself out of business?

2. The first great philosopher to make a living as a professor of philosophy was Immanuel Kant in the eighteenth century. These days, it seems, everyone who is considered a philosopher earns a living as a professor. Is there something odd, or inappropriate, about a philosopher being paid money to teach philosophy? If Socrates is right that no one can teach anyone else wisdom, what is it that philosophers teach?

3. The great seventeenth- and eighteenth-century philosophers all thought that a study of human nature could reveal the limits and foundation of our knowledge of nature. How would they have responded to the possibility that there are rational, nonhuman forms of life in the universe that have knowledge, but not a human nature?

4. It is pretty clear what you hope to get out of studying French, or physics, or history, or business administration. What can you hope to get out of studying philosophy? How can you tell whether you are getting out of philosophy what you hope to get? Is your grade in this course a good indicator? Why? Why not?

The Primary Source: Philosophical Readings and Commentary

Aristotle: *Metaphysics*

Augustine, St.: *City of God*

d'Holbach, Baron: *The System of Nature*

Descartes, Rene: *Meditations on First Philosophy*

DuBois, W.E.B.: *The Souls of Black Folk*

Epicurus: *Letter to Menoeceus*

Hume, David: *Treatise On Human Nature; An Enquiry Concerning Human Understanding*

Kant, Immanuel: *Fundamental Principles of the Metaphysics of Morals; Prolegomena to Any Future Metaphysics; Critique of Pure Reason*

Kierkegaard, Soren: *Philosophical Fragments*

Locke, John: *Essay Concerning Human Understanding*

Lucretius: *On the Nature of Things*

Marx, Karl: *The Communist Manifesto*

Nietzsche, Friedrich: *Beyond Good and Evil*

Plato: *The Republic; Theaetetus, Philebus, Sophist, Parmenides, Statesman, Timaeus*

Plotinus: *Enneads*

Rand, Ayn: *Philosophy: Who Needs It?; The Virtue of Selfishness*

Russell, Bertrand: *The Problems of Philosophy*

Sartre, Jean-Paul: *Man As Self Creator*

René Descartes

*R*ené Descartes (1596–1650) is universally recognized among philosophers as the first great figure of the modern age. Born in a small town in Touraine, France, Descartes was educated by the Jesuits, and he remained throughout his life a devoted Catholic. His early interest was principally in mathematics and physics, two fields in which exciting new work was being done by many Continental and English thinkers. In his early twenties, perhaps as the result of a dramatic trio of dreams, Descartes conceived the grandiose plan of formulating an entirely new system of science founded upon mathematics. Though he never accomplished this impossible task, his many contributions to mathematics and physics place him in the forefront of seventeenth-century science.

Descartes' primary concern throughout his life was with problems of methodology, justification, and certainty. His first work was entitled *Rules for the Direction of the Mind,* and in it he sought to establish the

proper procedures by which a question could be investigated without the danger of error or confusion. His most famous work, *Meditations on First Philosophy,* was immediately recognized as a dramatic challenge to all established philosophy and science. It was circulated widely throughout Europe and provoked a series of objections, to which Descartes wrote extended replies. In these objections and replies, we can see a number of profound and dramatic debates unfolding, in which such famous thinkers as Hobbes, Gassendi, and Arnauld locked horns with Descartes.

Although Descartes was deeply influenced by the scholastic philosophy that had preceded him, the problems he posed, the questions he raised, and the demands he made for absolute subjective certainty in knowledge served to undermine the influence of the 2,000-year-old tradition of Aristotelian philosophizing. Virtually all of the great philosophy written during the 150 years following Descartes' death can be seen as an attempt to answer the questions raised by the brilliant, iconoclastic Frenchman.

Theory of Knowledge

Descartes' Method of Doubt

As you work your way through this book carefully, reading and thinking, discussing the problems it raises with your teacher and your fellow students, you will get some feel for what philosophy is and how philosophers think. And if I am at all successful, then philosophy will seem a fairly sensible sort of business to you. Perhaps philosophical questions are not exactly what your mind would turn to if you had a few spare moments caught in a traffic jam or if you could not sleep late at night, but at least it is easy enough to understand how reasonable men and women might get genuinely worked up about them. What rules should I use to decide the hard moral choices that life poses for me? How should the wealth of a society be divided up among its members? Do I have an obligation to obey the state, even when I believe that its laws are unjust? These may not be everyone's questions, but they are surely questions worth asking. Some of them even get asked in political campaigns, in hospital emergency wards, in law courts, or in the front lines of a war.

In this chapter, the situation is dramatically different. We are going to take a look at the philosophical attempts to deal with questions that some of you may think are just plain crazy. Suppose a friend of yours asks whether you and he really did go to the movies last night or whether he just dreamed it. A little odd, perhaps, but people do have very lifelike dreams; I have myself on a couple of occasions had dreams so real that afterwards I was not entirely sure whether they had actually happened or not. You would not think your friend was being *philosophical,* but on the other hand you would not think he was crazy either. Suppose he went on to wonder, in absolute seriousness, whether everything that had ever happened to him was a dream, whether his childhood, his adolescence, his school days, his fights with his parents, his first romance, his first trip away from home, his coming to college, and his standing right there in front of you were *all just dreams.* If he were dead serious, not just kidding around or trying to get a rise out of you, then about now you would start edging toward the phone, trying to figure out how you could call the school psychiatrist without getting your friend too upset. People who really are not sure whether their whole lives have been dreams "need help," as the saying goes.

Suppose another friend said, as the two of you were waiting for an elevator, that she could not really be sure that she needed an elevator to get back down to the first floor. Maybe if she stepped out the window, she would be able simply to fly down. Suppose, indeed, that she expressed doubt about whether she could ever tell what would happen next—whether she would drown if she held her head under water, whether her finger would burn if she held it in a flame, whether her books would fall down or up if she let them go. She might even admit that she was not sure there was anyone else in the whole world besides herself, though of course there might be a lot of human-looking bodies that made speechlike noises and acted in peoplelike ways. Well, once again, you would probably think that either the whole act was a put-on, or that your friend was in the midst of a bad trip, or else that it was time for the shrink. You certainly would not think that she was simply doing philosophy!

From the beginning of the seventeenth century until the present day, some of the most brilliant thinkers ever to grace the cultural and intellectual life of Western civilization have devoted their best philosophical efforts to just such questions as the ones we have been imagining your friends to be asking. And though I would be the first to admit that philosophers have suffered their share of mental illness, there is no reason at all to suspect that any of these great thinkers was mentally unsound when he wrote his philosophy. (Rousseau was more than a little odd, but we will not be talking about him in this chapter.) The greatest challenge any teacher of philosophy faces is to present the epistemological theories of the seventeenth- and eighteenth-century theorists of knowledge in such a way that students not only understand the arguments but also understand why in heaven's name sane people worried about such peculiar problems.

The theory of knowledge is the heart and soul of the philosophy that has been written since the beginning of the seventeenth century. All of the most important philosophers—Descartes, Leibniz, Locke, Berkeley, Hume, and Kant—set epistemological investigations at the center of their work. If we cannot understand what made them take so seriously the questions that seem odd to us today, then we cannot really understand philosophy as it has been done during the past four centuries. The strange-seeming problems of the modern theory of knowledge (in philosophy, anything since 1600 is called "modern") connect directly with one of the dominant cultural and intellectual developments of the postmedieval world—namely, the steady movement toward a radical individualism in religion, in politics, in art, and in literature, as well as in philosophy. Though the epistemological puzzles of seventeenth- and eighteenth-century philosophy seem bizarre or unintuitive on first inspection, they have deeply influenced the way painters painted; the way poets wrote; the way theologians reinterpreted the Word of God; and even the way economists, political scientists, and sociologists have explained our collective social life. So like it or not, we are in for some complicated philosophy in this chapter.

By common agreement, the man who started the new theory of knowledge on its way in philosophy was a Frenchman, born in 1596, named René Descartes. Indeed, though Descartes wrote a number of important works during his fifty-four years, in which mathematics, physics, and other subjects as well as philosophy were discussed, we can even name the precise piece of philosophy that marks the beginning of modern philosophy as we study it today. That honor clearly belongs to a seventy-page work, entitled *Meditations on First Philosophy*, published by Descartes in 1641.

The seventeenth century was an age of scientific giants, and among the truly great thinkers whose efforts created what we know today as modern science, only the German Gottfried Leibniz and the Englishman Isaac Newton can stand with Descartes. You have probably already met Descartes, or at least spent some time working with one of his contributions to knowledge, for it was he who invented what is called analytic geometry. (That is why, when you draw a graph and plot points on it, you are said to be using "Cartesian" coordinates.)

Descartes was born three-quarters of a century after Martin Luther had begun the Protestant Reformation by nailing his famous theses to the church door in Wittenberg. Descartes himself was, and remained throughout his life, a Roman Catholic, and his early education was received from the Jesuits. Nevertheless, if the essence of the Protestant Reformation was the rejection of the religious authority of the institution of the Church and the emphasis on the primacy of individual conscience, then it is clear that Descartes was, intellectually and emotionally, an extreme Protestant. The keynote of his life's work was a thoroughgoing rejection of received opinion, established doctrine, and the authority of the ancients, and a thoroughly individualistic insistence upon accepting only those truths that his own reason could certify to be correct.

In his early twenties, Descartes' interest turned to mathematics and physics, fields which at that time were dominated by concepts and methods almost 2,000 years old. Exciting new work was being done in both areas, and Descartes, like many young scientific geniuses, moved immediately to the scientific frontier. On the night of November 10, 1619, Descartes, then twenty-three, had a series of three dreams which seem to have transformed his life. He spoke and wrote of them ever after as the turning point in his career. I am not going to try my hand at armchair dream interpretation. As Freud made very clear when he first described the psychoanalytic method of interpreting dreams, you cannot figure out what a dream meant to the person who had it unless you can get that person actually to talk to you about the dream. There is no code book of dream symbols in which you can look up the meaning of falling, or a mirror, or whatever. But Descartes himself interpreted his dreams as a sign that he was to spend his life establishing a new, unified theory of the universe based upon mathematics—what we today would call mathematical physics.

The important part of Descartes' plan, for our purposes, is not the new science he developed but his conception of the *method* by which he was to proceed. Descartes devoted a great deal of thought to problems of intellectual and scientific method, and his contributions in this field are, if anything, more revolutionary than his actual mathematical and scientific work itself. Descartes published nothing while he was young, despite the fact that he had made a number of important discoveries in his twenties and thirties. In 1637, when he was past forty, he brought out his first published work, appropriately

titled "Discourse on the Method of Rightly Conducting the Reason and Seeking for Truth in the Sciences." In this partly autobiographical, partly philosophical work, he lays down a set of four rules, which he claims are sufficient
to guide the mind in whatever inquiry it may undertake. Here are the rules, as
Descartes stated them:

> The first of these was to accept nothing as true which I did not clearly
> recognize to be so: that is to say, carefully to avoid precipitation and
> prejudice in judgments, and to accept in them nothing more than
> what was presented to my mind so clearly and distinctly that I could
> have no occasion to doubt it.
>
> The second was to divide up each of the difficulties which I ex-
> amined into as many parts as possible, and as seemed requisite in
> order that it might be resolved in the best manner possible.
>
> The third was to carry on my reflections in due order, commenc-
> ing with objects that were the most simple and easy to understand, in
> order to rise little by little, or by degrees, to knowledge of the most
> complex, assuming an order, even if a fictitious one, among those
> which do not follow a natural sequence relatively to one another.
>
> The last was in all cases to make enumerations so complete and
> review so general that I should be certain of having omitted nothing.

RENÉ DESCARTES,
Discourse on Method

René
Descartes, *Discourse on
Method,* Part II

They do not seem like much when you first read them, do they? Avoid
prejudice, do not take anything on faith, be careful, tackle questions one step
at a time, be orderly, and so forth. It sounds more like instructions to an army
filing clerk or the directions for assembling an outdoor barbecue grill than a
great revolution in philosophy. Indeed, Leibniz once remarked rather sarcasti-
cally that Descartes' famous "method" boiled down to saying, "Take what you
need, and do what you should, and you will get what you want." But first impressions often are wrong (as Descartes himself pointed out), and in this case,
Leibniz was being more clever than wise.

The real importance of Descartes' method lies in two of its features and
a consequence that follows from those two. Since what follows may be easier
to understand if you have some labels to attach to it, let me start by telling
you that Descartes' method is both a *method of inquiry* and a *method of doubt,*
and that the combined consequence of these two methods is to set into motion a philosophical transformation known as the *epistemological turn.* Now, if
you have carefully underlined these three terms in red or yellow or blue, we
can try to make some sense out of them.

First, Descartes' method is a method of inquiry. In other words, it is a
method for finding things out and making sure that you get them right; it is
not a method for proving what you already know, or for setting forth your
knowledge in the most systematic way. Think for a moment about traditional

Euclidean geometry. On the first page of a geometry book (at least this was so when I went to school), you find definitions, axioms, and postulates. These are the simplest, or the most fundamental part of the geometric theory, but they are hardly the first things that a real mathematician would think up if she were doing geometry. Then come the theorems, each one neatly set forth, step by step, from the axioms or previously proved theorems down to what is to be proved, Q.E.D. That may be the way Euclid rearranged his proofs once he had thought them up, but it surely is not the way he discovered them! Most likely, when he wanted to prove something (say, the theorem that the line bisecting the apex of an isosceles triangle is perpendicular to the base), he drew a diagram, fiddled around with the lines, looked to see whether there was anything that was equal to anything else, and worked his way up from the conclusion and down from the premises, until the proof finally fell into place. So his *method of inquiry*—his way of finding something out—was very different from his method of proof or exposition. Descartes' rules for the mind are obviously intended as guides for someone who is trying to solve a problem or analyze a phenomenon. In other words (and this is going to turn out to be very important indeed), he adopts the point of view of someone who does not yet know anything but is trying by the use of his or her intelligence to discover something, rather than the point of view of a teacher or an expert who is quite sure he or she knows something and is simply trying to explain it to someone else.

Second, Descartes' method is a method of doubt. His first rule is "to accept nothing as true which I do not clearly recognize to be so." Just how radical this rule will be depends on how we interpret the phrase "clearly recognize." If Descartes merely wants us to stop and think before we say we are sure, as a quiz show contestant might pause before answering the jackpot question, then obviously that rule is not going to produce any great intellectual revolution. But as you shall see in a few pages, when you read part of the *Meditations on First Philosophy,* Descartes had much more in mind. When he tells us not to accept anything unless we can "clearly recognize" it as true, he means that we should refuse to accept anything, however sure we once were of it, however many people believe it, however obvious it seems, unless we can be *absolutely certain that it is 100 percent right.* If there is the slightest, the wildest, the farthest-out chance that it just might be false, then we are not to accept it.

Now that opens up quite a can of worms! For example, I am quite sure that Washington, D.C., is the capital of the United States of America. If you ask me how I can be so sure, I will tell you that I have read it in history and government books, that I have heard Washington referred to a thousand times on television as "our nation's capital," that I have visited Washington and actually sat for a day in the visitors' gallery of the Senate, and so forth. But does that make it absolutely, 100 percent certain? Could I not be wrong? It is not likely that I am wrong, but is it logically possible? Maybe the books were wrong; maybe the television commentators were wrong; maybe I was actually in Philadelphia when I thought I was in Washington; indeed, maybe there is a great conspiracy afoot to fool me into thinking that Washington is the capital. I can not imagine why anyone would go to all that trouble, but it *is* possible. Put it this way: I could write a science fiction story about such a conspiracy; and although you might say it was not very plausible, you could not say that the story was a total impossibility.

Well, you protest, if Descartes is going to interpret "clearly recognize" like that, then just about everything anyone has ever believed will go out the window! I might as well doubt that there is even a United States, or an earth, or a human race, or space and time and the universe. If I am going to refuse to accept things like that, then maybe I ought to start doubting that two plus two is four. After all, if a giant conspiracy might be underway to trick me into believing that Washington is the capital of the United States, then maybe some mysterious, evil, powerful demon is reaching into my mind and tricking me into thinking that two plus two is four when really it is five. Maybe every time I take two objects and place them next to two more, that demon sneaks one of them away, so that as I count them up, I get only four instead of five, which is the right number.

Strange as it may sound, this is just what Descartes has in mind. When he says accept *nothing* that is not certain, he means *nothing*. But, you object, that is madness! We have to start somewhere. Why, if I am going to doubt everything that has even the most minute bit of possible uncertainty attached to it, then I might even have to doubt my own existence. Perhaps I do not exist either; maybe that evil demon is fooling me about myself as well as about simple arithmetic. No, says Descartes, with one of the most dramatic reversals in all philosophical literature. Doubt all else, but you cannot doubt your own existence. That, and nothing but that, is the true foundation, the unshakable first principle, the rock on which all the rest of your knowledge shall be raised up. How does he manage to prove that I cannot rationally doubt my own existence, when he has erected a standard of certainty so strict that literally everything else that I have ever believed fails to meet it? You shall see when you read the *Meditations*. I do not want to spoil the effect of the argument by giving it away. Descartes' proof of his own existence is one of the high points in the history of philosophy. It is also, in a way, the high point of unbridled individualism in Western civilization. Imagine a philosopher who proposes to base the entire edifice of scientific, mathematical, and religious knowledge *not* on the collective learning and wisdom of humanity, *not* on the evidence of the laboratory, *not* on the existence of God, *not even* on the first principles of logic, *but simply on the fact of his own existence!*

When the method of inquiry is combined with the method of doubt, a transformation in the central nature of philosophy is begun. That transformation, which I am calling the epistemological turn, took a century and a half to complete. Not until Kant's *Critique of Pure Reason* was the epistemological turn brought to its end; thereafter, all philosophy was so changed that the very questions philosophers asked, as well as the answers they gave, looked little like what was written before the *Meditations*. The epistemological turn is a very simple, but tricky, notion. Even after you have it, you find it slipping away from you. Like Einstein's notion of relativity, or a Picasso painting, it makes you see familiar things in an entirely new way.

The heart of the *epistemological turn* is a simple reversal in order of two basic questions. From the ancient pre-Socratic cosmologists up to the time of Descartes, philosophers put questions about what exists, about the nature of the universe, before questions about what I can know to exist, about what I can know the nature of the universe to be. That is to say, philosophers considered questions of *being* to take precedence over questions of *knowing*. Aristotle, for example, called the essays in which he discussed questions of being "essays on first philosophy." He did not mean that these very difficult, abstract essays were the first sorts of philosophy a student should read. He meant that questions about the nature of being were the logically first, most fundamental, or most basic questions to be dealt with.

To be sure, Aristotle and many of his predecessors and followers discussed the nature of knowledge. They talked about the nature of the mind, the role of the senses (sight, hearing, touch, and so forth) in knowledge, the role of reasoning, the limits of human knowledge, and countless other topics. But they considered these *epistemological* questions to be secondary, less important than questions about the nature of God, the reality of space and time, and all of the other topics dealt with in "first philosophy," or as we call it today, metaphysics. So we can sum up philosophy prior to Descartes by saying that in it, *metaphysics took precedence over epistemology.*

Descartes' two methods—the method of inquiry and the method of doubt—had the effect of reversing this order of precedence. Properly understood and carried out with a consistency and rigor that Descartes himself never achieved, these two methods forced philosophers to set aside questions of being until they had dealt with the questions of knowing. And that fact in turn changed the meaning of the questions about being, so that by the time the revolution begun by Descartes had run its course, old-style metaphysics was finished, and new-style epistemology had taken its place as "first philosophy." Let us see how Descartes' two methods began this transformation.

First, as we have noted, the method of inquiry tells us to adopt the point of view of someone who is ignorant but is trying to learn, rather than the point of view of someone who knows something and is trying to explain. What is more, it teaches us to take questions in an orderly manner, not moving on to the next until we have settled the first. There is an old case in the English common law, going back to the Middle Ages, which illustrates the hidden force of Descartes' rule. Jones sued Smith for damages, claiming that Smith had borrowed a water jug from him and had returned it broken. Smith's defense was a classic of what we now call "stonewalling." "First," he argued, "the jug does not exist; second, I didn't borrow it; third, it was whole when I returned it; and fourth, it was cracked when I borrowed it." Smith was not out of his mind. He was simply saying to Jones, "Before I am going to pay you any money, you are going to have to prove every single item in your story. You must prove that the jug even exists; then you must prove that I borrowed it; then you must prove that I didn't return it whole; and then you must prove that it wasn't cracked when I borrowed it, but was cracked when I returned it." Now the legal point of this story is that proving one of these points might be a good deal harder than proving another, and Jones must prove them all in order to collect damages. If he threw the jug away after it was returned broken, then he may have trouble proving that it ever existed. Even if he kept the pieces, he may have trouble proving that it was not already cracked when he lent it to Smith. And so on. When the defense in a court case agrees not to dispute some assertion by the prosecution about the facts of the case, it is called "stipulating." Descartes' first rule tells us not to stipulate anything.

For example, at the beginning of his book entitled *Physics,* Aristotle says that the subject matter of physics is motion, or rather things in motion. If anyone wants to deny that there is motion in the world (as some philosophers in fact had denied), then a book on physics is not the right place to argue with him or her. "We physicists," Aristotle writes, "must take for granted that the things that exist by nature are, either all or some of them, in motion. . . . No man of science is bound to solve every kind of difficulty that may be raised, but only as many as are drawn falsely from the principles of the science." But Descartes adopts the opposite view. Before we can do physics, we must prove that there are bodies in motion in space. Once we have established that, we can appeal to the experiments and observations, deductions and proofs, which scientists have developed in their study of nature. But until we have shown that nature exists—until we have, like Jones, proved that there is a jug—we must set aside such investigations. We shall not stipulate the universe.

The second half of Descartes' method—the method of doubt—makes things ten times worse, of course. Having refused to stipulate anything, even the existence of the world, Descartes now insists that the standard of proof be absolute certainty. In a court of law, the jury is asked whether the case has been proved "beyond a reasonable doubt." There is a whole lot of difference between absolute certainty and beyond a reasonable doubt. I am pretty sure that my car will not turn into a boa constrictor and squeeze me to death while I am putting on my seat belt. I am sure enough of it to bet my life on it every day when I drive somewhere. My conviction goes way beyond any reasonable doubt. But if Descartes asks me whether I can be *certain* that my car will not turn into a boa, I must answer that of course I cannot rule it out as absolutely impossible. I can, after all, imagine some weird planet across the galaxy in which cars turn into boa constrictors. In a way, that is not much stranger than the fact that caterpillars turn into butterflies.

Method of doubt ∨
method of
  inquiry

Combining the two methods seems to drive us into the corner that philosophers call "**Epistemological skepticism.**" If we cannot move on to point B until we have proved point A, and if in order to prove point A we must establish it with absolute certainty, then it looks as though we will have a very hard time proving any point at all. Instead of wandering all over the universe, studying the stars, the planets, the origins of life, the workings of the human body, the laws of society, or the movement of the tides, we are going to be huddled in a corner, trying to figure out how to take step A, so that we can take step B.

Now, if your car is working, you go on trips and look at the scenery. But if your car will not run, you open the hood and inspect the motor. So too, if your logical engine is in good working order, then you cruise through the world of knowledge, looking at one interesting field after another; but if your logical engine breaks down—if your rules of inquiry and proof do not permit you to move with ease from one truth to another—then you stop, raise the lid on your mind (which is, after all, your logical engine), and take a good hard look to see what is wrong. In short, you start analyzing and examining the process by which you come to know anything. Epistemology is the study of the way in which we know, the rules by which we reason, the limits of what we can know, and the criteria or standards we use for judging whether a supposed piece of knowledge really is knowledge. If we follow Descartes' rule, we cannot take a scientific or metaphysical trip through the universe until we have checked out our means of transportation—our knowing process itself— and made sure that it will take us where we want to go.

Descartes himself never realized the full magnitude of the revolution that his two methods were to produce. He thought of himself as laying the basis for a new, unified system of scientific knowledge, free of all reliance on tradition, the wisdom of the ancients, or the old concepts of Aristotelian metaphysics. But he seems still to have supposed that questions of being would take precedence over questions of knowing. In the *Meditations,* after the section that you are about to read, he went on to offer "proofs" for the existence of God, of the physical universe, and of all the other things he had so carefully doubted at the beginning of the essay. It remained for later philosophers, both on the continent of Europe and in Great Britain, to draw out the deeper implications of the process that Descartes started.

Here now are selections from the First and Second Meditations.

Epistemological Skepticism   The doctrine that no adequate justification can be given for any of our beliefs about the world, not even for apparently rock-solid beliefs that there is a physical world, that I have a body, that the sun will rise tomorrow, or that fire causes heat. The aim of epistemological skepticism is to focus our attention on the relationship between our beliefs and their justification, not actually to get us to stop believing.

Meditation I

It is now some years since I detected how many were the false beliefs that I had from my earliest youth admitted as true and how doubtful was everything I had since constructed on this basis; and from that time I was convinced that I must once and for all seriously undertake to rid myself of all the opinions which I had formerly accepted, and commence to build anew from the foundation, if I wanted to establish any firm and permanent structure in the sciences.

Now for this object it is not necessary that I should show that all of these are false—I shall perhaps never arrive at this end. But inasmuch as reason already persuades me that I ought no less carefully to withhold my assent from matters which are not entirely certain and indubitable than from those which appear to me manifestly to be false, if I am able to find in each one some reason to doubt, this will suffice to justify my rejecting the whole. And for that end it will not be requisite that I should examine each in particular, which would be an endless undertaking; for owing to the fact that the destruction of the foundations of necessity brings with it the downfall of the rest of the edifice, I shall only in the first place attack those principles upon which all my former opinions rested.

All that up to the present time I have accepted as most true and certain I have learned either from the senses or through the senses; but it is sometimes proved to me that these senses are deceptive, and it is wiser not to trust entirely to any thing by which we have once been deceived.

But it may be that although the senses sometimes deceive us concerning things which are hardly perceptible, or very far away, there are yet many others to be met with as to which we cannot reasonably have any doubt, although we recognize them by their means. For example, there is the fact that I am here, seated by the fire, attired in a dressing gown, having this paper in my hands and other similar matters. And how could I deny these hands and this body are mine, were it not perhaps that I compare myself to certain persons, devoid of sense, whose cerebella are so troubled and clouded by the violent vapours of black bile, that they constantly assure us that they think they are kings when they are really quite poor, or that they are clothed in purple when they are really without covering, or who imagine that they have an earthenware head or are nothing but pumpkins or are made of glass. But they are mad, and I should not be any the less insane were I to follow examples so extravagant.

At the same time I must remember that I am a man, and that consequently I am in the habit of sleeping, and in my dreams representing to myself the same things or sometimes even less probable things, than do those who are insane in their waking moments. How often has it happened to me that in the night I dreamt that I found

RENÉ DESCARTES,
Meditations on First Philosophy

myself in this particular place, that I was dressed and seated near the fire, whilst in reality I was lying undressed in bed! At this moment it does indeed seem to me that it is with eyes awake that I am looking at this paper, that this head which I move is not asleep, that it is deliberately and of set purpose that I extend my hand and perceive it; what happens in sleep does not appear so clear nor so distinct as does all this. But in thinking over this I remind myself that on many occasions I have in sleep been deceived by similar illusions, and in dwelling carefully on this reflection I see so manifestly that there are no certain indications by which we may clearly distinguish wakefulness from sleep that I am lost in astonishment. And my astonishment is such that it is almost capable of persuading me that I now dream.

Now let us assume that we are asleep and that all these particulars, e.g. that we open our eyes, shake our head, extend our hands, and so on, are but false delusions; and let us reflect that possibly neither our hands nor our whole body are such as they appear to us to be. At the same time we must at least confess that the things which are represented to us in sleep are like painted representations which can only have been formed as the counterparts of something real and true, and that in this way those general things at least, i.e. eyes, a head, hands, and a whole body, are not imaginary things, but things really existent. For, as a matter of fact, painters, even when they study with the greatest skill to represent sirens and satyrs by forms the most strange and extraordinary, cannot give them natures which are entirely new, but merely make a certain medley of the members of different animals; or if their imagination is extravagant enough to invent something so novel that nothing similar has ever before been seen, and that then their work represents a thing purely fictitious and absolutely false, it is certain all the same that the colours of which this is composed are necessarily real. And for the same reason, although these general things, to wit, [a body,] eyes, a head, hands, and such like, may be imaginary, we are bound at the same time to confess that there are at least some other objects yet more simple and more universal, which are real and true; and of these just in the same way as with certain real colours, all these images of things which dwell in our thoughts, whether true and real or false and fantastic, are formed.

To such a class of things pertains corporeal nature in general, and its extension, the figure of extended things, their quantity or magnitude and number, as also the place in which they are, the time which measures their duration, and so on.

That is possibly why our reasoning is not unjust when we conclude from this that Physics, Astronomy, Medicine, and all other sciences which have as their end the consideration of composite things, are very dubious and uncertain; but with Arithmetic, Geometry, and other sciences of that kind which only treat of things that are very simple and very general, without taking great trouble to ascertain whether they are actually existent or not, contain some measure of certainty and an element of the indubitable. For whether I am awake or asleep, two and three together always form five, and the square can never have more than four sides, and it does not seem possible that truths so clear and apparent can be suspected of any falsity [or uncertainty].

Nevertheless I have long had fixed in my mind the belief that an all-powerful God existed by whom I have been created such as I am. But how do I know that He has not brought it to pass that there is no earth, no heaven, no extended body, no magnitude, no place, and that nevertheless [I possess the perceptions of all these things and that] they seem to me to exist just exactly as I now see them? And, besides, as I sometimes imagine that others deceive themselves in the things which they think they know best, how do I know that I am not deceived every time that I add two and three, or count the sides of a square, or judge of things yet simpler, if anything simpler can be imagined? But possibly God has not desired that I should be thus deceived, for He is said to be supremely good. If, however, it is contrary to His goodness to have made me such that I constantly deceive myself, it would also appear to be contrary to His goodness to permit me to be sometimes deceived, and nevertheless I cannot doubt that He does permit this.

I shall then suppose, not that God who is supremely good and the fountain of truth, but some evil genius not less powerful than deceitful, has employed his whole energies in deceiving me; I shall consider that the heavens, the earth, colours, figures, sound, and all other external things are nought but the illusions and dreams of which this genius has availed himself in order to lay traps for my credulity; I shall consider myself as having no hands, no eyes, no flesh, no blood, nor any senses, yet falsely believing myself to possess all these things; I shall remain obstinately attached to this idea, and if by this means it is not in my power to arrive at the knowledge of any truth, I may at least do what is in my power [i.e. suspend my judgment], and with firm purpose avoid giving credence to any false thing, or being imposed upon by this arch deceiver, however powerful and deceptive he may be. . . .

Meditation II
The Meditation of yesterday filled my mind with so many doubts that it is no longer in my power to forget them. And yet I do not see in what manner I can resolve them; and, just as if I had all of a sudden fallen into very deep water, I am so disconcerted that I can neither

make certain of setting my feet on the bottom, nor can I swim and so support myself on the surface. I shall nevertheless make an effort and follow anew the same path as that on which I yesterday entered, i.e. I shall proceed by setting aside all that in which the least doubt could be supposed to exist, just as if I had discovered that it was absolutely false; and I shall ever follow in this road until I have met with something which is certain, or at least, if I can do nothing else, until I have learned for certain that there is nothing in the world that is certain. Archimedes, in order that he might draw the terrestrial globe out of its place, and transport it elsewhere, demanded only that one point should be fixed and immoveable; in the same way I shall have the right to conceive high hopes if I am happy enough to discover one thing only which is certain and indubitable.

I suppose, then, that all the things that I see are false; I persuade myself that nothing has ever existed of all that my fallacious memory represents to me. I consider that I possess no senses; I imagine that body, figure, extension, movement and place are but the fictions of my mind. What, then, can be esteemed as true? Perhaps nothing at all, unless that there is nothing in the world that is certain.

But how can I know there is not something different from those things that I have just considered, of which one cannot have the slightest doubt? Is there not some God, or some other being by whatever name we call it, who puts these reflections into my mind? That is not necessary, for is it not possible that I am capable of producing them myself? I myself, am I not at least something? But I have already denied that I had senses and body. Yet I hesitate, for what follows from that? Am I so dependent on body and senses that I cannot exist without these? But I was persuaded that there was nothing in all the world, that there was no heaven, no earth, that there were no minds, nor any bodies: was I not then likewise persuaded that I did not exist? Not at all; of a surety I myself did exist since I persuaded myself of something [or merely because I thought of something]. But there is some deceiver or other, very powerful and very cunning, who ever employs his ingenuity in deceiving me. Then without doubt I exist also if he deceives me, and let him deceive me as much as he will, he can never cause me to be nothing so long as I think that I am something. So that after having reflected well and carefully examined all things, we must come to the definite conclusion that this proposition: I am, I exist, is necessarily true each time that I pronounce it, or that I mentally conceive it.

But I do not yet know clearly enough what I am, I who am certain that I am; and hence I must be careful to see that I do not imprudently take some other object in place of myself, and thus that I do not go astray in respect of this knowledge that I hold to be the most certain and most evident of all that I have formerly learned.

That is why I shall now consider anew what I believed myself to be before I embarked upon these last reflections; and of my former opinions I shall withdraw all that might even in a small degree be invalidated by the reasons which I have just brought forward, in order that there may be nothing at all left beyond what is absolutely certain and indubitable.

René Descartes, *Meditations on First Philosophy,* Meditations I–VI

Rationalism and Empiricism: Two Responses to Cartesian Doubt

When Descartes summarized his proof for his own existence in Latin, he used the phrase *Cogito, ergo sum,* which means "I think, therefore I am." So his proof has come to be known in philosophical shorthand as the Cogito Argument. If you read the selection from the *Meditations* carefully, you will realize that "I think, therefore I am" is not exactly what Descartes says. Instead, he says something slightly but very significantly different, namely, "The proposition, I exist, is necessarily true each time I pronounce it." Pronouncing or asserting the proposition is crucial, because it is the asserting that guarantees its truth. The point is that if the proposition is being *asserted,* then someone must be doing the asserting, and if I am asserting it, then that someone must be me. Needless to say, I cannot use this proof to establish the existence of anyone else. Suppose, for example, that I try to prove my wife's existence by saying, "The proposition, She exists, is necessarily true each time I pronounce it." Well, that just will not work. The fact that I pronounce or assert that she exists in no way guarantees that she does. But it does guarantee that I exist! In fact, my asserting any proposition, true or false, about myself or about anything else, guarantees that I exist, because I am the subject, the asserter, the conscious thinker of the proposition. And—this is the key point—assertions cannot simply hang in midair with no one asserting them. When a proposition is asserted, it must be asserted *by* someone.

Incidentally, I hope you realize that Descartes' Cogito Argument only proves his existence to him; it does not prove his existence to you or to me. "The proposition, Descartes exists, is necessarily true each time I pronounce it" does not hold water at all. Descartes can use his new argument to prove his existence to himself, I can use his argument to prove my existence to myself, and each of you can use his argument to prove your own existence to yourself. But no one can use the argument to prove someone else's existence. This fact about the Cogito Argument has two important consequences for subsequent epistemology. First, it drives each philosopher into the position called **solipsism;** that is, the individual subject knows its own existence prior to, and better than, anything else and perhaps knows the existence of nothing but itself. Second, it turns the attention of philosophers away from the *objects* of knowledge, the things that we know about, and toward the *subject* of knowledge, the mind that does the knowing. Later in this chapter, we shall see that this pair of implications of the Cogito Argument is used by Kant in his effort to find a way out of the skepticism and solipsism of the Cartesian position.

Descartes got himself, and us, into the skeptical solipsist box in the First Meditation by doubting everything that was not known with certainty. He proceeded, you will recall, by adopting a criterion of certainty so strict that in the end, nothing, save the assertion of his own existence, could meet its requirements. In surveying the multitude of his beliefs, furthermore, Descartes divided them into two major groups: those which he thought he knew on the basis of the evidence of his own senses and those which he thought he knew on the basis of reasoning with general concepts. In this way, two central problems are raised by the argument in the First Meditation. The first is the problem of *certainty.* What criterion of truth should we adopt as the standard against which to measure our various knowledge claims? The second is the problem of the sources of knowledge. Insofar as we know anything, is our knowledge based upon the evidence of the senses, upon abstract reasoning, or upon some combination of the two? The philosophy of the 150 years following the publication of the *Meditations* was very largely a series of variations on these two themes.

Descartes himself offered preliminary answers to the questions of certainty and the sources of knowledge in the latter part of the Second Meditation. Before taking our leave of him and moving on to survey the attempts of his successors to deal with the problems he raised, perhaps we should see what he had to say about them. On the problem of certainty, he offered two criteria, two tests of the certainty of an assertion. Here is what he says:

> I am certain that I am a thing which thinks; but do I not then likewise know what is requisite to render me certain of a truth? Certainly in this first knowledge there is nothing that assures me of its truth, excepting the clear and distinct perception of that which I state, which would not indeed suffice to assure me that what I say is true, if it could ever happen that a thing which I conceived so clearly and distinctly could be false; and accordingly it seems to me that already I can establish as a general rule that all things which I perceive very clearly and very distinctly are true.

Solipsism   Literally, the belief that I am the only person in the universe. Somewhat more generally, solipsism is an extreme form of epistemological skepticism that refuses to acknowledge the existence of anything other than my own mind. Some philosophers have even argued that I cannot be sure of anything but my own mind *right now,* since my memories might also be mistaken.

Clearness and distinctness are not much as a hedge against the far-reaching skepticism fostered by the method of doubt. How can I be sure that I really perceive a proposition clearly or distinctly? It is no good saying that it really, truly *seems* clear and distinct to me. After all, it really, truly seems to me that I am awake, but as Descartes himself pointed out, I might nonetheless be mistaken. Later on, after using the clearness and distinctness test to prove the existence of God, Descartes turns around and uses the goodness of God as a proof that clearness and distinctness are adequate criteria of certainty. A good God, he argues, would not deceive me. Well, that is about as obvious a case of arguing in a circle as you will find in the writings of great philosophers, and I think we can agree that having posed the problem of certainty, Descartes did not really have a solution to it.

As for the sources of our knowledge, Descartes came down foursquare on the side of reason rather than the senses. That is what you would expect from someone whose dream it was to create a mathematical physics. In place of observation and the collecting of data from sight, smell, hearing, and touch, Descartes wanted a universal system of science derived from logical and mathematical premises and proved by rigorous deduction.

In order to persuade his readers of the primacy of reason in our acquiring of knowledge, Descartes uses what is called a "thought experiment." That is, he asks us to imagine with him a situation—in this case, that he is sitting near his fire with a piece of wax in his hand—and then he tries to get us to see, through an analysis of the situation, that our methods of reasoning or of acquiring knowledge must have a certain character. Philosophers frequently argue in this way when they are trying to establish some general proposition rather than to prove a particular fact. The thought experiment is not supposed to be evidence, in the modern scientific sense. Rather, it is merely a device for exploring the logical or conceptual relationships between different ideas. Here is Descartes' thought experiment to show that our knowledge comes from understanding or reason or the mind, rather than through the senses.

Let us begin by considering the commonest matters, those which we believe to be the most distinctly comprehended, to wit, the bodies which we touch and see; not indeed bodies in general, for these general ideas are usually a little more confused, but let us consider one body in particular. Let us take, for example, this piece of wax: it has been taken quite freshly from the hive, and it has not yet lost the sweetness of the honey which it contains; it still retains somewhat of the odour of the flowers from which it has been culled; its colour, its figure, its size are apparent; it is hard, cold, easily handled, and if you strike it with the finger, it will emit a sound. Finally all the things

RENÉ DESCARTES,
Meditations on First Philosophy

which are requisite to cause us distinctly to recognize a body, are met with in it. But notice that while I speak and approach the fire what remained of the taste is exhaled, the smell evaporates, the colour alters, the figure is destroyed, the size increases, it becomes liquid, it heats, scarcely can one handle it, and when one strikes it, no sound is emitted. Does the same wax remain after this change? We must confess that it remains; none would judge otherwise. What then did I know so distinctly in this piece of wax? It could certainly be nothing of all that the senses brought to my notice, since all these things which fall under taste, smell, sight, touch, and hearing, are found to be changed, and yet the same wax remains.

Perhaps it was what I now think, viz. that this wax was not that sweetness of honey, nor that agreeable scent of flowers, nor that particular whiteness, nor that figure, nor that sound, but simply a body which a little while before appeared to me as perceptible under these forms, and which is now perceptible under others. But what, precisely, is it that I imagine when I form such conceptions? Let us attentively consider this, and, abstracting from all that does not belong to the wax, let us see what remains. Certainly nothing remains excepting a certain extended thing which is flexible and movable. But what is the meaning of flexible and movable? Is it not that I imagine that this piece of wax being round is capable of becoming square and of passing from a square to a triangular figure? No, certainly it is not that, since I imagine it admits of an infinitude of similar changes, and I nevertheless do not know how to compass the infinitude by my imagination, and consequently this conception which I have of the wax is not brought about by the faculty of imagination. What now is this extension? Is it not also unknown? For it becomes greater when the wax is melted, greater when it is boiled, and greater still when the heat increases, and I should not conceive [clearly] according to truth what wax is, if I did not think that even this piece that we are considering is capable of receiving more variations in extension than I have ever imagined. We must then grant that I could not even understand through the imagination what this piece of wax is, and that it is my mind alone which perceives it. I say this piece of wax in particular, for as to wax in general it is yet clearer. But what is this piece of wax which cannot be understood excepting by the [understanding or] mind? It is certainly the same that I see, touch, imagine, and finally it is the same which I have always believed it to be from the beginning. But what must particularly be observed is that its perception is neither an act of vision, nor of touch, nor of imagination, and has never been such although it may have appeared formerly to be so, but only an intuition of the mind, which may be imperfect and confused as it was formerly, or clear and distinct as it is at present according as my attention is

René Descartes, *Meditations on First Philosophy,* Meditations I–VI more or less directed to the elements which are found in it, and of which it is composed.

The debate over Descartes' problems soon resolved itself into a conflict between two more or less unified schools of thought, the Continental rationalists and the British empiricists. (Since this makes it sound a bit like an international soccer match, let me explain that those are labels we put on the two groups today; they themselves did not go about wearing T-shirts saying "Continental Rationalist" or "British Empiricist.") The rationalists accepted Descartes' demand for certainty, agreed with his view that logic and mathematics were the model for all true knowledge, and sought to discover ways of establishing the principal propositions of science and metaphysics with as much certainty as the truths of the syllogism or geometry possessed. They sought proofs for the existence of God; they offered demonstrations of the fundamental principles of the new physics; and they pursued Descartes' dream of a universal system of knowledge. Like Descartes, they downgraded the senses as a source of knowledge and instead claimed that all valid knowledge claims must rest upon the operations of reason.

The empiricists also accepted Descartes' demand for certainty, but in progressively more sweeping attacks on the knowledge claims of the rationalists, they argued that nothing could meet that demand. David Hume, the most brilliant and thoroughgoing of the empiricists, produced devastating proofs that neither the theorems of science nor the beliefs of common sense could possibly qualify as knowledge when measured against Descartes' own standard of certainty.

The empiricists also challenged the rationalists' reliance upon reason as the sole source of knowledge. First John Locke, in his *Essay Concerning the Human Understanding,* and then Hume, in *A Treatise of Human Nature,* insisted that all the ideas in the human mind must ultimately be derived from the sights, sounds, smells, feels, and tastes of our sense organs. Reason, they argued, could do no more than rearrange and sort the materials provided to the mind by sensation. This subordination of reason to the senses was one of the most powerful weapons in the empiricists' assault on the systems of science and metaphysics erected by the rationalists.

If you have managed to follow our discussion of epistemology thus far, it should be obvious to you that there is much more to be discussed in the theory of knowledge than we can hope to touch on in the remainder of this chapter. Rather than mentioning everyone and everything without explaining anything, therefore, I shall limit myself to *three* areas. First we shall take a brief look at Gottfried Leibniz's attempt to deal with the criteria of certainty and his very important distinction between what he calls truths of reasoning and truths of fact. Then we shall examine David Hume's attempt to reduce all of the contents of the mind to data of the senses and his analysis of the criterion of certainty so that we can understand the full force of his skeptical attack on the claims of science and common sense. And finally I will try to explain how Immanuel Kant sought to overcome the division between the rationalists and the empiricists by compromising their dispute over the sources of knowledge and the criteria of certainty. If you can get all that under your belt, then you will have had quite enough philosophy for one chapter!

Leibniz and Rationalism

Descartes' tests of certainty were clearness and distinctness. These essentially psychological criteria tell us very little about the structure of knowledge, about the kinds of knowledge claims that can meet the test of certainty and the kinds that cannot. After all, any belief might, upon inspection, turn out to be conceived clearly and distinctly, or at least it might seem to be. I think I clearly and distinctly apprehend that two things added to two things make a total of four things; but I also think I clearly and distinctly apprehend that I am seated now at a desk in my office, with a computer in front of me and a chair under me.

In place of Descartes' psychological tests, Leibniz offered logical criteria of truth and certainty. All truths, he proposed, could be divided into two sorts. The first are truths that can be known merely by application of a fundamental principle of logic, called the *law of contradiction*. When we state some truth, we do so by making an assertion: "Two plus two equals four" is an assertion; "Washington, D.C., is the capital of the United States" is an assertion; "$E = mc^2$" is an assertion. Any declarative statement in its ordinary usage makes an assertion. If I have one assertion, I can make another, opposite assertion simply by denying the first. So from "Two plus two equals four," I can make "It is not the case that two plus two equals four." From "Washington, D.C., is the capital of the United States," I can make "It is not the case that Washington, D.C., is the capital of the United States." The denial of an assertion is called *negation,* and since "It is not the case that" is a little clumsy to keep repeating, philosophers and logicians shorten it to "not." The negation of "Two plus two equals four" would thus be "Not two plus two equals four," and so on.

If you think about it for a moment, you will see that a statement and its negation cannot both be true. Maybe Washington is our capital—maybe it is not—but there is just no way that it can both be and not be our capital. Logicians express this in very general form by saying that for any statement, it cannot be the case that both the statement and its negation are true. Because two statements are said to "contradict" one another if they cannot both be true, this general principle about statements and their negations is called the **law of contradiction.** There is another law of logic that usually goes along with the law of contradiction, according to which for any statement, either it is true or else its negation is true. There is no third possibility, no middle ground. This law is called the **law of the excluded middle.** So logic teaches us that no matter what statement we are thinking about, either it is true or its negation is true, but not both.

According to Leibniz, truths of reasoning are those statements that we can know to be true merely by using the law of contradiction (and the law of the excluded middle, although he does not mention it). For example, suppose a fast-talking door-to-door salesman tries to push a fifteen-volume encyclopedia on you. "This encyclopedia is absolutely free," he says, "You only pay ten dollars per volume." Now you don't have to know anything about encyclopedias to be certain that he is not telling you the truth. All you have to do is whip out your trusty law of contradiction and perform the following process of reasoning:

❚ Number one, you say this encyclopedia is absolutely free.
❚ Number two, you say I must pay ten dollars per volume for it.
❚ But "free" means "I don't have to pay."
❚ So you are saying that I don't have to pay, and I do have to pay.
❚ Or, as we logicians put it, I do have to pay and not I do have to pay.
❚ And that violates the law of contradiction, so it must be false. What is more, with a quick application of the law of the excluded middle, I can draw the absolutely certain conclusion that,
❚ Either I have to pay or I do not have to pay, so stop the fast talk and tell me which it is.

Truths of reasoning are nice, because we can know them to be certain merely by application of these two simple laws, but they leave a good deal to be desired. Thus, my bit of reasoning does not tell me whether I have to pay, it just tells me that either I have to or I do not, but not both. Truths that cannot be certified by appeal to the laws of logic are called truths of fact by Leibniz. They include most of what we ordinarily call *knowledge*. To establish their truth, we must appeal to a quite different principle, which Leibniz labeled the principle of sufficient reason. Here is the passage from his short summary work, *The Monadology,* in which he defined and distinguished the two sorts of truths.

The Law of Contradiction and the Law of the Excluded Middle   The two basic laws of formal logic. The *Law of Contradiction* states that a statement and its contradictory cannot both be true. For example, the statement, "Fire is hot" may be true, and it may be false. Its contradictory, "It is not the case that fire is hot" may be true, and it may be false. But it cannot be that *both* the statement *and* its contradictory are true. The *Law of the Excluded Middle* says that for any statement, either it is true or its contradictory is true. Thus, either fire is hot, or it is not the case that fire is hot.

**GOTTFRIED
LEIBNIZ,**
The Monadology

Our reasoning is based upon two great principles: first, that of Contradiction, by means of which we decide that to be false which involves contradiction and that to be true which contradicts or is opposed to the false.

And second, the principle of Sufficient Reason, in virtue of which we believe that no fact can be real or existing and no statement true unless it has a sufficient reason why it should be thus and not otherwise. Most frequently, however, these reasons cannot be known by us.

There are also two kinds of Truths: those of Reasoning and those of Fact. The Truths of Reasoning are necessary, and their opposite is impossible. Those of Fact, however, are contingent, and their opposite is possible. When a truth is necessary, the reason can be found by analysis in resolving it into simpler ideas and into simpler truths until we reach those which are primary.

There are finally simple ideas of which no definition can be given. There are also the Axioms and Postulates or, in a word, the primary principles which cannot be proved and, indeed, have no need of proof. These are identical propositions whose opposites involve express contradictions.

But there must also be a sufficient reason for contingent truths or truths of fact; that is to say, for the sequence of the things which extend throughout the universe of created beings, where the analysis into more particular reasons can be continued into greater detail without limit because of the immense variety of the things in nature and because of the infinite division of bodies. There is an infinity of figures and of movements, present and past, which enter into the efficient cause of my present writing, and in its final cause there are an infinity of slight tendencies and dispositions of my soul, present and past.

And as all this detail again involves other and more detailed contingencies, each of which again has need of a similar analysis in order to find its explanation, no real advance has been made. Therefore, the sufficient or ultimate reason must needs be outside of the sequence or series of these details of contingencies, however infinite they may be.

It is thus that the ultimate reason for things must be a necessary substance, in which the detail of the changes shall be present merely potentially, as in the fountainhead, and this substance we call God.

As you can see, Leibniz thought that when it came to truths of fact, such as the laws of physics or the facts of history, we could only certify them by an indirect appeal to God. The skeptical opponents of the rationalists had very lit-

Valid Arguments	
1. Major Premise	All dogs are mammals.
Minor Premise	All poodles are dogs.
CONCLUSION	(Therefore) All poodles are mammals.
2. Major Premise	No freshmen are frat members.
Minor Premise	Some band members are freshmen.
CONCLUSION	(Therefore) Some band members are not frat members.

Invalid Arguments	
3. Major Premise	Some affectionate animals are cats.
Minor Premise	Some dogs are affectionate.
CONCLUSION	(Therefore) Some dogs are cats.
4. Major Premise	All marmalade is made from oranges.
Minor Premise	Some preserves are not marmalade.
CONCLUSION	(Therefore) Some preserves are made from oranges.

The first two arguments are "valid"—that means that the conclusion follows from the premises. Can you figure out why they are valid? The second two arguments are not valid. The conclusion does not follow from the premises (even though, in the fourth argument, the conclusion happens to be true). How can we tell whether an argument is valid or invalid?

tle faith in the proofs for the existence of God, so you can imagine that they were not much impressed by this sort of justification for scientific theories. (Hume's objections to some of those proofs appear in Chapter 8.)

Hume and Empiricism

The first major assault on the Continental rationalists was launched by the Englishman John Locke, whose theory of the social contract you will encounter in Chapter 6. Locke hit upon a simple but very powerful strategy for attacking the claims by Descartes and others that reason alone could provide us with knowledge. Instead of examining our knowledge claims directly, Locke suggested, let us instead ask from what source we derive the ideas which we use in stating these knowledge claims. Scientists and metaphysicians had been accustomed to express their theories by statements using terms like "matter," "space," "time," "substance," "cause," "necessary," "possible," "object," and "self." In addition, of course, they used more familiar terms like "red," "hard," "round," and "sweet." If our knowledge claims make any sense at all, Locke argued, then these words must correspond to ideas in our minds. Otherwise, we will simply seem to be saying something, but really we will not be asserting anything at all. (This is what humorists do when they write nonsense verse. Lewis Carroll, the author of *Alice in Wonderland,* wrote a poem that begins, "Twas brillig, and the slithy toves did gyre and gimble in the wabe." That sounds as though it ought to mean something, but it doesn't, because "words" like "brillig" and "toves" don't correspond to any ideas in our minds.)

According to Locke, the mind is a blank tablet or **tabula rasa** when we are born. He compares it to a piece of white paper on which experience writes. Here, from his *Essay Concerning the Human Understanding* (Book II, Chapter 1), is his statement of this famous doctrine:

> Let us then suppose the mind to be, as we say, white paper, void of all characters, without any ideas;—How comes it to be furnished? Whence comes it by that wide store which the busy and boundless fancy of man has painted on it with almost endless variety? Whence has it all the *materials* of reason and knowledge? To this I answer, in one word, EXPERIENCE. In that all our knowledge is founded; and from it ultimately derives itself.

John Locke, *Essay Concerning Human Understanding*

That doesn't sound like such a brilliant philosophical strategy when you first hear it. Indeed, it sounds positively obvious. But in the hands of Locke, of George Berkeley, and especially of David Hume, it turned out to be a crusher. To see why this is so, think for a moment about all of the statements that philosophers and theologians have asserted over the ages about God. Every one of those statements uses the idea of God somehow. For example, one statement is that God exists; a second is that God is omnipotent; a third is that God has promised us eternal life if only we will obey His laws; and so forth. If we follow Locke's suggestion, instead of asking directly what evidence there is for these statements, we will instead ask, "Is there an *idea* of God in our minds corresponding to the word 'God' which is used in each of the statements?" And following Locke's theory of the blank white paper, we will ask whether the idea of God has come to us through our eyes, our ears, our fingertips, our noses, or our other sense organs. As soon as you put the question that way, it is obvious that we could not have derived the idea of God from any sensory sources. God is supposed to be infinite, but we can only see, hear, feel, and taste finite things. God is supposed to be eternal, but we cannot see or hear or feel something that exists outside of time, or even something that exists in time forever and ever. God is supposed to be omnipotent, but the most our senses could ever show us is something very powerful, not something infinitely powerful. So it would seem to follow simply and directly from Locke's strategy that *we do not really have an idea of God at all!* We have the word "God" and we make up what we think are meaningful statements using it, but all that talk about God turns out to have no more meaning than Lewis Carroll's poem about slithy toves. (Incidentally, Locke himself did not draw his antireligious conclusion from his theory of ideas, and he would have been horrified by it.)

Since the last paragraph may have whipped by a bit fast, let us stop a moment and be sure that we understand what the argument is really saying. Lewis Carroll's poem is not *false;* it is *meaningless,* because it uses "words" that do not correspond to ideas in our minds and hence have no meaning. A statement has to mean something before we can ask whether it is true or false. Philosophical books are full of arguments about the truth or falsehood of various theological, metaphysical, and scientific theories. But Locke's attack cuts these arguments off at the knees. Before two philosophers can even begin to argue about the existence of God, they must show that their words have meaning. According to Locke, that means showing that the words correspond to ideas in our minds that have been derived from the senses. So by his strategy of looking to the sources of our ideas, together with his doctrine of the mind as a blank sheet of paper written on by experience, Locke shifted the whole debate into a new channel.

Locke's weapon, incidentally, is a double-edged sword. If the theory proves that we do not even have a coherent idea of God, then one possible conclusion is that all of our talk about God is nonsense, and all of our theories of religion meaningless. But another possible conclusion is that since his theory implies such a ridiculous notion, it must itself be false! It comes down to deciding which is harder to believe. If I do have an idea of God, then it cannot have come through my senses, so I am going to have to explain how the mind can acquire ideas that it does not derive from sense experience; on the other hand, if all of my ideas are derived from sense experience, then I cannot have an idea of God, so I am going to have to explain why so many apparently reasonable people firmly believe that they have such an idea, and why people who talk about God think they are making sense and not nonsense.

The empiricist who carried Locke's strategy to its logical conclusion was David Hume. As you will recall from Chapter 1, Hume conceived the plan, when still a very young man, of writing a full-scale theory of the human mind along the lines of Isaac Newton's enormously successful theory

Tabula Rasa   Literally, blank tablet. The term was used by John Locke to summarize his claim that the mind comes into life blank, or empty, and is written on by experience as though it were a clay or wax tablet waiting to be marked by a writing stylus. Locke was arguing against the widely held view that the mind comes to experience with ideas that are built into it (or "hardwired," as computer types like to say).

of the physical universe. In the very opening pages of *A Treatise of Human Nature,* Hume adopts Locke's strategy and stakes out his own version of the "white paper" principle. In the following selection, remember that Hume uses the word "perception" to mean any content of the mind. He then divides perceptions into those which come directly from our senses and those which we form from our impressions by copying, rearranging, and otherwise altering them.

DAVID HUME,

A Treatise of Human Nature

Perceptions: Impressions and Ideas

All the perceptions of the human mind resolve themselves into two distinct kinds, which I shall call IMPRESSIONS and IDEAS. The difference betwixt these consists in the degrees of force and liveliness with which they strike upon the mind and make their way into our thought or consciousness. Those perceptions, which enter with most force and violence, we may name *impressions;* and under this name I comprehend all our sensations, passions and emotions, as they make their first appearance in the soul. By *ideas* I mean the faint images of these in thinking and reasoning; such as, for instance, are all the perceptions excited by the present discourse, excepting only, those

G E O R G E   B E R K E L E Y

George Berkeley (1685–1753) was an Irish philosopher and cleric who is remembered as the defender of a philosophical position known as "idealism." Berkeley's most important philosophical works, including his *Treatise Concerning the Principles of Human Knowledge* and *Three Dialogues Between Hylas and Philonus,* were all written before his thirtieth birthday. Berkeley defended the view that the only things that could be known to exist are human minds, the ideas in these minds, and God. This doctrine is opposed to the view, defended by Hobbes and others, that physical bodies are the only things that exist ("materialism").

Berkeley spent three years in the New World, seeking to found a college in the Bermudas. Though his plans were never carried out, he did leave his philosophical library to the then recently founded Yale College in New Haven, Connecticut.

which arise from the sight and touch, and excepting the immediate pleasure or uneasiness it may occasion. I believe it will not be very necessary to employ many words in explaining this distinction. Every one of himself will readily perceive the difference betwixt feeling and thinking. The common degrees of these are easily distinguished; tho' it is not impossible but in particular instances they may very nearly approach to each other. Thus in sleep, and in fever, in madness, or in any very violent emotions of soul, our ideas may approach to our impressions: As on the other hand it sometimes happens, that our impressions are so faint and low, that we cannot distinguish them from our ideas. But notwithstanding this near resemblance in a few instances, they are in general so very different, that no-one can make a scruple to rank them under distinct heads, and assign to each a peculiar name to mark the difference.

There is another division of our perceptions, which it will be convenient to observe, and which extends itself both to our impressions and ideas. This division is into SIMPLE and COMPLEX. Simple perceptions or impressions and ideas are such as admit of no distinction nor separation. The complex are the contrary to these, and may be distinguished into parts. Tho' a particular colour, taste, and smell are qualities all united together in this apple, 'tis easy to perceive they are not the same, but are at least distinguishable from each other.

Having by these divisions given an order and arrangement to our objects, we may now apply ourselves to consider with the more accuracy their qualities and relations. The first circumstance, that strikes my eye, is the great resemblance betwixt our impressions and ideas in every other particular, except their degree of force and vivacity. The one seem to be in a manner the reflexion of the other, so that all the perceptions of the mind are double, and appear both as impressions and ideas. When I shut my eyes and think of my chamber, the ideas I form are exact representations of the impressions I felt; nor is there any circumstance of the one, which is not to be found in the other. In running over my other perceptions, I find still the same resemblance and representation. Ideas and impressions appear always to correspond to each other. This circumstance seems to me remarkable, and engages my attention for a moment.

Upon a more accurate survey I find I have been carried away too far by the first appearance, and that I must make use of the distinction of perceptions into *simple and complex,* to limit this general decision, *that all our ideas and impressions are resembling.* I observe, that many of our complex ideas never had impressions, that corresponded to them, and that many of our complex impressions never are exactly copied in ideas. I can imagine to myself such a city as the *New Jerusalem,* whose pavement is gold and walls are rubies, tho' I never saw any such. I have seen *Paris;* but shall I affirm I can form such an idea of that city, as will perfectly represent all its streets and houses in their real and just proportions?

I perceive, therefore, that tho' there is in general a great resemblance betwixt our complex impressions and ideas, yet the rule is not universally true, that they are exact copies of each other. We may next consider how the case stands with our simple perceptions. After the most accurate examination, of which I am capable, I venture to affirm, that the rule here holds without any exception, and that every simple idea has a simple impression, which resembles it; and every simple impression a correspondent idea. That idea of red, which we form in the dark, and that impression, which strikes our eyes in sunshine, differ only in degree, not in nature. That the case is the same with all our simple impressions and ideas, 'tis impossible to prove by a particular enumeration of them. Everyone may satisfy himself in this point by running over as many as he pleases. But if any one should deny this universal resemblance, I know no way of convincing him, but by desiring him to shew a simple impression that has not a correspondent idea, or a simple idea, that has not a correspondent impression. If he does not answer this challenge, as 'tis certain he cannot, we may from his silence and our own observation establish our conclusion.

Thus we find, that all simple ideas and impressions resemble each other; and as the complex are formed from them, we may affirm in general, that these two species of perception are exactly correspondent. Having discover'd this relation, which requires no farther examination, I am curious to find some other of their qualities. Let us consider how they stand with regard to their existence, and which of the impressions and ideas are causes, and which effects.

The *full* examination of this question is the subject of the present treatise; and therefore we shall here content ourselves with establishing one general proposition. *That all our simple ideas in their first appearance are deriv'd from simple impressions, which are correspondent to them, and which they exactly represent.*

David Hume,
Treatise on Human Nature

Hume's style is not nearly as technical or forbidding as that of Aristotle, Descartes, Leibniz, or Kant, but you must not be misled into supposing that his arguments are therefore less powerful. The few simple principles that he lays down in the opening pages of the *Treatise* turn out to be more than enough to destroy some of the most impressive systems built up by his philosophical predecessors. There are three key points to notice in the passage you have just read. The first, of course, is Hume's adoption of the "white paper" theory. The second is what is sometimes called the copy theory of ideas. According to Hume, all of our ideas are either straight copies of sense impressions or combinations and rearrangements of copies of sense impressions. When we are confronted with some metaphysical statement, therefore, we need not ask immediately whether it is true or false. Instead, we may simply examine the words in which it is expressed and ask whether they correspond to ideas in our minds. If we do have such ideas, then either they will be copies of sense impressions or they will be constructed out of copies of sense impressions by combinations and rearrangements. We have already seen what a blow this doctrine can be to the claim that we have an idea of God. The third important point is that Hume has an "atomic" theory of the contents of the mind. That is to say, he conceives of the mind as containing little indivisible "atomic" bits of sensation, plus indivisible copies of those bits of sensation, plus what we might call "molecular" combinations of atomic sensations. But unlike chemical molecules, the combinations of atomic sensations do not have any properties that the atomic components lack.

Since all of the contents of the mind can be divided into atomic units, it follows that we can always distinguish one unit from another. In addition, Hume says, the mind has the power to "separate" two units of sensation from one another by imagining one away while keeping the other in mind. For example, when I look at a horse, I can distinguish my visual perception of its head from my visual perception of its body. Therefore, I can at least *imagine* the head without the body, or the body without the head. That power of "separating" impressions in imagination and then recombining the parts in new ways is of course what we all do when we imagine giants, or unicorns, or little green men, or anything else we have not actually seen. Hume summarizes this third point a bit later on in the *Treatise* in two principles:

A centaur being driven by a Bacchant; after an ancient painting found in the Herculaneum. (Undated engraving.) *(Source:* Corbis/Bettmann.*)*

Louis the XIV on horseback with the symbol of Victory; painting by P. Mignard. Castle Versailles. *(Source: Corbis/Bettmann.)*

1. Whatever objects are different are distinguishable.

2. Whatever objects are distinguishable are separable by thought and imagination.

By means of these two principles, which follow directly from his copy theory of ideas and his atomic theory of the contents of the mind, Hume constructs an argument that at one blow wipes out all metaphysics, all natural science, and just about all of our commonsense beliefs about the world. Here is the entire argument, as it appears in the *Treatise*.

DAVID HUME,
A Treatise of Human Nature

'Tis a general maxim in philosophy that whatever begins to exist, must have a cause of existence. This is commonly taken for granted in all reasonings, without any proof given or demanded. 'Tis suppos'd to be founded on intuition, and to be one of those maxims, which tho' they may be deny'd with the lips, 'tis impossible for men in their hearts really to doubt of. But if we examine this maxim by the idea of knowledge above-explain'd, we shall discover in it no mark of any such intuitive certainty; but on the contrary shall find, that 'tis of a nature quite foreign to that species of conviction.

All certainty arises from the comparison of ideas, and from the discovery of such relations as are unalterable, so long as the ideas continue the same. These relations are *resemblance, proportions in quantity and number, degrees of any quality, and contrariety;* none of which are imply'd in this proposition: *Whatever has a beginning has also a cause of existence.* That proposition therefore is not intuitively certain. At least any one, who wou'd assert it to be intuitively certain, must deny these to be the only infallible relations, and must find some other relation of that kind to be imply'd in it; which it will then be time enough to examine.

But here is an argument, which proves at once, that the foregoing proposition is neither intuitively nor demonstrably certain. We can never demonstrate the necessity of a cause to every new existence, or new modification of existence, without shewing at the same time the impossibility there is, that any thing can ever begin to exist without some productive principle; and where the latter proposition cannot be prov'd, we must despair of ever being able to prove the former. Now that the latter proposition is utterly incapable of a demonstrative proof, we may satisfy ourselves by considering, that as all distinct ideas are separable from each other, and as the ideas of cause and effect are evidently distinct, 'twill be easy for us to conceive any object to be nonexistent this moment, and existent the next, without conjoining to it the distinct idea of a cause or productive principle. The separation, therefore, of the idea of a cause from that of a beginning of existence, is plainly possible for the imagination; and consequently the actual separation of these objects is so far possible, that it implies no contradiction nor absurdity; and is therefore incapable of being refuted by any reasoning from mere ideas; without which 'tis impossible to demonstrate the necessity of a cause.

Accordingly we shall find upon examination, that every demonstration, which has been produc'd for the necessity of cause, is fallacious and sophistical. All the points of time and place, say some philosophers, in which we can suppose any object to begin to exist, are in themselves equal; and unless there be some cause, which is peculiar to one time and to one place, and which by that means determines and fixes the existence, it must remain in eternal suspense; and the object can never begin to be, for want of something to fix its beginning. But I ask; Is there any more difficulty in supposing the time and place to be fix'd without a cause, than to suppose the existence to be determin'd in that manner? The first question that occurs on this subject is always, *whether* the object shall exist or not: The next, *when* and *where* it shall begin to exist. If the removal of a cause be intuitively absurd in the one case, it must be so in the other: And if that absurdity be not clear without a proof in the one case, it will equally require one in the other. The absurdity, then, of the one supposition can never be a proof of that of the other, since they are both upon the same footing, and must stand or fall by the same reasoning.

The second argument, which I find us'd on this head, labours under an equal difficulty. Every thing, 'tis said, must have a cause; for if any thing wanted a cause, *it* wou'd produce *itself;* that is, exist before it existed; which is impossible. But this reasoning is plainly unconclusive; because it supposes, that in our denial of a cause we still grant what we expressly deny, *viz.* that there must be a cause; which therefore is taken to be the object itself; and that, no doubt, is an evident contradiction. But to say that any thing is produc'd, or to express myself more properly, comes into existence, without a cause, is not to affirm, that 'tis itself its own cause; but on the contrary in excluding all external causes, excludes *a fortiori* the thing itself which is created. An object, that exists absolutely without any cause, certainly is not its own cause; and when you assert, that the one follows from the other, you suppose the very point in question, and take it for granted, that 'tis utterly impossible any thing can ever begin to exist without cause, but that upon the exclusion of one productive principle, we must still have recourse to another.

'Tis exactly the same case with the third argument, which has been employ'd to demonstrate the necessity of a cause. Whatever is produc'd without any cause, is produc'd by *nothing;* or in other words, has nothing for its cause. But nothing can never be a cause, no more than it can be something, or equal to two right angles. By the same intuition, that we perceive nothing not to be equal to two right angles, or not to be something, we perceive, that it can never be a cause; and consequently must perceive, that every object has a real cause of its existence.

I believe it will not be necessary to employ many words in shewing the weakness of this argument, after what I have said of the foregoing. They are all of them founded on the same fallacy, and are deriv'd from the same turn of thought. 'Tis sufficient only to observe, that when we exclude all causes we really do exclude them, and neither suppose nothing nor the object itself to be the causes of the existence; and consequently can draw no argument from the absurdity of these suppositions to prove the absurdity of that exclusion. If every thing must have a cause, it follows, that upon the exclusion of other causes we must accept of the object itself or of nothing as causes. But 'tis the very point in question, whether every thing must have a cause or not; and therefore, according to all just reasoning, it ought never to be taken for granted.

They are still more frivolous, who say, that every effect must have a cause, because 'tis imply'd in the very idea of effect. Every effect necessarily pre-supposes a cause; effect being a relative term, of which cause is the correlative. But this does not prove, that every being must be preceded by a cause; no more than it follows, because every husband must have a wife, that therefore every man must be marry'd. The true state of the question is, whether every object, which begins to exist, must owe its existence to a cause; and this I assert neither to be intuitively nor demonstratively certain, and hope to have prov'd it sufficiently by the foregoing arguments.

David Hume,
Treatise on Human Nature

It does not take much imagination to see how deeply Hume's argument cuts. We can hardly get out of bed in the morning without implicitly relying on a host of causal beliefs. I believe that when I swing my legs over the side of the bed, they will naturally fall down toward the floor. (As astronauts have discovered, that is a belief that turns out to be false once we get away from the gravitational pull of the earth.) I believe that when I take a drink of water, it will cause my thirst to be abated. I believe that when I push the light switch, it will cause the lights to go on. The simplest propositions of physics, chemistry, and biology either are, or else depend upon, causal judgments.

Hume himself did not believe that it was psychologically possible for human beings to suspend their belief in causal judgments for very long. Although he was absolutely convinced that no adequate justification could ever be found for our beliefs, he also thought that we were naturally so constituted that we believe anyway. In a much-quoted passage from the end of the First Book of the *Treatise,* Hume tells how he disperses the clouds of gloom and doubt that settle over him when he follows out the logical conclusions of his powerful arguments.

> Most fortunately it happens, that since reason is incapable of dispelling these clouds, nature herself suffices to that purpose, and cures me of this philosophical melancholy and delirium, either by relaxing this bent of mind, or by some avocation, and lively impression of my senses, which obliterate all these chimeras. I dine, I play a game of backgammon, I converse, and am merry with my friends; and when after three or four hours' amusement, I wou'd return to these speculations, they appear so cold, and strain'd, and ridiculous, that I cannot find in my heart to enter into them any farther.

Kant's Resolution of the Rationalism/ Empiricism Debate

Immanuel Kant was not content to flee from the skepticism into which Hume had plunged philosophy by his wholesale destruction of causal beliefs. If Hume's arguments were accepted, then I could not even be sure that anything at all existed outside of my own mind. Descartes' fanciful notion that his whole life was a mere dream might be true, as far as philosophers could prove. It was, Kant said, a "scandal to philosophy and to human reason in general that the existence of things outside us . . . must be accepted merely on *faith,* and that if anyone thinks good to doubt their existence, we are unable to counter his doubts by any satisfactory proof." So Kant decided to return to Descartes' starting point, the Cogito, or "I think." He wanted to see whether he could derive directly from that fundamental premise an argument that would avoid the skepticism and solipsism that seemed to be implied by the powerful attacks of the British empiricists.

As we have seen, Descartes' philosophical investigation raised two basic problems: the problem of certainty and the problem of the sources of knowledge. But Kant realized that the Cogito argument raised an even more fundamental issue which both the rationalists and the empiricists had tended to ignore. The conclusion of Descartes' argument, you will recall, was the following:

> This proposition: I am, I exist, is necessarily true each time that I pronounce it, or that I mentally conceive it.

On the basis of this conclusion, Descartes went on to argue that he was essentially a "thing that thinks." Descartes' successors concentrated on the criteria to be used in judging the truths of what the mind thinks, and they concentrated on the sources of the ideas with which the mind thinks, but they paid much less attention to the central fact that the mind, in thinking, is *conscious.* Trees are not conscious, rocks are not conscious, even calculating machines are not conscious, but the mind is. It occurred to Kant that perhaps a proof of our scientific beliefs in the existence of physical objects and in causal connections between them could be based on the mere fact of consciousness. Such a proof would certainly be very hard to find, for the mere fact of consciousness is not much to go on in proving anything as large scale as the truth of science. But if he could find such a proof, Kant would have an answer to anyone who wanted to challenge the claims of reason, even someone prepared to go as far in the direction of skepticism as David Hume.

Descartes had simply accepted consciousness as an indisputable, directly observable, inexplicable fact. I know that I am conscious because I can think about my own thoughts and become aware of myself thinking about them. This self-awareness or self-consciousness is clearly central to the mind's operation; what is more, it is directly self-confirming. Even an evil demon could not trick me into thinking I was conscious when I was not, because if I thought anything at all, it would have to be the case that I was conscious. So instead of the premise "I think" as the starting point of all philosophy, Kant instead adopted the slightly different premise "I am conscious." But introspection reveals, and logical analysis confirms, that my consciousness has a certain basic structure or characteristic: it is unified into a *single* consciousness. All the thoughts, impressions, beliefs, expectations, hopes, and doubts that I have are *my* thoughts, and so on. They occur in *my* consciousness, and that consciousness is a single consciousness, or—to put it somewhat differently—the consciousness of a single subject, a single center of thought. Kant described this fundamental fact as the unity of consciousness. In order to show the connection between what he was doing and what Descartes had done, Kant invoked Descartes' language when he stated his own basic premise. In the central section of the *Critique of Pure Reason,* as he started the argument that he hoped would refute the skeptics and reinstate science as objectively justified, Kant stated his premise in the following way:

It must be possible for the "I think" to accompany all my representations.

Immanuel Kant, *Critique of Pure Reason*

This was his way of saying that all of the contents of my consciousness are bound up in a **unity of consciousness.**

Kant argued that the *unity* of my thoughts and perceptions could not be a given fact of my experience. The individual thoughts and impressions might just be brute facts of consciousness, but their unity could only be explained by some unifying act of the mind itself. Kant claimed that when my mind unifies its various thoughts and perceptions, when it holds them all together in a single consciousness and thinks of them all as *my* thoughts, it follows a certain set of *rules.* These rules are rules for holding thoughts together in the mind, and he gave them the technical name "categories." The only way in which I can think all of my thoughts as unified in a single consciousness is by following the rules or categories for holding thoughts together. Kant claimed that the categories are innate in the human mind; we are all born with them, he said, and we cannot change them.

What are these rules, or categories? Well, it turns out—if Kant is right—that they are just exactly those crucial concepts that play so large a role in the metaphysics, mathematics, and physics that Hume and the skeptics were attacking. Among the categories are such central concepts as substance, cause and effect, unity, plurality, possibility, necessity, and reality.

It may not look as though Kant moved very far toward an answer to Hume, but stop and reflect for a moment on what he is saying. Descartes claimed I could be conscious of my own thoughts, and even conscious of their unity *as* my thoughts, without knowing whether they were really accurate or

Unity of Consciousness   A phrase invented by Immanuel Kant to describe the fact that the thoughts and perceptions of any given mind are bound together in a unity by being all contained in one consciousness. Kant claimed that this fact—the *unity* of individual consciousness—could only be explained by postulating a fundamental mental activity of holding together, or "synthesizing," those thoughts and perceptions.

truthful thoughts about substances, causation, and a world independent of my mind. In other words, Descartes admitted that my subjective knowledge of my own thoughts was better established than any claims I might make about a world of objects. Locke, Hume, and other critics of the rationalists accepted Descartes' starting point—they agreed that I could know the contents of my own mind—but they threw doubt on all of Descartes' attempts to move from that purely subjective knowledge to anything further.

Kant turned the whole argument around by denying Descartes' first premise. I cannot know the contents of my own mind unless I first unify them into a single consciousness, he said. And that means that I must first have applied the categories to them, for those categories are the rules for unifying contents of consciousness. Now the categories are precisely the concepts (substance, cause, etc.) that we use in making objective judgments about the world outside of the mind. So Kant concluded that I could not even be subjectively conscious, à la Descartes, unless I had first put my thoughts and perceptions together in ways that would allow me to make objective judgments about them. Descartes' nightmare of life as an endless dream is an epistemological impossibility, Kant argued.

But Kant paid a price for his solution to the problem of skepticism. It might very well be that my objective concepts were guaranteed to apply to my experiences—it might, in short, be a sure thing that I would encounter substances related to one another causally—but such knowledge as I obtained through the use of the categories would not and could not be knowledge of the world as it really is in itself. Rather, my knowledge must be merely of a world of things as they appear to me.

We have already encountered the distinction between appearance and reality in the philosophy of Socrates and Plato, you will recall. But Plato claimed that we could, by the use of our reason, gain knowledge of true reality. Kant, in contrast, insists that we can only obtain knowledge of appearance, even though such knowledge is real knowledge, and not—as the skeptics claimed—error or unfounded belief.

The dispute between the rationalists and the empiricists was changed by Kant's new theory of the unity of consciousness. Even though many subsequent philosophers rejected his distinction between appearance and reality, they continued to ponder the problem of the nature of consciousness, a problem that Descartes had discovered and that Kant had substantially deepened by his arguments.

New Turns in Epistemology

The disagreement between rationalists and empiricists, the disagreement that Kant attempted to reconcile with his theory of the unity of consciousness, sometimes is couched in terms of a disagreement regarding the *source(s)* of knowledge. Thinking of the debate in this way, we say that rationalists rely on reason as the sole source of knowledge, empiricists—at least those who do not end up as utter skeptics—on experience. But the rationalism-empiricism debate also involves questions regarding the *foundations* of knowledge: upon what, ultimately, must genuine knowledge claims be founded? (It isn't clear that some thinkers, Locke, for example, were always clear about this distinction.) Again, the rationalists answered "reason," the empiricists, "experience." Still another way of casting the debate relies on talk of *justification:* What, in the final analysis, *justifies* my claim that I know that something is the case? This concern arises out of the traditional view that justified true belief is necessary for knowledge.

Now, although rationalists such as Descartes, empiricists such as Hume, and Kant, came up with different answers regarding the respective roles of reason and experience in knowledge, they implicitly agreed on the questions that epistemologists need to ask: "What are the sources of knowledge?" "How do we get from the sources to the knowledge?"

Some philosophers in the twentieth century have disagreed about what the questions should be.

We can't begin to summarize, in the space we have for this brief section at the end of our chapter on epistemology, all the work that has been done in the area since the time of Kant. But to give you an idea of the diversity of the work (and, I hope, to whet your appetite for further study in philosophy), we will take a brief look at three different approaches philosophers have taken at the end of the twentieth century.

Coherentism

This epistemological view is in direct contrast to the three we have been considering—rationalism, empiricism, and the Kantian view—all of which are *foundationalist*.

Foundationalism in epistemology is the view that knowledge must be viewed, to cite a famous metaphor, as a pyramid made up of building blocks the upper levels of which rest on a solid foundation which itself is basic and therefore needs no further support.[3]

Descartes, of course, sought the solid foundation in the "Cogito"; Locke sought the foundation in the ideas derived from sensation and reflection, that is, from experience. Casting their problem this way, they faced a major challenge in trying to explain the connection between the foundation and the beliefs it supposedly supports. We saw how the enterprise apparently trapped Descartes in a circle as he struggled with the problem of how to *even get started* bridging the gulf between his knowledge of his own existence, on the one hand, and the beliefs he was trying to rationalize—his belief in God, for example, and his belief in the external world—on the other. Hume despaired of bridging the gulf between our ideas and the external world which they supposedly represent: hence the significance of his observation that "an idea can only resemble another idea."

In contrast, coherentism holds that a body of beliefs may be known without an underlying foundation of certainty, but rather in virtue of the mutual support provided by the various parts, rather as we may know—to borrow philosopher Susan Haack's famous analogy—that we have correctly solved a crossword puzzle because of the way the interlocking parts fit together, even though we may be unsure of the entries considered one by one. (Haack used the crossword puzzle analogy in her discussion of *foundherentism*.)[4] Perhaps the most famous metaphor associated with coherentism is the Austrian philosopher Otto Neurath's image of a boat that must be reconstructed at sea: ". . . we are like sailors who on the open sea must reconstruct their ship but are never able to start afresh from the bottom." Thus coherentism is *holistic:* beliefs are not justified in isolation, but by their place in a coherent *system* of beliefs in which they must be both mutually consistent and interdependent. It is fallibilistic in that it allows for mistakes—"misfits"—in the system, but self-correcting in that when something doesn't fit quite right in the system, we tweak it to try to make it fit better; and if we find something that doesn't fit at all, we reject it.

One of the merits of coherentism is that it does not need to bridge the gulf between our beliefs, on the one hand, and a foundation for those beliefs that is different from beliefs—sensations, for example—on the other. A coherentist system *consists of*—to use still another famous metaphor—a web of beliefs.

Coherentism also seems to acknowledge that we do not acquire knowledge piece by piece, but within a mutually reinforcing framework.

But what about Descartes' evil genius? Isn't it possible that I might have a coherent system of beliefs, all of which are totally false? One response here, although not a direct answer to the questions, is to ask us to think very carefully about whether we *could* have a coherent system of beliefs, all of which are false. But what about people who live in a delusional world? There are, sadly, people who are quite mad and who live in a delusional world. Are their mutually consistent, interdependent beliefs to count as *knowledge?* "But," the coherentist might ask, "*are* their beliefs really mutually consistent?"

A return to pragmatism

Pragmatism is a distinctively American approach to philosophy, rooted in the work of Charles Sanders Peirce (1839–1914), William James (1842–1910), John Dewey (1859–1952), and George Herbert Mead (1863–1931), and characterized by Yankee toughmindedness and a practical, "But does it *work?*" attitude. Significantly, all four of the men just mentioned were engaged in fields other than philosophy, fields that some people call more "practical" in nature than philosophy—Peirce in mathematics, James in psychology (he is sometimes called "the father of American psychology"), Dewey in education (for decades, Dewey's name was inextricably tied to the philosophy of education), and Mead in sociology.

Pragmatism is a practice-oriented philosophy. In his essay, "Pragmatism," James wrote:

> [The pragmatist] turns away from abstraction and insufficiency, from verbal solutions, from bad *a priori* reasons, from fixed principles, closed systems, and pretended absolutes and origins. He turns towards concreteness and adequacy, towards facts, towards action and towards power. That means . . . the open air and possibilities of nature, as against dogma, artificiality, and the pretence of finality in truth. . . [Rather] Truth *happens* to an idea. It *becomes* true, is *made* true by events.

William James,
What Pragmatism Means

James' claim prompted a flurry of criticism, and James himself modified his stand in later years. But the pragmatic tone had been set: truth is not static, changeless, eternal, and waiting to be discovered like a Platonic Form. Rather, the ultimate test of the truth of an idea is its usefulness in practice—the truth of a claim is borne out in the way it works out *in practice*.

Pragmatism fell out of fashion in some of the leading graduate schools of philosophy in the middle part of the twentieth century, but there has been a resurgence of interest in pragmatism, in one form or another, in recent decades.

While it may be true, as someone has said, that "There are as many pragmatisms as there are pragmatists," there nevertheless are common themes among varieties of pragmatism, foremost among which is the pragmatic maxim that the meaning of a concept is to be found in the practical outcomes of its adoption—in its *practical results*. Other common themes are an antipathy toward grandiose metaphysical speculation and, in epistemology, a rejection of the Cartesian view that equates knowledge with absolute certainty. Rather, pragmatism connects knowledge with action: knowledge is action-guiding, instrumental, a tool for satisfactorily organizing the data of experience.

Contemporary pragmatists, or "neo-pragmatists," range from "reformists," those who reject the Cartesian requirement of absolute certainty for knowledge, but who still acknowledge the legitimacy of traditional epistemological questions, to "revolutionaries," those who call for the "Death of Epistemology," a rejection of the traditional epistemological program altogether: "Traditional epistemology was wrong to look for a pure essence of truth or an absolute method of knowledge beyond what is good or useful in the way of belief"[1]. Not only did Descartes, Hume, and Kant come up with the wrong answers; they didn't even ask the right questions!

The impact of cognitive science

Cognitive science seeks to provide an account for intelligent activity, whether exhibited by human beings or machines. (The word 'cognitive' means 'of or relating to mental processes connected with understanding, the formulation of beliefs, and the acquisition of knowledge'.) A product of the computer age, cognitive science emerged as an interdisciplinary enterprise during the mid-twentieth century, receiving input from psychology, artificial intelligence, linguistics, and philosophy, among other disciplines. Typically, cognitive science looks to information processing as its model for thinking about intelligent activity; basic underlying assumptions are that a human being is a kind of biological information processor, and that the human mind is best thought of as analogous to a computer. To this extent, cognitive science has stimulated new thinking in the area of philosophical psychology.

But some thinkers do not accept the model proposed by cognitive science, that the human mind is best thought of as a computer, or that information processing provides a model for human thought and understanding. In a famous thought experiment, the American philosopher John Searle introduced the metaphor of a Chinese Room to suggest dissimilarities between human understanding and the operations of a computer.[2] Imagine yourself, an English speaking person, closed in a room with a set of formal instructions for how to correlate sets of Chinese symbols. You do not understand spoken or written Chinese yourself, but your instructions are in English; they tell you how to identify the characters solely on the basis of their shape, which characters go together, and in what order. You are handed a card with Chinese characters on it and, using your instructions, write a different set of characters on another card, and hand it back. Unknown to you, your instructions provide all the rules for constructing grammatically correct conversational Chinese, so that if the incoming card says (in Chinese), "Do you understand me?" you write the appropriate symbols for, "Yes, thank you" (in Chinese). Of course, as someone who doesn't know Chinese, you have no idea of the content of the exchange that has taken place. But someone outside the room, seeing the results of the exchange, might think you do.

Searle believes that what you have done in the Chinese Room is precisely similar to what a computer does—take incoming data, manipulate it according to formal instructions (the program), and print out a result. But—and here is the point of the experiment—the computer doesn't *understand* any more of what it produces than you understand what you are producing in the Chinese Room. What Searle concludes is that information processing, of the kind a computer does, is not an adequate model for human cognition.

The contributions of cognitive science to epistemology as such are more indirect. One approach, taken by the American philosopher John Pollock, is to ask, "What can we learn about human cognition by looking at it from an information processing point of view?" Or, "What would we have to build into an information processing device—by way of hardware and software—to enable it to satisfactorily organize the data of experience, to cope *intelligently* with the world, the way humans do?" That is, how would we have to design an information processing device, to make it possible for it *to do what we do?* The idea here is that, by thinking about the way a machine would have to work in order to deal with the world the way we do, we may generate reasons

Philosophy and Popular Culture

The Matrix: Brains in a Vat

Imagine that you are in the movie *The Matrix.* Unfortunately, you are not Neo or Trinity. You are not a liberated human being who has become aware that most human beings are the equivalent of brains in a vat. You are not aware that most human beings have never used their eyes; instead, most human beings are connected to a matrix in which they only seem to be seeing, hearing, smelling, touching, and tasting. In fact, what they seem to sense is fed to them by machines that harvest them for the electricity their brains generate. Your role in *The Matrix* is not that of a hero; you are one of the huge number of human beings being lied to. The lie is that you are a human being who lives in a world in which you move around, interact with other free people, and use your senses. The reality is that for all of your life, including now, you lie in a vat and your brain is fed images and other senses by the machines.

Now imagine that *The Matrix* is not a movie, but reality. You seem to be sitting at home watching a DVD of *The Matrix*, but in reality the machines are feeding you sensory information that tells you that you are watching a

movie, not lying in a vat with electronic wires connected to your brain stem and spinal cord so the machines can make you think whatever they want you to think.

Questions To Consider

Is there any way for you to tell that what you seem to experience is not reality? Is there any way for you to figure out—without a hero, such as Morpheus, first disconnecting you from the matrix—that you are a brain in a vat?

for or against certain epistemological views. Pollock objects that all existing epistemological theories are *incomplete:* there simply would be more involved in creating an information processing machine that could do what we do, than current theories provide for.

A great deal has been written and said—for and against—the Chinese Room argument, and surely much more will be written and said. Work on epistemology from the point of view of cognitive science is in its infancy. We may discover that contributions to epistemology from the point of view of cognitive science are fundamentally flawed because they presuppose that human cognition is in fact *like* an information processing machine. Nevertheless, cognitive science surely will continue to stimulate exciting work in the area of epistemology well into the twenty-first century.

Notes

1. Richard Rorty, *Consequences of Pragmatism: Essays, 1972–1980,* Minneapolis, University of Minnesota Press, 1982, 164.
2. John Searle, "Minds, Brains, and Programs," *The Behavioral and Brain Sciences* (1980) 3, 417–424.
3. Ernest Sosa, "The Raft and the Pyramid: Coherence versus Foundations in the Theory of Knowledge." In *Midwest Studies in Philosophy 5: Studies in Epistemology,* eds. P. A. French *et al.* Minneapolis: University of Minnesota Press, 1980, 3–25.
4. Susan Haack, *Evidence and Inquiry: Towards Reconstruction in Epistemology.* Oxford, UK; Cambridge, USA: Blackwell, 1993.

The Main Points in Chapter Two

1. In the seventeenth century, the great French mathematician, scientist, and philosopher René Descartes changed the course of philosophy by raising a fundamental question about what we can know, and how we know it. Descartes' *method of doubt* called into question every belief that could not be demonstrated with absolute certainty. Descartes was able to show that most of our mathematical, scientific, religious, and everyday beliefs really cannot stand up to that kind of examination.

2. Descartes' systematic doubt brought to center stage a question that philosophers had discussed for a very long time: How do we learn about the nature of things, through our physical senses or by reasoning? Philosophers who think sensation is the source of knowledge are called *empiricists.* Philosophers who think reason is the source of knowledge are called *rationalists.* The seventeenth and eighteenth centuries saw a complicated debate between empiricists and rationalists, in which physics, mathematics, theology, and logic were called into play.

3. Descartes himself was a rationalist, as was the German Leibniz. The most original empiricists were a number of British philosophers, including John Locke, George Berkeley, and David Hume. These British empiricists pushed Descartes' skeptical arguments farther than he had himself and thereby called into question the validity of the proof for the existence of God, the basic propositions of physics, and even the theorems of mathematics.

4. The most radical of the empiricists was David Hume, whose *A Treatise of Human Nature,* published in 1739 to 1740, raised skeptical doubts about even the unity and existence of the self.

5. By the middle of the eighteenth century, the empiricists and rationalists had fought one another to a draw, philosophically speaking. At this point, the greatest philosopher since Plato and Aristotle, Immanuel Kant, came forward to try to resolve the conflict and to get philosophy out of the dead end it was in. Kant's great work, the *Critique of Pure Reason,* published in 1781, transformed philosophy by changing our understanding of knowledge, consciousness, the self, and the relation between what we know and the way things are.

6. Using the old Platonic distinction between *appearance* and *reality,* Kant argued that we in fact never have knowledge of reality but only of things as they appear to us, and that the mind itself contributes the form in which we know appearances. As Kant said in perhaps his most famous statement, "The mind is itself the lawgiver to nature."

7. In recent decades, a number of philosophers have challenged the claims of *rationality, universality,* and *objectivity.* They say that *what* we know is powerfully shaped by *who* we are.

Questions for Discussion and Review

1. These are strange times, what with *The National Enquirer* regularly featuring stories about people who say they have been kidnapped by aliens, and actress Shirley MacLaine reporting that in a previous life she was stomped to death by a white elephant. On the other hand, in recent decades we have also seen live television transmissions from the moon and electron microscope photographs of individual atoms. *How* can we tell the difference between truth and fiction? Are the people crazy who refused to believe their own eyes and said that the pictures of men on the moon were faked?

2. Reflect for a bit about all of the things you think you know: state capitals, historical events, details of the private lives of rock stars, the difference between reptiles and mammals, how much a Chevy sedan costs, what a Big Mac is really made of. How do you *know* these things? If you were forced to defend any of these beliefs, how would you go about it? Could you produce arguments, evidence, reasons, proof? If not, then is it sensible for you to believe them anyway?

3. The great epistemologists of the seventeenth and eighteenth centuries were, one must admit, a little mad, what with their dreams of settling

once and for all, by a philosophical investigation, the limits of human knowledge. Is there *any* way of determining whether there are limits beyond which human knowledge cannot go? Would it help us to know more about the structure and functioning of our sense organs? Would a deeper insight into computers make any difference?

4. Imagine that the virtual reality equipment eventually becomes so good that it can simulate sound, smell, taste, and touch as well as sight when you are wearing it. Imagine, too, that the programming becomes so elaborate that you can have week-long virtual reality experiences, not just brief encounters. Under those circumstances, would you be willing to give up real-world interactions with other people and settle for virtual reality fantasies? Why? Why not? What is there about an engagement with the real world that is missing from a virtual reality experience? Remember: everything we know about the world comes originally through our senses. Or does it?

5. Is anything that happens in a virtual reality experience moral or immoral? What about two-person virtual reality experiences? Suppose the equipment becomes so complex that a whole community could be hooked up to it. Would there be political implications? What is *reality* anyway?

The Primary Source: Philosophical Readings and Commentary

Aristotle: *Metaphysics; Categories; de Anima; On Interpretation; Physics; Poetics; Posterior Analytics; Prior Analytics; Rhetoric*

Berkeley, George: *A Treatise Concerning the Principles of Human Knowledge*

Descartes, Rene: *Discourse on Method; Meditations on First Philosophy*

Heraclitus: *Fragments*

Hume, David: *An Enquiry Concerning Human Understanding; Treatise on Human Nature*

James, William: *What Pragmatism Means*

Kant, Immanuel: *Critique of Judgment; Critique of Pure Reason; Prolegomena to any Future Metaphysics*

Leibniz, Gottfried: *Monadology*

Locke, John: *Essay Concerning Human Understanding*

Lucretius: *On the Nature of Things*

Peirce, Charles Sanders: *The Fixation of Belief; Clear Ideas*

Plato: *The Republic*

Thales: *Fragments*

ABCNEWS

CONTEMPORARY APPLICATION

Virtual Reality

Ever since Jules Verne published his great science fiction yarn, *Twenty Thousand Leagues Under the Sea,* about a boat that could actually submerge and travel for months without surfacing, the real world has been imitating the literary imagination. When I was a boy, many decades ago, the comic book detective Dick Tracy spoke into a wrist telephone. Today, as I drive down the highway, I see people carrying on telephone conversations while steering with one hand. Even that most impossible of all science fiction dreams, walking on the moon, is now a reality. Indeed, it happened so long ago that my students these days have heard about it from their parents.

For some time now, very sophisticated philosophers have been arguing about a quite fanciful, imaginary situation straight out of science fiction. It goes by the bizarre name of "brains in vats." Hilary Putnam, a distinguished philosopher of mathematics, asked what it would be like if an evil scientist removed my brain from my body and kept it alive in a tub of nutrient fluids, feeding sensory inputs to it through electrical connections. Putnam used this weird idea to explore some rather tricky issues in the philosophy of mind.

Another distinguished philosopher, Daniel Dennett, took issue with Putnam, arguing that the sort of complete hallucination Putnam was talking about would be impossible. The first two readings in this Contemporary Application are selections from the discussions by Putnam and Dennett.

But neither of these philosophers realized that hardly before the ink was dry on their articles, science would produce a device that goes a long way toward creating the brains-in-a-vat situation they were arguing about. The name for this device is "virtual reality," a futuristic helmet that projects images onto an internal visor and responds to movements of the eyes, hands, or body of the person wearing the device. The effect is to make it seem as though you have entered a television world. Looking straight ahead, perhaps, you see a tree-lined walk. Turn your head to the left and into view come the trees on your left. Walk two steps forward and the trees look larger, just as they would if they were really there. *Except that there is nothing there but images on the inside of the helmet visor!*

The latest wrinkle is a pair of virtual reality helmets that allow two people to enter the same imaginary space or virtual reality, and even to play ball in it. The makers promise that before too long, you will be able to climb into a body suit and make virtual love to an imaginary, but quite visible, partner. It sounds too much like the Holodeck on the Enterprise for comfort.

Our last selection discusses the new virtual reality devices directly. But this is one chapter where you must view the accompanying video to get the full flavor of the discussion. How about a virtual reality philosophy class in which you can carry on debates with an imaginary Socrates? If you ask a question the imaginary Socrates cannot answer, do you suppose the helmet would short out?

THE CASE OF THE BRAINS IN A VAT
Hilary Putnam

Here is a science fiction possibility discussed by philosophers: imagine that a human being (you can imagine this to be yourself) has been subjected to an operation by an evil scientist. The person's brain (your brain) has been removed from the body and placed in a vat of nutrients which keeps the brain alive. The nerve endings have been connected to a super-scientific computer which causes the person whose brain it is to have the illusion that everything is perfectly normal. There seem to be people, objects, the sky, etc; but really all the person (you) is experiencing is the result of electronic impulses travelling from the computer to the nerve endings. The computer is so clever that if the person tries to raise his hand, the feedback from the computer will cause him to "see" and "feel" the hand being raised. Moreover, by varying the program, the evil scientist can cause the victim to "experience" (or hallucinate) any situation or environment the evil scientist wishes. He can also obliterate the memory of the brain operation, so that the victim will seem to himself to have always been in this environment. It can even seem to the victim that he is sitting and reading

these very words about the amusing but quite absurd supposition that there is an evil scientist who removes people's brains from their bodies and places them in a vat of nutrients which keep the brains alive. The nerve endings are supposed to be connected to a super-scientific computer which causes the person whose brain it is to have the illusion that . . .

When this sort of possibility is mentioned in a lecture on the Theory of Knowledge, the purpose, of course, is to raise the classical problem of skepticism with respect to the external world in a modern way. *(How do you know you aren't in this predicament?)* But this predicament is also a useful device for raising issues about the mind/world relationship.

Instead of having just one brain in a vat, we could imagine that all human beings (perhaps all sentient beings) are brains in a vat (or nervous systems in a vat in case some beings with just a minimal nervous system already count as "sentient"). Of course, the evil scientist would have to be outside—or would he? Perhaps there is no evil scientist, perhaps (though this is absurd) the universe just happens to consist of automatic machinery tending a vat full of brains and nervous systems.

This time let us suppose that the automatic machinery is programmed to give us all a *collective* hallucination, rather than a number of separate unrelated hallucinations. Thus, when I seem to myself to be talking to you, you seem to yourself to be hearing my words. Of course, it is not the case that my words actually reach your ears—for you don't have (real) ears, nor do I have a real mouth and tongue. Rather, when I produce my words, what happens is that the efferent impulses travel from my brain to the computer, which both causes me to "hear" my own voice uttering those words and "feel" my tongue moving, etc., and causes you to "hear" my words, "see" me speaking, etc. In this case, we are, in a sense, actually in communication. I am not mistaken about your real existence (only about the existence of your body and the "external world," apart from brains). From a certain point of view, it doesn't even matter that "the whole world" is a collective hallucination; for you do, after all, really hear my words when I speak to you, even if the mechanism isn't what we suppose it to be. (Of course, if we were two lovers making love, rather than just two people carrying on a conversation, then the suggestion that it was just two brains in a vat might be disturbing.)

Source: "The Case of the Brains in a Vat" by Hilary Putnam. From *Reason, Truth, and History,* 1981, pp. 5–7. Reprinted with the permission of Cambridge University Press.

THE BRAIN IN THE VAT
Daniel Dennett

Suppose evil scientists removed your brain from your body while you slept, and set it up in a life-support system in a vat. Suppose they then set out to trick you into believing that you were not just a brain in a vat, but still up and about, engaging in a normally embodied round of activities in the real world. This old saw, the brain in the vat, is a favorite thought experiment in the toolkit of many philosophers. It is a modern-day version of Descartes's evil demon, an imagined illusionist bent on tricking Descartes about absolutely everything, including his own existence. But as Descartes observed, even an infinitely powerful evil demon couldn't trick him into thinking he himself existed if he didn't exist: *cogito ergo sum,* "I think, therefore I am." Philosophers today are less concerned with proving one's own existence as a thinking thing (perhaps because they have decided that Descartes settled that matter quite satisfactorily) and more concerned about what, in principle, we may conclude from our experience about our nature, and about the nature of the world in which we (apparently) live. *Might* you be nothing but a brain in a vat? Might you have *always* been just a brain in a vat? If so, could you even conceive of your predicament (let alone confirm it)?

The idea of the brain in the vat is a vivid way of exploring these questions, but I want to put the old saw to another use. In the standard thought experiment, it is obvious that the scientists would have their hands full providing the nerve stumps from all your senses with just the right stimulations to carry off the trickery, but philosophers have assumed for the sake of argument that however technically difficult the task might be, it is "possible in principle." One should be leery of these possibilities in principle. It is also possible in principle to build a stainless-steel ladder to the moon, and to write out, in alphabetical order, all intelligible English conversations consisting of less than a thousand words. But neither of these are remotely possible in fact and sometimes an *impossibility in fact* is theoretically more interesting than a *possibility in principle,* as we shall see.

Let's take a moment to consider, then, just how daunting the task facing the evil scientists would be. We can imagine them building up to the hard tasks from some easy beginnings. They begin with a conveniently comatose brain, kept alive but lacking all input from the optic nerves, the auditory nerves, the somatosensory nerves, and all the other afferent, or input, paths to the brain. It is sometimes assumed that such a "deafferented" brain would naturally stay in a comatose state forever, needing no morphine to keep it dormant, but there is some empirical evidence to suggest that spontaneous waking might still occur in these dire circumstances. I think we can suppose that were you to awake in such a state, you would find yourself in horrible straits: blind, deaf, completely numb, with no sense of your body's orientation.

Not wanting to horrify you, then, the scientists arrange to wake you up by piping stereo music (suitably encoded as nerve impulses) into your auditory nerves. They also arrange for the signals that would normally come from your vestibular system or inner ear to indicate that you are lying on your back, but otherwise paralyzed, numb, blind. This much should be within the limits of technical virtuosity in the near future—perhaps possible even today. They might then go on to stimulate the tracts that used to innervate your epidermis, providing it with the input that would normally have been produced by a gentle, even warmth over the ventral (belly) surface of your body, and (getting fancier) they might stimulate the dorsal (back) epidermal nerves in a way that simulated the tingly texture of grains of sand pressing into your back. "Great!" you say to yourself: "Here I am, lying on my back on the beach, paralyzed and blind, listening to rather nice music, but probably in danger of sunburn. How did I get here, and how can I call for help?"

But now suppose the scientists, having accomplished all this, tackle the more difficult problem of convincing you that you are not a mere beach potato, but an agent capable of engaging in some form of activity in the world. Starting with little steps, they decide to lift part of the "paralysis" of your phantom body and let you

wiggle your right index finger in the sand. They permit the sensory experience of moving your finger to occur, which is accomplished by giving you the kinesthetic feedback associated with the relevant volitional or motor signals in the output or efferent part of your nervous system, but they must also arrange to remove the numbness from your phantom finger, and provide the stimulation for the feeling that the motion of the imaginary sand around your finger would provoke.

Suddenly, they are faced with a problem that will quickly get out of hand, for just how the sand will feel depends on just how you decide to move your finger. The problem of calculating the proper feedback, generating or composing it, and then presenting it to you in real time is going to be computationally intractable on even the fastest computer, and if the evil scientists decide to solve the real-time problem by precalculating and "canning" all the possible responses for playback, they will just trade one insoluble problem for another: there are too many possibilities to store . . .

It is a familiar wall these scientists have hit; we see its shadow in the boring stereotypes in every video game. The alternatives open for action have to be strictly—and unrealistically—limited to keep the task of the world-representers within feasible bounds. If the scientists can do no better than convince you that you are doomed to a lifetime of playing Donkey Kong, they are evil scientists indeed.

There is a solution of sorts to this technical problem. It is the solution used, for instance, to ease the computational burden in highly realistic flight simulators: use *replicas* of the items in the simulated world. Use a real cockpit and push and pull it with hydraulic lifters, instead of trying to simulate all that input to the seat of the pants of the pilot in training. In short, there is only one way for you to store for ready access that much information about an imaginary world to be explored, and that is to use a *real* (if tiny or artificial or plaster-of-paris) world to store its own information! This is "cheating" if you're the evil demon claiming to have deceived Descartes about the existence of absolutely everything, but it's a way of actually getting the job done with less than infinite resources.

Descartes was wise to endow his imagined evil demon with *infinite* powers of trickery. Although the task is not, strictly speaking, infinite, the amount of information obtainable in short order by an inquisitive human being is staggeringly large. Engineers measure information flow in bits per second, or speak of the *bandwidth* of the channels through which the information flows. Television requires a greater bandwidth than radio, and high-definition television has a still greater bandwidth. High-definition smello-feelo television would have a still greater bandwidth, and *interactive* smello-feelo television would have an astronomical bandwidth, because it constantly branches into thousands of slightly different trajectories through the (imaginary) world. Throw a skeptic a dubious coin, and in a second or two of hefting, scratching, ringing, tasting, and just plain looking at how the sun glints on its surface, the skeptic will consume more bits of information than a Cray supercomputer can organize in a year. Making a *real* but counterfeit coin is child's play; making a *simulated* coin out of nothing but organized nerve stimulations is beyond human technology now and probably forever.[1]

One conclusion we can draw from this is that we are not brains in vats—in case you were worried. Another conclusion it seems that we can draw from this is that strong hallucinations are simply impossible! By a strong hallucination I mean a hallucination of an apparently concrete and persisting three-dimensional object in the real world—as contrasted to flashes, geometric distortions, auras, afterimages, fleeting phantom-limb experiences, and other anomalous sensations. A strong hallucination would be, say, a ghost that talked back, that permitted you to touch it, that resisted with a sense of solidity, that cast a shadow, that was visible from any angle so that you might walk around it and see what its back looked like.

Hallucinations can be roughly ranked in strength by the number of such features they have. Reports of *very* strong hallucinations are rare, and we can now see why it is no coincidence that the credibility of such reports seems, intuitively, to be inversely proportional to the strength of the hallucination reported. We are—and should be—particularly skeptical of reports of very strong hallucinations because we don't believe in ghosts, and we think that only a real ghost could produce a strong hallucination. . . .

But if *really* strong hallucinations are not known to occur, there can be no doubt that convincing, multimodal hallucinations are frequently experienced. The hallucinations that are well attested in the literature of clinical psychology are often detailed fantasies far beyond the generative capacities of current technology. How on earth can a single brain do what teams of scientists and computer animators would find to be almost impossible? If such experiences are not genuine or veridical perceptions of some real thing "outside" the mind, they must be produced entirely inside the mind (or the brain), concocted out of whole cloth but lifelike enough to fool the very mind that concocts them.

[1]The development of "virtual reality" systems for recreation and research is currently undergoing a boom. The state of the art is impressive, electronically rigged gloves that provide a convincing interface for "manipulating" virtual objects, and head-mounted visual displays that permit you to explore virtual environments of considerable complexity. The limitations of these systems are apparent, however, and they bear out my point: it is only by various combinations of physical replicas and schematization (a relatively coarse-grained representation) that robust illusions can be sustained. And even at their best, they are experiences of virtual surreality, not something that you might mistake for the real thing for more than a moment. If you really want to fool someone into thinking he is in a cage with a gorilla, enlisting the help of an actor in a gorilla suit is going to be your best bet for a long time.

COULD LIFE, SEX, AND DEATH BECOME JUST PART OF THE COMPUTER REVOLUTION, ASKS PAT COYNE

Computer graphics have become part of everyday life. Within a decade, they have invaded TV, the military, games, advertising, Hollywood, and even high Euro-art, with Peter Greenaway's *Prospero's Books*. From the most rudimentary beginnings—simulated ping-pong on the mono screens of machines like the Sinclair Z80 with a bare four kilobytes of memory—computer graphics programmes now run on some of the most powerful machines in the world, creating illusions that first mirror and then better reality. Take, for example, the $100-million movie, *Terminator 2: Judgment Day,* with its villain sliding between prison bars, melting and reforming into dozens of different shapes, all done not with the use of trick photography, but digital manipulation.

The buzzword now is interactive. It is not enough to sit passively and watch electronic wonders being displayed before your eyes. You must take part. At its simplest, this means computer games, a herd of demonic hedgehogs zipping through hoops and pipes in an effort to escape obliteration.

One step up is the home interactive system, such as the CD-i being marketed by Phillips, which combines all the electronic gadgets in the home—TV, video, CD player, camcorder—under the control of a computer. This allows the user to mix and match, pulling in pictures from the TV, adding graphics or video from the camcorder and music from the CD, speeding up or slowing the action and, at least in theory, allowing everybody to produce their own original electronic art.

But the real focus of interest is now virtual reality, the creation of whole new, sensory worlds. At its simplest, the subject is fitted with sensors to hands and body and provided with a helmet, inside which are two small TV screens that give him or her a stereoscopic view of the new reality. Inside that world, there need be no constraints. You can fly, jump impossible distances, perform incredible feats, visit Mars or Jupiter, do whatever pleases you.

At the moment, virtual reality graphics and action are relatively crude, but that is simply a function of computer powers. As computers become more powerful, and programs and sensors more sophisticated, the differences between actual and virtual reality will become smaller and smaller, perhaps ultimately vanishing. After all, what the brain experiences as sensations are actually electronic and chemical stimuli, which can, at least in principle, be duplicated.

What then? Why confine the sensors to limbs and head? The most obvious next step is virtual sex, or teledildonics as it is becoming known in the (as yet, virtual) trade. So far, computer porn has been confined to still pictures circulated on floppy disks or downloaded from bulletin boards, which, even at super-VGA resolutions, are fairly tame stuff. But now we have the possibility of the digital equivalent of the inflatable doll, infinitely more sophisticated and capable of being programmed to cater for the most exotic of tastes. Will we be able to rent the electronic versions of our favorite movie or TV actors to enjoy their bodies, just as we now rent their videos?

Indeed, teledildonics holds out the ultimate in choice—an infinite variety of safe sex. Turn your TV camera on a crowd, pick out someone that you fancy and allow the camera long enough to gather all the necessary data—shape, looks, colouring, body rhythms and so on. Perhaps do a vox pop interview to capture the modalities of voice and facial expression. Download the data to the computer and allow it to calculate all the necessary parameters, set your own passion levels, preferred positions, duration of activity, and timing of orgasm and then double-click the mouse cursor on the icon.

For those brave enough to seek the ultimate in virtual experience, there will be, sooner or later, the "snuff" program. Already, the computer games charts are stuffed with a huge variety of beat-'em-up and shoot-'em-up games, in which the players are encouraged to visit mayhem on their opponents using guns, missiles, fists, feet, and anything else capable of being pressed into service. Virtual reality offers the logical extension of such games. You can stalk your prey in the setting of your choice, armed with your favorite weapons (or use bare hands if that is your fancy). Aim a gun, and direction, trajec-tory, and recoil will all be faithfully calculated. The computer will be primed with the tensile strengths of flesh and bone and arterial systolic pressures to produce the most realistic simulation of wounds, rendered in 24-bit colour, with over 16 million shades, more than the human eye is capable of distinguishing. The screams of the victim will be synthesized in 20-channel stereo, and algorithms emulating the human metabolism will give a realistic prognosis—life or death. Mission accomplished, you can remove the helmet and relax with another part of your electronic emporium, perhaps a Chopin prelude. After all, it won't be real, will it?

Source: Coyne, Pat, *Dielectrics (Could life, sex, and death become just part of the computer revolution?)* New Statesman & Society v. 6, p. 31, March 19, 1993.

Thomas Hobbes

homas Hobbes (1588–1679) was (in my opinion) the most powerful political theorist and the most accomplished literary stylist ever to write philosophy in English. Born at the very moment when rumors were flooding England of a threatened attack by the powerful Spanish navy, Hobbes grew up in the age of Shakespeare and Queen Elizabeth I. In his earlier years, he served as tutor to the young Earl of Devonshire, and in his thirties, he met the great scientific philosopher Francis Bacon (see Chapter 4).

By the time Hobbes was approaching fifty, the political struggles between the Catholic House of Stuart and the Puritans were becoming more and more heated. Fearing for his life, Hobbes exiled himself to Paris in 1640, just as the English Civil War was breaking out. In 1651, with the English King Charles I executed by the Puritans and the royalist cause seemingly lost, Hobbes published his greatest work, *Leviathan,* in which he set forth in the most elegant and compact manner his theory of matter, perception, desire, the social contract, and the state.

At the end of 1651, Hobbes returned to England. Although he is commonly considered a supporter of the Stuart monarchy (which was restored in 1660), Hobbes actually managed to alienate both sides in the great struggle. The royalists viewed him with suspicion because he claimed that the absolute authority of the king is derived from the will of the people; the Puritans considered him an enemy because he taught that social peace can come only from an absolute submission to the will of a king.

After his return to England at the age of sixty-three, Hobbes lived another twenty-eight years, writing a series of major works that earned him great renown. He died in 1679, only a few years before the second great upheaval in English politics, the so-called Glorious Revolution of 1688. Hobbes is perhaps best remembered for his famous description of life in a society without a strong ruler as "solitary, nasty, brutish, and short." The political events of the twentieth century have made him once again a writer much looked to for insight into our social and political condition.

Metaphysics and Philosophy of Mind

What Is Metaphysics?

Hobbes' Materialism

Free Will and Determinism

The Mind and the Body

Contemporary Application: Do Computers Think?

What Is Metaphysics?

Some years ago, there appeared a listing in the Yellow Pages of the Manhattan telephone book, between "Metals" and "Meteorologists," for "Metaphysician." A gentleman who shall remain nameless had hung out his shingle in Greenwich Village and was apparently prepared to offer his metaphysical services for a fee to all comers. The listing has disappeared from subsequent editions of the Yellow Pages, but I continue to wonder just what services he offered and what his clients imagined they were going to get when they sought him out.

What *is* metaphysics? Or should we ask, What *are* metaphysics? The term itself is a sheer historical accident. The great Greek philosopher, Aristotle, wrote a set of essays on fundamental problems concerning the most basic classifications or categories of being and the most general concepts by means of which we can think about what is. He called his discussions *First Philosophy,* not because they were about things most easily understood but because they were about fundamentals. Several centuries after Aristotle's death, when other philosophers commented on Aristotle's arguments, they found that the essays on first philosophy came after the book on physics in the edition or manuscript with which they worked. Because the essays had no name, they were referred to in Greek as "*ta meta ta physika biblia,*" or "the books which come after the physics." Eventually, this was shortened to *The Metaphysics,* and the topics dealt with under this title were dubbed **"metaphysics."** Unfortunately, over the centuries the prefix "meta" has acquired the bogus sense of "super" or "going beyond" or "transcending sense perception." So metaphysics is thought somehow to deal with what transcends physics, with what is supernatural, occult, mysterious. Perhaps that is what our Greenwich Village metaphysician's clients expected—a touch of the beyond.

In philosophy, metaphysics is not really a single field or discipline, but rather a catchall for a number of problems whose scope and significance are so broad that they seem to have implications for virtually every other field of philosophy. Let me mention just a few of the questions that are dealt with by philosophers under the heading of "metaphysics." You will very quickly see why this branch of philosophy was for so long considered truly fundamental.

First there are the basic questions: What sorts of things are there? What are the categories into which whatever is can be sorted? Physical bodies in space? Minds? Properties of things, such as size, shape, color, smell, hardness, and taste? Events, such as the moving of a body from one place to another, or

---

Metaphysics   In modern philosophy, the study of the most fundamental principles of the nature of things. The term derives from an early description of the set of essays by Aristotle, called by him "First Philosophy," which came after the Physics in an edition of Aristotle's works (*ta meta ta physika,* or "after the Physics").

the growth of a tree from a seed, or the change in color of a leaf as it dies and browns? Ideas in a mind, thoughts, feelings, sense perceptions? How many different categories are there? Can some of these sorts of things be reduced to instances of other sorts? Is there one correct set of general categories for classifying things? What shall we say of peculiar things, like the number three, which does not seem to *exist*, in any ordinary sense, but on the other hand can hardly be said not to exist? (It would certainly sound odd to say that there is no such thing as the number three.)

Then there are more particular questions: What is space, and what is time? Are they dimensions? Containers in which things exist and happen? Relations among things? Forms of our perception of things? Can there be space in which nothing exists—a void, as it is called by philosophers and scientists? Can there be a stretch of time in which absolutely nothing happens? Could there be totally empty time, in which nothing happens and nothing even exists? What sense does it make to speak of "empty" time and "empty" space, as though they were huge boxes waiting to be filled up?

Is there such a thing as a soul? Is it made out of physical matter, and if not, what then is it? Is the soul the same as the mind? Can a soul exist without relation to a body? How? Do souls continue to exist after the body dies? Did they exist before they were associated with, or planted in, bodies? What *is* the relationship of the soul to the body? Is the mind the same as the brain? Is the body just an idea in the mind?

Does the past exist? If not, then does nothing exist save whatever there is right now at this very moment? If the past does exist, then where is it? Is there some other universe of past things? What about future things as well? Is there a whole assortment of possible worlds alongside this actual one that we live in? Does it make any sense at all to say that something has *possible* existence?

Are all of my actions absolutely causally determined by what has gone before, or am I free in some sense to choose among a variety of alternative actions available to me? If I am determined to act as I do, then can I also consider myself responsible for what I do? If I am free, what is the nature of my freedom? What sort of thing am I, that I should have this strange capacity to act freely?

Why is there anything at all in the universe? Why is there in general something and not nothing? Is the universe fundamentally absurd, or does it make some sort of rational sense? Was it created? Has it existed from all eternity? Can I even imagine a satisfactory *reason* for the universe? Does the universe stretch infinitely away from me in space? Will it go on existing forever?

And last, but of course hardly least: Is there an infinite, omnipotent, omniscient creator of all that is—a God?

Well, no one can accuse metaphysics of wasting its time on trivia! But how are we to get a handle on a field this vast in the confines of a single chapter? Following the practice of previous chapters, we shall begin by focusing on the life and thought of a single great philosopher, Thomas Hobbes, one of the most provocative thinkers ever to write in English. Although Hobbes wrote on many subjects, including the theory of the social contract and the nature of the state, we shall focus on his *metaphysical* theories, which we can describe in a word as materialism.

After getting a general idea of how Hobbes saw the world, and human beings in the world, we shall look at one of the oldest and most challenging metaphysical questions, the problem customarily referred to by philosophers as "free will and determinism." Hobbes, as we shall see, held a very controversial and uncompromising position on this question.

Finally, we shall take a brief look at the problem of the relationship between the mind and the body.

By the time we are done, you should have a pretty good idea of what metaphysics is and how some of the great thinkers have approached its most puzzling problems.

Hobbes' Materialism

The well-known American logician and philosopher Willard van Orman Quine, in one of his most famous essays, written more than half a century ago, begins with the following tongue-in-cheek observation.

> A curious thing about the ontological question is its simplicity. It can be put in three Anglo-Saxon monosyllables: "What is there?" It can be answered, moreover, in a word—"Everything"—and everyone will accept this answer as true. However, this is merely to say that there is what there is. There remains room for disagreement over cases; and so the issue has stayed alive down the centuries.

Quine is quite right; the issue has indeed stayed alive down the centuries. By and large, philosophers have argued not about particular *things,* but rather about what *sorts* of things there are. And simple as that little three-word question may look, it has turned out to be uncommonly difficult to find an answer that everyone can agree on.

Here are some of the sorts of things philosophers have said there are: physical bodies, including big ones like the stars and the planets, middle-sized ones like trees, houses, and the human body, and very small ones, such as atoms; minds, or souls, or spirits—not only the human mind, but also angels, devils, world-souls, and of course God; numbers, geometric shapes (triangles, squares, and so forth), logical relationships such as if-then, or, and not; sense perceptions, such as smells, tastes, sounds, sights, and feels; emotions, like anger, love, jealousy, and affection; properties or characteristics of bodies, such as softness, hardness, solubility, density, and elasticity; and even imaginary or fictional things, such as the Starship Enterprise, Superman, and Alf the alien.

If you look back over the past 2,500 years of Western philosophy, for each one of these kinds of things you can find at least one major thinker who argued for their existence. Democritus believed that physical bodies exist (as did lots of other philosophers, of course); Leibniz believed that minds or souls exist; Plato believed that numbers and logical relationships exist; Hume believed that sense perceptions exist; and Meinong believed that possible objects like Alf exist (in some curious sense of existing).

But simplifying for the sake of getting a handle on this confusion, we can say that there have been essentially three dominant positions in the whole history of the debate, to which philosophers have attached the titles *materialism, idealism,* and *dualism.* Materialism is the theory that physical objects in space are all there is—everything else, even mind or spirit, upon closer examination, turns out to be just combinations of physical objects. Idealism is the theory that minds or spirits are all there is—everything else, even the physical body, turns out upon closer examination to be just minds, or ideas in minds. Dualism (by now you should be able to figure this one out) is the theory that there are *two* fundamentally different kinds of things in the world—bodies and minds—neither of which can be reduced to, or analyzed into, the other.

The ancient Greek atomists, discussed briefly in Chapter 1, were materialists. They believed that everything, even soul or spirit, consists of very small, very fine bits of physical matter, which they called "atoms." Thomas Hobbes, writing 2,000 years after the time of those early philosophers, defended exactly the same theory. Hobbes was the most brilliant, insightful, consistent materialist since the time of ancient Greece. Let us begin by taking a look at Hobbes' materialism.

Hobbes has no serious difficulty explaining the physical universe in terms of atoms. Following the ancient thinkers, he describes the world as made up of very tiny atoms that are constantly moving about, bumping into one another like billiard balls. Allowing for 300 years of scientific advance, we still take essentially the same view today.

The problem for Hobbes or any other materialist is how to explain the human mind and its operations without ever appealing to anything except atoms in motion. How can we give a purely physical, atomistic explanation of desire, aversion, choice, deliberation, sensation, language, and such personality traits as courage, greed, or pride?

Hobbes's answer is both very modern and very puzzling. When light strikes my eye or sound strikes my ear, the atoms in the eye or ear begin to vibrate—to move. That motion is then communicated to the atoms next to them, and is passed along, by a chain reaction, until the atoms in the brain start to vibrate. The vibrating of the atoms in the brain is what we call sight or sound, seeing or hearing. When I think about something, all that happens is that certain atoms vibrate in a particular fashion.

Think, if you will, of Commander Data on the television show *Star Trek: The Next Generation.* Data is an android, and as we discover periodically when Geordie lifts up a flap on his head for repairs, he is essentially a very complicated, very sophisticated electronic machine. Many of the most provocative *Star Trek* episodes deal with the puzzling question, is Data alive? Is he a person? The last episode of the 1992–93 season even confronted the question, can Data feel emotions?

Hobbes' answer, if he were suddenly transported to the twentieth century, would be: Data is as alive as any of us, for we are all nothing more than very complicated machines.

Now, on the face of it, this does not sound quite right. We are surrounded today by extremely complicated machines, some of which—such as the computer on which I am writing these words—can perform wonders in a fraction of a second. But I do not think that my computer is alive, nor do I suppose that my car, my toaster, my VCR, or my telephone answering machine is alive. They are all very complicated machines, but they are not alive. What is more, I do not think that they get closer and closer to being alive, the more complicated they become.

The real test for a materialist like Hobbes is not explaining complicated machines—or, since there were no complicated machines in Hobbes' day, explaining complicated physical things like an eclipse, or combustion, or the human eye. No, the real test is explaining what seems most distinctively human, namely desires, aversions, choice, deliberation, and action. No one thinks a computer, however complicated, *desires* anything. It simply operates whatever programs are loaded into it.

Hobbes recognized that desire, deliberation, and choice—in a word, will—posed the greatest challenge to his philosophy, and he faced the problem head on. Here is a selection from his most important book, *Leviathan,* in which he undertakes to explain these most human of all of our capacities and characteristics.

> There be in Animals, two sorts of *Motions* peculiar to them: One called *Vitall;* begun in generation, and continued without interruption through their whole life; such as are the course of the *Bloud,* the *Pulse,* the *Breathing,* the *Concoction, Nutrition, Excretion,* &c; to which Motions there needs no help of Imagination: The other is *Animall motion,* otherwise called *Voluntary motion;* as to *go,* to *speak,* to *move* any of our limbes, in such manner as is first fancied in our minds. That Sense, is Motion in the organs and interiour parts of mans body, caused by the action of the things we See, Heare, &c;

And that Fancy is but the Reliques of the same Motion, remaining after Sense, has been already sayd in the first and second Chapters. And because *going, speaking,* and the like Voluntary motions, depend always upon a precedent thought of *whither, which way,* and *what,* it is evident, that the Imagination is the first internall beginning of all Voluntary Motion. And although unstudied men, do not conceive any motion at all to be there, where the thing moved is invisible; or the space it is moved in, is (for the shortnesse of it) insensible; yet that doth not hinder, but that such Motions are. For let a space be never so little, that which is moved over a greater space, whereof that little one is part, must first be moved over that. These small beginnings of Motion, within the body of Man, before they appear in walking, speaking, striking, and other visible actions, are commonly called ENDEAVOUR.

This Endeavour, when it is toward something which causes it, is called APPETITE, or DESIRE; the later, being the generall name; and the other, oftentimes restrayned to signifie the Desire of Food, namely *Hunger* and *Thirst.* And when the Endeavour is fromward something, it is generally called AVERSION.

That which men Desire, they are also sayd to LOVE: and to HATE those things, for which they have Aversion. So that Desire, and Love, are the same thing; save that by Desire, we alwayes signifie the Absence of the Object; by Love, most commonly the Presence of the same. So also by Aversion, we signifie the Absence; and by Hate, the Presence of the Object.

Of Appetites, and Aversions, some are born with men; as Appetite of food, Appetite of excretion, and exoneration, (which may also and more properly be called Aversions, from somewhat they feele in their Bodies;) and some other Appetites, not many. The rest, which are Appetites of particular things, proceed from Experience, and triall of their effects upon themselves, or other men. For of things wee know not at all, or believe not to be, we can have no further Desire, than to taste and try. But Aversion wee have for things, not onely which we know have hurt us; but also that we do not know whether they will hurt us, or not.

Those things which we neither Desire, nor Hate, we are said to *Contemne:* CONTEMPT being nothing else but an immobility, or contumacy of the Heart, in resisting the action of certain things; and proceeding from that the Heart is already moved otherwise, by other more potent objects; or from want of experience of them.

And because the constitution of a mans Body, is in continuall mutation; it is impossible that all the same things should alwayes cause in him the same Appetites, and Aversions; much lesse can all men consent, in the Desire of almost any one and the same Object.

> As, in Sense, that which is really within us, is (as I have sayd before) onely Motion, caused by the action of externall objects, but in apparence; to the Sight, Light and Colour; to the Eare, Sound; to the Nostrill, Odour, &c; so, when the action of the same object is continued from the Eyes, Eares, and other organs to the Heart; the reall effect there is nothing but Motion, or Endeavour; which consisteth in Appetite, or Aversion, to, or from the object moving.

Thomas Hobbes, *Leviathan*, Parts 1 and 2

Although Hobbes writes with great style, his English is of the seventeenth century, and you may therefore find it a bit hard to follow. Let me summarize what he is telling us in the passage you have just read.

There is nothing in the world but atoms moving about, and atoms, like all physical bodies, can move up or down, backward or forward, fast or slow—and nothing else. When I see a table with food on it, what is happening is that atoms from the food on the table (Hobbes did not know that light is a form of electromagnetic radiation) are moving into my eyes, where they start the atoms in my retinas and my optic nerves moving. Eventually, the atoms in a portion of my brain vibrate as a result of that motion in the eye, and that is what I call "seeing the food on the table."

Now, sometimes, these vibrations in my brain trigger vibrations in the nerves leading to my arms and legs; the muscles in my arms and legs contract, and I reach for the food, or start walking toward it. That, according to Hobbes, is what we call "desiring the food." On other occasions (perhaps because the food is rotting, and gives off a particular smell that agitates my nose), I start moving away from the food. That, says Hobbes, is what we call "having an aversion to the food," or perhaps "disliking the food."

Sometimes, of course, I vacillate between moving toward the food and moving away from it. Perhaps I am hungry, even though the food is rotting. So first the atoms in my brain agitate the nerves in such a way that I start to move toward it; then the atoms in my brain agitate the nerves in such a way that I start to move away from it. For a while, I go on like that, leaning toward it, leaning away from it, leaning toward it, leaning away from it. That, Hobbes says, is what we call "deliberating" or "deciding."

Finally, the atoms in my brain that are triggering movement toward the food get the better of the atoms in the brain that are triggering movement away, and my body makes a decisive move for the food on the table. That, says Hobbes, is what we call "willing," or "determining the will."

Stated as I just have, this all sounds horribly simpleminded. Surely desire, aversion, deliberation, and will are something more than that! But think about it for a minute. I can complicate the story considerably with some modern scientific jargon from the field of neurophysiology, and no doubt a complete explanation is going to be much, much more elaborate than anything Hobbes can tell us. But at bottom, won't it just be a story about atoms bumping into other atoms? Or, if you wish, electric currents passing along nerve pathways? Won't it be, when all is said and done, a *materialistic* explanation? After all, what else could the final explanation possibly be?

So in principle, Data *is* a human being. Or at least, he can become a human being once his neural circuitry gets complicated enough. The only real difference between Data and me is that Data's insides are wires and transistors, whereas mine are nerve cells and fluids. My body is wet and his is dry, as scientists these days like to say. But both Data and I—and you, of course—are physical beings, all of whose behavior must in principle be explainable in purely materialistic terms.

We are going to have a good deal more to say about this fascinating and troubling idea in the remainder of this chapter, but it might be a good idea right now to consider one of the principal objections to Hobbes' story, an objection we can label *the consciousness objection*.

The consciousness objection goes like this. The defining characteristic of all minds—the "essence," as some philosophers put it—is *consciousness*. I am aware of myself, of my own thoughts, feelings, pains, pleasures, hopes, fears, deductions, and sense impressions. As Descartes said in the *Meditations,* I am a thing that thinks. Now computers are not conscious. They are not aware of themselves. They are simply complicated combinations of transistors, circuitry, and other hardware. When I say that a computer is "calculating" something, or checking my grammar, I am speaking very loosely. I do the same sort of thing when I say that my car "doesn't want to start this morning." I do not actually suppose that my car sits there in the garage saying to itself, "It is cold outside. I think I won't turn over." I understand that the charge in the battery is low. I am just saying, in a sort of shorthand way, that the car is behaving *as though* it were conscious.

Exactly the same is true of a computer, although the physics of what is happening may be more complicated. When I type this sentence on my computer, I am actually causing a series of electric currents to be sent through the circuitry. Eventually, the cathode ray tube in the monitor sends a stream of particles to the screen in the shape of letters. But there is no consciousness in the computer of the words being formed, let alone of the ideas those words stand for.

So Data is not conscious; he (or it, as a character in one episode insists on saying) is simply a very advanced machine. We humans are conscious, no doubt the higher animals are conscious, and for all we know there are beings elsewhere in the universe who are conscious. And that shows that we, the higher animals, and those other beings, if they exist, *are not merely material things.*

That is the objection, and it certainly does have an initial plausibility. I *am* conscious, and I cannot see how that consciousness can simply be the same thing as a complicated electrical pattern in my nerve cells. But Hobbes, or any other materialist, has a very powerful comeback. If the mind is *not* some arrangement of matter, he may ask, what else could it possibly be? I started out as a nonconscious sperm fused with a nonconscious egg. As I grew and developed, I became more and more physically complicated. My organs and nervous system developed before I was born. At some point, either before or after birth (for this discussion, it does not matter which), I developed consciousness, and finally *self-consciousness*—an awareness of my own awareness.

I can always explain this development by appeal to the religious notion of a soul, but if I want a purely naturalistic, scientific explanation, my only option seems to be to explain consciousness as a certain level of complexity of my physical body. In short, Hobbes appears to be right.

Free Will and Determinism

We turn first to one of the oldest and most difficult problems in all of philosophy, the conflict between *free will* and *determinism*. The problem is this: I think of myself as free, at least within some limits, to choose what I will do, and how I will do it. Give me enough money to buy an ice cream cone, and I think of myself as free to choose vanilla, chocolate, or strawberry. Present me with a college course catalogue, and I deliberate about precisely which courses to enroll for. Even if I am confined to my bed with a broken leg, physically able to do little more than turn my head to the right or to the left, I think of myself as free to choose which way I will turn, or even whether I will turn at all.

The notion that I am free to choose is important to me when I am trying to decide what to do, for it would not make much sense to trouble myself with deciding unless I were really free to choose. It also is important when I am trying to judge whether I am responsible for what I do. I consider myself responsible for deciding to run a red light, because I am aware of having chosen to do it. But I do not consider myself responsible for the beating of my heart, because I do not think I could choose whether to have it beat or not.

So some things are within my choice, and some are not. I am free to choose among the things that are within my choice, and hence I can be held responsible for what I have chosen. Without this notion of freedom and choice, our whole legal system seems to make no sense, nor does any of our ethical and political deliberation.

But even as I tell myself that I am *free to choose,* I also am aware that I am a physical being like any other, and that the movements of my arms and legs, the sounds I utter, everything I do, can be traced to physical causes in my nervous system, my muscles, my bones, and my other organs. And I am accustomed to thinking of physical movements of that sort as *causally determined,* not free. If I trigger an electrical impulse in a nerve cell, the impulse travels along the cell and causes a muscle to contract. If I shine light on the retina of my eye, a series of physical reactions is set up that results in my seeing a colored light. I can "choose" to close my eye, of course, but even that is accomplished by a causal sequence that takes impulses from the brain and sends them to the muscles controlling my eyelids.

Hobbes, as we have seen, is a materialist. He argues that all things, including thoughts in our minds, consist of the motions of atoms. And the motions of atoms obey the universal laws of physics, in which there seems to be no room for *choice* or *freedom*. So Hobbes denies that there is any sort of free will, in the sense described above.

According to Hobbes, here is what actually happens. First, atoms from outside the body strike the various sense organs of the body (eyes, ears, etc.), setting up sympathetic vibrations in the nerve cells, which are carried to the brain. Then the brain atoms rattle about, bumping into one another, triggering little beginning motions toward or away from something outside of the body. These to-ings and fro-ings, these bumpings and reboundings, are what I call *thinking about what I am going to do,* or *deliberating.* So long as this process is going on, I am under the illusion that I am "free," because the motions are too small and quick for me to observe them. Eventually, the atoms bump into each other in such a way that a message is sent back down the nerve cells to the muscles, and I move (I go to the store and buy some chocolate ice cream, perhaps). I now tell myself that I have *freely chosen* to buy the chocolate ice cream, but in fact my "choice" is as rigorously determined by the law of physics as any movement of balls on a billiard table.

Perhaps I can make Hobbes' theory a bit clearer, and also a bit more believable, with the help of one of Hobbes' countrymen, Jonathan Swift, who published his great satire, *Gulliver's Travels,* just seventy-five years after Hobbes published *Leviathan.*

Do you remember that in *Gulliver's Travels,* Lemuel Gulliver travels first to a land of very small people, the Lilliputians, and then to a land of very big people, the Brobdingnagians? Swift is rather careful about his proportions, and while the Lilliputians are exactly one-twelfth the size of normal humans, the Brobdingnagians are exactly twelve times as big. So, in comparison to Gulliver, who is six feet tall, they are seventy-two feet tall.

Now let us suppose (this is not actually in the book, of course) that the Brobdingnagians played dominoes and were especially fond of setting up long rows of dominoes so that when the first was tipped over, each of the remaining dominoes would be knocked over in turn. (I assume you have all seen this sort of thing, or have even done it yourselves.) The Brobdingnagian dominoes, of course, would be enormous—three feet long. And let us also suppose that Gulliver has brought along a set of his own dominoes, which are the normal length—three inches each.

Gulliver, we may imagine, sets up a display of dominoes for the amusement of the Brobdingnagians, who also, by the way, do not have very good

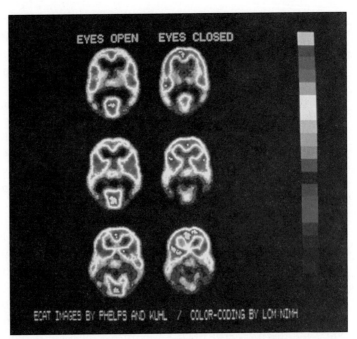

EYES OPEN   EYES CLOSED

ECAT IMAGES BY PHELPS AND KUHL / COLOR-CODING BY LOM:NIMH

Positron Image. The CAT scan (short for computerized axial tomography) has made it possible for physicians to get a three-dimensional picture of the brain—but not, of course, to get a picture of the mind. *(Source:* National Institute of Health.*)*

eyesight. In fact, while they can see their own dominoes well enough from their great height, Gulliver's dominoes are too small for them to be able to pick out.

Gulliver sets up a long row of big Brobdingnagian dominoes and then carefully arranges the last in the series so that when it falls, it just barely brushes the first of a long row of normal-sized dominoes. These are set to fall over, one after another, until the very last hits a hair-triggered big domino, which starts a second row of Brobdingnagian dominoes falling.

Okay. There is our imaginary experiment, all set up. A row of big dominoes, then a row of small ones, and then another row of big dominoes. The Brobdingnagians sit down on their enormous chairs and tell Gulliver to begin the demonstration. He shoves the first big three-foot domino over, and one by one the dominoes begin to fall.

Now what actually happens of course is that each domino is knocked over by the one just before it. *But that is not what the Brobdingnagians see.* They see the first run of big dominoes fall, but the middle run of small dominoes is too small for them to see, so for a while, as far as they can tell, nothing at all is happening. Then suddenly (or so it seems to them) the first big domino in the second run falls over, apparently without having been pushed, and the second run starts falling, one after the other.

To the Brobdingnagians, it looks as though the second run of dominoes started falling freely, spontaneously, without having been caused to fall. *And that is exactly the way our very own actions appear to us.* Because our eyes are not able to see the tiny brain atoms pushing and shoving, we mistakenly think that our movements are spontaneous, free, uncaused. In fact, they are just as rigorously determined by the previous movements of atoms as the second run of big dominoes was by the fall of the little dominoes in between.

To be sure, Hobbes admits that we use words like "freedom" and "choice" and "deliberation," but upon close examination, these words turn out to refer to physically determined motions of atoms, for that is all there is in the world. According to Hobbes, when I say that a man is *free,* all I mean is that nothing external to him stood in the way of his doing what he was inclined to do. But his inclination itself is of course causally determined, as is everything in the natural world. Here is how Hobbes explains "freedom."

LIBERTY, or FREEDOME, signifieth (properly) the absence of Opposition; (by Opposition, I mean externall Impediments of motion;) and may be applyed no lesse to Irrationall, and Inanimate creatures, than to Rationall. For whatsoever is so tyed, or environed, as it cannot move, but within a certain space, which space is determined by the opposition of some externall body, we say it hath not Liberty to go further. And so of all living creatures, whilest they are imprisoned, or restrained, with walls, or chayns; and of the water whilest it is kept in by banks, or vessels, that otherwise would spread it selfe into a larger space, we use to say, they are not at Liberty, to move in such manner, as without those externall impediments they would. But when the impediment of motion, is in the constitution of the thing it selfe, we use not to say, it wants the Liberty; but the Power to move; as when a stone lyeth still, or a man is fastned to his bed by sicknesse.

And according to this proper, and generally received meaning of the word, A FREE-MAN, *is he, that in those things, which by his strength and wit he is able to do, is not hindred to doe what he has a will to.* . . . From the use of the word Freewill, no liberty can be inferred to the will, desire, or inclination, but the liberty of the man; which consisteth in this, that he finds no stop, in doing what he has the will, desire, or inclination to doe.

Feare and Liberty are consistent; as when a man throweth his goods into the Sea for *feare* the ship should sink, he doth it neverthelesse very willingly, and may refuse to doe it if he will: It is therefore the action, of one that was *free:* so a man sometimes pays his debt, only for *feare* of Imprisonment, which because no body hindred him from detaining, was the action of a man at *liberty.* And generally all actions which men doe in Commonwealths, for *feare* of the law, are actions, which the doers had *liberty* to omit.

Liberty and *Necessity* are Consistent: As in the water, that hath not only *liberty,* but a *necessity* of descending by the Channel: so likewise in the Actions which men voluntarily doe; which (because they proceed from their will) proceed from *liberty;* and yet because every act of mans will, and every desire, and inclination proceedeth from some cause, and that from another cause, which causes in a continuall chaine (whose first link is in the hand of God the first of all causes) proceed from *necessity.* So that to him that could see the connexion of those causes, the *necessity* of all mens voluntary actions, would appeare manifest.

Thomas Hobbes, *Leviathan,* Parts 1 and 2

Although Hobbes was unusual among philosophers of the seventeenth and eighteenth centuries in defending materialism, he was by no means alone in denying that human beings have a will that is free of external determinations. David Hume takes the same view in his *Treatise of Human Nature,* although, as we shall see very shortly, he manages at the same time to get a dig in at Hobbes.

In Hume's day—the 1700s—it was commonplace for philosophers and scientists to grant the absolute determination of physical events but at the same time to claim that human actions are freely chosen. Hume pointed out that no one in actual practice really believes any such thing. We go through the day making predictions about the behavior of those around us and very often bet our lives on the accuracy of those predictions. When I drive down a two-way street (my example, of course, not Hume's), at every moment I am predicting that the people driving toward me will not suddenly decide to veer into my lane and crash into my car. When I fly in a commercial airplane, I bet my life that the pilot will perform in a totally expected fashion, taking off and landing in accordance with the rules and practices of safe navigation. When I buy a meal at a restaurant, I depend on the chef not to poison me.

All of these beliefs about the behavior of others are instances of causal judgments, Hume says, and we all consider them quite as reliable as our judgments about the boiling point of water or the properties of sodium. But that is just another way of saying that we consider the behavior of people to be causally determined, just as the behavior of physical bodies is. Hume puts the point this way:

Shou'd a traveller, returning from a far country, tell us, that he had seen a climate in the fiftieth degree of northern latitude, where all the fruits ripen and come to perfection in the winter, and decay in the summer, after the same manner as in *England* they are produc'd and decay in the contrary seasons, he would find few so credulous as to believe him. I am apt to think a traveller wou'd meet with as little credit, who shou'd inform us of people exactly of the same character with those in *Plato's Republic* on the one hand, or those in *Hobbes's Leviathan* on the other. There is a general course of nature in human actions, as well as in the operations of the sun and the climate. There are also characters peculiar to different nations and particular persons, as well as common to mankind. The knowledge of these characters is founded on the observation of an uniformity in the actions, that flow from them; and this uniformity forms the very essence of necessity.

David Hume,
Treatise on Human Nature

In the face of these arguments, it will obviously require a very strong counterattack to defend the notion of the freedom of the human will. The strongest response in the entire philosophical literature comes from Immanuel Kant.

At the end of Chapter 2, we saw that Kant tried to resolve the conflict between the empiricists and the rationalists by appealing to the old distinction between appearance and reality. Our scientific and mathematical knowledge, he said, is knowledge only of appearance, not of independent reality. Even mathematical physics gives us knowledge only of how things appear to us in space and time. How they are in themselves is forever a closed book to us.

Confronted by the conflict between the determinism of science and morality's demand for freedom and responsibility, Kant adopts a similar position. The realm of appearance, the world of mathematics and science, is through and through determined, he argues. Thus far, Kant agrees completely with Hobbes and Hume. But the realm of independent reality stands outside of the chain of natural causation. In that realm, a different kind of determination holds sway, what Kant calls "rational determination." And in that realm— or, as he sometimes puts it, from that standpoint—we are free, not causally determined.

To be sure, our freedom is not license or a mere absence of determination. That, Kant insists, is impossible. But in the realm of independent reality, we are self-determined, obeying only laws that our reason gives to itself. We are thus lawgivers to ourselves, or *autonomous* ("the Greek auto-nomos" means "giving law to oneself"). Here is Kant's clearest statement of his position:

If appearances were things in themselves, and space and time forms of the existence of things in themselves, the conditions would always be members of the same series as the conditioned; and thus, in the present case, as in the other transcendental ideas, the antinomy would arise, that the series must be too large or too small for the understanding. But the dynamical concepts of reason, with which we have to deal in this and the following section, possess this peculiarity that they are not concerned with an object considered as a magnitude, but only with its existence. Accordingly we can abstract from

IMMANUEL KANT,
Critique of Pure Reason

Immanuel Kant. Kant tried to resolve conflict between empiricists and rationalists by appealing to the distinction between appearance and reality. *(Source:* Courtesy of Library of Congress.)

the magnitude of the series of conditions, and consider only the dynamical relation of the condition to the conditioned. The difficulty which then meets us, in dealing with the question regarding nature and freedom, is whether freedom is possible at all, and if it be possible, whether it can exist along with the universality of the natural law of causality. Is it a truly disjunctive proposition to say that every effect in the world must arise *either* from nature *or* from freedom; or must we not rather say that in one and the same event, in different relations, both can be found? That all events in the sensible world stand in thorough-going connection in accordance with unchangeable laws of nature is an established principle of the Transcendental Analytic, and allows of no exception. The question, therefore, can only be whether freedom is completely excluded by this inviolable rule, or whether an effect, notwithstanding its being thus determined in accordance with nature, may not at the same time be grounded in freedom. The common but fallacious presupposition of the *absolute reality* of appearances here manifests its injurious influence, to the confounding of reason. For if appearances are things in themselves, freedom cannot be upheld. Nature will then be the complete and sufficient determining cause of every event. The condition of the event will be such as can be found only in the series of appearances; both it and its effect will be necessary in accordance with the law of nature. If, on the other hand, appearances are not taken for more than they actually are; if they are viewed not as things in themselves, but merely as representations, connected according to empirical laws, they must themselves have grounds which are not appearances. The effects of such an intelligible cause appear, and accordingly can be determined through other appearances, but its causality is not so determined. While the effects are to be found in the series of empirical conditions, the intelligible cause, together with its causality, is outside the series. Thus the effect may be regarded as free in respect of its intelligible cause, and at the same time in respect of appearances as resulting from them according to the necessity of nature.

Immanuel Kant, *Critique of Pure Reason*

The Mind and the Body

People who report so-called out-of-body experiences sometimes recall that they felt their consciousness had removed itself from their body, distancing from it or hovering over it. My mother once told me that as she was gaining consciousness after a surgical procedure she had the sensation that her consciousness was floating near the ceiling of the hospital room, watching the medical personnel tending to her body. She interpreted the experience to indicate that she had been near death. Reports like these have been common in recent years—a recent Google search produced nearly a million and one-half hits.

Such experiences often are associated with the paranormal, the occult, or the mystical—in the same category as astrology, fortune telling, and UFOs. Web sites proclaim "Astral Flight," "Astral Projection," "Near Death Experiences," "Ouija Mysteries," "Alien Abduction," and so on. This may be a reason that some scientifically oriented people are reluctant to talk about them. Yet the September 19, 2002, edition of ABCNEWS.com contained an article, "Mind Over Body: Neurologist Finds Way to Trigger Out-of-Body Experiences." The reference was to an article in the journal *Nature* in which Swiss scientists described " . . . how they were able to trigger bizarre, out-of-body experiences in a 43-year-old female epileptic patient while analyzing her brain with electrodes." The article in *Nature* is significant because it reported that " . . . the sensation [had] been captured in the controlled setting of a laboratory." Here were reputable scientists joining in on the conversation.

Some people claim that reports of out-of-body experiences yield "amazing conclusions"—proof, among other things, that our consciousness can, or does, exist quite apart from our body. As students of philosophy, we perhaps may be forgiven for doubting that such experiences prove any such thing: we can accept the truthfulness of those who describe these experiences, and still wonder how the experiences are best explained. For example, I certainly believe that my mother described her experience there in that hospital room truthfully; all my life I found her to be a very truthful woman. But clearly her sensation, that her consciousness was floating near the ceiling, out of her body, did not prove that it was. I have had the sensation that I was falling when I was not falling, for example. Perhaps a more coherent explanation for her experience would be that as she was regaining consciousness she was in a dream-like state, or imagining things. Nevertheless, it seems to me that reports of such experiences do *reinforce* a prevalent view about the nature of minds and bodies and the relationship between the two, a view so prevalent that the English philosopher Gilbert Ryle[1] called it "the official view."

According to this view as Ryle characterized it, every human being, with the possible exception of infants and those who are severely mentally retarded, has (or is) both a body and a mind. During the human being's lifetime, the body and the mind ordinarily are linked together into a working unit; but the mind can survive and function after the body dies. This is of course a species of dualism, a position you met earlier in this chapter. But attractive—and familiar—as the distinction is, trying to make sense out of it has been one of the thorniest problems in modern philosophy, the **mind-body problem.** As with so many problems in philosophy, it was Descartes who formulated the mind-body problem for the modern era.

As we saw in the last chapter, Descartes convinced himself that he could be certain of his own existence, "I am," but not certain that he had senses and a body. That at least was where his thinking led him in the first two of the *Meditations*. However, by the time he reached *Meditation VI,* he had concluded that he was a being composed of a mind *and* a body:

> From the very fact that I know with certainty that I exist, and that I find that absolutely nothing else belongs necessarily to my nature or

Mind-Body Problem   The *Mind-Body Problem* is the problem of explaining exactly what the relationship is between our minds and physical bodies in space. There are really *three* problems lumped together under this heading: First, do minds and bodies causally interact with one another, and if so, how? Second, how, if at all, can I (i.e., my mind) gain knowledge about bodies—indeed, can minds really know anything at all about bodies, or do minds only know about themselves? And third, what is the special relationship between *my* mind and *my* body? In the twentieth century, the Mind-Body Problem led philosophers to a related problem, the *Problem of Other Minds:* How, if at all, can I know of the existence and contents of minds other than my own? Is there anyone out there, or am I alone in a world of mere bodies?

essence except that I am a thinking being, I readily conclude that my essence consists solely in being a body which thinks or a substance whose whole essence or nature is only to think. And although perhaps, or rather certainly, . . . I have a body with which I am very closely united, nevertheless, since on the one hand I have a clear and distinct idea of myself in so far as I am only a thinking and not an extended being, and since on the other hand I have a distinct idea of body in so far as it is only an extended being which does not think, it is certain that this "I"—that is to say, my soul, by virtue of which I am what I am—is entirely and truly distinct from my body and that it can be or exist without it.

René Descartes, *Meditations on First Philosophy*, Meditations I-VI

Descartes had at least two motivations for developing the official view. One of his motivations was scientific: as we saw in the last chapter, he believed that he was to spend his life establishing a new, unified theory of the universe based upon mathematics.

The physical theories developed by Aristotle and refined by countless philosophers during the many centuries following placed great emphasis upon the purposive order of nature. Aristotle himself conceived of nature as exhibiting an inherent purpose that need not be traced to the conscious intentions of a divine creator. Later philosophers in the Christian tradition tended to appeal, at some point in their arguments, to such a divine purpose. But whether religiously based or not, physical theories relied heavily upon notions of goal, end, purpose, and rational order, usually associated with the operations of conscious agents. As we have seen, Descartes focused his attention entirely on the self-conscious self or mind at the outset of philosophical deliberations. But when he came to develop his theory of the physical universe, he rejected entirely any appeal to properties, concepts, or modes of explanation associated with the mental or the conscious. The material universe, he argued, was characterized by such properties as extension and motion. All explanation in science must be couched in terms of size, shape, density, velocity, and the like.

This exclusion of the mental from the sphere of physical explanation was prompted by the fact that extension and motion could be quantified and treated mathematically, whereas purpose, end, goal, intention, or rational order could not be. The tools of arithmetic and analytic geometry were inapplicable to the notions that Aristotle and his followers had employed in their physical explanations. So it was the search for a mathematical science that led Descartes to exclude all "mentalistic" characteristics from his physical theories. But having thus shunted aside the mental, Descartes was forced to ask himself what relationship there was between the physical realm of extension and motion to which the new science applied, and the realm of thought, purpose, and reason. Here was the scientific motivation.

Another motivation, stemming from Descartes' Roman Catholicism, is apparent in the letter of dedication that Descartes wrote to the Dean and Doctors of the Sacred Faculty of Theology of Paris as a preface to the copy of the *Meditations* that he sent to them:

> My reason for offering you this work is so logical, and after you have learned its plan you will also, I am sure, have so logical a reason to take it under your protection, that I believe nothing will recommend it to you more than a brief statement of what I herein propose to do.
>
> I have always thought that the . . . [question] . . . of the soul [was among] the principal questions . . . that should be demonstrated by rational philosophy rather than theology. For although it may suffice us faithful ones to believe by faith that . . . the human soul does not perish with the body, certainly it does not seem possible ever to persuade those without faith to accept any religion . . . or expectation of another life . . . unless they can be shown [this] by natural reason.

Thus Descartes faced two challenges: first, to find a place in physical, mathematically describable nature for a nonphysical, nonquantitative mind; and second, to demonstrate by rational philosophy that the soul survives bodily death. Descartes found that metaphysical theories already in circulation seemed to provide him the philosophical materials he needed to meet these challenges—that is, to develop a theory to explain the relationship between the realms of consciousness and physics, and at the same time show how the soul continues to survive after the body dies.

Descartes' proposal was relatively simple: he argued that minds and bodies are two different kinds of *substances*. Minds (or souls—Descartes did not distinguish between the mind and the soul) are immaterial, unextended, simple conscious substances, and bodies are material, extended, composite, nonconscious substance. A human being is thus a combination of a material substance—the body—and a spiritual substance—the mind.

(Source: By permission of Johnny Hart and Creators Syndicate, Inc.)

In metaphysics, the term "substance" is a technical one, and notions surrounding the term have a convoluted and complex history. But two features concern us here. First, according to the traditional theory, the substance of a thing is its essence, or that which remains the same throughout all changes in its characteristics or properties. To use an example from Aristotle, a man (substance) may be suntanned at one time, fair at another; hot at one time, cold at another; bad at one time, good at another; but throughout he remains the same man, although at the different times he exhibits the different properties of darkness, fairness, etc. According to Descartes, the fundamental property of material substance is extension in length, width, and depth. Other properties are size, shape, location, movement, and divisibility. The fundamental property of mental substance is thinking. Minds are indivisible, not extended in length, breadth, and depth, and do not participate in any of the qualities of bodies.

Second, substance is that which can exist by itself and does not need something else for its existence, as characteristics or properties do: substance is that which *has* the characteristics or properties, or that in which the characteristics or properties "inhere." For example, there are many green objects—or square figures, or tall people—but something has to be there to *be* green, or square, or tall. The objects, or figures, or people, are the substances which exhibit the properties or characteristics—green, square, tall—and upon which the properties or characteristics depend for their existence. Destroy the green leaf beneath your heel, and its greenness is destroyed with it. Other green things remain in the world, of course, but that leaf's greenness is gone with the leaf. Lewis Carroll's Cheshire cat that goes away leaving nothing behind but its grin is a wonderfully amusing fictional personage, but we know that a grin can't just remain behind all by itself. A grin is a configuration of a face, or a mouth. Without a face or a mouth there can't be a grin. Thus in the context of the metaphysical theories of his time, and having set out to show that the soul can exist independently of the body—that it can exist by itself—Descartes in his theory *had* to categorize the soul as a substance.

You probably have noticed that, according to this feature of the traditional theory, the only substance—that which can exist by itself and needs nothing else for its existence—would be God! Descartes was aware of this implication of the theory; he argued that minds and bodies are the two kinds of *created* substances.

Nevertheless, Descartes held, although mind and body are entirely and truly distinct from one another, they do interact in a relationship of cause and effect. The causal link works both ways—body to mind, and mind to body. For example, when I drink an alcoholic beverage, the alcohol causes changes in my body chemistry (a bodily change), and this in turn may lead to fuzzy thinking (a mental condition): this is a body-to-mind causal link. Similarly, if I daydream about my sweetheart (a mental process), I may find that my palms become sweaty, my breathing becomes heavier, and so on (bodily changes), and this despite the fact that I am only daydreaming: here the causal link is mind-to-body. All this of course is consistent with common experience.

Descartes' dualistic theory of a universe with a spiritual realm alongside a physical realm, each composed of a substance with its own unique properties, each having its place in nature, but causally interacting, seemed to respond to both his challenges. It accommodated, on the one hand, the seventeenth century world view of a physical realm of extension and motion to which the new science applied, and, on the other hand, the Christian world view that included a nonphysical, nonquantitative realm of souls able to exist independently of the material realm. If you go on to study the *Meditations* in detail you will discover that Descartes did not deliver on his promise to the Paris University Faculty of Theology to demonstrate the immortality of the soul; but his theory, *dualistic interactionism,* laid the theoretical foundation for that possibility. And as far as I know, Descartes never claimed to have had out-of-body experiences; but again, his theory probably would allow for them.

But a problem seems to be lurking here: If spiritual substance and material substance really are as radically different as Descartes suggests, neither one participating in any of the qualities of the other, how can there be any interaction between them? A mind can interact with a mind, a body can interact with a body, but how can a nonmaterial, unextended substance be touched, moved, altered, or affected by a material, extended substance? And how can a simple, unextended, conscious substance touch, move, alter, or affect an extended, material substance?

Contemporaries of Descartes were quick to point out a paradox: If Descartes' two-substance theory were true, the causal interaction so consistent with common experience apparently would be impossible! Here is the

---

Three Mind Body Theories

1. **Idealism:** the theory that everything in the universe is either minds, or else ideas in minds (hence, "*idealism*"). Bodies, according to the idealist, are simply particular collections of ideas. Thus, a table is simply the interconnected set of all of the ideas—concepts, images, feels, sights, sounds, and so on—that I think of as *ideas of* a table.
2. **Materialism:** the theory that everything in the universe is matter (hence, "materialist"). Minds, according to the materialist, are simply collections of very small bodies, or structures and organizations of bodies (such as nerve cells in the brain). Perceptions, to the materialist, are particular sorts of interactions between bodies, and so are thoughts, emotions, and feelings of pleasure and pain.
3. **Psycho-Physical Dualism:** the theory that minds are one kind of substance and bodies are another. The defining characteristic of mind, according to the dualist, is consciousness or thought. The defining characteristic of body is spacial extension (and sometimes also force or impenetrability). For the dualist, the major problem is to explain how mind and matter interact and affect one another.

heart of the "Cartesian Problem," the problem of attempting to find a way out of the morass into which Descartes' dualistic interactionism led him.

There have been countless attempts to solve the problem of the nature and relationship of mind and body, and in an introductory text of this kind, it would be folly to try to lay them all out for you. Nevertheless, I would like to introduce you to a few of them as examples of philosophical thinking and method, and of how, if a problem seems thorny enough, almost any solution, however bizarre it may seem to us, may appeal to even a great thinker.

The two aspects of Descartes' theory that lead to the Cartesian Problem are (a) its dualism, and (b) its interactionism. Some attempts to resolve the problem retained the theory's dualism while rejecting its interactionism; others rejected its dualism.

Taking a cue from Descartes' scientific world view of parallel realms— a material realm of bodies in space governed by physical laws and describable in mathematical terms, and a radically different mental realm of nonphysical, nonquantitative consciousness—one alternative to Descartes' dualistic interactionism was *parallelism,* according to which the material and mental realms, being composed of different substances, never actually causally interact but operate in tandem in such a way that there seems to be a causal interaction. Since the appearance of a causal connection is so compelling, the apparent interaction nevertheless seems to call for an explanation of some kind. Using a famous two-clocks analogy, Leibniz suggested that, in creating a human being, God programs that person's mental and physical lives in advance so that they always function harmoniously in *pre-established harmony:* just as two perfectly timed clocks always tick and chime in perfect unison without there ever being any interaction between them, so do a person's mental and physical lives function harmoniously without causal interaction. Another form of parallelism that was seriously advanced in the seventeenth century was *occasionalism.* This is the theory that an event in a person's physical history provides an occasion for God's intervention to bring about an appropriate event in the person's mental history, and vice versa. Both these forms of parallelism pose formidable problems for many modern thinkers, who find the theology upon which they are based at least as mysterious, if not more so, than the mind-body problem itself.

Other thinkers attempted to avoid the Cartesian Problem by rejecting Descartes' two-substance view altogether and opting instead for varieties of *monism,* or one-substance theories. *Materialism* (not to be confused with an excessive desire for money), advocated by Hobbes, among others, is the view that everything in the universe is a body, and that minds are to be analyzed as collections of, or aspects of, or configurations of, bodies. *Idealism* (also not to be confused with a belief in high principles or the flag), developed by George Berkeley, among others, is the one-substance theory that everything in the universe is mental in nature, and that bodies are to be analyzed as collections of, or aspects of, or thoughts in, minds. *Neutral monism,* sometimes associated with *double-aspect* theories, is the doctrine that the universe consists of only one underlying substance which is itself neither mental nor physical but of which mind and body are two manifestations, aspects, or emanations. *Epiphenomenalism* is the view that mental states are causal by-products of physical processes, but denies that mental events ever cause changes in the body or any part of it. An analogy is that of the incandescent light bulb. Physical changes in the filament excited by electricity cause the filament to glow, thus producing light; but the light emitted by the bulb has no causal effect back on the filament.

In a book published in 1949, *The Concept of Mind,* the English philosopher Gilbert Ryle argued that Descartes' theory, "the official view" (or "Descartes' myth" as Ryle called it), as well as most of the other theories we have mentioned, suffer from a fundamental logical confusion, a confusion Ryle labeled a "category mistake." A category mistake is either the placing of something in a category in which it does not belong, or attributing a property to something that is the wrong kind of thing to have that property. One of Ryle's examples of the former concerns a visitor to a university who, after having been shown classrooms, the library, a laboratory, faculty offices, playing fields, and residence halls, says, "Thank you for the tour; but where is the university?" The visitor has made a category mistake, the mistake of placing the university in the same logical category as a classroom, the library, etc. The visitor doesn't understand that the classroom, library, laboratories, etc. just *are what make up* the university. Examples of the other kind of category mistake are "Caesar was prime [a prime number]" and "My dream was polysyllabic." Numbers may be prime or not, but persons are not the kind of things that can be prime; and although words may be polysyllabic, dreams can't—they are the wrong kind of thing to have that property.

Ryle argued that Descartes' mistake was to treat the terms, "minds" and "bodies," as if they were of the same logical type–substances—whereas (according to Ryle) they are of different logical types. At the same time, Ryle did not deny that there occur mental processes: "Doing long division is a mental process and so is making a joke. But I am saying that the phrase 'there occur mental processes' does not mean the same sort of thing as 'there occur physical processes'." To say of a person that she has a brilliant mind is not to say that she possesses some occult substance—a mind, a "thing"—that is lodged in some mysterious location in her body, a thing that has the property of being brilliant in the same way that her body may have the property of being five feet tall. It is, rather, to say that she possesses certain capabilities or capacities in an especially striking way.

When two terms belong to the same logical category, it makes sense to construct sentences conjoining them, as in "She bought a right hand glove and a left hand glove," or contrasting them, "She bought a green lawn chair or an orange one, but not both", but it doesn't make sense when the terms belong to different categories, as in "She bought a right hand glove and a left hand glove, *and* a pair of gloves," or "She bought a right hand glove and a left hand glove, or a pair of gloves, *but not both*". Thus idealists and materialists are as guilty of a category mistake as Descartes was when they make such claims as, "Either there exist minds [idealists] or there exist bodies [materialists], but not both." Both are attempting to contrast terms of different logical types in an illegitimate way.

Ryle's program in *The Concept of Mind* was largely critical—to dispel what he called "Descartes' myth." His constructive theory has been called a form of *philosophical behaviorism:* he attempted to analyze mental processes and states in terms of capacities or dispositions to behave in characteristic ways. On this account, to say that a person knows something (to be in a certain mental state) is to say, among other things, that she is able to do certain things—to solve quadratic equations, for example; and to say that a person believes something is to say, among other things, that he is disposed to behave in certain ways in certain circumstances—to fetch his umbrella before going outside when he believes it is raining, for example. Critics were quick to attack Ryle's behaviorism (some raised the consciousness objection that had plagued Hobbes' materialism, for example) but Ryles's critique of Cartesian dualism, and of traditional idealism and materialism, stimulated attempts to find alternative approaches to the mind-body problem.

One striking feature of recent literature on the mind-body problem is that very few philosophers still frame the problem in terms of substances. In this regard Ryle's critique has been largely successful. Most thinkers, even those who agree with Descartes that the mental is not physical, have stopped thinking of the mind as a *thing*-that is, as an elusive, nonmaterial object of the same logical type as a body—opting instead to approach the mind-body problem in terms of categories such as physical and mental processes, states, events, or properties. Indeed, on some views, there is no such thing as a mind at all. Donald Davidson, the late emeritus professor of philosophy at the University of California at Berkeley, wrote:

> There are no such things as minds, but people have mental properties, which is to say that certain psychological predicates are true of them. These properties are constantly changing, and such changes are mental events. Examples are: noticing that it is time for lunch, seeing that the wind is rising, remembering the new name of Cambodia, deciding to spend next Christmas in Botswana, or developing a taste for Trollope. Mental events are, in my view, physical (which is not, of course, to say that they are not mental).[2]

Much of the recent literature on the mind-body problem has been highly technical, involving concepts from neurophysiology and esoteric branches of logic, and the arguments in support of competing theories are complex, as you might imagine. But in closing this section, I would like to give you some sense of the direction of recent debate by briefly outlining an approach taken in the past few years, the *identity theory* of the mental and the physical.

The basic idea underlying the identity theory—or rather, the various identity theories—is that every mental phenomenon (state, event, or process) is identical to some physical phenomenon; that is, that every phenomenon that has a mental description—such as noticings, rememberings, itches, and hopes do—also has a physical description, a description in the vocabulary of physics. For example, identity theorists claim that a mental event, such as a sudden feeling of pain, identically is a physical event, such as a neural firing in the brain: here are two different ways of describing the same event, much as you might describe the breaking of your arm in terms of broken bones and lacerations, on the one hand, or in terms of the pain and distress it caused you, on the other. But there are no mental events that are not identical to some physical event. Notice that the views we are discussing are not of the crude, "The mind just is the brain," variety; and although I think it is fair to characterize identity theories as varieties of materialism, or "physicalism," they certainly are not wedded to what some writers describe as "the billiard-ball physics"of the nineteenth century.[3] These more sophisticated varieties of materialism embrace the quarks, leptons, and hadrons of modern physics, as well as energy and electro-magnetic fields. What they deny is that there are any non-physical entities such as minds or souls, although as we have seen in the quote from Davidson, they acknowledge that persons exhibit mental characteristics.

How could this be? To be sure, my thoughts, feelings of pain, decisions, and so on, may be closely associated in some way with functions of my body. There may be some close causal connection that modern techniques of brain surgery, neurophysiology, and the like can discover. But the most that a brain surgeon can demonstrate, surely, is that when she puts an electrode in my brain and sends a little current through it, then I feel or hear or see or taste something. Does that prove that my feeling, hearing, seeing, or tasting identically is the physical response to the movement of the electrical current along my nerve paths?

While identity theorists probably would not want to claim that this experiment *proves* that my feeling, hearing, seeing, or tasting identically is the physical response to the movement of electrical current, they would want to claim that an identity theory provides the most philosophically satisfactory explanation, in light of all our experience, of what is going on. Remember how, in the old TV series, attorney Perry Mason usually managed to win, not by directly proving his case, but by providing such a compelling reconstruction of what probably had happened that he provoked a courtroom confession from the guilty party? Well, we are not likely to get a courtroom confession that will resolve the mind-body problem debate in philosophy; but identity theorists do believe that theirs is the most compelling of the reconstructions of the relationship between the mental and physical.

As early as the late nineteenth century, philosophers and scientists were exchanging views and participating in panel discussions on "the physical basis of mind." By the 1930s, medical discoveries linked mental illness to physical imbalances, studies related loss of mental function to physical injuries or abnormalities, stress related mental problems resulting from World War I, such as shell shock, were indicted in physical malfunction, and the term "psychosomatic" came into common usage (although actually coined somewhat earlier) to denote physical ailments caused by mental or emotional disturbance; the journal, *Psychosomatic Medicine,* was founded in 1939. It was becoming apparent that the mental is inextricably tied to the physical. Yet mental phenomena continued to resist capture in the net cast by cruder forms of materialism such as Hobbes'.

Philosophers began to think in terms, not of trying to explain away the apparent causal interaction of the mental and the physical in an attempt to salvage Cartesian dualism, as the parallelists had, but of beginning with psycho-physical interaction as a datum and trying to construct a metaphysical theory that would enable them to account for the interaction. Identity theories seemed to hold promise that the interaction could be accounted for at the level of events under their physical descriptions.

But what of the consciousness objection? Well, in one of the classics of the identity theory literature, philosopher U. T. Place posed the question, "Is Consciousness a Brain Process?" and answered in the affirmative. While not denying that human beings experience consciousness, or counseling that we eliminate such terms as "consciousness" from the vocabulary of the mind-body problem, Place urged the view that consciousness just identically is a process of the brain, much as lightning just identically is a certain form of electrical discharge.

One point underlying the identity theorist's claim needs clarification, namely, the kind of identity that he has in mind when he maintains that states of consciousness just identically are states of the brain. Some identity claims are such that you can test them immediately and conclusively simply by examining their structure or the meanings of their component parts. After all, when I say "John Smith identically is John Smith," I can tell that it is true merely from the logical fact that in general anything is identical to itself. Similarly, when I say "Bachelors just identically are unmarried men," I can tell that it is true by examining the words and realizing that "bachelor" means "unmarried man." The kind of identity involved here is identity of *meaning* or identity of *sense*. But not all identity claims are of this kind. When I say "Mark Twain identically is Samuel Clemens," what I am saying is true, but I can't tell that—or explain it to you—simply by examining the structure of the sentence or the meanings of the words or phrases that are its component parts. (Indeed, some writers use a pseudonym for the very reason that they do not want their true identity known.) To know that Mark Twain just identically is Samuel Clemens requires some knowledge of the history of American literature, not merely the meanings of words or phrases. The reason is that two words or phrases may refer to one and the same thing—identity of *reference*—even though that fact may not be revealed by their meanings. Let me give you a simple example, originally from the influential German mathematician and philosopher Gottlob Frege, that has become famous in recent philosophy. As some of you may have noticed, it is sometimes possible to see what looks like a very bright star in the heavens just before sunset. From ancient times, that body has been referred to as "the evening star." It also is sometimes possible to see what looks like a very bright star in the heavens just after sunrise: that has long been called "the morning star." The ancients did not know exactly what those two heavenly bodies were, and because they appeared in different parts of the sky (one in the west, one in the east), it was assumed that they were different bodies. We now know that both the evening star and the morning star are the planet Venus, which is large enough and close enough to the earth to be visible in morning or evening light at certain times in its movements around the sun.

Now think what this means. If a medieval astronomer had said, "the evening star just identically is the morning star," he would have been right, but he would not have been able to show that he was right merely by examining the words and phrases in his assertion. That would have required the use of telescopes and other modern astronomical instruments. The object named "the evening star" is identical with the object named "the morning star," but that fact was a discovery of science; it cannot be deduced merely from the meanings of the words. Philosophers refer to this as a *contingent identity.*

How is all of this relevant to our assessment of the identity theory? Well, some critics have argued that the identity theory cannot be correct because the claim, " 'state of consciousness *X*' identically *means* 'brain state *X*'," is clearly false. To this the identity theorist agrees; but then goes on to claim that although the phrase "state of consciousness X" *refers* to identically the same object or state of affairs as the phrase "brain state X," the identity in question is a contingent one, thus one that must be tested by methods of the sciences, and not merely by examining the meanings of words and phrases.

Other critics argue that if there is a contingent identity between mental phenomena (states, events, or processes) and physical phenomena, then a particular mental event, such as noticing that it is time for lunch, should

Philosophy and Popular Culture

Existenz: Questions About Reality

As a character in *Existenz,* a movie written and directed by David Cronenberg, you are given the opportunity to be among the first few players of a highly advanced virtual reality game named eXistenZ. You don the virtual reality apparatus, and while your body sits still in a chair, your mind roams widely in the game, and you seem to be doing all the things that you do in real life—walking, running, talking—but you know that the things that seem to be real are not. Of course, the things that happen to you in the game are frequently more interesting than the things that happen to you in real life. For example, when the character named Allegra is shot, you dig out the bullet from her shoulder. However, you discover that the bullet is not a bullet—it is a tooth. Later in the game, you order the special at a restaurant, and after devouring the flesh of an animal, you discover that the animal's bones are oddly shaped. In fact, one bone seems designed to connect with another bone, and another bone seems designed to connect with the first two bones, and so on. When you are finished connecting the bones, you have a functional gun—a gun that shoots teeth.

Questions to Consider

In real life, do you ever perceive physical matter? Or do you perceive only things that are perceptible by the mind, such as colors, textures, and shapes? After all, even your perception of a brain consists only of things that are perceptible by the mind. To explain reality, do you need to assume that matter exists? Or could reality consist of minds only and no matter?

Further, consider how you would ever know you have ended the virtual reality game and returned to real life. It may seem that you have won the game, thus ending it and returning to your real life. But what if you have merely won the first level of the game, and the second level begins by pretending that you have ended the game and returned to your real but boring life?

have all the properties of the physical event—presumably a brain event—with which it is claimed to be contingently identical. But, the critic continues, since brain events have a specific location in space and it does not make sense to assign spatial locations to mental events, mental events cannot be identical with brain events. To this the identity theorist may reply that the critic has begged the question, since if mental events identically are brain events, then every property of a mental event certainly *is* shared by some brain event: if mental events just are events in the brain, and if it makes sense to ask where brain events occur, then it makes sense to ask where mental events occur. Besides, the argument from spatial location is not as clear cut as the critic claims. Smith's drowning is surely a physical event, but to ask where it occurred is to ask where Smith was at the time he drowned, not a request to pinpoint a specific location in his body where it occurred; come to think of it, where precisely in one's body *does* a drowning occur? Similarly, my suddenly remembering that tomorrow is my son's birthday is a mental event, but surely it would make sense for my analyst to ask where it occurred, and, similarly, the correct answer would be just where I was when I remembered.

Still other critics argue that the kind of contingent identity the identity theorist depends on is a fantasy. Relying on advanced developments in logic, they argue that the examples the identity theorist uses to bolster his case, such as "lightning identically is a certain kind of electrical discharge," "water identically is H_2O," and "clouds identically are collections of water droplets," are not examples of contingent identity at all, but are necessarily true. Moreover, if the identity between mental phenomena and physical phenomena is genuinely contingent, there should be some scientific test or experiment to verify the identity; yet no such test has been designed, nor, does it appear, is one forthcoming.

And the debate goes on. The mind-body problem has not been solved. Nevertheless, I hope that by now you see some of the drift the debate has taken over the past three and one-half centuries, and that it has not realized Descartes' dream of a unified theory of the universe that both would find a place in physical, mathematically describable nature for a nonphysical, nonquantitative mind, and demonstrate by rational philosophy that the soul survives bodily death. It seems to me that recent developments come closer to realizing the first part of Descartes' dream than the second, since they do promise to find a place in physical, mathematically describable nature for the *mental*. As far as the second part of Descartes' dream is concerned, remember that a few philosophers still are trying to develop a coherent theory of substance dualism that would allow for the kind of immortality Descartes evidently had in mind; and perhaps more recent theories, such as identity theories, leave open the possibility that a kind of immortality may be achieved through a resurrection of the body.

Notes

1. Gilbert Ryle, *The Concept of Mind,* University Paperback, Barnes and Noble, New York, Fourth printing 1962, Copyright, 1949, by Gilbert Ryle, pp. 11ff.
2. Donald Davidson, entry on "Donald Davidson," *A Companion to the Philosophy of Min d,* Samuel Guttenplan, ed., one of the Blackwell Companions to Philosophy, Basil Blackwell, Oxford, Copyright, 1994, p. 231.
3. (See e.g. J. J. C. Smart, "Materialism," *The Journal of Philosophy* 60 (1963), pp. 651–62.)

The Main Points in Chapter Three

1. *Metaphysics* is the philosophical study of the fundamental nature of the things that exist. In the seventeenth century, Hobbes put forward a modern version of the ancient theory that the universe is composed of tiny indivisible bits of matter, or atoms. By means of his atomic theory of matter, Hobbes sought to explain the way human beings think, feel, choose, and act.

2. One of the central problems posed by the relation between mind and body is *freedom of the will.* Hobbes was a determinist, arguing that all of our actions are determined by the motions of atoms. Kant used the distinction between appearance and reality to try to show that the determinism of science could be made compatible with the freedom demanded by morality.

3. There are three main theories of the relation between the mind and the body: dualism, idealism, and materialism. Using sophisticated logical analysis, some modern philosophers have defended a version of traditional materialism.

Questions for Discussion and Review

1. What *are* minds? It is easy enough to find objections to the leading philosophical theories, but very hard indeed to come up with an alternative. Does it make any sense to say that my mind is a substance with neither spatial location nor mass? On the other hand, does it make sense to identify my mind with the brain, the heart, the nervous system, or some other anatomical structure?

2. Let us suppose, for the sake of argument, that one or another of the three theories of mind/body relation discussed in the chapter is true.

How could we go about deciding which one it was? Would scientific evidence help us? Logical analysis? Inner reflection?

3. Every time we decide that there is some distinctively human capacity that computers cannot imitate, someone invents a way for computers to imitate it! By the time you are my age (seventy at this writing), computers may very well be walking, talking, designing houses, writing music, and who knows what else! At what point down the road do we have to start worrying about whether computers should have the vote?

4. Can computers *feel?* Can they love, hate, desire, yearn? Suppose we can build a computer that *imitates* all of these human emotional responses and *looks* rather human besides. Should we be allowed to marry computers? Kill them (that is, turn them off)? Hire them? Should we pay them at least minimum wage? Why? Why not?

The Primary Source: Philosophical Readings and Commentary

Aristotle: *Metaphysics; Categories; de Anima; On Interpretation; Physics; Poetics; Posterior Analytics; Prior Analytics; Rhetoric*

Augustine, St.: *City of God*

Berkeley, George: *A Treatise Concerning the Principles of Human Knowledge*

Berkeley, George: *Three Dialogues*

Descartes, Rene: *Discourse on Method; Meditations on First Philosophy*

Freud, Sigmund: *Outline of Psychoanalysis*

Heraclitus: *Fragments*

Hobbes, Thomas: *Leviathan*

Hume, David: *Treatise On Human Nature; An Enquiry Concerning Human Understanding*

James, William: *Consciousness*

Kant, Immanuel: *Critique of Judgment; Critique of Pure Reason; Prolegomena to any Future Metaphysics; Critique of Practical Reason*

Leibniz, Gottfried: *Mondadology*

Locke, John: *Essay Concerning Human Understanding*

Lucretius: *On the Nature of Things*

Mencius: *Human Nature*

Milindaphana: *The Simile of the Chariot*
Peirce, Charles Sanders: *The Fixation of Belief; Clear Ideas*
Plato, *Phaedo; Meno; Symposium; Cratylus; Phaedrus; The Republic*
Ryle, Gilbert: *The Concept of Mind*
Thales: *Fragments*

CONTEMPORARY APPLICATION

Do Computers Think?

According to Aristotle, man is a rational animal. Rationality, he argued, is the distinguishing mark of human beings, the "specific difference" that sets us off from all other animals. In the 2,000 years since Aristotle offered his definition, philosophers have called attention to a number of other characteristics that seem to set humans apart: the fact that we play games, that we laugh, that we kill members of our own species, and of course the fact that we speak. Nevertheless, again and again one returns to rationality, for being able to think, to reason, does seem to be what makes us most fully human.

Descartes says, "I am a thing that thinks," thereby making thought his defining characteristic. Animals, he holds, are merely machines, for they have no consciousness, no thought processes. For most philosophers, it is the power of thought that has distinguished us from all other beings, and thought most often means some form of reasoning.

What do I mean when I say that I am rational? Well, one answer is that I can calculate. I can count objects, I can do sums, multiply two numbers together, or divide one by the other, or add or subtract them. The ability to perform computations has always seemed to philosophers to be central to what we mean when we say we are rational.

A second answer, closely associated with the first, is that I can perform logical deductions. Tell me that all men are mortal, and that Socrates is a man, and I can work it out that Socrates is mortal. From the premise that no woman has ever been elected president, and the premise that Zachary Taylor was the twelfth president, I can deduce that Zachary Taylor was not a woman. Many philosophers, impressed by the similarities between this sort of reasoning and arithmetic computations, have tried to find some way to represent logical deductions as a sort of calculation.

A third answer is that I learn from experience. I observe, I remember, and I generalize from past experiences so that I am better prepared to face the future. The first time I see fire, I may reach out to touch it, but very quickly I will learn that fire burns, and from then on I will be careful with it.

Over time, I and my fellow humans acquire elaborate, complex systems of knowledge based on observation and generalization, with the aid of which we can transform the world around us.

Yet a fourth answer is that I can act in accordance with rules rather than merely behaving instinctively or in response to immediate stimuli. To be rational is to be able to follow a plan, play a game, or conform to directions. Or, some philosophers have argued, to be rational is to be able to make up new rules, devise new games, or formulate new plans, in the service of some end or goal or purpose.

Finally, to be rational, philosophers like Kant have said, is to be self-aware, self-conscious, capable not only of thinking but also of thinking that one is thinking.

For two millennia, philosophers have puzzled over the nature of rationality without having to worry very much about whether humans are the only rational creatures in the universe. To be sure, God was assumed to possess reason to the highest degree, and angels, if one included them in one's world, also were rational. But among the things of this world, only human beings could be said to calculate or compute, to make logical deductions, to learn from experience, to make and follow rules, or to be self-conscious.

All of this has changed drastically in the past twenty years or so with the invention of the high-speed, sophisticated computer. Computers also can calculate faster, more accurately, and with greater precision than humans ever could. Computers also can perform logical deductions. Indeed, the basic structure of a computer is modeled on a branch of logic known as Truth Function theory, or the First Order Predicate Calculus (believe it or not, those of you who know how to write simple computer programs, in BASIC or FORTRAN or Pascal, actually know quite a lot of logic without realizing it). Computers can learn from experience, and they follow rules with great success. Computers are now capable of playing chess as well as a Grandmaster, which means better than all but one-tenth of 1 percent of the serious tournament players in the United States.

Or so it seems. Do computers actually perform arithmetic calculations? Well, they look as though they do. If I punch in "5" and " + " and "7" and hit the appropriate button, the computer prints "12" on the screen. Hasn't it added five and seven to get twelve? What else is there to doing arithmetic calculations?

One answer that springs to mind is consciousness. When I do a sum, I think to myself, "five plus seven, that's twelve." I am aware of what I am doing. Indeed, I am *self*-aware. That is, I am aware that I am aware. And that, as Descartes and Kant agreed, is what distinguishes me from a mere machine.

Can we be sure, then, that a computer is *not* self-aware, not conscious? We could ask it, of course, but what would we do if it assured us that it *was* quite aware of what it was doing? This is the point at which the

British mathematician and logician Alan Turing steps into the picture. Turing specialized in thinking up hypothetical situations—"thought experiments," they are called—that help us reason about questions that puzzle or confuse us.

Steven Pinker is a computer scientist at Massachusetts Institute of Technology. Danny Hillis is a computer inventor who works for Disney. John Horgan is a writer for Scientific American. In these three short selections, they debate the question of computer intelligence. Incidentally, in the ABC video that accompanies this chapter, the Chess Grandmaster, Patrick Wolff, who appears, is my son.

CAN A COMPUTER BE CONSCIOUS?
Steven Pinker

In one of the first episodes of *The Twilight Zone,* a man named James Corry is serving a 50-year sentence in solitary confinement on a barren asteroid. Allenby, the captain of a supply ship, takes pity on him and leaves behind a crate containing "Alicia," a robot that looks and acts like a woman. Corry, of course, soon falls deeply in love. A year later the captain returns with the news that Corry has been pardoned and that he has come to get him—and a maximum of 15 pounds of gear. Alicia, unfortunately, weighs more than that. When Corry refuses to leave, Allenby shoots Alicia in the face, exposing a tangle of smoking wires. He tells a devasted Corry, "All you're leaving behind is loneliness."

The horrifying climax raises two vexing questions. Could a mechanical device ever duplicate human intelligence—the ultimate test being whether it could cause a real human to fall in love with it? And if such a machine could be built, would it actually be conscious? Would dismantling it be the snuffing out of a sentient being that we felt we witnessed on the small screen?

Pose the first question to experts in the field of artificial intelligence, and you'll get one of two answers: "Lifelike robots are just around the corner," or "It will never happen." It is almost certainly a mistake to believe either kind of prediction. These are the kinds of experts who a few decades ago were predicting that nuclear powered vacuum cleaners were in our immediate future—and that humans would never reach the moon. Certainly computers will continue to get smarter, as the recent defeat of Gary Kasparov reminds us. Today's computers can converse in English on restricted topics, control mechanical arms that weld and spray-paint, and duplicate human expertise in dozens of areas from prescribing drugs to diagnosing equipment breakdowns. Artificial intelligence has jumped from the laboratory to everyday life. Most people today have had their speech recognized by telephone directory assistance systems, and many have used intelligent search engines on the World Wide Web or bought mutual fund portfolios selected by artificial neural networks.

Better than a snail. Still, today's computers are not even close to a 4-year-old human in their ability to see, talk, move, or use common sense. One reason, of course, is sheer computing power. It has been estimated that the information processing capacity of even the most powerful supercomputer is equal to the nervous system of a snail—a tiny fraction of the power available to the supercomputer inside the bloated human skull.

But the kinds of processing are different, too. Computers find it easy to remember a 25-digit number but find it hard to summarize the gist of Little Red Riding Hood; humans find it hard to remember the number but easy to summarize the story. One well-recognized reason for that difference is that computers have a single, reliable processor (or a small number of them) working very, very fast; the brain's processors are slower and fuzzier, but there are hundreds of billions of them, each connected to thousands of others. That allows the human brain to recognize complicated patterns in an instant. Computers have to reason out every niggling detail one step at a time.

Human brains also have the advantage of sitting inside human beings, where they can soak up terabytes of information over the years as the humans interact with other humans and with the environment. And brains have the benefit of a billion-year research-and-development effort in which evolution equipped them with cheat sheets for figuring out how to outmaneuver objects, plants, animals, and other humans.

So how well will tomorrow's machines do? Technological progress, like scientific discovery, is notoriously unpredictable. When it comes to replacement parts for the body, for example, no one foresaw that artificial hips would become commonplace and artificial hearts elusive. And when it comes to the performance of duplicates of the mind, the most reasonable answer is that computers will probably retain their uneven competence for quite some time. They are likely to do a lot better than they do now for some kinds of thinking, and they will probably not do as well as a human being for other kinds.

But let's return to science fiction and assume that someday we really will have Alicia-class robots. Will they be "conscious"? It all depends on what you mean by the word. Woody Allen once wrote a hypothetical course catalog with a listing for Introductory Psychology that read, "Special consideration is given to a study of consciousness as opposed to unconsciousness, with many helpful hints on how to remain conscious." We laugh because we realize that the word consciousness has at least two meanings.

One of them is Freud's famous distinction between the conscious and unconscious mind. I say, "A penny for your thoughts." You reply by telling me the content of your daydreams, your plans for the day, your aches and itches, and the colors, shapes, and sounds in front of you. But you cannot tell me about the enzymes secreted by your stomach, the current settings of your heart and breathing rate, the projections on your retinas, the rules of syntax that order words as you speak, or the sequence of muscle contractions that allows you to pick up a glass. This shows that information processing in the nervous system falls into two pools. One pool can be accessed by the brain modules responsible for verbal reports, rational thought, and deliberate decision making. The other pool, which includes gut responses, the brain's calculations for vision, language, and movement, and repressed desires and memories—if there are any—cannot be accessed by those modules. Sometimes information can pass from one pool to the other. When we first learn how to use a stick shift, every motion has to be thought out, but with practice the skill becomes automatic. With intense concentration and biofeedback, we can focus on a hidden sensation like our hearbeat.

If you have to ask . . . Will computers ever become conscious, in this sense of access to a subset of the information in the whole system? In a way, they already are. The operating system of your computer is designed so that certain kinds of information are available to the programmer or user—opening and saving files, sending documents to the printer, displaying directories—and others are not, such as movements of the disk drive head, or the codes sent by the keyboard. That's because any information system, computer or brain, has to work in real time.

A device in which every morsel of information had to be easily available at all times to every process would be perpetually lost in thought. It would have to calculate whether the price of tea in China was relevant to which foot should be put in front of the other one next. Only some kinds of information are relevant to what the system is doing at a given time, and only that information should be routed into the system's main processors. Even robots of the future, with their thousands of processors, will need some kind of control system that limits what goes in and out of the individual processors. So in that sense, computers, now and in the future, are built with a distinction between "conscious" and "unconscious" processing.

But it's a very different sense of the word that captivates people. That sense is sentience: pure being, subjective experience, raw feels, first-person present tense, "what it is like" to see red or feel pain or taste salt. When asked to define consciousness in this sense, we have no better answer than Louis Armstrong's when a reporter asked him to define jazz: "Lady, if you have to ask, you'll never know."

So, many philosophers reject the very idea of sentience and insist the only meaningful definition of consciousness is the operational one: Consciousness is access to information that makes a difference in behavior. How could we ever know for certain what another mind, even an electronic one, is experiencing? How could we ever know whether there's "anyone home" behind Alicia's camera-eyes? No matter how smart she acts, no matter how responsive, no matter how vehemently she says she is conscious, the supply-ship captain can always insist that she's just a very fancy stimulus-response machine programmed to act as if she were sentient. Try as hard as you like, but you will not come up with an experimental test that will refute him.

Tell it to Plato. Perhaps it is some consolation to know that our befuddlement here is not just a technological puzzle but is of a piece with some of the deepest problems in philosophy. If I can't know whether Alicia is sentient, how can I know whether you are sentient? I think you are,

and I'm not so sure about Alicia, but maybe I'm just chauvinistic about creatures that are made out of meat rather than metal. How can I be so confident that consciousness is secreted by the brain tissue in my skull, rather than lurking in the software that my brain is running—and that Alicia's computer could run just as well?

Lest you think that the answer is obvious one way or another, ponder these thought experiments. Suppose surgeons replaced one of your hundred billion neurons with a microchip. Presumably you would feel and behave exactly as before. Then they replace a second one, and a third one, and so on, until more and more of your brain becomes silicon. The chips do what the neurons did, so your behavior and memory never change. Do you even notice the difference? Does it feel like dying? Is some other conscious entity moving in with you? Suppose that the transporter in *Star Trek* works as follows: It scans in a blueprint of Kirk's body, destroying it in the process, and assembles an exact duplicate out of new molecules on the planet below. When Kirk is beamed down, is he taking a nap or committing suicide?

The head spins in confusion; it's hard to imagine what a satisfying answer to these questions would even look like. But they are not just brain-teasers for late-night, college-dorm-room bull sessions. The imponderables also drive our intuitions about right and wrong. Was the supply ship captain guilty of destruction of property, or of murder? Does a newborn boy feel pain when he is circumcised, or is his crying just a reflex? What about a lobster boiled alive, or a worm impaled on a fishhook?

These problems won't be solved anytime soon. Perhaps the entire question of sentience is meaningless and we have been deluded by misleading verbiage into taking it seriously. Perhaps some unborn genius will have a thunderbolt of insight and we will slap our foreheads and wonder why the problem took so long to be solved.

But perhaps the human mind, a mere product of evolution of one species on this planet, is biologically incapable of understanding the solution. If so, our invention, the computer, would present us with the ultimate tease. Never mind whether a computer can be conscious; our own consciousness, the most obvious thing there is, may be forever beyond our grasp.

Source: From: "Can A Computer Be Conscious?" by Steven Pinker. Mysteries of Science Section, August 18, 1997/August 25, 1997. Copyright, August 18/August 25, 1997, U.S. News & World Report.

Steven Pinker is director of the Center for Cognitive Neuroscience at the Massachusetts Institute of Technology and author of *The Language Instinct*. His new book, *How the Mind Works,* will be published in October by Norton.

CAN THEY FEEL YOUR PAIN?
Danny Hillis

When I was an 8-year-old, I read a story about a boy who built a robot out of junkyard scraps. The robot in the story could move, talk, and think, just like a person. For some reason, I found the idea of building a robot very appealing, so I decided to build one of my own. I remember optimistically collecting body parts: pipes for arms and legs, motors for muscles, light bulbs for eyes, and a big tin can for the head, fully expecting to assemble the pieces into a working mechanical man. After nearly electrocuting myself a few times I began to get my parts to move, light up, and make noises. I felt I was making progress. If I only had the right tools and the right parts, I was sure that I could build a machine that could think.

I never completed my childhood project to build a mechanical friend, but I never really gave up on it, either. As I grew up, I learned that my efforts followed a long tradition. Aristotle speculated on constructing a device that would "understand the will of its master." "Barring that," he wrote, "there will always be slavery." In the 1500s, several philosophers and magicians were rumored to have built mechanical men, including Friar Bacon's talking brass head and the Rabbi of Prague's human-like automation. In the 17th century, philosopher Gottfried Wilhelm von Leibniz actually described in some detail how a thinking machine could work, but mindful of the church, he was careful to point out that it would not have a soul. He phrased his speculations carefully, asking whether "God could at least join the faculty of thought to a machine which was made ready for it."

The issue that Leibniz so delicately avoids is at the heart of our fascination and our fear: if a machine can think, then what does that say about us? We humans have always favored theories that seem to put us comfortably apart from and above the rest of the natural world. Historically, we liked the idea that our Earth was at the center of the universe. The problem with tying our sense of self-importance to such theories is that we feel diminished when they turn out to be wrong. Galileo's telescope seemed to make us less special. So did Darwin's version of our family tree.

In the past, our ability to reason seemed to make us unique. We could deal with Darwin's message by assuring ourselves that our noble rationality separated us from the beasts. Today we feel threatened, not by the beasts but by the machines. Already, computers can keep track of details better than we can. They can prove theorems that we cannot. They beat us at chess. They are not yet as clever as we are, but they are getting smarter—and getting smarter faster than us. Our monopoly on rationality is in peril, and it is time to move our sense of self-worth to a higher perch.

So, if reason is no longer a uniquely human attribute, how do we separate ourselves from machines? These days, many philosophers are placing their hopes on consciousness as a uniquely human attribute. According to this latest version of human-superiority theory, machines may become intelligent, but they will never feel. If this is so, we have a convenient distinction to justify our intuition that we are a cut above machines. My own guess is that this is another case of wishful thinking. There is no scientific reason to suspect that consciousness is unique to humans. Animals are probably conscious, at least a little. Intelligent machines will probably be conscious, too.

A few decades ago, the prospect of a computer's beating humans at chess would have seemed shocking. Today we take it as a matter of course. We get used to things. Chess is still a fun game. We still enjoy each other's company. It turns out that being the best at chess wasn't such a definitive element of being human after all. Life goes on. Fortunately for the human ego, it is unlikely that machines will suddenly become as intelligent as people in every way. Intelligence is complicated and multifaceted; it is not a single magic principle. Machine intelligence will emerge gradually, improving decade by decade, giving us time to get accustomed to it.

Although I believe that we will someday build thinking machines, I am much less confident that we will ever really understand the process of thought. This may sound like a contradiction. How can we build a mechanism that does something that we do not understand? Actually, we do it all the time. Anyone who has written a complicated computer program realizes that there is a difference between understanding the parts and understanding the consequences of how they interact. Even a state-of-the-art computer like Deep Blue can surprise its designers. Computers a few decades from now will be thousands of times faster and more complicated. Their thoughts will be correspondingly more difficult to predict and understand.

Some people find this prospect of inscrutable machines disturbing, but I assume we will get used to it. After all, how many people today really understand the workings of the telephone system, the Internet, or even a single personal computer? We understand how to get along with them, and that is enough. Humans are long accustomed to living with other organisms without knowing how they work. Since the Garden of Eden, we have been surrounded by mysteries. We humans will continue, no doubt, to worry, to hope, to love, and to wonder, surrounded by the garden of our own machines.

Source: Hillis, the inventor of massive parallel computing, is a Disney Fellow at the Walt Disney Co.

SMARTER THAN US? WHO'S US?
John Horgan

Even before the world chess champion Gary Kasparov faced the computer Deep Blue yesterday, pundits were calling the rematch another milestone in the inexorable advance of artificial intelligence, the effort to create machines that mimic human thought. Computers will soon become "smarter than us," the supercomputer designer Danny Hillis asserted in a *Newsweek* essay.

Actually, the contest, whatever its outcome, only underscores what a flop artificial intelligence has been, especially relative to its founders' goals. The naivete of Marvin Minsky of the Massachusetts Institute of Technology and other pioneers in the field is legendary. In 1966, Professor Minsky gave an undergraduate, Gerald Sussman, the task of building an object-recognition device out of a computer and a television. Object recognition is what you do when you're having lunch with a prospective employer and you suddenly realize that the person at the next table with his back to you is your current employer. Bald spot, blazer, jowls. Yup, it's him.

Mt. Sussman did not fulfill his assignment (although he eventually became a prominent researcher). Since then, computers have become unimaginably fast. But their ability to recognize a face or conduct a conversation, activities that humans perform almost, well, thoughtlessly, remains primitive. Computers can do very well in situations with simple, clear-cut data, rules and goals. They do very poorly in situations with complicated or ambiguous data, rules, and goals—that is, in real life.

Chess is tailor-made for computers, and Deep Blue is prodigiously powerful, capable of examining hundreds of millions of positions a second. If this silicon monster must strain so mightily to beat a mere human, what hope is there that computers will ever, say, replace diplomats in negotiating weapons treaties?

Sure, some programs can "hear" a limited number of words. Banks use neural networks to weigh the merits of loan applications. The immigration service plans to test face-recognition software at borders. But these achievements are paltry compared with the dreams of artificial intelligence enthusiasts.

As recently as 1993, Hans Moravec, a roboticist at Carnegie Mellon University, assured me that by the middle of the next century, robots would be intelligent enough to usurp the roles of doctors and C.E.O.'s. Professor Minsky fantasizes about converting human personalities into strings of ones and zeros and "downloading" them onto machines.

More sober sorts roll their eyes. "Anyone who expects any human-like intelligence from a computer in the next 50 years is doomed to disappointment," Philip Anderson, the physicist and Nobel laureate, asserted in the journal *Science* two years ago. For the foreseeable future—and perhaps forever—HAL, the murderous machine in *2001: A Space Odyssey,* and Data, the charming cyborg from *Star Trek: The Next Generation,* will remain creatures of science fiction.

One day, if not this month, a computer will surely be world chess champion, proving that the game, like loan analysis, is reducible to number-crunching. But the most essential aspects of human thought will continue to elude scientists. As the linguist Noam Chomsky has said, we will probably always learn more about ourselves from novels than we will from science. The question is, should that shortcoming be cause for consternation or celebration?

Source: From: "Smarter Than Us? Who's Us?" by John Horgan, Section 4, p. 15, Column 1, Editorial Desk, May 4, 1997. Copyright © 1997 by *The New York Times.* Reprinted by permission.

John Horgan, a senior writer at *Scientific American,* is the author of "The End of Science."

Francis Bacon

Francis Bacon (1561–1626) was both a major figure in the early modern development of science and an important player in English politics during the reigns of Queen Elizabeth I and King James I. Bacon was related to influential public figures on both his mother's and his father's side. After pursuing studies at the University of Cambridge and in Paris, he returned to England to take up a career in law. Throughout his life, Bacon remained involved with legal matters, rising eventually to hold two of the most important legal positions in the nation: Solicitor General and Attorney General. In addition, Bacon sat as a member of Parliament for four different constituencies. In the turbulent politics of Elizabethan and Jacobean England, where a wrong move could literally cost you your head, Bacon managed to survive, and to flourish, until 1621, when charges of bribery and mismanagement of funds drove him from public life. He died in 1626 without ever obtaining from the king the full pardon he sought.

Bacon's published works were many and quite varied, including literary essays as well as scientific and philosophical works. He conceived a systematic work on a grand scale, called the *Instauratio Magna,* which was intended to reestablish all human knowledge on a sound foundation. In the first part of the *Instauratio,* called the *Novum Organum,* or *New Organon,* Bacon set down the method which, in his view, would provide a satisfactory basis for the expansion of our knowledge of nature. It is this work, more than any other, that influenced subsequent thinkers and secured Bacon's reputation as a major figure in the philosophy of science.

Bacon has achieved a second sort of fame, posthumously, in the strange world of Shakespearean scholarship. Odd as it may sound, there are serious students of Elizabethan literature who claim that, in addition to his many other accomplishments, Francis Bacon wrote the plays and sonnets attributed to William Shakespeare. If it were true, it would undoubtedly make him the most artistically gifted philosopher in the long history of the subject!

Philosophy of Science

The Place of Science in the Modern World

The four modern thinkers whose works, more than those of any others, have made our world what it is today are Charles Darwin, Karl Marx, Albert Einstein, and Sigmund Freud. Darwin, whose theory of evolution threw nineteenth-century European society into turmoil with its claim that human beings had descended from lower orders of animals, laid the foundations for modern biology. Marx was the greatest of the nineteenth-century socialist theoreticians (although not the only one, by any means) and the inspiration for the communist movement that has played a central role in the economics and politics of half of the world. Einstein was the mathematical and scientific genius whose theories of special and general relativity created modern physics, paving the way for atomic energy, nuclear weapons, and modern speculations about the origins and shape of the universe. And Sigmund Freud was a medical doctor who single-handedly created psychoanalysis and gave to the modern world the concept of the unconscious and a clinically grounded theory of the psychosexual development of the human personality.

There are a great many things we might say about these four giants of the nineteenth and twentieth centuries. All four of them were men. All four were white (which is to say, Caucasian—very few people are actually *white!*). Three of them—Marx, Einstein, and Freud—spoke German as their native language. The same three were Jewish by background (although Marx's father converted to Christianity, for career reasons, before Karl was born). Two of them had the first same name ("Karl" and "Charles" are the same name in different languages). And no two of them knew each other, even though there was a brief period of three years, from 1879–1882, when all four were alive.

But what is most striking about this quartet of world-shaking figures is that three of them—Darwin, Einstein, and Freud—were scientists, and the fourth—Marx—thought that "scientific" was the highest word of praise he could apply to his economic, historical, and political theories.

It probably will not surprise you, at first, that three of the four dominant thinkers of the past century have been scientists. We have grown accustomed to the domination of science in our lives. Whether as an endless source of new technological miracles (such as the home computer on which I am writing these words) or as the force that brought nuclear weapons into the world to terrify us, science shapes, directs, and consumes our lives.

But it has not always been that way. Indeed, the rise of science to this position of pre-eminence is really only about a century old. If you had asked an Athenian of the fourth century B.C., or a Chinese mandarin of the eighth century of the modern era, or the king of France in the thirteenth century, or, indeed, if you had asked any of the Founding Fathers of the American Republic in the 1780s, who the thinkers were who had most decisively formed their eras, they would almost certainly have named religious and ethical figures, such as Jesus, Confucius, or Calvin; or, perhaps, political leaders—Pericles,

Caesar Augustus, Charlemagne, Genghis Khan: or possibly great artists, such as Homer, Sophocles, or Shakespeare. They might *even* have named philosophers. But scientists? There weren't any, to speak of, and those thinkers who engaged in what we today would call scientific speculation were more likely to be known for something other than their "science."

What *is* science? How does it achieve the extraordinary successes that have set it above all other disciplines and activities in the modern world? What sort of knowledge, if any, does science give us, and in what way does it operate? How do we know what is genuine science, and what is not? A look at your college catalogue will give you a list of what are today accepted as *sciences:* physics, chemistry, zoology, botany, microbiology, and the rest. But what about some of the activities, bodies of knowledge claims, disciplines— call them what you will—that do not turn up in a college catalogue? What of astrology, phrenology, dianetics, *I Ching,* freemasonry, Zoroastrianism, and all of those other odd affairs that are advertised in the back pages of not-quite-respectable magazines?

In this chapter, we are going to try to get at least a preliminary understanding of the nature of science by looking at the debates that have raged during the past four centuries over the nature of this central activity of the modern world. We will start back in the time of Queen Elizabeth I, when William Shakespeare was writing his plays and sonnets, for that is where our story begins. Very quickly, however, we shall find ourselves in the twentieth century, for as science has come to dominate our lives, the debates over its nature have grown steadily more vigorous and wide-ranging.

We have now entered the first decade of the third millennium of the modern era. It is absolutely certain that your lives will be transformed by science many times over as the twenty-first century unfolds. Your encounter with philosophy in this book will be a success if it leaves you thinking about what science is and what it will become.

Francis Bacon and the Foundations of Scientific Method

The late sixteenth and early seventeenth centuries were a time of dramatic developments in our understanding of the universe and of the place of the earth in that universe. In 1543, Nicholas Copernicus scandalized the learned world by asserting that the sun, and not the earth, is the center of the solar system. The planets, he said, revolve about the sun, which remains unmoving at the center. Copernicus was by no means the first thinker to put forward this claim, but ever since the time of Aristotle, in the fourth century before Christ, it had been almost universally agreed that the earth was the hub about which the sun, the moon, the planets, and the stars rotated. Indeed, this theory had become a part of the official doctrine of the Roman Catholic Church, with the result that Copernicus and later astronomers found themselves in religious hot water, not merely intellectual hot water, for their revolutionary hypothesis.

Within less than a century, a flood of other astronomical works appeared in which ever more powerful and astonishing theories of the heavens were put forward. The Danish astronomer, Tycho Brahe, conducted observations in the late 1500s, which his even more brilliant student, Johannes Kepler, published early in the new century. Kepler himself formulated several general propositions, or laws, about the motions of the planets, including the revolutionary claim that the planets actually travel in elliptical orbits, not circular orbits, around the sun. In 1632, the Italian physicist and astronomer Galileo Galilei published a set of Dialogues in which he defended Copernicus's claim about the revolution of the planets around the sun.

I want you to try to think your way back to the way things were in the late sixteenth and early seventeenth centuries. Today we have seen so many television pictures of the earth from satellites and space shuttles and so many diagrams of the solar system and of the galaxy of which it is a part that it is very hard for us to imagine what it was like to live at a time when even the brightest scientists could not really tell which was the truth—the earth going around the sun, or the sun going around the earth.

At first there were tremendous disputes about these new theories. Without sophisticated instruments like modern telescopes and space vehicles, it was unclear just what the truth was. It is not at all surprising, therefore, that along with the arguments about the nature of the universe, a new kind of debate began—about what *method* we should use to investigate the universe. In short, questions of *scientific method* began to play an important part, along with questions about *scientific fact*.

The most important contributor to this growing debate, at the beginning of the seventeenth century, was an extraordinary Englishman named Francis Bacon. Bacon was a man of many parts, as they used to say. He was a learned scholar of the law; a skilled politician in the very complicated and dangerous world of Queen Elizabeth and her successor, King James; a polished and witty essayist; and the holder of several of the most important political offices in the England of his day. Strange though it may sound, he is actually thought by some to have been the real author of the three dozen plays attributed to William Shakespeare. But most important of all, Bacon was a systematic thinker who undertook to lay the methodological foundations for the new science of his day. He pulled together all of his speculations on scientific method in a great work which he called the *Novum Organum* (in English, *The New Organon*). An organon is a system of scientific investigation, a method for discovering truths about the world, and Bacon thought he could state, once and for all time, how such investigation should be carried out.

The secret to scientific investigation, Bacon claimed, was to make a systematic collection of observations about the world and then to tabulate them and arrange them in ways that would enable us to discover the hidden nature of the phenomena we wish to understand. In this day of federally funded science, when the newspapers casually report the expenditure of billions of dollars for a supercollider and hundreds of millions of dollars for genetic research, it may not come as much of a surprise to you to hear that Bacon believed in *observation*. What else, you might ask. But in Bacon's day, very few students of nature thought that the way to learn about the world was patiently to collect observations. Indeed, the greatest intellectual successes up to that time had been in fields like mathematics and logic, in which observation played no role at all.

We also must remember that for Bacon, observation meant looking, listening, tasting, smelling, and touching with our unaided senses. The time of elaborate scientific *instruments* was still far in the future. The primitive telescopes that were beginning to come into use were so weak and unreliable that it was an open question how much better they were than the naked eye.

In Book I of *The New Organon,* Bacon laid out for us the fundamental controversy that dominated discussion about scientific method for the next two centuries. "There are and can be only two ways of searching into and discovering truth," he said.

> The one flies from the senses and particulars to the most general axioms, and from these principles, the truth of which it takes for settled and immovable, proceeds to judgment and to the discovery of middle axioms. And this way is now in fashion. The other derives axioms from the senses and particulars, rising by a gradual and unbroken ascent, so that it arrives at the most general axioms last of all. This is the true way, but as yet untried.

If we recall the discussion in Chapter 2, we can see that Bacon is presenting us with the old and fundamental conflict between *rationalism* and *empiricism.* In his view, the rationalists move immediately to very general axioms, which are set forth systematically as the starting point for elaborate deductions. This is exactly what happens in mathematics, where the method works very well indeed. For example, those of you who studied geometry in high school will remember that first you were given some definitions, axioms, and postulates, and then you began deducing conclusions, or propositions, such as the proposition that the interior angles of a triangle equal two right angles.

But successful though this method may be in mathematics, Bacon was convinced that it was all wrong in the exploration of nature. Instead, he said, we must start from the evidence of our senses and proceed very, very slowly, from particular observations to tentative generalizations or hypotheses. Then, instead of rushing into deductions and elaborate system building, we must go back to nature and test our generalizations with more evidence of the senses. Eventually, if we are careful (and lucky), we will arrive at the end of this process at some general truth that we can hang onto with confidence.

To show us exactly what he has in mind, Bacon sets out an elaborate example, designed to arrive at a scientific understanding of *heat*. Here is how he introduces his examination in *The New Organon:*

> The investigation of forms proceeds thus: a nature being given, we must first of all have a muster or presentation before the understanding of all known instances which agree in the same nature, though in substances the most unlike. And such collection must be made in the manner of a history, without premature speculation or any great amount of subtlety. For example, let the investigation be into the form of heat.

What is Bacon saying here? Well, first of all, Bacon believes that in nature there are certain *forms,* such as heat, light, whiteness, heaviness, hardness, and so forth. The job of science is to learn exactly what these forms are and thereby to gain the ability to change and manipulate nature so that it can be used to satisfy human needs. "A nature being given"—that is to say, once we have posed the question, What is *heat?* (for example)—we begin by systematically collecting all of the examples we can find of that form—what Bacon calls a "muster or presentation." If heat is what we are trying to understand, we collect as many examples as possible of heat, from the widest possible variety of situations: hot metal, hot water, the hot sun, a hot forehead of someone who is sick, a hot ember from a dying fire, a stick that becomes hot after it is rubbed very hard with another stick, and so on.

Once we have made our collection, Bacon says, we make a list of all of the instances of heat and contrast it with another list of as many examples as we can find of lack of heat—an ice cube, a chilly day, a cold wind, water fresh from a spring, and so on.

With these two lists before us, we now try out a series of guesses, or hypotheses, about what heat is, checking them against our two lists to see whether they fit the facts.

For example, suppose someone offers the suggestion that heat is a kind of fluid that is in things that are hot. Well that certainly fits the case of hot water, which is liquid, and it might even fit the case of the hot forehead of a sick person, because she might have a hot fluid inside her. But it does not fit the case of the hot, dry sand of the desert, so that guess is contradicted by the evidence and rejected.

Little by little, according to Bacon, we zero in on the true nature of heat by checking and rechecking what he calls the Tables of Presence and Absence (i.e., presence of heat and absence of heat). We can then take a next step and make up what Bacon calls Tables of Increase and Decrease (lists of cases in which things get hotter [increase] or colder [decrease]). Suppose we are working with the guess that heat is somehow connected with things getting smaller. We check this against our Table of Increase and find that as a volume of air is heated in a balloon, it gets bigger. That is sufficient to rule out the theory that heat is connected with things getting smaller.

Well, you get the idea. Eventually, after a good many pages, Bacon comes up with the following theory about heat, which, as it happens, is pretty close to the mark:

> If in any natural body you can excite a dilating or expanding motion, and can so repress this motion and turn it back upon itself that the dilation shall not proceed equably, but have its way in one part and be counteracted in another, you will undoubtedly generate heat.

There are three important things to notice about what Bacon says in this little passage. All of them will turn out to be crucial to the discussion of this chapter.

First: The "forms" whose nature science investigates are, according to Bacon, familiar, everyday characteristics of things that are readily accessible to the five senses. Heat, weight, solidity, whiteness—these are the *subjects* of scientific discovery. Compare this to modern science, which investigates things—atoms, genes, galaxies, electricity—which we cannot see with the naked eye and would not even know about without complicated scientific equipment and even more complicated theories.

Second: The "muster or presentation"—that is, the list of instances of what we are investigating—is to be "made in the manner of a history, without premature speculation or any great amount of subtlety." What Bacon means is that the scientist is to make up the list by just *describing* the instances of heat without any prior scientific assumptions about what heat is, or where it is likely to be found. As much as possible, the scientist is to approach experience with an open mind, recording whatever presents itself to her senses. The point of this procedure is to avoid prejudicing the outcome by unintentionally building any of the scientist's presuppositions into the list of facts.

To see why Bacon thinks that this is so important, consider a controversy that has raged in the world of television sports reporting for years. Careful monitoring of broadcasts of professional football games reveals that descriptions like "smart," "clever," "savvy," "intelligent," "always in there thinking," and the like are regularly applied to *white* ball players who make good plays, while *black* star players are equally regularly described as "natural athletes," "very physical," and so forth. The prejudice of the sportscasters leads them to see instances of intelligence in the play of white athletes but not in the play of black athletes. If someone watching these broadcasts were to make up Tables of Presence and Absence of intelligence from these descriptions, he would come to the completely incorrect conclusion that intelligence in sports is somehow connected with race. The problem would lie *not* with his reasoning but with the original muster of facts on which that reasoning was based.

So, Bacon insists, the initial collection of facts must be made "in the manner of a history, without premature speculation."

Third: The purpose of the entire scientific investigation, as Bacon's conclusion about heat makes clear, is to use knowledge to gain the power to change nature. Bacon does not tell us what heat *is*. He tells us how to *generate* heat—in other words, how to produce it. He tells us "The true and lawful goal of the sciences is none other than this: that human life be endowed with new discoveries and powers."

Let us take a closer look at the second of these three points, for it came to be central to subsequent debates about scientific method. The collection of observations with which scientific theorizing begins is to be made, as far as possible, in an unprejudiced manner. The facts are to be set down by observers who do not allow their own prior beliefs or expectations, their own scientific theories, to color their descriptions. For example, even if a physicist firmly believes that the temperature of a gas *increases* as it is compressed into a smaller volume, he must not allow that belief to alter the way he reads the thermometer when he compresses a gas and observes its temperature. An astronomer may be absolutely certain, on the basis of some prior theory, that an eclipse of the sun will occur at precisely 10:04 A.M. on June 13, 2001, but as she carefully observes the onset of the eclipse and checks the time against her watch, she must not allow her expectations to affect her report of the time at which the eclipse starts.

Now here is the point of these apparently innocuous remarks. If observations are unaffected or uncolored by the theories of the scientists who make them, then those observations will continue to serve as a legitimate basis for theorizing *even after the theoretical beliefs of the original observers have been disproved.* If the observations are, as we now say, theory neutral, which means that they are completely independent of any theories about what makes the world tick, then scientists even centuries later can continue to use those observations as part of the collection or muster on which they base their own theorizing.

Quite clearly, the immediate implication of this "theory neutrality" is that the pile of observations will grow steadily bigger over time, as more and more new observations are added to the list, *and none are thrown out.* And so we can conclude that science will progress toward a greater and greater understanding of nature in a steady, unbroken, upward direction. Today's scientists will have available to them everything that previous generations of scientists have observed, plus whatever new observations they add to the collection. And tomorrow's scientists will be better off still, for they will add new observations to the ever-growing store.

This sort of one-directional progress, onward and upward, is certainly not typical of other spheres of human activity. I daresay very few serious students of politics, art, or religion would be prepared to claim that those fields exhibit steady upward progress. Are we in the United States confident that today's politicians are superior to Abraham Lincoln or the Founding Fathers? Would many Christians claim that today's religious leaders are superior to

Jesus, the Disciples, and St. Paul? Does anyone think today's composers are a distinct improvement over Beethoven and Bach, or that today's playwrights have advanced beyond Sophocles or Shakespeare?

And yet, when it comes to science, we all automatically assume that even mediocre scientists today know vastly more than the most brilliant scientists of only a generation ago. Francis Bacon had the great foresight to see, at the very beginning of the modern scientific era, that this claim of unidirectional progress in science must rest firmly on the base of an ever-expanding body of theory-neutral, unbiased observations.

Now turn this idea around. Suppose it should turn out that theory-neutral observation is impossible—that every observer, no matter how honest, objective, and careful, unavoidably brings to the process of observation a set of theoretical presuppositions that shape and color the observations. In *that* case, it may turn out that science is rather more like religion, art, or politics than we thought—changing, but not unambiguously progressing to better, more inclusive theories of the world.

The Relation Between Theory and Observation

The great scientific advances of the early modern period—the late fifteenth to the early eighteenth centuries—were capped by the greatest achievement of classical physics and by one of the handful of truly immortal accomplishments of the human mind: Sir Isaac Newton's *Mathematical Principles of Natural Philosophy* (in Latin, *Philosophiae Naturalis Principia Mathematica*), usually referred to simply as the *Principles*. It is obviously impossible to summarize a work of this sort, although if you have studied physics in high school or college, you have certainly encountered Newton's theories in one form or another. Galileo had worked out a theory that described the motions of bodies on the earth—a theory, as physicists put it, of terrestrial motion. Kepler, as we have noted, propounded a number of laws that described the motions of planets around the sun—a theory of celestial motion. From ancient times up to the seventeenth century, philosophers and physicists believed that objects on earth were fundamentally different from heavenly bodies—made of a different stuff, obeying different laws. Newton proved that *both* Galileo's laws of terrestrial motion *and* Kepler's laws of celestial motion could be derived mathematically from the very same set of three elementary principles, using a new mathematics that he had invented, known today as calculus.

This extraordinary theoretical achievement had a profound effect on the methodological debate over the proper role of observation and pure theory in the study of nature, for Newton proceeded in his *Principles* by abstract mathematical deduction, not by what Bacon had called a "muster" of observational data. The balance was thus tilted in favor of the rationalist side of the debate.

To be sure, the rationalists freely acknowledged that observation of nature had a role to play, but they insisted that observation must be *guided* by theory. It was not enough, they argued, just to collect data and pile it up into vast Tables, as Bacon proposed. Instead, the observations had to take the form of what we today call "experiments."

The word "experiment" comes from a Latin word meaning "to try," and that sense of a trial, a test, conveys just exactly how experiments are different from mere observations. When I perform an experiment, I already have in mind some theory or hypothesis that I am testing. That tentative idea guides me in making the test and focuses my attention on the particular aspects of the situation that I suspect are important. When I merely observe, however, with no theory in mind, I have no guide to tell me what to pay attention to and what to ignore.

Suppose, for example, that I planted a rose bush in my garden last fall, and now, after the winter, it has died. I want to figure out why. I can simply *observe* the plant and the garden and write down everything I notice. But in that case, I am likely to end up with an enormous number of observations and no way of sorting them out. I will jot down the condition of the soil, the average number of cars that pass by on the road each day, whether there is a Democrat or a Republican in the White House, how much it snowed last win-

SIR ISAAC NEWTON

Sir Isaac Newton (1642–1727) was the greatest physicist of the modern age. Newton did revolutionary work on the laws of optics in addition to inventing calculus and achieving a theoretical unification of the theories of Galileo and Kepler.

ter, what species of birds are nesting in nearby trees, how much it has rained this spring, and so forth. Even with Bacon's Tables of Presence and Absence, I am not likely to figure out why my rose bush has died.

When I do an *experiment,* on the other hand, I start with a hypothesis—some idea in mind that I want to test. For example, I may guess that the survival of the rose bush depends on how acidic the soil is. I then compare the acidity of my soil with the acidity of the soil of my neighbor, whose rose bushes did not die. I may even alter the acidity of half of my rose bed and leave the other half alone, to perform what scientists today call a "controlled experiment." I am still observing, notice, but now my observations are guided and shaped by a prior theory.

Karl Popper and Falsifiability

In his book, *The Logic of Scientific Discovery,*[1] Sir Karl Popper, the Austrian-born Professor of Logic and Scientific Method at the London School of Economics, called into question some of the most hallowed claims of science. The book had been published in an obscure German printing in 1934, but it was the English translation published in 1959 that brought Popper's views to the attention of a wide audience.

Otto von Guericke's most celebrated experiment on air pressure utilizing the Magdeburg hemispheres to demonstrate the power of a vacuum before Emperor Ferdinand III in 1657. Copper engraving from his *Experiments Nova,* Amsterdam, 1672. *(Source:* The Granger Collection.*)*

While still a young man, Popper was impressed by the risk inherent in Einstein's theory of relativity in physics, in the sense that it was possible to deduce consequences from the theory that, if proven false, would falsify the theory itself. He noticed that this risk was in sharp contrast to, for example, the allegedly scientific psychoanalytic theories of Freud and Adler that seemingly were immune to falsification, since no matter what objections were raised to the theories, there always seemed to be some way to accommodate them into the theory. This apparent immunity to falsification had been considered a strength of these theories, and in some circles is still considered a strength of a theory or position. (How often have you heard someone say, in the context of a religious or political debate, "You can say anything you want to about my position on X, but *you can't prove me wrong!*"?) But Popper saw that this apparent ability to accommodate any and all challenges was not a strength of a scientific theory but a critical *weakness,* since a theory that is compatible with any and all *possible* situations cannot distinguish, in its predictions, between which possible situations will *actually* occur and which will not.

For Popper, then, *falsifiability* became the line of demarcation between genuine science and *pseudo-science,* between those theories with genuine predictive power, and those that only pretend to predict. Consider the soothsayer, for example, whose predictions are so ambiguous that virtually any outcome can be interpreted to be consistent with her claims, as in the case of the prophecy of the ancient Oracle of Delphi, who told the Lydian monarch Croesus that if he attacked the Persians he would destroy a great empire. On the basis of this advice Croesus attacked the Persians and was defeated, thus destroying his own empire—not at all what he expected. Of course, the oracle's prophecy was true, but it would have been borne out given either outcome; and even if the battle had been drawn in a tie, the claim could always be made that Croesus' attack at least weakened the empires, so that when one of them eventually fell, its fall could be attributed to Croesus' attack. It is in this sense that the oracle's prophecy was not falsifiable, and thus, on Popper's view, not scientific.

Popper argued moreover that in fact scientific progress does not work the way that Bacon's model describes, that is, by accumulating more and more evidence in support of general scientific principles, but that it is based on attempts to falsify daring hypotheses. Thus *resistance to falsification* replaces confirmation as the test of scientific theories. In practice, the scientific researcher finds herself confronted with a puzzle, has a hunch, makes a guess—hypothesis—as to what the solution might be, and then sets out to test the hypothesis against further observation. The hypothesis itself is as much a product of imagination or intuition as observation, although of course it is cast in light of what has been observed. But on Popper's view, if she is a genuine scientist and not a "pseudo-scientist," she sets out not merely to find instances that confirm her hypothesis (Popper thought that it would be easy to find evidence that supports her hypothesis); rather, she sets out to try to falsify it. When she is lucky, she discovers that her hunch bears the test of observation. The nature of a successful scientific theory is that, although it is *falsifiable,* it has not yet been *falsified.*

An unsettling feature of Popper's views on falsifiability is that while every genuinely scientific claim can be tested and falsified, it can never be conclusively *verified.* A famous example illustrating this point is the generalization, "All swans are white." For thousands of years before the exploration of Australia, all of the swans that Europeans had seen had been white, and indeed "All swans are white" was a textbook example of a generalization confirmed by millions of instances. But when Westerners began to explore Australia they discovered black swans. Of course they could have insisted that the black birds they were seeing were not really swans, but some other kind of bird very like a swan but not white, and this would have been one way to make their generalization immune to falsification. But that maneuver would have stripped the generalization of any information that it might convey about *birds,* since it would have involved merely a semantic shift, changing the significance of "All swans are white" to "All *white* swans are white"—undoubtably true, but not very interesting. Instead, the Westerners acknowledged that the birds in Australia were swans, and that their textbook claim, "All swans are white," was in fact false. The point of the example is this: however long a theory has been tested, however many hundreds of thousands or millions of confirming instances have been found to support it, it is always possible—if the theory is genuinely scientific—that at some time it may be falsified. And this seems to call into question one of the proudest boasts of science, that science gives us the *truth* about what nature really is. According to Popper we should view scientific theories not as the truth, but as provisional, to be retained until they have been falsified (if indeed they ever are) or until they have been replaced by better theories.

Popper also challenged the traditional, Baconian view that scientific observations must be *theoretically neutral,* with the observer approaching experience without presupposition or prejudice and recording whatever presents itself to her senses. Popper argued that observation simply is not like that. When the researcher sets out to record her observations, her observations are selective. She is looking for something, and her observations are influenced by what she is looking for. I remember being frustrated by my first experience with a microscope in a laboratory science class. The teacher said, "Focus your microscope, and in your lab manual, draw what you see!" But I saw all sorts of things, squiggles and blobs and what looked like eyelashes! What was I supposed to be focusing *on?* Without an idea of what I was supposed to be looking *for,* I was quite at sea. In a similar vein, I have wasted a lot of time and energy looking for misplaced articles when I was "looking for the wrong thing"—a book that I thought had a blue cover that in fact had a white cover, for example. I might have passed over it a dozen times, when it was right there in front of me, but because I was looking for "the wrong thing," I missed it completely. Popper argued that all observation is selective, "theory laden." With all due deference to Bacon, there are no pure or theory-neutral observations. And what this suggests is that science may be, like religion, art, or politics, shaped and colored by the presuppositions of the scientific observer.

Thomas Kuhn's Theory of Scientific Revolutions

Thus far, we have said a good deal about how scientists *ought* to proceed (Bacon's "muster of known instances"), but very little at all about how real, working scientists actually go about doing their scientific research, day by day. Strange as it may seem, despite the fact that many of the classical and modern philosophers of science were themselves accomplished scientists, sometimes even major scientific figures of their age, until recently very little was written about the real conduct of science.

One problem, which shows up again and again, is the tendency of philosophers of science to assume, without argument, that the scientists in past debates who turned out to be right were, in their own time, obviously the best scientists, and that their opponents were just dodos. For example, we now know that the earth is round (or, more precisely, an oblate spheroid—flattened at the poles), and that the earth revolves around the sun. That is what Copernicus said in the sixteenth century. His opponents were the supporters of the so-called Ptolemaic theory, named after the ancient Egyptian astronomer Ptolemy, according to which the earth is fixed in the heavens and does not move. Since we know that all of the arguments and evidence are now on Copernicus's side, it is natural for philosophers of science to suppose that the Ptolemaists were just bad scientists who could not recognize sound arguments and clear evidence when they saw it.

But the truth is actually very different, as modern historians of science began to realize when they took a careful look at the documents of the time and reconstructed the debates as they actually took place. If you think about it, it is not really surprising to learn that the supporters of the Ptolemaic system were, by and large, a serious, intelligent, careful group of people who had some good arguments and facts on their side. As a matter of historical fact, given the rather primitive state of astronomical observation in the early sixteenth century, the Ptolemaists actually did a slightly *better* job of predicting and explaining the observed positions of heavenly bodies than did the Copernican system.

Very much the same sort of situation turned up again and again as historians of science began to do detailed studies of scientific debates in earlier times. For example, in the great debate over the nature of combustion between the British chemist Joseph Priestley and the French chemist Antoine Lavoisier, Priestley's theory of "phlogiston" lost out to Lavoisier's "oxygen."

We now know that Lavoisier was right, but Priestley's experiments were just as careful, just as scientific, just as reasonable as were Lavoisier's.

Historians of science also began to notice that scientific development did not exhibit quite the sort of slow, steady, straight-line upward progress that philosophers of science seemed to describe. Instead, in any given science, the historical evidence suggested a more uneven process, with long periods of quiet, incremental development being punctuated with brief, dramatic periods of change in which, within a very short time, the whole picture with which scientists were working apparently was transformed.

Putting these historical results together with some of his own research, the American historian of science, Thomas Kuhn, startled the philosophical and scientific world in 1962 with a short monograph entitled *The Structure of Scientific Revolutions.* Ranging over 2,000 years of scientific history, but focusing especially on the developments in theoretical physics and chemistry of the past four centuries, Kuhn painted an extremely persuasive picture of the shape and course of scientific development which differed dramatically from virtually everything that countless philosophers of science had been saying. Kuhn's book itself revolutionized the philosophy of science and called into question the two proudest boasts of science: first, that science gives us the *truth* about what nature really is; and second, that science, unlike art, philosophy, religion, or politics, is *progressive,* securing an ever-greater store of truths about nature and building steadily on the work of past scientists.

Antoine Laurent Lavoisier, 1743–1794. French chemist. Lavoisier experimented to determine the composition of water by igniting a mixture of hydrogen and oxygen with an electric spark. Line engraving, French, nineteenth century. *(Source:* The Granger Collection.*)*

Kuhn tells his story with the aid of three interconnected concepts: Normal Science, Paradigm, and Scientific Revolution. Here is how Kuhn introduces the first two of these ideas.

THOMAS KUHN,
The Structure of Scientific Revolutions

In this essay, "normal science" means research firmly based upon one or more past scientific achievements, achievements that some particular scientific community acknowledges for a time as supplying the foundation for its further practice. Today such achievements are recounted, though seldom in their original form, by science textbooks, elementary and advanced. These textbooks expound the body of accepted theory, illustrate many or all of its successful applications, and compare these applications with exemplary observations and experiments. Before such books became popular early in the nineteenth century (and until even more recently in the newly matured sciences), many of the famous classics of science filled a similar function. Aristotle's *Physica,* Ptolemy's *Almagest,* Newton's *Principia* and *Opticks,* Franklin's *Electricity,* Lavoisier's *Chemistry,* and Lyell's *Geology*—these and many other works served for a time implicitly to define the legitimate problems and methods of a research field for succeeding generations of practitioners. They were able to do so because they shared two essential characteristics. Their achievement was sufficiently unprecedented to attract an enduring group of adherents away from competing modes of scientific activity. Simultaneously, it was sufficiently open-ended to leave all sorts of problems for the redefined group of practitioners to resolve.

Achievements that share these two characteristics I shall henceforth refer to as "paradigms," a term that relates closely to "normal science." By choosing it, I mean to suggest that some accepted examples of actual scientific practice—examples which include law, theory, application, and instrumentation together—provide models from which spring particular coherent traditions of scientific research. These are the traditions which the historian describes under such rubrics as "Ptolemaic" astronomy (or "Copernican"), "Aristotelian dynamics" (or "Newtonian"), "corpuscular optics" (or "wave optics"), and so on. The study of paradigms, including many that are far more specialized than those named illustratively above, is what mainly prepares the student for membership in the particular scientific community with which he will later practice. Because he there joins men who learned the bases of their field from the same concrete models, his subsequent practice will seldom evoke overt disagreement over fundamentals. Men whose research is based on shared paradigms are committed to the same rules and standards of scientific practice. That commitment and the apparent consensus it produces are prerequisites for normal science, i.e., for the genesis and continuation of a particular research tradition.*

Notice the difference between the way Bacon speaks about science and the way Kuhn speaks about it. For Kuhn, science is something done by real men (and women, though he does not say so)—people who are born into a particular culture at a particular time, learn their science out of textbooks and in classrooms, and then practice what they have learned in laboratories. Kuhn is interested in the human processes by which real scientists learn their craft and pass it on to others.

Kuhn's picture of real-world science (not science as we find it in textbooks or in the writings of philosophers of science) is this: in each branch or sub-branch of science, such as astronomy, during times of "normal science," there are a few models ("paradigms") of actual scientific work that are so striking, so successful in solving the problems that scientists in that field are working on, so persuasive as pictures of how to do science, that all of the ordinary scientists in the field imitate those models and try to solve the puzzles that remain by applying or adapting the methods that the author of the paradigm introduced. When they are first getting into the field, these everyday, average scientists (many of whom, of course, may be very gifted and brilliant men and women) either study those models in school or read them on their own. These paradigms come to be the accepted picture of what the world is like and how to study it.

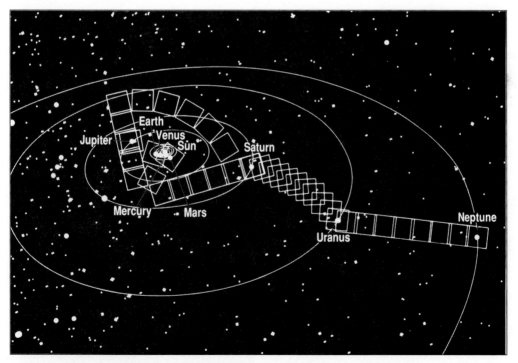

A computerized composite photo of the solar system produced by the Voyager space probe as it left the solar system, showing all but the outermost planet. We are now able to see that our system has the structure postulated by Copernicus, Galileo, and Newton. *(Source: NASA Headquarters.)*

Normal scientists are puzzle solvers, working out answers to problems that no one has yet solved. Normal science is based upon paradigms, or models, which are precise and clear enough to tell scientists what the world should look like, but which are not so complete and finished as to leave no unsolved puzzles for normal scientists to tackle. If they are too loose and ill defined, they fail to create the context of expectation and investigation within which normal science can proceed. But if they are too finished off, too closed, they will generate no new problems for solution and attract no followers.

Notice that Kuhn talks about paradigms attracting followers, not about theories being proven right by logic or evidence or both. Science, he is telling us, is a human activity like any other. A theory succeeds, takes hold, and becomes a paradigm for future work by attracting supporters, followers, and adherents. Kuhn is deliberately using a language to talk about science that is usually reserved for historical descriptions of political, religious, or artistic movements.

But first we must introduce the third key term in Kuhn's story— "scientific revolutions." Scientific revolutions, Kuhn suggests in *The Structure of Scientific Revolutions,* are "noncumulative developmental episodes in which an older paradigm is replaced in whole or in part by an incompatible new one." In this passage, excerpted from two different sections of Kuhn's work, we get his account of the process by which this "paradigm shift" occurs.

THOMAS S. KUHN

Thomas S. Kuhn (1922–1996) was educated at Harvard University, where he spent three years as a junior fellow and five years as a member of the faculty. He also held teaching positions at the University of California at Berkeley, Princeton University, and at the Massachusetts Institute of Technology. In addition to his major work *The Structure of Scientific Revolutions,* Kuhn published *The Copernican Revolution: Planetary Astronomy in the Development of Western Thought* (1957) and *Black-Body Theory and the Quantum Discontinuity, 1894–1912* (1978).

Anomaly and the Emergence of Scientific Discoveries

Normal science is a highly cumulative enterprise, eminently success-ful in its aim, the steady extension of the scope and precision of sci-entific knowledge. In all these respects it fits with great precision the most usual image of scientific work. Yet one standard product of the scientific enterprise is missing. Normal science does not aim at novel-ties of fact or theory and, when successful, finds none. New and un-suspected phenomena are, however, repeatedly uncovered by scientific research, and radical new theories have again and again been invented by scientists. History even suggests that the scientific enterprise has developed a uniquely powerful technique for producing surprises of this sort. If this characteristic of science is to be recon-ciled with what has already been said, then research under a para-digm must be a particularly effective way of inducing paradigm change. That is what fundamental novelties of fact and theory do. Produced inadvertently by a game played under one set of rules, their assimilation requires the elaboration of another set. After they have become parts of science, the enterprise, at least of those specialists in whose particular field the novelties lie, is never quite the same again.

The Response to Crisis

Let us then assume that crises are a necessary precondition for the emergence of novel theories and ask next how scientists respond to their existence. Part of the answer, as obvious as it is important, can be discovered by noting first what scientists never do when con-fronted by even severe and prolonged anomalies. Though they may begin to lose faith and then to consider alternatives, they do not re-nounce the paradigm that has led them into crisis. They do not, that is, treat anomalies as counterinstances, though in the vocabulary of philosophy of science that is what they are. In part this generalization is simply a statement from historic fact, based upon examples like those given above and, more extensively, below. These hint what our later examination of paradigm rejection will disclose more fully: once it has achieved the status of paradigm, a scientific theory is declared invalid only if an alternate candidate is available to take its place. No process yet disclosed by the historical study of scientific development at all resembles the methodological stereotype of falsification by direct comparison with nature. That remark does not mean that sci-entists do not reject scientific theories, or that experience and experi-ment are not essential to the process in which they do so. But it does mean—what will ultimately be a central point—that the act of judg-ment that leads scientists to reject a previously accepted theory is al-ways based upon more than a comparison of that theory with the world. The decision to reject one paradigm is always simultaneously the decision to accept another, and the judgment leading to that

THOMAS KUHN,
The Structure of
Scientific Revolutions

decision involves the comparison of both paradigms with nature and with each other.

Though history is unlikely to record their names, some men have undoubtedly been driven to desert science because of their inability to tolerate crisis. Like artists, creative scientists must occasionally be able to live in a world out of joint. But that rejection of science in favor of another occupation is, I think, the only sort of paradigm rejection to which counterinstances by themselves can lead. Once a first paradigm through which to view nature has been found, there is no such thing as research in the absence of any paradigm. To reject one paradigm without simultaneously substituting another is to reject science itself. That act reflects not on the paradigm but on the man. Inevitably he will be seen by his colleagues as "the carpenter who blames his tools."*

*From *The Structure of Scientific Revolutions* by Thomas S. Kuhn. © University of Chicago Press. Reprinted with permission from the publisher.

As Kuhn notes, it is extremely difficult for a scientist who has grown up in one paradigm to shift over to a new one. Those of us who are not scientists at all may have trouble understanding why this is so difficult, but that is because we have not adopted the habits of thought, the manual skills, the very body language that characterize one paradigm or the other. Changing one's paradigm, for a scientist, must be at least as difficult as changing one's backhand for a professional tennis player, or one's bowing arm for a violinist. It may be almost as difficult as, say, giving up the law as a profession and becoming a doctor. What is called for is not so much learning new things as adopting an entirely new way of looking at the world. It is hardly surprising, then, that during times of dramatic paradigm conflict in a branch of science, it is the young apprentices who most easily take up a newly proposed paradigm. Nor should we be surprised that some scientists, even very great ones, steadfastly refuse to the end of their lives to adopt a new paradigm, even after it has virtually swept the field. Perhaps the best recent example of this phenomenon is the great physicist Albert Einstein, who found the Quantum Theory of his contemporary Max Planck so fundamentally contrary to his way of conceiving the world that he refused to consider it an acceptable new theory, choosing instead to treat it as a temporary ad hoc approximation until a satisfactory "classical" interpretation could be found.

In a postscript to his book, written seven years after its first publication, Kuhn responded to critics who accused him of portraying scientific change as an irrational process, determined by subjective factors rather than by evidence and argument. Kuhn rejected this criticism, pointing out that in his view, paradigm change occurs in response to experimental evidence or theoretical calculation and is carried out by argument, reasoning, counterargument, and new experimentation—precisely the sorts of activities that his critics presumably considered appropriate scientific behavior.

But Kuhn acknowledged—indeed, he insisted—that precisely because paradigm *change* does not take place *within* a single paradigm but instead consists of a struggle between competing paradigms, the arguments between proponents of the opposed paradigms cannot possibly appeal to the clearly defined rules of a common paradigm to resolve their dispute.

Kuhn's critics were not entirely wrong, however, for it is clear that his conception of science differed radically from the tradition we looked at in the earlier sections of this chapter. The crucial theme, as I noted when we were discussing Bacon, is that what counts as scientific *facts* is independent of the theories a scientist advances to explain or predict the facts. Hence the foundation of observation on which scientific theory builds is solid and ever growing. But Kuhn rejected this basic tenet of the modern philosophy of science, arguing instead on the basis of the historical evidence that when a paradigm shift takes place, there is actually a corresponding shift in what counts as a scientific fact as well.

The result is that if there are two competing paradigms, we can no longer say that whichever one explains all of the facts that the other explains, and more besides, wins. The most we can say—and this, I think, is what really has unsettled so many of Kuhn's readers—is that after a time, one paradigm wins the allegiance of virtually all the new young scientists, while those who used to adhere to the other paradigm retire, die, or are redefined as "not scientists."

Science as a Social Institution

In the last section, Thomas Kuhn introduced the idea that science is a social practice, an activity carried on by groups of men and women whose interactions with one another in the classroom, in the laboratory, and through their publications shape who they are and what they believe. We saw him talking about times of scientific crisis and controversy, when some scientists choose one paradigm, much as if they were supporting a political party, and other scientists choose a competing paradigm which they defend with their research.

This recognition, that science, like politics, the economy, marriage, art, and religion, is a *social* institution, is the distinctive mark of the most recent work being done in the philosophy of science. Let us conclude this chapter by taking a look at some of the implications of the fact that science is a social institution.

First of all, what do we *mean* by calling science a "social institution"? We mean that science is an activity or a practice that is organized into social roles, such as research scientist, science student, science professor, science journal editor, laboratory assistant, and so forth. We mean, too, that science is carried on in established places—the laboratory, the research institute, the university—and is regulated, paid for, and run by bureaucratic structures—committees, professional associations, international congresses, state and federal bureaus, and university departments. There are certain marks or symbols by which participants in the institution of science recognize one another and are recognized by outsiders—Ph.D. degrees, lab coats, "nerd packs" (the uncomplimentary slang name for the little plastic pen holders that engineers especially use to keep ink from staining their shirt pockets).

We also mean that science as a social institution has certain norms or standards of behavior that are passed on from established to novice scientists and are enforced, officially or unofficially, by members of the profession.

But we mean something much deeper and more important than all of this, for at base, what we mean is that the character, performance, accomplishments, and role of an individual scientist can only be properly understood and evaluated when seen in the context of the total social practice of which he or she is a part.

Suppose, for example, that we are trying to evaluate the performance of an individual scientist—to decide whether she is doing good science, as it were. Following Bacon, we might look at how she assembles her muster of facts and what sorts of conclusions she derives from them. Kuhn introduces a *social* consideration by asking whether she is engaged in normal science within a paradigm or is struggling to formulate a revolutionary new paradigm. But this does not tell us how her relationship to other scientists bears on the value or scientific propriety of her apparently individual research. We have not yet captured the *social* dimension of the scientific enterprise.

To see exactly how the social aspect of science might enter into our evaluation and understanding of the performance of an individual scientist, but without going into the elaborate detail of a real scientific research project, let us choose a *non*scientific example, which will make the very same point. (I am indebted to Robert J. Ackermann for this very useful illustration.) Imagine that a little brother and sister have gotten themselves lost in the woods and that the whole town in which they live has turned out to search for them. (I want to compare the lost children to a fact that a group of scientists is trying to discover, and the town searchers to the scientific community engaged in research in this area of science.)

How should the anxious townspeople undertake a search for the lost children? One thing is perfectly obvious: they *should not* do it as isolated, individual searchers. Instead, they should organize a *group* search based on a plan for the whole town. If each man or woman in the town sets out by him- or herself to search for the children, the result will probably be something like this: Mr. Jones will say to himself, "The most likely place for those kids to have gone is the old swimming hole in the north quadrant of the woods, so I will look there." Ms. Smith will say to herself, "The most likely place for those kids to have gone is the old swimming hole in the north quadrant of the woods, so I will go there," and so on, until the whole town is hunting in the same little corner of the woods! Now, the old swimming hole may very well *be* the *most* likely place, but it surely is not the *only* place. So it would obviously be better for at least some of the townspeople to try the less likely places, just in case one of them is where the children are. Indeed, if there are enough searchers, it would make sense to send at least someone to the *least* likely place, just to make sure.

There are several different ways in which the searchers can be spread out through the woods in accordance with the probabilities of where the children are. One way is for the mayor to get a map of the woods, divide it up into sections, make some estimates of the probability that the children are in each segment (after consulting with the Boy Scout troop leader, the fire captain, and a few other town bigwigs), and then assign searchers to different segments as they report for the search. Another way is simply to let people sign up for segments as they arrive and leave it to latecomers to select segments of the woods that are not yet spoken for. In this case, instead of getting official estimates of the probabilities, the search organizers will rely on the common knowledge in the town of the nature of the woods. There will, of course, be significant differences of opinion among the townspeople about which the likeliest segments are, and that will affect who goes where.

Some parts of the woods will be much easier to get to than others, and it may be necessary to motivate people to try the more inaccessible segments, either by a cash reward for the person who finds the children or simply by the promise of publicity and general praise. Those setting out relatively late in the search may decide to gamble on trying a very unlikely piece of woods, thinking to themselves that if they head for the old swimming hole, they will be stumbling over other searchers and probably not get credit for finding the children even if that is where they are.

Now let us suppose that the search is successful, and the children are found, *not* by the old swimming hole, perhaps, but at the campgrounds, which was everybody's second choice as the likeliest place. When Molly Johnson emerges from the woods, leading the two exhausted children, everyone starts to cheer, the TV cameras capture the moment, microphones are shoved in Molly's face, and nobody even bothers to say thank you to all of the weary searchers who straggle out of remote segments of the woods after the flares are set off announcing that the children have been found.

The town reporter, writing the story for the news wires, might very well ask himself the following obvious, but totally inappropriate, question: What were the special techniques that Molly used that distinguished her from all of the unsuccessful searchers and enabled her to find the children? What can we learn from her success for future searches?

The answer, of course, is *nothing!* Molly did not use any special techniques; she was not privy to secrets of the search that enabled her to be the one to find the children. She just happened to be looking in the segment of the woods where the children actually were. In a very real sense, it was not Molly who was successful, it was the whole search, of which she was simply one part.

Now if the search was organized by the mayor, then it makes a certain amount of sense to give him the credit. But suppose the town used the second

Search. When organizing a search for children lost in the woods, the best plan is to send searchers into all parts of the woods, not just into the part where the children are most likely to be. Similarly, when scientists are trying to solve a problem, it makes sense to have researchers working on a wide variety of solutions, not just on the one that is most promising. It is really the entire search party that finds the lost children, not just the particular searcher who happens to stumble upon them. *(Source:* Drawn for Robert Paul Wolff by Prentice Hall.*)*

method of organization mentioned above—suppose individual searchers took their cues from those who set out before them, without any organization or even much communication among the searchers. In that case, the only thing we can say is that the structure of the *institution* of the search was successful, that the search as a social practice was effectively arranged to maximize the likelihood of finding lost children.

Two final points before we return to the subject of science as a social institution: First, even though we cannot reasonably conclude that Molly was doing something special that enabled her rather than any of the other searchers to find the children, nevertheless we certainly can make judgments about whether she was following proper procedures in searching. We can observe that she made marks on the trees as she proceeded so as to be able to tell whether she was doubling back on herself, that she observed safety precautions so that she herself would not get hurt, and so forth. This does not distinguish her from most of the other searchers, of course, since they did the same thing, and it does not at all explain why *she* found the children. But it does serve to distinguish her and the other genuine searchers from some foolish thrill seekers who blundered into the woods unprepared and had themselves to be rescued when they got lost.

Second, the search could, of course, have had an unhappy outcome. The children might, against all the odds, have wandered into the *least* likely place of all, to which only one searcher went, and they might therefore have been overlooked until they died of exposure. That failure, however, would not by itself prove that the search was poorly organized or based on the wrong search principles, nor surely would it show that any particular searcher had in any way searched incorrectly. When you are dealing with probabilities, unhappy outcomes are an unavoidable fact of life. What is more, we cannot even say that a successful search *must* have been properly conducted! After all, even if all of the townspeople rushed to the old swimming hole and left the rest of the woods unsearched, if that was where the children actually were, they would have been found; and everyone would have been happy, even though any sensible person could see that the search, as a search, was a shambles.

Well, by now, the relation of this long story to science must be obvious. A group of researchers, looking, let us suppose, for a cure for AIDS, is like a town searching in the woods for lost children, except that the researchers cannot even be sure that there is a cure to be found. The sensible way to organize the scientific search for a cure for AIDS is to put relatively more researchers and research dollars into the most promising areas, but still to put some money and some research teams into even the least likely areas, on the off chance that that is where the cure lies. The search for a cure must be seen as a large social effort, not as a collection of individual efforts, and any philosophical or methodological evaluation of the scientific efforts of particular AIDS researchers can only be carried out in the context of an evaluation of the entire social effort to find a cure.

The task of distributing resources to different research projects can be guided centrally, perhaps by the National Institutes of Health, or it can be left to the choices of individual researchers, who make their decisions in part on the basis of the prior choices by other research teams already in the field. In practice, of course, a combination of these two different methods is always at work in the real world of modern science.

When cures finally are found—as we all hope and pray they will be—inevitably the particular research teams who make the discoveries will receive public acclaim, perhaps the Nobel Prize, certainly lasting fame. But, like Molly Johnson, they may simply be good, solid, competent searchers who happened to be looking in the right place. And where they are looking *may* be the result of their shrewd insight and scientific judgment, or it may simply be a result of the fact that when they came on the scene, that was a spot for which no other team had yet headed. Only a conception of science as a social institution can guide us to the correct evaluations of individual scientific efforts.

But if you have been reading carefully, you may have noticed that our elaborate searching-the-woods example still does not do justice to what is, perhaps, the most controversial element in Thomas Kuhn's theory. If scientific research is like looking for lost children in the woods, then the implication is that there really are facts to be discovered (just as there really are children to be found), and that we can unambiguously known when we have found them (just as we can surely tell whether the children have been rescued). Where is there room, in this example, for the idea of competing paradigms? The children-in-the-woods example fits Kuhn's description of normal science, with its focus on puzzles to be solved (children to be found), but it does not seem to fit his account of paradigm shifts.

Rather than trying to fuss with the example, stretching it and cutting it here and there to fit Kuhn's theory, it would be best just to recognize that to understand the social dimensions of paradigm shifts, we need different examples. We can say that when a paradigm shift takes place, one of the things up for grabs is the very definition of what will count as a problem, what will count as a scientific fact, and what will count as a solution to a problem.

The most unsettling and controversial element in all of this is the notion that social factors can play a role in determining what is and what is not a scientific fact. Bacon clearly thought that a scientific fact is simply a careful, biasfree observation, made either with our unaided senses or with such simple devices as telescopes or magnifying glasses. We might be able to increase the usefulness of our muster of facts by arranging experiments in a laboratory, but even then, there could be no dispute about whether something *is* a fact, only a disagreement about what the fact means, or whether it is important.

Nothing in the methodological speculations of Bacon or Kuhn fundamentally challenges the independent reality of scientific facts, although some of Kuhn's remarks come very close. But some recent work in the philosophy and history of science is changing that four-centuries-old assumption, and it might be appropriate to conclude this chapter by saying a few words about this truly unsettling new thinking.

How does something come to be established as a fact in science? The outsider, not initiated into the actual practices of modern scientific research, might quite naturally suppose that the correct answer goes like this: a statement about the world comes to be established as a scientific fact by its being

shown to be a description of a state of affairs (e.g., the electrical charge on an ion, the boiling point of water, the molecular structure of DNA), which is confirmed by the observations, calculations, and theoretical interpretations of a number of competent scientists, working independently of one another in the same field of investigation.

But the truth is rather significantly different. What happens, it now appears, is something like this: a scientist writes a research report in the socially appropriate fashion (right sorts of footnotes, correct tone and language, proper credentials as a research investigator, etc.) and submits it to a recognized, refereed journal—a periodical publication that other scientists consider respectable, which publishes papers only after they have been sent to other respectable scientists who read the papers anonymously and judge whether they are worthy of publication.

Once the paper is published, it is either cited in the papers written by other researchers in the same field, or it is not. If it is not, the statements in it drop out of sight and do not become scientific facts. If it *is* cited, then there is a chance that the statements in it will become scientific facts. A while later, new papers on the same subject are written by other researchers who, along the way to staking *their* claims about what is and is not a fact, cite the paper we are considering. They may report that they have replicated the original experiments, with the same results, or they may simply cite the paper in support of further claims that they are advancing.

If the future research continues in a direction that incorporates the claim we are considering, eventually through repeated citations it acquires the status of a *fact* and is henceforth used by other researchers, perhaps even without citation, as the basis for their own experiments and analyses.

What you will see immediately from this description is that it is a matter of *social* convention whether something is a scientific fact. There is no other test, save acceptance by the scientific community, as signalled by citation, replication, and eventual incorporation into the canon of well-known "facts." But surely airplanes fly, lightbulbs light, heart transplant operations work, and atomic bombs explode! That is a matter of fact, not of convention, agreement, or social determination.

To be sure. But the fact that atomic bombs explode does not, of itself, settle the debates in atomic physics, any more than the fact that sixteenth-century sailors made it home to port while navigating by the stars proved that their astronomical theories were correct.

Voices Beyond Popper and Kuhn

The views we have just been discussing are largely a product, at least in their present form, of an intellectual climate that arose in the wake of the social, political, and intellectual ferment of the 1960s, a time during which voices

were raised against established orders of the day, challenging the power structures that had led the world into the crises of the mid-twentieth century, and often framing their issues in terms of the class struggles of Marxist rhetoric. Associated with this ferment were movements of protest such as the Civil Rights movement, the anti-Vietnam War movement, and the Women's Liberation movement. In this context, conflict frequently was seen in political terms—in terms of a power struggle between entrenched political, social, and intellectual orthodoxies, between conservative and progressive, between Caucasian and African American, between men and women, between those established in positions of rank and privilege, on the one hand, and those struggling to have their voices heard, on the other. Some protestors argued that even the academic, intellectual, and scientific ideals of rationality, objectivity, and fair-mindedness are merely shabby subterfuges designed to enable an entrenched elite to retain power over scientific and other intellectual enterprises—including philosophy. Once again we were hearing challenges, of the kind that we noted in Chapter 1, to the ideals of rationality, universality, and objectivity. Quite apart from the merits of Kuhn's arguments, it is no wonder that his work, challenging as it did the establishment image of science as the bastion of objective knowledge, found a receptive audience.

By the mid 1970s, writers inspired by the reception given Kuhn's work began to stretch some of Kuhn's insights to lengths beyond those which Kuhn himself had taken them, some even arguing that there are no clearly defined rules of a common paradigm to resolve disputes between proponents of competing scientific paradigms, there is no general standard that gives the scientific paradigm priority over the paradigms of voodoo, astrology, or myth, and reiterating the claim that acceptance of a body of theory is determined by power relations and social convention. In a famous paper, "How to Defend Society Against Science," philosopher Paul Feyerabend argued that it is *ideological pressures* that "make us listen to science to the exclusion of everything else," and pronounced, "I want to defend society and its inhabitants from all ideologies, science included . . . [S]cientists will not play any predominant role in the society I envisage. They will be more than balanced by magicians, or priests, or astrologers."

We saw in Chapter 1 that, even in Plato's time, some thinkers were propounding a philosophy of power: Thrasymachus tried to reduce justice to a question of power, "the interest of the stronger," for example. But in the modern era—since the time of Bacon and Descartes—the canons of scientific research have emphasized the importance of objectivity and rationality, among other methodological ideals, as antidotes against the pressures of power or fashion. This mind set is what makes it so unsettling when sociologists, historians, and even some philosophers reflecting on the nature of the scientific enterprise argue that scientific objectivity and rationality are myths, and that even the progress of scientific knowledge is a matter of political allegiance and social convention.

But we also saw that, in his argument with Thrasymachus, Socrates led Thrasymachus to admit that, according to the principle Thrasymachus himself was advancing, people should obey their rulers only when the rulers are issuing orders that really are in their own interest. That is, it isn't just *who* makes the pronouncements; there are *criteria of acceptance* to be applied to the pronouncements of even those in power. What reasons do the powerful have to give to you and me for why we should accept their claims? That they are charismatic and have powerful personalities? That they will ridicule us—or kill us—if we don't? Maybe the question, rather, is "What is it about the claim itself that makes it worthy of our assent? Against what criterion or criteria of acceptance are we to evaluate *it*?"

While acknowledging that social factors play a role in the acceptance of scientific theory, some contemporary philosophers of science nevertheless are unwilling to concede that acceptance by the scientific community *alone* is enough to establish something as a scientific fact, or that *all* knowledge is covertly political, or that scientific knowledge is *merely* a matter of social convention. Some argue that there are criteria against which we can make some headway in comparing competing paradigms—or theories within competing paradigms—that are not themselves part of either paradigm, but that transcend them. (On a personal note, it was just this promise that there are things that can be said for or against competing claims in light of criteria that are external to either claim—in my case, it was competing religious claims—that excited me into pursuing the study of philosophy.)

More or less traditional criteria for evaluating competing scientific theories are standard fare in logic textbooks. Here is a sample set, from Copi and Cohen's *Introduction to Logic, Tenth Edition:*[2]

1. *Relevance:* a theory should be relevant to the facts it is proposed to explain;

2. *Testability:* for scientific theories, this is *empirical* testability; although the theory may not be *directly* testable, there must be *some kind* of observations that tend to support or discredit the theory—meter readings or lines on a photographic plate, for example;

3. *Compatibility with Previously Well-established Theories:* this criterion is consistent with science's aim to establish a *body* of scientific theory, and is operative in what Kuhn called "Normal Science;" a scientific revolution may overthrow previously well-established theories, of course;

4. *Predictive or Explanatory Power:* given two competing theories both of which satisfy the above criteria, choose the one with the greater range of predictions actually borne out by observation;

5. *Simplicity:* if rival theories satisfy the first four criteria equally well, choose the simpler one!

These are only sketches of the criteria. Volumes have been written attempting to clarify or formalize them, and it is generally conceded that they probably do not provide algorithmic rules for adjudicating between competing theories. However, a more troubling claim, *the underdetermination thesis,* is that empirical data never are sufficient to conclusively determine the choice among competing theories in any rational, objective way.

In its simplest form, the underdetermination thesis merely underscores one of the common frustrations of scientific research: sometimes there are alternative theories that seem to be equally well supported by available evidence, as, in the sixteenth century, were Ptolemy's theory that the heavenly bodies revolve around the earth and Copernicus' theory that the earth and other planets revolve around the sun. In such cases the scientists' task becomes one of developing observations and experiments that will enable them to choose one theory over the other, as Galileo began to do in the seventeenth century. But according to the underdetermination thesis in its more radical form, any theory can be reconciled with any body of empirical evidence—if we are willing to make suitable adjustments—and thus we cannot rationally distinguish between *any* competing theories on the basis of such criteria. Obviously the thesis seriously undercuts the ideals of rationality and objectivity in scientific inquiry.

Studies from the early 1980s that attempted to determine whether there is a causal link between prenatal hormone levels and so-called gender-typical childhood behavior, provided an alleged example of underdetermination that has played a prominent role in literature for the past twenty years or so. Here is the background: researchers had observed that girls exposed prenatally to high levels of androgens, particularly testosterone, tend to exhibit tomboyish preferences and activities at an early age; this is especially pronounced in cases of a genetic disorder that results in the masculinization of the external genitalia. How are we to account for this behavior? One theory was that there is a direct causal connection between prenatal hormone levels and the girls' preference for toys and modes of play typically preferred by boys. The theory seemed to receive support from later studies that involved obtaining blood samples from pregnant women and analyzing them for levels of testosterone, and then doing follow-up studies on the children at age three and one-half to try to correlate the blood tests with gender-typical, or -atypical, behavior. Researchers confirmed a correlation between high testosterone level in mothers and tomboyish behavior exhibited by their daughters, and some concluded that such behavior is caused by the hormonal factors. "Tomboys made, not born–by testosterone," trumpeted one headline. Other researchers found a correlation between hormonal exposure and right hemisphere brain development that might account for the phenomenon that boys typically exhibit significantly better performance on the mathematics SAT than girls do.

Critics, including feminists, were quick to challenge the studies, which they thought might be used to attempt to demonstrate a biological basis for

such differences in behaviors and thereby bolster claims that men just "naturally" are better than women at mathematics, spatial ability tests, and leadership, while women are better suited to engage in domestic affairs, childbearing, and husband nurturing, and so on, thus reinforcing prevalent patriarchal views of male superiority. They offered a different theory to account for the behavioral differences, a theory that gave more significance to experience, self-image, and social factors. They pointed out, for example, that the girls who had unusually high levels of prenatal testosterone—especially those who had experienced abnormal genital development—usually were aware of their medical histories; this alone could make them self-conscious and insecure about their sexual identities, and thus inclined to exhibit boisterous behavior. Even if the girls themselves were not aware of this history, their mothers were, and might therefore project their perceptions of their daughters' ambiguous sexuality onto their daughters. Moreover, the tomboyish behavior might be accounted for by the fact that muscle development enhanced by increased levels of testosterone could stimulate the need for vigorous exercise. The upshot was that the empirical data seemed to be insufficient to determine conclusively the choice of either theory. So how do theorists decide which theory is correct? Upon what criteria do they base their choice? Underdeterminists argued that they make their choice, consciously or unconsciously, in the light of assumptions, including nonrational preferences and agendas, that they carry with them as they approach the studies.

Philosopher P. D. Magnus does not believe that the hormone research example in fact provides a genuine case of underdetermination; he argues that we can imagine experiments that could eliminate one of the rival theories. The details of the experimental design are sophisticated and complex, as you might imagine, but here is a rough outline. Imagine a situation in which researchers, using blind tests, treat in utero one each of pairs of identical twins with hormones. The researchers never tell the twins which one has been treated, never even tell the twins that they are part of an experiment, but monitor the twins' growth in terms of muscle development, judge whether their playing preferences are boyish or girlish, and then determine whether prenatal hormone levels correlate with behavior. Or if this design seems to leave too much room for error, perhaps researchers could harvest identical twins and raise them in a clinical facility (a la *Matrix*?) to allow for full control of their history. Such an experiment might be prohibitively expensive, or, more importantly, so monstrous as to be morally unacceptable, but *if* we were willing to do it, Magnus claims, it *could* decide between the competing theories. Or could it? I think you can see that even here further objections could be raised, about the influence of the harvesting process itself, for example, or the emotional coldness of the clinical setting, that would challenge the claim that empirical data conclusively determine the choice of either theory. Are there really no rational or objective criteria against which to evaluate scientific theories?

Philosopher of science Larry Laudan is one of the most forceful, if cautious, defenders of scientific objectivity and rationality. Regarding Kuhn, Laudan writes,

> [Kuhn] asserts that all the standards which scientists use are ambiguous and that 'individuals may legitimately differ about their application to concrete cases.' 'Simplicity, scope, fruitfulness and even accuracy can be judged differently . . . by different people.' He is surely right about some of this. Notoriously, one man's simplicity is another's complexity; one may think a new approach fruitful, while a second may see it as sterile. But such fuzziness of conception is precisely why most methodologists have avoided falling back on these hazy notions for talking about the empirical warrant for theories. Consider a different set of standards, one arguably more familiar to philosophers of science:
>
> • prefer theories which are internally consistent;
> • prefer theories which correctly make some predictions which are surprising given our background assumptions;
> • prefer theories which have been tested against a diverse range of kinds of phenomena to those which have been tested only against very similar sorts of phenomena.
>
> Even standards such as these have some fuzziness around the edges, but can anyone believe that, confronted with *any* pair of theories, and *any* body of evidence, these standards are so rough-hewn that they could be used indifferently to justify choosing either element of the pair? Do we really believe that Aristotle's physics correctly made the sorts of surprising predictions that Newton's physics did? Is there any doubt that Cartesian optics, with its dual insistence on the instantaneous propagation of light and that light traveled faster in denser media than in rarer ones, violated the canon of internal consistency?[3]

Taking a somewhat different tack, philosopher Philip Kitcher suggests—urging due caution in its application—a *success* criterion:

> Many people are impressed by the fact that current sciences are extremely successful in predicting future events and in enabling us to intervene in our environments. . . . Success is naturally taken to betoken truth: the predictions of particle physicists and the organisms manufactured by molecular biologists inspire us to ask how we could obtain agreement to ten or so decimal places or breed mice with tissue characteristics made-to-order unless our theoretical claims were at least approximately true. . . . A theory is not successful for a group of people simply in virtue of the fact that members of that group can

use it to attain their goals. Groups can set their sights low and obtain facile "successes"; conversely, successes can be available, whether or not they harmonize with the contingent goals of some cluster of people. On [our] conception, a science is successful when it provides the means to hypothetical ends, ends which are numerous, diverse, and individually difficult to achieve.[4]

While conceding limitations of the success criterion and acknowledging that "appraisals of success are fallible, . . ." Kitcher continues,

The next step is to generalize, claiming that the success that people collectively enjoy in predicting the behavior of objects that exist independently of all of us and in adjusting our actions to them indicates that our most successful ways of representing the world are approximately correct. . . .

Philosophy and Popular Culture

The X-Files: Questions About Evidence

Has Fox Mulder gone completely wacko? Alien abductions, monsters, conspiracy theories—you name it, and this guy believes it. Mulder may be the best crime investigator in the FBI, but people are starting to call him "Spooky" because he is obsessed by the supernatural and the paranormal. What's the FBI to do?

The answer is to bring in a partner for Mulder, a partner who is known to be completely rational. That partner is Dr. Dana Scully (a physician), whose scientific and medical credentials are impeccable. Scully can keep an eye on Mulder and report on his work. As a rational scientist, Scully will be able to examine the evidence and answer this question: Is Mulder doing something substantial, or is he a wild-eyed conspiracy theorist? If Scully's reports support the latter finding, the X-Files can be closed down—*forever.*

Questions to Consider

What kind of evidence would be sufficient to convince you that alien abductions are real? What kind of evidence would be sufficient to convince a completely rational scientist?

I conclude that neither the fact that major scientific controversies are protracted nor our inability to delineate a precise account of scientific evidence should undermine our confidence that the resolution of scientific debate on the basis of evidence is possible.[5]

My own position on this debate occupies something of a middle ground. On the one hand, I have seen scientific claims overinflated and over-canonized. When I was in high school, our science textbooks (and some of our science teachers) smugly and piously proclaimed that it was a scientific fact that there are exactly three subatomic particles—protons, electrons, and neutrons—and the periodic tables that hung in our chemistry classrooms reflected that view. Nowadays we hear talk of quarks, leptons, hadrons, and so on, and some of my humanities colleagues and I no longer can make sense of the periodic tables displayed in the science lecture halls near my campus office. Moreover, sometimes I have questions about our country's priorities in its allocation of funds. I have seen public funds allotted to giant telescopes and the exploration of space while children in Appalachia were going hungry. In the universities, science departments and faculties routinely receive ample funding while English departments are underfunded and nursing programs are eliminated. I believe that there is something to the view that science became the religion of the twentieth century, not to be questioned, *the* dispenser of Truth with a capital 'T'. I believe moreover that such deference was in many respects unhealthy, and that therefore some of the recent demystification of science has been therapeutic.

On the other hand, it was not Feyerabend's magicians, or priests, or astrologers, who effectively rid the world of smallpox, or that saved millions of children from the crippling effects of polio, but Edward Jenner, whose *scientific* investigations led to the discovery of the smallpox vaccine, and Jonas Salk, who discovered the polio vaccine, *scientifically*. Maybe, as we inquire into the nature of theory confirmation and the possibility of developing criteria to adjudicate among competing paradigms, there is a lesson to be learned there.

Notes

1. Karl R. Popper, *The Logic of Scientific Discovery*, Basic Books, New York, 1959.
2. Irving M. Copi and Carl Cohen, *Introduction to Logic*, Tenth Edition, Prentice Hall, Upper Saddle River, Copyright, 1998, 1994, by Prentice Hall, Inc.
3. Larry Laudan, *Beyond Positivism and Relativism: Theory, Method, and Evidence*, Westview Press, Boulder, 1996.
4. Philip Kitcher, *Science, Truth, and Democracy*, Oxford University Press, Inc., New York, Copyright, 2001, by Philip Kitcher, pp. 16–17.
5. *Ibid.*, p. 141.
6. Richard Rudner, "The Scientist *qua* Scientist Makes Value Judgments," *Philosophy of Science* (20), 1953.

7. Edward Goldsmith, Lewis Wolpert, Exchange of letters, *The Ecologist,* 22 April, 2000.
8. Ronald W. Clark, *Einstein: The Life and Times,* The World Publishing Company, New York and Cleveland, Copyright 1971 by Ronald W. Clark, p. 620.
9. James Sterngold, "Torch Being Passed to Younger Scientists," *The San Francisco Chronicle,* 23 June, 2003.

The Main Points in Chapter Four

1. Francis Bacon proposed to lay a solid foundation for our scientific study of nature by beginning with a theory-neutral "muster" of observations, on which theories could then be built. Bacon's method is central to the school of philosophy called empiricism. According to Bacon, science can progress to greater and greater knowledge because it rests on an ever-growing foundation of observations.

2. Thomas Kuhn rejected the traditional picture of science as progressing steadily and evenly toward ever greater knowledge, arguing instead that science changes by a series of revolutions, in which old pictures or paradigms lose out to new ones. On Kuhn's view, it is quite unclear whether there is one-direction progress in science, since the change from old paradigms to new ones is so great that there is no common ground between them on which to base a judgment.

3. Recent work in the philosophy of science has emphasized the social and institutional structure of science, rather than portraying science as something done by isolated individuals. Judgments about the value of scientific research are ultimately social judgments rather than logical ones.

4. While recognizing the social dimensions of science, some contemporary philosophers argue nevertheless that there are limited standards of scientific objectivity and rationality.

Questions for Discussion and Review

1. Suppose you were part of a space exploration team that had landed on a distant planet where you had no idea what the local conditions were like, whether there was anything alive, what life would look like if you found it. How would you go about learning something about this entirely new environment? How would you interpret your instrument readings? How would you check to see whether the physical and chemical laws you knew from earth worked there?

2. Thomas Kuhn published *The Structure of Scientific Revolutions* in 1962. Have there been any "scientific revolutions" in the three decades since

that time? Is the development of computers a "revolution," in Kuhn's terms? What about space travel? Why? Why not?

3. If the final test of a scientific theory is its acceptance by the community of men and women who are called "scientists," does that mean that *anything* is acceptable science as long as enough of the right people agree with it? Does that mean there is no such thing as scientific *truth*? How, if at all, does science differ from politics, art, or religion, in that case?

ABCNEWS

C O N T E M P O R A R Y
A P P L I C A T I O N

Is Science Value-Neutral?

In 1953 the scholarly journal *Philosophy of Science* (20) published an article by American philosopher Richard Rudner entitled "The Scientist *qua* Scientist Makes Value Judgments," one of Rudner's contributions to a debate on the topic, "Is Science Value-Neutral?"[6] The debate concerned claims about the objectivity of science, claims that science *qua* science—that is, science *as such*—is concerned with facts, not values. Some writers had defended these claims; critics questioned them.

Some critics were quick to point out that from the point of view of *academic* values, science—at least scientific research—certainly is not value-neutral. We expect the scientific researcher to be honest in reporting her findings, meticulous in crediting her sources, etc. But Rudner went further. He wrote, "Any adequate analysis or (if I may use the term) rational reconstruction of the method of science must comprise the statement that the scientist *qua* scientist accepts or rejects hypotheses; and further that an analysis of that statement would reveal it to entail that the scientist *qua* scientist makes value judgments."

Whether the scientific researcher is expected to conform to *social and moral* values in her research was another question. In the paper cited, Rudner did not speak directly to this point, although he did write, "To refuse to pay attention to the value decisions which *must* be made, to make them intuitively, unconsciously, haphazardly, is to leave an essential aspect of scientific method out of control. . . . [A] science of ethics is a necessary requirement if science's progress toward objectivity is to be continuous." At one end of the debate's spectrum, advocates of "scientific neutrality" claimed that the task of the scientist *qua* scientist is to seek truth through the methods of the empirical sciences; it is up to policy makers to determine the uses to which scientific discovery may be put—whether, that is, the use of the research, and in what ways it is used, conform to societal values. Of course, in other areas of her life—in her roles as citizen, friend, colleague, wife, and mother, for example—the scientific researcher is not exempt from social and moral constraints simply because she is,

professionally, a scientist. But, according to this point of view, in her role as scientist she should leave her social and moral values out of her work. At the other end of the spectrum, advocates of "social responsibility" claimed that there are certain areas of scientific research that simply ought not be pursued because of potentially disastrous results or the moral impermissibility of doing the experimentation.

Sometimes one and the same person experiences the tension between the two points of view. Among the most famous examples are Albert Einstein and J. Robert Oppenheimer, both scientists, and both involved in one way or another with the development of the atomic bomb.

In 1939 a group of scientists asked Einstein to sign a letter to U.S. President Franklin D. Roosevelt urging that an atomic bomb be developed. They thought that Einstein, the scientist who had formulated the famous equation "$E = mc^2$" to express the concept that a small amount of matter could release a large amount of energy, could command the attention needed to persuade President Roosevelt to initiate the project. Although Einstein thought of himself as a pacifist, he was concerned about the growing Nazi menace in Europe and had been alarmed to learn that in 1938 German scientists had succeeded in splitting the uranium atom. He agreed to sign the letter. After he learned of the devastation that atomic bombs had caused in the Japanese cities of Hiroshima and Nagasaki, Einstein had second thoughts.

"I made one great mistake in my life," he lamented near the end of his life, "when I signed the letter to President Roosevelt recommending that atom bombs be made; but there was justification—the danger that the Germans would make them."

A prominent physicist at Cal Tech, Oppenheimer was tapped in 1942 to head the "Manhattan Project", an effort to find a way to harness nuclear energy for military purposes. A result was the atomic bomb, developed at a laboratory in Los Alamos, New Mexico. Oppenheimer later opposed the development of the hydrogen bomb, and as a result lost his security clearance, becoming a victim of the McCarthy era anti-Communist hysteria of the 1950s. He became a worldwide symbol of the scientist struggling to resolve the moral dilemmas arising from scientific discovery, and spent the rest of his life working out ideas on the relationship of science and society.

The following articles reflect this continuing tension. The first, which appeared in the British periodical *The Ecologist,* contains an exchange of letters between British biology professor Lewis Wolpert and environmentalist and *Ecologist* founder Edward Goldsmith, and has as its focus the question of the value-neutrality of science, although in passing the writers touch on many of the topics we have discussed in Chapter 4; I have retained the British spellings throughout. (The "GM foods" mentioned several times in the letters are genetically modified foods, foodstuffs that have been modified in the laboratory, rather than through selective breeding, to enhance

desired traits such as drought-resistance or resistence to insect larvae.) The second, a clear call for renewed thinking about ethical criteria for scientific activities, comes from a Pugwash Workshop on Science, Ethics and Society sponsored by the Pugwash Conferences on Science and World Affairs, co-recipient of the 1995 Nobel Peace Prize. In the article from the *San Francisco Chronicle,* interviewees express some of the ambivalence that characterizes the ongoing debate.[7]

Introduction

Following our articles in April's issue examining the independence of the scientific world, we here invite developmental biologist Professor Lewis Wolpert to debate the neutrality of science with environmentalist and *Ecologist* founder Edward Goldsmith.

Dear Professor Wolpert:

One thing that modern science is not and cannot be is neutral—or, for it comes to the same thing, objective.

To begin with, scientific knowledge is empirical—founded on observation or perception. But perception is subjective. It begins with the detection of data, which is an active rather than a passive process, data being detected, rather as a mine is detected and not just passively received. It is then interpreted in the light of one's mental model of our relationship with the world around us. A perception is thus no more than a hypothesis based on a 'paradigm' developed during the course of our upbringing within our cultural group, whose values and beliefs it will reflect. That the human mind is simply not designed to entertain objective knowledge is acknowledged by enlightened philosophers of science. Michael Polanyi, for instance, considered that only someone brought up in total isolation from human society could entertain such knowledge, and Karl Popper described objective knowledge as 'knowledge without a

knower,' though he thought it possible to build objective 'logical constructs'.

It is further argued by those who see science as objective that a scientific proposition is one that has been 'verified' or 'falsified' empirically. However, as Thomas Kuhn pointed out in *The Structure of Scientific Revolutions,* modern scientists are generally more concerned with 'problem solving' than they are with fundamental issues. And because today's scientists believe unquestioningly in the same overall paradigm, it is only the details that are tested, while the paradigm, and hence the scientists' fundamental beliefs, are never tested 'and could be guaranteed to emerge unscathed' even if they were.

Michael Polanyi considered that 'the test of proof or disproof is . . . irrelevant to the acceptance or rejection of fundamental beliefs'. To the modern scientist, for example, the belief that man is a rational, as opposed to rationalising, being, that evolution proceeds by natural selection from random variations, and that all benefits are the product of science, technology and industry, is fundamental. It would be difficult to imagine a test that could persuade them otherwise. Hence Max Planck's oft-repeated saying that 'a new scientific truth does not triumph by convincing its opponents, and making them see the light, but rather because its opponents eventually die, and a new generation grows up that is familiar with it.'

It is reasonable to trace the origins of modern science to Francis Bacon (which is not to play down the roles played by Galileo and Descartes). He was the first to insist that science be methodically separated from values so as to make it truly 'neutral'. In reality he did nothing of the sort. His 'scientific knowledge', instead of being value-free, set out explicitly and purposefully to give humanity power over nature. 'Truth and utility are perfectly identical,' he wrote in his *Novum Organum,* and 'that which is most useful in practice is most correct in theory'. In effect he merely replaced the old 'subjective' values of 'good' and 'evil' with the values of 'useful' and 'useless', or more precisely 'of contributing or not contributing to man's domination over or transformation of the natural world'. There were to be no limits to this transformation. His goal was explicitly stated. It was to 'achieve all things achievable'. At least he was honest enough to admit it.

Modern science has followed Bacon's lead to the letter but does not admit it. It serves two purposes. The first is to provide the knowledge that will enable technologists and industrialists to transform the planet. As such it is reductionistic, since a holistic science could not conceivably lead to the development of pesticides, antibiotics, genetically modified crops or atom bombs.

The second is to rationalise, and hence legitimise, such endeavours by accentuating their apparent short-term benefits. Again, a truly holistic science would be undesirable as it would reveal the intolerable biological, social and ecological implications of such endeavours.

Edward Goldsmith

Dear Edward Goldsmith,

Science is the best way of understanding how the world works and has been astonishingly successful in doing so; and I disagree with almost everything that you write in your letter. Contrary to your view, I claim that reliable scientific knowledge is morally and ethically neutral, and ethics only enter when science is applied to making a product, for example, GM foods. If we are not at the centre of the universe, and genes are responsible for determining some of our behaviour, that is the way the world is—it is neither good nor bad. Knowledge can be used for both good and evil. Of course scientists in their work have the responsibilities of all citizens to do no harm and be honest.

Their additional responsibility is to put their work and its possible applications in the public domain. But one must distinguish between scientific knowledge and its application—technology. It is the very nature of science that it is not possible to predict what will be discovered or how these discoveries could be applied.

The idea that science is not objective and does not tell us how the world works is a philosophical problem that bears no relation to reality. Do you really not believe that we are made of cells or that the heart pumps blood or that DNA is the genetic material? Practising scientists have not the slightest interest in the philosophy of science, and, in the historian Gerald Holton's phrase, view philosophy of science as a 'debilitating befuddlement'. In his book, *Dreams of a Final Theory,* the distinguished physicist Weinberg has a whole chapter entitled 'Against Philosophy'. He describes himself as 'an unregenerate working scientist who finds no help in professional philosophy,' and continues, 'I am not alone in this; I know of no one who has participated actively in the advance of physics in the postwar period whose work has been significantly helped by the philosophers'. This is also true of biology and the tremendous success of genetics and molecular biology. Philosophers of science have contributed nothing that helps us understand the scientific process. The oft-quoted counter-example is Karl Popper's famous book *The Logic of Scientific Discovery.* Popper claimed to have solved the problem of induction by arguing that science proceeds by a sequence of bold conjectures rather than being based on observations, and that then these conjectures are replaced when they are falsified.

Falsification is all and verification irrelevant. This view completely ignores the nature of discovery in science, and fails to explain how one knows that a falsification is correct. He goes so far as to say, 'Our science is not knowledge; it can never claim to have attained truth, or even a substitute for it, such as probability. . . We do not know; we can only guess'. What nonsense—DNA is the genetic material and codes for proteins.

The so-called 'fundamental beliefs' of science you claim are largely your invention. I have no knowledge that scientists as a group believe man (no women?) to be rational. Most do believe that evolution works by natural selection on changes in organisms due to random changes in their DNA, and the evidence for this is overwhelming.

I admire Kuhn, but he does not use science as only 'problem solving' in your pejorative sense. Scientists deal with the most fundamental of problems relating to how nature functions. Planck's point about scientists being unwilling to change their minds emphasises that science is a communal process in which the views and contributions of the individual are in the long run irrelevant . One should not give up one's ideas too easily.

It is to Archimedes and Galileo that we should point to the origins of modern science—Bacon discovered nothing, and was all talk. Truth and utility are not the same. I do not understand what 'holistic' science means. It must be true that all phenomena in the universe are controlled by the same set of fundamental physical laws. I cannot believe that you would disagree. But that is not the same as wanting to explain everything in terms of physics.

There are different levels of organisation, long recognised by biologists, and the reductionist approach is to try and account for the phenomena at one level in terms of the properties of the components of the next level down. It is unnecessary to go down to further levels but there must be nothing in one's explanations that contradict laws that hold at lower levels, like, for example, the laws of physics. The trick is to find the right level at which to try and explain the phenomena. No one would attempt to deal with economics in terms of the behaviour of molecules, but that is exactly what has been so brilliantly successful with cell and developmental biology. The language of cells is, as Sydney Brenner once put it, molecules.

There are few cases where scientists as a group have behaved immorally, the main example being the false claims of eugenics. As Robert Oppenheimer made clear in relation to the bomb, the duty of scientists is to understand how the world works; but how this knowledge is used ultimately lies, in a democracy, with the people's elected representatives. Moreover, scientists rarely have power in relation to applications of science; this rests with those with the money—industry and government. The way scientific knowledge is used raises ethical issues for everyone involved, not just scientists.

Professor Lewis Wolpert,
University College London

Dear Lewis,

Thanks for your interesting letter. For you, science such as that involved in mapping the human genome is neutral, though not the use that is made of it by 'those with the money—industry and government'. But scientists cannot live in a void: they must take into account the realities of the world they live in. And in today's world it could not be more predictable that work on the genome project must lead to such things as the development of GM foods.

The position you take is very much that of the U.S. gun lobby. While they actively supply an increasingly unstable American population with guns, they deny any responsibility for the use to which they are put.

For you, the philosophy of science is of no value. You appear not to be concerned about scientists working in a void. But the philosophy of science serves above all to relate scientific information to other forms of information such as that contained in a genome, an ecosystem or a society's cultural pattern—which is essential in order to understand what science really is, and hence to make scientists aware of the social, ecological and moral implications of the work they do.

In my book *The Way* I document the moral ideas of leading Darwinians and neo-Darwinians. Though their views of evolution vary considerably, they all share the same fundamental beliefs, for instance that morality consists in building up objective scientific knowledge, that moral ideas have to be chosen rationally, that they have to be flexible and constantly changing, and above all that they must promote individualism rather than social values and 'progress'. The basic underlying values of these biologists are thus indistinguishable, and I would argue, not by chance, from those of industrial mass society.

I do not accept your contention that there is 'overwhelming evidence' for the neo-Darwinian thesis. Such 'evidence' consists in noting that adaptation has occurred and then taking such adaptation as constituting evidence of natural selection at work. On the subject of the Galapagos finches that so impressed Darwin, Michael Ruse writes, 'we find that all the different species show the effects of selection . . . peculiar characteristic after peculiar characteristic has some special adaptive function . . . There are beaks for cactus eating, beaks for insect eating on the wing . . . One species has even developed the ability to probe with twigs for insects in hollow parts of trees'. In this passage, Ruse's identification of selection with adaptation is quite explicit. The fact that Ruse is assuming what he set out to prove could not be more evident.

Many critics have noted that natural selection is little more than the biological version of Adam Smith's 'invisible hand'—a fundamental belief of modern economists that serves to rationalise and hence legitimise today's social and economic priorities. As for the 'random changes' that you also believe in, what evidence is there that they are really random? How do you know that they are not part of an orderly pattern that you have not been able to identify? It was Lamarck who said, 'the word randomness only expresses our ignorance of causes'.

Edward Goldsmith

Dear Edward,

There was nothing inevitable about genetics leading to GM foods until the techniques were developed in genetic research. And what is wrong with GM foods? In all the hysteria I have yet to read a single reasoned argument about the supposed dangers as compared to foods developed during the green revolution. Did you know that those foods were developed by irradiating plants with X-rays and then selecting the mutants for the desired properties? Are you happy with that approach? And do we not need new plants to feed the world's increasing population? Greenpeace and those like them are almost religious fundamentalists with no interest in evidence or science. Scientists who developed the genetic techniques for manipulating genes are not responsible for GM foods—that rests with the large and rich industrial companies. The techniques were developed in relation to pure research and cannot be compared to guns. It is worth noting that there are very few objects in the world that cannot be put to evil use—I could do terrible damage to you with my glasses. Please do not confuse knowledge with its application.

In a democracy we must all, through our government, take the responsibility for controlling any abuses and dangers. I fail to see why you should want to give so much power to scientists by allowing them to make ethical decisions about the applications of their work. They have neither the right nor the skills.

I cannot accept that the moral values of scientists have a significant influence on their scientific ideas. Scientists deal with the real world and if history were to be rerun, given enough scientists they will come up with the same ideas. DNA will still be the genetic material and water H_2O, though both may be given different names. It is relativistic nonsense propagated by the sociologists of science that science is a social construction with particular validity, just another set of myths. If you really believe that then why bother about applications of science?

I have no strong views on how we should base our moral values but I am sure our evolutionary history plays a role. I am surprised at your rejection of Darwinism and your example is not persuasive; is not Ruse a philosopher? For evolution you should go to Maynard Smith, Bill Hamilton and Dawkins. I am a developmental biologist. Embryos are the key component in the evolution of animals and plants. The only thing that changes from generation to generation is the DNA inherited by the fertilised egg and this controls how the embryo develops. Changes in the DNA lead to changes in adult form and function and this is the material of natural selection acts—the fittest survive.

Surely you are not a Lamarckian—or do you have a hidden religious objection to Darwinism? Randomness is common in nature, the molecules in a gas move randomly as do those in a diffusing chemical in a liquid. It may well be true that certain changes in DNA are more likely

than others—I am not an expert on that—but the fundamental principle is the same. Drug resistance is a lovely example of bacterial evolution. It is also true that development puts a constraint on what can evolve—we could not by natural selection evolve wings like an angel, for example, but we could evolve an angelic disposition; this is due to the number of small changes in DNA required that could lead to forms and behaviours that could be selected for.

Lewis Wolpert

Dear Lewis,

I too disagree with just about everything you say. Let's face it our debate is above all a head-on conflict between two opposed and unreconcilable world views.

For a start you regard the opposition to GM foods as public 'hysteria'. Sir Robert May, our Government's chief scientist refers to Doctor Pusztai's important work on the effects of GM potatoes on rats as 'garbage'. Doctor William Bean insisted in the Archive of Internal Medicine in 1962 that Rachel Carson's exposure of the intolerable effects of DDT was 'so much hogwash'. Professor Lord Zuckerman, who in the early 1970s was also the British government's chief scientist, referred to the Club of Rome's Limits To Growth as 'arbitrary speculation', and 'unscientific nonsense'.

My first reaction to these outbursts is that they don't say much for 'scientific neutrality' or 'objectivity'. They suggest instead that scientists like May, Bean, Zuckerman and yourself are little more than the priests of the modern cult of scientific progress, and that you feel duty-bound to discredit any heretics who dare suggest that this insidious process might not be entirely beneficial.

Like other members of your cult, you have swallowed the neo-Darwinian thesis hook line and sinker. As I have already pointed out, the 'overwhelming evidence' that you refer to is based on the assumption that evolution and natural selection are synonymous. You reject the example I cite of this sleight of hand on the grounds that its author is a philosopher not a scientist. But Charlesworth is a scientist and he is equally guilty. He tells us that 'probably the most generally relevant prediction of the theory of natural selection is that episodes of rapid evolution should coincide with periods when the direction of selection is changing'.

Among the examples Charlesworth cites is that 'insecticide resistance evolves in populations exposed to a new insecticide'. Quite true, but how does this prove that the resistance is the product of natural selection? Why for instance can it not equally be attributed to cognitive and metabolic changes that can eventually be fixed genetically and that are part of the adaptive stock-in-trade of the highly dynamic and creative creatures that mosquitoes, for example, are known to be? Does this latter interpretation not fit in very much better with the way mosquitoes have actually adapted to DDT?

I remind you that some mosquitoes simply learned not to alight on the walls of huts sprayed with DDT. Others developed a thick cuticle through which the DDT could not penetrate. Still others got much fatter so that the DDT could be sufficiently diluted, while others went so far as to develop an enzyme that broke down DDT into a perfectly harmless substance. Does natural selection provide a plausible explanation for these incredibly diverse and creative responses?

In any case, natural selection is a purely mechanistic process. Like the sorting of envelopes in a post office into two heaps—one for those to be posted (the fit), and the other for those to be returned to their senders (the unfit). The trouble is that envelopes don't evolve. As Ludwig von Bertalanffy (like you a developmental biologist) noted 'selection presupposes self-maintenance, adaptability, reproduction etc. of the living organism. These therefore cannot be the effects of selection'. They can clearly only be the effects of a very much more sophisticated process.

This suggests that natural selection is generally accepted not because there is 'overwhelming evidence' for it, but because it fits in so perfectly with our mechanistic and reductionistic world view in terms of which we see the natural world as random rather than orderly, and committed to perpetual change (progress) rather than overall stability.

Edward Goldsmith

Dear Edward,

Yours is a very peculiar world view which you never make clear. There is no doubt that individual scientists have said things that are reprehensible and that they have been wrong but that in no way undermines the scientific enterprise. Science is the best way to understand the way the world works and Pusztai and others can and should be criticised on scientific grounds—the essence of science is peer review. Scientists are not a homogeneous group, they vary enormously in their views, and expertise.

It is of little use to insult the scientists you refer to as priests of a cult—if anything you are a bit cult-like with your holism and totally unsubstantiated rejection of evolutionary theory.

It is not a scientific argument to say that natural selection and genetic variation cannot account for the ability of mosquitoes to develop resistant strategies to DDT. You are a Lamarckian who believes that acquired characteristics can be inherited, and ignores the enormous evidence against this idea. I wonder if there is any science that you believe to be reliable and which you would trust or do you really think like some sociologists of science that it is just another religion, another set of myths.

Like you I care about the environment and it is only through a scientific understanding of nature that we will be able to protect it. For example, it is science that has warned us about ozone holes and global warming. That has to be important.

Lewis Wolpert

PUGWASH WORKSHOP ON SCIENCE, ETHICS AND SOCIETY
27-29 June 2003
Paris, France

Introductory Remarks

The social responsibility of scientists has been a central topic on the Pugwash agenda since the first Conference in Pugwash, in 1957. Indeed over a period of thirty or forty years there has been a major change in the attitude of scientists towards public discussion of ethical issues. Nowadays, the noteworthy feature of Pugwash is that it provides a forum for collaboration between social and natural scientists, while retaining the methodology of the natural sciences.

The present world goes through parallel and contrasting processes of globalisation (no country alone is responsible for scientific research) and fragmentation. The research is being privatised in certain areas (biotechnology for example), the researchers are not so free in private firms as compared with public institutions, and therefore their sense of responsibility may diminish.

The threat of global destruction seem more remote, and therefore the issue of the scientists' responsibility is not so prominent as in the case of the development of nuclear weapons. However, smaller arms are being developed, such as non-lethal weapons or arms which cannot be defined as weapons of mass destruction although they may inflict enormous damages, or chemical or biological weapons. Moreover, we are thus faced with a daunting dilemma. As part of cultural evolution, science should be allowed to develop freely, with no restrictions put on it. But can we afford the luxury of uninhibited research—which may lead to an even greater potential for total destruction—in a world in which war is still a recognized social institution?

The pace of advances is science is such now that applications follow very soon fundamental research. Indeed, practical applications often follow immediately after scientific discoveries, and are often pursued by the same people. Science is changing rapidly, not only in its research techniques and organisational structures but also in its relationships with society at large. Science becomes more closely embedded in society and these changes reveal ethical dilemmas which could previously be glossed over.

All these new developments make necessary a renewed thinking on ethical criteria for scientific activities. The fact that many scientists and other professionals continue to subscribe to a belief in the value-neutrality of science, and deny that the introduction of new insights and technologies inevitably has a social impact, forms a considerable obstacle to the establishment of ethical and moral norms. Even where potential negative effects cannot be denied, the argument of 'neutrality' is often heard. This is moreover encouraged by the increasing disciplinary specialisation. Traditional modes of ethical analysis cannot deal adequately with the values, norms and interests activated by present-day technoscience without reference to its sociological, political and economic dimensions. Each community, each country, as well as the world community have the responsibility to understand the ethical issues at stake and implement means to control the scientific activities and their potential negative outcomes. Developing new ethics norms should be the result of a multilateral stand on responsibility: that of the scientific community with respect to other values present in the society, and those of other social institutions (economic, political, religious, etc.) with respect to the rights of science.

The increasing gulf between the public and scientists is a threat to the support of science, to rational discussion of scientific issues in the public debate and policy making. There is a need to have a much more interactive process of communisation between scientists, the policy makers and the public. The vast whole of problems raised by the communication with various publics, of the objectives and results of a scientific research should constitute a large chapter of the ethics of the work of science. There is a real need to work out an ethics of scientific information. It required there to develop an informative democracy, because science needs also to become, in adapted forms, appropriable by all, so that the knowledge is raised in culture. The whole of the citizens has right to this knowledge and this culture. It is therefore most important that science improves its public image, that it regains the respect of the community for its integrity, trust in its pronouncements.

Scientists should address the larger context of their work and, at the same time, they should create or re-create the conditions to practice their social responsibility.

TORCH BEING PASSED TO YOUNGER SCIENTISTS[9]
James Sterngold
Chronicle Staff Writer

Bruce Goodwin admits he often meets with puzzled stares when he tells young people he designs nuclear bombs for a living and tries to recruit promising scientists, as though he had emerged from an outdated science fiction fantasy.

"People will say to us, 'My God, you still work on nuclear weapons?' " said Goodwin, the head of the weapons program at the Lawrence Livermore National Laboratory in the East Bay. "I would say, 'Yes, we do.' But it is still a surprise."

"It has become more difficult over the past 10 years to attract the right people."

The Cold War may be over and the once-anxious nuclear standoff with the Soviet Union a hazy memory.

But the Bush administration and congressional Republicans recently succeeded in repealing the decade-old ban on research into new types of low-yield nuclear weapons, and they are pushing ahead on the development of a bunker-busting warhead—giving momentum to a quiet renaissance for the complex of facilities where warheads are designed, built and maintained.

As billions of dollars are being spent rebuilding production capabilities, a new generation of weapons designers—most of them newly minted Ph.D.s or post-doctoral researchers—are being recruited and trained by Lawrence Livermore and its sister lab, the Los Alamos National Laboratory in New Mexico, both managed by the University of California.

Because of the extensive academic training required, these scientists are often in their 30s and even 40s—a couple of decades younger than the Cold War weaponeers. But they face dramatically different circumstances, with the threats to the United States less clear and the kind of nuclear arsenal it needs a matter of intense debate.

Live testing has been banned for a decade, so most weapons work is done using computer simulations. The scientists say their work has become more theoretical than hands-on. They come in contact only rarely with actual weapons or the missiles and bombers that deliver them to targets. Those who do say the experience can be sobering, if not jarring.

"It's their size," said Charles Nakhleh, 36, a brash, combative physicist at Los Alamos. "It's pretty amazing, because they're not that big. You realize these are practical, engineered objects. They have tolerances. We don't get that otherwise."

Labs Now Under a Cloud

Another big change from the past is that the labs themselves—once secretive, highly respected and generally considered beyond reproach—are now under a cloud because of continuing management problems that have tarnished their image.

Energy Secretary Spencer Abrahams recently told UC that if it wants to continue running Los Alamos when its contract expires in two years, the university will have to enter a competition. There are concerns Abrahams may do the same with Livermore.

At least for now, the controversies do not seem to be affecting these young designers, whose ranks include many women and minorities—another contrast with the older, mostly white male scientists.

During interviews at both labs, a dozen young designers discussed what drew them into the field and how they view their work in a world in which it is no longer clear who might be the target of a nuclear attack or what role these uniquely destructive weapons would play when U.S. policy is to prevent new members in the world's nuclear club.

The designers all seemed motivated in equal parts by patriotism and the thrill of knotty scientific challenges. Goodwin said that, since the Sept. 11 attacks, there has been a stronger sense of mission among designers.

Yet the word "fascinating" popped up constantly.

"To me it's really a fascinating realm of physics," said John Scott, 31, a Los Alamos designer who recently entered the lab's intensive training program, called the Theoretical Institute for Thermonuclear and Nuclear Studies, or Titans. "They're never going to go away. We might as well capitalize on the positive aspects."

Most of the lab scientists sought to deflect questions about whether they had concerns regarding producing such destructive weapons, saying they had no control over arms policy.

"I was born into a world with tens of thousands of nuclear weapons," said Robert Canaan, 37, a nuclear engineer from the University of Texas, who is now at Livermore. "I'd rather that people who know what they're doing are designing them and maintaining them."

Most of the young designers objected to the notion that nuclear arms are different from other kinds of weapons, a reality that was central to America's Cold War strategy and diplomacy for decades.

"Sometimes I think it's a little irrational to say there are good ways to destroy things and bad ways to destroy things," said Omar Hurricane, 35, a Livermore physicist. "It's sort of arbitrary."

Some resisted the notion that they are designing weapons at all.

See Weapons As Deterrents

"I don't look at issues of design as involving weapons of mass destruction," said Mary Jane Lindquist, 43, an expert in applied mathematics at Livermore. "I look at them as deterrents. I don't really look at it as if I'm designing something with the object of killing people. The whole point is that they don't get used."

Alan Wan, 45, a Livermore physicist, echoed that view, arguing that the weapons made this country safer. "My job is to make our deterrent so credible that no one will challenge us," he said. "I'm very proud of what I do."

Most of the young researchers said they had grappled quietly, and on their own, with any moral qualms they might have had about working on nuclear weapons—the labs had never encouraged an airing of the subject, they said. For many, their concerns centered on their families and educating their children. Several said they had chosen work at a weapons lab because it was a well-paid job that fit in with a spouse's move.

Raymond Jeanloz, a physics professor at UC Berkeley and a member of a high-level university panel that oversees the scientific work at the labs, called weapons design an attractive career choice.

The labs often permit more interdisciplinary work than do universities, where research tends to be more compartmentalized, and the young designers have a sense they are contributing to the nation's security, Jeanloz said. He added that lab scientists tend to be better paid—with salaries starting at $80,000 or so—than young academics on university faculties, and they are given more responsibility sooner.

The scientists who join the programs undergo lengthy apprenticeships, either with the Titans program at Los Alamos or a mentoring system at Livermore.

While much of what they do is highly theoretical, Michael Bernardin, who runs Los Alamos' Titans program, noted that there are some practical exercises. One assignment, he said, is "to compute what kind of explosive yield would take out Los Angeles."

Scant Knowledge of History

Though computers have given the new generation a better understanding than their elders of the abstruse physics of thermonuclear explosions, their knowledge of Cold War history, current policy debates and the human impact of nuclear warfare seemed scant, at best.

Few said they followed the recent battle in Congress on whether the decade-old ban on developing low-yield nuclear warheads should be repealed.

"I'm not a news buff," said Livermore's Lindquist. "I'm really bad that way. I have so much to do and I have so many deadlines. There are only so many hours in the day."

None of them had accurate knowledge of the toll taken by history's lone instance of nuclear warfare, which ended World War II.

The first several generations of weapons designers generally found the bombings in 1945 of Hiroshima and Nagasaki, Japan, an emotional experience that influenced their subsequent work, along with seeing the power of the weapons in later tests. But those bombings are little discussed now.

The only designer who was close to knowing the number of deaths was Canaan, who said he believed something on the order of 100,000 had been killed by each blast—a significant understatement, according to experts. But, when asked, he noted, "I haven't especially studied those two tests."

He was not alone. Neither lab includes study of the bombings—the sole opportunity to understand the political, military and human impact of nuclear warfare in its training program.

"Students are exposed to the great destructive effects of the nuclear explosion" through test data, Bernardin said, but the bombings in Japan "are not part of what we study, really."

Juliana Hsu, 40, a weapons physicist at Livermore, said she did not know how many died in the bombings, except that the attacks forced Japan's surrender and ended the war.

According to John Dower, a history professor at MIT and a respected scholar of the U.S. war with Japan, the bombing of Hiroshima killed about 140,000 people in 1945, and 70,000 to 75,000 died within the first few months of the strike on Nagasaki. Other experts generally agree that the toll rose considerably by 1950 because of radiation poisoning and other bomb-related injuries, to as many as 200,000 in Hiroshima and 140,000 in Nagasaki.

But most of the young designers stressed that America's nuclear arsenal had prevented another war of the magnitude of World War II.

Nakhleh, the Los Alamos physicist, said he worked for a time in arms control and retains an interest in the area, but he does not advocate getting rid of nuclear weapons.

"I would submit that the advent of nuclear weapons has made warfare on that old scale obsolete," he said. "I would argue you can't get away from nuclear weapons."

Immanuel Kant

Immanuel Kant (1724–1804) was born, lived out his life, and died in the provincial city of Königsberg in Prussia. Kant's early studies were concentrated in the areas of natural science, mathematics, and philosophy. At the University of Königsberg, he learned the philosophical theories of Leibniz, as interpreted by a widely read German philosopher, Christian Wolff. After graduating from the university, Kant took a number of jobs as a tutor to children in the houses of Prussian aristocrats. Finally he returned to the university to become what was called a *privatdozent*. This meant that he was licensed by the university to offer lectures, which the students could attend. But he was not paid by the university; instead, he had to collect fees from the students. The more popular he was, the more money he made! For more than a dozen years, Kant lectured as much as twenty-one hours a week on virtually every subject imaginable, from mathematics and logic to geography and history. At last, in 1770, he was ap-

pointed to the position of Professor of Logic and Metaphysics.

Kant was already well known throughout Germany for his writings on physics, astronomy, and metaphysics, but his important work was still far in the future. For eleven years, from 1770 until 1781, he published virtually nothing. All that time he was struggling with fundamental problems of human knowledge, but in 1781, there appeared the book that was to revolutionize all philosophy: his *Critique of Pure Reason*. During the next ten years, book after book flowed from his pen. After the *Critique*, Kant published *Prolegomena to Any Future Metaphysics* (1783), *The Groundwork of the Metaphysic of Morals* (1785), *Metaphysical Foundations of Natural Science* (1786), *Critique of Practical Reason* (1788), and *Critique of Judgment* (1790).

Kant continued writing and revising his theories until finally, at the age of eighty, shortly after the start of the new century, he died. Though he had never left his native Königsberg, his mind had spanned all time and all space, and he had left an indelible mark on the thought of his civilization.

Ethical Theory

THE VARIETIES OF ETHICAL THEORY

Kant and the Commands of Duty

Irwin Edman, a well-known early-twentieth-century Columbia University professor of philosophy, is said to have stopped a student on the street one day. "Excuse me," Edman said. "Can you tell me whether I am walking north or south?" The startled student replied, "You are walking south, Professor." "Ah, good," Edman replied. "Then I have already eaten lunch."

Well, it is not much of a joke, and it has been told of half the professors in America, but it does capture the popular impression of philosophy professors as rather unworldly characters, out of touch with the real world—people, as American businesspeople are fond of saying, who have "never met a payroll."

Immanuel Kant is the greatest philosopher to live and write since the ancient times of Plato and Aristotle; he is the first great philosopher in modern times (after the end of the Middle Ages) to make his living as what we would call a professor of philosophy; and he is also about as close as any great philosopher has ever come to the standard caricature of the professor. Kant is said to have lived so regular and retiring a life that the townspeople of Königsberg, his lifelong home, could set their clocks by him as he went on his daily walk. One would expect a professorial type like Kant to make contributions to such abstruse technical fields as cosmology, metaphysics, or the theory of knowledge, and so he did. But it is rather surprising to discover that Kant also wrote profound, powerful, and deeply moving books on the problems of morality. Despite the uneventful regularity of his own private life, Kant was able to confront and grapple with the great issues of duty, right, justice, and virtue that have troubled the human soul since the ancient times recorded in the Old Testament. The contrast between Kant's outer life and his inner thoughts serves as a reminder to us that the greatness of a philosopher's insights cannot readily be measured by the external excitements of his or her life or times.

Kant was born on April 22, 1724, to a north Prussian family of modest means in the port city of Königsberg on the North Sea. Two centuries earlier, Luther had turned Central Europe upside down with his Reformation of the Catholic Church, and out of Luther's challenge to the institution of the papacy and to the rituals of medieval Christianity had sprung a number of Protestant sects. Kant's family belonged to the sect known as Pietism, an extremely individualistic form of Protestant Christianity that rejected the mystery, ritual, and ceremony that the Catholic Church had interposed between the ordinary Christian and his God. Pietism emphasized the direct, inner relationship of the individual worshiper to God. It placed a strong inner conscience and a stern self-control at the center of its religious doctrine. Kant's mother was particularly devout, and it was universally said of him that he owed both his religious faith and his overpowering sense of moral duty to her influence.

Although he was a believing Christian, Kant rejected the notion that religious doctrine could provide a foundation for morality. Quite to the contrary, he insisted that our moral principles must be established on purely rational grounds, open to criticism and capable of a defense as solid as that which philosophers offered for the principles of pure logic itself.

For Kant, the central question of morality was not, "What should I do?" This he firmly believed was perfectly well known to every decent man and woman, whether a peasant or a professor. As he remarked at one point in his moral writings, the truths of **ethics** had been known for thousands of years, so a moral philosopher could hardly expect to discover something *new* in ethics. Rather, Kant saw the real moral problem in the way that most Puritans and other individualistic Protestants did, as the constant struggle to do what we know is right in the face of temptations and distractions. The soldier who knows that his duty requires him to stand fast even as his fear tempts him to run; the merchant who knows that she should give honest measure for honest measure in the marketplace, but nevertheless secretly wishes to tilt the scales in her own favor; the good husband who knows that his marriage vow is absolutely binding but feels the temptation of adultery—these and others like them are the men and women Kant has in mind when he writes on moral questions.

Kant was a student of the new science of Newton as well as a deeply committed Pietist. He saw a fundamental conflict between the scientific explanation of natural events, which emphasized their subordination to causal laws, and the moral assumption that we are free to choose our actions and hence are morally responsible for what we do. How can we demand that a person resist temptation and hold to the moral law if every action is merely another causally determined event in the universal natural order? How can we conceive of persons as free, responsible beings and yet also acknowledge their place in the system of events and objects studied by science?

Equally important to Kant, how can we prove, absolutely and without the slightest room for doubt or uncertainty, that the fundamental moral beliefs shared by all right-thinking persons are true, and not merely public opinion? As we saw in the first chapter, Kant insisted that even religion and morality submit to the spirit of *criticism*. The simple peasants and proud professors of

---

Ethics   In philosophy, the systematic study of how we ought to act, both toward ourselves and to others; and also the study of what things, character traits, or types of persons are good, estimable, admirable, and what kinds are bad, reprehensible, worthy of being condemned. Ethics deals both with general rules or principles, and also with particular cases.

north Prussia might believe that they knew the truth about ethics, but until they could produce a valid proof of their beliefs, they would have no argument to offer against the skeptic, the relativist, the doubter who said that all opinions are equally good, or even that there is no truth about ethics to be known at all.

Kant had some ideas about how to handle these two problems. He thought that he could work out a philosophical truce between ethics and science that would give each its rightful place in the totality of human knowledge; at the same time, he hoped to provide a proof of the fundamental principles of ethics. In this way, he would bring all the parts of his own life and work into harmony with one another. In his philosophical system, there would be a place for the devout faith imparted to him by his mother, a proof of the moral maxims he had grown up with and which to his death he never doubted, and a conceptual framework for the great new achievements of science and mathematics that so dominated the intellectual world of his day, to which he devoted so much of his own life and work.

Kant's struggle to achieve a harmonious accommodation among his scientific interests, his moral convictions, and his religious faith was a model for many later struggles by other philosophers. Today more than ever, science seems to encroach upon religion and morality. New developments in behavioral psychology threaten our age-old belief in moral freedom. Though many philosophers have challenged Kant's solution, few would deny that he saw deeply into the problem and forced the rest of us to confront it as philosophers.

Three Reasons to Think About Ethics

Having read this far into a chapter on ethics, some of you may have the feeling that you do not quite recognize the subject as one that you can relate to. Perhaps Kant knew perfectly well what was right, but many of *us* are filled with doubts. Furthermore, you may want to say, his single-minded emphasis on duty, on conscience, on doing the *right* thing, misses the real flavor of much of our thinking about how to live our lives. The fact is that although this book contains only one chapter titled "Ethics," there are many quite different sorts of problems that have been discussed under that name since the time of the ancient Greeks. There is hardly enough room in a single book, let alone in one chapter, to talk about all of these problems, but at least *three* are important enough to demand some extended examination.

Kant has already introduced us to the first reason that people worry about what is called ethics—namely, a desire to discover an absolutely certain, irrefutable proof of the moral principles that we are already convinced are true. This proof serves two purposes: first, it answers the skeptic, who denies that there are any moral truths at all; and second, it answers the relativist, who says, in effect, "Everyone's opinions are as good as everyone else's."

A second reason people worry about ethics is that sometimes we get into situations in which we want to do the right thing but really do not know what it is. For example, a woman may find out that she is pregnant and feel that to have a baby will simply turn her life inside out. Perhaps she wants to continue her studies in order to prepare for a career; perhaps the pregnancy is the result of a casual affair with a man whom she does not love; perhaps she and her husband already have as many children as they want and feel they can care for. Should she have an abortion? Part of her says that abortion is morally wrong; another part tells her that to have the baby would be wrong. She wants to do what is right, but she just does not know what *is* right in the situation.

Or, a young man wants to leave home and start a life of his own, despite his parents' pleas that he remain with them and care for them. On the one hand, he feels love for his parents and a debt of gratitude and loyalty for all of the years they have given to him. On the other hand, he knows that this is his only life, and that it is wrong for him to sacrifice it to the needs or demands of his parents. Again, he wants to do what is right, but he does not know whether he really has an obligation to stay at home, and if he does, for how long.

In philosophy, cases such as these are sometimes called "hard cases." They are real-life moral dilemmas in which ordinary moral opinions are either hopelessly contradictory or else just confused. Many philosophers have sought some method or rule by which we could decide hard cases, either by a process of moral reasoning or even by a sort of calculation. Genuine confusion rather than temptation is the motivation here, and frequently the emphasis is less on an absolutely rock-solid *proof* of things we already believe than it is on some genuinely new insight into an otherwise unsolvable dilemma.

But the oldest tradition of ethical reflection in Western thought has nothing to do with rights and duties, temptations and their denial, hard cases and tortured choices. For Plato, for Marcus Aurelius, for the ancient Stoics, and for countless philosophers since their time, ethics has been concerned with the definition, analysis, search for, and achievement of the *good life.* Our stay on this earth is brief, the years pass faster and faster as we grow older, and all too soon we are forever dead. As we grow up and grow old, how shall we live our lives? What set of precepts, what style of inner feelings and outer relationships, what set of commitments will make us truly happy during the short passage of our lives? Should we strive to pile wealth upon wealth? Fulfill our talents? Aim for power and fame? Retire to quiet contemplation? Taste every experience, pleasurable or not, before death comes? Can reason and philosophy even help us in this choice? Or is the life of the mind itself just one path among many, and not the happiest at that?

Sometimes when we say that someone lived a "good life," we mean that he or she experienced a great deal of pleasure—ate, drank, made merry. As it is said in Italian, such a person lived *la dolce vita,* the "sweet life." But just as often, we mean that the life was one of virtue, of service, of honor and dignity, that it was a life in which there was goodness. Many philosophers deliberately preserve this ambiguity because they believe that a truly happy life must also be a virtuous life, a life of goodness. Plato is perhaps the philosopher most often associated with this claim. But many other philosophers have, in one way or another, made the same claim, among whom are such unlikely bedfellows as Confucius and Karl Marx.

Here, then, are three reasons for thinking about ethics—or better, three searches that are usually grouped under the heading "ethics": the search for absolutely certain, universally valid first principles of conduct that can stand against the challenges of the skeptic and the relativist; the search for a method or process of reasoning to help us in deciding hard cases and other real-world moral choices; and the search for the good life, the life that combines virtue and happiness in true human fulfillment. Most of the remainder of the first half of this chapter will be devoted to a deeper examination of these three approaches to the subject of ethics.

Ethical Disagreement and the Categorical Imperative

When we are very little, our parents stop us from doing things we should not do—hitting our baby brother, eating paint, touching a wall plug—by physically pulling us away and saying "No!" in a loud, firm voice. You cannot have a philosophical discussion with a two-year-old, as I was forced very quickly to recognize with my own two sons. As we grow older, we internalize those "No's" in the form of some set of rules, or norms, some conception of what is right and wrong. For a very long time, we simply accept these rules as given, a part of the world just as trees and tables or our parents and friends are part of the world. Pretty early on, of course, we discover that not everyone abides all the time by the rules that our parents have taught us, but we can handle that fact, conceptually, by means of the category "bad." "Why can't I hit my brother? Tommy does." "Because it is wrong. Tommy is a bad boy, and I don't want you to be a bad boy like him."

So we grow older, with a more or less coherent moral code as part of our mental equipment. There are bad guys, naughty children, villains, criminals, but they are the "others," the ones who are not nice, the sort of people we do not want to be like.

Then, one day, somewhere, there comes the great shock. It may be when we are still children, or when we go away to college, or when we move from a tight, little, homogeneous neighborhood to a big, heterogeneous city. It may simply be something we see on television. But all of a sudden, we encounter a whole group of people who seem to be good, decent, respectable, law-abiding, and upright, except that they call good what we call bad! We think it is good to fight for our country, and they think it is wicked. We think homosexuality is a perfectly acceptable lifestyle, and they think it is evil. They think abortion is a sensible technique for rational family planning and population control, and we call it murder.

This discovery, in whatever form it comes, is a genuine shock. The problem does not lie in the realization that some people do bad things. Ever since we saw Tommy hit his brother, we have known that. The real problem is that these people doing "bad" things and living by the "wrong" rules are *good* people. They are responsible; they are respected by their friends and neighbors. They may even be held up to children as models of virtue. And yet they do bad things! A man comes home from a war in which he gunned down 200 defenseless women and children in a village, and he is paraded along Main Street as a hero. A mother and father refuse to allow their baby to receive medical treatment, the baby dies, and they are praised in their church as pillars of rectitude. A governor calls out the National Guard to shoot striking prison inmates, and he is immortalized in marble in front of the state capital.

If it is unsettling to encounter men and women within our own society whose moral codes differ markedly from our own, think how much more unsettling it is to discover whole cultures or civilizations in which what we call virtue is despised as vice, and what we condemn as wicked is celebrated as noble. Even a study of the history of the literate civilizations of the East and West provides countless examples of this sort of variation in moral beliefs. When the anthropologists' experiences with nonliterate cultures are added to our stock of information, it begins to appear that there is no single rule, precept, or moral belief that has been accepted by decent men and women everywhere. War? Torture? Child murder? Adultery? Suicide? Theft? Lying? Every single one has been condemned by some cultures and accepted, approved, or even praised by others.

There are basically three ways in which a philosopher can deal with the troublesome problem of the variation in moral codes from person to person, group to group, and culture to culture. The first way is to deny that the variation exists, despite appearances to the contrary. The second way is to admit that the variation exists and conclude that there are therefore no universally valid moral norms applicable to all persons in all places at all times. The third way is to acknowledge the variation but insist nonetheless that some moral principles are true and other supposed principles are false, no matter how many people believe them. Those who take this last route then do their best to provide some sort of proof for the principles they believe to be valid.

How can philosophers possibly maintain that there is no real disagreement about norms and moral principles, when the evidence of personal and cultural variation is all around them? Essentially, their tactic is to argue that when two people or two cultures seem to disagree about what is right or good, they are *really* only disagreeing about some of the facts of the case. If they could settle that disagreement, then it would turn out that they actually make the same moral judgments. For example, the Christian Scientist, like the nonbeliever, wants what is best for his sick child. But he firmly believes that the body is not real and that salvation depends upon holding firm to that belief. So for him to consent to an operation for his child would be as irresponsible (on his assessment of the facts) as for another parent to give a diabetic child all the candy she wants. To take another example, the culture that condemns abortion may believe that the fetus is already a person; the culture that approves of abortion does not think the fetus is a person until after it is born. Both condemn murder, defined as the willful killing of a person, but they disagree on the factual question of whether the fetus is a person.

A number of philosophers have taken this line, including the Scotsman David Hume. Anthropologists have actually carried out cross-country surveys of norms in an effort to discover any constants. Although it does appear that the ban or taboo on incest is widespread, the effort has essentially been a failure. There are no broad moral principles of justice, charity, equity, or benevolence that can be discovered in the moral systems of all cultures. (There is a much deeper question which we have not touched on yet. Even if there *were* universally accepted norms, what would that fact prove? Does everybody believing something make it right? Do we not need some justification for our moral convictions that goes beyond saying, "Everybody agrees with me?" This problem troubled Kant a great deal, and a bit later in this chapter we shall see how he tried to deal with it.)

The second response to moral disagreement—the denial of objective, universal moral norms—has actually been relatively rare in the history of Western ethical theory, but it has had its defenders from the time of the ancient Greeks to the present day. There are two forms of this position: *ethical skepticism* and ***ethical relativism.*** Ethical skepticism denies that we can have the slightest certainty about questions of the right and the good. Sometimes the ethical skeptic says that words like "right," "good," "ought," and "duty" just do not have any meaning; sentences containing them are a bit like incantations or cheers of approval or perhaps just plain gibberish. Because the very words we use to make moral judgments have no meaning, our moral judgments can hardly be called true or false, valid or invalid. At other times, the ethical skeptic merely points out that no valid argument can be found for any

Ethical Relativism   The theory that whether an act is right or wrong depends on—is relative to—the society in which one lives. Sometimes ethical relativists merely claim that we must take social contexts and rules into account, but sometimes they assert that one and the same act is right for men and women in one society and wrong for men and women in another. Frequently confused with *Ethical Skepticism,* which doubts that any acts are right or wrong, and *Ethical Nihilism,* which denies that any acts are either right or wrong.

particular moral principle. If I doubt that murder is wrong, you cannot find an argument that will prove to me that it is. If I cannot see why I should help another person in distress, there is no way it can be demonstrated to me that I should. Philosophers who take either of these lines frequently think that science and scientific language are the models on which we should base all of our knowledge. They point to the nondescriptive character of moral statements (they do not tell us how things are, they claim to tell us how things ought to be). They contrast the orderly experimentation and examination of data in the sciences with the haphazard, intuitive, unfactual character of moral disputes. Sometimes they suggest that moral arguments really come down to disagreements over matter of taste, and as the old saying has it, *de gustibus non disputandem est* (there is no disputing in matters of taste).

The *ethical skeptic* is sometimes joined in the fight against objective moral principles by the ethical relativist. How often, in a bull session, have we heard someone say, "Oh well, it's all relative!" Sometimes that means "Everyone *has* her own opinion." Sometimes it means, "Everyone is *entitled* to her own opinion." But sometimes it means "Everyone's opinion is true to her, even though it may not be true for someone else." As a student said to me once in class when I asked whether he thought that Hitler had been wrong to kill millions of people in death camps, "Well, it wouldn't be right for me, but I guess it was right for him."

In the following passage, the American anthropologist Ruth Benedict draws on her wide knowledge of the varieties of human culture to argue for the fundamental relativity of moral judgments. There is something very unsettling about the fact that a scientist who has seen so much of human culture and society in all of its forms should come to a relativist position.

No one civilization can possibly utilize in its mores the whole potential range of human behavior.

Every society, beginning with some inclination in one direction or another, carries its preference farther and farther, integrating itself more and more completely upon its chosen basis, and discarding those types of behaviors that are uncongenial. Most of those organizations of personality that seem to us more incontrovertibly abnormal have been used by different civilizations in the very foundations of their institutional life. Conversely the most valued traits of our normal individuals have been looked on in differently organized cultures as aberrant. Normality, in short, within a very wide range, is culturally defined.... The very eyes with which we see the problem are conditioned by the long traditional habits of our own society.

It is a point that has been made more often in relation to ethics than in relation to psychiatry. We do not any longer make the mistake of deriving the morality of our own locality and decade directly

RUTH BENEDICT,
Anthropology and the Abnormal

from the inevitable constitution of human nature. We do not elevate it to the dignity of a first principle. We recognize that morality differs in every society, and is a convenient term for socially approved habits. Mankind has always preferred to say, "It is morally good," rather than "It is habitual," and the fact of this preference is matter enough for a critical science of ethics. But historically the two phrases are synonymous.

Ruth Benedict, *Anthropology and the Abnormal*

Immanuel Kant is the strongest opponent of the ethical relativist position. A major aim of Kant's philosophical efforts was to provide an absolutely solid, totally universal proof of the validity of that moral principle which he considered the foundation of all ethics, the principle which he called the **Categorical Imperative.** Kant was well aware that there were serious ethical disagreements among philosophers on particular questions of moral judgment, though he was not so impressed as Hume had been by the systematic cultural differences that appeared to divide "cultivated" peoples. But Kant was extremely concerned about the lack of solid foundations for even those ethical beliefs that are more or less broadly agreed upon. In a number of profound and very difficult treatises on ethics, Kant undertook to lay those foundations.

(A cautionary word: Kant tried to think in a totally universal way about ethics, and yet, as we have seen, he gave voice to some vicious racist prejudices that were commonplace in his day. It might make us wonder what views we hold now, unthinkingly, that later generations will find appalling.)

Saying just a few words about Kant's philosophy is like saying just a few words about quantum mechanics or the theory of relativity. Nevertheless, some of the key notions of Kant's moral philosophy can be understood pretty well without plunging into the depth of his argument, and in the remainder of this section, I shall introduce you to those notions through a combination of my exposition and Kant's own words.

Kant first set out his moral philosophy in a little book called *Groundwork of the Metaphysic of Morals* (a rather imposing title). He intended the book to be just an introduction to his theory, and shortly thereafter he published another, longer work called *Critique of Practical Reason*. But as often happens, the short "introductory" book took on a life of its own, and today it is widely viewed as the finest statement of Kant's position.

The aim of *Groundwork* is to discover, analyze, and defend the fundamental principle of morality. As you know, Kant did not think that he had dis-

Categorical Imperative   A term invented by Immanuel Kant to refer to a command that orders us to do something unconditionally—that is, regardless of what we want or what our aims and purposes are. According to Kant, we experience the principles of morality as Categorical Imperatives. The term is also used, by Kant and those following him, to refer to one particular moral principle, which Kant calls the Highest Moral Law.

Varieties of human culture. Crowd scene. *(Source:* Joel Gordon Photography.*)*

covered a *new* principle, and he liked to say that his Categorical Imperative was nothing more than a philosophically more precise statement of the old Golden Rule: Do unto others as you would have others do unto you. Here is the way in which Kant revised and restated that rule:

> Act only on that maxim through which you can at the same time will that it should be a universal law.

The Categorical Imperative

That does not *look* much like the Golden Rule, but Kant thought it contained the same basic notion, which is that we ought to put aside our own private interests and act instead on the basis of rules that would be equally reasonable for all moral agents to adopt as their own. "Do unto others as you would have others do unto you" does not mean, "Go ahead and steal from your neighbor as long as you don't squawk when he steals from you." It means something more like, "Treat other people with the same respect and dignity that you expect to be treated with." As we shall see, the idea of human dignity plays a central role in Kant's moral philosophy.

There are three ideas that lie at the heart of Kant's ethics. If we can understand something about each of them, we can form at least a preliminary notion of his theory. The ideas are, first, that persons are rational creatures, capable of thinking about the choices they face and selecting among them on the basis of reasons; second, that persons have an infinite worth or dignity that sets them above all merely conditionally valuable things in this world, that they are what Kant calls ends-in-themselves; and, third, that persons, as rational ends-in-themselves, are the *authors* of the moral law, so their obedience to duty is not an act of slavish submission but an act of dignified *autonomy*. Persons, as rational agents, as ends-in-themselves, and as autonomous—these are the basic building blocks out of which Kant constructs his proof of the Categorical Imperative.

When Kant asserts that persons are rational agents, he means more than merely that they are capable of making judgments about the nature of

Moses coming down from Mount Sinai. Kant believed that the Golden Rule, "Do unto others as you would have others do unto you," is a summary statement of the Ten Commandments, and that his Categorical Imperative is simply a philosophical restatement of the Golden Rule. (Woodcut by Gustave Dore.) *(Source: Corbis/Bettmann.)*

the world, or inferences from one set of propositions to another. A rational agent is a person who is capable of *moving himself or herself to act* by reason. David Hume, like many other philosophers, had thought that reason was incapable of moving us to action. Hume argued that *desire* moves us to act; reason merely points out the most efficient path to the goal that desire chooses. So Hume said, in a much-quoted passage, that "reason is, and ought only to be the slave of the passions, and can never pretend to any other office than to serve and obey them" (*A Treatise of Human Nature,* Book III). Kant replied that if we are to make any sense at all of our condition as creatures capable of choice and deliberation, we must acknowledge that we can be moved by *reasons,* not merely by *desires.*

If Kant is right, that we can be moved by reason, then it makes sense to ask whether we have acted wisely or foolishly, whether we have reasoned consistently in our choice of ends and means. It makes sense also to ask whether, in our reasoning, we have taken special account of our own particular wishes and interests, or instead have limited ourselves only to reasons that would be compelling reasons for any person in the same circumstances. In short, it makes sense to ask whether we have acted *rationally.*

This notion of "reasons good for all rational agents" is a difficult one to grasp. Perhaps one way to get some idea of Kant's meaning is to compare a moral agent to a mathematician doing a geometry problem. Suppose the mathematician is trying to show that the square of the hypotenuse of a right triangle is equal to the sum of the squares of the other two sides (the so-called Pythagorean theorem that some of you studied in high school). Now the first thing she does in developing the proof is to draw a triangle, and because every triangle has to be some size and shape or other, the particular triangle the mathematician draws will be some particular size (maybe 4½ inches by 6 inches by 7½ inches), and it also will be some particular color (depending on the color of the paper she draws it on), and so forth. But of course she is not supposed to pay any attention to the actual size and color of the triangle. They are there, all right, but she is supposed to ignore them. The only thing she is allowed to count in her proof is the fact that the triangle has a right angle in it. If our imaginary mathematician constructs her proof by using only the fact that her triangle is a right triangle, then her conclusions, when she gets them, will apply to *all* right triangles, not just to the one she actually drew.

In the same way, Kant claims that moral agents, when they reason about what they ought to do, should ignore all of the particular facts about their own interests, special desires, individual circumstances, and so on and concentrate just on those facts that hold for *all* rational agents as such. If they do that, he says, then the conclusions they come to will be valid for all rational agents, not just for themselves. In short, their conclusions will be universal laws, not just personal rules. Kant uses the word "maxim" to mean a personal rule on which we actually base our decisions. (In the following selection, he also uses the term "subjective principle" with this meaning.) So he is telling us that when we make our decisions, we, like the mathematician, should restrict ourselves to rules, or maxims, that could just as well serve any rational agent. In other words, he tells us to restrict ourselves to maxims that could serve as universal laws. That is what he is trying to say in the Categorical Imperative: Act only on that maxim through which you can at the same time will that it should become a universal law.

If we do succeed in acting in a genuinely rational way, Kant says, we show ourselves to possess a dignity that sets us above everything else in the world. Indeed, the statement that moral agents, as persons, have an infinite worth or dignity is, according to Kant, just another way of saying what has already been said in the Categorical Imperative. Here is the famous passage in which Kant develops the notion that persons are ends-in-themselves. Difficult as Kant's argument is, I think you will be able to see in it something of the grandeur and profundity that has so impressed generations of readers:

IMMANUEL KANT,
Groundwork of the Metaphysic of Morals

Now I say that man, and in general every rational being, *exists* as an end in himself, *not merely as a means* for arbitrary use by this or that will: he must in all his actions, whether they are directed to himself or to other rational beings, always be viewed *at the same time as an end.* All the objects of inclination have only a conditioned value; for if there were not these inclinations and the needs grounded on them, their object would be valueless. Inclinations themselves, as sources of needs, are so far from having an absolute value to make them desirable for their own sake that it must rather be the universal wish of every rational being to be wholly free from them. Thus the value of all objects that can *be produced* by our action is always conditioned. Beings whose existence depends, not on our will, but on nature, have none the less, if they are nonrational beings, only a relative value as means and are consequently called *things.* Rational beings, on the other hand, are called *persons* because their nature already marks them out as ends in themselves and consequently imposes to that extent a limit on all arbitrary treatment of them (and is an object of reverence). Persons, therefore, are not merely subjective ends whose existence as an object of our actions has a value for *us:* they are *objective ends*—that is, things whose existence is in itself an end, and indeed an end such that in its place we can put no other end to which they should serve *simply* as means; for unless this is so, nothing at all of absolute value would be found anywhere. But if all value were conditioned then no supreme principle could be found for reason at all.

If then there is to be a supreme practical principle and a categorical imperative, it must be such that from the idea of something which is necessarily an end for every one because it is an *end in itself* it forms an *objective* principle of the will and consequently can serve as a practical law. The ground of this principle is: *Rational nature ex-*

ists as an end in itself. This is the way in which a man necessarily conceives his own existence: it is therefore so far a *subjective* principle of human actions. But it is also the way in which every other rational being conceives his existence on the same rational ground which is valid also for me; hence it is at the same time an *objective* principle, from which, as a supreme practical ground, it must be possible to derive all laws for the will. The practical imperative will therefore be as follows: *Act in such a way that you always treat humanity, whether in your own person or in the person of any other, never simply as a means, but always at the same time as an end.*

Immanuel Kant, *Fundamental Principles of the Metaphysics of Morals*

Hume had described reason as the "slave" of the passions, subservient to their direction. If my reason is the slave of my passions, then I forfeit the dignity that I possess in virtue of being an end-in-myself. There is no honor in subservience to passion, any more than in subservience to a king or emperor. In the inner life of each man and woman, as in the public life of the state, honor is to be found only in submission to self-made laws. The citizen of a republic, who makes the laws to which he bows his head, loses no dignity by his obedience, for he is obeying only himself when he abides by the law. His obedience is an act of responsibility rather than of servitude.

The same principle, Kant thought, holds true within the individual soul. When reason bows to passion, it forfeits its claim to honor and dignity. But if reason can itself legislate the laws to which it submits, if reason can itself write the Categorical Imperative that binds it, then it will preserve its freedom in the very act of submission. To give laws to oneself is, following the Greek, to be *autonomos*—giver of law to oneself—in short: autonomous. The principle of the autonomy of reason is, Kant says, yet another version of the Categorical Imperative.

Having set forth three key principles—(1) the rationality of the will, (2) the infinite worth of persons as ends-in-themselves, and (3) the self-legislating, or autonomous, character of reason—Kant now pulls them all together in the notion of a society of moral agents, all of whom govern their actions by reason, all of whom are ends-in-themselves, and all of whom are autonomous. He calls this society a *kingdom of ends,* and we can imagine it as an ideal community of upright, responsible, rational men and women who base their actions on universally valid laws that they autonomously lay down for themselves. It is a community that lives according to the Categorical Imperative. In our last passage from Kant, we see all of these themes united:

In the kingdom of ends everything has either a *price* or a *dignity.* If it has a price, something else can be put in its place as an equivalent; if it is exalted above all price and so admits of no equivalent, then it has a dignity.

IMMANUEL KANT, *Groundwork of the Metaphysic of Morals*

What is relative to universal human inclinations and needs has a *market price;* what, even without presupposing a need, accords with a certain taste has a *fancy price (Affektionspreis);* but that which constitutes the sole condition under which anything can be an end in itself has not merely a relative value but has an intrinsic value—that is, *dignity.*

Now morality is the only condition under which a rational being can be an end in himself; for only through this is it possible to be a lawmaking member in a kingdom of ends. Therefore morality, and humanity so far as it is capable of morality, is the only thing which has dignity. Skill and diligence in work have a market price; wit, lively imagination, and humour have a fancy price; but fidelity to promises and kindness based on principle (not on instinct) have an intrinsic worth. In default of these, nature and art alike contain nothing to put in their place; for their worth consists, not in the effects which result from them, not in the advantage or profit they produce, but in the attitudes of mind which are ready in this way to manifest themselves in action even if they are not favoured by success. Such actions too need no recommendations from any subjective disposition or taste in order to meet with immediate favour and approval; they need no immediate propensity or feeling for themselves; they exhibit the will which performs them as an object of immediate reverence; nor is anything other than reason required to *impose* them upon the will, nor to *coax* them from the will—which last would anyhow be a contradiction in the case of duties. This assessment reveals as dignity the value of such a mental attitude and puts it infinitely above all price, with which it cannot be brought into reckoning or comparison without, as it were, a profanation of its sanctity.

What is it then that entitles a morally good attitude of mind to make claims so high? It is nothing less than the *share* which it affords to a rational being in the *making of universal law,* and which therefore fits him to be a member in a possible kingdom of ends. For this he was already marked out in virtue of his own proper nature as an end in himself and consequently as a maker of laws in the kingdom of ends—as free in respect of all laws of nature, obeying only those laws which he makes himself and in virtue of which his maxims can have their part in the making of universal law (to which he at the same time subjects himself). For nothing can have a value other than that determined for it by the law. But the law-making which determines all value must for this reason have a dignity for the appreciation of which, as necessarily given by a rational being, the word "*reverence*" is the only becoming expression. *Autonomy* is therefore the ground of the dignity of human nature and of every rational nature.

Immanuel Kant, *Fundamental Principles of the Metaphysics of Morals*

Utilitarianism and the Calculation of Pleasures and Pains

How shall we deal with those terrible situations in which we want very much to do the right thing but simply cannot figure out what it is? Sometimes, there are two different and conflicting things, both of which seem right in the situation. Sometimes the situation is such a tangle that we are just at a loss. The source of our uncertainty is not temptation, or skepticism, or relativism but the genuine moral difficulty of the case itself. One of the most ancient attempts to deal with such hard cases, and also to lay down a rule for action that will always tell us what we ought to do, is the moral philosophy that these days goes under the name of *utilitarianism*. In this section, we are going to take a look at several varieties of utilitarianism, see what the theory says and how it works, and also consider some serious objections to it.

Utilitarianism is simply the rule that we should always try to make as many people as possible as happy as possible. Indeed, it is sometimes called The Greatest Happiness Principle for this reason. The cosmologist Lucretius was a utilitarian, and so was the man whose teachings he followed, Epicurus. In the modern world, the most famous utilitarian, generally credited with establishing the doctrine as a serious contender in moral philosophy, was the eighteenth-century Englishman Jeremy Bentham.

Bentham argues that however people may appear to use the words "good" and "evil," they really just mean "pleasant" or "painful": "Pleasant" when they say "good" and "painful" when they say "evil." More good is better than less, which is to say that more pleasure is better than less. And, of course, less pain is better than more. The only good reason for doing anything is to increase the amount of pleasure that human beings experience, or at least to reduce the amount of pain. What is more, pleasures and pains can, in a manner of speaking, be added to and subtracted from one another. I can ask myself, "Which gave me more pleasure: the good movie I saw last week or the mediocre movie I saw last night plus the really good pizza I had afterward?" I can also ask myself, "Which will be more painful: three dentist's visits now, complete with drillings, or a toothache followed by an extraction followed by the annoyance of a missing tooth later?" If the mediocre movie plus the pizza gave me more pleasure, then the next time I have to choose between a good movie and no pizza or a mediocre movie and pizza, I ought to take the mediocre movie plus the pizza. And, more seriously, if the dentist's visits, bad as they are, add up to less pain than the rotting of my tooth, then I ought to go to the dentist even though I do not want to, because the only rational thing to do is to minimize the total amount of pain in my life.

Bentham announced the doctrine now known as utilitarianism in a book entitled *An Introduction to the Principles of Morals and Legislation,* first printed in 1780 and formally published in 1789. Here is a selection from the opening chapter. Notice the complete identification of pleasure with good and pain with evil. This is the heart and soul of Bentham's utilitarian doctrine.

JEREMY BENTHAM,
An Introduction to the Principles of Morals and Legislation

Nature has placed mankind under the governance of two sovereign masters, *pain* and *pleasure*. It is for them alone to point out what we ought to do, as well as to determine what we shall do. On the one hand the standard of right and wrong, on the other the chain of causes and effects, are fastened to their throne. They govern us in all we do, in all we say, in all we think: every effort we can make to throw off our subjection, will serve but to demonstrate and confirm it. In words a man may pretend to abjure their empire: but in reality he will remain subject to it all the while. The *principle of utility* recognizes this subjection, and assumes it for the foundation of that system, the object of which is to rear the fabric of felicity by the hands of reason and law. Systems which attempt to question it, deal in sounds instead of sense, in caprice instead of reason, in darkness instead of light.

But enough of metaphor and declamation: it is not by such means that moral science is to be improved.

The principle of utility is the foundation of the present work: it will be proper therefore at the outset to give an explicit and determinate account of what is meant by it. By the principle of utility is meant that principle which approves or disapproves of every action whatsoever, according to the tendency which it appears to have to augment or diminish the happiness of the party whose interest is in question: or, what is the same thing in other words, to promote or to oppose that happiness. I say of every action whatsoever; and therefore not only of every action of a private individual, but of every measure of government.

By utility is meant that property in any object, whereby it tends to produce benefit, advantage, pleasure, good, or happiness (all this in the present case comes to the same thing) or (what comes again to the same thing) to prevent the happening of mischief, pain, evil or unhappiness to the party whose interest is considered: if that party be the community in general, then the happiness of the community; if a particular individual, then the happiness of that individual.

The interest of the community is one of the most general expressions that can occur in the phraseology of morals: no wonder that the meaning of it is often lost. When it has a meaning, it is this. The community is a fictitious *body*, composed of the individual persons who are considered as constituting as it were its *members*. The interest of the community then is, what?—the sum of the interests of the several members who compose it.

It is in vain to talk of the interest of the community, without understanding what is the interest of the individual. A thing is said to promote the interest, or to be *for* the interest, of an individual, when it tends to add to the sum total of his pleasures: or what comes to the same thing, to diminish the sum total of his pains.

An action then may be said to be conformable to the principle of utility, or, for shortness sake, to utility (meaning with respect to the community at large) when the tendency it has to augment the happiness of the community is greater than any it has to diminish it.

A measure of government (which is but a particular kind of action, performed by a particular person or persons) may be said to be conformable to or dictated by the principle of utility, when in like manner the tendency which it has to augment the happiness of the community is greater than any which it has to diminish it.

Jeremy Bentham, *An Introduction to the Principles of Morals and Legislation*

The crucial step in Bentham's argument is his move from the total pleasure and pain experienced by one person to the total pleasure or pain experienced by all of the members of the community taken together. This is the device that permits Bentham to extract a moral principle from his theory. The point is that whenever I do anything at all, my action has effects that impinge on the lives of other people. Sometimes I cause them pleasure, sometimes I cause them pain, and sometimes of course I cause some of them pleasure and others pain. For example, if the young man we mentioned earlier decides to stay at home with his parents rather than leave and set out on his own, he will probably cause himself pain and his mother and father pleasure. That is precisely why he does not know what to do! If his staying at home caused his parents pain too (they, after all, might want to live their own lives), then the decision would be an easy one for him.

Whenever we face hard choices, Bentham tells us, we can translate an impossible moral dilemma into a problem of addition and subtraction. For the young man, the choice is between staying home with his parents and leaving. He adds up all of the pleasure and pain (negative values for pain, of course) that anybody in the situation will experience as the result of his staying and compares it with the total pleasure and pain that everyone will experience as a result of his leaving home. He then chooses the alternative with the highest positive total (or, if it is one of those "least of evils" situations, the alternative with the smallest negative total). For example, suppose that the young man desperately wants to leave home. Then we can assume that he will suffer great pain if he must stay, and he will gain great pleasure if he goes. Let us also assume that his parents would like him to stay at home, but they are not dead set on it. They will manage all right if he leaves. Now we have great pain plus moderate pleasure on the side of staying and great pleasure plus moderate pain on the side of going. Obviously this adds up to a decision to go.

JEREMY BENTHAM

Jeremy Bentham (1748–1832) was the founder of the ethical doctrine now known as utilitarianism. He began his long life during the reign of King George II and died in the year of the Reform Bill that extended the franchise to virtually all of middle-class England. He lived through the American Revolution, the French Revolution, the Napoleonic wars, and the rise of parliamentary government in England, and he nearly survived into the reign of Queen Victoria. He was the godfather of John Stuart Mill, son of his friend and colleague James Mill. John Stuart Mill was, in his own turn, the godfather of Bertrand Russell, the great English philosopher who near the end of his own long and distinguished life led the British campaign for nuclear disarmament in the 1960s. So in three generations of great English philosophers, we move from the mid-eighteenth-century world of wigs, carriages, and kings, to the mid-twentieth-century world of jets, nuclear weapons, and popular democracy.

Bentham's primary concern as a philosopher was with legal and social reform. The law in the eighteenth century was a crazy quilt of precedents, quibbles, hanging offenses, and rank injustices. Several of Bentham's books were devoted to the attempt to sort things out and to find some rational system of principles to put in place of the tangle that had grown up over so many centuries. He hoped that his simple, intuitively appealing principle of utility—the Greatest Happiness of the Greatest Number—would serve as the basis for a thoroughgoing reform of the law.

A great many objections can be raised to utilitarianism, and I am about to raise several of the more serious ones. But before we start chopping this theory down, it is worth taking a few moments to look at its very considerable strengths. In the first place, utilitarianism assumes that everyone wants to be happy, and it is hard to argue with that. But even more important, utilitarianism explains happiness in terms that everyone can understand. It does not say that happiness is oneness with the infinite, or self-fulfillment, or the integration of adult roles with childhood ego formation, or what have you. It says that happiness is pleasure, unhappiness is pain, and the more pleasure or the less pain the better.

Nor does utilitarianism demand strange, painful sacrifices from its believers. Kant believed, for example, that we should keep our promises and tell the truth no matter who gets hurt. That is a dark saying, fraught with potentiality for terrible choices where lives are lost or hideous pain is inflicted simply because someone will not violate an absolute moral rule. But Bentham says nothing of that sort. By all means lie, he says, if the total pain produced by the truth is greater than that produced by the lie. Make sure to add in the side effects of the lie, such as the likelihood that the next time you tell the truth it will not be believed. But when all of those long-term, short-term, direct, and indirect effects have been calculated, then just choose the course promising the greatest happiness for the greatest number of people.

The most impressive strength of utilitarianism is its ability to transform seemingly impossible problems of moral deliberation into manageable empirical problems of investigation and addition. To see what that means, imagine that we lived a long time ago in an agricultural society that had not yet discovered geometry. Each year, as the flood waters from the river receded, it would become necessary to divide up the land again for the spring planting. The plots all must be triangular (owing to some religious belief, we may suppose). The high priest would stake out each family's land, and then the arguing would begin over whose plot was bigger, and who had been slighted in the dividing up. The wise men would gather, great deliberations would ensue, with much prayer and meditation, and in the end no one would really be satisfied with the high priest's decisions. Now just think what it would mean, in such a society, for someone to discover the simple geometric theorem that the area of a triangle is equal to one-half the base times the height. All of those moral and religious disputes would be dissolved in an instant into a process of calculation. The royal surveyor would just measure the bases of the family plots, multiply by their heights (the plots', not the families'), and then make adjustments until each family had the same area. It would put the royal moral philosopher and the royal priest out of business.

Well, Bentham had hopes that his Greatest Happiness Principle would do the same for the modern wizards who in his own society did the job of the ancient priests and moral philosophers—namely, the judges and lawyers. He believed that rational legislators, with the principle of utility to guide them,

To Leave Home or Not to Leave Home: A Utilitarian Calculation

If I Leave	Units of Pleasure	If I Don't Leave	Units of Pleasure
1. Independence	+ 1000	1. Lack of independence	−1000
2. Loneliness	− 200	2. Parents' happiness	+ 2000
3. Parents' unhappiness	−1000	3. No personal growth	− 600
4. New experiences	+ 350	4. Family wrangling	− 250
5. Setting a good example for younger sister	+ 400	5. Financial burden on parents	− 400
The utility of leaving	+ 550	The utility of staying	− 250
	+550 IS GREATER THAN −250. THEREFORE I LEAVE.		

According to Bentham, the rational person will choose the alternative that offers the greatest total of pleasure. Does anyone ever make an important decision this way? Would you?

Egypt: Surveying. Measuring of fields by royal supervisor and his staff. Cords are being used as measure units. The ancient Egyptians were forced to re-survey their fields each year after the Nile River overflowed its banks. This practical problem led them to make important advances in mathematics. (Undated fresco) *(Source:* Corbis/Bettmann.*)*

could replace the hideous tangle of laws and punishments of the English common law with a single reasonable schedule of punishments designed to produce the greatest happiness for the greatest number. Where the legislators lacked enough facts to make a sensible decision, instead of digging around in their law books for precedents and corollary cases, they could go out and collect some facts to settle the matter.

Utilitarianism has probably had more words written about it than all of the other moral theories put together. It is a clear, simple, natural-sounding moral philosophy, and it has a thousand things wrong with it as a theory! That is a perfect formula for a philosophical argument. Two sorts of objections turn up over and over again in philosophical discussions. First, critics say that al-

Act Utilitarianism/Rule Utilitarianism   The moral theory that holds that everyone—private individuals or lawmaking governments—should always seek to produce the greatest happiness for the greatest number of people. *Act Utilitarianism* asserts that each of us should use this rule in choosing every single act that we perform, regardless of whether we are private citizens or legislators making general laws for a whole society. *Rule Utilitarianism* says that governments should use this rule in choosing the general laws they enact, but then should simply treat individuals fairly according to the existing rules, with like cases handled in a like manner.

though utilitarianism looks clear and simple, it is actually so confused that we cannot tell exactly what it says. And, second, these same critics argue that even after we have decided what utilitarianism says, we find that it tells us to do things that most of us would consider deeply immoral. Let us take a look at both of these objections.

What does utilitarianism say? Very simple: maximize happiness. But what exactly does that mean? The most natural answer is, add up all of the pleasure experienced by all of the people in the world, subtract all of the pain they suffer, and that is the total. Then anything that increases the total is good, anything that decreases it is bad, and if two actions promise to increase the total, the one that offers a bigger increase is just that much better. What could be clearer?

Ah well, a little philosophy teaches us that a trap very often lurks in even the simplest-looking statement. If *total* happiness is all that counts, then a world with a *billion* slightly happy people will be morally better than a world with a *million* extremely happy people. The point is that if the very happy people are only 500 times happier than the marginally happy people, then one billion times the small happiness in the first world will be a bigger total than one million times the tremendous happiness in the second world. Something is obviously wrong with that conclusion. In an already overcrowded world, it makes no sense to go on increasing the population as long as each additional person can be said to experience a slight balance of pleasure over pain. Surely Bentham was not merely arguing for a population explosion.

So maybe what he really meant was to maximize the *average* happiness experienced by the people already on this earth. That makes a good deal more sense. A world of a million very happy people is obviously preferable to a world of a billion marginally happy people, because in the first world, the *level* of happiness—in other words, the average—is higher. And it is the level of happiness we are really interested in.

But once again, serious problems arise. Suppose we can make some people very happy indeed by making other people miserable. That is not an implausible hypothesis at all. Slavery is a social system that lays the burden of work and suffering on one group—the slaves—so that another group—the masters—can lead easy, comfortable lives. (So is capitalism, but we shall get to that later.) Is Bentham really in favor of slavery?

Bentham has an answer, of sorts. His principle, he claims, calls for "the greatest happiness of all those whose interest is in question." Because everyone (even a slave) is someone whose interest is in question, it follows that utilitarianism calls for the greatest possible happiness for everyone, not just the greatest happiness for the slave owners, the capitalists, or the rulers. Now the trouble with this interpretation of the Principle of Utility is that on closer examination, it turns out not to be any sort of rule at all.

Sometimes life offers me a way to make everybody happier at the same time, and obviously when a chance like that comes along, I take it. Too often,

Scene at an eighteenth-century trial. Bentham hoped to correct the abuses of the English legal system. (Undated illustration) *(Source: Corbis/Bettmann.)*

life offers me a way to make everybody unhappier at the same time, and if I have any sense at all, I stay away from chances like that. But most of the time, what I do will make some people happier and other people unhappier. Remember the young man trying to decide whether to leave his parents? His first choice, to stay home, makes his parents happier and him unhappier. His second choice, to leave, makes him happier and his parents unhappier. There just is no way to make all of them happier at the same time. That is precisely why it is a hard case. Now, we do not need Bentham to tell us what to do on those rare occasions when we can make everyone happier simultaneously. But utilitarianism is supposed to give us a rule, a method, for handling just the hard-to-decide cases in which one person's happiness has to be balanced against another person's unhappiness. Plausible as "the greatest happiness for the greatest number" sounds, it does not work out in practice to be a rule that is going to settle any hard cases for us.

Suppose we go back th   atest average happiness. (Notice, by the way, t   stable, working for the greatest average happine   as working for the greatest total happiness, so   iam had in mind.) How does that stand up as   At least it is unambiguous; if we have enough   utcomes of our actions, then we can add up   ains, divide by the total population, and get s   we run into the second sort of objection to u   tells us to do things that seem immoral.

Once again, the prol   suffer so that others may be happy. Let me ske   will help to make this point. Suppose that Amer   ns, positively enjoyed watching people being to   umption is totally contrary to the real facts, bec   , television shows, and novels shows that we are   pathetic creatures who hate the sight of violence   y believe that torture is an evil to the person wh   ul, and pain is evil. But the pleasure that a grou   the torture is good, for pleasure, says Bentham,   torture can be justified when the total pleasure   ain produced, including side effects, long-run ef   ore, if torture produces, in total and on balance,   ther alternative open to us, then it is the positiv   to utilitarianism.

We shall therefor   lled *Torture of the Week*. This is a live show in w   tortured. (Sadists get little or no pleasure fror   ) The victims are simply snatched off the stree   asochist is going to offer himself as a victim, a   watching masochists undergo torture). Accord   are enough viewers who are ecstatic at the sig   easure must outweigh the pain suffered by the   on television has anything resembling its high r   that putting on the torture show is not only justi   igatory!

Just to handle   lso assume that a board of social psychologists   how does not increase the probability of violen   , it may even decrease such crime by offering ar   short, assume that from any point of view, this to   n of the Principle of Utility.

What is wron   t tell me that there are not enough people arol   w. The point of the example was to show that,   show *would* be right if there *were* such people i   always increase the pleasure product by beamir   adists all over the world could watch it. And do not tell me that the pain of the victim's suffering outweighs the pleasure of millions of sadistic viewers. That is implausible, and what is more, I can always adjust the torture inflicted on the victim downward until the pleasure of the viewers outweighs it.

No, what really convinces me that my proposal is immoral (and I suspect many of you feel the same way) is that society has *no right* to make one man or woman suffer for the mere amusement of others. This is one of those cases, something inside me says, where adding up pleasures and pains is the wrong way to find out what we ought to do. If America's sadists have to suffer the pain and frustration of losing their favorite show, then so much the worse for them!

We have opened up a very large and complicated subject with this appeal to the notion of *rights,* and a few words can only begin to indicate some of its ins and outs. Nevertheless, let us explore if for a bit, just to see what makes Bentham's pleasure-pain calculus seem such an inadequate expression of our moral convictions. To begin with, we must not go overboard and say that society *never* has the right to derive benefits from the suffering of one of its members. Leaving aside obvious but controversial cases like wars, we can simply recall that every time a major bridge or tunnel is built, several workers lose their lives. It may seem callous when we put it into words, but all of us employ a rough utilitarian calculation in judging the social desirability of large-scale public works. We try hard to minimize the loss of life in heavy construction, but we refuse to bring building to a dead halt simply because we know that men and women lose their lives on the job. If a project is going to cost hundreds of lives, we will probably veto it. If only a few are likely to be killed, we will give it the go-ahead. Are we not weighing one person's life against the convenience of the motorists who will use the bridge? How does that differ from weighing the pain of the victim against the pleasure of the sadistic viewers?

Well, one answer is that the construction workers choose voluntarily to work on the bridge, knowing that it is a risky job, whereas the torture victim is forced into his or her role. That certainly is part of the difference, for I imagine we would take a *somewhat* different view of the show if we knew that the victims were volunteers.

But there still seem to be other differences. The motorist benefits from the work of the construction worker, to be sure. And the worker is injured (suffers) while performing that work. But that suffering is not the *object* of the motorist's pleasure. The sadist, on the other hand, takes pleasure in the victim's pain. Now it seems to me that there are some pleasures that are evil in and of themselves. They are bad pleasures, pleasures that people should not have; and pleasure taken in the pain of another person is one of those evil pleasures. So the torture example suggests, at least to me, that Bentham's original assumption was wrong. Not all pleasures are equal, save for quantity or intensity. And "good" does not simply mean "pleasant." So when we perform Bentham's social arithmetic, adding up pleasures and pains in order to evaluate a social policy, we most certainly ought not to put the sadist's pleasure on the plus side. He or she does not have a right to that pleasure, and if it is to be weighed at all, it ought to be put on the negative side with the pains. (Needless to say, there may be some pains that ought to go on the positive side. As you can see, this subject gets more and more complicated the deeper into it you go.)

It may even be, as Immanuel Kant thought, that there are some considerations more important than pleasure and pain—considerations of justice and freedom. Kant would argue that the torture show degrades both the victim and the viewers, that it treats them—in his famous phrase—as means merely and not as ends-in-themselves.

consideration of justice & freedom

But when all is said and done, when examples like the torture show have been brought forward to refute utilitarianism, when the unclarities in the very meaning of the principle have been exposed to view, there still remains a natural appeal of Bentham's theory that will not go away. In Chapter 6, when we meet John Stuart Mill, Bentham's most famous follower, we shall try once again to discover the kernel of truth that seems to lie inside of the moral philosophy of utilitarianism.

Virtue Ethics

The ethical theories of Immanuel Kant and Jeremy Bentham represent the two major approaches to the philosophy of morals that have dominated philosophical thought during most of the past two centuries. Kant's theory, sometimes called an "ethics of duty," concentrates on what it is our *duty* to do. Bentham's theory concentrates on how best to maximize *value* (or goodness)—in Bentham's case, pleasure. Since the last three or four decades of the twentieth century, however, a different approach to ethical theory has commanded the attention of an increasing number of philosophers, *virtue ethics*. As the name suggests, its focus of concentration is on virtue, that is, on character (the kind of person one is) rather than on behavior (what one does). Contemporary proponents of virtue ethics ("virtue theorists") find a major source of inspiration in the moral thinking of the ancient Greeks, especially in the philosophy of Aristotle (*Nicomachean Ethics*).

Aristotle believed that the aim of human life is *eudaimonia,* usually translated—perhaps unfortunately—as "happiness." (Some writers prefer "well-being"; in the work of contemporary virtue theorists we see the term "human flourishing" used a lot. While discussing Aristotle, I shall continue to use "happiness.") Aristotle observed that happiness is the one thing that all humans strive for, and it is the one that would, in and of itself, make life worth living; and he defined 'happiness' as 'an activity of the soul in accordance with virtue'. Moreover, any action is "well performed" when it is performed in

human flourishing

accordance with virtue. Here the central role that virtue plays in the ethics of Aristotle is apparent.

We need to mention in passing that Aristotle made a distinction between intellectual virtues, such as philosophic wisdom and understanding and practical wisdom, on the one hand, and moral virtues, such as liberality and temperance, on the other. We acquire intellectual virtue through the teaching of others, but we acquire moral virtue by doing virtuous things until they are habitual; and Aristotle's ideal person is one who makes the right choices by habit, or one for whom making the right choice is second nature. Ethical theory is concerned primarily with moral virtue.

According to Aristotle's analysis, virtue is "...a settled disposition of the mind determining the choice of actions and emotions, consisting essentially in the observance of the mean, relative to us, this being determined by principle, that is, as a man of practical wisdom would determine it." The definition may make you feel a little dizzy at first; it isn't really all that formidable, however.

A disposition is a tendency to choose to act, or react, in a certain way in a given set of circumstances. For example, when faced with a schoolyard bully, you may be disposed (have the tendency) to muster your courage to find a way to stand up to him and yet avoid an all-out confrontation. Or, faced with an awkward question, "Just how did you do on that examination, young lady?" you may be disposed (have the tendency) to reply honestly, even if the truth is embarrassing. For you to actually possess the virtues of courage and honesty, however, your disposition to act in these ways must be settled, not just a momentary whim, or an attempt to live up to a New Year's resolution for at least two weeks, or to win a bet.

The claim, that virtue consists "essentially in observance of the mean," reflects Aristotle's doctrine that all virtues, including moral virtues, strike a balance between two extremes, one of excess and the other of deficiency. Among Aristotle's many examples we find courage, the virtue that is between the mean of recklessness (excess) at one extreme and cowardice (deficiency) at the other. And truthfulness is the virtue that is the mean between boastfulness at one extreme, and self-depreciation at the other. It's probably because of the doctrine of the mean that some people mistakenly associate Aristotle with the slogan, "Everything in moderation." Aristotle was careful to point out, however, that some activities—such as adultery, theft, and murder—admit of no moderation because they are bad by their very nature.

The mean is also relative to us. Aristotle used the example of the diet an athletic trainer orders for his client: the diet that is appropriate for a seasoned athlete may be inappropriate for a beginner. But we can apply the notion to the moral realm as well. The courage that is appropriate for a schoolboy is not appropriate for a warrior. And how much courage is it appropriate to expect? Just the amount that a man of practical wisdom would determine. As Aristotle said elsewhere, "The rest is up to perception." Not just anybody's perception, but the perception of a man of practical wisdom—a man who understands the proper ends of life and who is skillful in determining the means needed to attain those ends.

Contemporary virtue theorists agree with Aristotle that the virtues are central to an adequate account of morality and the moral life; virtue theorist Rosalind Hursthouse even describes contemporary virtue ethics as "the sort of ethical theory derived from Aristotle." Here is the way she outlines the "bare bones" of her version of virtue theory:

Premise 1:   An action is right if and only if it is what a virtuous agent would characteristically (i.e., acting in character) do in the circumstances.

Premise 1a: A virtuous agent is one who has, and exercises, certain character traits, namely, the virtues.

[Premise 2]: A virtue is a character trait a human being needs for *eudaimonia,* to flourish or live well.

Hursthouse concedes that [Premise 2] is very complicated in its explication, but she regards it as encapsulating the following requirements:

1. The virtues benefit their possessor. (They enable her to flourish, to be, and live a life that is, *eudaimon.*)

2. The virtues make their possessor a good human being. (Human beings need the virtues in order to live well, to flourish as human beings, to live a characteristically good, *eudaimon,* human life.)

3. The above two features of the virtues are interrelated.[1]

At first glance, these three approaches to ethical theory—Kant's, Bentham's, and virtue theorists'—seem to reflect very neatly the three searches, usually grouped under the heading "ethics", that we outlined at the beginning of this chapter:

1. Kant was concerned to discover an absolutely certain, universally valid principle of conduct that can stand against the challenges of the skeptic and the relativist.

2. Bentham thought he had developed a method or process of reasoning to help us in deciding hard cases and other real-world moral choices.

3. And advocates of virtue ethics concentrate on the search for the good life, the life that combines virtue and happiness in true human fulfillment.

However, to fully understand the focus of the debate among Kantians, utilitarians, and virtue theorists such as Hursthouse, we need to spend a little more time on some subtleties of ethical theory.

Let's begin by observing that all three—Kant, Bentham, and Hursthouse—are concerned, each in his or her own way, with all of the central questions of ethical theory that we outlined at the beginning of this chapter.

First, all three are concerned to discover a valid first principle of conduct that can stand against the challenges of the skeptic and the relativist. The first principle of conduct that Kant proposed is the Categorical Imperative, or what Kant called the Highest Moral Law; Bentham thought he had discovered the first principle in the Principle of Utility: "Maximize Happiness!" And we might articulate Hursthouse's first principle as follows (although I haven't found her stating her position just this way): "Be a Virtuous Person!" Earlier we said that this search is for an absolutely certain, universally valid first principle, and Kant thought he found such certainty because his principle is grounded in reason, that is, in logic alone. Indeed, he believed that the principle is binding on all rational creatures, so presumably even non-human aliens and angels, if there are any, are bound by the Categorical Imperative, as well as human beings. The first principles of Bentham and Hursthouse do not rest on reason alone, but on the contingencies of human psychology. Thus they cannot aspire to the certainty that Kant claimed for his first principle. But Bentham nevertheless believed that his principle commanded absolute universal validity, that is, for all human beings, who are psychologically constituted to seek pleasure and avoid pain. And for Hursthouse, the first principle is grounded in what is required for human flourishing.

Second, all three are concerned to articulate a method or process of reasoning to help us in deciding hard cases and other real-world moral choices. As we have seen, Bentham advocated the method of calculating pleasure and pain. Later utilitarians, as well as critics, have pointed out all sorts of problems with the method, and Bentham himself admitted that it wouldn't be practical for the method to be strictly pursued before every moral judgment, or every legislative action. He recommended, however, that the method should always be kept in view, as a sort of backdrop for moral judgment and legislative action.

Kant believed that the method he recommended is implicit in the Categorical Imperative, and he gave us some examples of how the method works—or how he thought it works. Many of my former students have found that his example based on the lying promise is the clearest and easiest to understand, so I will use it to illustrate Kant's method for deciding real-world moral choices.

Kant asked us to consider the case of a man forced by necessity to borrow money. The man knows that his circumstances are such that there is no way that he will be able to repay the money; but he also knows that unless he promises to pay, no one will lend him the money. So here is his problem: he desperately needs to borrow the money, but he will have to sign a promissory note to get it, knowing at the very moment he signs the note, that he has no intention of repaying it. What should he do? Kant thought that the man probably already believed that he shouldn't make the lying promise, but in case he needed to reinforce that belief, Kant says that the man should call to mind the Categorical Imperative:

> Act only on that maxim through which you can at the same time will that it should be universal law.

So the man needing the money should ask himself the question,

> Can I will it to be universal law that, whenever a man needs to borrow money, he will go ahead and do it, and promise to repay it, although he knows that he can never do so?

This question, "Can I will it to be universal law?" is the *universalizability* test.

As is often the case, Kant's language is somewhat forbidding here, so let's recast the question in simpler terms: "What if everyone did that?" Think about it. What *would* happen if everyone who needed to borrow money went ahead and did it, and signed notes promising to repay the loans, without ever intending to repay, even at the very moment they sign the note?

Well, as my students in the past have been very quick to point out, if everyone went around signing promissory notes that they never intended to repay, it wouldn't be long before lenders would refuse to lend money at all. And if that happened, the world would become a pretty miserable place very quickly. And of course this is correct. But this response is one Bentham would have pointed out; and that's why, Bentham would have said, lying promises are wrong: because they are not conducive to human happiness.

But Kant's point here is much more subtle, and it illustrates the genius of Kant's insight: because Kant saw that the lying promise involves a contradiction—in Kant's words, it "would necessarily contradict itself." Kant saw that the man *cannot* consistently will the maxim, "Whenever a man needs to borrow money, he ought to go ahead and do it—and promise to repay it, although he knows that he can never do so," because in trying to do so he wishes out of existence the very thing he wants: that is, if *everyone* made lying promises, he *couldn't do it himself!*

As I have hinted already, Kant thought that the man probably already believed that he shouldn't make the lying promise. But frequently we are faced with moral choices where our intuitions speak less clearly, or not at all. In those cases, the universalizability test provides a method for moral decision making.

Many readers find Kant's other examples, of how the universalizability test is supposed to work, less persuasive than the lying promise example. But at least the lying promise example clearly illustrates the method for deciding hard cases that Kant advocated.

Hursthouse's decision procedure is to ask herself, "What would the virtuous person do?" Not, she elaborates, as some people might imagine, just picking your favored candidate, Mother Teresa, maybe, or Socrates, and asking yourself, "What would he/she do in these circumstances?" but "If I were to do such and such now, would I be being kind or unkind, honest or dishonest, fair or unfair [and so on]?" Even if I consider myself less than fully virtuous and do not fully trust my moral intuitions, I still have some idea of what a virtuous person would do, according to Hursthouse: the virtuous person is one who "characteristically does what is honest, charitable, true to her word, etc. and not what would be dishonest, uncharitable, untrue to her word" (*ibid.* page 36), for example. Let's try it. Suppose in a job interview you see that by lying about your job related experience you could gain an advantage over another applicant. Do you really need a Benthamite calculation of pluses and minuses of projected pleasures and pains, or a Kantian universalizability test, to determine what you ought to do? Isn't it enough to see that in your circumstances lying would be both dishonest and unfair? Or suppose you see a wounded stranger by the roadside. You could stop to help him, or you could simply pass by on the other side of the road, maybe pretending not to notice—he has no claim on you, after all. Again, isn't it enough to see that stopping to help would be charitable, and passing on the other side would be callous? And if you're really stumped and don't see your way clear, suggests Hursthouse, go to someone whom you admire as being kinder, or more honest, or more fairminded than yourself, and ask her what she would do in your circumstances.

Third, Kant, Bentham, and Hursthouse, each in his or her own way, has, or at least implies, a program for the good life, the life that combines virtue and happiness in true human fulfillment. For Bentham, this was the life of happiness. For Kant, it was the life, devoted to duty, that *deserves* happiness. For Hursthouse, it was *eudaimonia*.

For Bentham, the virtues would be those character traits that best tend to dispose one to make the decisions that contribute to maximizing happiness; in Kant's case, the virtues would be those character traits that best tend to dispose one to do one's duty. In this way, their accounts of the virtues are derivative; that is, their approach to the virtues is, in effect, to define them in terms of maximizing happiness or doing one's duty. But their interests were only indirectly focused on the virtues.

With virtue theorists like Hursthouse, this focus changes, and this is one of the most obvious differences between virtue ethics and the ethics of Kant and Bentham. But there is a deeper, more fundamental, theoretical difference in focus.

We have been attending to questions of universal principles, method, and virtue. But at a more theoretical level, ethical theorists also have been concerned to respond to such questions as, "What *makes* right acts right?" and "What *makes* a state of affairs good, or one state of affairs better than another?" That is, what characteristic—or maybe it's a complex set of characteristics—do all and only right acts have, by virtue of which they are right, and do all and only good states of affairs have, by virtue of which they are good?

I suspect that some of you are thinking that these questions are abstruse, if not downright silly. But the motivation behind them is reflected in a lot of our moral discourse. For example, if a resident counselor suggests to us that a new university policy that has been proposed, a policy that we think is a very bad idea, is a good policy, we may ask, "What's good about it?" The counselor may explain that as things have been, some students have been unfairly discriminated against in the allocation of campus resources—something we didn't know about—and that the new policy will correct that. Sometimes we are surprised when parents or teachers object to something we or friends are doing, and we ask, "What's wrong with it?" Maybe, unknown to us, the activity has hidden dangers for our health. In these cases we are asking what makes the policy good, or the activity wrong, and we are told that, in this case, what makes the policy good is that it will correct unfairness (or at least the counselor thinks it will), and that what makes the activity wrong is that it is hazardous to health.

The point here is that in cases of moral judgment—indeed, in cases of any evaluative judgment—it is always appropriate to ask, "You say X is good (or bad); what's good (or bad) about it?" Or, "You say X is wrong (or right); what's wrong (or right) with it?" That is, it is always appropriate to ask for an identification of good-making (or bad-making), or wrong-making (or right-making) characteristics: thus, the philosopher's questions, "What makes good states of affairs good?" and "What makes right acts right?"

In particular cases like the ones we have been discussing, sometimes one kind of answer seems to be appropriate; other cases seem to call for a different kind of answer. A dream of the philosopher working in the area of ethics is to discover a universally valid principle of conduct that is at once general enough, but also precise enough, that it will cover all cases. Some people think this is a pipe dream, but it has motivated much of the work in ethical theory. Kant thought he had discovered the universally valid principle in his Categorical Imperative, and with it the basis for his ethics of duty. Bentham thought it was his Principle of Utility, and with it the basis for utilitarianism. For Kant, the answer to the question, "What makes right acts right?" is that they conform to what it is our duty to do. For Bentham, the answer is that they maximize value. For Hursthouse's virtue theory, however, the answer is that an action is right if it is what a virtuous agent would characteristically do in the circumstances.

Here, then, is the crux of the debate: Which is theoretically more fundamental, duty, value, or virtue? At first glance this may seem to be a pretty abstract, theoretical question that surely can't make much difference to us. But recall some of the objections that we made to Bentham's utilitarianism. One of the reasons we were so uncomfortable with the advice Bentham's theory would give the young man wondering whether to leave home is that we believe we have a duty to respect, or least consider, our parents' wishes. And we were uncomfortable with the idea that torturing people for the entertainment of others is morally acceptable, at least in part because we recoil at the thought that decent (that is, virtuous) people would enjoy such things. And must we always tell the truth, as Kant claims, regardless of the consequences for good or ill, even when doing so means that innocent lives will be lost, or horrible pain inflicted? Do we really want to insist that the members of the Dutch family, who lied in order to harbor the family of Anne Frank, were acting immorally, as Kant's theory claims? Maybe the tensions among duty, value, and virtue aren't so abstract and theoretical, after all.

We have considered criticisms of Kant's theory and utilitarianism. Virtue ethics has its critics, too, who point out what they believe are fundamental objections to virtue ethics.

Some critics contend that virtue ethics is circular. That is, they claim that virtue ethics maintains that an action is right if it is what a virtuous agent would do in the circumstances, but then turns around and defines a virtuous agent as the one who does the right thing in those circumstances! This is an objection that some critics have leveled against Aristotle's theory, where, critics claim, the virtuous mean is defined in terms of a man of practical reason, and the man of practical reason in terms of one who is able to perceive the virtuous mean. Most Aristotelians deny this charge; in any case Hursthouse attempts to avoid the circle by grounding virtue in human flourishing. We still may want to ask whether in modern society there any generally accepted standards of what constitutes human flourishing.

Other critics argue that virtue ethics has no helpful answer to the question, "What should I do?" To this Hursthouse replies, as we have seen, "Do what a virtuous person would do!" And she might ask, as well, if this is really any less satisfactory than Bentham's utilitarian calculation or Kant's Categorical Imperative test.

Still other critics maintain that virtue ethics has no first principle of conduct that can stand against the challenges of the skeptic and the relativist. To this charge Hursthouse replies that skeptics and relativists continue to challenge other ethical theories, too, so that this problem is not one for virtue ethics alone.

What more can be said in support of virtue ethics?

Proponents claim that virtue ethics has certain advantages over rival theories. For one thing, they claim, it addresses important topics, such as motivation and moral character, that are not adequately treated in either Kantian (or neo-Kantian) ethical theory or utilitarianism. Indeed, they continue, without virtue a moral agent can't even adequately apply the principles advocated by alternative theories.

For another thing, proponents argue, virtue ethics offers a more complete and coherent picture of the moral life than does its rivals, going beyond mere right action to include good character, desires, life goals, likes and dislikes, and the kind of person one wants to be.

Of special interest to us is a strong connection between virtue ethics and some of the concerns voiced by feminist philosophers. Significantly, among the first twentieth century philosophers to decry the aridity in modern ethical theory were two women. In an influential paper, "Modern Moral Philosophy,"[2] which appeared in 1958, Elizabeth Anscombe argued that moral philosophy in the tradition of Bentham and Kant is philosophically bankrupt because it attempts to find a foundation for morality in legalistic concepts such as obligation, and these, Anscombe argued, make sense only relative to a lawgiver. Since many of us no longer believe in God, we need to turn to virtue to find a foundation for morality. In the introduction to her 1978 collection of essays, *Virtues and Vices*,[3] Phillipa Foot suggests that "a sound moral philosophy should start with a theory of the virtues and vices." I once heard her lament the stagnation of modern moral philosophy: "The moral life is so *rich*," she exclaimed; "but can you imagine a discussion about utilitarianism without a reference to promising?"

While Anscombe and Foot are not usually considered to be at the forefront of late twentieth century feminist philosophy, they have been an inspiration to many younger women working in the field. We turn now to a distinctly feminist critique of ethics.

The Feminist Critique of Ethical Theory

From the time of the ancient Greeks to Kant and Bentham, ethics—and philosophy in general—was dominated by male thinkers. The central problems of ethics—and philosophy in general—were those seen by male thinkers in male-dominated societies. The virtues seen as intellectual virtues—rationality, objectivity, impartiality, universality—were those associated with male-dominated thinking. Those virtues seen as moral virtues were the character traits exhibited by and admired by men who engaged in the almost exclusively male pursuits of public life, commerce, and warfare. We have virtually no record of philosophy done by, for, or about women until the nineteenth century, and very little even then. Women philosophers, including those working in the area of ethics, are essentially a product of the twentieth century.

That women have *not* been doing philosophy all this time is perhaps symptomatic of the attitudes toward women that have been dominant in Western history—attitudes that women, their interests, capacities, values, and ways of approaching things, are inferior to and less important than those of men: "What would a mere woman have to say about important issues?"

Moreover, philosophy is a luxury of the affluent. Men—and women—who are grubbing day to day for their next meal may wonder why God makes life so hard for them, or why God is punishing them; but they do not have the luxury of time or resources to reflect on the good, the true, and the beautiful. And women, whose lives have been dominated by caring for and responding to the needs of others, have been simply too occupied with their tasks, and too exhausted at the end of the day, to do philosophy.

What *if* women had been doing philosophy all this time? Would the very history of the discipline be different? Would women's philosophy be different, not only in perspective, but in content, from the kinds of philosophy we have been discussing in this book? Would their approaches to ethical theory be different from those of men like Aristotle, Kant and Bentham?

We call the Athens of Socrates, Plato, and Aristotle "democratic," but we need to remember that its economy was based on slave labor, and that Athenian citizenship was restricted to adult, native-born males, and systematically excluded slaves, anyone who was not Athenian by birth, and women. Women were confined to the home to manage a household and bear and raise children. Their virtues—caring, nurturing, love, sensitivity to the needs of others—did not find their way into moral philosophy. The traditional Athenian virtues—wisdom, courage, temperance, and justice—were associated with men and their pursuits.

Aristotle accepted, uncritically, the Athenian view that women are inferior to men, physically, intellectually, and morally. Aristotle even taught that women's courage, temperance, and justice are different from, and inferior to, men's. He argued that women are incomplete men, much as Freud did in the twentieth century, in that women lack something which men have:

> The male and the female differ from each other in the possession of an ability and the lack of an ability. The male is able to concoct, formulate and to ejaculate the sperm which contains the origin of the form . . . , the initiating formative principle. The female, on the other hand, is that which receives the seed but is unable to formulate or ejaculate it. (*Generation of Animals* 765b, 9-16)

 Aristotle, *Generation of Animals*

Further

> [A good wife] will serve [her husband] more assiduously than if she had been a slave bought and taken home. For he has indeed bought her with a great price. (*Oikonomikos*)[4]

Kant wrote, "The virtue of a woman is a *beautiful virtue*. That of the male sex should be *noble virtue*," thus suggesting that women's virtues are not only different from but morally inferior to men's.

Women in England at the time of Bentham were essentially the chattel of their fathers or husbands, or if they were widows with male offspring, their sons. They could not vote or own property; indeed, any property women might inherit became the property of their husbands when they married. And even Bentham, who believed in women's suffrage as a matter of principle, did not advocate it because he was afraid that injecting the topic into the British political debates of the early nineteenth century would detract from his program for extending *male* suffrage.

Of course we need not look to earlier centuries to uncover sexually biased attitudes. Even now we treat boys and girls differently almost from birth. Most parents of my generation gave their little daughters dolls and their little sons toy trucks, without really thinking very much about which toy would please which child most. (In their defense, I hasten to add that many did make sure their daughter had a well supplied tool chest to take along when she went off to college!) We expect different behavior from boys and girls in the classroom: we expect the boys to be boisterous, but the girls to be "ladylike." Of course the children learn this very quickly; they know what kind of behavior will be rewarded. Sexual roles are clearly defined and reinforced. Boys play sports; girls wearing short skirts cheer them on.

The prevalent attitude toward women, among the men I grew up with, was "Keep 'em barefoot, pregnant, and in the kitchen!" reminiscent of the slogan in 1930's Germany, "Kinder, kuchen, kirchen" (children, kitchen, church) that defined the role of German women during the Nazi era. Even those of us who were respectful of women's ambitions for careers outside the home thoughtlessly joined in on the "joke" (smirk, smirk), thus helping to perpetuate the attitude. And then there was the notorious double standard of sexual behavior. Men bragged about, and were admired for, their sexual conquests. Women were condemned, ostracized, and called ugly names. Despite the recent popularity of the TV series, *Sex and the City*, those attitudes are still prevalent in the part of the country where I grew up.

Even after the Second World War, when more and more women were working outside the home, about the only professions open to women were teaching, nursing, and secretarial work. It took years of activism to open the doors of real estate, medicine, and law, for example, to women. It was generally accepted that women even think differently from men. When asked about her professional standards, one of the most inspirational teachers of my early graduate school years replied, "Well, some people say I think like a man."

Although the past thirty or forty years have seen significant changes on these fronts, even today women earn significantly less than men do in comparable professions. Women's athletic programs in schools and colleges fight to receive funding comparable to the funding that is readily available to men's athletic programs. Conservative social groups still insist, "A woman's place is in the home!" Even my mother, who in later years ran her own business, and served on the school board, didn't like it when she found me washing dishes in my kitchen. That wasn't a man's work!

It isn't just that these received attitudes perpetuate different roles and ways of doing things for women: they perpetuate the notion that women's roles and ways of doing things are inferior or subservient to men's. It's the guys out there on the gridiron who are doing the important work. The role of the gals is to support them.

The insidious thing about these culturally entrenched attitudes toward women, their capacities, values, and ways of approaching things, is that in many cases they are subliminal. They have been so much a way of thinking that it simply never occurs to many of us to examine them, just as it never occurs to us to examine so many of our culturally received attitudes. Thomas Jefferson, the author of the words, "We hold these truths to be self-evident, that all men are created equal," was a slave owner. John Stuart Mill, author of *Liberty,* the famous defense of individual liberty, was his entire wage-earning life an employee of the East India Company, a major force in nineteenth century British imperialism, arguably the most oppressive institution of the era. I wonder what cultural norms and attitudes, that we embrace so uncritically, will baffle people of the twenty-second century.

Feminism is an intellectual, social, and political movement united in an effort to combat and change institutions and attitudes that have oppressed women and the oppression of women that they have engendered. Although there are feminists of many different persuasions, they share a common conviction that important intellectual, social, and political institutions have been dominated by men and have been based on an exclusively male viewpoint— sometimes overt but more frequently insidiously covert—that considers only men to be fully human. Feminists argue that these institutions need to be reevaluated from a point of view that appreciates the experiences, interests, styles, values, insights, and sensitivities of women as well as men. *Feminist philosophy* applies a specifically and self-conscious feminist viewpoint to the traditional problems and practices of philosophy. Feminist approaches to ethics, often called *feminist ethics,* "...are distinguished by an explicit commitment to correcting male biases they perceive in traditional ethics, biases that may be manifest in rationalizations of women's subordination, or in disregard for, or disparagement of, women's moral experience".[5]

To be sure, as early as 1798 a few voices were speaking out against the subservient position of women:

1. In *A Vindication of the Rights of Women* (1798), Mary Wollstonecraft (the mother of Mary Shelley, author of *Frankenstein*) argued that women's position in society was the result of lack of educational opportunity and social strictures, not inferior rational or moral powers. While granting that women in her day were typically inferior to men in most respects, she insisted that their inferiority was due to the kind of education they received—or hadn't received—and the environment in which they lived, rather than in any innate sexual inferiority. If women were given the same educational opportunities, their equality with men would be apparent.[6]

2. John Stuart Mill's essay *The Subjection of Women* (1869),[7] was an impassioned protest against the nineteenth century social subordination of women. The opening paragraph presents its fundamental argument:

> The object of this Essay is to explain as clearly as I am able grounds of an opinion which I have held from the very earliest period when I had formed any opinions at all on social political matters, and which, instead of being weakened or modified, has been constantly growing stronger by the progress reflection and the experience of life. That the principle which regulates the existing social relations between the two sexes—the legal subordination of one sex to the other—is wrong itself, and now one of the chief hindrances to human improvement; and that it ought to be replaced by a principle of perfect equality, admitting no power or privilege on the one side, nor disability on the other.

The second chapter presents an argument against the 19th century subordination of women in marriage, which Mill compared to slavery. The third presents evidence of the competence of women to do many of the jobs from which they were by custom (and law, in some cases) barred.

3. Frederick Engels' *The Origin of the Family, Private Property and the State* (1884)[8] contains this claim:

> The first class opposition that appears in history coincides with the development of the antagonism between man and woman in monogamous marriage, and the first class oppression coincides with that of the female sex by the male.

4. And Simone de Beauvoir, the existentialist thinker and companion to Jean-Paul Sartre, concluded her 1949 bombshell, *The Second Sex,* as follows:

> To emancipate woman is to refuse to confine her to the relations she bears to man, not to deny them to her; let her have her independent existence and she will continue none the less to exist for him also: mutually recognising each other as subject, each will yet remain for the other an other. The reciprocity of their relations will not do away with the miracles—desire, possession, love, dream, adventure—worked by the division of human beings into two separate categories; and the words that move us—giving, conquering, uniting—will not lose their meaning. On the contrary, when we abolish the slavery of half of humanity, together with the whole system of hypocrisy that it implies, then the 'division' of humanity will reveal its genuine significance and the human couple will find its true form. . . . It is for man to establish the reign of liberty in the midst of the world of the given. To gain the supreme victory, it is necessary, for one thing, that by and through their natural differentiation men and women unequivocally affirm their brotherhood.[9]

These writers are feminists (although some feminists might object to my calling them such), and their writings, feminist classics. But despite their more or less isolated protests, it was only in the latter half of the twentieth century that the philosophical reflections of women came to be an important part of the total philosophical scene.

Feminist ethics received a significant boost with the publication of Carol Gilligan's early work in moral psychology, *In a Different Voice: Psychological Theory and Women's Development* (1982).[10] Gilligan reported that her empirical findings revealed a strong correlation between gender and response to moral situations. Men tend to be preoccupied with rights, justice, and autonomy, and in their moral thinking tend to rely on rules and seek a universal perspective. Women, in contrast, are more concerned with personal relationships and wanting not to hurt others. They tend to avoid abstract principles and concentrate rather on interpersonal empathy. (So far her findings are consistent even with the teachings of the sexist Aristotle!) Where Gilligan believes thinkers have gone wrong is in their assumption that female moral reasoning is inferior or deficient.

Gilligan's research has been called into question—for one thing, her subjects were white, middle class, and heterosexual—but her contributions to the development of feminist ethics are generally agreed to be significant. Moreover, moral psychology is an empirical science, and philosophy is not: philosophical issues can't be resolved by "looking to the facts." But most modern philosophers nevertheless have wanted their philosophical theories to be *consistent* with empirical evidence.

Feminist philosopher Alison Jaggar identified five main headings under which feminist criticisms of the tradition of modern Western moral theory may be grouped. First, Western moral theory reveals a lack of concern for women's interests, as when it prescribes to women "...allegedly feminine virtues such as obedience, silence, and faithfulness." Second, it neglects women's issues, such as those that arise in the home, and downplays the significance and creativity of women's work in the home. Third, it denies the moral agency of women, describing them as inferior to men in the area of moral reason. Fourth, it favors values traditionally associated with men, such as independence, autonomy, intellect, domination, reason, war, and death, over the supposedly female-associated values of interdependence, community, emotion, sharing, joy, peace, and life. Fifth, it devalues the moral experience of women, who are more likely than men to resolve moral dilemmas by relying on feelings rather than rules and abstract principles. Needless to say, not all feminist philosophers endorse all these criticisms, although Jaggar believes that most would agree on the first three.[11]

Are these perceived shortcomings a result of a failure in *application* of ethical theory to address women's concerns, as I believed when I was first confronted by feminist criticism of modern ethical theory? Or are they a bias inherent in the theory itself? Feminist responses to these questions vary widely. At one end of the spectrum, some feminists aim to work within the general framework of existing ethical theory, attempting to correct male bias within that framework. At the other end, radical feminists insist that the framework is so deeply flawed that it must be utterly rejected, and a completely new philosophy—and ethical theory—rewritten from a female point of view.

In "Feminism in Ethics," an article that reflects some of her more recent thinking, Alison Jaggar charts something of a middle course. She meticulously points out what she perceives to be flaws in the Western tradition in ethical theory, while concurring with certain features of it (*Feminism in Philosophy,* Cambridge, 2000):[12]

Feminists have identified several male-biased assumptions that are not held idiosyncratically by a few isolated philosophers but that instead infect a whole tradition of thinking about moral justification. This is the liberal tradition descending from the European Enlightenment.

1. First, 'the' moral subject of this tradition appears to be generic but in fact reflects a specific social type: he is a western male head of household, upper or middle class, and therefore probably white. The motivations and style of reasoning characteristic of this social type are ascribed to all rational moral subjects, despite the overwhelming empirical evidence that many people have different motivations and employ alternative styles of reasoning.

2. When this social type is taken as the moral norm, people whose thinking deviates from his are presented as deficient in moral rationality. Idealizing his mode of thinking is thus covertly authoritarian because it invalidates the moral thinking of many women as well as of male members of subordinated groups.

3. The sphere of moral reason is arbitrarily limited so as to exclude matters of intimate and family relations.

4. In consequence, numerous issues that have special importance for women's lives become morally undecidable; there is no conceptual space for criticizing many practices oppressive to women.

5. The foregoing points together entail that mainstream conceptions of moral justification deny the conceptual resources that would permit women and male members of subordinated groups to express their own moral perspectives in their own terms.

6. Despite the impartiality and universality claimed by these conceptions of moral justification, they are in fact self-serving and circular because they rationalize the views of the philosopher who invokes them while silencing dissenting voices.

For these reasons, the very conceptual tools that purport to guarantee moral objectivity are biased in favour of the privileged.

Implicit in feminists' criticisms of mainstream ethics is an expectation that any adequate account of moral justification must not only be able to distinguish justified moral claims from both subjective desires and established conventions; it must also fulfill the following conditions:

1. Its conception of the moral subject must be carefully scrutinized to eliminate covert bias on the basis of race, class, gender or any other axis of domination.

2. Therefore, it must take care not to discredit or disregard the moral narratives, vocabularies and styles of thinking characteristic of women, lower-class and marginalized persons.

3. It must be practically available for use by all moral subjects, including those with little formal education; thus, it should not be highly technical nor rely on overly idealized, counter-factual assumptions.

4. It must not exclude from moral scrutiny aspects of life that are of special concern to women or to male members of disadvantaged and marginalized groups.

In short, a feminist account of moral justification must be non-elitist and truly unbiased; it must not privilege the perspective of the powerful nor assign disproportionate moral authority to their voices. The next section sketches some feminist work that moves in the direction of meeting these conditions.

Liberal moral theory has typically discussed moral subjects at a high level of abstraction, presenting them as generic rational agents who are essentially—though not empirically—solitary. The classic liberal theorists were certainly aware that empirical subjects are embodied members of specific communities, but they dismissed people's bodies and community memberships as 'accidental' properties, inessential to their moral subjectivity. Some may have supposed that treating moral subjects as indistinguishable was required by the Enlightenment commitment to the equal moral value of every human individual. By focusing on people's commonalities and ignoring their differences, liberalism implies that moral subjects are indiscernible in all theoretical respects. . . .

Over the past twenty-five years, the liberal conception of the moral subject has been challenged from many directions. Communitarian critics have been particularly vocal in insisting that moral subjects are essentially embodied, thereby entailing that they are 'embedded' in communities and 'encumbered' by particular loyalties and obligations that constitute essential aspects of their identities. Many feminist accounts of moral subjects resemble communitarianism in emphasizing bodies, communities and relationships, but feminist work is distinguished by its attention to inequality. Feminist discussions of embodiment, for instance, typically treat the body neither merely as an individuator of persons nor merely as a universal condition of human life but as a bearer of contingent and varying social meanings which locate bodies and their persons not only in particular communities but also in specific structures of privilege and power. Similarly, feminists not only present moral subjects as constituted by particular relations but also assert that these relations invariably involve dimensions of systematic dominance and inequality. Finally, feminists typically focus on those aspects of moral subjects' identities that are constituted by their membership in distinct—though overlapping—social collectivities defined not only by history and geography but also by categories such as gender, class and race, in which power inequalities are inherent.

Feminists do not deny that moral subjects are alike on some level of abstraction, but their consciousness of the many false humanisms that have purveyed generalizations about specific populations as universal truths of human nature motivates them to highlight human differences over human commonalities. Nor do feminists dispute the equal moral worth of each individual but, when individuals are so differently situated, they insist that a genuine commitment to moral equality requires sensitivity to actual inequalities.... Such disparities and inequalities create obstacles to projects of imaginative identification and even to productive discussion. To recognize these obstacles is to challenge mainstream assumptions that there is a single correct model of moral reason, and that moral subjects are interchangeable....

Many feminists argue that recommendations that moral agents think from the standpoint of others, reverse perspectives with them, and so on, are not only disrespectful of others but epistemically incoherent. There exists no substitute for listening to real people explain their moral perspectives in their own terms....

A full theory of moral rationality must include an account of individual rationality but, ... feminists' positive work on moral rationality has focused more on social processes than on individual capacities.... One theme running throughout this work is that dominant philosophical accounts of individual moral rationality are biased by gender, class, race and ethnicity insofar as they reflect and rationalize the culturally specific values held by modern, western, bourgeois, men. However, few feminists believe that the remedy for existing bias is to replace one singular model that covertly represents moral rationality as bourgeois and masculine with another singular model that has more features considered characteristically feminine; there no more exists a representative or generic woman than a generic human or a representative man. Instead, many feminists argue that the remedy is to reconstrue moral rationality as a characteristic primarily of social processes....

A considerable number of feminists, including myself, broadly concur with the long western philosophical tradition, stretching from Plato through Locke and Kant, to Rawls and Habermas, that holds moral conclusions to be rationally justified when they are reached by rational people through discursive processes that are open, inclusive and egalitarian. But even though philosophers in this tradition are aware that real people are not all alike, they have ignored the practical and theoretical problems posed for egalitarian discourse by systematic difference and inequality. Feminists, by contrast, have been deeply troubled by those problems; in response, they have developed an extensive literature on discursive communication, including its ethical and political aspects. . . .

Mainstream accounts of domination-free discourse require that each participant equally have an opportunity to speak and be heard; however, they neglect to examine the conditions necessary for such opportunities to be real rather than merely formal. Speaking requires a language but dominant vocabularies may lack the resources necessary to express the perspectives of subordinated groups; as a young woman, for instance, I was unable to articulate many vague and confused feelings and perceptions because the language necessary to do so had not yet been invented. The vocabulary I needed included such terms as: 'gender' (applied beyond grammar to social norms and identities); 'sex role'; 'sexism'; 'sexual harassment'; 'the double day'; 'sexual objectification'; 'heterosexism'; 'the male gaze'; 'marital, acquaintance and date rape'; 'emotional work'; 'stalking'; 'hostile environment'; 'displaced homemaker'; and 'double standard of aging'. Because language is essentially public, creating new vocabularies is necessarily a collective rather than an individual project. In order that alternatives to dominant moral vocabularies may be developed, I have recently argued that, if discourses are to be open and inclusive for some, they may have to be closed to and exclusive of others. . . .

Feminist models of moral discourse include a number of other characteristic features, in addition to their reinterpretations of equality, openness and inclusiveness. Among those features are a commitment to the collective moral evaluation of participants' emotions and a conception of moral discourse as a nurturing rather than an adversarial practice. For feminists, moral discourses are not neutral procedures in which people withdraw from the real world to debate moral concerns; instead, they are activities within the world and themselves are liable to moral and political evaluation. Done well, moral discourse has a value that is intrinsic and not merely instrumental. . . .

Western philosophers have often construed moral justification as the attainment of 'the moral point of view', a grandiose expression that hints heavily at a transcendent moral reality. In the twentieth century, they have interpreted the expression through such metaphors as a god's eye view, the perspective of an ideal observer or an archangel, an Archimedean point, a view from nowhere or a view from everywhere. The aim of these metaphors is to designate an imagined perspective that is precisely not a specific point of view, what might be called the father of all points of view, and contemporary feminists typically regard such metaphors as misleading. For most feminists, moral justification cannot be achieved by an individual appeal to transcendent ideals or absolute principles; instead, it consists in the on-going evaluation of individual actions and social practices by people in actual communities of discourse who collectively construct historically specific ideals, norms and values. On this understanding, moral justifications are socially developed and contingently situated; 'the' moral point of view loses its transcendent status and becomes not single but multiple, rooted in the social world rather than floating above or outside it.

Rejecting moral realism, construed as the postulation of a mind-independent moral reality, does not commit feminists to embracing relativism, interpreted as the claim that all moral points of view are equally valid. Indeed, relativism is inconsistent with feminism's non-negotiable moral commitment to opposing male dominance. The work surveyed here directs us to understand moral justification in terms of discursive processes that are open, inclusive and egalitarian. Since openness, inclusivity and equality are moral and epistemic ideals that are only ever met imperfectly, to a greater or lesser extent, the warrant for accepting particular moral assertions will be stronger or weaker according to the degree to which the ideals are realized. The conclusions of moral dialogues thus are always provisional and fallible rather than final or absolute and always dependent on a discursive social context that determines what count as good reasons. . . .

Several features of Jaggar's work deserve careful attention. First, she points out that the perspective of the liberal tradition in modern moral philosophy is that of a Western male head of household, upper or middle class, and therefore probably white. From this perspective, the points of view and the moral sensibilities of others—including women and males of subordinated groups—are seen as defective or inferior. Second, she questions the values of universality, individuality, and disinterestedness that have constituted the theoretical ideal in the modern liberal tradition. Third, she rejects the model of the moral philosopher as a solitary contemplator in his study (remember Kant?), and recommends rather the model of moral agents engaged in communal moral discourse. Fourth, she eschews the idea that moral justification is the attainment of the 'moral point of view', the point of view of an ideal observer, or an Archimedean point. All of these objections point to fundamental flaws in the modern liberal tradition.

However, Jaggar agrees with some features of the Western philosophical tradition from the time of Plato to the twentieth century. She agrees that moral conclusions can ". . . be rationally justified when they are reached by rational people through discursive processes that are open, inclusive and egalitarian." And she agrees—even with Plato—in rejecting relativism (although she rejects Plato's absolutist version of a response to relativism as well).

Jaggar's work, challenging as it is, is theoretical and programmatic. How would a feminist approach a practical moral issue? In the following selection,

"Pornography, Civil Rights, and Speech," law professor Catharine MacKinnon
supplies a critique of pornography within a distinctively feminist perspective
on the condition of women:[13]

> ...Once power constructs social reality, as I will show pornography
> constructs the social reality of gender, the force behind sexism, the
> subordination in gender equality, is made invisible: dissent from it
> becomes inaudible as well as rare. What a woman is, is defined in
> pornographic terms; is what pornography *does*. If the law then looks
> neutrally on the reality of gender so produced, the harm that has
> been done *will not be perceptible as harm*. It becomes just the way
> things are.
>
> ...Substantively considered, the situation of women is *not really
> like anything else*. Its specificity is due not only to our numbers—we
> are half the human race—and our diversity, which at times has ob-
> scured that we are a group with an interest at all. It is, in part, that
> our status as a group relative to men has almost never, if ever, been
> changed from what it is. Women's roles do vary enough that gender,
> the social form sex takes, cannot be said to be biologically deter-
> mined. Different things are valued in different cultures, but whatever
> is valued, women are not that.
>
> ...There is a belief that this is a society in which women and
> men are basically equals. Room for marginal corrections is conceded,
> flaws are known to exist, attempts are made to correct what are con-
> ceived as occasional lapses from the basic condition of sex equality.
> Sex discrimination law has concentrated most of its focus on these
> occasional lapses. It is difficult to overestimate the extent to which
> this belief in equality is an article of faith for most people, including
> most women, who wish to live in self-respect in an internal universe,
> even (perhaps especially) if not in the world. It is also partly an ex-
> pression of natural law thinking: if we are inalienably equal, we can't
> "really" be degraded.
>
> This is a world in which it is worth trying. In this world of pre-
> sumptive equality, people make money based on their training or
> abilities or diligence or qualifications. They are employed and ad-
> vanced on the basis of merit. In this world of just deserts, if someone
> is abused, it is thought to violate the basic rules of the community. If
> it doesn't, victims are seen to have done something they could have
> chosen to do differently, by exercise of will or better judgment.
> Maybe such people have placed themselves in a situation of vulnera-
> bility to physical abuse. Maybe they have done something provoca-
> tive. Or maybe they were just unusually unlucky. In such a world, if
> such a person has an experience, there are words for it. When they
> speak and say it, they are listened to. If they write about it, they will
> be published. If certain experiences are never spoken about, if cer-

tain people or issues are seldom heard from, it is supposed that silence has been chosen. The law, including much of the law of sex discrimination and the First Amendment, operates largely within the realm of these beliefs.

Feminism is the discovery that women do not live in this world, that the person occupying this realm is a man, so much more a man if he is white and wealthy. This world of potential credibility, authority, security, and just rewards, recognition of one's identity and capacity, is a world that some people do inhabit as a condition of birth, with variations among them. It is not a basic condition accorded humanity in this society, but a prerogative of status, a privilege, among other things, of gender.

I call this a discovery because it has not been an assumption. Feminism is the first theory, the first practice, the first movement, to take seriously the situation of all women from the point of view of all women, both on our situation and on social life as a whole. The discovery has therefore been made that the implicit social content of humanism, as well as the standpoint from which legal method has been designed and injuries have been defined, has not been women's standpoint. Defining feminism in a way that connects epistemology with power as the politics of women's point of view, this discovery can be summed up by saying that women live in another world: specifically, a world of *not* equality, a world of inequality.

Looking at the world from this point of view, a whole shadow world of previously invisible silent abuse has been discerned. Rape, battery, sexual harassment, forced prostitution, and the sexual abuse of children emerge as common and systematic. . . .

. . . In pornography, there it is, in one place, all of the abuses that women had to struggle so long even to begin to articulate, all the unspeakable abuse: the rape, the battery, the sexual harassment, the prostitution, and the sexual abuse of children. Only in the pornography it is called something else: sex, sex, sex, sex, and sex, respectively. Pornography sexualizes rape, battery, sexual harassment, prostitution, and child sexual abuse; it thereby celebrates, promotes, authorizes, and legitimizes them. More generally, it eroticizes the dominance and submission that is the dynamic common to them all. It makes hierarchy sexy and calls that "the truth about sex" or just a mirror of reality. Through this process pornography constructs what a woman is as what men want from sex. This is what the pornography means.

Pornography constructs what a woman is in terms of its view of what men want sexually, such that acts of rape, battery, sexual harassment, prostitution, and sexual abuse of children become acts of sexual equality: Pornography's world of equality is a harmonious and balanced place. Men and women are perfectly complementary and perfectly bipolar. . . .

...There, women substantively desire dispossession and cruelty. We desperately want to be bound, battered, tortured, humiliated, and killed. Or, to be fair to the soft core, merely taken and used. This is erotic to the male point of view. Subjection itself, with self-determination ecstatically relinquished, is the content of women's sexual desire and desirability: Women are there to be violated and possessed, men to violate and possess us, either on screen or by camera or pen on behalf of the consumer. On a simple descriptive level, the inequality of hierarchy, of which gender is the primary one, seems necessary for sexual arousal to work. Other added inequalities identify various pornographic genres or subthemes, although they are always added through gender: age, disability, homosexuality, animals, objects, race (including anti-Semitism), and so on. Gender is never irrelevant.

What pornography does goes beyond its content: it eroticizes hierarchy, it sexualizes inequality: It makes dominance and submission into sex. Inequality is its central dynamic; the illusion of freedom coming together with the reality of force is central to its working. Perhaps because this is a bourgeois culture, the victim must look free, appear to be freely acting. Choice is how she got there. Willing is what she is when she is being equal. It seems equally important that then and there she actually be forced and that forcing be communicated on some level, even if only through still photos of her in postures of receptivity and access, available for penetration. Pornography in this view is a form of forced sex, a practice of sexual politics, an institution of gender inequality.

From this perspective, pornography is neither harmless fantasy nor a corrupt and confused misrepresentation of an otherwise natural and healthy sexual situation. It institutionalizes the sexuality of male supremacy, fusing the erotization of dominance and submission with the social construction of male and female. To the extent that gender is sexual, pornography is part of constituting the meaning of that sexuality: Men treat women as who they see women as being. Pornography constructs who that is. Men's power over women means that the way men see women defines who women can be. Pornography is that way: Pornography is not imagery in some relation to a reality elsewhere constructed. It is not a distortion, reflection, projection, expression, fantasy, representation, or symbol either. It is a sexual reality.

...Pornography participates in its audience's eroticism through creating an accessible sexual object, the possession and consumption of which is male sexuality, as socially constructed; to be consumed and possessed as which, is female sexuality, as socially constructed; pornography is a process that constructs it that way.

The object world is constructed according to how it looks with respect to its possible uses. Pornography defines women by how we look according to how we can be sexually used. Pornography codes how to look at women, so you know what you can do with one when you see one. Gender is an assignment made visually, both originally and in everyday life. A sex object is defined on the basis of its looks, in terms of its usability for sexual pleasure, such that both the looking —the quality of the gaze, including its point of view—and the definition according to use become eroticized as part of the sex itself. This is what the feminist concept "sex object" means. In this sense, sex in life is no less mediated than it is in art. Men have sex with their image of a woman. It is not that life and art imitate each other; in this sexuality, they *are* each other.

To give a set of rough epistemological translations, to defend pornography as consistent with the equality of the sexes is to defend the subordination of women to men as sexual equality. What in the pornographic view is love and romance looks a great deal like hatred and torture to the feminist. Pleasure and eroticism become violation. Desire appears as lust for dominance and submission. The vulnerability of women's projected sexual availability, that acting we are allowed (that is, asking to be acted upon), is victimization. Play conforms to scripted roles. Fantasy expresses ideology, is not exempt from it. Admiration of natural physical beauty becomes objectification. Harmlessness becomes harm. Pornography is a harm of male supremacy made difficult to see because of its pervasiveness, potency, and, principally, because of its success in making the world a pornographic place. Specifically, its harm cannot be discerned, and will not be addressed, if viewed and approached neutrally, because it *is* so much of "what is." In other words, to the extent pornography succeeds in constructing social reality, it becomes invisible as harm. If we live in a world that pornography creates through the power of men in a male-dominated situation the issue is not what the harm of pornography is, but how that harm is to become visible.

Obscenity law provides a very different analysis and conception of the problem of pornography. In 1973 the legal definition of obscenity became that which the average person, applying contemporary community standards, would find that, taken as a whole, appeals to the prurient interest; that which depicts or describes in a patently offensive way—you feel like you're a cop reading someone's Miranda rights—sexual conduct specifically defined by the applicable state law; and that which, taken as a whole, lacks serious literary, artistic, political or scientific value. Feminism doubts whether the average person gender-neutral exists; has more questions about the content and process of defining what community standards are than it does about deviations from them; wonders why prurience counts but powerlessness does not and why sensibilities are better protected from offense than women are from exploitation; defines sexuality, and thus its violation and expropriation, more broadly than does state law; and questions why a body of law that has not in practice been able to tell rape from intercourse should, without further guidance, be entrusted with telling pornography from anything less. Taking the work "as a whole" ignores that which the victims of pornography have long known:

legitimate settings diminish the perception of injury done to those whose trivialization and objectification they contextualize. Besides, and this is a heavy one, if a woman is subjected, why should it matter that the work has other value? Maybe what redeems the work's value is what enhances its injury to women, not to mention that existing standards of literature, art, science, and politics, examined in a feminist light, are remarkably consonant with pornography's mode, meaning, and message. And finally—first and foremost, actually—although the subject of these materials is overwhelmingly women, their contents almost entirely made up of women's bodies, our invisibility has been such, our equation as a sex with sex has been such, that the law of obscenity has never even considered pornography a women's issue.

Obscenity, in this light, is a moral idea, an idea about judgments of good and bad. Pornography, by contrast, is a political practice, a practice of power and powerlessness. Obscenity is ideational and abstract; pornography is concrete and substantive. The two concepts represent two entirely different things. Nudity, excess of candor, arousal or excitement, prurient appeal, illegality of the acts depicted, and unnaturalness or perversion are all qualities that bother obscenity law when sex is depicted or portrayed. Sex forced on real women so that it can be sold at a profit and forced on other real women; women's bodies trussed and maimed and raped and made into things to be hurt and obtained and accessed, and this presented as the nature of women in a way that is acted on and acted out, over and over; the coercion that is visible and the coercion that has become invisible—this and more bothers feminists about pornography. Obscenity as such probably does little harm. Pornography is integral to attitudes and behaviors of violence and discrimination that define the treatment and status of half the population. . . .

What might defenders of the liberal tradition of modern ethical theory say in response to the feminist critique? Are feminist theorists right when they say that the tradition is flawed by patriarchal thinking and oblivious to the experiences and insights of women? Do the ethical writings of feminist philosophers introduce distinctively new themes and a genuine alternative to the tradition of Western ethical theorizing, discussed in the earlier part of this chapter?

Obviously this is not a question of fact, such as "What is the capital of South Dakota?" to which I can simply supply an answer. It is a question of judgment and interpretation, to which different philosophers will give different answers. But let me give my own view of the matter, and in your classroom discussions, you can develop other answers as well.

First, it seems to me that the primary target of feminist ethical theorists is the Kantian tradition—an ethical theory of rules, rationality, autonomy, obligation, and individualism. This has undoubtedly been a dominant theme in Western ethical writings for the past two centuries or so, but it is by no means the dominant theme in Western ethical theory as a whole. If you read the works of Plato from cover to cover, you will find little or nothing about duty, obligation, rules, and universal reason—although you *will* find a great deal about *reason* in a wider, more inclusive sense. The feminist emphasis on the integration of feeling and thought, on the importance of the particular context of action, on the special importance of relationships between people —all of that fits in rather comfortably with the ancient Greek approach to the moral dimension of life, even though Greek society severely restricted the lives of women and treated them, in a variety of ways, as inferior beings.

Even in recent philosophical history, when the Kantian point of view has been so widely accepted, we find many writers who think and write about personal relationships and the role of feelings in the good life. Karl Marx writes that way, even though in his personal life he exploited the women closest to him (and, as it happens, the men as well). So does the great Russian novelist Tolstoy, the American philosopher John Dewey, the American social scientist and philosopher George Herbert Mead, and the French writer and philosopher Jean-Paul Sartre.

In my judgment, the feminists are right that the *practice* of ethical theory, and of philosophy in general in the Western tradition, has reflected an ingrained and mostly unexamined bias against women. The very same criticism can justly be made of philosophy's treatment of the nonwhite portion of the human species. What must still be determined is whether correcting those biases requires a change in the fundamental *conception* of philosophy as well as in its *practice.*

I am thinking here of ethical *principles,* on the one hand, and the *application* of ethical principles, on the other. Let me elaborate. Is there something fundamentally flawed about the Kantian principle, that morality requires us always to treat human beings as ends in themselves and never simply as a means to an end? Or is the problem that the Kantian principle has not been appropriately applied, inasmuch as, in Western culture, women and men of subordinated groups have not been considered as fully human beings, ends in themselves, but rather as means to the end of serving the interests of privileged, white men?

Recall the utilitarian principle, "The greatest happiness for the greatest number, where *each is to count for one but only one.*" Is the problem, from the point of view of feminist critique, with the principle itself; or is it rather that, in Western culture, women and men of subordinated groups have *not* counted for one—their share of happiness has not been included in the calculation of pains and pleasures—whereas privileged white men have each counted for a lot more than one? Similarly, is the problem with virtue ethics the principle that we morally ought to strive to be virtuous? Or is the problem, rather, that the virtues traditionally viewed as masculine virtues have been overvalued, while the virtues of women and men of subordinated groups have been undervalued or even denigrated?

Philosophy and Popular Culture

Ai No Corrida (translated as In the Realm of the Senses): Questions About Sex

The theater darkens, and the movie starts. You are here at college to experience new things, and if that means watching films with subtitles, such as *In the Realm of the Senses,* so be it.

    The theme of the movie is becoming clear. This movie is about sexual passion and sexual obsession. Wait a minute! That looks like a scene from a hard-core pornographic movie! Has the film projectionist made a mistake and started showing a reel from a pornographic movie instead of the intended reel from *In the Realm of the Senses?* The answer is no. At one time, nudity in films was shocking, but actresses and actors started taking off their clothes when they felt that nudity was integral to the movie's plot and theme. For *In the Realm of the Senses,* director Nagisa Oshima believed that sex was integral to the movie's plot and theme, so his main actor and actress are really engaging in various sexual acts.

Questions to Consider

Is it moral for film actors and actresses to actually have sex when the film's plot and theme revolve around sex? Is such sex aesthetically necessary? Does the sex automatically make In the Realm of the Senses *a pornographic film? What counts as pornography?*

    Let me add a personal note here if I may. When I began the study of philosophy almost half a century ago, it never occurred to me to question the unexamined assumption that the story of philosophy could be told entirely in the voices of the men whose works dominate this, or any other, philosophy text. It never occurred to me to ask whether the insights and perspectives of the nonwhite majority of the world could safely be ignored. If anyone had asked me, I think I would have said, "Of course, we must listen to everyone's voice," but that is just the point: No one ever asked me, and I never thought to ask myself! Now in Chapter 1 we heard Socrates teach us that the unexamined life is not worth living. Well, as I am sure he would agree, it also is true that the unexamined assumption is not worth holding. What you see in this ninth edition of this book is my ongoing effort to examine my own previously unexamined assumptions, and thereby, perhaps, to get just a little bit closer to the truth. If I live to be 100, and this book goes through twenty editions, I am sure there will still be questions I have not yet asked, and unexamined assumptions I have not yet subjected to criticism. Our philosophical understanding must always be a work in progress. This book will be a success if you learn nothing else from it.

Notes

1. Rosalind Hursthouse, *On Virtue Ethics,* Oxford University Press, Oxford, Copyright, 1999, by Rosalind Hursthouse.
2. Elizabeth Anscombe, "Modern Moral Philosophy," *Philosophy* (33), 1958.
3. Philippa Foot, *Virtues and Vices and Other Essays in Moral Philosophy,* Berkeley and Los Angeles, University of California Press, Copyright, Philippa Foot, 1978.
4. Aristotle, *The Generation of Animals,* many editions, e.g., The Loeb Classical Library, Harvard University Press.
5. Alison Jaggar, "Feminist Ethics," in *Encyclopedia of Ethics,* Lawrence C. Becker and Charlotte B. Becker, eds., Garland Publishing, Inc., New York & London, 1992, vol. 1, pp. 361–370.
6. Mary Wollstonecraft, *A Vindication of the Rights of Women,* Penguin Books Ltd., London, Reprinted 1992. First published 1792.
7. John Stuart Mill, *The Subjection of Women,* M.I.T. Press, Cambridge, Massachusetts, and London, England, Tenth printing, 1985, Original edition published in London in 1869 by Longmans, Green, Reader and Dyer.
8. Frederick Engels, *The Origin of the Family, Private Property and the State,* International Publishers, New York, Copyright 1942, International Publishers Co., Inc.
9. Simone de Beauvoir, *The Second Sex,* Vintage Books, 1989. Copyright 1952 by Alfred A. Knopf, Inc. Copyright renewed 1980 by Alfred A. Knopf, Inc.
10. Carol Gilligan, *In a Different Voice, Psychological Theory and Women's Development,* Harvard University Press, Cambridge, Massachusetts, and London, England, 1982, Copyright 1982 by Carol Gilligan.
11. (Becker and Becker, op. cit., p. 364).
12. Alison Jaggar, "Feminism in ethics: Moral Justification," in *The Cambridge Companion to Feminism in Philosophy,* Cambridge University Press, Cambridge, Copyright Cambridge University Press 2000.
13. Catharine MacKinnon, "Pornography, Civil Rights, and Speech," Harvard Civil Rights-Civil Liberties Law Review, Vol. 20, Number 1, Winter, 1985, pp. 1–70. ©(1985) by the President and Fellows of Harvard College and the Harvard Civil Rights-Civil Liberties Law Review.

The Main Points in Chapter Five, Part One

1. The eighteenth-century Prussian philosopher Immanuel Kant tried to find a way to make the science of Newton compatible with the strict moral beliefs of his Protestant upbringing and also to provide a rigorous logical proof of the fundamental principles of morality.

2. When philosophers talk about ethics, there are really three very different questions they ask, namely:

   a. How can I be certain that my moral beliefs are correct?
   b. How can I decide moral hard cases?
   c. How can I live a good life?

3. Kant put forward a moral principle called the Categorical Imperative as the absolutely right principle for all persons in any situation. Ethical relativists *and* ethical skeptics deny that there is any such universally valid principle.

4. To decide hard cases, defenders of utilitarianism, such as Jeremy Bentham and John Stuart Mill, offer the Principle of the Greatest Happiness for the Greatest Number. Utilitarianism is the most widely debated moral theory of modern-day philosophy.

5. Inspired especially by the ethical writings of Aristotle, some recent philosophers have developed theories of ethics using virtue, rather than duty or happines, as their basis.

6. Feminist critics of the Western tradition of ethical theory have argued that the various main theories all embody a male or patriarchal point of view and fail to express the experiences and insight of women.

Questions for Discussion and Review

1. Think back over your life and pick the hardest choice you ever had to make. Was it a moral choice? Did it involve a decision about what is right and wrong? If the answer is yes, ask yourself whether it would have helped you to carry out a utilitarian-style calculation of pleasures and pains to yourself and others. Would Kant's rule—The Categorical Imperative —have helped you at all? How did you make the decision?

2. A central thesis of virtue ethics is that virtues are character traits needed to live well. While it probably is true that, generally speaking, people who live fulfilling, rewarding lives are truthful, humane, just, and so on, is it possible for someone to live well without being truthful, or humane, or just? Who comes to your mind when you think of a virtuous person? Do you think that person lives well? Who comes to your mind when you think of a person who lives well? Do you think of that person as virtuous?

3. What do you think Kant's ethical theory tells us about the morality or immorality of abortion? Is it clear what utilitarianism tells us? Is it reasonable to pick your moral theory on the basis of what it tells you about issues, like abortion, on which you already have fixed views? Why? Why not? If you leave out any religious considerations, where do you think the truth lies on the question of the morality of abortion?

4. Are the moral experiences of women and men fundamentally different in ways that would affect their interpretation and evaluation of choices and actions? If you have studied child development in a psychology course, can you draw on what you learned there to help clarify the dispute between the traditional moral theorists and feminist theorists like Jaggar? How would you develop an analogous critique based on racial differences?

ABCNEWS

CONTEMPORARY APPLICATION

Same-Sex Marriage

There are some subjects that seem to get people worked up all out of proportion to their larger importance in the overall scheme of things. Forty years ago, when the Beatles burst onto the cultural scene, people were simply outraged by the fact that they wore their hair shoulder length, even though they also appeared neatly dressed in ties and jackets. Just last year, Janet Jackson bared a breast on national television during the Super Bowl halftime show, and the United States Congress held hearings. Poverty, domestic violence, racial oppression, and even war did not get folks as totally worked up as the length of the hair on the heads of four popular musicians or the brief undress of a pop singer. It seems that what have come to be labeled "cultural values" and "family values" hit some of us with a force that cannot easily be explained.

This past year, absolutely nothing—not even a war in Iraq—has stirred people up quite as much as the idea that two gay men or two lesbian women might go through a marriage ceremony and be considered by the State to be legally married. The downfall of Western Civilization [or of all civilization, for that matter] has confidently been predicted as the result of such an event. *Same-sex marriage,* the shorthand code name for such events, clearly triggers the most powerful of feelings in scores of millions of Americans.

It is not hard to understand why gay and lesbian Americans want the right to enter into legal marriages. Aside from the emotional, moral, and spiritual significance of such ceremonies, there are a great many legal and economic benefits of marriage that are now denied to homosexual partners. For example: in most health insurance plans, an employee can claim medical benefits for his or her spouse, but not for someone with whom there is no legal marital relationship. Child custody, home ownership, credit availability, tax exemptions, legal rights in trials, and countless other extremely important rights, benefits, and privileges are tied to marriage, and hence are unavailable to gay and lesbian couples because they are not permitted to enter into formal matrimony. One of the most painful and poignant problems is the attempt by the partners of dying AIDS sufferers to be with them at their bedside in the last hours, a right that would automatically be granted a husband or wife but is frequently denied the life partner of a gay or lesbian AIDS patient.

When I wrote these lines five years ago, a state judge in Hawaii was poised to rule in favor of a suit brought by gay and lesbian couples who claimed that the denial of marriage violated the state constitution. In the end, the court did not rule in their favor, but just last year, the Supreme Judicial Court of Massachusetts did, in fact, rule that the State Constitution required that gay and lesbian residents of the state be offered the right to marry. After a wait of several months, during which the legislature feverishly debated an amendment to the State Constitution, same-sex couples were permitted to obtain marriage licenses, and as of this moment, it is indeed legal for gay and lesbian couples to be legally married in Massachusetts. A number of members of the U.S. House of Representatives are busy crafting amendments to the United States Constitution for the purpose of making same-sex marriages unconstitutional—which, were it to succeed, would of course trump Massachusetts and outlaw same-sex marriages everywhere in America. I am writing now as we are in the midst of a political campaign in which this issue is being debated at the presidential level.

Pretty clearly, this issue raises all manner of ethical questions, the resolution of which requires us to think deeply about many of the theoretical themes discussed in the first part of this chapter. What is a person? Do all persons have the same rights, duties, privileges, and obligations? What is the source or ground of our morality—agreements among men and women, a divine law-giver, or a Natural Law written into the structure of the universe? In trying to come to some resolution of the fight over same-sex marriage, should we weigh the happiness and unhappiness likely to be produced by alternative policies, or should we ask what general principle comports with the dictates of reason itself? Or, perhaps, should we ask whether same-sex marriage [or any sort of marriage, for that matter] can be a component of the good life?

One personal word, by way of full disclosure. I am not at all neutral on this issue. My younger son, Tobias, who appears in the video associated with this end-of-chapter Contemporary Application, is a gay man—indeed, he is a leading gay legal rights expert and at the moment is a principal advisor on these issues to the presidential campaign of John Kerry. I look forward with great anticipation to attending his wedding to the man of his choice, just as I attended the wedding of his older brother to the woman of his choice. I must confess that I resent bitterly the attempt by politicians to deny me that fatherly pleasure.

On April 28, 2004, the Pew Forum hosted a debate on the issue of same-sex marriage between Andrew Sullivan, a well-known gay political commentator, columnist, and former editor of *The New Republic,* and Gerard Bradley, a professor of law at the University of Notre Dame. The speakers were introduced by E. J. Dionne.

E.J. DIONNE, JR.: Thank you, Luis, and thanks to everybody who worked on putting this together. We'll get to that at the end. When Luis talked about the Forum's trademark tone of civility, I was thinking maybe someday we should just stage a brawl for a change, but then I was thinking that on this discussion especially, brawls are so common that there is an awful lot of room for the kind of discussion we are going to have today between two incredibly thoughtful people.

Andrew is one of the most theologically sophisticated people I know, and this may be the only debate on this topic ever where both sides may invoke St. Augustine, Thomas Aquinas, John Courtney Murray, and Cardinal Ratzinger. I think it is very possible that that could happen in the course of this debate.

Andrew is a senior editor at *The New Republic,* a magazine he edited from 1991 to 1996. He is also a columnist for *Time,* the Washington correspondent for the *Sunday Times of London* and a political blogger at andrewsullivan.com. In fact, I think you were one of the very first of the bloggers in the country. His book *Virtually Normal,* published in 1995, subtitled *An Argument About Homosexuality* was one of the best selling books on gay rights, was translated into five languages and it is really, for those of you who have not read it, a magnificent book. Parts of that book show what I mean when I talk about Andrew's theological sophistication.

He is also the author of *Love Undetectable: Notes on Friendship, Sex and Sur-* *vival,* and he is the editor of the just published "Same-Sex Marriage: Pro and Con: A Reader." He has also written for the *New York Times,* the *Wall Street Journal,* the *Washington Post,* and he has appeared on more than 100 radio and television talk shows, and he is still here to tell the tale.

Born in England, he holds a B.A. in modern history and modern languages from Oxford University. His Ph.D. in political science is from Harvard University where he taught moral and political theory for several semesters. Outspoken on gay rights, he testified before Congress on the Defense of Marriage Act in 1996.

We're also very, very honored to have Gerard Bradley here today. He is a professor of law at Notre Dame University, where he has taught since 1992. A noted scholar in constitutional law, as well as in the area of law and religion, he teaches in Notre Dame's trial advocacy program, long considered to be among the top 10 such programs in the country. His publications include *Catholicism, Liberalism and Communitarianism, Church-State Relations in America,* and many articles in law journals and in the National Review.

Recently he authored the amicus brief in the *Lawrence v. Texas* sodomy case on behalf of Focus on the Family and the Family Research Council. He helped draft the proposed constitutional amendment defining marriage, and he is co-editor of *Same-Sex Attraction: A Parent's Guide.* He served as director of Notre Dame's Natural Law Institute and as co-editor of the institute's *American Journal of Jurisprudence.* He has served there since 1996. His wonderful list of achievements includes being the former president of the Fellowship of Catholic Scholars, vice president of the American Public Philosophy Institute, a member of the board of advisers of the Cardinal Newman Society, chair of the

Federalist Society's Religious Liberties Practice Group—I could go on and on, but you get the picture.

This is an excellent pair. What we'll do here is have each one talk for about 15 minutes, I'm going to pose a couple of annoying questions to each of them, and then we will very quickly go to the audience. We very much want you to join this discussion early on, and I will just reserve the right to continue to ask annoying questions as we go along.

Andrew, bless you for being here. Thank you very much.

ANDREW SULLIVAN: Excuse me for my hobbling. I normally attribute my inconsistencies and incoherencies to general muddleheadedness and human imperfection, but today I have another culprit: Vicodin. I just had a hernia "repaired," the most euphemistic term I've heard in my life—(laughter)—and they promised me, "Oh, you'll be up and running within a couple of days." And here I am. I can't even blog, let alone run. Those of you who know how addicted I am to blogging will understand how profound a sacrifice that has been. And I wondered, Gerry (sp), could you possibly pass me the water just so that I can—thank you so much.

I want to make today just a few brief arguments in the small time allotted and then hope to have a conversation. Most of the arguments I'm going to discuss, I think, are going to be what could broadly be called conservative arguments. This debate has become polarized in the last year or so between what has been described as a conservative camp and a liberal camp, and I think that it is a much more complicated and interesting topic than that would imply. I come at this from a variety of viewpoints, but one of the viewpoints I do come from is definitely a conservative one, and I believe that the ability to integrate homosexual citizens and family members into their own society and into their own families is an absolutely critical moral challenge for this generation and for future ones. This is fundamentally the argument for allowing all citizens to enter the institution of civil marriage. It is at root a very pro-family argument.

People tend to think that homosexuals are born under a Guthrie bush somewhere near Castro Street in San Francisco. They pop up out of the womb already in a leather harness on the back of a motorbike, or pop out of the womb with an absolutely unerring sense of what drapes will go with which wallpaper. But the reality, of course, is that gay people are born everywhere. It's a remarkable fact of this minority that it is absolutely endemic to the society and, in fact, endemic to every society that has ever existed. Gay people come from and live in and grow up in heterosexual families. Unlike any other minority, they are absolutely integrated into the broader society from the minute that they are born.

The notion that these people should leave their homes at a certain point to go out into the broader world and then find that their parents have actually changed the locks and thrown away the keys, and when they want to come back into their own families as fully-fledged members of those families, as married couples, they're denied entrance back in. To tear families apart in this way, to tell one sibling among many that they cannot have the same ritual, the same process of integration into their own family, is a terribly destructive element in the stability and maturity and love that every family, I believe, should uphold.

It's also, alongside many other traditionally conservative arguments, an argument for integration, not for Balkanization. I'm one of those people who don't believe that human beings should be cordoned off into certain categories by their identity, whether it be black, or female, or Latino, or Jewish, or gay, or any of the other appellations that we have managed to bring to this complicated debate about identity. I think, in general, that so far as we possibly can, we should treat people as individuals, regardless of their attributes, regardless of their identities, and that our entire political system traditionally has insisted upon treating people as individuals before we treat them as gay people.

I made a point once of talk of a new phenomenon called "as-a's." These people are people who start every sentence with the word "As-a," as in "As a gay person I'd like to say," "As a black lesbian disabled person, I'd like to say," "As a white male I'd like"—Well, as a human being, I believe that all human beings are made in the image of God, and, as citizens, deserve simply the same treatment from their own government that every other citizen demands and assumes. I see no reason why every citizen shouldn't be treated the same way, and I see very many good reasons why a whole group of citizens should not be not just denied this, but cordoned off in the very Constitution and told that they do not and can never have the same rights as everybody else.

I also don't believe in setting up institutions that require different standards from different people. I don't believe in setting up fake or euphemistic institutions like civil unions or domestic partnership that somehow demand fewer responsibilities and fewer rights than traditional marriage. There's a phrase for having lower standards for particular minorities; it's a phrase coined by the president of the United States. It's called "the soft bigotry of low expectations." I do not see why any group in our society should be subjected to that soft bigotry.

There are some who argue that marriage alone is the exception to all these general principles because marriage is about procreation, and, by definition, homosexuals, or two homosexuals, whether they be two women or two men, cannot procreate and therefore are barred from marriage. But, of course, as every court that's had to deal with this has recognized, the minute you bring that up in a civil context, you find that the state already does give marriage licenses willy-nilly to people who cannot procreate, do not wish to procreate, have never procreated, and are not interested in procreating. The loophole in this law is so big you could drive a huge lesbian Mack truck right through it.

The point is also that this is not some tiny fringe of exceptions. If you look at married households in the United States, you will find a majority of married households, a small majority, are households without children. Also, a quarter of same-sex couples already have children. It seems to me that the procreation argument falls apart legally as soon as you recognize it is not a criterion for civil marriage upheld for heterosexuals. It fails socially and culturally because in our culture at this time, procreation is not understood to be an essential part of what it is to be married.

I'd like to appeal also to simple common sense among conservative people. Gay people exist. They have always existed. They always will exist. They are a fact of human society, of human life, of human nature. It just so happens that it's taken millennia for this tiny minority, excluded by a very fundamental fact, to have managed to screw up their courage to talk about who they actually are, why they're not freaks, why they are human beings, why the same need for love, and companionship, and friendship, and support, and institutional structures applies to them as human beings, too.

These people are around. They exist; they're in your families, they're among your friends. They're not ashamed anymore.

They've been through enormous trials over the last few years. They've been through one of the most horrifying epidemics that any community has suffered in a very long time, losing up to a third of a million people in a small community. And through all of this, rather than seeking further radicalization, rather than succumbing to the possibilities of bitterness and anger, this group has said, "Let us turn this experience into one that is positive, let us rejoin families, let us become fully part of our society. Let us contribute as equals to the country and society in which we all belong."

And this burgeoning group of people, this natural constituency for people of conservative bent, for people who believe in small government, and freedom, and treating people equally and with dignity, they're told by those very people, "Sorry, go away. We don't want you. We don't need you. You sicken us. You appall us. The very concept that you might be able to commit yourself to one another in love and fidelity is so sickening and outrageous to us that we're prepared to amend the very Constitution of the United States to make sure you are never under the illusion that you are an equal person or an equal citizen."

It strikes me as one of the great tragedies of our current society that a group with so many aspirations, so much potential, so much eagerness to become a part of this family, should have the door slammed, violently in some instances, in their faces.

I would like, very briefly, in conclusion, to deal with the federal marriage amendment. It is absolutely, under any circumstances, it seems to me, unnecessary. In this country, the states have always historically dealt with the matter of civil marriage. No other institution, except for the egregious example in 1996 with the Defense of Marriage Act, has ever deemed it necessary to intervene in every state's right to define marriage. I thought that conservatism was about defending the rights of states. Not today's conservatism, which holds hostage all its old principles about limited government, about states' rights, and about protecting the Constitution in order to placate a very small minority of religious people.

Secondly, it strikes me that the Constitution should only be amended under extreme circumstances. It should only be amended if very obvious constitutional and procedural matters are at stake, things like who is in line for the presidency, things like how do we arrange the Senate, things that have to do with the constitutional structure that we live in. To resolve extremely emotional, divisive, and polarizing social questions by trying to force them into the Constitution itself is to do damage not only to the fabric of our society, it is to do terrible damage to the Constitution by using it as an instrument of social policy. We all know the polls on this issue. The country is divided very evenly and very deeply about whether to amend the Constitution of the United States. That in itself is an argument not to do it, that in itself is an argument not to use the Constitution to divide a country where a Constitution is precisely designed and required to bring it together.

Moreover, there is no danger of one state's civil marriages being forced upon other states against their will. There has always been a policy in this country called the "public policy exception," in which individual states can say they do not recognize the marriages from another state, insofar as those marriages violate the public policy of the second state. That has always been the case. That's why for over a hundred years we had a patchwork of laws throughout the country on interracial marriage where an interracial couple could travel across the country, be married, unmarried, married, unmarried, married, unmarried, depending which state line they crossed. We allowed that to happen for over a hundred years, and the society didn't fall apart. Those laws and that understanding still exist.

If you aren't secure in that understanding, there is something called the Defense of Marriage Act in which the Congress of the United States stamped its foot in 1996 and said not only is this already the case, we emphatically underline that in federal law.

Thirdly, 37 individual states have already passed their own Defense of Marriage Acts to make it absolutely clear what their public policy exception is. The notion that we should advance an amendment to the federal Constitution when not even in the beginning of this process through the courts has begun to take place, when we don't have a single case yet of a civil marriage license in this country applying from one state to another, when we don't yet have a single case of a single civil marriage existing in one state, when in that one state there's a potential after two years of those civil marriages being converted into civil unions anyway, such a move is not only extraordinarily radical, it is extraordinarily unnecessary.

So I finish by saying this: On the principle of family, on the principle of equality, on the principle of constitutional protection, on the principle of allowing democracies to debate openly and fully and in good time the consequences of a major and important social change, there is every reason to support including everybody in the American family and every reason to oppose writing into the very Constitution of the United States—a Constitution that upholds equality for all citizens—that one group of citizens— this is the transcript of a talk—this is what he said. Think how chilling this would be for

anybody, if one group of citizens would be denied fundamental, basic constitutional rights. Using the Constitution to single out a group of people for discrimination; it really is the most radical attack upon the Constitution of the United States that we've seen, certainly in our lifetimes, and it's one that I think all people, regardless of how they feel about the question of same-sex marriage, need to stand up against and fight with every fiber of their being.

Thank you.

(Applause.)

MR. DIONNE: Thank you so much, Andrew. Now, Gerard Bradley.

GERARD V. BRADLEY: Well, I move to the microphone rather quickly–not to prove to you that I've not had a hernia operation, at least not recently, but I haven't had one recently. But, actually, I'd like to hurry through my remarks because, frankly, I can't wait to hear some of E.J.'s annoying questions, and also because who knows what'll happen during the question period. Perhaps that brawl that he so wistfully imagines will actually break out then.

But I am grateful for the opportunity, the invitation from the Pew Forum, because it promises a bit of a respite for me. Like Andrew Sullivan, I've not been too shy about tackling, in public forums such as this, the question of same-sex marriage head on: Should we have it or not? I've even criticized Andrew Sullivan's views here and there, and he's kindly returned the favor. In one article—one of his columns in *The New Republic* several months ago, perhaps as much as a year ago—he described myself and my friend and collaborator at Princeton, Robert George, as—and this is close to a quote—two of the most orthodox Catholic scholars on the planet. Now, however it was intended—

MR. DIONNE: That was a compliment from Andrew. (Laughter.)

MR. BRADLEY: Well, we haven't rehearsed this, but however it was intended, I took it as a compliment. Now, more recently Andrew looked at the authors of the Federal Marriage Amendment and described them as "radical natural-law jurisprudes." I confess, again, I find myself complimented.

So I proceed to the body of my remarks, but noting that today's conversation is really more a conversation about the same-sex debate, a conversation you might call a second-order conversation about certain kinds of arguments, certain kinds of contributions to the same-sex marriage debate, and those elements or second-order features are really having to do with religion: theological argument, what are the religious convictions lying behind positions people take on this issue, and whether, or what role religious pluralism should play in this debate.

So I turn to a second-order conversation, this conversation for analyzing the conversation about same-sex marriage. Now, the questions that are posed to me in the invitation are important questions. Probably the substance of them has been at the heart of English-speaking political philosophies since World War II. The substance of these questions—religion, public argument, civil law—those things have been at the heart or near the heart of constitutional law since World War II as well.

Now, my judgment is that with specific reference to the same-sex marriage question, second-order conversational constraints or doctrines or norms about religion, the public square, civil law, don't have much traction upon the debate. I know that these matters, these second-order constraints, are often conceived with the view of protecting some divisive moral question from a head-on confrontation with political processes, and that is to insulate the body politic from such divisive questions that sometimes these second-order constraints are called into being. But I don't think it works here. I don't think there's any way to escape a confrontation with the question about the reality of marriage, what really is marriage, if marriage is really something at all.

But back to the matters at hand. Religious convictions which lie behind deeply held beliefs about marriage, to answer the question descriptively, would require much more time and an encyclopedic knowledge of American religion. I leave that aside. I should like to make two points that are less descriptive about this question, posed to me in the invitation—the convictions behind deeply held beliefs about marriage.

It seems to me we can say that characteristically—again, characteristically, not universally—but characteristically, religious believers, at least the believers that we see in our society, think of religion and marriage as a matter of value added—transcendent value added; that is to say, to the natural reality of the common understanding of what they think is noble about marriage by virtue of reason and experience, they find in their religious belief some additional significance, meaning, or point.

Now, take the Catholic Church, for example. Catholics understand marriage as a kind of natural moral reality but also as a type or representation of Jesus' fidelity to his church, the idea of Christ the bridegroom. But again, I think characteristically, believers add something to what is naturally knowable by marriage, some additional significance, some transcendent matter or some other kind of signification that arises from their beliefs. Now, in our constitutional order, such additional significance as transcendent value added really is supposed to be invisible to the lawmaker. It's beyond the competence of public authority to really care about. That is to say, even under free exercise doctrine, just to speak about the law in particular for a moment, if a matter is generally permitted it may not be treated differently for those people who attach some religious significance to it, and if a matter is generally prohibited, people aren't allowed to do it because of the religious significance they attach to it.

Okay, second, I don't think the transcendent attributes of marriage that I'm describing in very general terms are any part of the political program or the public arguments made by believers in favor of preserving traditional marriage. At least as far as I can tell, in the self understanding of those people making the arguments in public about traditional marriage, they do not understand themselves to be making theological arguments. They understand themselves to be making arguments based upon reason and experience. They could be wrong about what reason and experience show, but they certainly do offer their arguments as matters of reason and common experience.

Okay, second question: more generally, theological arguments in the public square. It seems to me that in the last 20 years or so, after very heady times from between around '75 to '85, and during that time there were many comprehensive doctrines about keeping religion out of the public square found in scholarly journals, even high journalism, and it was probably the high tide—that is, 1985 or so was the high tide of a privatization project in the United States Supreme Court. Again, I think 1985 marked the high watermark of the Supreme Court's attempt to keep religion out of public life, to make religion private, and in that sense to have a secular public realm.

Over the last 20 years or so, not only in court but also in political philosophy and in high journalism, we've seen a retreat from that sort of zenith of privatization. I think now what we can say about theological argument in the public square, we can say only about gross or clear cases, and I'll offer a few norms for theological argument in the public square taken more or less faithfully from Supreme Court doctrine, but a few norms about theological argument.

One I've already mentioned, that where people make arguments in the public square that they offer on the basis of reason and experience, but arguments about which they hold some theological convictions as well, I think those theological convictions operate not at all in the public square. This is more or less the meaning of our Free Exercise Clause. The mere coincidence of some legal norm with religious convictions of even a great number—even a majority of people—is neither here nor there. It is mere coincidence of religion and civil law—it is meaningless. Also, a law should be deemed to have a secular basis—that is, a constitutionally permissible basis—unless the basis for it is entirely religious. That is to say—and this I think is a faithful rendition of Supreme Court doctrine as it presently stands—if there is a secular basis for a law, then it is constitutionally permissible. It is impermissible only if it is entirely rooted in theology.

Then finally, as a special category of acts—and you might say norms about acts that are intrinsically or entirely religious—that is to say, in the law there is a special category in norms about prayer, worship, other acts which have no secular or non-religious analogue. But I believe that none of these rules for conversation in the public square, none of these norms about theological argument, have any traction on the debate about same-sex marriage. It seems to me again that in the course of the public argument over same-sex marriage, defenders of traditional marriage are not relying upon what might be called strictly religious sources or entirely religious reasons, just to illustrate a little bit more, or explain by way of illustration.

I don't think believers in the public square are appealing to the authority of private knowledge, including revelation, or to the authority of religious texts, or to the authority of a particular religious figure. Now, to the extent you do see that in the public square, I think what one wants to say in that context is not so much that it violates a norm of conversation but rather that those are not reasons at all. In other words, we don't need a rule that excludes such reasons, so called, from serious consideration because such appeals have no force upon the minds of people who don't already share the commitment to that authority: the sacred book, the high religious figure. That is to say, such appeals to private sources of knowledge or to authority just aren't reasons at all. And I think that's an adequate response to such arguments in the public square.

Finally, I think the third question posed in the program, the invitation, goes something like this: it's about pluralism and how it affects our decisions concerning change and marriage laws. I render the third question, at least in substance, this way: does our increasing religious pluralism influence—I suppose I should say, should it influence, and if so, how—our resolution of the marriage question before the House, the same-sex marriage question.

Again, I think the third question in substance is, "Should our increasing religious pluralism influence our resolution of this matter, and if so, how?" Well, the answer is, I think not at all—none, nada, zilch. And that's because I doubt whether our religious pluralism is increasing in any significant way, and I'm almost sure that no such increase in religious pluralism is at the root of our debate over marriage.

How do I say that, or why do I say that? Well, the movement to change marriage laws to allow for same-sex marriage is at least a decade old. I think it's surely not more than 20 years old. It burst on the scene in a big way about 10 years ago. For discussion's sake, let's stipulate it goes back 20 years. I don't see that there's been any significant increase in religious pluralism during that time, and surely none at the root of the movement, whether the movement began in 1993 or 1983.

Now, at the root of the movement to legally recognize same-sex marriage is not religion but rather culture. More specifically, the argument that I take most seriously is the argument posed by Andrew Sullivan in his remarks today. It's an argument that anybody defending traditional marriage has to reckon with. It's an argument from culture and it's an argument from law, but the argument goes something like this: given what marriage has already become in our law, what it already is in our law, and how it is lived, how marriage is lived, inhabited, carried out, by a very large number of married couples in our society, it is unfair to exclude same-sex partners from that legal status.

This argument builds not upon religion or even upon some peculiarly gay ideology, but rather begins with what you might call the straight world's rebellion against marriage. That's a rebellion that began probably in the mid-1960s and continues to the present day. People look at the way many married couples act and seem to think about their marriages, and people look at what many homosexual partners can do and may think about their relationships. You see that many married men and women think of their relationships mainly as an emotional, financial, and sexual partnership involving the mutual conferral of important individual benefits. Proponents of same-sex marriage say that homosexuals and lesbians are quite capable and have demonstrated their capability of entering into such relationships. Such proponents of same-sex marriage conclude that opposition to same-sex marriage is an arbitrary exclusion of persons from the straight marriage club.

Okay, after this short march through the three questions presented in the invitation, I aim to close and get to the annoying part of the program. I may be bold at this point to question the invitation's summary description of our encounter today. The summary description that I have in mind is this: about the legal and policy implications of religiously informed arguments on same-sex marriage; again, the invitation's reference to the legal and policy implications of religiously informed arguments on same-sex marriage.

I submit in closing it might well be better to put it the other way around. Why not think, rather, that norms about religiously informed arguments are the passengers and not the engine of the train? What I mean is this: if the outcome one is seeking, in politics or law—in a controversy about stem cell research, or cloning, or abortion, or laws against non-marital sexual activity, or some controversy about including non-Darwinian accounts of human origins in public school curricula, or a controversy about pornography or same-sex marriage—within that controversy one's own position can be advanced against opposition, which can be plausibly styled to be religious. One is certainly tempted to develop side constraints, second-order norms, about religious arguments. This need not be rank opportunism, but it could be more than that. This could be also a way of thinking about the development of the whole idea of a secular public square, whether going back to World War II and its immediate aftermath.

What the idea then was—I think it was that our democracy, our democratic way of life, is actually not a reference to political mechanisms but really to a political culture, to the kind of person who would live and come to be reared in that political culture. One might find, going back, that a theory of democracy gave us, shortly after the war, a secular public ground, because it was thought then that democracy presupposed a kind of pragmatic spirit, a kind of commitment to scientific ways of understanding the world, and relativism and morals. And during that time, many people—I think many people on the Supreme Court saw in religion, especially the Roman Catholic Church, an authoritarian personality wed to a deep and unwavering commitment to immutable or objective moral norms.

So I submit to you that going back to the war, shortly thereafter secularism was midwifed by a democratic theory or a theory of democracy, and perhaps more recently—and this is my final comment—our understanding of how to justify, sustain, maintain liberty now seems to be at odds with deep and abiding commitment to objective morality, which commitment probably is much more commonly associated with traditional religious roots.

Think back to '92 when the Casey abortion case decision and the so-called mystery passage in which the heart of liberty is a very deep and strong subjectivism and morals, the idea of making up your own moral universe—now, a theory of liberty of that sort is going to have implications for the role of religion in public life insofar as one makes the additional judgment, which I think is a safe one to make, that at least traditional religious people are more or less committed to an objective morality and do indeed reject subjectivism and morals.

THE ETHICAL DIMENSIONS OF MEDICINE
The Ethical Dimensions of Medical Decisions

As you may have read in the papers or seen on television, jobs are scarce in the academic world, especially for scholars in fields like philosophy. You do not see many ads these days looking for epistemologists or logicians. But strange as it may seem, in recent years, we *have* begun to see help wanted ads for *ethicists,* specifically for *medical ethicists*. Mind you, these are not ads placed by out-of-work Ph.D.'s in philosophy, hoping to snag some sort of employment in the health or business world. These are ads placed by serious hospitals or health maintenance organizations that say they will pay good money—very often more than you can make teaching philosophy—for men and women who are professional ethics experts. In a minute, we will try to figure out what sort of expertise an ethicist might possibly have that anyone would want to pay good money for. But first, let us try to understand why those hospitals and health maintenance organizations are so eager to put an ethicist on the payroll.

As we have just seen in the first part of this chapter, philosophers who write ethical theory talk rather abstractly about the moral dilemmas we face. When they do mention particular moral choices, the examples tend to be rather hastily made up, and very far from real life—the little story I invented about the young man deciding whether to leave home, for instance. That is, I guess, a genuine moral decision that many young people have to make, but surely no one faced with that choice has ever made up a table of plus and minus pleasures and pains like the one on page 176. Just to give you an idea of how far out the examples can get in academic ethical theory, let me tell you about one that is all the rage these days in philosophy journals.

Suppose—these authors ask us—you found yourself in a situation in which you could save five lives by killing one person. Should you do it? For example, imagine you are standing on a little hill, overlooking a trolley line, and you see a trolley careening out of control and about to go over a cliff. You can see that the only way to stop the trolley and save those five people is to throw something onto the tracks to derail the trolley before it gets to the cliff. You look around for something big enough to throw, and the only thing you see is an innocent little five-year-old girl. If you pick her up and throw her onto the tracks, you will kill her and save the five lives. If you do nothing, she will live and the five will die. Which should you do?

No kidding. This really is the sort of thing ethical theorists talk about! Now most of us never find ourselves in this sort of situation. I guess maybe someone, somewhere, has actually faced such a choice, but it is not your average, everyday, make-a-decision-and-go-home-to-dinner sort of choice. So I personally would be inclined to say that ethical theory written about "examples" like that one cannot be taken seriously.

But the strange thing is that there *are* real decisions just as weird, just as impossible, just as gut wrenching as that one, and there are thousands upon thousands of people who face them every day of their professional lives. I am speaking, of course, about doctors.

Let us talk about a real example, not a kooky, made-up one. Consider the problems faced daily by the hospital committee charged with deciding which patient will be put on the list for kidney dialysis when a slot opens up. This is not a hypothetical philosophical exercise conducted in a classroom for the purpose of illustrating certain general principles of ethical theory. It is a regular committee decision that results in one patient getting a chance to live, and other patients being forced to wait, and in some cases, to die. How shall such a committee make its decisions? What should it take into account, and what should it ignore?

Should the committee pay any attention to the age of the patient? For example, should a fourteen-year-old boy, with maybe sixty-five years of life ahead of him, get preference over a seventy-year-old woman who, under the best of circumstances, has only ten years or so left? Should whites be given preference over African Americans, or African Americans over whites? Should rich people be offered a chance to buy their way to the head of the line, perhaps by paying off the poor people ahead of them on the list? If one of the patients has lived a virtuous life and another has been a bad person, should the good person get preference? Should the committee strive for a gender, ethnic, religious, and racial balance? Should they simply say first come, first served? How much weight should be given to the purely medical estimates of the likelihood that the dialysis will keep the patient alive? Suppose a young, virtuous, admirable candidate has little chance of surviving, even with the dialysis, while an old, vicious reprobate has a good chance? Should the patients themselves have some voice in the committee? What about their families? The community at large?

Throughout the 1960s, individual physicians, patient selection committees, and hospitals thus were forced to deal with the medical-moral dilemma of selecting a limited number of medically eligible candidates to receive dialysis, knowing that those patients not chosen would soon die unless a transplant was possible. The type of decision that recurrently had to be made—what many involved ruefully called "playing God"—was as follows: This month our hospital's dialysis unit has space for one new dialysis patient, but there are four medically eligible candidates. How do we select the recipient? Those responsible

RENEE C. FOX, JUDITH P. SWAZEY, AND ELIZABETH M. CAMERON,
Problems in the Treatment of Renal Disease Patients?*

---

*From "Social and Ethical Problems in the Treatment of End-Stage Renal Disease Patients," by Renee C. Fox, Ph.D., Judith P. Swazey, Ph.D., and Elizabeth M. Cameron R.N. © Churchill Livingstone, Philadelphia. Reprinted by permission of the publisher.

for allocating dialysis used a variety of selection methods, which were based on one or more of six principles of social justice that can be used to provide a moral basis for distributing scarce resources.

1. A *meritarian* concept of social justice allocates limited goods or resources to individuals on the basis of their merits or deserts. Merits or deserts, in turn, can be defined by the distributors—for example, a dialysis selection committee—in many ways, such as a person's conduct, achievement, or contributions to society.

2. A *needs* principle seeks to justly allocate a limited resource such as dialysis according to the essential needs of individuals, leaving for further definition the question of what constitutes "essential needs."

3. An *ability* principle distributes a scarce resource on the basis of various criteria concerning an individual's ability. For example, in a fee-for-service system, ability to pay can be the determinant of who receives care, and a selection committee thus could narrow a pool of dialysis candidates by eliminating those who cannot afford to pay for treatment.

4. A principle of *compensatory justice* would distribute resources to those who have previously suffered social wrongs that deprived them of those resources, such as a lack of access to medical care because of a low socioeconomic status. (This is the principle of social justice underlying Medicaid insurance.)

5. A *utilitarian "ethometrics"* principle seeks to provide the greatest benefit or good for the greatest number of persons. This is the principle behind quantitative cost-benefit analyses for the provision of various forms of health care, which often founder in efforts to define what variables should constitute the "greatest good"—for example, economic, personal, social—and to quantitatively calculate noneconomic "goods" such as health status.

6. An *egalitarian* principle of social justice, in American society, is often viewed as the most morally acceptable way to distribute scarce resources. There are, however, many ways to formulate egalitarian principles, and it is seldom easy to specify just what is meant by them and consequently how one should act on them. In the arena of medical care, for example, many hold that we should "provide similar treatment for similar cases," which then leads to a panorama of questions about how one defines "similar treatment" and "similar cases." During the 1960s, a number of dialysis facilities selected patients by random lottery, believing that this form of egalitarian distribution was the fairest, most neutral way of determining who might live when not all could live.

As this brief discussion of the principles of social justice underlying the allocation of dialysis during the 1960s suggests, the need to make such decisions involves a host of complex, painful, medical, moral, and social issues. None involved in selecting dialysis recipients welcomed their task, or were comfortable with the selection methods they adopted. All felt there was no really good way to make such decisions; rather, they sought to find what they felt was the "least worst" selection method.

Needless to say, rationing kidney dialysis is not the only medical problem that raises ethical questions. Let me list just a few of the types of everyday, real-life decisions in which doctors, nurses, patients, family members, hospital administrators, and others are called on to think about the moral dimensions of their situation.

- Rationing scarce medical care of all sorts
- Deciding which patients get heart, kidney, or lung transplants when they become available
- Deciding whether to keep a terminally ill patient alive, even when the patient will never regain consciousness
- Deciding whether to tell a seriously ill patient the truth about his or her medical condition
- Deciding whether to have an abortion
- Deciding whether to perform an abortion
- Deciding whether to assist a patient who wants to die
- Deciding whether to use aborted fetuses for medical research that will save the lives of other patients
- Deciding whether to screen patients for genetically inherited diseases, and whether to tell them the results of the screening
- Deciding whether to use genetic techniques to influence the sex or other characteristics of a fetus
- Deciding whether patients should play a role in choosing their treatment

I think I can say with confidence that *every single person reading this chapter* will face one or more of these situations sometime in his or her life, either personally or in connection with a family member. What can ethical theory tell us that will help us and the medical professionals make better decisions?

Well, let us get one thing clear right away. Philosophers specializing in ethical theory cannot make any of these decisions for us. When your sink is clogged up, you can call a plumber, step back, and let her unclog it. When your battery dies on a winter day, you can call the AAA and have them give you a jump start. But if you are an intensive-care-unit physician trying to decide whether to keep a terminally ill patient alive by heroic means, you cannot call the local university and have it send over an ethicist to take care of the matter.

This should not surprise us. Remember what we learned from Socrates in Chapter 1. *The unexamined life is not worth living.* That is a snappy way of saying that each of us must make his or her own life choices, based on the clearest, most reflective, most critical thinking we can muster. No philosopher, minister, guru, or political ruler can make our life choices for us. And what is true of life in general also is true of the critical life-and-death choices that regularly arise in medicine. What a philosopher can do for us, as Socrates had the great wisdom to recognize almost 2,500 years ago, is to assist us to think better about the choices we must make. As he put it, the philosopher can act as a midwife, assisting at the birth of ideas, but not herself actually producing those ideas. In the remainder of this chapter, I am going to try to play exactly that role. With the help of some selections from the writings of men and women who have thought deeply about the ethical dimensions of medicine, I am going to see whether I can help you to think a bit more clearly about a few of the many critical decisions that we must make in the field of medicine and biotechnology. You will not find any definitive answers here. Instead, if I am successful, you will begin to develop your own ability to look at a problem of medical ethics and see some of the complexities of it. Later in life, when you face one or another of these choices for yourselves, your parents, your children, or your partners, perhaps you will be able to think about it a bit more clearly. That is the most philosophy can do for you, but if the truth be told, that is a great deal.

One brief observation before we begin. Philosophers have been thinking and writing about ethics for two and a half millennia, but the literature devoted to medical ethics is no more than half a century old. There is a good reason for that odd fact. For most of human history, men and women have not been able to do more than say a prayer and hope when serious injury or illness strikes. That is why doctors have from time immemorial taken it as their first principle to do no harm. If you cannot cure the patient, which for most of human history doctors could not, then at least do not make the patient worse.

In this century, however, medical science has suddenly advanced to a point where doctors can very definitely cure patients, whether with antibiotics and other wonder drugs, or with extraordinary surgical procedures, radiation therapy, and other miracles of modern medicine. That is why the average life expectancy for people in relatively wealthy societies has almost doubled in the past century. Now, once you *can* do something, there is no avoiding the question of whether you *should* do it. If a patient in an irreversible coma is going to die, regardless of what you do, then there is nothing for it but arrange for the funeral. But if medical science can keep an irreversibly unconscious patient alive for years, as it now can, then we are forced to ask whether it should do so. And immediately, the hard questions about cost, scarce medical resources, the feelings of the family, and all the rest come up and just will not go away. So, in an odd way, medical ethics is a by-product of medicine's great success.

Now let us turn to some case studies. I have chosen three quite different sorts of problems to suggest something of the scope of the subject of medical ethics. These are: Is it ever morally right to withhold food and water from a hopelessly ill patient, which raises the issue of the moral principles that should guide the caregiver; Should we allow the purchase and sale of human organs for organ transplants, which raises many questions about the sanctity of the human body and the limits of the marketplace; and What should the doctor tell the patient, which raises issues of the rights of the patient and the responsibilities of the physician.

Withholding Food and Water

Doctors, nurses, orderlies, and hospital administrators are all trained to be care*givers.* When a patient is admitted to a hospital, they are supposed to bring all their knowledge, skill, and energy to bear on caring for that patient—curing him or her if possible, but at the very least alleviating pain and suffering. No doubt doctors and nurses sometimes fall short of that ideal. Anyone who has ever spent time as a patient in a hospital will have stories to tell of bad stretches in the middle of the night when no one answered the call button for what seemed like hours, or unfeeling attendants who were insensitive to one's pain. Nevertheless, I think we can all agree that hospitals, doctors, nurses, and attendants at least try to live up to their ideal of being caregivers. No ordinary doctor or nurse *tries* to make a patient worse, after all.

So what are we to think of the many, many cases in which the caregivers of a terminally, hopelessly ill patient decide to withhold care, so that the patient can die? And, what is even more important, what are the caregivers themselves to think of situations in which withholding care seems to be the right thing to do? Can it ever be right to withhold something as basic as food and water? Are there cases in which doctors should literally starve a patient to death? If medical science knows how to keep a patient alive, should it not do so?

First of all, let us be absolutely clear about the nature of the cases. We are talking, for example, about a newborn infant who lacks organs necessary for survival and can be kept alive only by continual, heroic, life-saving measures. We are talking about a terminally ill brain tumor patient who has slipped into an irreversible coma. We are talking about a patient so severely burned over so much of her body that doctors are unable to perform skin grafts or other procedures and cannot even find a way to keep the patient alive without terrible pain for very long. We are very definitely *not* talking about a conscious, coherent, viable patient who is capable of communicating that he or she wants to be kept alive.

What sorts of ethical considerations arise in cases like these? Let me briefly sketch just a few of the ethical questions that doctors and nurses must ask themselves as they decide what to do.

a. First, there is the issue of *trust*. Hospitals are social institutions that exist for the purpose of caring for the sick. When you enter a hospital as a patient, you expect—you have a *right* to expect—that everyone in that hospital will try to help you get well, or at least that they will do what they can to enable you to suffer less. Even if you are brought into the hospital unconscious—say, after a car accident—you have a right to assume that the doctors and nurses will be caregivers, regardless of the fact that you were not able to talk to them and tell them that you want to be cared for. Now, there is nothing in caregiving more basic than providing food and water. The doctors may not know how to treat whatever is wrong with you, but at least they can give you the food and water you need to stay alive. So it would seem that a hospital and its caregivers violate a fundamental principle of trust when they deliberately withhold food and water from a patient.

b. Second, there is the issue of *knowledge*. In my description of the cases, I assume that doctors know with certainty that a patient cannot survive. I talk about a "terminally ill" patient in an "irreversible coma." But the most any doctor can honestly say is that it is extremely probable that the patient is terminally ill, and highly unlikely that the patient will come out of the coma. Is it right for doctors to withhold food and water from a patient on the basis of what is, after all, imperfect and incomplete knowledge?

c. Third, there is the issue of *professional principles*. Doctors and nurses undergo long and rigorous training as caregivers. They are taught to make truly heroic personal sacrifices in order to provide care to their patients. Doctors are taught to work long hours when patients need them. Nurses are taught to check and recheck medications, in order to make absolutely certain that a patient is not harmed by a mistaken dosage. As they study and prepare for careers as caregivers, they learn to take personal pride in their dedication to the welfare of their patients. All of us grumble from time to time about our doctors, but when someone collapses in a public place and the call goes up "Is there a doctor here?" we all feel that inner relief when a woman steps forward and says, quietly, "I am a doctor." Now men and women who have been trained in this way feel a deep inward conflict when called upon to deny care rather than to give it. If society tells them that it is all right to withhold something as basic as food and water, will we be damaging the very professional principles that we admire so much in doctors and nurses? Will we be undermining the training on which all of us rely when we become patients?

So there are a number of very powerful moral reasons for condemning the withholding of food and water, even in cases that appear terminal, irreversible, hopeless. These reasons involve just the sort of autonomy and respect for persons that we saw Kant emphasizing so strongly. But there are also a number of very powerful moral considerations that weigh on the other side, in favor of the withholding of food and water. And here too, some of the abstract issues of ethical theory that we took a look at in the first part of this chapter come into play. Consider just a few of them:

a. First, we must confront, once again, the problem of *allocating scarce resources*. Terminally ill patients require a great deal of skilled care just to keep them alive. The hospital beds they occupy, the nursing care they use, the doctor's time they need—all of those resources could be used to treat some other patient who has a chance of recovering. So long as we focus just on the terminally ill patient, it may seem heartless or even immoral to withhold the food and water needed for a few more days or weeks of life. But health care professionals know all too well that there are other patients waiting to be treated, and they have responsibilities to those people as well.

b. Second, we must recognize the finiteness, *the limitations of medical science*. The great successes of the past century have made it easier for all of us to forget how little we can really do in the face of inevitable death. All people die, regardless of the heroic efforts of doctors and nurses. Isn't it better to accept that fact and find ways to make death dignified, even meaningful? Desperately keeping alive an infant born without the internal organs needed for survival is not *caregiving*. It is a kind of arrogance, a refusal to acknowledge the human condition. If doctors are being taught to keep patients alive at all costs, regardless of the patient's prospect for survival, then perhaps we should change medical education to include a dignified, resigned recognition of human mortality.

c. Third, we must pay more attention to the *needs of the loved ones*. All human life is a cycle of childhood, adulthood, old age, and death. True human maturity, as Erik Erikson observed in his classic work *Childhood and Society,* is the recognition that "an individual life is the accidental coincidence of but one life cycle with but one segment of history; and that for [us] all human integrity stands or falls with the one style of integrity of which [we] partake." In some situations, the very best thing a doctor can do for the patient's family and friends is to help them accept the death as an inevitable part of life, so that they can learn from the death and live their own lives with greater dignity and integrity.

All of these powerful considerations, pro and con, confront medical professionals each time they must deal with a patient for whom they can do no more. Set out like this in a textbook, (a) (b) (c) on one side, (a) (b) (c) on the other, they may look abstract and theoretical. But when you are a doctor or a nurse, standing in an intensive care unit looking down at a woman in a coma, or a hopelessly burned man, or an infant on a respirator, these are anything but abstract and theoretical.

What follows is an extended excerpt from a widely read treatment of the problem of withholding food and water, written by a professor of medicine at Dartmouth Medical School and a professor of religious studies at the University of Virginia. As you will see, they are painfully conscious of the arguments on both sides of the issue, although they are not afraid to draw some conclusions at the end.

JOANNE LYNN AND JAMES F. CHILDRESS,

Must Patients Always Be Given Food and Water?*

Many people die from the lack of food or water. For some, this lack is the result of poverty or famine, but for others it is the result of disease or deliberate decision. In the past, malnutrition and dehydration must have accompanied nearly every death that followed an illness of more than a few days. Most dying patients do not eat much on their own, and nothing could be done for them until the first flexible tubing for instilling food or other liquid into the stomach was developed about a hundred years ago. Even then, the procedure was so scarce, so costly in physician and nursing time, and so poorly tolerated that it was used only for patients who clearly could benefit. With the advent of more reliable and efficient procedures in the past few decades, these conditions can be corrected or ameliorated in nearly every patient who would otherwise be malnourished or dehydrated. In fact, intravenous lines and nasogastric tubes have become common images of hospital care.

Providing adequate nutrition and fluids is a high priority for most patients, both because they suffer directly from inadequacies and because these deficiencies hinder their ability to overcome other diseases. But are there some patients who need not receive these treatments? This question has become a prominent public policy issue in a number of recent cases. In May 1981, in Danville, Illinois, the parents and the physician of newborn conjoined twins with shared abdominal organs decided not to feed these children. Feeding and other treatments were given after court intervention, though a grand jury refused to indict the parents.[1] Later that year, two physicians in Los Angeles discontinued intravenous nutrition to a patient who had severe brain damage after an episode involving loss of oxygen following routine surgery. Murder charges were brought, but the hearing judge dismissed the charges at a preliminary hearing. On appeal, the charges were reinstated and remanded for trial.[2]

In April 1982, a Bloomington, Indiana, infant who had tracheoesophageal fistula and Down syndrome was not treated or fed, and he died after two courts ruled that the decision was proper but before all appeals could be heard.[3] When the federal government then

*From: "Must Patients Always Be Given Food and Water?" by Joanne Lynn and James F. Childress. From Part IV:2: *Terminating Treatment for the Terminally Ill* in *Life Choices: A Hastings Center Introduction to Bioethics,* pp. 201–203 and 211. Edited by Joseph H. Howell and William F. Sale. © Georgetown University Press. Reprinted with permission from the publisher.

moved to ensure that such infants would be fed in the future,[4] the Surgeon General, Dr. C. Everett Koop, initially stated that there is never adequate reason to deny nutrition and fluids to a newborn infant.

While these cases were before the public, the nephew of Claire Conroy, an elderly incompetent woman with several serious medical problems, petitioned a New Jersey court for authority to discontinue her nasogastric tube feeding. Although the intermediate appeals court had reversed the ruling,[5] the trial court held that he had this authority since the evidence indicated that the patient would not have wanted such treatment and that its value to her was doubtful.

In all these dramatic cases and in many more that go unnoticed, the decision is made to deliberately withhold food or fluid known to be necessary for the life of the patient. Such decisions are unsettling. There is now widespread consensus that sometimes a patient is best served by not undertaking or continuing certain treatments that would sustain life, especially if these entail substantial suffering.[6] But food and water are so central to an array of human emotions that it is almost impossible to consider them with the same emotional detachment that one might feel toward a respirator or a dialysis machine.

Nevertheless, the question remains: should it ever be permissible to withhold or withdraw food and nutrition? The answer in any real case should acknowledge the psychological contiguity between feeding and loving and between nutritional satisfaction and emotional satisfaction. Yet this acknowledgment does not resolve the core question.

Some have held that it is intrinsically wrong not to feed another. The philosopher G.E.M. Anscombe contends: "For wilful starvation there can be no excuse. The same can't be said quite without qualification about failing to operate or to adopt some courses of treatment."[7] But the moral issues are more complex than Anscombe's comment suggests. Does correcting nutritional deficiencies always improve patients' well-being? What should be our reflective moral response to withholding or withdrawing nutrition? What moral principles are relevant to our reflections? What medical facts about ways of providing nutrition are relevant? And what policies should be adopted by the society, hospitals, and medical and other health care professionals?

In our effort to find answers to these questions, we will concentrate upon the care of patients who are incompetent to make choices for themselves.

Patients who are competent to determine the course of their therapy may refuse any and all interventions proposed by others, as long as their refusals do not seriously harm or impose unfair burdens upon others.[8] A competent patient's decision regarding whether or not to accept the provision of food and water by medical means such as tube feeding or intravenous alimentation is unlikely to raise questions of harm or burden to others.

What then should guide those who must decide about nutrition for a patient who cannot decide? As a start, consider the standard by which other medical decisions are made: one should decide as the incompetent person would have if he or she were competent, when that is possible to determine, and advance that person's interests in a more generalized sense when individual preferences cannot be known. . . .

Our conclusion—that patients or their surrogates, in close collaboration with their physicians and other caregivers and with careful assessment of the relevant information, can correctly decide to forego the provision of medical treatments intended to correct malnutrition and dehydration in some circumstances—is quite limited. Concentrating on incompetent patients, we have argued that in most cases such patients will be best served by providing nutrition and fluids. Thus, there should be a presumption in favor of providing nutrition and fluids as part of the broader presumption to provide means that prolong life. But this presumption may be rebutted in particular cases.

We do not have enough information to be able to determine with clarity and conviction whether withholding or withdrawing nutrition and hydration was justified in the cases that have occasioned public concern, though it seems likely that the Danville and Bloomington babies should have been fed and that Claire Conroy should not.

It is never sufficient to rule out "starvation" categorically. The question is whether the obligation to act in the patient's best interests was discharged by withholding or withdrawing particular medical treatments. All we have claimed is that nutrition and hydration by medical means need not always be provided. Sometimes they may not be in accord with the patient's wishes or interests. Medical nutrition and hydration do not appear to be distinguishable in any morally relevant way from other life-sustaining medical treatments that may on occasion be withheld or withdrawn.

The Buying and Selling of Human Organs

There have always been ways of making up for the loss of a leg, by means of crutches, or even of a hand, by means of the sort of metal hook that Captain Hook sported. But until quite recently, there has been nothing that medical science could do to provide some sort of substitute for one of the many vital internal organs the body needs to live. If a kidney, a lung, a liver, or a heart failed, the patient either died, or, if the body had two of them (such as a kidney), got along with the remaining organ. If both of a patient's kidneys failed, then life depended on the dialysis machine forever.

In recent years, however, all that has changed. Miraculous as it seems to someone my age, who can remember a time when transplants were a matter of science fiction and fantasy, doctors can now actually take a functioning kidney, heart, liver, or lung out of one person and put it into a patient whose own organ has failed. In countless cases, men, women, and even tiny babies have received organ transplants that allow them to live reasonably full, functioning lives. No longer is it only the mad Dr. Frankenstein, in his Transylvanian castle, who snatches body parts from cadavers and constructs a monster out of them. Now we see medical technicians rushing to a helicopter and transporting a still-warm heart to a hospital hundreds of miles away where it is put into the chest of a dying patient and sewn up.

Well, as we have already observed, once doctors know how to do something heroic and technologically extraordinary, questions arise for which we seem to have no very good answers. Organ transplants are no exception. Here are just some of the previously unimaginable questions that must now be confronted and dealt with by doctors, nurses, hospital administrators, and legislators on a daily basis:

- Should we permit organ transplants?
- Who should get an organ when it becomes available?
- Should individuals be permitted, encouraged, even required to consent to the donation of their organs after they die?
- Should a market price be put on human organs?
- Should individuals be permitted to sell their organs to those needing transplants?
- Should doctors be permitted to harvest organs from dead people without their prior consent? (I really hate that use of the word "harvest," but that is the way people talk about organ transplants.)

All of these questions pose profound ethical problems, but the ones that trouble me the most concern the buying and selling of body parts. There is something obscene about the idea of a market in livers or the going price for hearts. I think it is morally admirable for a man or a woman to choose to be an organ donor, declaring by a formal statement that his or her corneas, heart, liver, kidneys, and lungs can be removed at death and offered to patients who need them (even though, at this writing, I still have not actually taken the step of getting and signing an organ donor card). But selling my body parts? Should I even be allowed to leave a little nest egg for my children by stipulating that they sell off parts of me before what is left gets buried?

If that does not bother you, how about allowing poor people to sell spare body parts to rich people who need transplants? Can it possibly be right to permit a desperately poor father to provide for his family by selling one of his two kidneys to a wealthy patient suffering from renal failure? Slavery seems benign by comparison!

And yet, and yet. Right now homeless men keep alive by selling their blood to blood banks for twenty dollars a pint. Surrogate mothers sell the use of their wombs to childless couples seeking a nurturing home for their fertilized ovum. Why should I not be allowed to sell parts of my body, either before or after I die. It is my body, isn't it?

This is a perfect example of the point I have made several times—that modern medicine, by making previously unimaginable things possible, poses ethical dilemmas for which we simply are not prepared. Most of us—even ethical theorists—rely on our settled intuitions, or gut feelings (which is the same thing) to guide us through difficult ethical terrain. Those intuitions are the product of the accumulated experience of thousands of years of human history, during which men and women facing hard choices have struggled, puzzled, prayed, and argued about what to do. We have very strong intuitions about the relationships between husbands and wives, parents and children, the young and the old, the sick and the well. These intuitions are not always right—indeed, much of the most important ethical theory consists of challenges to those ancient intuitions. But they do give us somewhere to start, some fund of experience to draw on.

Organ transplants, however, are so new, so recent, that we have neither experience nor intuition concerning them. We are forced, therefore, to try to reason our way to decisions, with all the uncertainty and contradiction that seems to produce. Consider just a few of the arguments for and against the buying and selling of body parts that come to mind.

The first argument in favor of permitting the selling of organs is simply that my body is mine and I have a right to do with it what I choose. I have a right to be a body builder, developing exaggerated muscles, and I also have a right to be a couch potato (though I may not have a right to expect society to give me medical care if I fail to look after myself). I have a right to dye my hair, to cut my fingernails (or to grow them long), to risk my health in dangerous sports, and even—or so some people would say—to commit suicide. I have a right to choose to be embalmed (so long as the process does not pose a health hazard to someone else), and I also have the right to be cremated at my death. Now if I have a right to do all of those things to and with my body, both before and after my death, then surely I also have the right to sell part of my body to someone willing to pay me for it. Unless it wants to invoke religious reasons for stopping me, what possible grounds could the state have for denying me the right to dispose of all or part of my body as I wish?

If I have the right to dispose of my body as I choose at my death, surely I have the right to give (i.e., donate) a part of my body to someone whose life it will save. And if I have the right to give my liver, lungs, or heart to a needy patient, why can I not sell the part and make some money in the transaction? No doubt it would be morally preferable for me to make a free gift of my body organs, just as it would be morally admirable for me to give away a large portion of my income to those in need. But however admirable either of those free gifts might be, surely I am not morally required to be generous, am I?

The second argument for permitting the buying and selling of body parts is that it would increase the number of available organs for transplanting. I am sure we can all agree that it would be better if millions of people agreed to donate their organs at death, but the hard fact is that they do not. As a result, tens of thousands of patients die who could be saved by a timely transplant. Does it not make sense at least to try marketing organs, in order to see whether it would stimulate an increase in donations? If you are still put off by the idea of the going price for a heart, imagine explaining to the parents of a dying child that her life could be saved by a transplant, and a heart could be made available if it were permissible to sell organs, but you are going to allow the child to die because you find the idea of buying and selling organs "troubling." Is it really more troubling than watching a patient die whom modern medicine could save?

But of course the arguments are not all on one side. If they were, this would be a no-brainer. Perhaps the most powerful argument against the buying and selling of organs is the danger that such a practice would put unbearable pressures on the poor. Poverty itself is a moral outrage in a society that is capable of adequately feeding and housing everyone—at least some people would say that (and I am one of them). But the hard fact is that there are tens of millions of poor people in this society, and the way things are going, we shall see more poor people, not fewer, as the years go by. Once people are confronted with the threat that they and their children will starve, the offer of money for their body parts is simply too tempting to turn down, even for some who are deeply offended by the idea. Markets have many advantages, but one of the worst disadvantages is that they put the poor at the mercy of the rich. It is bad enough that the rich can eat, drink, and be merry while the poor struggle to survive. Should the rich also have the right to bribe the poor to give up parts of their own bodies?

A second problem with buying and selling organs is that it turns a medical decision into an economic decision. A rich patient whose need for a transplant is not so desperate will go to the head of the line, while a less wealthy patient in urgent need of the transplant will have to wait. A poor donor whose health really does not permit the giving up of a kidney will be led to make a medically unwise decision by the offer of large amounts of money. If organs are for sale, companies will spring up to make a profit out of the transactions, and the doctor's medically informed control over this heroic procedure will be lost to executives whose concern is the bottom line. Health care is already big business. Do we really want the financial pages of our newspapers to list the daily spot market prices for hearts, lungs, and livers?

It should be obvious even from this brief discussion that there are all sorts of legal as well as medical and ethical questions that spring up as soon as we begin to think about the sale of body parts. Judges often try to settle disputes about the selling of organs by applying the laws that govern ordinary property disputes, but that just seems to raise as many issues as it settles. In what sense, if any, is my body something I own? If I own my body, can I sell it to someone else? Does that make me a slave? If I can sell my kidney, can I also sell my heart, even though it will literally kill me to complete the transaction? If brain transplants ever become possible, should I be permitted to sell my brain? When I agree to sell my brain to a buyer and have it transplanted into her body, who emerges from the operation, the buyer or me?

Well, enough science fiction! When Mary Shelley wrote *Frankenstein* more than a century ago, organ transplants were a matter of fictional imagination. By the time this edition grows old, brain transplants may be on the horizon.

What Should the Doctor Tell the Patient?

We have been discussing problems that are posed by the extraordinary medical advances of the past century, but there are some moral dilemmas facing doctors, nurses, and patients that have been with us for millennia. One of the most difficult is this: What should the doctor tell the patient? Even before doctors were actually able to do much in the way of curing disease, they had acquired expert knowledge that enabled them to tell, better than the patients themselves, what was likely to be the outcome of a bout of illness. A doctor who cannot cure tuberculosis, relieve a stroke, or repair a dysfunctional kidney may nevertheless recognize how serious the patient's condition is. So for as long as there have been doctors and patients, doctors have struggled with the decision of what to tell the patient and the family gathered around the sickbed.

The problem is most urgent when the doctor can see that the patient's condition is never going to improve—that he or she is dying. When the test results come back from the lab and the news is terminal cancer, should the doctor tell the patient, "You have three months to live"? Does a doctor have a right to withhold vital information from a patient or family members? If she does have that right, are there any circumstances in which she should exercise it? Or do patients have an absolute right to an honest answer when they ask, "How bad is it, Doc?"

This is one of those many cases in which a Utilitarian, dedicated to maximizing happiness, is likely to say one thing, whereas a Kantian, committed to truth telling and individual autonomy, might say another. But there are, as always, complications. Twenty-five years ago, my physician saw a shadow on my lung x-ray, and he made a provisional diagnosis that I had something called sarcoidosis. He sent me to New York City for some fancy tests, and sure enough, the experts said I had "asymptomatic sarcoidosis." That meant I did not have any symptoms—no pains, no fever, nothing but the shadow on the x-ray. No treatment was indicated. My doctor just said he would monitor it yearly with chest x-rays, and in all probability it would go away of itself.

Well, I was much reassured, and promptly stopped worrying. Sure enough, the shadow disappeared after several years, and I never felt a thing. Some years later, I was sitting in a specialist's office, waiting for my wife, and I happened to pick up a big thick book lying on a shelf. It was a sort of medical encyclopedia of diseases. Out of curiosity, I looked up "sarcoidosis," and to my horror, discovered that in 17 percent of cases it is fatal! I very nearly had a retroactive heart attack.

Now did my doctor do the right thing or the wrong thing by keeping from me the statistical fact that a significant percentage of sarcoid cases are fatal? He had already done everything that was medically indicated, sending me to specialists and allowing them to decide whether treatment was called for. There was nothing else I could have done had I known how serious the condition might be. Had he told me, I would have suffered the tortures of the damned, to no useful effect whatsoever. There are even cases in which patients have suffered real heart attacks and other terrible consequences from being told the truth about their condition in plain English.

But there are at least some people—philosophers or not—who would argue that I had a right to know, and my doctor had a duty to tell me, regardless of the consequences. Interestingly, the first philosopher to comment on this issue was Plato, who argued that doctors should seek to educate their patients about medicine as part of their treatment, so that the patients can make rational choices when faced with medical prescriptions.

In this selection, two philosophers, Tom Beauchamp and Lawrence Mc-Cullough, explore some of the moral, legal, and medical issues intertwined in a real case, that of Bernard Berkey.

A Case Study: Herniated Disc Injury*

The following "informed consent" case was ultimately decided in a Los Angeles courtroom in 1970.

In 1961, Bernard Berkey suffered a neck injury, which became aggravated in 1962. Dr. Frank M. Anderson treated him on both occasions and conducted a neurological examination that revealed no obvious problem in the leg or back. Dr. Anderson thought the problem was probably in the neck and suggested a myelogram[9] to see if there was damage to the spinal cord. He said, "We have to get to the bottom of this." Mr. Berkey, according to his sworn and uncontested testimony, asked Dr. Anderson whether the myelogram would be similar to the electromyograms[10] he had undergone. Dr. Anderson responded that myelograms were done for diagnostic and exploratory purposes. He said that patients experience minor discomfort when strapped to a cold table, which then is tilted in various directions to determine the extent of damage to the spinal system. Dr. Anderson was otherwise quite reassuring about the procedure; he said Mr. Berkey would "feel nothing" and promised to order an injection of a pain killer to eliminate any possible discomfort. There was little more to the patient-physician interchange during this discussion. Dr. Anderson did not mention that a myelogram involves a spinal puncture, which is *not* performed in electromyograms.

Dr. Robert E. Rickenberg performed the myelogram procedure, and Mr. Berkey later testified that the following events transpired during the procedure: He first felt a few innocuous "sticks." Then suddenly he felt an excruciating pain, as if someone were jamming an ice pick into his lower spine. Mr. Berkey said he had never experi-

* From *Medical Ethics* by Beauchamp/McCullough, © 1984. Adapted with permission of Prentice-Hall, Inc., Upper Saddle River, NJ.

enced anything comparable to this pain, which then shot with intensity over his left side and left leg. He "let out a yell," as he later reported, but was told the pain would pass and was sent to rest for 24 hours. When he first stood up he found that he had what he called a "rubber leg": His leg buckled whenever he put weight on it. The next few weeks brought no significant improvement, and he was diagnosed as having "foot drop."[11]

He was examined by several doctors during this period, including Dr. Anderson. One physician, Dr. Faeth, noticed a compression of a nerve, which he judged to be "most probably" caused by a herniated disc.[12] Other possible causes, he later testified, included a tumor, adhesions around the nerve trunk, and the formation of a spur at the margin of the bone. Dr. Anderson was asked in court whether such a herniated disc injury could result from a myelogram. He responded that it could, but only under special circumstances such as "repeated injury with a large bore needle." Dr. Rickenberg testified that he had never heard of anyone developing foot drop as a result of a myelogram.

Mr. Berkey said that nothing whatever had been mentioned to him about the possibility of these levels of pain, injury, and subsequent loss of function. Neither Dr. Anderson nor Dr. Rickenberg had discussed their possible occurrence with Mr. Berkey. Neither physician denied Mr. Berkey's claim to this effect, except to note that they had told him it was a very important diagnostic procedure. Mr. Berkey sued them both—Dr. Rickenberg for negligent performance of the myelogram and Dr. Anderson for a failure to obtain informed consent before ordering the myelogram. The California court that heard an appeal in the case noted that different issues were involved in assessing each physician's actions, but that in each case the court's interest was exclusively in possible damages caused to Mr. Berkey by the responsible physician's action or inaction: "Regarding Dr. Anderson, the questions are whether he obtained the informed consent of his patient before ordering the myelogram and if not, what damages proximately resulted; and as to Dr. Rickenberg, whether there was negligence in administering the myelogram and, if so, whether the injury suffered was the proximate result of such negligence."[13]

The court noted, with regard to the suit against Dr. Anderson, that it is the "duty of a doctor" to explain fully the contemplated procedure and its possible consequences, as well as to obtain the patient's informed consent. If the patient proffered no consent whatever to the myelogram, this omission "would constitute a technical *battery*."[14] If Mr. Berkey had consented, but on the basis of an inadequate disclosure, then Dr. Anderson would be guilty of *negligence*.[15]

Dr. Anderson . . . held that other practicing physicians would not have explained such a remote risk of spinal injury under the circumstances and would have routinely ordered the diagnostic procedure. Dr. Anderson and his lawyer argued that this general standard of what other physicians routinely disclose establishes what *should* have been disclosed. Mr. Berkey and his lawyer, by contrast, argued that "the reasonable person's" needs for information set the standard, not simply what the community of physicians actually discloses. The court sided primarily with Mr. Berkey: "A physician's duty to disclose is not governed by the standard practice of the physicians' community, but is a duty imposed by law.... To hold otherwise would permit the medical profession to determine its own responsibilities to the patients in a matter of considerable public interest. Further,... Dr. Faeth testified that it was not standard practice in obtaining a patient's consent to a myelogram not to inform him that it involves a spinal puncture."[16]

Even their goal of helping or curing patients could not justify this apparent disrespect for patient autonomy....

The Risks and Benefits of Disclosure

In modern medicine the nature and quality of communication in the patient-physician relationship tend to vary with the duration of prior contact, the state of the patient, and how well the physician relates to his or her patient and the patient's family. A patient's right to information ("to know the truth") and the physician's obligation to provide it have traditionally been thought to depend heavily on such situational factors. Most physicians believe that time constraints and other pressing obligations justify departures from such abstract, oversimplified principles as "Don't lie," "Don't deceive," or "Always tell the truth," when used as guides to determine appropriate levels of disclosure.... [A] strategy of nondisclosure or partial disclosure enjoys a prominent place throughout the history of medical ethics....

The principal worry expressed in these historical writings about disclosures is that information might be harmful rather than helpful to seriously ill patients. For example, patients may become agitated as a consequence of full disclosure, sometimes leading to more complicated courses of recovery. This venerable hypothesis has its contemporary adherents, as the following influential statement by Elizabeth F. Loftus and James F. Fries indicates:

A considerable body of psychological evidence indicates that humans are highly suggestible. Information has been found to change people's attitudes, to change their moods and feelings, and even to make them believe they have experienced events that never in fact occurred. This alone would lead one to suspect that adverse reactions might result from information given during an informed consent discussion.

An examination of the medical evidence demonstrates that... not only can positive therapeutic effects be achieved by suggestion, but negative side effects and complications can similarly result. For example, among subjects who participated in a drug study after the usual informed consent procedure, many of those given an injection of a placebo reported physiologically unlikely symptoms such as dizziness, nausea, vomiting, and even mental depressions. One subject given the placebo reported that these effects were so strong that they caused an automobile accident. Many other studies provide similar data indicating that to a variable but often scarifying degree, explicit suggestion of possible adverse effects causes subjects to experience these effects. Recent hypotheses that heart attack may follow coronary spasm indicate physiological mechanisms by which explicit suggestions, and the stress that may be produced by them, might prove fatal. Thus, the possible consequences of suggested symptoms range from minor annoyance to, in extreme cases, death.

If protection of the subject is the reason for obtaining informed consent, the possibility of iatrogenic harm [harm caused by a physician's treatment] to the subject as a direct result of the consent ritual must be considered.[17]

A recent Presidential Commission investigated such claims and concluded as follows: "Despite all the anecdotes about patients who committed suicide, suffered heart attacks, or plunged into prolonged depression upon being told 'bad news,' little documentation exists for claims that informing patients is more dangerous to their health than not informing them, particularly when the informing is done in a sensitive and tactful fashion.... There is much to suggest that therapeutic privilege has been vastly overused."[18]

Despite this cloud over the claims, physicians continue to report that many of their sick and dependent patients often find extensive disclosures of potential hazards frightening and incomprehensible. For example, Dr. Robert M. Soule, in response to Sissela Bok's views on lying to patients, argues as follows:

She states there is no evidence that total candor does any harm to patients. Clinical experience simply doesn't bear this out.... Through the years I have seen too many examples of the lethal effect of total candor, including mental breakdowns and suicides by patients given a cold-turkey diagnosis.

Years ago a Harvard report documented fatal ventricular fibrillation brought on by fright in healthy people. And a letter in the May 12, 1977, New England Journal of Medicine *cited two heart attacks—one fatal—after patients with no history of cardiac disease had been given full information for consent to noncardiac surgery. The authors said patients often complained they "could not sleep all night before their procedure because of preoccupation and concern."...*

Many times a conference with the family suggests a patient needs to be protected from the "whole truth."...

In a crisis many people would prefer compassion to total frankness, which can have a devastating emotional impact.[19]

It is a matter of overwhelming importance that any generalizations...about physician behavior and patients' attitudes reflect the type of illness and degree of morbidity, as well as the context in which disclosures are made and the background of the patients involved. If a healthy patient wants information about the side effects of a prescribed drug or a parent seeks the results of a pediatrician's examination of a young child, we would not expect and would quickly condemn nondisclosure of relevant information. In such instances, a physician can relate to a patient or parent without the degree of emotional dependence that inevitably accompanies the state of sickness. Information can be freely dispatched without fear of undue alarm, let alone terror.

However, many patients with diseases such as metastatic cancer or endstage kidney disease face life-threatening circumstances that may inherently involve choices among alternative courses of treatment, each carrying terrifying risks. Here, any physician must employ managerial skills, taking into account the patient's need for information and ability to deal with it—as, for example, when the terminally ill cancer patient cannot accept the fact that his or her death is imminent, and thus refuses palliative treatment. Is it a primary responsibility of the physician to inform the patient that he or she has but a few months to live? Or is this only a rather wooden way of discharging legal responsibilities while failing the patient at a deeper moral level—for example, failing to help the patient come to grips with his or her mortality and the impact of his or her death on family and friends?

Both empirical evidence and philosophical argument suggest that considerations of risks and benefits of disclosure, as understood through the beneficence model, play an appropriate role in the physician's determination of moral responsibility. The perspective of medicine is invoked to determine the relative weight of harm full disclosure causes to some patients: They might refuse needed diagnostic or therapeutic interventions, suffer unnecessarily, or have more complicated courses of recovery. The physician assumes an obligation to avoid these harms while providing the benefits of medical care. Dr. Anderson's behavior in the diagnosis of Mr. Berkey's condition reflects this approach, even if his execution of it is flawed.

Review of argument and evidence on both sides...indicates that the basic issue in the management of medical information is how the physician should balance the goods and harms of various levels of disclosure. Under the professional community standard, as invoked by Dr. Anderson, the rationale is that of the beneficence model: Medicine's perspective should be used to determine the weight of the harms and goods of disclosure. By contrast, the *Berkey* court insisted that the perspective of the informed patient should determine the appropriate weighting—an approach that reflects the autonomy model. Because both perspectives have merit, we should expect that neither the law nor medical ethics will settle finally on a single directive. As we shall now see, the legal history of which *Berkey* is a key part does *not* result in the complete triumph of the patient-based perspective over the professionally based one. The result, instead, is a delicate tension in the law between the two perspectives.

Philosophy and Popular Culture

The West Wing: Questions About Ethics and Medicine

It's a shocking scene. President Jed Bartlett is on TV telling the nation that he suffers from and has suffered from multiple sclerosis but had kept it secret. Of course, he is not the only one who had kept it secret. Obviously, his doctor knew about the multiple sclerosis, but his doctor—who happens to be his wife—kept it secret as well.

But should this be kept a secret? The President of the United States has a finger on the nuclear button and makes decisions that affect the entire world, so shouldn't the President's health be the concern of the nation? Or should doctors respect the confidentiality of the doctor-patient relationship, no matter what?

Questions to Consider

Is medical knowledge private even when it could affect millions of people? For example, if you were the President's doctor and discovered that the President was in the beginning stages of Alzheimer's Disease, would you tell the nation?

Notes

1. John A. Robertson, "Dilemma in Danville," *The Hastings Center Report* 11 (October 1981), 5–8.
2. T. Rohrlich, "2 Doctors Face Murder Charges in Patient's Death," *L.A. Times,* August 19, 1982, A–1; Jonathan Kirsch, "A Death at Kaiser Hospital," *California* 7 (1982), 79ff; Magistrate's findings, *California v. Barber and Nejdl,* No. A 925586, Los Angeles Mun. Ct. Cal., (March 9, 1983); Superior Court of California, County of Los Angeles, *California v. Barber and Nejdl,* No. AO 25586, tentative decision May 5, 1983.
3. *In re Infant Doe,* No. GU 8204–00 (Cir. Ct. Monroe County, Ind., April 12, 1982), writ of mandamus dismissed sub nom. *State ex rel. Infant Doe v. Baker,* No. 482 S140 (Indiana Supreme Ct. May 27, 1982).
4. Office of the Secretary, Department of Health and Human Services, "Nondiscrimination on the Basis of Handicap," *Federal Register* 48 (1983), 9630–32. [Interim final rule modifying 45 C.F.R. #84.61]. See Judge Gerhard Gesell's decision, *American Academy of Pediatrics v. Heckler,* No. 83–0774, U.S. District Court, D.C., April 24, 1983; and also George J. Annas, "Disconnecting the Baby Doe Hotline," *The Hastings Center Report* 13 (June 1983), 14–16.
5. *In re Claire C. Conroy,* Sup. Ct. NJ (Chancery Div-Essex Co. No. P-19083E) February 2, 1983; *In re Claire C. Conroy,* Sup. Ct. NJ (Appellate Div. No. 4-2483-82T1) July 8, 1983.
6. The President's Commission for the Study of Ethical Problems in Medicine and Biomedical and Behavioral Research, *Deciding to Forego Life-Sustaining Treatment* (Washington, D.C.: Government Printing Office, 1982).
7. G.E.M. Anscombe, "Ethical Problems in the Management of Some Severely Handicapped Children: Commentary 2," *Journal of Medical Ethics* 7 (1981), 117–124, at 122.
8. See e.g., the President's Commission for the Study of Ethical Problems in Medicine and Biomedical and Behavioral Research, *Making Health Care Decisions* (Washington, D.C.: Government Printing Office, 1982).
9. "Myelogram" literally means "graph of the spinal cord." During the myelogram, a large gauge, 2_-inch needle is inserted into the lumbar area (lower mid-back) of the spine, while the patient is prone and harnessed on a fluoroscopic table. Eight to ten cc's of spinal fluid are tapped for laboratory analysis, with the needle inserted into the subarachnoid space (just beneath a major covering membrane). An opaque substance (panopaque) is then introduced into the spinal canal through the needle. Tilting the table causes a flow of the substance in the spine, and this flow is captured by x-rays.
10. An electromyogram is a procedure used to study electrical activity in the muscle to diagnose a variety of disorders. The procedure involves inserting needle electrodes into muscle tissue. This involves some discomfort, but poses only minor risks.
11. "Foot drop" means a falling of the foot because of paralysis of the ankle.
12. In a herniated disc, the pulpy body at the center of the disc protrudes through the surrounding fibrocartilage, forming a small sac.
13. *Berkey v. Anderson,* App. 82 Cal. Rptr. 67, p. 72.
14. Battery is an unconsented to physical violence or constraint inflicted by one person on another.
15. Negligence is the omission of (or doing of) something that a reasonable person in the circumstances would do (or not do).
16. *Berkey v. Anderson,* p. 78.
17. Elizabeth F. Loftus and James F. Fries, "Informed Consent May be Hazardous to Health," *Science* 204 (6 April 1979): 11. The position and argument of Loftus and Fries have been subjected to important criticism. See Ruth Barcan Marcus, Bruce Kuklick, and Sacvan Bercovitch, Letter, *Science* 205 (17 August 1979): 644. These authors have shown its logical flaws, while important empirical limitations have been pointed to by Ruth Faden et al., "Disclosures of Information to Patients in Medical Care," *Medical Care* 19 (July 1981): 718–33, esp. p. 731, and Ruth Faden et al., "Disclosure Standards and Informed Consent," *Journal of Health Politics, Policy, and Law* 6 (1981): 255–84. Faden et al. show that there exists better evidence for the Loftus-Fries position than they themselves adduce, but that there exists equally powerful counterevidence.
18. President's Commission for the Study of Ethical Problems in Medicine and Biomedicine and Behavioral Research, *Making Health Care Decisions: The Ethical and Legal Implications of Informed Consent in the Patient-Practitioner Relationship* (Washington: U.S. Government Printing Office, 1982), vol. 1, p. 96.
19. Robert M. Soule, "The Case Against 'Total Candor'," *Medical World News* 20 (14 May 1979): 94.

The Main Points in Chapter Five, Part Two

1. The dramatic advances in medicine over the last century have raised new and difficult ethical questions for doctors, nurses, and health professionals. Ethical theory can assist them in making their decisions, but cannot provide them with ready-made answers for the difficult questions they now must confront.

2. When trying to decide whether to withhold food and water from terminally ill and unconscious patients, doctors and nurses must weigh the sanctity of life and their professional commitments as caregivers against both the suffering of the families and the need for scarce resources to be allocated to other curable patients.

3. The development of organ transplant technology has forced the medical and legal professions to ask whether it is morally right, legal, or professionally acceptable for individuals to sell and buy human organs for transplant. The autonomy of the individual comes into conflict with the indirect, unintended market effects of the practice of selling organs.

4. One of the most ancient moral dilemmas faced by doctors is what to tell the patient. The moral autonomy of the individual seems to call for complete disclosure by the doctor. But the doctor's commitment to caring for the patient and his or her well-being may conflict with that autonomy.

Questions for Discussion and Review

1. Have you or your family ever faced a really serious and difficult medical decision that raised ethical questions? How did you go about deciding what to do? Did you consider the relative value of alternative consequences [the Utilitarian approach], or did you focus on the rights of the different people involved [the Kantian approach]?

2. Do you think doctors and hospitals should consider whether patients have been good or bad persons when deciding who should get the next available heart or liver for transplant? Should they consider the age of the patients? How much they can contribute to society? Or should the organ transplants be distributed on a first-come first-served basis? Why?

3. If you were dying of an incurable disease, would you want to be told? Should you tell a friend or relative who has such a disease? Who has the right to make that decision?

4. As modern genetic techniques improve, doctors become more and more capable of determining who is at risk for various diseases, such as cancer, Alzheimer's, and multiple sclerosis. If doctors can predict who will become sick, but cannot cure the diseases or do anything to ward them off, do they have an obligation to give the information to their patients? Should they give that information to insurance companies or employers?

5. In this section of Chapter 5, we have focused on the ethical dimensions of medical decisions, but similar ethical questions arise in other areas of human experience, such as business, the military, government, and education. See whether you can identify the sorts of ethical dilemmas that might come up in those areas, and try to figure out how the ethical theories you have studied could be applied to them.

The Primary Source: Philosophical Readings and Commentary

Aristotle: *Nicomachean Ethics; de Anima*

Benedict, Ruth: *Anthropology and the Abnormal*

Bentham, Jeremy: *An Introduction to the Principles of Morality and Legislation*

Camus, Albert: *Absurdity and Suicide; The Myth of Sisyphus*

de Spinoza, Benedict: *Ethics*Epictetus: *Enchiridion; Discourses*

Hume, David: *Inquiry Concerning Principles of Morals*

James, William: *The Will to Believe*

Kant, Immanuel: *Fundamental Principles of the Metaphysics of Morals*

Kierkegaard, Soren: *Concluding Unscientific Postscript; On the Dedication of "That Single Individual"*

King, Martin Luther, Jr.: *Letter from a Birmingham Jail*

Nietzsche Friedrich: *Beyond Good and Evil*

Plato: *The Republic*

Rachels, James:. *Elements of Moral Philosophy*

Rand, Ayn: *The Virtue of Selfishness; Philosophy: Who Needs It?*

Singer, Peter: *Animal Liberation*

ABCNEWS

CONTEMPORARY APPLICATION

The Ethics of Cloning Human Beings

As we have already seen, the astonishing scientific advances in medical technology create serious ethical problems for the doctors who control that technology. Nowhere are these ethical problems more starkly drawn than with regard to what is called "cloning." A clone is an exact copy. In genetic terms, a clone is an organism with exactly the same DNA, exactly the same genetic code as the original. When British scientists succeeded in cloning a sheep from the cell of a living mature sheep, all hell broke loose in the public press, with even the president and Congress getting into the act.

The cloning of sheep was not the issue. No one much cared about that. But the success of the British scientists raised the spectre of the cloning of human beings. Let us be clear what we are talking about, so that we do not wander down blind alleys. We are *not* talking about a Transporter malfunction aboard the Enterprise, with Captain Picard stepping onto the transporter platform and *two* Captain Picards emerging on the surface of a planet. That really would pose problems of a sort that no philosopher wants to contemplate. We are talking about genetically replicating a human being, in much the same way that nature does every time identical twins are born.

As of this writing, the technology to clone a human being does not exist, but we have all learned in the past generation that there is a shorter and shorter lag between the conception of a scientific innovation and the announcement of its achievement. It would not surprise me at all if the first successful cloning of a human being from the cell of a mature person takes place before this edition of *About Philosophy* has run its course, so we had better start thinking about the ethical implications now, before it is too late.

As the debate in these selections makes clear, cloning raises religious as well as ethical questions. Several of the authors find it impossible to separate the two. But cloning also raises legal issues discussed by well-known constitutional scholar Lawrence Tribe. Any law permitting or banning the cloning of humans will have legal implications for other sorts of activities involved with human reproduction.

As the third millennium unfolds, we shall have to face such complex issues as "designer babies"—fetuses deliberately crafted by medical technology so as to have certain genetic components, such as gender, hair color, skin color, height, weight, and perhaps—though this is much less clear—even musical talent or athletic ability. Already efforts are underway to remove from fetuses genes that cause fatal or debilitating hereditary diseases. Cloning seems to be a logical next step.

Before those of you reading this book have finished your childbearing years, cloning may be one of the options available to you. Imagine a couple trying to decide whether to clone one partner or the other! That is an ethical and a human nightmare I am glad I will never have to face—but I would not be surprised if my sons confront it.

STOP CLONING AROUND: IN THE FLURRY OF SCIENTIFIC BOUNDARY BREAKING, LET'S REMEMBER THAT HUMANS ARE NOT SHEEP
John F. Kilner

Cigar, the champion racehorse, is a dud as a stud. Attempts to impregnate numerous mares have failed. But his handlers are not discouraged. They think they might try to have Cigar cloned.

If a sheep and a monkey can be cloned—and possibly a racehorse—can human clones be far behind? The process is novel, though the concept is not.

We have long known that virtually every cell of the body contains a person's complete genetic code. The exception is sperm or egg cells, each of which contains half the genetic material until the sperm fertilizes the egg and a new human being with a complete genetic code begins growing.

We have now learned that the partial genetic material in an unfertilized egg cell may be replaced by the complete genetic material from a cell taken from an adult. With a full genetic code, the egg cell behaves as if it has been fertilized. At least, that is how Dolly, the sheep cloned in Scotland, came to be. Hence, producing genetic copies of human beings now seems more likely.

We have been anticipating this possibility in humans for decades and have been playing with it in our imaginations. The movie *The Boys from Brazil* was about an attempt to clone Adolf Hitler. And in Aldous Huxley's novel *Brave New World,* clones were produced to fulfill undesirable social roles. More recently the movie *Multiplicity* portrayed a harried man who jumped at the chance to have himself copied—the better to tend to his office work, his home chores, and his family relationships. It all seems so attractive, at first glance, in our hectic, achievement-crazed society.

The Costs of Clones

But how do we achieve this technologically blissful state? *Multiplicity* is silent on this matter, implying that technique is best left to scientists, as if the rest of us are interested only in the outcome. But the experiments of Nazi Germany and the resulting Nuremberg Trials and Code taught us long ago that there is some knowledge that we must not pursue if it requires the use of immoral means.

The research necessary to develop human cloning will cause the deaths of human beings. Such deaths make the cost unacceptably high. In the process used to clone sheep, there were 277 failed attempts—including the deaths of several defective clones. In the monkey-cloning process, a living embryo was intentionally destroyed by taking the genetic material from the embryo's eight cells and inserting it into eight egg cells whose partial genetic material had been removed. Human embryos and human infants would likewise be lost as the technique is adapted to our own race.

Goal Rush

Yet, as we press toward this new mark, we must ask: Is the production of human clones even a worthwhile goal? As movies and novels suggest, and godly wisdom confirms, human cloning is something neither to fool around with nor to attempt.

Cloning typically involves genetically copying some living thing for a particular purpose—a wheat plant that yields much grain, a cow that provides excellent milk. Such utilitarian approaches may be fine for cows and corn, but human beings, made in the image of God, have a God-given dignity that prevents us from regarding other people merely as means to fulfill our desires. We must not, for instance, produce clones with low intelligence (or low ambition) to provide menial labor, or produce clones to provide transplantable organs (their identical genetic code would minimize organ rejection). We should not even clone a child who dies tragically in order to remove the parents' grief, as if the clone could actually *be* the child who died.

All people are special creations of God who should be loved and respected as such. We must not demean them by fundamentally subordinating their interests to those of others.

There is a host of problems with human cloning that we have yet to address. Who are the parents of a clone produced in a laboratory? The donor of the genetic material? The donor of the egg into which the material is transferred? The scientist who manipulates cells from anonymous donors? Who will provide the necessary love and care for this embryo, fetus, and then child—especially when mistakes are made and it would be easier simply to discard *it*?

The problems become legion when having children is removed from the context of marriage and even from responsible parenthood. For instance, Hope College's Allen Verhey asks "whether parenting is properly considered making children to match a specific design, as is clearly the case with cloning, or whether parenting is properly regarded as a disposition to be hospitable to children as given." Clearly, from a biblical perspective, it is the latter.

Further, the Bible portrays children as the fruit of a one-flesh love relationship, and for good reason. It is a context in which children flourish—in which their full humanity, material and nonmaterial, is respected and nourished. Those who provide them with physical (genetic) life also care for their ongoing physical as well as nonphysical needs.

As Valparaiso University's Gilbert Meilaender told *Christianity Today*, this further separation of procreating from marriage is bad for children. "The child inevitably becomes a product," says ethicist Meilaender, someone who is made, not begotten.

"To beget a child is to give birth to one who is like us, equal in dignity, for whom we care, but whose being we do not simply control. To 'make' a child is to create a product whose destiny we may well think we can shape. Hence, the 'begotten, not made' language of the creed is relevant also to our understanding of the child and of the relation between the generations.

"If our purpose is to clone people as possible sources of perfectly matching organs," says Meilaender, "that clearly shows how we could come to regard the clone as a being we control—as simply an 'ensemble of parts or organs.'"

Xeroxing Michael

It is all too easy to lose sight of the fact that people are more than just physical beings, Meilaender's ensembles of organs. What most excites many people about cloning is the possibility of duplicate Michael Jordans, Mother Teresas, or Colin Powells. However, were clones of any of these heroes to begin growing today, those clones would not turn out to be our heroes, for our heroes are not who they are simply because of their DNA. They, like us, were shaped by genetics and environment alike, with the spiritual capacity to evaluate, disregard, and at times to overcome either or both. Each clone would be subject to a unique set of environmental influences, and our loving God would surely accord each a unique personal relationship with him.

The problem with cloning is not the mere fact that technology is involved. Technology can help us do better what God has for us to do. The problem arises when we use technology for purposes that conflict with God's. And, as C. S. Lewis argued, technology never merely represents human mastery over nature; it also involves the power of some people over other people. This is as true in the genetic revolution as it was in the Industrial Revolution. When human cloning becomes technically possible, who will control who clones whom and for what ends? Like nuclear weaponry, the power to clone in the "wrong hands" could have devastating consequences.

There is wisdom in President Clinton's immediate move to forestall human cloning research until public debate and expert testimony have been digested and policies formulated. But there is even greater wisdom in never setting foot on the path that leads from brave new sheep to made-to-order organ donors, industrial drones, and vanity children.

Source: *Christianity Today:* April 28, 1997, V. 41. Christianity Today, Inc., 465 Gunderson Drive, Carol Stream, IL 60188.

John F. Kilner is director of the Center for Bioethics and Human Dignity, Bannockburn, Illinois.

PAUSE FOR PHILOSOPHICAL 'SPEED BUMPS' ON CLONING
Paul Ginnetty

The breathtaking momentum of assisted reproductive technology seems to have whisked us beyond a number of traditional cultural and moral milestones. Confronted with ovum brokers, frozen embryos, and now the theoretical possibility of *human cloning,* one senses the need for a philosophical speed bump or two along the way to protect whatever wisdom we had accumulated about the meaning of personhood, of the life cycle, of family and, for those of a theistic bent, of creation and creaturehood.

The putative technology for *human cloning* raises profound issues about the integrity, dignity, and uniqueness of the person. The ethically troublesome notion of exploiting clones for fetal tissue implants or organ transplants gained an eerie aura of relevance with the recent genetic engineering of a headless tadpole, a prototype—some have suggested—of future anencephalic humans from which we could gleefully "harvest" spare parts.

Did I hear somebody calling Dr. Frankenstein? Even in more benign cloning scenarios, what happens to the concept of personal autonomy and individuation if people actually start replicating themselves, spawning their own (delayed) genetic twins? As a psychologist, I've worked with many young people suffering from deficient senses of identity and differentiation of self from a parent. I shudder to think of the therapeutic work that would be entailed if the patient's sense of being too much "a chip off the old block" needed to be taken in an all too literal sense!

Just as there is value in the person being one of a kind, there probably also is wisdom in having the eras of our life span remain unique and unrepeatable. Any sense of there being a "season" for everything is fairly well stood on its head with the advent of 63-year-old gestational mothers. Increasingly, you're only as old as your donated ovum (or your own time-encapsulated frozen one). So much for the biological imperative; now women too can enjoy Tony Randall-style deferred parenting. But, asks bioethicist Daniel Callahan, is it fair to children or sufficiently responsive to the implied social contract about sticking around long enough to take care of one's offspring? Some would say we already do a dubious job in this department.

Much of the poignancy—but also nobility—of human experience involves coming to terms with limitation and the irreversibility of loss within our span of years. We naturally seek to avoid the tragic. Might not the new biotechnologies seduce us into attempts to mitigate or reverse the tragic in ways that would be at best unseemly, at worst grotesque?

Ethicist Arthur Caplan cites the recent case of a woman who sought to extract sperm from her suddenly deceased husband, hoping through posthumous procreation to offset the enormity of her loss. Understandable, perhaps. But what of the proposed use of cloning to replace a dying child? I'm reminded of Stephen King's *Pet Semetary,* which explores the unnatural, ghoulish lengths to which one might be tempted to go to reclaim a child from the dead. The ensuing horror suggests there are some things worse than even the worst natural tragedies. Again, people probably are best thought of as irreplaceable, unrepeatable events.

And how is all this technology affecting our collective consciousness about family and relationships? Fatherhood, already somewhat marginalized, is in some cases reduced to sperm donation. The greeting card bards will be working overtime in this brave new era of ovum donation. Imagine the inscription: "To my gestational mother who is also my part sibling, the daughter of my ovum donating grandmother." Weren't family roles complicated enough before all this high-biotech?

Finally, these developments raise questions about what some still consider the ineffable mystery of life and its origins. Within this more spiritual perspective, do we have a right to clone ourselves or otherwise usurp that level of the authorship of life? Freud once spoke of "the narcissism of small differences," the tendency to think of ourselves as superior to others because of some laughably superficial and nonessential feature such as wealth, race, or gender.

I wonder if the somewhat arbitrary differentiations commonly made between pre- and post-viability in fetuses (and lately of "partial" vs. full birth) might not someday strike us all as having been distinctions without real difference, the arrogance of the already born.

A biotechnology that becomes unhinged from a humane vision of person, family, and life cycle becomes morally bankrupt in its expediency. Modern-day Prometheuses, we have raided godly realms and returned with powers more precious than fire. Ironically, the name Prometheus means "forethought," something that will serve us far better than regrets.

Source: From: "Pause for Philosophical 'Speed Bumps' on Cloning" by Paul Ginnetty. Originally appeared in *Newsday,* April 14, 1998. © 1998 by Paul Ginnetty. Reprinted from *Newsday.*

Paul Ginnetty, who holds graduate degrees in divinity and clinical psychology, is an associate professor at St. Joseph's College in Patchogue, N.Y.

SECOND THOUGHTS ON CLONING
Laurence H. Tribe

Some years ago, long before human cloning became a near-term prospect, I was among those who urged that human cloning be assessed not simply in terms of concrete costs and benefits, but in terms of what the technology might do to the very meaning of human reproduction, child rearing, and individuality. I leaned toward prohibition as the safest course.

Today, with the prospect of a renewed push for sweeping prohibition rather than mere regulation, I am inclined to say, "Not so fast."

When scientists announced in February that they had created a clone of an adult sheep— a genetically identical copy named Dolly, created in the laboratory from a single cell of the "parent"—ethicists, theologians, and others passionately debated the pros and cons of trying to clone a human being.

People spoke of the plight of infertile couples; the grief of someone who has lost a child whose biological "rebirth" might offer solace; the prospect of using cloning to generate donors for tissues and organs; the possibility of creating genetically enhanced clones with a particular talent or a resistance to some dread disease.

But others saw a nightmarish and decidedly unnatural perversion of human reproduction. California enacted a ban on human cloning, and the President's National Bioethics Advisory Commission recommended making the ban nationwide.

That initial debate has cooled, however, and many in the scientific field now seem to be wondering what all the fuss was about.

They are asking whether human cloning isn't just an incremental step beyond what we are already doing with artificial insemination, in vitro fertilization, fertility enhancing drugs, and genetic manipulation. That casual attitude is sure to give way before long to yet another wave of prohibitionist outrage—a wave that I no longer feel comfortable riding.

I certainly don't subscribe to the view that whatever technology permits us to do we ought to do. Nor do I subscribe to the view that the Constitution necessarily guarantees every individual the right to reproduce through whatever means become technically possible.

Rather, my concern is that the very decision to use the law to condemn, and then outlaw, patterns of human reproduction—especially by invoking vague notions of what is "natural"— is at least as dangerous as the technologies such a decision might be used to control.

Human cloning has been condemned by some of its most articulate detractors as the ultimate embodiment of the sexual revolution, severing sex from the creation of babies and treating gender and sexuality as socially constructed.

But to ban cloning as the technological apotheosis of what some see as culturally distressing trends may, in the end, lend credence to strikingly similar objections to surrogate motherhood or gay marriage and gay adoption.

Equally scary, when appeals to the natural, or to the divinely ordained, lead to the criminalization of some method for creating human babies, we must come to terms with the inevitable: the prohibition will not be airtight.

Just as was true of bans on abortion and on sex outside marriage, bans on human cloning are bound to be hard to enforce. And that, in turn, requires us to think in terms of a class of potential outcasts—people whose very existence society will have chosen to label as a misfortune and, in essence, to condemn.

One need only think of the long struggle to overcome the stigma of "illegitimacy" for the children of unmarried parents. How much worse might be the plight of being judged morally incomplete by virtue of one's man-made origin?

There are some black markets (in narcotic drugs, for instance) that may be worth risking when the evils of legalization would be even worse. But when the contraband we are talking of creating takes the form of human beings, the stakes become enormous.

There are few evils as grave as that of creating a caste system, one in which an entire category of persons, while perhaps not labeled untouchable, is marginalized as not fully human.

And even if one could enforce a ban on cloning, or at least insure that clones would not be a marginalized caste, the social costs of prohibition could still be high. For the arguments supporting an ironclad prohibition of cloning are most likely to rest on, and reinforce, the notion that it is unnatural and intrinsically wrong to sever the conventional links between heterosexual unions sanctified by tradition and the creation and upbringing of new life.

The entrenchment of that notion cannot be a welcome thing for lesbians, gay men, and perhaps others with unconventional ways of linking erotic attachment, romantic commitment, genetic replication, gestational mothering, and the joys and responsibilities of child rearing.

And, from the perspective of the wider community, straight no less than gay, a society that bans acts of human creation for no better reason than that their particular form defies nature and tradition is a society that risks cutting itself off from vital experimentation, thus losing a significant part of its capacity to grow. If human cloning is to be banned, then, the reasons had better be far more compelling than any thus far advanced.

From: "Second Thoughts on Cloning" by Laurence H. Tribe, Editorial Desk, December 5, 1997. Copyright © 1997 by *the New York Times*. Reprinted by permission.

Laurence H. Tribe is a professor of constitutional law at Harvard Law School.

THERE'S NO REASON TO FEAR CLONING
Harry Binswanger

The recent cloning of mice brings much closer the prospect of cloning human beings.

Human cloning—everyone seems to tremble at the prospect. Why?

After all, we are not talking about a weapon of mass destruction, just the ability to produce a baby who exactly resembles, physically, someone else—a godsend for infertile couples.

Where's the threat?

The fear is only partly explained by misconceptions resulting from Hollywood's treatment of cloning. In films like *Multiplicity,* cloning is presented as a sort of super-photocopying: you stand in one chamber, lights flash, and in another chamber your exact double appears. But an actual clone is not an adult but an egg cell implanted in a woman to begin a normal pregnancy.

If you were cloned today, nine months from now a woman would give birth to a baby with your genetic endowment. The cloned baby would be your identical twin, delayed a generation.

Twins of the same age do not frighten us, so why should twins separated by a generation?

Some fear the spectre of mass cloning of one individual, especially cloning of sadistic monsters, as in *The Boys of Brazil,* Ira Levin's nightmarish projection of cadres of young Hitlers spawned from the dictator's genes.

The error here is philosophical: equating a person with his body. A person's essential self is his mind—that in him that thinks, values and chooses. It is one's mind, not one's genes, that governs who one is. Man is the rational animal. One's basic choice is to think or not to think, in Ayn Rand's famous phrase, and the conclusions, values, and character of individuals depend upon the extent and rationality of their thinking.

Genes provide the capacity to reason, but the exercise and guidance of that capacity is up to each individual, from the birth of his reasoning mind in infancy through the rest of his life.

Neither genes nor environment can implant ideas in a child's mind and make him accept them. Only his own self-generated thinking—or his default on that responsibility—will shape his soul. Cloning the body will not clone the mind. A mind is inescapably under the individual's own control. *The Boys of Brazil?* It was not Hitler's genes but his choices that made him a monster.

Yes, the technology of cloning can be misused. Any technology can be. In particular, parents might treat a cloned child not as a unique, separate individual, but as if he were a reincarnation of the person he resembles. But the same wrong has always been possible: some parents attempt to relive their own lives through their children.

Worry about this kind of problem cannot account for the virtual panic over human cloning, nor for the fact that the anti-cloning clique opposes human cloning across the board, in any quantity, for any reason.

The actual opposition to human cloning springs from something primordial, the fear of the unknown, the fear captured in the catchphrase: "We can't play God." But why can't we? We can and we must.

A surgeon "plays God" whenever he removes a cancer or an infected appendix rather than letting the patient die. We "play God" any time we use our intelligence to improve the "natural" course of events. Natural? It is man's nature to "play God" by reshaping matter to produce the food, shelter, tools, cars, and power stations that sustain and enhance our existence. Not to "play God" in this way means to abandon the struggle for human life and submit uncomplainingly to whatever happens.

Human cloning, in particular, would emancipate not only infertile couples but also those fearing birth defects inherited from one partner. It would extend prospective parents' control of the reproductive process, which is precisely why it is feared by the familiar phalange of Luddites, religionists, and the merely confused.

Further, progress in cloning technology is linked to progress in other life-enhancing biomedical applications, such as new weapons against cancer and aging. Restricting one technology retards all.

At the threshold of a wide range of exciting biomedical advances, we must not let irrational fears slow progress in the battle to enhance and extend human life.

Source: Knight Ridder Tribune Information Services.

John Stuart Mill

*J*ohn Stuart Mill (1806–1873) was the most important English philosopher during the 125 years between the death of David Hume in 1776 and the turn of the twentieth century. Trained from his youth by his father, James Mill, to be a defender of the utilitarian doctrine of Jeremy Bentham and the Philosophical Radicals, Mill devoted his early years to an unquestioning support of his father's principles. After undergoing a severe emotional crisis in his twenties, Mill gave up the narrow doctrine of Bentham and became instead an eclectic synthesizer of the views of such diverse schools as the French utopian socialists and the German romantics.

Mill was active in the public life of England, first as an officer (and eventually head) of the great East India Company, a principal instrument of English economic expansion during the nineteenth century, and later as a member of Parliament. In addition to the

books on moral and political topics that have established him as one of the leading advocates of liberalism, Mill also wrote a number of highly influential works on logic and the theory of knowledge, including *A System of Logic* and *An Examination of Sir William Hamilton's Philosophy*.

As a young man, Mill befriended Mrs. Harriet Taylor, with whom he maintained a close relationship until, after her husband's death, they were married in 1851. Mill believed Mrs. Taylor to be an enormously gifted thinker, and he was convinced that she would have made her mark on English letters had it not been for the powerful prejudice against women that operated then, as it does now. His relationship with Mrs. Taylor made Mill sensitive to the discrimination against women, with the result that he became one of the few philosophers to speak out on the matter. His discussion of the problem appears in a late work, *The Subjection of Women*, published four years before his death.

Social and Political Philosophy

Mill and Classical Laissez-Faire Liberalism

Some, it is said, are born great; some achieve greatness; and some have greatness thrust upon them. To that saying we might add—and some are trained from birth for greatness. Of all the philosophers who have won for themselves a place in the ranks of the great, none was more carefully groomed, schooled, prodded, and pushed into greatness than the English empiricist and utilitarian thinker of the nineteenth century, John Stuart Mill. Never has a child been given less chance to "do his own thing," and never has a man defended with greater eloquence the right of every man and woman to be left free from the intrusions of well-meaning parents, friends, and governments. Though it would be wrong to reduce Mill's mature philosophical views to the level of mere psychological reflections on his childhood experiences, the temptation is irresistible to see in his adult career a reaction to the pressures of his youth.

Mill was born in 1806, a time when a strong movement was developing to reform the political life of England. The intellectual leader of the movement was the same Jeremy Bentham whose utilitarian doctrines you encountered in Chapter 5. We took our first look at utilitarianism in its guise as a moral philosophy designed to lay down a principle for calculating what actions are right for an individual facing a decision. But Bentham's primary interest was in social issues, not in private morality. He conceived the Principle of Utility as a weapon in the attack on the traditions, privileges, laws, and perquisites of the English upper classes. So long as courts and governments could hide behind precedent, or immemorial custom, it was extremely hard to force them to admit the injustices and irrationalities of the social system. But once those ancient customs were put to the test of the Principle of Utility, it was immediately clear how badly they had failed to produce the greatest happiness for the greatest number.

One of Bentham's close friends and associates in the reform movement was the philosopher James Mill. Mill was a thinker of considerable distinction, although he has long since been eclipsed by his more famous son. His writings on economics and moral philosophy erected a system, on Benthamite foundations, which served as a fortress from which the Philosophical Radicals, as they were called, sallied forth to do battle with the last remnants of the aristocratic hosts. Shortly after the birth of his son John Stuart, James Mill met Bentham and joined forces with him. Mill decided to train his son as a soldier in the reform movement, and no medieval squire ever had a more rigorous preparation for combat. Little John Stuart began studying Greek at the age of three. His father surrounded him with Latin-speaking servants, so that by the age of eight, he could dig into that other ancient tongue. Logic was young John Stuart's fare at twelve, to be followed shortly by the study of the new science of political economy. Formal religion was deliberately omitted

JAMES MILL

James Mill (1773–1836) was a close friend and colleague of Jeremy Bentham, the founder of the doctrine known as utilitarianism. Mill led a group of English political reformers who believed that social justice and wise government required a broadening of the franchise to include the industrial middle classes in England, and a thoroughgoing overhaul of the antiquated laws and governmental machinery which, in Mill's day, strongly favored the landed interests in England. Mill and the Philosophical Radicals, as his circle of supporters was called, succeeded in generating enough support to carry through a number of major reforms, culminating in the sweeping Reform Bill of 1832. Mill's son, the great John Stuart Mill, had this to say about his father's position in *The Autobiography of John Stuart Mill:*

"So complete was my father's reliance on the influence of reason over the minds of mankind, whenever it is allowed to reach them, that he felt as if all would be gained if the whole population were taught to read, if all sorts of opinions were allowed to be addressed to them by word and by writing, and if by means of the suffrage they could nominate a legislature to give effect to the opinions they adopted."

from the curriculum, but the poor lad may be forgiven for having somewhat formed the notion that he was being raised by an orthodox utilitarian.

By the time he reached adulthood, John Stuart Mill was a brilliant, finely honed logical weapon in the armory of his father's political battles. He wrote attacks on the antiquated legal and political institutions of England, defending his points with straight utilitarian dogma.

Not surprisingly, Mill finally broke under the strain of this rigid doctrinaire discipline. At the age of twenty, he suffered an internal emotional crisis and began what was to be a lifelong reevaluation of the Benthamism of his father and his father's allies. Though it is always a mistake to sum up a great philosopher's work in a single phrase, we can get some general overview of Mill's subsequent intellectual development by saying that he spent his life struggling to broaden, deepen, and complicate the extremely simple philosophical theory into which he was initiated as a boy.

The doctrine of the reformers was clear, coherent, and attractively free from the mystifications that clouded the writings of the conservative defenders of the old order. As Bentham had laid it down, the only good in this world is pleasure; the only evil, pain. Human actions are goal oriented, purposeful actions. Our desires determine what objects or experiences we choose as our goals, and reason aids us in discovering the most efficient path to those goals. The question "What ought I to do?" is either a question of goals—"What should I desire?"—or it is a question of means—"How can I reach my goal most easily?" But there is no point in disputing about desires. We either want something or we do not, and whatever pleasure we experience comes to us as the result of satisfying a desire. So the only questions worth debating are factual questions of means: "Is this the best way to satisfy my desire, or would that way be quicker, cheaper, easier?"

If abstruse questions of natural rights and absolute goodness are to be disputed, then common men and women will be hard put to keep up with trained philosophers, lawyers, or theologians. But if Bentham is right, then the fundamental moral question is simply, "Does it feel good?" "Is this experience pleasurable?" Now each one of us is the best judge of whether he or she is feeling pleasure or pain, so utilitarianism has the effect of eliminating expertise and putting all men and women on an equal footing in moral debates. What is more, Bentham insisted, the only morally relevant distinction between pleasures and pains is a quantitative distinction of more and less. As Bentham put it, pushpin (a child's game) is as good as poetry, as long as it gives you an equal amount of pleasure. This doctrine too had the effect of leveling the social distinctions between the high and low born, for it had been easy for the cultivated upper classes to insist that they were privy to joys and sorrows too refined for the lower classes even to imagine. In these ways—by making each person the judge of his or her own happiness and by making quantity the only significant variable—utilitarianism provided a philosophical justification for a democratic social program.

All persons are basically prudent, rationally self-interested actors. That is to say, we seek to satisfy our desires in the most extensive and pleasurable way, and we use the resources available to us—money, talent, power—in the most efficient manner possible. But there are two great obstacles to fully rational self-interested action. The first of these, the target of the eighteenth-century enlightenment, is superstition. So long as people falsely believe that they have no right to satisfy their desires; so long as religion, ancient custom, or class distinctions inhibit common men and women from using the resources they have for the achievement of their own happiness; so long, in short, as the reasoning power of the mind is clouded by fear, awe, and false belief—then just so long will the injustices and inequalities of society continue. The second obstacle is the ignorance that even enlightened men and women suffer of the facts of science and public affairs, ignorance of the most efficient means for pursuing legitimate satisfactions.

Education was the weapon utilitarians aimed at these twin enemies, superstition and ignorance. Education was to perform two tasks: first, to liberate enslaved minds from the superstitious religious and political dogmas of the past and, second, to introduce the liberated minds to the facts of science and society. An educated population could then be counted on to support wise public policy, for such policy would aim at the greatest happiness of the greatest number, and that simply meant their own happiness as private citizens. Thus utilitarianism combined a psychological theory of individual motivation with a moral theory of the good and an educational theory of enlightenment to produce what we today call a political theory of liberal democracy.

It remains to mention one last element of the utilitarian system an element that may well have been the most important of all, namely the **laissez-faire** economic theory created by Adam Smith and David Ricardo and deployed by James Mill and his son in the great debates over public policy. This is not an economics textbook, and philosophy is hard enough all by itself, but at least a few words must be said about the laissez-faire theory in order to fill out Mill's position and set the stage for the powerful attacks that Karl Marx launched against it a very few years later.

The major fact of the end of the eighteenth century and the beginning of the nineteenth was, of course, the growth of mercantile and industrial capitalism. The key to the new capitalism was the systematic investment of accumulated wealth, or "capital," for the purpose of producing goods that could be sold at a profit in the marketplace. The individual who set the economic activity in motion was called an "entrepreneur," which is French for "undertaker" and means someone who undertakes to do something, not someone who buries someone (although critics of capitalism might have argued that there was indeed a connection between the two meanings). The capitalist undertook to rent the land, hire the labor, buy the raw materials, and bring together these factors of production in a process that resulted in finished goods. The goods were put on sale in a market where no law fixed the prices that must be paid or the profits that could be made. Adam Smith, in his famous treatise *The Wealth of Nations,* argued that if everyone were permitted to do the best he could for himself—worker, capitalist, merchant, and consumer—then the net result would be the most efficient use of the resources of the nation for the production of goods designed to satisfy human desires. The consumers would spend their money in the marketplace in such a way as to get the greatest pleasure for value. If one sort of product rose too high in price, they would shift to another, for paying all your money for a single piece of meat would be

Laissez-Faire   Literally, allow to do. Laissez-faire is the system of free market exchanges, with an absolute minimum of government control, which nineteenth-century liberals believed would result in the most efficient use of resources and the greatest material well-being for society. *Laissez-faire capitalism* refers to the early stage in the development of capitalism, when firms were small, owner-run, and controlled both in their purchases and in their sales by market pressures.

foolish when the same money could buy you fish, eggs, shoes, and a coat. The capitalists would pull their capital out of areas where too much was being produced, because as supply exceeded demand, they would be forced to drop their prices in order to unload their inventory, and profits would tumble. In the same way, if there were customers clamoring for a commodity that was not being produced, they would bid up the price in the market, drive up profits in that branch of business, and attract profit-seeking capitalists who would open new factories to "capitalize" on the unsatisfied demand.

Since happiness is pleasure and pleasure results from the satisfaction of desire, and consumers buy goods to satisfy desires, it follows that the capitalists trying to make a profit are at the same time actually working to make the consumers happy. They are not *trying* to make them happy, of course! The capitalists, like all men and women, are rationally *self*-interested pleasure maximizers. But the genius of the new capitalist free market system was precisely that each person, seeking only his or her own good, automatically advanced the good of others. Thus selfishness could be counted on to do rationally and efficiently what altruism never quite managed—namely, to produce the greatest happiness possible for the greatest number of people. Here is how Adam Smith puts it in a passage that is much quoted and copied. Smith is actually in the midst of a discussion of restrictions on imports, but the thesis he enunciates has a quite general application:

ADAM SMITH,
The Wealth of Nations

Adam Smith,
*The Wealth of Nations,
Books I and II*

But the annual revenue of every society is always precisely equal to the exchangeable value of the whole annual produce of its industry, or rather is precisely the same thing with that exchangeable value. As every individual, therefore, endeavours as much as he can both to employ his capital in the support of domestic industry, and so to direct that industry that its produce may be of the greatest value; every individual necessarily labours to render the annual revenue of the society as great as he can. He generally, indeed, neither intends to promote the public interest, nor knows how much he is promoting it. By preferring the support of domestic to that of foreign industry, he intends only his own security; and by directing that industry in such a manner as its produce may be of the greatest value, he intends only his own gain, and he is in this, as in many other cases, led by an invisible hand to promote an end which was no part of his intention. Nor is it always the worse for the society that it was no part of it. By pursuing his own interest he frequently promotes that of the society more effectually than when he really intends to promote it. I have never known much good done by those who affected to trade for the public good. It is an affectation, indeed, not very common among merchants, and very few words need be employed in dissuading them from it.

Mill read widely in authors whose views were far removed from those of Bentham and his father. He learned from the Romantic critics of the reform movement even as he sought to counter their arguments. He studied the writings of such acute conservative observers as Alexis de Tocqueville, and even absorbed the lessons of the French socialists, though he seems not to have read or appreciated the more powerful theoretical assault mounted by the great German socialist Karl Marx. The breadth of his learning and his personal dissatisfaction with the narrow dogma of his father led Mill to doubt or even to deny some of the central tenets of utilitarian philosophy and social policy. Nevertheless, to the end of his life, his mind remained trapped within the confines of the principles he had been taught as a youth.

In at least *three* important ways, Mill questioned the theses of the orthodox reform doctrine. First, he denied Bentham's egalitarian insistence that any pleasure, in and of itself, is as good as any other (which, as we have seen, is a roundabout way of saying that any person is as good as any other). As far back as Plato, philosophers had argued that some pleasures are simply finer, higher, morally better than other pleasures. Usually, as we might expect, they claimed that the pleasures of the mind are superior to the pleasures of the

ADAM SMITH

Adam Smith (1723–1790) was born in Scotland at a time when that small country was one of the liveliest intellectual centers in Europe. Like his countryman, David Hume, Smith wrote on a wide variety of problems, in what we would now call the social sciences. His masterwork was a long, difficult, revolutionary study of the foundations of economic activity in a free market capitalist economy, entitled *Inquiry into the Nature and Causes of the Wealth of Nations*. With this book, Smith created the field of economics and laid the theoretical basis for the doctrine of laissez-faire, which still has wide support two centuries later. The *Wealth of Nations* was published in 1776, just at the time when the American colonies were declaring their independence of the English crown; and it is fitting that history should have linked these two events, for the Founding Fathers were deeply imbued with the laissez-faire spirit of individual freedom, minimal government, and the pursuit of rational self-interest.

body. Bentham was prepared to admit that some pleasures are more intense, or more long lasting, or had more pleasant after-effects than others. A quart of bad wine might give less pleasure than a sip of fine brandy. A night of drinking might be followed by such a horrendous morning after that the total experience would add up to a minus rather than a plus. Some pleasures, like some foods, might be acquired tastes, requiring knowledge and long practice before they could be properly appreciated. But after all this had been taken into account—and Bentham carefully did take it into account—utilitarianism still insisted that only quantity and not quality of pleasure mattered. Mill could not accept this teaching, fundamental though it was to the philosophy he had been trained to defend. He was stung by the critics of utilitarianism who made it out to be a brutish or degraded philosophy, a philosophy of the base appetites. In replying to their charge, he drew a distinction between higher and lower pleasures that fundamentally altered the significance and logical force of utilitarianism. Here is the passage, taken from an essay called "Utilitarianism," which Mill first published in a magazine and later as a short book.

Gin Lane by William Hogarth (1697–1765). Hogarth's famous engraving illustrates rather forcefully the negative consequences of a night of drinking! *(Source:* The Metropolitan Museum of Art.*)*

Higher and Lower Pleasures

Now such a theory of life excites in many minds, and among them in some of the most estimable in feeling and purpose, inveterate dislike. To suppose that life has (as they express it) no higher end than pleasure—no better and nobler object of desire and pursuit—they designate as utterly mean and groveling, as a doctrine worthy only of swine, to whom the followers of Epicurus were, at a very early period, contemptuously likened; and modern holders of the doctrine are occasionally made the subject of equally polite comparisons by its German, French, and English assailants.

When thus attacked, the Epicureans have always answered that it is not they, but their accusers, who represent human nature in a degrading light, since the accusation supposes human beings to be capable of no pleasures except those of which swine are capable. If this supposition were true, the charge could not be gainsaid, but would then be no longer an imputation; for if the sources of pleasure were precisely the same to human beings and to swine, the rule of life which is good enough for the one would be good enough for the other. The comparison of the Epicurean life to that of beasts is felt as degrading, precisely because a beast's pleasures do not satisfy a human being's conceptions of happiness. Human beings have faculties more elevated than the animal appetites and, when once made conscious of them, do not regard anything as happiness which does not include their gratification.

It is quite compatible with the principle of utility to recognize the fact that some kinds of pleasure are more desirable and more valuable than others. It would be absurd that, while in estimating all other things quality is considered as well as quantity, the estimation of pleasure should be supposed to depend on quantity alone.

If I am asked what I mean by difference of quality in pleasures, or what makes one pleasure more valuable than another, merely as a pleasure, except its being greater in amount, there is but one possible answer. Of two pleasures, if there be one to which all or almost all who have experience of both give a decided preference, irrespective of any feeling of moral obligation to prefer it, that is the more desirable pleasure. If one of the two is, by those who are competently acquainted with both, placed so far above the other that they prefer it, even though knowing it to be attended with a greater amount of discontent, and would not resign it for any quantity of the other pleasure which their nature is capable of, we are justified in ascribing to the preferred enjoyment a superiority in quality so far outweighing quantity as to render it, in comparison, of small account.

Now it is an unquestionable fact that those who are equally acquainted with and equally capable of appreciating and enjoying both do give a most marked preference to the manner of existence which

JOHN STUART MILL, *Utilitarianism*

employs their higher faculties. Few human creatures would consent to be changed into any of the lower animals for a promise of the fullest allowance of a beast's pleasures; no intelligent human being would consent to be a fool, no instructed person would be an ignoramus, no person of feeling and conscience would be selfish and base, even though they should be persuaded that the fool, the dunce, or the rascal is better satisfied with his lot than they are with theirs. They would not resign what they possess more than he for the most complete satisfaction of all the desires which they have in common with him. If they ever fancy they would, it is only in cases of unhappiness so extreme that to escape from it they would exchange their lot for almost any other, however undesirable in their own eyes. A being of higher faculties requires more to make him happy, is capable probably of more acute suffering, and certainly accessible to it at more points, than one of an inferior type; but in spite of these liabilities, he can never really wish to sink into what he feels to be a lower grade of existence.

John Stuart Mill, *Utilitarianism*

There are a number of tricky logical problems with the position Mill defends here, the complete analysis of which would carry us into some rather dry and technical regions of the theory of utility. But one problem springs instantly from the page at us. If not all pleasures are equal in quality, if some persons of more refined sensibility are better able to judge of the quality of pleasures, then the basic democratic one-person-one vote thrust of utilitarianism is lost. Instead of giving every person, however low in station or meager in education, an equal voice in the choice of the ends of social policy, special weight shall have to be accorded to the opinions of that educated minority who have tasted the elevated pleasures of the mind—to those who claim, from the height of their culture, that Bach is better than rock and cordon bleu better than cheeseburgers. The fact is that Mill does indeed exhibit just such an aristocratic bias in his political writings, both in regard to the privileged position of the upper classes within England and also in regard to England's privileged position in her colonies vis-à-vis the "subject races" not yet raised to her own level of culture. The cultural imperialism of Mill, as we may call it, is of course interesting as a fact about the man and his times. But it also is a firstrate example of the way in which an apparently trivial philosophical argument about a technical point can carry with it very large consequences for the most practical questions of politics.

Mill's second revision of his father's faith concerned the rationality and predictability of the laborers, capitalists, and consumers who interact in the marketplace. The doctrine of laissez-faire, with its emphasis on limited government intervention in the market and a removal of all regulations on trade and commerce, depends upon two assumptions, as we have already seen. The first is that economic actors can be counted on to behave in a rationally self-interested manner, buying as cheaply as possible, taking the highest

wages available, always looking for a profit; the second, which depended for its plausibility on the first, is that an economy run along laissez-faire lines and populated by rationally self-interested persons will maximize growth and production and thereby create the greatest happiness possible, within the limits of natural resources and technology, for the greatest number of people. In one of his major works, *Principles of Political Economy,* Mill denied the first of these two assumptions and thereby laid the theoretical groundwork for the rejection of the second.

First let us look at Mill's argument. Then we will consider its significance.

JOHN STUART MILL, *Principles of Political Economy*

Under the rule of individual property, the division of the produce is the result of two determining agencies: Competition and Custom. It is important to ascertain the amount of influence which belongs to each of these causes, and in what manner the operation of one is modified by the other.

Political economists generally, and English political economists above others, have been accustomed to lay almost exclusive stress upon the first of these agencies; to exaggerate the effect of competition, and to take into little account the other and conflicting principle. They are apt to express themselves as if they thought that competition actually does, in all cases, whatever it can be shown to be the tendency of competition to do. This is partly intelligible, if we consider that only through the principle of competition has political economy any pretension to the character of a science. So far as rents, profits, wages, prices, are determined by competition, laws may be assigned for them. Assume competition to be their exclusive regulator, and principles of broad generality and scientific precision may be laid down, according to which they will be regulated. The political economist justly deems this his proper business: and as an abstract or hypothetical science, political economy cannot be required to do, and indeed cannot do, anything more. But it would be a great misconception of the actual course of human affairs, to suppose that competition exercises in fact this unlimited sway. I am not speaking of monopolies, either natural or artificial, or of any interferences of authority with the liberty of production or exchange. Such disturbing causes have always been allowed for by political economists. I speak of cases in which there is nothing to restrain competition; no hindrance to it either in the nature of the case or in artificial obstacles; yet in which the result is not determined by competition, but by custom or usage; competition either not taking place at all, or producing its effect in quite a different manner from that which is ordinarily assumed to be natural to it.

Since custom stands its ground against competition to so considerable an extent, even where, from the multitude of competitors and the general energy in the pursuit of gain, the spirit of competition is strongest, we may be sure that this is much more the case

> where people are content with smaller gains, and estimate their pe-
> cuniary interest at a lower rate when balanced against their case or
> their pleasure. I believe it will often be found, in Continental Europe,
> that prices and charges, of some or of all sorts, are much higher in
> some places than in others not far distant, without its being possible
> to assign any other cause than that it has always been so: the cus-
> tomers are used to it, and acquiesce in it. An enterprising competitor,
> with sufficient capital, might force down the charges, and make his
> fortune during the process; but there are no enterprising competitors;
> those who have capital prefer to leave it where it is, or to make less
> profit by it in a more quiet way.

Mill is saying that although the behavior of men and women in the market may be *predictable,* it is not *calculable.* The difference is fundamental, so
perhaps we should take a moment to explain it more clearly. Suppose I want
to open a snack shop, and I am trying to decide whether to locate downtown
or in a new mall being built on the edge of town. I know that the mall will
have a number of discount outlets selling well-known brands at very low
prices. If I can assume that consumers will be motivated solely by a desire to
minimize their expenditures for the goods they buy, then I can *calculate* (without any special information about shopping habits in this area) that the mall
will be crowded with bargain hunters. Since I want my snack shop to be
where the shoppers are, I will choose the mall.

But if Mill is right (as in fact he is), then a certain proportion of the shoppers will go on shopping downtown, whether out of habit or because they
care enough about such nonmonetary things as the familiarity of the stores.
There is no way in the world that I can foresee just how many shoppers will
be influenced enough by these factors to go downtown instead of to the mall.
I can observe shopping behavior in other towns and extrapolate to this case,
or do an opinion survey of shoppers, or in some other fashion try to base my
prediction on experience. With enough data, I may be able to *predict* what the
shoppers will do, so that I can decide where to put my snack shop. But there
is no way that I can *calculate* their behavior.

As long as economic actors in the marketplace act in a rationally self-
interested way, I can calculate their actions without any prior knowledge of
their individual character, without elaborate collections of information about
their past behavior. All I need know is that (1) they seek to maximize profits
or enjoyments and (2) they will make use of the available information in a rational attempt to achieve that maximization. I can then carry out in my own
head the same calculation they will carry out, and so I can calculate their actions. But if they are influenced by what Mill calls *custom,* which is to say by
irrational tastes, habits, and preferences that deviate from the strict rationality
of profit maximization, then I can only predict their behavior on the basis of
vast quantities of systematically collected data about their past behavior. I
cannot count on the "invisible hand" of the marketplace to direct their eco-

nomic activities into the most productive areas. Capitalists may refrain, out of irrational habits or aversions, from shifting their capital into sectors of unmet market demand. Consumers may go on shopping at a more expensive store when identical goods are offered more cheaply next door. Workers may fail to quit low-paying jobs and move to better-paying jobs in labor-short industries.

The result will be a breakdown of the automatic mechanisms of the market and a need for scientifically controlled management of the economy by a central authority possessing both the information and the power to implement its judgments. In short, the slight revision that Mill makes in the classical theory of laissez-faire leads directly, although not immediately, to the modern managed economy of welfare-state capitalism.

Mill's third alteration in the radical philosophy of James Mill follows directly from the first and concerns the government's right to interfere with the private lives of its citizens. In his famous essay, *On Liberty,* Mill argues for an absolute ban on all state or social intervention in the inner life of thoughts and feelings. But in the last chapter of the *Principles,* he takes a somewhat different line. To be sure, he says, *"Laissez-faire* . . . should be the general practice: every departure from it, unless required by some great good, is a certain evil." But in considering permissible departures, Mill concedes a very great deal indeed. Listen to him in this suggestive passage:

We have observed that, as a general rule, the business of life is better performed when those who have an immediate interest in it are left to take their own course, uncontrolled either by the mandate of the law or by the meddling of any public functionary. The persons, or some of the persons, who do the work, are likely to be better judges than the government, of the means of attaining the particular end at which they aim. Were we to suppose, what is not very probable, that the government has possessed itself of the best knowledge which had been acquired up to a given time by the persons most skilled in the occupation; even then, the individual agents have so much stronger and more direct an interest in the result, that the means are far more likely to be improved and perfected if left to their uncontrolled choice. But if the workman is generally the best selector of means, can it be affirmed with the same universality, that the consumer, or person served, is the most competent judge of the end? Is the buyer always qualified to judge of the commodity? If not, the presumption in favour of the competition of the market does not apply to the case; and if the commodity be one, in the quality of which society has much at stake, the balance of advantages may be in favour of some mode and degree of intervention, by the authorized representatives of the collective interest of the state.

Now, the proposition that the consumer is a competent judge of the commodity, can be admitted only with numerous abatements

JOHN STUART MILL,
Principles of Political Economy

and exceptions. He is generally the best judge (though even this is not true universally) of the material objects produced for his use. These are destined to supply some physical want, or gratify some taste or inclination, respecting which wants or inclinations there is no appeal from the person who feels them; or they are the means and appliances of some occupation, for the use of the persons engaged in it, who may be presumed to be judges of the things required in their own habitual employment. But there are other things of the worth of which the demand of the market is by no means a test; things of which the utility does not consist in ministering to inclinations, nor in serving the daily uses of life, and the want of which is least felt where the need is greatest. This is peculiarly true of those things which are chiefly useful as tending to raise the character of human beings. The uncultivated cannot be competent judges of cultivation.

We have been speaking thus far of Bentham, James Mill, and John Stuart Mill as "liberals," and that is indeed how they spoke of themselves. But as often happens in politics, as in other fields, words shift their meanings as time passes. No word shows this tendency more strikingly than the word "liberal."

"Liberal" comes from the same Latin root as "liberate," which means "to set free." The original, late eighteenth-century and early nineteenth-century liberals criticized the old order for its lack of "liberty," both political and economic. Men and women were not politically free to speak as they chose, to worship in their own manner, to assemble, to participate in the selection of their government, to help make the laws by which they were ruled. And they were also not free to buy and sell as they wished, to take jobs anywhere they could find them, to start businesses and sell their goods at whatever price they thought best.

Bentham and the Mills believed that these two kinds of unfreedom were connected. They argued, by means of their doctrine of utilitarianism, that the citizens of a nation should be free, "liberated," both to conduct their private lives as they chose *and* to conduct themselves in the marketplace, as employers or employees, buyers or sellers, consumers or producers, just as they saw fit. They argued that if the government would interfere as little as possible in either realm, men and women would be happier, and society as a whole would be better off.

Despite all his qualifications and revisions in the utilitarian creed, Mill remained faithful to its spirit. But powerful intellectual attacks were mounted on laissez-faire liberalism and utilitarianism. In the next section of this chapter, we shall listen to some of the voices of dissent. The attacks began as soon as industrial capitalism and its liberal defenders appeared. In the very first decades of the nineteenth century, Romantic conservative critics of industrialism and socialist critics of the capitalist organization of that industrialism appeared in England and on the Continent. But I do not want you to think that this is an ancient dispute, buried in dusty books written by men long dead. The very same argument continues today.

The Socialist Attack on Capitalism

The misery of the workers in the early factories, the squalor of the slums in which they and their families suffered, and the gross contrast between their poverty and the wealth of the entrepreneurs provoked a flood of scathing condemnations of the new industrial order. Some of the criticisms were merely cries from the heart, but especially in France a number of philosophers and economists made an effort to discover the underlying causes of the suffering created by capitalism. It was the German Karl Marx, however, who mounted the most sustained, thoroughgoing, and intellectually impressive critique of the institutions, economic theories, and philosophical rationalizations of industrial capitalism.

The genius of Marx's critique was that it met the liberal philosophy head on at its strongest point and turned its own arguments against itself. Liberalism and laissez-faire claimed to be rational doctrines, stripped of all superstitious mystification. Conservatives denied the primacy of reason and attempted instead to elevate imagination or tradition to the first place. But Marx accepted the challenge of liberalism. Industrial capitalism, he insisted, is not rational. Instead, it is profoundly irrational, and its claims to rationality, expressed in its economic theory and in its philosophy, are no more than an ideological rationalization designed to conceal the inner illogic of capitalism and thereby preserve a system that favors the interests of a few at the expense of the lives of many.

Marx begins his criticism of capitalism with an analysis of it. How does capitalism work? What is Marx's conception of the social and economic organization of a capitalist country? Upon first inspection, society at any one time seems an unorganized beehive of multifarious activities, without any system, pattern, or rationale. Agriculture, the arts, science, industry, government, religion, entertainment, marketing, war, charity, crime—the things men and women do—are endless in number and variety. Merely to list all of the categories of jobs being performed by someone or other is to lose oneself in a confusion of diversity. But Marx saw order in the chaos. He argued that in order to make sense of social life, we must distinguish a certain group of activities that are basic to the survival and reproduction of the human race. Each day, men and women work to transform nature into the food, clothing, and shelter they need to live. These economic activities form the base, or foundation, on which all else in the society rests. To distinguish the productive economic activities from the philosophical theorizing that his German idealist predecessors had made so much of, Marx called the productive elements of society its *material base*. In calling the base "material," he did not mean to suggest that it consisted of physical bodies rather than human thoughts, purposes, and plans, for even productive activities are intelligent, purposeful activities involving "ideas." Rather, Marx wanted to emphasize the fundamental role of economic production as opposed to philosophy, religion, or art.

The material base of a society consists of three layers. The first is the *means* of production—the raw materials, land, and energy resources with which men and women work. The second layer—the *forces* of production— includes the factories, machinery, technology, industrial knowledge, and accumulated skills of those who transform the means of production by their labor. The third and by far the most important layer of the material base is what Marx called the *social relationships of production*. Since everything in Marx's theory depends on this last element, we must take a few paragraphs to explain it in some detail.

Human beings are productive creatures, to be sure. But according to Marx, they are *socially* productive creatures. Men and women divide the labor among themselves, differentiating the process of production into a series of subjobs or specialties and then parceling out these pieces of the total productive process among different workers. Some people raise grain, others dig iron ore out of the ground. Others bake the grain into bread, and still others work the ore into tools and weapons. This *division of labor* also requires a system of exchange, for no one can live on the products of his or her own labor alone. The farmer needs the products of the carpenter, the carpenter needs the products of the metal worker, and the metal worker needs the grain grown by the farmer. The market is the system by which a never-ending chain of trades, or purchases and sales, distributes the products of labor among the members of society.

Although productive activity is cooperative, in the sense that there is a division of function and an exchange of products, it is by no means harmonious, equitable, or universally beneficent. Very early in human history, according to Marx, some men by force of arms succeed in seizing control over the vital means of production. They take the land, the streams, the mines, and the forests, and they prevent others from using them. Once these men have successfully asserted ownership of the means of production, they are in a position to extract a ransom from the rest of the men and women in the society. Pay me half of all you grow, the landholder says to the farmer, or I will not allow you to farm the land. The farmer has no choice, for if he does not farm, he starves. So two classes of people crystallize out of the social situation: the ruling class, which controls the means of production; and the underclass, which is forced to give up a part of the product of its labor in order to survive.

At first, of course, the naked force that holds the underclass down is obvious to all. But as time passes and generations succeed one another, sheer custom and familiarity confer legitimacy on what was originally mere might. The rulers pass on the control of the means of production to their sons and daughters, who grow up believing that it is theirs by right. The free time that the rulers have—because they eat and drink and wear what they do not have to produce—permits them to develop a culture and style of life quite different from that of the laboring majority. Small wonder that even those in the underclass soon come to believe that the rulers are "different." They may not have

Marx's theory of the structure of society. *(Source:* Drawn for Robert Paul Wolff by Prentice Hall.*)*

been originally, but their descendants have certainly become so. As regular patterns of work, exchange, land ownership, and personal subordination develop, the rulers hold periodic courts to settle disputes that may have arisen in the enactment of those patterns. The decisions of these courts become the law of the land. Needless to say, the decisions rarely threaten the interests of the rulers, for it is they who convene the courts, they who sit on the bench, and they who enforce the orders of the courts with their soldiers. Nor is it surprising that the religious men and women of the society bless the rulers and their dominance. Churches are economically unproductive institutions, and they can survive only by sharing in that portion of the product that the rulers have taken from the laborers.

The system of relationships connecting those who control the means of production and those who do not is called by Marx the social relationships of production. It is the basic fact about a society, and from it grow such other, secondary facts as the structure of the law, and the dogmas of the dominant religion, and the underlying themes of the art and literature. Marx calls these subordinate or secondary features of a society its *superstructure,* conveying by this metaphor the notion that a society rests on, or is built upon, that portion of it that is the "base." A more modern way of putting the same idea would be to say that the means, forces, and social relationships of production are the independent variables in a society, and that the law, politics, art, religion, and philosophy are the dependent variables.

In the superstructure, the state occupies a central place, for it is the instrument the ruling class uses to maintain its domination of the rest of the society. As the character of the social relationships of production changes, so does the character of the state. Under feudalism, which is a system of production based on ownership of land, the state is controlled by the landed aristocracy, which employs it to maintain control of the agricultural workers (or "serfs") and to regulate the relationships between the great landholders (or "lords") and their subordinate tenants (or "vassals"). This same system of landholding also forms the basis for the military organization of the society, thereby combining the control of the means of production with the supply of the force to maintain that control. In an industrial system of production, where capital rather than land is central to the productive process, the class that owns the capital (the "capitalists") also controls the state. As Marx and his lifelong collaborator Friedrich Engels say in their most famous work, *The Communist Manifesto,* "The executive of the modern state is nothing but a committee for managing the common affairs of the whole bourgeoisie."

How, according to Marx, do societies change over time? At any given moment, we may speak of the ruling class and the underclass. In our society, these are the **bourgeoisie** and the **proletariat.** But as new technology develops, as the division of labor is carried farther and farther, slow shifts take place in the material base. Within the feudal order, capitalism begins to grow. New ways of production and exchange give rise to new systems of relationships. At first, the changes seem minute by comparison with the overwhelming preponderance of economic activity. But little by little, more men and women are drawn into the new patterns of economic activity. The economically progressive group, or class, is at first disadvantaged, for the rules have all been made to favor the dominant class. However, as the real economic power of the progressive class grows, it begins to demand a place in the ruling circles of the society. It wants laws changed to help rather than hinder its economic interests. It wants a share of the power that comes from controlling the means of production.

Bourgeoisie and Proletariat   The *bourgeoisie* is the middle class consisting of factory owners, shopkeepers, bankers, financiers, and their associates. "Bourgeoisie" comes from the medieval term *bourg,* meaning "walled city." Burghers, or bourgeois, were the inhabitants of a walled city—by extension, the merchants and master craftsmen who formed the economic elite of the city, as opposed to the aristocracy, whose wealth and power were based on landholdings. In Marx's writings, the *proletariat* is the urban population of wage-earning workers. "Proletariat" comes from the old Latin word for the lowest class of people in Rome.

Now Marx was an optimist, if by that we mean that he thought the human race was heading toward better times. But he was not a fool. It was perfectly obvious to him that whenever a growing class challenges the dominance of a ruling class, there is going to be violence. There was no way that capitalists could compromise their interests with the landed aristocrats of the old order; one of them was going to have to go. According to Marx, the two centuries of civil war and social upheaval, beginning with the English Civil War, continuing on through the French and American revolutions, and ending with the American Civil War, were simply the protracted struggle between the landed aristocracy of the precapitalist order and the capitalist class that controlled the new industrial means of production.

This, in a very brief summary, is Marx's *analysis* of capitalism—how it emerged from feudalism, how it works, and what makes it change. This is the case with what has come to be known as **Marxism.** Now we can take a look at his *criticism* of capitalism—what he thinks is wrong with it. As I suggested earlier, Marx's basic complaint against capitalism is that it is *irrational*. Indeed, Marx claims that industrial capitalism is irrational in two different ways. First, it is instrumentally irrational. That is to say, it systematically chooses inefficient means to attain the ends it claims to set for itself. The triumphant claim of Adam Smith and the other capitalist apologists had been that a free market profit system would make maximally efficient use of the resources and technology available to a society at any moment and that it would generate new economic production more expeditiously than any system of government management or tradition. Marx agreed that capitalism is unequaled at the task of production, but the very same capitalism is unable to solve the even more important problem of distributing what its factories have produced. In a capitalist system, production is for profit, not for use. If the capitalist cannot make a good return on his investment, he is forced to close up shop, even though there may be men and women in the society crying for the goods he produces. By the same token, as long as he is making a good

Marxism   The economic, political, and philosophical doctrines first set forth by Karl Marx and then developed by his disciples and followers. Although Marx himself considered his theories scientific, his followers have often treated them as a form of secular religion. The principal doctrines are: first, that capitalism is internally unstable and prone to fall into economic crises; second, that the profits of capitalist enterprises derive from the exploitation of the workers, who receive in wages less than they produce; third, that as capitalism develops, workers will tend to become more self-aware of their situation—and hence more likely to overthrow capitalism by force; and fourth, that the society that comes into existence after capitalism is destroyed will be socialist and democratic in its economic and political organization.

K A R L   M A R X

Karl Marx (1818–1883) is the founder of modern socialism. Born in Prussia, he studied philosophy and in his twenties joined a circle of young radical social critics and philosophers known as the Young Hegelians. After a number of years as a pamphleteer and intellectual agitator in Germany and France, Marx moved to London to escape political persecution. Once in England, he settled into a rather quiet life of scholarship, reflection, writing, and political organization. Throughout a lifetime of collaboration with Friedrich Engels (1820–1895), Marx systematically elaborated a full-scale economic, political, philosophical, historical, and moral critique of the industrial capitalist system that had developed first in England and then throughout the rest of Europe.

As a young man, Marx was inflamed with the revolutionary conviction that the capitalist order was on the brink of total collapse. After the failure of the workers' uprisings in 1848 and the reactionary turn of most Continental governments, Marx developed a deeper and more long-term analysis of the internal weaknesses of capitalism. Though his writings fill many volumes, there can be no doubt that the masterpiece of his life was the book called, simply, *Capital*.

Unlike many of his followers, Marx was always ready to alter his theories in the face of new evidence. Although he was certain in his youth that socialism could come only through a violent revolutionary overthrow of capitalist society and government, later in his life he concluded that, in countries such as England and America, socialism might come through the relatively peaceful avenue of political agitation and election.

profit, he goes on churning out goods, regardless of whether they are high on society's list of genuine needs. The market is the distribution mechanism, which means that only consumers with cash in hand can buy what the capitalists have produced. But in order for the capitalist to make a high profit, he must keep his wages down, for—Marx argues—profits come out of the difference between the value of what the workers produce and the wages they are paid by their employers. So the same capitalist who cuts his workers' wages to the bone finds no one in the market with money to buy his products.

Competition with other capitalists pushes each producer to cut prices and to increase volume in an attempt to seize a larger share of the market. The result is a cycle of overproduction, leading to layoffs, recession, depression, general misery, and then an upswing into new overproduction. Now ever since people have been on the earth, natural disasters have afflicted them, blighting their crops, flooding their homes, striking them down with disease. But the depressions produced periodically in the nineteenth and twentieth centuries by capitalism are not natural disasters; they are man-made disasters, arising out of the inner irrationality of the capitalist system. Hunger has resulted not from crop failures but from the inability of the market system to distribute what is produced. There has been famine in the midst of plenty; in America, during the Great Depression of the 1930s, farmers were literally forced to plow piglets under with their tractors while millions hovered on the brink of malnutrition and actual starvation. These "inner contradictions" of capitalism, as Marx called them, are living evidence of the irrationality of that social system the utilitarians had proclaimed the reign of reason.

Even this terrible instrumental irrationality of capitalism, however, is merely a means, as it were, to the substantive irrationality, the debasing inhumanity of capitalism as it is actually lived by industrial workers. You have all heard the term **alienation**. These days it has become a catchword and is used to apply to everything from psychic disorder to mere boredom. The term was first used by the German philosopher Georg F. W. Hegel and was taken over by Marx to describe what happens to men and women who labor under capitalism. Marx held that humans are by nature productive animals who live in this world by intelligently, purposefully transforming nature, in cooperation with their fellow humans, into commodities that can satisfy their needs and desires. In the process of production, men and women "externalize" themselves—that is, they make what was first a mere idea in their minds external to themselves in the form of an object or state of affairs that they create by their labor. The most important act of such self-externalizing creation is birth itself, but the same structure of creativity can be seen in the farmer's planning, planting, tending, and harvesting of a field of grain, in the carpenter's conceiving, cutting, fashioning, and finishing a piece of furniture, and also in an artist's sculpting of a statue or a poet's forming of a sonnet.

Men and women need productive, fulfilling labor to be truly happy, Marx thought. He rejected the utilitarian notion that happiness consists simply in the satisfaction of desire. But the process of "externalization," by which men and women embody themselves in their creations, in their transformations of nature, and in their interactions with one another, can be corrupted and

Alienation   According to Marx, the condition of being at war with one's own nature, the products of one's labor, and one's fellow workers. Marx argued that capitalism undermines the human capacity for creative and productive work, making men and women unhappy in their work, dissatisfied in their leisure, and unable to fulfill their human potential. Marx derived the concept of alienation from German philosophers of the early nineteenth century.

perverted. If the products of our labor are taken out of our control, if the very laboring process itself is turned into a kind of submission to superior force, then what we make will come to appear to us not as fulfillments of our needs but as oppressive enemies thwarting our human nature. What has been externalized will become *alien*. In short, healthy externalization will become destructive *alienation*.

Capitalism systematically frustrates our need for satisfying labor in every possible way, according to Marx. There is plenty of labor, to be sure. But it is not autonomous labor, it is not labor directed at satisfying genuine human needs, it is not healthful, fulfilling labor. It is competitive labor that sets worker against worker, worker against capitalist, and capitalist against capitalist. The very productivity of capitalism makes it a hell on earth, for at the moment in history when we first achieve the technology to raise ourselves above famine, sickness, and misery, the inner contradictions of our system of property plunge us into depths of suffering worse than anything that was known in the Middle Ages.

Here is just a short selection from Marx's essay on alienated labor from the unpublished and unfinished papers that are known today as the *Economic-Philosophic Manuscripts of 1844*.

KARL MARX,
Economic-Philosophic Manuscripts of 1844

What constitutes the alienation of labour? First, that the work is *external* to the worker, that it is not part of his nature; and that, consequently, he does not fulfill himself in his work but denies himself, has a feeling of misery rather than well-being, does not develop freely his mental and physical energies but is physically exhausted and mentally debased. The worker, therefore, feels himself at home only during his leisure time, whereas at work he feels homeless. His work is not voluntary but imposed, *forced labour*. It is not the satisfaction of a need, but only a means for satisfying other needs. Its alien character is clearly shown by the fact that as soon as there is no physical or other compulsion it is avoided like the plague. External labour, labour in which man alienates himself, is a labour of self-sacrifice, or mortification. Finally, the external character of work for the worker is shown by the fact that it is not his own work but work for someone else, that in work he does not belong to himself but to another person.

What can be done about the irrationality and dehumanization of capitalism? Marx's answer, as you all know, was a revolution, a socialist revolution made by the workers against the capitalists. The revolution, Marx believed, would accomplish several things. First, it would overthrow the system of ownership of the means of production which, under capitalism, places in the hands of a few the accumulated technology, factories, raw materials, and machinery that have been produced collectively by the labor of generations of working men and women. Second, it would replace the system of production for profit in the marketplace by a system of production for the satisfaction of human needs. Men and women would collectively determine what they need and put their talents to work to produce it. The mere accident of profitability would no longer be permitted to govern decisions about capital investment and economic growth. It might be, for example, that a large profit can be made in the United States by building luxury housing for which there was no burning need, but that little or no profit can be made from the production of well-made, gracefully designed, low-cost housing. No matter. If the low-cost housing were needed, it would get first call on the available building materials and construction workforce. Finally, the capitalist system of distribution through the market would be replaced by a rational and humane system of distribution for human need. Under capitalism, the ruling slogan might be "From each as much as you can get; to each as little as you can get away with giving." Under **socialism**, however, the ruling slogan would be "From each according to his ability; to each according to his work." When the final stage of communism is reached, Marx said, the slogan on society's banner would be "From each according to his ability; to each according to his need."

Collective ownership of the means of production, production for use rather than for profit, distribution for need rather than for ability to pay—with these changes, socialism would overcome the instrumental and substantive irrationality of capitalism and eliminate the alienation of human beings from their product, their labor, their own human nature, and their fellow workers.

Marx wrote in the middle of the nineteenth century, and it is now more than 140 years later. The last major depression was sixty-five years ago. In the major industrial nations, despite continuing inequalities of wealth, the workers enjoy a standard of living beyond Marx's wildest dreams. Governments have stepped in with active policies of budget management and monetary control to dampen the boom-to-bust swings that Marx saw as proof of the unstable inner nature of capitalism.

Earlier in the twentieth century, it looked to many people as though the world was going in the direction Marx predicted, although many modern

---

Socialism   An economic and social system based on collective social ownership of the means of production, rational planning of economic investment and growth, roughly equal distribution of goods and services, and production for the satisfaction of human need rather than for private profit. Modern socialism dates from the teachings of the French socialists of the early nineteenth century, but the leading socialist philosopher is the German, Karl Marx.

socialists deny that the Soviet Union and its empire were truly socialist. But the Soviet Union is no more, and the nations of Eastern Europe are competing with one another to see which one can become truly capitalist the fastest. To be sure, China, with one-fifth of the world's population, calls itself Marxist, but even in that great country, the most rapid economic growth is taking place along the coast in cities that have been permitted by the government to follow a capitalist economic path. So it would seem that Marx's dream of socialism is just one more outmoded fantasy, one more bit of nineteenth-century German metaphysics.

And yet, Marx's criticism of capitalism seems still to have some truth to it. In the United States, wealthiest of all the capitalist countries, millions of homeless men and women sleep on the streets, while entire buildings stand vacant because they do not have paying tenants. The government pays farmers billions of dollars *not* to grow food, while children go to bed hungry. Every day we are told by newspaper reporters, politicians, and economists that the only way to get our country to grow economically is for all of us to go into the stores and buy "on credit" things we cannot pay for. Meanwhile, half of America's black teenagers cannot find work, and this generation of young people has discovered that they will not even be able to live as well as their parents have.

The gap between rich and poor in wealthy countries like the United States is exceeded by the even bigger gap between rich and poor nations in the world as a whole. If we think of the entire planet Earth as a single society—a way of looking at things that comes naturally to those of us who have seen pictures of Earth from space—then the contrast between rich and poor, well fed and hungry, hopeful and hopeless is as dramatic, as compelling, as overwhelming as the same contrast was for Marx in London, England, in the 1860s.

Perhaps socialism, as Marx conceived it, is not the *answer,* but the *question* he raised remains with us: how can men and women work together to create a world in which *all* people, not just the favored few, can live decent, meaningful lives? Even though the Cold War is over, it remains to be seen whether capitalism can provide a satisfactory answer to that question.

Rousseau and the Theory of the Social Contract

Thus far, we have been looking at some of the ways in which philosophers have answered the general question, what is the good society? We saw that moral problems of the just distribution of wealth are central to this subject. In a way, social philosophy, as Plato suggested long ago, is ethics writ large—it is ethics in a social, rather than an individual, setting. But there is a very special set of questions associated with the study of the *state,* and it is to these questions that we now turn. Before we go any farther, we had best determine what we mean by a *state* and what philosophical problems are raised by states. Everywhere we look, across historical time and around the globe, men and women are organized into social groupings within defined territorial limits or borders. Within each one of these geographical units, there is some smaller group of people who rule, give orders, run things, and use force to get others to obey—some group who make and enforce laws. This smaller group is what we call the state. Sometimes the group that rules consists of a single person and his or her personal followers: a king or queen, a general or dictator, a priest or pope, plus a group of loyal underlings. Sometimes the group consists of a hereditary class, such as a military aristocracy. The group may be a political clique or party that has led a successful revolution against the previous rulers. It may even, as in our own country, be a large group of men and women who have been chosen in an election by a much larger group of citizens. But whoever makes the laws, gives the commands, and enforces them on everyone living within that territory *is* the state.

States may exist for any number of purposes: to carry out the tenets of a religious faith, to maintain general peace and security, to see to the well-being of some or all of the people within the territory, or to ensure justice and tranquility. The state may even exist merely for the purpose of lining the pockets and satisfying the desires of itself, regardless of what the rest of the population wants or needs. There are so many different purposes for which states have existed that it is not much use to look for some basic or underlying function that all states perform insofar as they are states. Philosophers express this fact by saying that the state cannot be defined teleologically. That simply means that we cannot explain what a state is in terms of the goals (*telos* is Greek, meaning "end" or "goal") at which it aims. But all states, regardless of who comprises them and no matter what purposes they pursue, have *two* characteristics in common. Once you understand these two characteristics, you will know what a state *is* and also what the fundamental problem of political philosophy is.

First, states everywhere and always use force to obtain obedience to their commands. Sometimes force takes the form of armed troops, police, jails, and death rows. And sometimes merely the threat of force is enough to bring recalcitrant citizens into line. Economic threats can be used as effectively as the whip or the club, but behind the judge there always stand the police, and they are not there for ceremony only.

Force alone does not make a group of people into a state, however; for a band of robbers, an invading army, even a lone gunman holding you up on a dark street all use force to make you obey, and no one would call robbers, an army, or a mugger "the state." The second, more important, mark of the state is that as it issues its commands and shows its sword, it also claims to have the *right* to command and the *right* to be obeyed. Now a mugger does not claim the *right* to rob you. He says, "Your money or your life!"; he does not

"First of all, I would like to express my gratefulness to all
of those wonderful ancestors of mine who helped make
this glorious day possible." (Drawing by W. Miller, 1960)
(Source: The Cartoon Bank*)*

say, "Your money, for I have a right to it." But when the state sends you a bill
for taxes, or commands you to report for induction into the armed forces, or
orders you to stop at red lights and drive only with a valid license, it claims to
have a right to your obedience. In the language of political philosophy, the
state claims to be *legitimate.*

There is a wonderful scene in one of Shakespeare's plays *(Henry IV, Part 1)*
in which a group of conspirators is planning its attack on the forces of the
king. One of the group is a flamboyant Welsh chieftain named Glendower,
who claims to have some magical powers in addition to some usable troops.
At one point, in an effort to impress his fellow conspirators with the wonder-
fulness of his powers, he brags, "I can call spirits from the vasty deep." The
leader of the conspiracy, Hotspur, is not very impressed, and he answers,
"Why so can I, and so can any man/but will they come when you do call
them?" The point, of course, is that it is one thing to make a claim and quite
another to get anybody to believe it.

The really remarkable thing about human beings is that they are so
prone to accept the claims of legitimacy made by states that rule the territories in which they live. From time to time, people rebel against the state, and
a few philosophers called anarchists have denied the state's claim to have a
right to rule. But by and large, when states make laws and claim the right to

Signing of The Constitution by **Albert Herter.** The United States was the first country to actually be brought into existence by a social contract. *(Source:* Brown Brothers.*)*

enforce them, people believe their claim and obey *even when they are not actually being forced to do so.* Those last few words are crucial, of course, for most of us "obey" a gunman who holds us up or an army that invades our city and points its guns at us. We "obey" because we do not want to get shot. Cynics might say that that is really the only reason anyone ever obeys the law, but all the historical and sociological evidence points in the opposite direction. Save in the most unusual circumstances, men and women obey the law more faithfully than the threat of punishment requires. They obey from habit, to be sure, but they also obey because they genuinely believe that the state has the right to command them. After all, they think, it is *the law.* How often has each of us done something or refrained from doing something merely because the law says that we must or must not? How, save by playing on this belief in the legitimacy of the law, could a single official or police officer control the behavior of a large crowd? How could several thousand overworked employees of the Internal Revenue Service collect taxes from 200 million Americans? How could a lieutenant lead a platoon of frightened soldiers into withering enemy fire? How, indeed, could an old, feeble king bend young, vigorous, ambitious dukes, princes, and generals to his will?

The belief in the **legitimate authority** of the state is the glue that holds a political society together. It is, even more than armies or police or jails, the means by which the state gets its laws obeyed. So we may sum up the universal characteristics of states by saying that the state is *a group of people who claim the right to enforce obedience to their commands within a territory and succeed in getting most of the people in the territory to accept that claim.* A group of people who make a claim of this sort are said to be claiming *political authority.* So a state is a group of people who claim political authority and have their claim accepted by most of those against whom the claim is made.

Well, states claim political authority, and they get their claims accepted. But it is one thing to get other people to accept something you say; it is quite another to be right. I may claim to be a doctor, and if enough people believe me, I can open an office and start prescribing medicine. But that does not make me a doctor. My "patients" may fail to notice that I am not curing them, but even that does not make me a doctor. So too, a group may claim the right to rule, and the people may accept their claim, but that does not make their claim *true.*

The fundamental question of all political philosophy is obviously this: when does a group calling itself the state really have a *right* to command? Or, since that way of putting the question seems to assume that states sometimes have such a right, we can ask: does any group of persons ever have the right to command?

The same question can be turned around to focus our attention on the person doing the obeying rather than the people doing the commanding. From my point of view as a citizen, a state is a group of people who command me. If I believe that I have an obligation to obey their commands, then I consider them as constituting a legitimate state. Otherwise, I consider them tyrants. To the citizen, the fundamental question of political philosophy is: do I ever have an obligation to obey the commands issued by some group calling itself the state?

In ancient and medieval times, the citizen's obligation to the ruler was considered to be limited and conditioned upon the ruler's just performance of his or her sovereign duties. But in the sixteenth and seventeenth centuries, in response to fundamental shifts in the relative power of the aristocracy, the monarchy, and the new middle class, the theory began to be put forward that

Legitimate Authority   The right to give commands that others have a moral obligation to obey. States claim legitimate authority when they say that they have a right to pass laws that citizens or subjects *ought* to obey, regardless of whether they are in danger of being caught for not obeying. Democratic states base their claim to legitimate authority on the fact that they are elected by the people whom they rule and, therefore, speak with the voice of the people.

Devout Catholic kissing the ring of Pope John Paul II. The Roman Catholic Church demands obedience from its communicants, as did the absolute monarchs of their subjects. The distinctive mark of eighteenth-century social contract theorists is their rejection of such demands for obedience. *(Source:* Corbis/Sygma. Photo by Fabian.*)*

the authority of the ruler is absolute. The king, it was said, is the sole possessor of the ultimate political authority—sovereignty, as it was called. All others in the society are unconditionally obligated to obey his commands. Usually a religious justification was advanced for this claim—the king was considered God's representative on earth—but sometimes the theory of an original agreement or contract was also appealed to.

The unqualified claim of absolute kingly authority was unacceptable to the philosophers of the Enlightenment. A person who bows his head to God or his knee to the king merely makes himself the slave of another. In the words of Immanuel Kant, submission to the commands of another means a loss of autonomy, a denial of one's own reason.

So far the political philosophers of the seventeenth and eighteenth centuries, the question of obligation to the state became a new and more complicated question: is there any way in which I can submit to the commands of a legitimate state without giving up my freedom and autonomy?

The man who asked this question more clearly and forcefully than anyone in the history of Western philosophy was the eighteenth-century Swiss thinker Jean-Jacques Rousseau. Judgments differ among philosophers as much as they do among the compilers of all-time baseball or football teams, but in my personal judgment, Jean-Jacques Rousseau is the greatest political philosopher who has ever lived. His claim to immortality rests upon one short book, *Of the Social Contract,* an essay scarcely more than 100 pages long. In that brief, brilliant work, Rousseau formulates the fundamental question of the philosophy of the state and makes a valiant, although ultimately unsuccessful, effort to solve it. Why such fame, you might ask, if he failed to solve the problem? In philosophy, as in the sciences, the most important step frequently is to ask the right question, and although philosophers had been analyzing the nature of the state for more than 2,000 years before Rousseau, he was the first to see exactly what the problem was and to recognize how difficult it would be to solve.

For the philosophers of the state who struggled with the question of legitimate authority in the seventeenth and eighteenth centuries, the standard solution to the problem was the device that they call the **social contract**. The authority of the state, it was argued, can only be founded upon an agreement among all of the persons who are to be ruled by the state. The idea of a contract, of course, was taken from the law, where it applied to an agreement between two parties for their mutual advantage. A buyer and seller in the marketplace make a contract with one another, according to which the seller will supply goods in such and such a quantity, and of so and so quality, and the buyer will pay so much money for them at a particular time. The heart and soul of a contract is what the lawyers call a *quid pro quo,* or a "this for that"; each side must stand to benefit from the deal in order to make the contract binding. The right of either party to have the contract enforced on the other derives from two things: first, each party has freely promised to abide by the contract and so is bound by his or her word; second, each party benefits from the contract and so has an obligation to return the benefit to the other according to the agreed-upon terms.

The social contract theorists, as they have become known, conceived the idea of tracing political obligation back to a contract or social agreement among all the members of the society. If each citizen could be imagined to have actually made such an agreement, then the riddle of legitimate state au-

Social Contract   A voluntary, unanimous agreement among all the people of a society to form themselves into a united political community and to obey the laws laid down by the government they collectively select. In seventeenth- and eighteenth-century political theory, the legitimacy claims of the state are said to rest on an actual or hypothetical social contract.

JEAN-JACQUES ROUSSEAU

Jean-Jacques Rousseau (1712–1778) is one of the most paradoxical figures in modern European letters. Born in Geneva, Switzerland, he spent his early years in a succession of homes (his mother having died only a few days after his birth). At age sixteen, he converted to Catholicism, though he seems not to have been devout in any orthodox manner. After trying his hand at such tasks as music teacher and tutor, Rousseau finally found his true calling, which was to be a writer, a man of letters.

Rousseau's writings fall into two groups, which seem entirely to contradict each other in their teachings. His autobiographical *Confessions,* his novels *Émile* and *La Nouvelle Heloise,* and his *Discourse on the Sciences and the Arts* all set forth in the most moving and powerful way the sentimental doctrine that our nature is inherently good, that civilization is the great corrupter, that feeling rather than reason is the proper guide to life, and that men and women will be naturally moral if only the impediments of cultivated life can be cleared away. But in his greatest work, *Of the Social Contact,* Rousseau argues in a spare and rigorously logical way for the proposition that the just state and morality itself arise from the exercise of our rational powers. Rousseau is thus an apostle both of sentiment—of feeling, of tears and sympathy—and also of reason.

It was the special genius of Rousseau that he saw the central question of political philosophy more clearly than anyone before him, and he expressed it with greater precision and force. Here are the words in which he framed the problem, taken from the sixth chapter of *Of the Social Contract:*

> Where shall we find a form of association which will defend and protect with the whole common force the person and the property of each associate, and by which every person, while uniting himself with all, shall obey only himself and remain as free as before?

thority would be solved. First, it would then be possible to explain why, and under what conditions, the citizen has a duty to obey the law. Very simply, he would have a duty to obey laws made by a state that he had freely contracted or agreed to bring into existence. If he says to the judge, "Who are you to command me? Who are you to threaten me with punishment if I fail to obey?" the judge will answer, "I am a representative of that state which you yourself promised to obey when you signed the social contract." And if the citizen, still resistant, goes on to ask, "What have I received from my fellow citizens that I should keep the agreement I made with them?" the judge can answer, "You have received peace, social order, even-handed justice, and the benefits of a civilized society."

But even more important, if the citizen asks, "How can I obey this state I have brought into existence without forfeiting any autonomy and giving up my freedom?" the judge can answer, "In this state, and only in this state, those who obey remain free. For the state that makes the laws consists not of *some* of the people who live in this nation but of all the people. The commands you obey are the very commands that you, as a citizen, have issued in your role as a lawmaker. In this state, the law obeyers and the lawmakers are one. Through the device of a social contract, the people become the rulers." Indeed, since the traditional word for ruler is "sovereign," the social contract theory is a doctrine of people's sovereignty, or, as it is usually known, popular sovereignty. (That does not mean that people like it; it means that the people are sovereign. This is what Abraham Lincoln meant when he said that we live under a government that is by the people, as well as of and for the people.)

Here is how Rousseau describes the social contract.

JEAN-JACQUES ROUSSEAU,
Of the Social Contract

The articles of this contract are so unalterably fixed by the nature of the act that the least modification renders them vain and of no effect; so that they are the same everywhere, and are everywhere tacitly understood and admitted, even though they may never have been formally announced; until, the social compact being violated, each individual is restored to his original rights, and resumes his native liberty, while losing the conventional liberty for which he renounced it.

The articles of the social contract will, when clearly understood, be found reducible to this single point: the total alienation of each associate, and all his rights, to the whole community; for, in the first place, as every individual gives himself up entirely, the condition of every person is alike; and being so, it would not be to the interest of any one to render that condition offensive to others.

Nay, more than this, the alienation being made without any reserve, the union is as complete as it can be, and no associate has any further claim to anything: for if any individual retained rights not enjoyed in general by all, as there would be no common superior to decide between him and the public, each person being in some points his own judge, would soon pretend to be so in everything; and thus would the state of nature be continued and the association necessarily become tyrannical or be annihilated.

Finally, each person gives himself to all, and so not to any one individual; and as there is no one associate over whom the same right is not acquired which is ceded to him by others, each gains an equivalent for what he loses, and finds his force increased for preserving that which he possesses.

If, therefore, we exclude from the social contract all that is not essential, we shall find it reduced to the following terms:

Each of us places in common his person and all his power under the supreme direction of the general will; and as one body we all receive each member as an indivisible part of the whole.

From that moment, instead of as many separate persons as there are contracting parties, this act of association produces a moral and collective body, composed of as many members as there are votes in the assembly, which from this act receives its unity, its common self, its life, and its will. This public person, which is thus formed by the union of all other persons, took formerly the name of "city," and now takes that of "republic" or "body politic." It is called by its members "State" when it is passive, "Sovereign" when in activity, and whenever it is compared with other bodies of a similar kind, it is denominated "power." The associates take collectively the name of "people": and separately, that of "citizens," as participating in the sovereign authority, and of "subjects," because they are subjected to the laws of the State. But these terms are frequently confounded and used one for the other, and it is enough that a man understands how to distinguish them when they are employed in all their precision.

Two problems arise immediately. First, it is going to be difficult to get everyone together when laws need to be made. How can the people obey only themselves if they do not personally make the laws? The usual solution both in political theory and in political practice is to institute a system of elected representatives. But Rousseau will have none of that. If the state is not kept small enough for everyone to participate in lawmaking, then so far as he is concerned, tyranny replaces liberty. Of course, that means that all citizens, and not just a few professionals, are going to have to pay attention to public affairs. But that is the price of freedom, Rousseau insists. As he says later on in *Of the Social Contract:*

As soon as men cease to consider public service as the principal duty of citizens, and rather choose to serve with their purse than with their persons, we may pronounce the State to be on the very verge of ruin. Are the citizens called upon to march out to war? They pay soldiers for the purpose, and remain at home. Are they summoned to council? They nominate deputies, and stay at home. And thus, in consequence of idleness and money, they have soldiers to enslave their country, and representatives to sell it.

It is the hurry of commerce and of the arts, it is the greedy thirst of gain, and the effeminate softness and love of comfort that occasion this commutation of money for personal service. Men give up a part of the profits they acquire in order to purchase leisure to augment them. Give money, and you will soon have chains. The word "finance" is a term of slavery; it is unknown in the true city. In a State truly free, the citizens do all with their own arms and nothing with their money; and, instead of purchasing exemption from their duty, they would even pay for fulfilling it themselves. My ideas on this subject are indeed very different from those commonly received; I even think the *corvées* [unpaid labor on roads and highways, required of French peasants before the revolution] are less an infringement upon liberty than taxes.

The better a State is constituted, the more do public affairs intrude upon private affairs in the minds of the citizens. Private concerns even become considerably fewer, because each individual shares so largely in the common happiness that he has not so much occasion to seek for it in private resources. In a well-conducted city, each member flies with joy to the assemblies; under a bad government, no one is disposed to bend his way thither, because no one is interested in proceedings where he foresees that the general will will not prevail, and in the end every man turns his attention to his own domestic affairs. Good laws lead on to better, and bad ones seldom fail to generate still worse. When once you hear some one say, when speaking of the affairs of the State, "What is it to me?" you may give over the State for lost.

It was the decline of patriotism, the activity of private interest, the immense extent of States, the increase of conquests, and the abuses of government that suggested the expedient of having deputies or representatives of the people in the assemblies of the nation. These representatives are the body to which, in certain countries, they have dared to give the name of the "Third Estate," as if the private interest of the two other orders deserved the first and second rank, and the public interest should be considered only in the third place.

Sovereignty cannot be represented for the same reason that it cannot be alienated; its essence is the general will, and that will must speak for itself, or it does not exist: it is either itself or not itself: there is no intermediate possibility. The deputies of the people, therefore, are not and cannot be their representatives; they can only be their commissioners, and as such are not qualified to conclude anything definitively. No act of theirs can be a law, unless it has been ratified by the people in person; and without that ratification nothing is a law. The people of England deceive themselves when they fancy they are free; they are so, in fact, only during the election of members of parliament: for, as soon as a new one is elected, they are again in chains, and are nothing. And thus, by the use they make of their brief moments of liberty, they deserve to lose it.

The second problem is how to make decisions when there is disagreement. The natural solution that springs to our minds is to take a vote and let the majority rule. We have become so accustomed to deciding questions by majority vote that it sometimes seems as though little children learn to vote

"Revolutionary tribunal in the Abbaye." A meeting of the Jacobin club, a radical group that ruled France for a time during the Revolution. Maximilien Robespierre, the most famous revolutionary, was a leader of the Jacobin club from 1791 to 1792. *(Source:* North Wind Picture Archives.*)*

in school before they learn how to count the votes. But Rousseau had the clarity of mind to see that majority rule presents a very serious obstacle to freedom. I may promise, in the original unanimous contract, to abide by the vote of the majority. However, in so doing, I seem simply to be agreeing to a sort of voluntary slavery. If I vote against a proposed law, believing that it is a bad law, contrary to the national interest, then how can I be said to "obey only myself and remain as free as before" when I am forced to submit to it? Rousseau has an extremely subtle answer to this question. First read what he has to say, and then we can talk about it a bit.

> There is one law only which, by its nature, requires unanimous consent; I mean the social compact: for civil association is the most voluntary of all acts; every man being born free and master of himself, no person can under any pretense whatever subject him without his consent. To affirm that the son of a slave is born a slave is to pronounce that he is not born a man.
>
> Should there be any men who oppose the social compact, their opposition will not invalidate it, but only hinder their being included: they are foreigners among citizens. When the State is instituted, residence constitutes consent; to inhabit a territory is to submit to the sovereignty.
>
> Except in this original contract, a majority of votes is sufficient to bind all the others. This is a consequence of the contract itself. But it may be asked how a man can be free and yet forced to conform to the will of others. How are the opposers free when they are in submission to laws to which they have never consented?
>
> I answer that the question is not fairly stated. The citizen consents to all the laws, to those which are passed in spite of his opposition, and even to those which sentence him to punishment if he violates any one of them. The constant will of all the members of the State is the general will; it is by that they are citizens and free. When any law is proposed in the assembly of the people, the question is not precisely to enquire whether they approve the proposition or reject it, but if it is conformable or not to the general will, which is their will. Each citizen, in giving his suffrage, states his mind on that question; and the general will is found by counting the votes. When, therefore, the motion which I opposed carries, it only proves to me that I was mistaken, and that what I believed to be the general will was not so. If my particular opinion had prevailed, I should have done what I was not willing to do, and, consequently, I should not have been in a state of freedom.

Something very tricky is going on in this passage. How can I be free when I do not get what I voted for? Earlier, in *Of the Social Contract,* Rousseau put his point even more dramatically. A citizen who refuses to obey **the general will,** he said, must be compelled to do so. "This in fact only forces him to be free." What on earth can Rousseau have meant?

The full answer would take a book by itself, but we can say a few things to clear away some of the mystery. Rousseau believed that the people have a right to make laws only as long as they are genuinely attempting to legislate in the public interest rather than in their own individual and private interests. Now if the majority could be counted on always to be right about the general good, then no one in the minority would want his or her view to become law. For if I want what is for the general good, and if the majority is always right about the general good, and if I am in the minority, then what I mistakenly wanted is *not* for the general good, and hence not what I really want. And if freedom is getting what you really want, then only by being forced to abide by the majority can I really be free!

There is a flaw in the argument, of course. The majority may always aim at the general good, but it does not always aim accurately. More often than not, even when every citizen is seeking what is best for all, the truth will be seen only by one citizen or a few. Rousseau confused aiming at and hitting the target.

Americans have a vested interest in the theory of the social contract, with all its flaws, because we are the first nation ever actually to bring itself into existence as a state by means of a real, historical, explicit contract. We call it our Constitution, but what the Founding Fathers actually wrote was the first operative social contract. When it was ratified in 1788, there came into being for the first time in Western history a state truly founded upon a contract.

Although the theory of the social contract has dominated liberal political theory since the seventeenth century, it has been subjected to a number of powerful criticisms. The most obvious objection is that, save for the special case of the United States, no actual state has ever been brought into existence by such an explicit contractual agreement among the citizens to be. Hence the theory does not provide any justification at all for the claims of even the most "democratic" governments.

But the mere historical absence of a contract is not the worst of the problems confronting social contract theories. Even if a group of men and

The General Will   A term invented by Jean-Jacques Rousseau to describe the decision by the citizens of a republic to set aside their private and partisan concerns and instead collectively aim at the general good. According to Rousseau, to say that a society "has a general will" is to say that all of the members of the society are public-spiritedly aiming at the general good in their political actions and deliberations. Rousseau was very pessimistic about the possibility of ever achieving a general will.

women have indeed contracted together, some time in the dim past, to submit themselves to the collective will of all, that still leaves those of us in the present generation without any reason for obeying the commands of the state. After all, I am not bound by the marriage contracts or the business contracts made by my ancient ancestors; why should I be bound by whatever political contracts they may have made?

To this, the social contract theorists answer that each of us, upon reaching the legal age of adulthood, implicitly signs his or her own name to that original contract by remaining in the country, living under its laws, and entering actively into its legal arrangements. John Locke, the spiritual father of our Constitution, especially emphasizes the owning of property in this selection from his most famous political work, the *Second Treatise of Government.*

JOHN LOCKE,
Second Treatise of Government

Every man being, as has been shown, naturally free, and nothing being able to put him into subjection to any earthly power but only his own consent, it is to be considered what shall be understood to be sufficient declaration of a man's consent to make him subject to the laws of any government. There is a common distinction of an express and a tacit consent, which will concern our present case. Nobody doubts but an express consent of any man entering into a society makes him a perfect member of that society, a subject of that government. The difficulty is, what ought to be looked upon as a tacit consent, and how far it binds, i.e., how far any one shall be looked on to have consented, and thereby submitted to any government, where he has made no expressions of it at all. And to this I say that every man that hath any possession or enjoyment of any part of the dominions of any government doth thereby give his tacit consent, and is as far forth obliged to obedience to the laws of that government during such enjoyment as any one under it; whether this his possession be of land to him and his heirs for ever, or a lodging only for a week; or whether it be barely traveling freely on the highway; and in effect it reaches as far as the very being of any one within the territories of that government.

To understand this the better, it is fit to consider that every man when he at first incorporates himself into any commonwealth, he, by his uniting himself thereunto, annexes also, and submits to the community those possessions which he has or shall acquire that do not already belong to any other government; for it would be a direct contradiction for any one to enter into society with others for the securing and regulating of property, and yet to suppose his land, whose property is to be regulated by the laws of the society, should be exempt from the jurisdiction of that government to which he himself, and the property of the land, is a subject. By the same act, therefore, whereby any one unites his person, which was before free, to any

President Clinton gestures while giving his State of the Union address, Thursday, January 23, 1996, on Capitol Hill. (Photo by Greg Gibson) *(Source: AP Wide World Photos.)*

commonwealth, by the same he unites his possession, which was before free, to it also; and they become, both of them, person and possession, subject to the government and dominion of that commonwealth as long as it hath a being. Whoever therefore from thenceforth by inheritance, purchases, permission, or otherwise, enjoys any part of the land so annexed to, and under the government of that commonwealth, must take it with the condition it is under, that is, of submitting to the government of the commonwealth under whose jurisdiction it is as far forth as any subject of it.

But since the government has a direct jurisdiction only over the land, and reaches the possessor of it (before he has actually incorporated himself in the society), only as he dwells upon, and enjoys that: the obligation any one is under, by virtue of such enjoyment, to submit to the government, begins and ends with the enjoyment; so that whenever the owner, who has given nothing but such a tacit consent to the government, will by donation, sale, or otherwise, quit the said possession, he is at liberty to go and incorporate himself into any other commonwealth, or to agree with others to begin a new one *(in vacuis locis)* in any part of the world they can find free and unpossessed. Whereas he that has once by actual agreement and any express declaration given his consent to be of any commonwealth is perpetually and indispensably obliged to be and remain unalterably a subject to it, and can never be again in the liberty of the state of nature; unless, by any calamity, the government he was under comes to

John Locke,
Second Treatise of Government

be dissolved, or else by some public acts cuts him off from being any longer a member of it.

You may wonder how a person can enter into a contract by "tacit consent." Don't I have to actually *say* that I am making a contract in order to do so? Locke here is relying on the ancient legal principle that when a person, over a period of time, acts in such a way as to give other persons a reasonable expectation that she will continue so to act, and if she benefits from that unspoken understanding, then she has made a "quasi-contract," which the law will enforce just as it will an explicit, spoken contract.

But Locke's argument depends on the assumption that a citizen can pick up and leave if he or she is dissatisfied with the laws of the state under which he or she lives. In Locke's day (the late 1600s) that was still thought to be possible. The Pilgrims who came to America, and many millions who followed them, thought they were exercising precisely that option. Today, emigration requires visas and passports, no matter where you want to go. Every square foot of inhabitable earth is claimed by some state or other, so that the most anyone can do is to go from the rule of one state to the rule of another. Under this condition, it is harder and harder to see what truth there is in the theory of the implicit, or tacit, contract.

The Pluralist Theory of the State

The theory of the social contract takes for granted that the political world is made up of individuals and of the state—nothing more. Rousseau and the classical liberal social contract theorists think that the individual comes first, and that it is many individuals, acting together, who create the state by their social contract. They see a direct relationship between the individual and the state—a relationship of the sort philosophers call "immediate" or sometimes "unmediated." Both words—"immediate" and "unmediated"—convey the same idea, which is that there is nothing in between "mediating" the individual and the state.

In the late nineteenth and twentieth centuries, however, a new view was put forward of the relationship between the individual and the state. According to this view, all of us, children and grown-ups, men and women, old and young, belong to many different *groups,* such as neighborhoods, churches, labor unions, fraternities, women's groups, gun enthusiasts' groups, farmers' groups, chambers of commerce, ethnic groups, hobbyists' groups, and so on. No one ever actually confronts the state as an individual, except perhaps when he or she is on trial in a court of law. It is always groups of people who work, as groups, to influence legislation, persuade judges, sway presidents, and in general to get the state to favor their needs, interests, or desires.

JOHN LOCKE

John Locke (1632–1704) had a philosophical career that was, in a sense, the reverse of David Hume's. Locke's great works were not published until close to his sixtieth year, and they were received almost immediately with great acclaim. During the troubled times in England that followed the restoration of the Catholic monarchy (in 1660) after the English Civil War, Locke sided with the moderate faction, which sought to limit the power of the king and bring the throne under some control by Parliament. In 1689, one year after the so-called Glorious Revolution, which established a limited monarchy in England, Locke published a pair of long essays on the subject of the foundations of the authority of the state. The second of these essays, known now as the *Second Treatise of Government,* is the most important single document in the literature of constitutional democracy. Appearing when it did, the *Second Treatise* naturally was interpreted as a justification for the new regime of William and Mary, for it defended the sort of limited monarchy, hedged round with parliamentary restraints, that the English people adopted as their form of government in 1688. Actually, we now know that the two *Treatises* were written in the early 1680s, some years before the change in government took place.

The next year, 1690, Locke published a massive work on the foundations of human knowledge, the *Essay Concerning the Human Understanding.* The *Essay* is the foundation of the school of philosophy known as empiricism. Locke's arguments profoundly affected Berkeley, Hume, and the other British philosophers who followed him. The work was soon translated into French and had a major influence as well on Continental thought. A century later, Immanuel Kant was to acknowledge it as one of the most important influences on his own thinking.

So society is really made up of groups, in this view, not individuals. Even the state is a group, like any other. Indeed, the state is actually many groups, not just one. It is the career civil servants in the state capital or Washington; it is the members of Congress; it is the men and women who serve as judges in the federal, state, or municipal courts; it is the leaders and workers of the political parties; it is the staffers who work for members of Congress, and who keep their jobs only so long as their bosses get reelected.

To understand politics, this pluralist or group theory of the state says that you must study the way in which groups are formed and the way they interact. Just reading social contract theorists or the Constitution will not help you to understand what really goes on—how decisions are made, how power is wielded, and who really governs.

One of the clearest statements of the pluralist theory was set forth in *The Group Basis of Politics* by a professor of government, Earl Latham. Here is how he summarizes this theory in the first chapter of his book:

> The chief social values cherished by individuals in modern society are realized through groups. The number is countless, and the variety of these social groupings is abundant and complex. No aspect of the life of the individual is untouched by them. Modern man is literally conducted from the cradle to the grave by groups, for he is born in a family, goes to school in organized classes, goes to church, perhaps, plays with boyhood gangs, joins fraternities, works for a corporation, belongs to various associations, cultural, civic, professional and social, and is carried off to his immortal reward by a business enterpriser with the solemnity appropriate to such ceremonies.
>
> The utilitarians made the same assumptions about the nature of the political community that they made about the nature of the economic community. The liberal philosophy of a John Stuart Mill rejected the doctrines of natural law and right that were so familiar to the eighteenth century but retained the feeling that the chief political problems were those that involved the singular individual on the one hand and the "state" on the other. All other and intermediate associations and groupings were dissolved, blanked, and obscured—a kind of sunken hinterland between two dominating mountainous battlements. This exaggerated individualism not only abstracted man from his social environment; it made him more sentient, more responsive to the gentle but compelling dictates of reason, more enlightened about his affairs than the facts justified.
>
> But utilitarian theories did not entirely dominate the field of political speculation.
>
> The principal attack, in England at least, upon the political speculations of the philosophic idealists was made by a group of writers professing pluralist doctrines. . . . The state, said the pluralists, is merely one association among a host of associations both as fact and right, which, far from absorbing the entire allegiance of the individual, has to compete with conflicting group loyalties, some of which are invincible. Most people think of themselves first as members of their clubs, lodges, unions, or parishes, and only incidentally as members of the state. The state, therefore, is merely one group among many, without superior right to dominate other associations.
>
> The apparatus of the state, through its manifold offices—legislatures, councils, agencies, departments, courts, and other forums—maintains a system of instrumentalities for the writing and enforcement of the formal rules by which society is governed. But all

of these instrumentalities are themselves groups, and they possess a sense of group belonging and identification which is very strong. In what respect are these groups different from the more numerous groups outside the structure of public government? In a political sense they are not different at all, but are the same. They exhibit all the internal social and political characteristics of group forms in that infinite universe of plural forms outside the state apparatus.

The legislature referees the group struggle, ratifies the victories of the successful coalitions, and records the terms of the surrenders, compromises, and conquests in the form of statutes. Every statute tends to represent compromise because the process of accommodating conflicts of group interest is one of deliberation and consent. The legislative vote on any issue tends to represent the composition of strength, i.e., the balance of power, among the contending groups at the moment of voting. What may be called public policy is the equilibrium reached in this struggle at any given moment, and it represents a balance which the contending factions of groups constantly strive to weight in their favor. In this process, it is clear that blocs of groups can be defeated. In fact they can be routed. Such groups do not possess a veto on the proposals and acts that affect them. What they do possess when they are defeated is the right to make new combinations of strength if they are able to do so, combinations that will support a new effort to rewrite the rules in their favor. This process is fully in accord with the American culture pattern which rates high in the characteristics of optimism, risk, experimentalism, change, aggressiveness, acquisitiveness, and a colossal faith in man's ability to subdue and bend nature to his desire. The process is dynamic, not static; fluid, not fixed. Today's losers may be tomorrow's winners.

Latham's description of politics certainly sounds a good deal more like what goes on in the United States than what Rousseau and Locke have to say. But there remains a very important question to which he provides no answer: This may be the way things *do* work in this country, but is it the way they *should* work? Is a pluralist political system a good thing?

The Founding Fathers—the men who wrote our Constitution—did not think so. In fact, in a famous essay published during the debates over the ratification of the Constitution, James Madison, later our fourth president, condemned as *factions* what Latham calls "interest groups." Madison actually thought that one of the greatest advantages of the new Constitution was precisely that it would undermine the effects of factions. "Among the numerous advantages promised by a well-constructed Union," Madison wrote in the Tenth *Federalist Paper,* "none deserves to be more accurately developed than its tendency to break and control the violence of factions." By a faction, he went on "I understand a number of citizens, whether amounting to a majority or minority of the whole, who are united or actuated by some common impulse or passion, or of interest, adverse to the rights of other citizens, or to the permanent and aggregate interests of the community." This is exactly what Latham means by an interest group.

What did Madison have against factions? Very simply, they are out for their own particular interest rather than for the larger interest of the community as a whole. Farmers want laws that help farmers, regardless of who else must pay. The same can be said for entrepreneurs, workers, gun owners, importers, exporters, Southerners, Northerners, Easterners, and Westerners. So long as citizens think, act, and vote as members of interest groups rather than as members of the whole community, the true interests of the society will be ignored in the struggle for partisan advantage.

Now Latham was perfectly well aware of Madison's objections to factions. The Tenth *Federalist Paper* is one of the most widely read texts of American political theory. So was he simply describing the way government now works? Or is there an argument *in favor* of interest group politics that can respond to Madison's fears?

Let me suggest just such an argument, based on a combination of the traditional contract belief in the sovereignty of the people and the modern story about the role of interest groups in American politics.

According to the social contract theorists, the people speak every two or four years at election time. But the business of governing goes on daily, week in and week out, year after year. Thousands of important decisions are made, many of them about issues that never even arise during the election campaign. If voters only get to express their will on election day, how can their representatives know, between elections, what their will is? And if the elected representatives do not know the will of their constituents, how can they truly be *representatives?*

The interest group theory steps in at this point to fill the gap between elections. In a democracy like ours, citizens are politically active every day, not just on election day. Through their letter writing, lobbying, political fundraising, and other activities, groups of citizens communicate their desires to their representatives, who are then able truly to *represent* their constituents.

Television pundits may look down their noses at lobbying and letterwriting campaigns, but these are, according to the pluralist theory of democracy, the legitimate and essential means by which the will of the people is translated into the law of the land. Wipe out "factions"—put a stop to interest group politics—and true democracy dies. All that remains is a token, meaningless, once-every-four-years vote.

The argument in favor of the interest group theory is even stronger. When I vote in an election, all I can do is vote "yes" or "no." Now there are some proposals I do not care very much about, even though on balance I may be in favor. Others matter deeply to me, so much so that I might consider them life-or-death issues. I cannot express the intensity of my preference through a vote, because my "yes" counts no more and no less than your "no," even if for you it is life or death and for me it is no big deal.

But there *is* a way I can express the intensity of my feeling about an issue, and that is by the amount of money I am willing to give or the amount of time I am willing to spend on that issue. If gun control is the heart and soul of my political life, I can spend all my spare time working for a gun control law (or against it, as the case may be). At the same time, if I care only a little bit about the environment, I can pay my annual twenty-five-dollar dues to the local environmentalist club and forget about it until next year.

Thus interest group politics permits me to give effective expression to the *complexity, specificity,* and *intensity* of my interests, something mere electoral politics can never do.

If interest group politics has this much going for it, what can be said against it? At least one thing, quite important. In order to express the intensity of your interest through political action, you must have resources to make that intensity known to your representatives. You must have the money, the time, and the skill to bring pressure to bear on a senator or representative, a mayor, or a governor. But as we all know, the resources in our society are very unevenly distributed. If you own a newspaper, or have a job that permits you to take time off for lobbying; if you have enough money to make a big donation to a political campaign; in short, if you are one of the affluent members of society, then your interests are going to get a much more attentive hearing from the elected representatives. And this will distort the process of interest expression, giving some people an advantage that outweighs the greater intensity of interest of the poorer people opposed to you.

So the pluralist theory of democracy does not make place for a fair expression of the interests of all. And that, you will recall, was precisely what the utilitarians claimed democracy would accomplish.

Nevertheless, the pluralist theory clearly takes into account the way American democracy actually works in the modern world, and it answers at least some, but certainly not all, of James Madison's objections to *factions*.

The Racial Critique of the Social Contract Theory of the State

Since the eighteenth century, the theory of the social contract has been the leading philosophical story in Western thought about the nature, origin, and justification of the state. Our own nation was organized by the Founding Fathers on the principle of Consent of the Governed—which means that those who seek to rule must have the consent of those whom they claim to rule. The social contract is supposed to embody that consent.

In the early days of the social contract theory, some philosophers actually talked as though they thought people had gathered together and made a formal agreement with one another—in a clearing in the woods maybe. But for the most part, the social contract was conceived of either as an ideal—what *would* be the case if everything was exactly as it should be—or merely as a way of expressing the central principle that the rulers must have the consent of the governed if their rule is to be legitimate. It is this belief that lies behind the modern emphasis on democracy and free elections. There seems to be very broad agreement throughout the world that states must go to the people for approval and endorsement if they are to be legitimate.

Social contract theory is really very simple and straightforward, or so it seems. A group of people living together in some part of the world decides that it would be mutually beneficial for them to get together and set up a government—perhaps to protect the whole community against outside attack, perhaps to provide common social services, such as fire and police protection, perhaps to launch some collective projects too big for any private individuals to undertake, like the building of a national highway network, or the exploration of space. They agree to unite their forces and submit themselves to a common government. If they need laws, they, or their representatives, enact them. Periodically, the people review the performance of their representatives and tell them, in elections, whether they can continue serving the public. If a majority of the people believes that their representatives have been doing a good job, they give them another turn. If they are dissatisfied, they turn them out and replace them with a new set of representatives.

From time to time, people from other parts of the world may ask permission to live in the community. If they want to settle permanently, then they can become citizens, which means joining themselves to the contract along with those already included. If they are just visiting, then they must agree to abide by the laws the community has established for as long as they stay.

All this sounds lovely—clear, simple, persuasive. But a growing number of critics have started to point out that this lovely picture does not actually correspond at all to what goes on in the real world. The most powerful critique I know is the one advanced by a young West Indian philosopher, Charles Mills, who currently teaches at the University of Illinois in Chicago. Mills' criticism of social contract theory takes the form of a competing story, which he calls the racial contract This racial contract, he says, comes a great deal closer to describing the way the world really works. According to Mills, the theory of the social contract is actually a bit of camouflage designed to conceal from view what has been going on in the world since the seventeenth century.

To put Mills' story in a nutshell, the theory of the social contract conveniently forgets to mention the people of color—slaves, colonials, original inhabitants—over whom the participants in the social contract exercise forcible control. The Founding Fathers made a contract with one another, but it was not merely a contract about how they would behave toward one another. It also was an agreement that they would own slaves who were not permitted to participate in this "contract" at all. In addition, it was an agreement that they would together drive the Native Americans out of the land where they had been living, land that the Founding Fathers had decided would be theirs. Mills writes: "The racial contract is obviously not a contract to which the nonwhite subset of humans can be a genuinely consenting party (though, depending on the circumstances, it may sometimes be politic to pretend that this is the case). Rather, it is a contract *between* those categorized as white *over* the non-whites, who are thus the objects rather than the subjects of the agreement."

Sometimes this racial contract is open, aboveboard, and completely explicit. The Constitution of the United States, for example, states for all to see that a slave does not count for as much as a free man, but instead counts for three-fifths of a free man or woman. In South Africa, under the apartheid regime that has finally been overthrown, nonwhites were officially denied the vote, citizenship, the right to own property, and even the right to remain within the limits of the white cities after sundown. In this century, throughout the world, one could see signs posted that read "No natives or dogs allowed."

At other times, the racial contract has been invisible to the white majority (although never to people of color, who knew quite well what was going on in the world). Right now, our own Supreme Court hands down decisions outlawing affirmative action on the grounds that differentiations according to race or color have no place in American society, as though it was not obvious to anyone with eyes to see that America is elaborately segregated and sorted by skin color. Mills insists that it "would be a fundamental error to see racism as *anomalous,* a mysterious *deviation* from Enlightenment European humanism. Rather, he says, "it needs to be realized that *European* [and American—RPW] *humanism usually meant that only Europeans were human.*"

Those of us who are white find it hard to imagine how the world looks to someone who is black, brown, red, or yellow. (I use these terms as a short-hand for referring to the various categories into which people are currently classified, but of course there is something a little bit weird about describing people as black, brown, white, red, or yellow. Only the stick figures in children's crayon drawings are really those colors. But that is one more example of what Mills is talking about.) It is hard for all of us to become self-aware of the ways in which the racial definition of the world by European/American whites has shaped our thinking. Perhaps I can begin to help you to see it by talking about something we all share—movies.

How many of you have seen one of those marvelous old voyage-to-darkest-Africa movies, complete with wild animals, impenetrable jungles, and stiff-upper-lip British types maintaining their upper-class calm in the midst of savage darkness? My all-time favorite is *King Solomon's Mines* with Stewart Granger and Deborah Kerr. (I actually saw the movie when it first came out, but I am hoping some of you have seen it on late-night cable somewhere. A much more sophisticated, upscale version, which came out only a few years ago, is the modern remake of the old Tarzan movies, called *Greystoke.*)

All those movies have the same plot basically. A safe, secure, middle-class man or woman starts out in safe, secure, thoroughly manageable England (for some reason it is always England) and launches on a long, difficult, dangerous trip to the heart of darkest Africa. The first part of the trip, by boat or plane, is easy, getting as far as a city on the East Coast of Africa. Then the adventurer hooks up with a white Big Game Hunter or guide who is an old Africa hand and speaks some Swahili. He rounds up some bearers, who then set off, singing their native songs, carrying all manner of junk into the bush. The adventurer, despite looking very healthy, carries nothing, except maybe a rifle. The farther into the jungle they go, the harder the going gets, with bearers deserting for unnamed superstitious reasons, wild animals turning up to threaten the party, and menacing natives surfacing in fearsome headdresses and war paint. Eventually, after many trials and tribulations, during which they become thoroughly exhausted and almost die, they reach their destination, which is either a fabulous treasure or else the remains of the adventurer's husband or brother. Then the whole party turns around and makes its way back to civilization. The closer they get to the coastal city from which they began, the easier the going gets, until finally, everyone is back in England, safe and secure, and then the movie ends.

Now when you stop and think about it, there is something very odd about this scenario. East Africa is no more or less hospitable to the people who live there than London is to the people who live *there*. To be sure, if you grew up in East Africa, you would find London traffic hard to get used to and London streets utterly confusing. But East Africa would not be confusing, dark, ominous, or impenetrable to you. It would be your *home*. You would be able to move about in it with the same ease with which a native Londoner makes her way through the streets of London. Everyone in the world is born and brought up somewhere, and to each of us, that place is home—familiar, manageable, and unmysterious. The movie, by presenting London as safe and secure and East Africa as mysterious, reinforces the assumptions on which the racial contract is founded. The movie is telling you that Londoners are civilized, while the Masai are savages. It is telling you that the very physical space of London is safe, familiar, and within the social contract, while the physical space of East Africa is wild, savage, and outside the contract.

If you are white, all of this may come as a total shock. Indeed, you may think it must be an exaggeration, an emphasizing of something that was important 100 years ago, but surely does not make that much difference anymore. If you are black or brown or yellow or red none of this will come as any surprise at all. The only surprise may be that someone bothers to put it in a college textbook, as though it was news. That divide, separating those of us who are white from everyone else in the world, is part of what Charles Mills (who is black) is talking about.

The following excerpts come from a new book, called *The Racial Contract,* by Mills. Perhaps it will get a good argument going in your class.

The Racial Contract manifests itself in white resistance to anything more than the *formal* extension of the terms of the abstract social contract (and often to that also.) Whereas before it was denied that nonwhites *were* equal persons, it is now pretended that nonwhites *are* equal abstract persons who can be fully included in the polity merely by extending the scope of the moral operator, without any fundamental change in the arrangements that have resulted from the previous system of explicit de jure racial privilege. Sometimes the new forms taken by the Racial Contract are transparently exploitative, for example, the "jim crow" contract, whose claim of "separate but equal" was patently ludicrous. But others—the job discrimination contract, the restrictive convenant—are harder to prove.

Nonwhites then find that race is, paradoxically, both everywhere and nowhere, structuring their lives, but not formally recognized in political/moral theory. But in a racially-structured polity, the only people who can find it psychologically possible to deny the centrality of race are those who are racially privileged, for whom race is invisible precisely because the world is structured around them, whiteness as the ground against which the figures of other races—those who, unlike us, are raced—appear. The fish does not see the water, and whites do not see the racial nature of a white polity because it is natural to them, the element in which they move.

The Racial Contract shows us that we need another alternative, another way of theorizing about and critiquing the state: the *racial,* or white-supremacist state, whose function inter alia is to safeguard the polity *as* a white or white-dominated polity, enforcing the terms of the Racial Contract by the appropriate means and, when necessary, facilitating its rewriting from one form to another.

The liberal-democratic state of classic contractarianism abides by the terms of the social contract by using force only to protect its citizens, who delegated this moralized force to it so that it could guarantee the safety not to be found in the state of nature. (This was, after all, part of the whole point of *leaving* the state of nature in the first place.) By contrast, the state established by the Racial Contract is by definition *not* neutral, since its purpose is to bring about conformity to the terms of the Racial Contract among the subperson population, which will obviously have no reason to accept these terms voluntarily, since the contract is an exploitation contract.

Now by its relative silence on the question of race, conventional moral theory would lead the unwary student with no experience of the world—the visiting anthropologist from Galactic Central, say—to think that deviations from the ideal have been contingent, random,

Philosophy and Popular Culture

Fahrenheit 9/11: Questions About Democracy and Free Speech

No matter what your politics are, you will probably agree that Michael Moore's documentary, *Fahrenheit 9/11,* makes George W. Bush and his administration look incompetent, if not worse.

For example, the movie shows footage of President Bush saying, "I call upon all nations to do everything they can to stop these terrorist killers. Thank you." He then brandishes a golf club and says, "Now, watch this drive" before swinging at and hitting the ball. The movie also shows happy Iraqi children laughing and playing before war begins, then it shows dead and mutilated Iraqi children—as well as dead and mutilated American soldiers. The narrator, Michael Moore, points out, 'While Bush was busy taking care of his base and professing his love for our troops, he proposed cutting combat soldiers' pay by 33% and assistance to their families by 60%. He opposed giving veterans a billion dollars more in health care benefits, and he supported closing veteran hospitals. He tried to double the prescription drug costs for veterans and opposed full benefits for part-time reservists. And when Staff Sergeant Brett Petriken from Flint was killed in Iraq on May 26th, the army sent his last paycheck to his family, but they docked him for the last five days of the month that he didn't work because he was dead." The movie also shows President Bush sitting in a classroom of children reading *My Pet Goat* for seven minutes after being informed that a second plane has hit the World Trade Center in New York City on September 11, 2001. His expression is odd and does not seem to communicate strength and resolution. Finally, an aide whispers to President Bush and he leaves the classroom.

Questions to Consider

Should citizens during wartime unquestioningly accept whatever their rulers tell them, and refrain from criticizing presidents or members of Congress, even when they are convinced that they are being lied to and manipulated for political ends? Or should they speak out against policies they consider misguided, despite the fact that men and women in uniform are dying in battle?

theoretically opaque, or not worth the trouble to theorize. Such a visitor might conclude that all people have generally tried to live up to the norm but, given inevitable human frailty, have sometimes fallen short. But this conclusion is, in fact, simply false. Racism and racially structured discrimination have not been *deviations* from the norm; they have *been* the norm, not merely in the sense of de facto statistical distribution patterns but, as I emphasized at the start, in the sense of being formally codified, written down and proclaimed *as such*.

What does it require for a subperson to assert himself or herself politically? To begin with, it means simply, or not so simply, claiming the moral status of personhood. So it means challenging the white-constructed ontology that has deemed one a "body impolitic," an entity not entitled to assert personhood in the first place. In a sense one has to fight an internal battle before even advancing onto the ground of external combat. One has to overcome the internalization of subpersonhood prescribed by the Racial Contract and recognize one's own humanity, resisting the official category of despised aborignal, natural slave, colonial ward. One has to learn the basic self-respect that can casually be assumed by Kantian persons, those privileged by the Racial Contract, but which is denied to subpersons. Particularly for blacks, ex-slaves, the importance of developing self-respect and demanding respect from whites is crucial. Frederick Douglass recounts "how a man was made a slave," and promises "you shall see how a slave was made a man."[1] But a hundred years later this struggle is still in progress. *"Negroes want to be treated like men,"* wrote James Baldwin in the 1950s, "a perfectly straightforward statement, containing only seven words. People who have mastered Kant, Hegel, Shakespeare, Marx, Freud, and the Bible find this statement utterly impenetrable."[2]

The Main Points in Chapter Six

1. John Stuart Mill devoted his life to applying the principle of utilitarianism to social questions. In the course of his writings, he revised the principle in three ways:

   a. He distinguished lower and higher pleasures.
   b. He recognized the role of habit or custom in economic life.
   c. He denied the right of the state to interfere in the private lives of men and women.

---

[1] Frederick Douglass, *Narrative of the Life of Frederick Douglass, An American Slave* [New York: Viking Penguin, 1982], p. 107.
[2] James Baldwin, *Nobody Knows My Name: More Notes of a Native Son* [1961. Reprint. New York: Vintage International, 1993], pp. 67–68.

2. The utilitarians defended the free market or laissez-faire principle that consumers and producers should be free to make bargains in the marketplace without government interference.

3. Socialists like Karl Marx criticized capitalism for exploiting the working class, for corrupting the work process so that it became a source of pain and suffering rather than fulfillment, and for driving the economy into evergreater business crises. Marx claimed that a socialist revolution would put an end to capitalism by placing ownership and control of the society's means of production in the hands of the working class.

4. The pluralist theory of American democracy takes into account the interest group political activity that goes on between elections. It claims that through such political activity, the complexity and intensity of the interests of citizens are given expression.

5. Classical social contract theory and its modern variants completely ignore the white domination and exploitation of nonwhite peoples, which has been a central fact of world history for the past four centuries. An alternative model of the state, called the Racial Contract by Charles Mills, seeks to capture and understand that fact.

Questions for Discussion and Review

1. According to Mill, we should judge public policies on the basis of their tendency to produce the greatest happiness for the greatest number. Select one of the issues currently being debated in the United States—drug policy, abortion policy, the balanced budget—and try to analyze it in terms of the tendency of the competing proposals to promote the greatest happiness. Is it possible to analyze public policies in this way? What are some of the problems? Does Mill's way of thinking clarify the issues for you?

2. Mill claims that we, the public, are good judges of consumer goods, but poor judges of cultural and intellectual goods, such as books, music, and art. Do you agree? Is it, in your experience, easier for you to judge the value of a consumer good such as a car, a VCR, or a quart of milk? Or is it easier to judge the value of a novel, a movie, or a CD record? In this age of advertising, with millions of competing consumer goods, do we need government regulation to protect us? What about medicines and drugs? Are we, as consumers, good judges of their value? If we turn over the job of evaluating commodities to the state, how do we guarantee that the state will protect us?

3. In the United States today, barely half of the eligible voters bother to vote in a general presidential election. In non-presidential years, the turnout

is even smaller. What would Rousseau or Locke say about this fact? Does it call into question the legitimacy of the officials who are elected? If I do not bother to vote, am I morally bound to obey the laws passed by the representatives who get elected?

4. Underlying the justification of representative democracy is the assumption that individual voters sometimes get what they want and sometimes do not. But suppose some voters, for example black or Latino voters, are permanent losers. They vote, but their candidates never get elected because everyone votes along racial lines and they are in the minority. Are they still morally bound to obey the laws passed by the representatives who do get elected? If you think the answer is no, what changes in the system of elections might give all segments of a society a chance to be represented?

5. Charles Mills claims that there is a racial contract among white people to oppress and exploit non-white people. If your philosophy class has both white and non-white students in it, have a discussion in which each student is asked to describe how he or she experiences American society. See whether Mills is right that the perceptions of white and non-white people are radically different. How do you think Rousseau and Locke would respond to Mills' thesis?

The Primary Source: Philosophical Readings and Commentary

Aristotle: *The Politics*

Dewey, John: *Democracy and Education*

DuBois, W. E. B.: *The Souls of Black Folks*

Hegel, Georg: *The Philosophy of History*

Hobbes, Thomas: *Leviathan*

Locke, John: *Second Treatise of Government*

Marx, Karl: *The Communist Manifesto*

Mill, John Stuart: *On Liberty; Utilitarianism*

Okin, Susan Moller: *Justice, Gender, and the Family*

Plato: *The Republic, The Laws*

Rawls, John: *A Theory of Justice*

Smith, Adam: *The Wealth of Nations*

Wollstonecraft, Mary: *A Vindication of the Rights of Women*

CONTEMPORARY APPLICATION

Affirmative Action

Almost a century ago, W. E. B. DuBois wrote, "The problem of the Twentieth Century is the problem of the color line." That prophetic statement, uttered more in sadness than in bitterness, has proved to be all too true. The century that has just drawn to a close has been as twisted and tortured by racial oppression and division as the century that preceded it. With a new millennium dawning, America remains divided by race. I have visited South Africa a number of times over the past fifteen years. At first, what impressed and troubled me most was the legal oppression of people of color, the laws forbidding Africans even to sleep in the big white cities unless they were house servants (and even then, required by law to live in little huts not physically connected to the house in which the white people live). But after I had traveled back and forth a few times, it began to dawn on me that America is as racially divided and segregated as South Africa. There really is no more mingling of the races here than there—less, indeed, in some respects.

Over many years, the United States Government has taken a number of steps to remove some of the legal obstacles placed in the way of African Americans. People of color were guaranteed the right to vote—a right granted to them shortly after the end of the Civil War and then forcibly taken away again in little more than a decade. The armed forces were integrated by a presidential executive order, and the government's own rules segregating federally funded housing were rescinded. Eventually, in a historic decision of the Supreme Court emerging from decades of legal struggle by black lawyers and plaintiffs, segregated schools were declared unconstitutional.

But despite these victories, for which many men and women gave their lives, deep inequities in employment, housing, and education continued to distort American society. To correct some of these inequities, the government, some thirty years ago, began to require colleges, universities, corporations, and public agencies to take positive steps to correct the imbalance in the opportunities accorded people of color. Because these steps went beyond merely the removal of legal barriers, requiring employers and others to be pro-active in the redressing of racial imbalances, they came to be called "affirmative action." The idea behind the phrase was that those in a position to open doors to people of color must act affirmatively by offering opportunities, not merely negatively by removing barriers.

From the outset, there has been enormous opposition to affirmative action. Those of you only beginning to become aware of the public world must not make the mistake of supposing that affirmative action was ever universally accepted or endorsed. But for several decades, the weight of the federal government was put behind a variety of affirmative efforts to rectify racial imbalances and inequities. And to a considerable extent, the programs had at least some success. Countless African Americans, Latinos, and Asian Americans have secured educations and jobs that could only have been opened to them by the sorts of governmental programs labeled "Affirmative Action."

In recent years, however, opposition to affirmative action has been growing stronger. With the shift of both the judiciary and the federal government toward the more conservative end of the political spectrum, a number of affirmative action programs have either been cut back or terminated. In the four selections included here, we can hear the debate as it is now being conducted all across this country. Speaking for affirmative action is a well-known professor of literature, Stanley Fish. James Q. Wilson, an expert on urban sociology, takes what we can call a modified negative position, arguing that under some circumstances there are good reasons for limited affirmative action. The strongly negative position is presented first by Thomas Sowell, a conservative economist, and then by Linda Chavez, director of the U.S. Commission on Civil Rights during the Reagan administration.

REVERSE RACISM OR HOW THE POT GOT TO CALL THE KETTLE BLACK*
Stanley Fish

In America "whites once set themselves apart from blacks and claimed privileges for themselves while denying them to others," the author writes.

"Now, on the basis of race, blacks are claiming special status and reserving for themselves privileges they deny to others. Isn't one as bad as the other? The answer is no."

I take my text from George Bush, who, in an address to the United Nations on September 23, 1991, said this of the UN resolution equating Zionism with racism: "Zionism . . . is the idea that led to the creation of a home for the Jewish people . . . And to equate Zionism with the intolerable sin of racism is to twist history and forget the terrible plight of Jews in World War II and indeed throughout history." What happened in the Second World War was that six million Jews were exterminated by people who regarded them as racially inferior and a danger to Aryan purity. What happened after the Second World War was that the survivors of that Holocaust established a Jewish state—that is, a state centered on Jewish history, Jewish values, and Jewish traditions: in short, a Jewocentric state. What President Bush objected to was the logical sleight of hand by which these two actions were declared equivalent because they were both expressions of racial exclusiveness. Ignored, as Bush said, was the *historical* difference between them—the difference between a program of genocide and the determination of those who escaped it to establish a community in which they would be the makers, not the victims, of the laws.

Only if racism is thought of as something that occurs principally in the mind, a falling-away from proper notions of universal equality, can the desire of a victimized and terrorized people to band together be declared morally identical to the actions of their would-be executioners. Only when the actions of the two groups are detached from the historical conditions of their emergence and given a purely abstract description can they be made interchangeable. Bush was saying to the United Nations, "Look, the Nazis' conviction of racial superiority generated a policy of systematic genocide; the Jews' experience of centuries of persecution in almost every country on earth generated a desire for a homeland of their own. If you manage somehow to convince yourself that these are the same, it is you, not the Zionists, who are morally confused, and the reason you are morally confused is that you have forgotten history."

A Key Distinction

What I want to say, following Bush's reasoning, is that a similar forgetting of history has in recent years allowed some people to argue, and

argue persuasively, that affirmative action is reverse racism. The very phrase "reverse racism" contains the argument in exactly the form to which Bush objected: In this country whites once set themselves apart from blacks and claimed privileges for themselves while denying them to others. Now, on the basis of race, blacks are claiming special status and reserving for themselves privileges they deny to others. Isn't one as bad as the other? The answer is no. One can see why by imagining that it is not 1993 but 1955, and that we are in a town in the South with two more or less distinct communities, one white and one black. No doubt each community would have a ready store of dismissive epithets, ridiculing stories, self-serving folk myths, and expressions of plain hatred, all directed at the other community, and all based in racial hostility. Yet to regard their respective racisms—if that is the word—as equivalent would be bizarre, for the hostility of one group stems not from any wrong done to it but from its wish to protect its ability to deprive citizens of their voting rights, to limit access to educational institutions, to prevent entry into the economy except at the lowest and most menial levels, and to force members of the stigmatized group to ride in the back of the bus. The hostility of the other group is the result of these actions, and whereas hostility and racial anger are unhappy facts wherever they are found, a distinction must surely be made between the ideological hostility of the oppressors and the experience-based hostility of those who have been oppressed.

Not to make that distinction is, adapting George Bush's words, to twist history and forget the terrible plight of African Americans in the more than 200 years of this country's existence. Moreover, to equate the efforts to remedy that plight with the actions that produced it is to twist history even further. Those efforts, designed to redress the imbalances caused by long-standing discrimination, are called affirmative action; to argue that affirmative action, which gives preferential treatment to disadvantaged minorities as part of a plan to achieve social equality, is no different from the policies that created the disadvantages in the first place is a travesty of reasoning. "Reverse racism" is a cogent description of affirmative action only if one considers the cancer of racism to be morally and medically indistinguishable from the therapy we apply to it. A cancer is an invasion of the body's equilibrium, and so is chemotherapy; but we do not decline to fight the disease because the medicine we employ is also disruptive of normal functioning. Strong illness, strong remedy: the formula is as appropriate to the health of the body politic as it is to that of the body proper.

At this point someone will always say, "But two wrongs don't make a right; if it was wrong to treat blacks unfairly, it is wrong to give blacks preference and thereby treat whites unfairly." This objection is just another version of the forgetting and rewriting of history. The work is done by the adverb "unfairly," which suggests two more or less equal parties, one of whom has been unjustly penalized by an incompetent umpire. But blacks have not simply been treated unfairly; they have been subjected first to decades of slavery, and then to decades of second-class citizenship, widespread legalized discrimination, economic persecution, educational deprivation, and cultural stigmatization. They have been bought, sold, killed, beaten, raped, excluded, exploited, shamed, and scorned for a very long time. The word "unfair" is hardly an adequate description of their experience, and the belated gift of "fairness" in the form of a resolution no longer to discriminate against them legally is hardly an adequate remedy for the deep disadvantages that the prior discrimination has produced. When the deck is stacked against you in more ways than you can even count, it is small consolation to hear that you are now free to enter the game and take your chances.

A Tilted Field

The same insincerity and hollowness of promise infect another formula that is popular with the anti-affirmative-action crowd: the formula of the level playing field. Here the argument usually takes the form of saying "It is undemocratic to give one class of citizens advantages at the expense of other citizens; the truly democratic way is to have a level playing field to which everyone has access and where everyone has a fair and equal chance to succeed on the basis of his or her merit." Fine words—but they conceal the facts of the situation as it has been given to us by history: the playing field is already tilted in favor of those by whom and for whom it was constructed in the first place. If mastery of the requirements for entry depends upon immersion in the cultural experiences of the mainstream majority, if the skills that make for success are nurtured by institutions and cultural practices from which the disadvantaged minority has been systematically excluded, if the language and ways of comporting oneself that identify a player as "one of us" are alien to the lives minorities are forced to live, then words like "fair" and "equal" are cruel jokes, for what they promoted and celebrate is an institutionalized unfairness and a perpetuated inequality. The playing field is already tilted, and the resistance to altering it by the mechanisms of affirmative action is in fact a determination to make sure that the present imbalances persist as long as possible.

One way of tilting the field is the Scholastic Aptitude Test. This test figures prominently in Dinesh D'Souza's book *Illiberal Education* (1991), in which one finds many examples of white or Asian students denied admission to colleges and universities even though their SAT scores were higher than the scores of some others—often African Americans—who were admitted to the same institution. This, D'Souza says, is evidence that as a result of affirmative-action policies colleges and universities tend "to depreciate the importance of merit criteria in admissions." D'Souza's assumption—and it is one that many would share—is that the test does in fact measure *merit,* with merit understood as a quality objectively determined in the same way that body temperature can be objectively determined.

In fact, however, the test is nothing of the kind. Statistical studies have suggested that test scores reflect income and socioeconomic status. It has been demonstrated again and again that scores vary in relation to cultural background; the test's questions assume a certain uniformity in educational experience and lifestyle and penalize those who, for whatever reason, have had a different experience and lived different kinds of lives. In short, what is being measured by the SAT is not absolutes like native ability and merit but accidents like birth, social position, access to libraries, and the opportunity to take vacations or to take SAT prep courses.

Furthermore, as David Owen notes in *None of the Above: Behind the Myth of Scholastic Aptitude* (1985), the "correlation between SAT scores and college grades...is lower than the correlation between weight and height; in other words you would have a better chance of predicting a person's height by looking at his weight than you would of predicting his freshman grades by looking only at his SAT scores." Everywhere you look in the SAT story, the claims of fairness, objectivity, and neutrality fall away, to be replaced by suspicions of specialized measures and unfair advantages.

Against this background a point that in isolation might have a questionable force takes on a special and even explanatory resonance: the principal deviser of the test was an out-and-out racist. In 1923 Carl Campbell Brigham published

a book called *A Study of American Intelligence,* in which, as Owen notes, he declared, among other things, that we faced in America "a possibility of racial admixture...infinitely worse than that faced by any European country today, for we are incorporating the Negro into our racial stock, while all of Europe is comparatively free of this taint." Brigham had earlier analyzed the Army Mental Tests using classifications drawn from another racist text, Madison Grant's *The Passing of the Great Race,* which divided American society into four distinct racial strains, with Nordic, blue-eyed, blond people at the pinnacle and the American Negro at the bottom. Nevertheless, in 1925 Brigham became a director of testing for the College Board, and developed the SAT. So here is the great SAT test, devised by a racist in order to confirm racist assumptions, measuring not native ability but cultural advantage, an uncertain indicator of performance, an indicator of very little except what money and social privilege can buy. And it is in the name of this mechanism that we are asked to reject affirmative action and reaffirm "the importance of merit criteria in admissions."

The Reality of Discrimination

Nevertheless, there is at least one more card to play against affirmative action, and it is a strong one. Granted that the playing field is not level and that access to it is reserved for an already advantaged elite, the disadvantages suffered by others are less racial—at least in 1993—than socioeconomic. Therefore shouldn't, as D'Souza urges, "universities...retain their policies of preferential treatment, but alter their criteria of application from race to socioeconomic disadvantage," and thus avoid the unfairness of current policies that reward middle-class or affluent blacks at the expense of poor whites? One answer to this question is given by D'Souza himself when he acknowledges that the overlap between minority groups and the poor is very large—a point underscored by the former Secretary of Education Lamar Alexander, who said, in response to a question about funds targeted for black students, "Ninety-eight percent of race-specific scholarships do not involve constitutional problems." He meant, I take it, that 98 percent of race-specific scholarships were also scholarships to the economically disadvantaged.

Still, the other two percent—nonpoor, middleclass, economically favored blacks—are receiving special attention on the basis of disadvantages they do not experience. What about them? The force of the question depends on the assumption that in this day and age race could not possibly be a serious disadvantage to those who are otherwise well positioned in the society. But the lie was given dramatically to this assumption in a 1991 broadcast of the ABC program *Prime Time Live*. In a stunning fifteen-minute segment, reporters and a camera crew followed two young men of equal education, cultural sophistication, level of apparent affluence, and so forth around St. Louis, a city where neither was known. The two differed in only a single respect: one was white, the other black. But that small difference turned out to mean everything. In a series of encounters with shoe salesmen, record-store employees, rental agents, landlords, employment agencies, taxicab drivers, and ordinary citizens, the black member of the pair was either ignored or given a special and suspicious attention. He was asked to pay more for the same goods or come up with a larger down payment for the same car, was turned away as a prospective tenant, was rejected as a prospective taxicab fare, was treated with contempt and irritation by clerks and bureaucrats, and in every way possible was made to feel inferior and unwanted.

The inescapable conclusion was that alike though they may have been in almost all respects, one of these young men, because he was black, would lead a significantly lesser life than his white counterpart: he would be housed less well and at greater expense; he would pay more for services and products when and if he was given the opportunity to buy them; he would have difficulty establishing credit; the first emotions he would inspire on the part of many people he met would be distrust and fear; his abilities would be discounted even before he had a chance to display them; and, above all, the treatment he received from minute to minute would chip away at his self-esteem and self-confidence with consequences that most of us could not even imagine. As the young man in question said at the conclusion of the broadcast, "You walk down the street with a suit and tie and it doesn't matter. Someone will make determinations about you, determinations that affect the quality of your life."

Of course, the same determinations are being made quite early on by kindergarten teachers, grade school principals, high school guidance counselors, and the like, with results that cut across socioeconomic lines and place young black men and women in the ranks of the disadvantaged no matter what the bank accounts of their parents happen to show. Racism is a cultural fact, and although its effects may to some extent be diminished by socioeconomic variables, those effects will still be sufficiently great to warrant the nation's attention and thus the continuation of affirmative-action policies. This is true even of the field thought to be dominated by blacks and often cited as evidence of the equal opportunities society now affords them. I refer, of course, to professional athletics. But national self-congratulation on this score might pause in the face of a few facts: A minuscule number of African Americans ever receive a paycheck from a professional team. Even though nearly 1,600 daily newspapers report on the exploits of black athletes, they employ only seven full-time black sports columnists. Despite repeated pledges and resolutions, major-league teams have managed to put only a handful of blacks and Hispanics in executive positions.

Why Me?

When all is said and done, however, one objection to affirmative action is unanswerable on its own terms, and that is the objection of the individual who says, "Why me? Sure, discrimination has persisted for many years, and I acknowledge that the damage done has not been removed by changes in the law. But why me? I didn't own slaves; I didn't vote to keep people on the back of the bus; I didn't turn water hoses on civil-rights marchers. Why, then, should I be the one who doesn't get the job or who doesn't get the scholarship or who gets bumped back to the waiting list?"

I sympathize with this feeling, if only because in a small way I have had the experience that produces it. I was recently nominated for an administrative post at a large university. Early signs were encouraging, but after an interval I received official notice that I would not be included at the next level of consideration, and subsequently I was told unofficially that at some point a decision had been made to look only in the direction of women and minorities. Although I was disappointed, I did not conclude that the situation was "unfair," because the policy was obviously not directed at me—at no point in the proceedings did someone say, "Let's find a way to rule out Stanley Fish." Nor was it directed even at persons of my race and sex—the policy was not intended to disenfranchise white males. Rather, the policy was driven by other considerations, and it was only as a byproduct of those considerations—not as the main goal—that white males like me were rejected. Given that the institution in question has a high percentage of minority students, a very low percentage of minority faculty, and an even lower percentage of minority administrators, it made perfect sense to focus on women and minority candidates, and within that sense, not as the result of

prejudice, my whiteness and maleness became disqualifications.

I can hear the objection in advance: "What's the difference? Unfair is unfair: you didn't get the job; you didn't even get on the short list." The difference is not in the outcome but in the ways of thinking that led up to the outcome. It is the difference between an unfairness that befalls one as the unintended effect of a policy rationally conceived and an unfairness that is pursued as an end in itself. It is the difference between the awful unfairness of Nazi extermination camps and the unfairness to Palestinian Arabs that arose from, but was not the chief purpose of, the founding of a Jewish state.

The New Bigotry

The point is not a difficult one, but it is difficult to see when the unfairness scenarios are presented as simple contrasts between two decontextualized persons who emerge from nowhere to contend for a job or a place in a freshman class. Here is student A; he has a board score of 1,300. And here is student B; her board score is only 1,200, yet she is admitted and A is rejected. Is that fair? Given the minimal information provided, the answer is of course no. But if we expand our horizons and consider fairness in relation to the cultural and institutional histories that have brought the two students to this point, histories that weigh on them even if they are not the histories' authors, then both the question and the answer suddenly grow more complicated.

The sleight-of-hand logic that first abstracts events from history and then assesses them from behind a veil of willed ignorance gains some of its plausibility from another key word in the anti-affirmative-action lexicon. That word is "individual," as in "The American way is to focus on the rights of individuals rather than groups." Now, "individual" and "individualism" have been honorable words in the American political vocabulary, and they have often been well employed in the fight against various tyrannies. But like any other word or concept, individualism can be perverted to serve ends the opposite of those it originally served, and this is what has happened when in the name of individual rights, millions of individuals are enjoined from redressing historically documented wrongs. How is this managed? Largely in the same way that the invocation of fairness is used to legitimize an institutionalized inequality. First one says, in the most solemn of tones, that the protection of individual rights is the chief obligation of society. Then one defines individuals as souls sent into the world with equal entitlements as guaranteed either by their Creator or by the Constitution. Then one pretends that nothing has happened to them since they stepped onto the world's stage. And then one says of these carefully denatured souls that they will all be treated in the same way, irrespective of any of the differences that history has produced. Bizarre as it may seem, individualism in this argument turns out to mean that every-one is or should be the *same*. This dismissal of individual difference in the name of the individual would be funny were its consequences not so serious: it is the mechanism by which imbalances and inequities suffered by millions of people through no fault of their own can be sanitized and even celebrated as the natural workings of unfettered democracy.

"Individualism," "fairness," "merit"—these three words are continually misappropriated by bigots who have learned that they need not put on a white hood or bar access to the ballot box in order to secure their ends. Rather, they need only clothe themselves in a vocabulary plucked from its historical context and made into the justification for attitudes and policies they would not acknowledge if frankly named.

*From "Reverse Racism or How the Pot Got to Call the Kettle Black" by Stanley Fish. *Atlantic Monthly,* November 1993, Vol. 272, No. 5, pp. 128–136. Reprinted with permission from Stanley Fish, professor of English and Law, and executive director of the Duke University Press.

SINS OF ADMISSION*
James Q. Wilson

Good Affirmative Action and Bad

Affirmative action—by which I mean selecting persons based on their group membership—is not one program but many and has consequences that range from acceptable to intolerable. We understand these distinctions intuitively. When a television commercial displays white and black actors or when a political party endorses candidates from a variety of ethnic backgrounds, no one complains—even though this is, literally, affirmative action. But should someone suggest that the musicians in a major symphony orchestra or the players in the National Basketball Association be chosen to create a specific racial balance, most people would be outraged.

The difference, of course, has to do with the purposes of the organizations. Television commercials and party candidates are chosen chiefly to attract support from customers and voters. Everyone expects organizations trying to sell something to cater to the preferences of those who might buy. But top-ranked musicians and athletes are selected exclusively on the basis of merit.

The debate over affirmative action in contracts, university admissions and public employment is in large measure a debate over what set of standards ought to govern achievement in these enterprises. The strongest defenders of affirmative action argue that these organizations have a representative as well as a technical function, while the toughest critics claim that the latter greatly outweighs the former.

Consider undergraduate admissions. A plausible proposal might run as follows: given the growing importance of college education in the life of the nation and the uncertainty attached to conventional measures of merit, one might defend the modest use of racial preferences as a way of increasing participation of underrepresented groups in educated society without doing serious harm to the quality of the university. One might, by the same token, take into account other nonintellectual attributes like athletic or musical ability.

But as one moves up through the university experience—to medical and law schools and onto a faculty—academic ability becomes the dominant criterion. Excellence at teaching and research are overwhelmingly important tests for faculty recruitment; no one proposes that law or medical schools admit athletes or musicians. Furthermore, three or four years of college training ought to have given students with natural abilities but subpar elementary and secondary educations a chance to catch up.

This guideline—race and ethnicity as a factor for 18 year olds but not after—might provide a reasonable basis on which to "mend, not end" affirmative action. Unfortunately, preference programs, as administered today, make no such distinctions—affirmative action is at least as pervasive in admissions to law and medical schools as in college, if not more so.

UCLA's undergraduate admissions are based on two sets of criteria: academic (grades, test scores) and supplemental ("socio-economic or educational disadvantage"). For each, students are ranked from one (the highest) to six (the lowest). The admissions office admits between 40 and 60 percent of the student body strictly on academic grounds. The next group consists of people whose combined academic and supplemental ranking gives them a high total score. In this combined mark, being disadvantaged may count for more than being smart; a student can have an academic ranking as low as five and still get in if his or her disadvantage

rating is at the top. The final group—the "read" group, meaning their files are closely read—are those whose rankings, academic and supplemental, are low.

In 1994, UCLA admitted 6,801 students as part of its academic-only criteria. Of these, seventy-seven, or about 1 percent, were African Americans. The African-American students admitted in the first academic group had an average SAT score nearly 300 points higher than blacks admitted in the latter two groups, and their high school grades were half a grade higher. Among those not chosen on purely academic grounds, 19 percent were African Americans, and another 51 percent were Latino. These second two categories have effectively become ethnicity driven.

The evidence is equally clear for the fall of 1995. Eighty-one percent of Asians and Caucasians admitted had academic rankings of one or two, but only 10 percent of the Asians and 1 percent of the Caucasians were in the top two supplemental ranks. For Mexican-American and African-American applicants, less than 13 percent of those admitted had academic ranks of one or two, but more than 97 percent were in the top two supplemental ranks.

Once admitted, disparities remain. Among white and Asian-American students, at least 80 percent graduate within five years. Among African-American students, less than half do so. In the UCLA class admitted in 1990, Caucasians had an average grade of just over a "B," while African Americans averaged just above a "C."

A common defense of these disparities is that athletic ability or alumni connections already count in admissions and, therefore, race should, too. But this misses the point. Race, according to the Supreme Court, is a suspect classification subject to strict scrutiny. Athletic prowess (or musical ability, or rich parents) are not suspect classifications and do not require strict judicial scrutiny. If these traits were treated legally the same as race, then I could sue the Boston Red Sox for denying me my lifelong ambition of playing second base for them simply because I can't hit, an untalented violinist could sue the New York Philharmonic to get a seat in the string section, and rich parents could demand scholarships for their children. One cannot easily correct this problem by abandoning the judicial protection given race; to do that would permit colleges and employers to discriminate against blacks. To the extent race deserves special constitutional protection, it cannot be equated with other principles of classification.

The famous opinion of Justice Lewis Powell in the *Bakke* case, decided in 1978, is still supposedly the basis for racial preference in American law: race, despite its special status, can be a "plus factor" in admissions so long as it is not the decisive one. Yet, at the University of California today, strictly academic admissions would admit a 1 percent black student body (down from 7 percent currently), while the supplemental categories admit students of whom only a tiny fraction are white or Asian. The contrast between the two systems is not a "plus" factor. It is decisive.

The evidence from medical school is the same. Ellen and Jerry Cook—she teaches at the University of California at San Diego (UCSD)—have compared graduates of UCSD who applied to that university's medical school between 1987 and 1993. The *only* students admitted with MCAT scores below the sixtieth percentile or with college grades below 3.0 were from affirmative action groups. Furthermore, a separate study showed that students from poorer families received no advantage per se; the only criteria for preference was race and ethnicity. The result was that UCSD admitted students based on two different distributions of abilities—one curve consisted of almost all the affirmative action students, another (barely overlapping) curve consisted mostly of whites and Asians. This

although both had access to the same undergraduate education.

Much the same pattern exists in law schools. If you have an LSAT score below the ninetieth percentile and college grades below 3.5, you are vastly more likely to be admitted into UCLA Law School if you are black or Hispanic than if you are white or Asian. One study, done unofficially by a student who cracked the law school's secrecy codes, suggests that the grades received by black students during their first year are significantly lower than those received by whites.

The costs of professional school racial preference are greater than those of undergraduate colleges, in part because 18 year olds have a wider range of available opportunities. High-school students wanting to enter a good university have more choices than do those wanting to enter the considerably smaller number of good law or medical schools. By the same token, the costs to society of admitting less qualified students into these select institutions is greater.

In California, four Under-Represented Minority groups (URMs) are generically entitled to affirmative action: African Americans, Native Americans, Mexican Americans and mainland Puerto Ricans. Let us suppose for a moment that African Americans belong there because of past discrimination and the legacy of slavery. But on what grounds are Mexican Americans on the list and other Hispanics numerous in California—Guatemalans, El Salvadorans, Cubans—not? At one time Asians were the object of the bluntest possible discrimination in California—many could not own land or serve on a jury—and Japanese Americans were exiled to inland camps during World War II. Yet Asians do not make the list and, indeed, lose space in universities owing to the preferences given to URMs. The Vietnamese came to this country poor after a war in which we were a major participant, but URM graduates applying for admission to

California medical schools were 2.7 times as likely to be accepted as Vietnamese students despite the fact that the grades of most of the rejected Vietnamese were higher than those of most of the accepted URMs.

One argument often cited in favor of university affirmative action is its support among faculty. And, indeed, last year the UCLA faculty legislative assembly did vote by a margin of six to one to criticize the State Regents for abandoning racial preferences. (Although when the assembly's vote was sent out on a mail ballot to all faculty members, support for its position fell from six to one to three to two, and to even lower margins at other UC campuses.) But even this does not prove faculty support for racial preference, since some faculty may have objected to the *way* the Regents made their decision, rather than to the principle of color-blindness itself. In 1995 the California Association of Scholars polled faculty opinion in the nine California public universities. Designed by the Roper Center for Public Opinion Research, the central question was this: Should the university "grant preferences to women and certain racial and ethnic groups in admissions, hiring and promotions?" Most faculty said no.

Just as affirmative action is more costly for professional schools than undergraduate colleges, it is more problematic at some colleges than others. At Harvard, with its pick of the country's top high-school students, white and black, the racial gap on college entrance scores was modest. But the scarcity of academically prepared blacks means that the best universities skim off the top. The result is that other universities—including the very good public universities in California—take a chance admitting students who may be unprepared to tackle college-level work, and may not graduate at all.

Affirmative action has lost its moorings. Colleges legitimately want a diverse student body, but their definition of diversity is limited to ethnicity, excludes ideology and favors some but not other ethnic groups. Law and medical schools want to produce more attorneys and physicians of certain ethnicities, but they can only do this by denying—not modifying, but denying—equal access to more talented applicants, thereby lowering the quality of the professionals they produce. This inevitably has consequences for consumers of medicine and legal assistance.

As universities become more competitive overall while lowering the standards by which they admit certain students, they increasingly produce anger and frustration among those hardworking young people who have upheld demanding standards themselves and expect their universities to do the same. Even worse, the very professional schools that have long made a special claim to excellence have abandoned that claim—to the dismay of all those who once believed them.

*From "Sins of Admission" by James Q. Wilson. *The New Republic,* July 8, 1996, Vol. 215, No. 2, Issue 4, pp. 12–16. Reprinted with permission from *The New Republic.* James Q. Wilson, a professor at the University of California-Los Angeles, is author of *The Moral Sense* (The Free Press).

THE "Q" WORD*
Thomas Sowell

Affirmative Action Produced Polarization and Violence in Some Countries, Including Civil War in Sri Lanka

Now that affirmative action is coming under fire politically and may be outlawed in some states, or perhaps even nationally, look for lots of word games by its advocates as they try to confuse the issues.

The big word game is denial that affirmative action means group quotas. Historically, it began meaning something else—but so did such terms as Catholic, communist and magazine. What matters is not these excursions down memory lane but what it is that people are for or against today.

What people are opposed to are group quotas instead of decisions based on individual performance. But of course the word "quota" has set off its own round of evasive word games.

The clever alternative to quotas is "goals," a more flexible version of quotas. By shifting the issue to flexibility versus rigidity, advocates of affirmative action evade the fundamental question: whether applicants for jobs, colleges, or a thousand other things are to be judged according to their own individual qualifications or according to some numerical standard of group representation.

Old-fashioned name-calling is another word game often invoked in discussions of affirmative action. "Racist" has long been tried and true in this role, but its overuse has weakened its sting and sometimes produces more boredom than anything else.

A related charge against minority critics of affirmative action is to claim that they have themselves benefited from affirmative action and are narrow and selfish in wanting to deny those benefits to others like themselves. Since it is impossible to prove a negative, supposedly this kind of word game should always be successful.

But, for the sake of argument, let us assume that this charge is 100 percent correct in all cases. What follows? If I have benefited from a war, should my position on issues of peace and war be determined forever after by what benefited me personally, rather than by what is best overall? This would be raising personal bias to the level of a principle.

One of the many unfortunate consequences of affirmative action has been that many minorities and females have no definitive way to know whether, or to what extent, they got where they are by their own efforts. Those of us old enough to have begun our careers before affirmative action began may be spared this particular burden, but, by and large, group quotas stigmatize even legitimate achievements.

Just recently a black youngster in a California high school who had received early admission to a prestigious college was told by a white classmate that this was due to racial preferences. The white classmate had been turned down—and had lower SATs than the black student. Just as "racism" has become a blanket excuse for individual failure available to minorities, so affirmative action has become a blanket excuse for individual failure available to white males.

The word "preferences" spawns a whole family of word games.

"There were once preferences for white males," we are told. So why such an objection now to preferences that offset that?

If it was wrong to have preferences for white males, then two wrongs do not make a right. And if it is all right to have preferences for various other groups now, why was it wrong to have had preferences for white males in the past?

In academia, the argument is that preferential admission for alumni children, football players and the like all preceded preferences for minority applicants to college. This might be a reasonable argument if the issue were whether minority students are benefiting too much in college.

The tragic fact, however, is that three-fourths of minority students are failing to graduate, often from colleges where they should never have been admitted in the first place. These include youngsters with test scores and other qualifications that would make them candidates for the dean's list in the average American college. They are simply going to the wrong schools.

Perhaps the most fraudulent of all the word games has been the claim that affirmative action is a "temporary" measure. Such claims have been made for affirmative action in countries around the world. Yet group preferences have not only persisted but spread over time to encompass more activities, more institutions and more groups.

By and Large, Group Quotas Stigmatize Even Legitimate Achievements

Even where explicit cut-off dates were written into the law, as in India and Pakistan, these laws were extended again and again, long past the original cut-off date. South Africa is the only country that has ended racial preferences—for whites, in this case—and that after more than a century.

That is not most people's idea of "temporary." Nor do Americans need to go to the brink of civil war before repealing a policy that has produced polarization and intergroup violence in other countries, including even civil war in Sri Lanka.

*From: "The 'Q' Word" by Dr. Thomas Sowell, *Forbes*, April 10, 1995, p. 61. Reprinted by permission of FORBES Magazine. © 1999 Forbes 1995.
Dr. Thomas Sowell is an economist and a senior fellow at the Hoover Institution in Stanford, Calif.

PORK BARREL QUOTAS*
Linda Chavez

When my oldest son graduated from high school a few years ago, he was inundated with college recruitment letters. Several offered him generous scholarships *without even seeing* his school transcripts or getting any idea of his financial need. His zip code alone should have told them he lived in an affluent suburban community. He was unlikely to have encountered any social or economic disadvantage. But the colleges' only interest was that he would make their Hispanic numbers look good. The irony is that he is just one-quarter Hispanic.

(We turned down all the offers.)

My family's experience as middle-class beneficiaries of affirmative action is not exceptional. Senate majority leader Bob Dole recently ordered a study by the Congressional Research Service of 168 federal affirmative action programs. The service found there were no fewer than 19 separate programs just to benefit minority bankers. Other programs included set-asides for minority contractors who run multimillion-dollar businesses. This is nothing more than pork barrel politics with a fancy name—affirmative action.

As affirmative action begins to unravel, after nearly 30 years of virtually unquestioned acceptance by the Washington elite, the rhetoric of those who want to save the programs has reached hysterical pitch.

"When the trains come, you'll be shoved right in there with me. And your political views won't protect you either," the Reverend Jesse Jackson warned me as we sat waiting to tape a TV show on affirmative action. At first, I thought it was the kind of barb I've grown used to getting from the civil rights establishment since the days when I was a Reagan Administration official. Then I realized he was serious. He really believes the current national mood on affirmative action means an American Kristallnacht is near for minorities.

Jackson is not alone. Representative Charles Rangel (D–N.Y.) says, "When I compare this to what happened in Germany, I hope that you will see the similarities to what is happening to us." Representative Major Owens (D–N.Y.), referring to Republican critics of affirmative action, says: "[They] are practicing genocide with a smile; they're worse than Hitler." Pulitzer Prize-winning author Toni Morrison, commenting on the possible dismantling of affirmative action, says, "...the descent into a final solution is not a jump. It's one step and then another and then another."

This grotesque hyperbole will have less effect than it would have had even a few years ago. The civil rights establishment has lost the moral high ground in the debate over racial justice.

America today is not the Deep South of 1963, when civil rights leaders were beaten, hosed down and sometimes killed for the right to sit at a lunchroom counter. And most Americans know it.

It's not surprising, given the passions aroused by the subject, that some politicians want to figure out a way to save affirmative action without incurring the political risk that defending it would cost them. In a series of meetings with civil rights leaders in mid-March, President Clinton was said to be looking for a "third way" between defending the status quo and abolishing all race- and sex-based preferences.

I have news for him. There is no "third way." Compromise on this issue is impossible. Quotas are a zero-sum game. Any effort to preserve them will leave their victims injured and mad.

Since there is no third way, there are only two alternatives: Get rid of quotas or preserve them pretty much as they are. Therefore, a terrific fight is shaping up. Defenders of affirmative action will throw up as many roadblocks as they can. They are not without resources.

Recently, California Assembly Speaker Willie Brown told me on CNN & Co. that he expects to defeat the California Civil Rights Initia-tive, which would bar all racial preferences in the state, if it makes it to the ballot next year. I was incredulous. I offered to fly to California and buy him a steak dinner if he did block the measure. On air, I asked if he was serious.

Brace Yourself for Extreme and Divisive Rhetoric as the Fight Over So-called Affirmative Action Heats Up

"Wait until Levi Strauss and Bechtel weigh in," he said. "They're committed to diversity." He may be right about corporate support for the quota system. Many in the corporate world long ago made their Faustian bargain with racial preferences.

But they should reconsider. So long as we continue to count by race, ethnicity and gender and to distribute benefits and preferences accordingly, civil rights will be a hollow and corrupt substitute for equal opportunity.

*From: "Pork Barrel Quotas" by Linda Chavez, *Forbes,* April 24, 1995, p. 112. Reprinted by permission of FORBES Magazine. © 1999 Forbes 1995.
Linda Chavez is president of the Center for Equal Opportunity and former director of the U.S. Commission on Civil Rights, under Ronald Reagan.

Plato

*P*lato (427?–347 B.C.) is one of the immortal geniuses of philosophy. Born in Athens to a wealthy and politically influential aristocratic family, he was closely associated as a young man with Socrates, who died when Plato was in his late twenties. When the democracy was restored, Plato's family fell out of favor, and his hostility to democratic government is reflected in a number of his works. At some time after Socrates' death, perhaps as much as fifteen years or more, Plato started to write dialogues in which moral, political, religious, cosmological, logical, and other subjects were explored. In the early Dialogues, Socrates is always the principal speaker, and there is some reason to suppose that Plato's picture of Socrates' personality and doctrines bears a close resemblance to the actual historical man who was his teacher. Later on, however, the Dialogues clearly come more and more to reflect Plato's own philosophical investigations, and in the works that he composed last, Socrates disappears altogether as a character.

Retreating from public life, Plato founded a school at his home in Athens, called the "Academy," and the word has since then meant a school or university. Many of the most gifted philosophers of the day worked or studied at the Academy, including the other great genius of ancient thought, Aristotle. Eventually, the Academy became an independent institution, and it continued in existence for almost 900 years before it was finally closed by the Roman emperor Justinian in A.D. 529.

Plato's greatest work was the *Republic,* a dialogue on the nature of justice, but much of his work in later life was devoted to mathematics and cosmology, and members of the Academy made significant contributions to formal logic and to such mathematical fields as solid geometry.

Philosophy of Art

Plato's Attack on the Poets

Aristotle's Defense of the Poets

Marcuse and the Uses of Negation

Arthur C. Danto's Theory of Artistic Identification

Contemporary Application: Pornography, Art, and Censorship

Plato's Attack on the Poets

Here is a short parable: There was a singer with a clear, strong, beautiful voice, whose songs were so lovely that people would come from miles around to hear him sing. The singer was a thoughtful, compassionate man whose heart was troubled by the poverty and misery of the people for whom he sang. After much reflection, he concluded that the people should rise up and change their condition. And he realized that his songs, because of their loveliness, were a distraction to the people, making them forget for the moment the real causes of their misery. He decided to tell the people what he had discovered, but alas, they would only listen to him when he sang. So he wrote a song about the misery of the people and the dangerousness of lovely songs. But because he was a great singer, his song was a lovely song, and the people, listening to it, were soothed and distracted from their misery, and so did nothing.

Plato was just such a singer of philosophical songs, and nothing is more poignant or paradoxical than his attitude toward the great works of art that he himself created. You have several times met Socrates in these pages, always in his role as the principal character in Plato's Dialogues (his "philosophical songs"). But Plato, the artist himself, is not to be confused with the dramatic character who sometimes speaks for him in his Dialogues, any more than the real historical Socrates should be confused with that character. Socrates wrote nothing himself, as Plato's own portrait of him tells us; but Plato wrote a great deal, and so he was forced to ask himself, as every artist must, whether artistic creation is good or evil, whether a life spent in the forming of artworks is a life well spent, what indeed the function of art is in human life and society, and whether there is a place for art in the good society.

Since Plato's Dialogues, at least as we encounter them today, are classified as philosophical works rather than as works of art, it might be worth saying a few words about what sets them off from all of the other philosophical works that no one would dream of calling "artistic." A philosophical dialogue is easy enough to write, if all you care about is getting the arguments down on paper. Just put your own theories in the mouth of one character—call her Ms. Wise—and whatever objections you can think of in the mouth of a second character—"The Fool," perhaps—and then write the whole thing down as though it were a play. The result will not exactly be beautiful, but as long as it has two characters in it, you can call it a dialogue. A number of great and not-so-great philosophers have actually written some of their philosophy in roughly this way, including the seventeenth-century Dutch metaphysician Baruch Spinoza, who was no artist at all, and the eighteenth-century Irish cleric George Berkeley, who was not either.

But Plato's Dialogues are quite another thing altogether. Their artistic brilliance results from Plato's ability to do three things at the same time, and to do them all superbly. First, his Dialogues are not shadowboxing, or put-up jobs. Plato constructs real arguments, in which Socrates' opponents score points and make philosophical moves that are genuinely persuasive. Second, the characters in the Dialogues are not cardboard figures, two-dimensional pop-ups with name tags attached. They are fully realized human beings, with feelings, passions, and characteristic ways of speaking. Some of them run on in great long speeches; others are mulish, grudging, giving nothing in an argument and resisting even the most obvious implications of their own statements. Some are dignified old men, full of years and self-confident in an awareness that they are nearing the end of life with their honor unsullied; others are eager, ambitious young men, out to score a quick knockout over Socrates and make their reputations. Most of the characters in the Dialogues were apparently modeled after real people, and the original readers presumably could judge how skillfully Plato had caught their characters in his portraits. But for those of us who read the Dialogues two millennia later, it matters only that they are completely successful artistic creations.

Finally, Plato accomplishes the most difficult creative feat of all—he makes the personalities and speech of his characters actually exemplify, and thereby provide evidence for, the philosophical theories he is trying to expound. His characters are not merely believable; they are just what they ought to be, given the philosophy they are expressing, if Plato's own theories are true. This fit between character and belief is designed by Plato as an expression of the central thesis of his philosophy: the doctrine that the metaphysical order of the universe is mirrored in the inner psychic order of the soul. Plato bases his philosophy upon a distinction between *appearance* and *reality,* a distinction that turns up over and over in many different guises throughout his works (indeed, we can quite accurately say that although the distinction *appears* in many different forms, it is *really* always the same distinction, and that is just one more example, Plato would say, of the distinction between appearance and reality). For example, a straight stick looks bent when half of it is put into water (because of the refraction of light). Sugar may seem good to a diabetic even though it would really make him sick. A tricky argument may look correct, but really be invalid. A devil may appear to be an angel of the Lord but really be a messenger from Satan. It may seem smart to cheat on an exam, even though it is really dumb. Popular opinion may sound wise but really be foolish.

In all of these cases, and countless others besides, there is an image, a belief, an action, a feeling, which seems to be right, true, good, accurate, veridical, or healthy but is really wrong, false, evil, misleading, fallacious, or harmful. The ability to tell the difference between the two is always, according to Plato, a matter of some sort of knowledge, and the power or part of the soul whose job it is to make that distinction is *reason*. Reason tells us that the stick is really straight, even though it looks bent; reason tells the diabetic not to eat the apparently good sugar; reason finds the flaw in the valid-looking argument; and reason shows us when the easy way—cheating, or going along with popular opinion—is in the end the harmful, destructive way.

As these examples suggest, knowledge of reality, and the ability to distinguish it from misleading appearance, is more than just "book learning." You can study the principles of optics in the classroom, but you need some common sense and the power of observation to tell you when to apply the formulas to a real stick in some real water. The diabetic patient can carefully write down his doctor's instructions not to eat candy, but he needs a quite different kind of knowledge and a much stronger power of reason to apply those instructions when temptation appears in the guise of a rich, tasty dessert. Socrates needed more than just a "philosophical" understanding of justice to resist the chance to escape from his punishment by the Athenians and instead remain, calm and resigned, to drink the hemlock.

According to Plato, a woman who has some true opinions but does not really understand what makes them true will *look* wise as long as she does not get into morally difficult or complicated situations, but she will not *really be* wise. We are liable to confuse her good habits and her true opinions with real knowledge until we see her come unstuck in a crunch. Then we will realize that we were deceived and that what we took for real wisdom was only its appearance. So too, a man who mouths current arguments without really having thought them through for himself will sound very knowledgeable until we press him with some hard questions. Then we will discover that his knowledge is only appearance. Worst of all, according to Plato, a person who has no systematic grasp of the true good for humanity will not be able to tell what is going to make her truly happy and so will do what looks pleasant but is ultimately harmful. She will allow herself to be flattered into betraying a trust, or beguiled away from the hard work that brings real satisfaction, or frightened by imagined evils into shameful or dishonorable deeds.

Plato weaves his philosophical theory about appearance and reality together with his psychological insights into human character to produce a series of persuasive and fundamentally true portraits in his Dialogues. (Needless to say, he deliberately intends the dramatic persuasiveness of his characters—their appearance—to reveal, rather than conceal, the truth about their souls—their reality.)

One example may make all this a bit clearer. In the Dialogue *Gorgias,* there are three characters who argue with Socrates. The first is the title character, a traveling public speaker and teacher named Gorgias; the second is a young disciple named Polus; and the third is the hot-headed, brilliant Callicles. Now Plato sees Gorgias as one of those decent human beings who personally would not do anything shameful or wicked but who does not really have rational knowledge of the right moral principles. In fact, although in his own life he is an upright person, the philosophy he expounds is totally false. Plato thinks that Gorgias is dangerous, because his pupils tend to do as he says, not as he does. Instead of imitating the decency and honorableness of

Gorgias' private life, his pupils listen to his relativistic moral arguments and act on them in the law courts and public life of Athens. Plato presents Gorgias as a man who is stuffily self-confident, easily trapped into logical contradictions, but personally horrified at the thought that anyone would take his philosophy as an excuse for dishonorable behavior. Plato lets him off rather easily in the Dialogue, because he respects Gorgias' personal decency as a human being, while nevertheless condemning the confusion of his thought. When Polus, the young disciple, enters the argument in Gorgias' place, the tone changes immediately. Polus is one of those impressionable young men who have been misled by Gorgias' statements and insufficiently impressed by Gorgias' actual character. Polus argues better than Gorgias, because he is not restrained—as Gorgias is—by a well-developed sense of what it is fitting and proper to maintain in a moral argument. Gorgias cannot bring himself to say something he knows to be wrong merely to make a point in a debate, but Polus is not so hesitant. Nevertheless, since he is merely repeating things he has heard in current conversation, without any deep thought, he is easily refuted by Socrates. But Plato permits Socrates to make fun of Polus, thereby expressing his moral evaluation of Polus as compared to Gorgias. When Callicles jumps into the debate to replace Polus, a real tension develops between him and Socrates. Callicles really believes, as he says, that might makes right, that there are no universal rational principles binding the weak and the strong, the ordinary and the extraordinary, to a single standard of conduct. This total confusion (as Plato sees it) is mirrored in the disorder of Callicles' soul. He rants, he shouts, he grows abusive, he loses whatever dignity he may have possessed. In short, his personality exhibits precisely that breakdown of true reason that his philosophy also reveals. The Dialogue becomes, at one and the same time, an argument between two philosophies and a contrast between two personalities. The truth of Socrates' position is shown as much by his composure, his ironic self-deprecation, his inner peace, as it is by the forcefulness of his arguments.

Now let me connect the parable at the beginning of the chapter with Plato's theory of appearance and reality and this long example from the *Gorgias* of Plato's artistic skill. Strange and paradoxical as it may seem, Plato actually believed, on the basis of his theoretical distinction between appearance and reality, that artistic creations were *appearances* and that as such they led us away from knowledge and away from a proper inner harmony of the soul. And like the singer in the parable, Plato expressed this conviction in a series of artistic works of such beauty that the attention of his audience is turned away from the message rather than toward it.

Our first selection in this chapter is, once again, from the *Republic*. It contains Plato's reasons for believing that art is misleading and harmful and, therefore, that it ought not to be permitted a place in the ideal society that he is sketching. In much of this selection, Plato seems to be talking about what philosophers call "metaphysics," or the study of the forms and nature of

Plato criticized art for misrepresenting reality. Here are three paintings by the Frenchman Auguste Renoir, the American Jackson Pollock, and the Spaniard Pablo Picasso. All three would claim that they are successfully capturing some aspect of reality that a photograph fails to reveal.

Left: Auguste Renoir, French (1841-1919) "Oarsmen at Chatou." *Canvas, 32 x 39½ (0.813 x 1.003)* *(Source:* National Gallery of Art, Washington, D.C.)

Above: Jackson Pollock, "Echo (Number 25, 1951)." *Enamel on unprimed canvas, 7 ft. 7 ⅞ in. x 7 ft. 2 in. (233.4 x 218.4 cm.). (Source:* Art Resource/The Museum of Modern Art)

Above: Pablo Picasso, Spanish, 1881–1973. "The Three Musicians," summer 1921. *Oil on canvas, 6 ft. 7 in. x 7 ft. 3 ¾ in. (200.7 x 222.9). (Source:* Art Resource/The Museum of Modern Art)

being, as much as about art. This interconnection of the different branches of philosophy is typical of the work of the great philosophers, and you should not be misled by the organization of this book into supposing that philosophy consists of a number of separate subfields locked away in watertight compartments. Indeed, the distinction between appearance and reality also bears directly on John Stuart Mill's claim, in Chapter 6, that some pleasures are higher or truer or better than others. Plato held the same view, and he defended it precisely by saying that some pleasures are *more real* than others.

Plato's objections to art focus on two distinct but related questions: First, does art give us knowledge, or does it mislead us about the nature of reality? Second, does art help us achieve a proper, harmonious inner psychic order, or does it stir up our emotions and destroy the rule of reason within the personality? Plato convicts art on both counts. Art leads us away from reality rather than toward it, he claims, and it destroys our psychic harmony rather than reinforces it. These twin issues, of the truthfulness of art and the psychological effect of art on the audience, run through all the philosophies of art that we shall be examining in this chapter.

Plato's Philosophy of Art

PLATO,
Republic

Can you tell me what is meant by representation in general?

...shall we proceed as usual and begin by assuming the existence of a single essential nature or Form for every set of things which we call by the same name?

Then let us take any set of things you choose. For instance there are any number of beds or of tables, but only two Forms, one of Bed and one of Table.

And we are in the habit of saying that the craftsman, when he makes the beds or tables we use or whatever it may be, has before his mind the Form of one or other of these pieces of furniture. The Form itself is, of course, not the work of any craftsman.

Now what name would you give to a craftsman who can produce all the things made by every sort of workman?

He would need to have very remarkable powers!

Wait a moment, and you will have even better reason to say so. For, besides producing any kind of artificial thing, this same craftsman can create all plants and animals, himself included, and earth and sky and gods and the heavenly bodies and all the things under the earth in Hades.

That sounds like a miraculous feat of virtuosity.

Are you incredulous? Tell me, do you think there could be no such craftsman at all, or that there might be someone who could create all these things in one sense, though not in another? Do you not see that you could do it yourself, in a way?

In what way, I should like to know.

There is no difficulty; in fact there are several ways in which the thing can be done quite quickly. The quickest perhaps would be to take a mirror and turn it round in all directions. In a very short time you could produce sun and stars and earth and yourself and all the other animals and plants and lifeless objects which we mentioned just now.

Yes, in appearance, but not the actual things.

Quite so; you are helping out my argument. My notion is that a painter is a craftsman of that kind. You may say that the things he produces are not real; but there is a sense in which he too does produce a bed.

Yes, the appearance of one.

And what of the carpenter? Were you not saying just now that he only makes a particular bed, not what we call the Form or essential nature of Bed?

Yes, I was.

If so, what he makes is not the reality, but only something that resembles it. It would not be right to call the work of a carpenter or of any other handicraftsman a perfectly real thing.

We must not be surprised, then, if even an actual bed is a somewhat shadowy thing as compared with reality.

True.

Now shall we make use of this example to throw light on our question as to the true nature of this artist who represents things? We have here three sorts of bed: one which exists in the nature of things and which, I imagine, we could only describe as a product of divine workmanship; another made by the carpenter; and a third by the painter. So the three kinds of bed belong respectively to the domains of these three: painter, carpenter, and god.

Yes.

Now the god made only one ideal or essential Bed, whether by choice or because he was under some necessity not to make more than one; at any rate two or more were not created, nor could they possibly come into being.

Why not?

Because, if he made even so many as two, then once more a single ideal Bed would make its appearance, whose character those two would share; and that one, not the two, would be the essential Bed. Knowing this, the god, wishing to be the real maker of a real Bed, not a particular manufacturer of one particular bed, created one which is essentially unique.

So it appears.

Shall we call him, then, the author of the true nature of Bed, or something of that sort?

Certainly he deserves the name, since all his works constitute the real nature of things.

And we may call the carpenter the manufacturer of a bed?

Yes.

Can we say the same of the painter?

Certainly not.

Then what is he, with reference to a bed?

I think it would be fairest to describe him as the artist who represents the things which the other two make.

Very well, said I; so the work of the artist is at the third remove from the essential nature of the thing?

Exactly.

The tragic poet, too, is an artist who represents things; so this will apply to him: he and all other artists are, as it were, third in succession from the throne of truth.

Just so.

We are in agreement, then, about the artist. But now tell me about our painter: which do you think he is trying to represent—the reality that exists in the nature of things, or the products of the craftsman?

The products of the craftsman.

As they are, or as they appear? You have still to draw that distinction.

How do you mean?

I mean: you may look at a bed or any other object from straight in front or slantwise or at any angle. Is there then any difference in the bed itself, or does it merely look different?

It only looks different.

Well, that is the point. Does painting aim at reproducing any actual object as it is, or the appearance of it as it looks? In other words, is it a representation of the truth or of a semblance?

Of a semblance.

The art of representation, then, is a long way from reality; and apparently the reason why there is nothing it cannot reproduce is that it grasps only a small part of any object, and that only an image. Your painter, for example, will paint us a shoemaker, a carpenter, or other workman without understanding any one of their crafts; and yet, if he were a good painter, he might deceive a child or a simple-minded person into thinking his picture was a real carpenter, if he showed it to them at some distance.

. . . the content of this poetical representation is something at the third remove from reality, is it not?

Yes.

On what part of our human nature, then, does it produce its effect?

What sort of part do you mean?

Let me explain by an analogy. An object seen at a distance does not, of course, look the same size as when it is close at hand; a straight stick looks bent when part of it is under water, and the same thing appears concave or convex to an eye misled by colours. Every sort of confusion like these is to be found in our minds; and it is this weakness in our nature that is exploited, with a quite magical effect, by many tricks of illusion, like scene-painting and conjuring.

. . . Instead of trusting merely to the analogy from painting, let us directly consider that part of the mind to which the dramatic element in poetry appeals, and see how much claim it has to serious worth. We can put the question in this way. Drama, we say, represents the acts and fortunes of human beings. It is wholly concerned with what they do, voluntarily or against their will, and how they fare, with the consequences which they regard as happy or otherwise, and with their feelings of joy and sorrow in all these experiences. That is all, is it not?

Yes.

And in all these experiences has a man an undivided mind? Is there not an internal conflict which sets him at odds with himself in his conduct, much as we were saying that the conflict of visual impressions leads him to make contradictory judgments? However, I need not ask that question; for, now I come to think of it, we have already agreed that innumerable conflicts of this sort are constantly occurring in the mind. But there is a further point to be considered now. We have said that a man of high character will bear any stroke of fortune, such as the loss of a son or of anything else he holds dear, with more equanimity than most people. We may now ask: will he feel no pain, or is that impossible? Will he not rather observe due measure in his grief?

Yes, that is nearer the truth.

Now tell me: will he be more likely to struggle with his grief and resist it when he is under the eyes of his fellows or when he is alone?

He will be far more restrained in the presence of others.

Yes; when he is by himself he will not be ashamed to do and say much that he would not like anyone to see or hear.

Quite so.

What encourages him to resist his grief is the lawful authority of reason, while the impulse to give way comes from the feeling itself; and, as we said, the presence of contradictory impulses proves that two distinct elements in his nature must be involved. One of them is law-abiding, prepared to listen to the authority which declares that it is best to bear misfortune as quietly as possible without resentment, for several reasons: it is never certain that misfortune may not be a blessing; nothing is gained by chafing at it; nothing human is matter for great concern; and, finally, grief hinders us from calling in the help we most urgently need. By this I mean reflection on what has happened, letting reason decide on the best move in the game of life that the fall of the dice permits. Instead of behaving like a child who goes on shrieking after a fall and hugging the wounded part, we should accustom the mind to set itself at once to raise up the fallen and cure the hurt, banishing lamentation with a healing touch.

Certainly that is the right way to deal with misfortune.

And if, as we think, the part of us which is ready to act upon these reflections is the highest, that other part which impels us to dwell upon our sufferings and can never have enough of grieving over them is unreasonable, craven, and faint-hearted.

Yes.

Now this fretful temper gives scope for a great diversity of dramatic representation; whereas the calm and wise character in its unvarying constancy is not easy to represent, nor when represented is it readily understood, especially by a promiscuous gathering in a theatre, since it is foreign to their own habit of mind. Obviously, then, this steadfast disposition does not naturally attract the dramatic poet, and his skill is not designed to find favour with it. If he is to have a popular success, he must address himself to the fretful type with its rich variety of material for representation.

Obviously.

We have, then, a fair case against the poet and we may set him down as the counterpart of the painter, whom he resembles in two ways: his creations are poor things by the standard of truth and reality, and his appeal is not to the highest part of the soul, but to one which is equally inferior. So we shall be justified in not admitting him into a well-ordered commonwealth, because he stimulates and strengthens an element which threatens to undermine the reason. As a country may be given over into the power of its worst citizens while the better sort are ruined, so, we shall say, the dramatic poet sets up a vicious form of government in the individual soul: he gratifies that senseless part which cannot distinguish great and small, but regards the same things as now one, now the other; and he is an image-maker whose images are phantoms far removed from reality.

Quite true.

One final word on the paradox of the parable of the singer before we move on to the views of other philosophers. Plato feared that art would lead us away from reality rather than toward it. Considering how famous Plato has become, how widely his works have been read and studied in both the West and the East, it is tempting to dismiss his fears as foolish. But the fact is that in a peculiar way, Plato's own success is evidence that he was right. Through the dramatic power of Plato's art, Socrates has become an immortal figure of Western thought. When we read the Dialogues today, all of us—students and trained philosophers alike—instinctively cast Socrates as the hero and his opponents as the villains of the drama. This encourages us to accept Socrates' (and Plato's) doctrines without properly criticizing them or evaluating them. In other words, we treat Socrates in exactly the way that the ancient Athenians treated Gorgias and the other popular speakers. We are swayed by Plato's art rather than persuaded by his arguments. Now Socrates took what we today would call a conservative political position, and his opponents—at least according to some scholars—were the "liberals" of their society. Strange as it may seem, many modern philosophers whose own political opinions are liberal still treat Socrates as the good guy and Gorgias or Protagoras or Thrasymachus or Callicles as the bad guys. In short, they are so beguiled by the beauty of Plato's song that they do not reflect, calmly and rationally, on its words. That is just the danger Plato saw and warned of when he banned the artists from his ideal Republic.

Aristotle's Defense of the Poets

Plato was not yet thirty when Socrates died. Later in life, he founded a school or center for mathematical, cosmological, and philosophical investigation called the Academy. Far and away the most distinguished "student" at the Academy, if we can speak of students at all, was a man named Aristotle. There are many students of philosophy who consider Aristotle the greatest philosopher of all. St. Thomas Aquinas, the medieval theologian who figures so prominently in the development of Catholic doctrine, had so high an opinion of Aristotle that he referred to him simply as "the philosopher," as though there were no other. When you think about it, the odds must be simply astronomical against such a sequence of teachers and students as Socrates, Plato, and Aristotle.

Aristotle was not at all gifted artistically as Plato was, though in his youth he tried his hand at writing some dialogues. His temperament was rather that of a scientist, and the writings that we have today by him are actually treatises or lecture notes for the teaching he did at the Academy. Because they were written for a specialized audience rather than for the general public, they are very condensed, rather dry, and sometimes hard to follow if you are not already pretty well up on what Aristotle is talking about. The range of Aristotle's investigations was simply staggering. In addition to his great work in logic, he wrote of systematic comparative political science, moral philosophy, cosmology, psychology, biology, astronomy, and physics, and he even developed several proofs for the existence of a "prime mover," or God. In Athens, at that time, the public theater was an important part of the religious and civic as well as the cultural life of the people, and the annual performances of the tragedies written by the great Greek playwrights were a focus of public interest. Aristotle wrote a short treatise on the subject of tragedy. We know that little work today as *Poetics,* and despite its brevity, it is much read and quoted, for it has had a wide and deep influence throughout the ages on philosophical theories about art.

For our purposes, Aristotle's treatise is interesting because of its defense of art against the twofold attack of his teacher Plato. Recall the charge that Plato had leveled against poetry: it leads us away from truth, and it disorders the soul. Aristotle does not say a great deal about these two criticisms, but he indicates rebuttals to both. First, consider the claim that art misleads us by offering nothing more than imperfect copies of the world of the senses, which is itself no better than an imperfect copy or realization of the ideal standards of beauty, goodness, and justice that Plato calls the Forms or Ideas. If I want to know the true nature of a circle, I had better turn my eyes away from physical objects and reflect instead upon the pure definitions of mathematical forms. It is bad enough that my inadequate intelligence sometimes needs the aid of wheels, coins, and other imperfectly round objects that I encounter in life. I will simply stray farther from the truth if I fix my eyes on a picture of a wheel. The same is true for the knowledge of the human soul. True or ideal justice has never been achieved by a living man or woman, so I can learn very little about the eternal standard of justice through an examination of the lives of even the noblest men and women. What can a tragedian do, save conjure up for me on the stage an admittedly imperfect imitation of an admittedly imperfect character. I might as well try to get a feel for fine cowhide by looking at a photograph of imitation leather!

Not so, Aristotle replies. Plato is right in insisting that we should seek a knowledge of the unchanging, universal forms of justice, beauty, and goodness, but he is wrong in supposing that art merely provides us with imperfect copies of particular instances of those universal forms. Great artists have the ability, through their art, to grasp the universal that lies within the particular, and to present it to us in such a way that we achieve a greater knowledge than we would otherwise have. When Shakespeare creates for us the character of Hamlet (needless to say, this is my example, not Aristotle's), he shows us, through the particularities of the vacillations and inner conflicts of one young prince, some universal truths about fathers and sons, sons and mothers, intellect and will, thought and action. Plato, to the contrary notwithstanding, we are wiser for seeing a performance of *Hamlet* than we would be were we to travel back in time and meet the real man on whom the play is based.

The dispute between Plato and Aristotle is partly a disagreement about art, of course, but it is, at a deeper level, a disagreement about metaphysics. Plato seems to have held that the universal, eternal, unchanging Forms actually exist independently of the particular, time-bound, changing objects and events that fitfully and inadequately embody them. (I say, "seems to have held," because this is a subject on which scholars differ.) In other words, Plato believed that there is a reality that transcends the appearances of the senses and the world of space, time, and physical things. True knowledge was for him, therefore, a rational understanding of that transcendent realm of universal Forms. Aristotle, on the other hand, held that the universal Forms are completely embodied in the particular things of the world of space and time. True

A R I S T O T L E

Aristotle (384–322 B.C.) is the most influential figure in the history of Western philosophy. Born in Stagira, a Greek colony on the Aegean Sea, he came to Athens as a very young man to study with Plato in the school known as the Academy. He remained a student and member of the Academy for twenty years, leaving only in 347 B.C. upon Plato's death. Eventually he founded his own school, where he lectured on a range of subjects so broad that he must have been virtually a one-man faculty. In addition to his major philosophical discoveries in the fields of logic, metaphysics, and the theory of knowledge, Aristotle did an enormous amount of empirical work on problems of astronomy, biology, comparative politics, and anatomy.

Aristotle is remembered today for his philosophy, but during his middle life, after leaving Plato's Academy and before founding his own school, he spent seven years as a tutor to the young prince who was to become Alexander the Great. Alexander, heir to the throne of Macedonia, eventually conquered the entire Greek world and pushed his military campaigns as far east as India. Aristotle persuaded Alexander to send back biological specimens and other data from his explorations.

Although much of Aristotle's work has been surpassed by later investigators in the 2,000 years and more since his death, some of his writings, particularly those in the areas of psychology and the theory of art, remain as suggestive and useful today as they were in ancient times.

knowledge does indeed consist of a grasp of those forms, and Plato was certainly right that we must penetrate the changing particularity of this and that moment or event in order to get at the universal truths. But because the universals are embodied in the particulars—because true circularity is to be found within actual circular things, true rationality within actual rational creatures, true beauty within actual works of art, our attention should be focused even more intently on those particular instances rather than directed entirely away from them toward an independent realm of eternal Forms.

Aristotle's answer to Plato's second charge rests on a point of psychology rather than metaphysics. Plato was afraid that tragedy would arouse uncontrollable passions in the audience and thereby disarrange the proper harmony of the soul. It would weaken the ascendency of the rational forces within the personality and release erotic and aggressive elements that are destructive and deluding. Aristotle argued that just the opposite is the case.

Since those harmful passions are present anyway, far better to release them in the controlled setting of the drama than to bottle them up entirely. In art, we experience those terrible feelings vicariously, through our identification with the characters in the play. When they suffer, triumph, love, hate, rage, and mourn, we in the audience also do. When the play ends, we experience a **catharsis** and are purged of the pentup passions without having expressed them in the terrible deeds that the playwright has depicted on the stage. We leave the theater calmed, not aroused.

All this seems thin, bloodless, "academic," until we realize that exactly the same debate now rages in America about violence and sex in our movies and television shows. Does the portrayal of violence make our children more prone to act violently in their real lives, or does it drain away the violence that lies within all of us, giving it a safe, harmless outlet? Does sado-masochistic pornography stimulate its viewers to commit sex crimes, or does it divert passions that otherwise would lead to rape or mutilation?

The following brief selections from Aristotle's *Poetics* will give you some sense of his approach to the analysis and justification of art, but they will hardly settle such a host of difficult and controversial questions. In the remainder of this chapter, we shall take a look at two other conceptions of the nature and rationale of art. Perhaps somewhere in this debate you will find your own answer to Plato's question: Does art have a legitimate place in the good society?

Aristotle's Philosophy of Art

From what we have said it will be seen that the poet's function is to describe, not the thing that has happened, but a kind of thing that might happen, i.e., what is possible as being probable or necessary. The distinction between historian and poet is not in the one writing prose and the other verse—you might put the work of Herodotus into verse, and it would still be a species of history; it consists really in this, that the one describes the thing that has been, and the other a kind of thing that might be. Hence poetry is something more philosophic and of graver import than history, since its statements are of the nature rather of universals, whereas those of history are singulars.

ARISTOTLE,
Poetics

Catharsis   Literally, a cleansing or purging. Aristotle uses the term to describe the effect on us of powerful dramatic performances. By watching a play whose events arouse fear and pity within us, he thought, we are purged of those emotions, so that we leave the theater liberated or cleansed. The opposing view is that such plays (and, by extension, movies and television programs) arouse in us feelings we otherwise would not have, and should not have, such as certain aggressive and sexual feelings.

A tragedy, then, is the imitation of an action that is serious and also, as having magnitude, complete in itself; in language with pleasurable accessories, each kind brought in separately in the parts of the work; in a *dramatic,* not in a narrative form; with incidents arousing pity and fear, wherewith to accomplish its catharsis of such emotions.

We assume that, for the finest form of Tragedy, the Plot must be not simple but complex; and further, that it must imitate actions arousing fear and pity, since that is the distinctive function of this kind of imitation. It follows, therefore, that there are three forms of Plot to be avoided. (1) A good man must not be seen passing from happiness to misery, or (2) a bad man from misery to happiness. The first situation is not fear-inspiring or piteous, but simply odious to us. The second is the most untragic that can be; it has not one of the requisites of Tragedy; it does not appeal either to the human feeling in us, or to our pity, or to our fears. Nor, on the other hand, should (3) an extremely bad man be seen falling from happiness into misery. Such a story may arouse the human feeling in us, but it will not move us to either pity or fear; pity is occasioned by undeserved misfortune, and fear by that of one like ourselves; so that there will be nothing either piteous or fear-inspiring in the situation. There remains, then, the intermediate kind of personage, a man not pre-eminently virtuous and just, whose misfortune, however, is brought upon him not by vice and depravity but by some error of judgment, of the number of those in the enjoyment of great reputation and prosperity; e.g., Oedipus, Thyestes, and the men of note of similar families. The perfect Plot, accordingly, must have a single, and not (as some tell us) a double issue; the change in the hero's fortunes must be not from misery to happiness, but on the contrary from happiness to misery; and the cause of it must lie not in any depravity, but in some great error on his part; the man himself being either such as we have described, or better, not worse, than that.

The tragic fear and pity may be aroused by the Spectacle; but they may also be aroused by the very structure and incidents of the play—which is the better way and shows the better poet. The Plot in fact should be so framed that, even without seeing the things take place, he who simply hears the account of them shall be filled with horror and pity at the incidents; which is just the effect that the mere recital of the story in *Oedipus* would have on one. To produce this same effect by means of the Spectacle is less artistic, and requires extraneous aid. Those, however, who make use of the Spectacle to put before us that which is merely monstrous and not productive of fear, are wholly out of touch with Tragedy; not every kind of pleasure should be required of a tragedy, but only its own proper pleasure.

The tragic pleasure is that of pity and fear, and the poet has to produce it by a work of imitation; it is clear, therefore, that the causes

A portrait of a scene from William Shakespeare's *Hamlet*. Hamlet speaks to the skull of Yorick. Undated portrait. Terrible though the events of the play are, Aristotle would claim that in watching them unfold, we are purged of powerful and potentially destructive emotions. *(Source:* Corbis/Bettmann.*)*

should be included in the incidents of his story. Let us see, then, what kinds of incident strike one as horrible, or rather as piteous. In a deed of this description the parties must necessarily be either friends, or enemies, or indifferent to one another. Now when enemy does it on enemy, there is nothing to move us to pity either in his doing or in his meditating the deed, except so far as the actual pain of the sufferer is concerned; and the same is true when the parties are indifferent to

Aristotle,
Poetics

one another. Whenever the tragic deed, however, is done within the family—when murder or the like is done or meditated by brother on brother, by son on father, by mother on son, or son on mother— these are the situations the poet should seek after.

Marcuse and the Uses of Negation

Plato says that art is negative, disruptive, antirational and, therefore, that it should be banned from the good society. Aristotle says that good art is positive, constructive, and should play an important role in social life. Our next theory of art turns these views upside down in a startling, apparently contradictory way. Herbert Marcuse argues that great art is negative, destructive, irrational and, *therefore,* a valuable element in human life. Why on earth would anyone praise art for having precisely the qualities that other philosophers have considered worthy of condemnation? To put the question in its most paradoxical form, what is positive about being negative?

Marcuse begins his argument with a puzzle that does not at first seem to have anything to do with art. Why is it that the most dramatic, outrageous, powerful words and ideas so rapidly become domesticated and acceptable in

HERBERT MARCUSE

Herbert Marcuse (1898–1979) was born in Berlin. He was one of the original members of the famous Frankfurt School of Social Research, which flourished in Germany in the years before World War II. After fleeing to the United States to escape the Nazis, Marcuse became a major voice on the Left. During the 1960s, he was the most widely quoted radical critic of American capitalist society. His best-known books include *Eros and Civilization* and *One-Dimensional Man.*

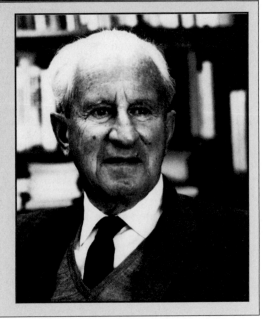

America today, *without changing anything along the way?* Sixties' radicals called America imperialist, and decent people everywhere were horrified. Several years later, Senator J. William Fulbright referred in passing to America's imperialist foreign policy on a television interview program, and none of the newscasters thought it worth commenting on. Black militants shout "Power to the people!" and "nice folks" cringe in their beds. Next season, "Power to the people!" is a liberal Democratic campaign slogan, and soon thereafter, a Richard Nixon campaign promise. Avant-garde artists violate every canon of artistic sensibility in a last-ditch effort to repudiate the plastic culture of Madison Avenue capitalism, and Madison Avenue reproduces their most outrageous productions as decorations for its advertisements. Woodstock begins as a cry of protest against Middle America and ends as the name of a bird in *Peanuts.* How can this be? Is nothing sacrilegious? Can modern American society absorb anything into itself without changing? Must every protest turn into this year's fad and next year's ancient history?

To answer these questions, Marcuse draws on the psychological theory of the origins of the ego and of civilization, which Sigmund Freud set forth in *Civilization and Its Discontents,* and which Marcuse revised and developed in *Eros and Civilization.* Freud argued that the objective, "un-get-over-able" constraints of the real world force each infant to, as he put it, substitute the reality principle for the pleasure principle. Because the physical world will not always fit itself to our desires, and also because we all inevitably get into interpersonal conflicts, particularly those fueled by sexual desire, we are forced to regulate or deny entirely some of our strongest desires. The psychic means for the regulation, Freud suggested, are **repression, sublimation,** and fantasy, of which repression is the first and most important. Thus is generated the realm of the "unconscious," populated by wishes, impulses, desires, loves, and hatreds that cannot be expressed and acted out in the real world. Civilization itself, our organized collective life, rests upon a foundation of repression, for not even the most miraculous technical wonders or the most flexible so-

Repression/Sublimation Two terms from the psychological theories of Sigmund Freud, referring to the primitive operations of the human mind. *Repression* is the forcible pushing out of consciousness of desires, wishes, thoughts, or feelings that the mind considers bad, dangerous, or otherwise unacceptable. According to Freud, what is repressed does not go away, but remains, with all of its emotional power, in the unconscious portion of the mind. *Sublimation* is the redirecting of sexual or aggressive energies into socially or morally acceptable channels—for example, aggressive energies directed away from physical violence and into philosophical arguments, or sexual energies diverted from immediate sexual activity into flirting.

cial arrangements can gratify the infantile wishes that lie beneath the conscious surface in every adult man and woman.

Two features of the content and structure of the unconscious are crucial to Marcuse's analysis. First, the unconscious is timeless. The thwarted desires and fears that reside there retain their power across decades of real-world time, returning again and again, irrespective of changes in the world that originally thwarted them. A mother who loses her child grieves, mourns, and eventually becomes reconciled to the loss. Time heals her wounds, and the objective passage of events places the loss further and further behind her. The child whose mother dies before he or she can cope with the loss may repress the grief and anger, so that half a century later, the anger at the mother's desertion will recur as strongly, albeit in transmuted forms. In particular, all of us carry with us unrelinquished infantile desires for the sorts of total, immediate, ecstatic satisfaction that as tiny babies we imagined we could, in our omnipotence, command.

Second, the content of the unconscious has a thoroughly ambivalent character. In the unconscious is to be found everything that reality (either natural or social) has decreed to be bad, inefficient, worthless, dirty, ugly, hostile, and shameful. But the wishes and desires that fill the unconscious retain their power, even though they have been denied fulfillment. Part of the self—the part that identifies with society, reality, adulthood, and the world—hates, loathes, and feels shame for what is repressed. That is the part of the self that cannot acknowledge a fascination with its own feces, or sexual desire for objects deemed socially inappropriate, or laziness, or messiness, or the urge to inflict pain and suffering. But another part of the self secretly delights in the content of the repressed. And what is more, it delights in the repressed *because* it is repressed. So we have the men and women who can only enjoy illicit sex; or, rather less dramatically, we find the familiar folk character of the perpetual child who refuses to grow up—Pan, Till Eulenspiegel, and Peter Pan.

Marcuse accepts Freud's fundamental claim that repression is essential to civilization. But in a brilliant deployment of one of Marx's key notions, he revises Freud's theory of repression by introducing a distinction between necessary repression and surplus repression. Necessary repression is simply that kind and amount of repression that is required at any stage of social development in order to carry on the struggle for existence. It involves, for example, denying ourselves part of the harvest even when we are hungry so that we have seed for the next planting; it involves forcing ourselves to continue laboring at painful tasks because of our rational recognition that hunger, disease, danger, and death may result if we let up too soon. But some repression, Marcuse argues, is not required by the objective constraints of reality. Rather, it is required by the specific system of domination and submission that exists in society at that moment in history. In short, some repression serves only to protect the favored position of the rulers by restraining the subjects from rising up and overthrowing their masters. That repression is "surplus repression," and human progress consists in eliminating surplus repression while simultaneously decreasing the amount of necessary repression through technological advance. Indeed, Marcuse argues, at a time when our technology should permit us considerably to relax the bonds of necessary repression, through the shortening and lightening of the workday, through the relaxation of work discipline, and so forth, surplus repression grows greater and greater so that the total burden of repression suffered in modern industrial society is not appreciably lighter than that suffered in technically less advanced societies. The purpose of that ever-increasing portion of surplus repression is, Marcuse claims, to maintain the ever more manifestly unjustifiable dominance of the ruling sectors of our society.

The concept of surplus repression is one of those brilliant insights that too often are rejected by hard-headed social scientists because they prove difficult to quantify or operationalize. How would we measure the relative proportions of necessary and surplus repression in an individual psyche? Indeed, how could we ever show of a single instance of repression that it was unnecessary, and hence surplus? I do not know the answer to these questions, but I remain convinced that Marcuse has his finger on a fundamental fact here, and that to the extent that it is fuzzy or imprecise, we should struggle to clarify it rather than use the unclarity as an excuse for rejecting it.

Now with the notion of surplus repression and the theory of the unconscious, we can sketch Marcuse's theory of the function of negative thinking and thereby approach his analysis of the function of art. Briefly, his position is this: The repressed content of the unconscious in all of us exists as a permanent psychic pool or source of opposition to the established order of society. We all construct powerful defenses against this repressed content within ourselves, using such familiar mechanisms as denial, projection, and transference. When a rebellious member of society violates some taboo by uncovering a part of the body that is supposed to be concealed; or by using, in public, language that is supposed to be used only in private; or by defying canons of dress, decorum, or deference, he or she provokes a response that is exaggerated all out of proportion. The rest of us recoil from the temporary and perhaps insignificant breach of the rules of repression because it provokes the ever-present desire within us to liberate ourselves from the same rules, and we can control that desire only by clamping down on the transgressor. A struggle over bare nipples or long hair or even an insolent, slouching way of standing becomes a struggle between the repressed content and the forces of civilization.

If all the actual repression were necessary repression, then it would be clear that the rebel should be contained, however sympathetically we might acknowledge that he or she speaks for a part of each of us. Marcuse's claim, however, is precisely that not all of the repression is necessary, that some of it is surplus, unnecessary, and that in the interest of human happiness, it should be eliminated. But—and this is the key to his entire theory—in order to generate sufficient emotional energy in enough people to conquer the surplus repression inflicted by our society, it is necessary to tap the ubiquitous, irrational, infantile desire for a release from all repression. To put it bluntly, you must promise people an impossible liberation from necessary repression in order to get them to struggle for the elimination of the merely surplus repression. To get us to the barricades, it is not enough to say, "Workers of the world, unite! After the revolution you shall suffer only necessary repression." Instead you must say, "Workers of the world, unite! After the revolution you shall be free." And each projects his or her own fantasy of absolute freedom, a daydream both inevitable and unfulfillable.

The revolutionary role of negative, oppositional styles of artistic expression is precisely to tap the reservoir of repressed desires, to draw on the permanent opposition within us to necessary repression, and thereby to fuel the fight against surplus repression. The artist's image of liberation is necessary, and illusory. The particular content of the rebellion against the established order of aesthetic canons is not crucial. In one social setting, the expletive "damn" will have as much effect as total nudity in another. The point is that no matter what is permitted, there remains both a repressed content that is denied and a longing to express it that can be tapped. The fight always appears to be about the particular artistic rule that has been broken, but it is always really about the existence of repression itself. If the rebellion is successful, surplus repression is reduced, but that success is always perceived as a failure by the participants themselves, because they must sooner or later relinquish their fantasy of total liberation.

The social function of art is thus to keep alive the possibility of what Marcuse calls transcendence. By transcendence, he does not mean, as Plato might, the passing from this world of space, time, and objects to a higher, eternal realm of forms or ideal entities. Rather, he means the imaginative leap beyond the given social world, with its repressions, oppressions, and reality-oriented sacrifices, to the conception of possible future social orders in which some of the repressed libidinal energy has been liberated. In thus adding a second "dimension" to our existence, Marcuse claims, art helps us escape the one-dimensionality of present society. But it is not art's job to draw us blueprints of the future. It must simply keep alive those repressed dreams of liberation and gratification whose energies, blocked but not diminished, will fuel the revolutions that reduce surplus repression and bring us closer to conditions of genuine human happiness.

In this selection, we listen to Marcuse talking about the "negative" function of great art. Despite the difficulty of his philosophical language, I think you will be able to see here some of the themes I have been discussing in the last few pages.

The Negative Function of Art

The achievements and the failures of this society invalidate its higher culture. The celebration of the autonomous personality, of humanism, of tragic and romantic love appears to be the ideal of a backward stage of the development. What is happening now is not the deterioration of higher culture into mass culture but the refutation of this culture by the reality. The reality surpasses its culture. Man today can do more than the culture heros and half-gods; he has solved many insoluble problems. But he has also betrayed the hope and destroyed the truth which were preserved in the sublimations of higher culture. To be sure, the higher culture was always in contradiction with social reality, and only a privileged minority enjoyed its blessings and represented its ideals. The two antagonistic spheres of society have always coexisted: the higher culture has always been accommodating, while the reality was rarely disturbed by its ideals and its truth.

Today's novel feature is the flattening out of the antagonism between culture and social reality through the obliteration of the oppositional, alien, and transcendent elements in the higher culture by virtue of which it constituted *another dimension* of reality. This liquidation of *two-dimensional* culture takes place not through the denial and rejection of the "cultural values," but through their wholesale incorporation into the established order, through their reproduction and display on a massive scale.

In contrast to the Marxian concept, which denotes man's relation to himself and to his work in capitalist society, the *artistic alienation* is the conscious transcendence of the alienated existence—a "higher level" or mediated alienation. The conflict with the world of progress, the negation of the order of business, the antibourgeois elements in bourgeois literature and art are neither due to the aesthetic lowliness of this order nor to romantic reaction—nostalgic consecration of a disappearing stage of civilization. "Romantic" is a term of condescending defamation which is easily applied to disparaging avant-garde positions, just as the term "decadent" far more often denounces the genuinely progressive traits of a dying culture than the real factors of decay. The traditional images of artistic alienation are indeed romantic in as much as they are in aesthetic incompatibility with the developing society. This incompatibility is the token of their truth. What they recall and preserve in memory pertains to the future: images of a gratification that would dissolve the society which suppresses it.

The tension between the actual and the possible is transfigured into an insoluble conflict, in which reconciliation is by grace of the oeuvre as *form:* beauty as the "promesse de bonheur." In the form of the oeuvre, the actual circumstances are placed in another dimension where the given reality shows itself as that which it is. Thus it tells the truth about itself; its language ceases to be that of deception,

HERBERT MARCUSE,
One-Dimensional Man

ignorance, and submission. Fiction calls the facts by their name and their reign collapses; fiction subverts everyday experience and shows it to be mutilated and false. But art has this magic power only as the power of negation. It can speak its own language only as long as the images are alive which refuse and refute the established order.

Whether ritualized or not, art contains the rationality of negation. In its advanced positions, it is the Great Refusal—the protest against that which is. The modes in which man and things are made to appear, to sing and sound and speak, are modes of refuting, breaking, and recreating their factual existence. But these modes of negation pay tribute to the antagonistic society to which they are linked. Separated from the sphere of labor where society reproduces itself and its misery, the world of art which they create remains, with all its truth, a privilege and an illusion.

In this form it continues, in spite of all democratization and popularization, through the nineteenth and into the twentieth century. The "high culture" in which this alienation is celebrated has its own rites and its own style. The salon, the concert, opera, theater are designed to create and invoke another dimension of reality. Their attendance requires festive-like preparation: they cut off and transcend everyday experience.

Now this essential gap between the art and the order of the day, kept open in the artistic alienation, is progressively closed by the advancing technological society. And with its closing, the Great Refusal is in turn refused; the "other dimension" is absorbed into the prevailing state of affairs. The works of alienation are themselves incorporated into this society and circulate as part and parcel of the equipment which adorns and psychoanalyzes the prevailing state of affairs. Thus they become commercials—they sell, comfort, or excite.*

*From *One Dimensional Man* by Herbert Marcuse. Copyright © 1964 by Herbert Marcuse. Reprinted by permission of Beacon Press, Boston.

Arthur C. Danto's Theory of Artistic Identification

Although Plato, Aristotle, and Marcuse advanced profoundly different views on the nature, value, and functions of art, they seemed to take it for granted that when they spoke of art we would know what they were talking about. Plato evidently had the arts of painting and poetry in mind; at least he used the examples of the painter who in his painting represents a bed and the tragic poet who in his dramas represents the actions and fortunes of human beings together with the feelings of joy or sorrow they experience. But clearly he intended his attack on painters and poets to extend to other arts—and in fact in the *Republic* he explicitly warned us against the seductive power of music to stir unmanly emotions in the soul. As the title of *Poetics* suggests, Aristotle's concern was primarily with dramatic poetry, particularly tragedy, although his philosophy of art surely has application to other arts as well. Marcuse writes of the ways in which things "are made to appear, to sing and sound and speak," and he cites in particular the salon, concert, opera, and theater; but it is the uses of negation in art in general that form the thrust of his argument that art is important to human life.

Alas, in the twenty-first century we no longer can be so certain of just what is to count as art. It isn't merely that a painter may explicitly depict a part of the body that we think should be covered in public, or that a poet may use language that by any conventional standards of decency is obscene, or that a composer may use wildly unconventional and discordant tonalities, all of which may disgust us or shock our artistic sensibilities. What galleries hang, or poetry reading organizers program, or concert impresarios schedule, may strike us as offensive or bad or tasteless or insulting art, but most of the time we at least recognize that what they are presenting is—or least is supposed to be—art. Rather, it's no longer clear what counts as a painting, or a piece of music, or a piece of sculpture.

New forms have claimed their place in the world of art, and work long considered the stuff of handicrafts now is accepted as art. Major art museums mount shows of photography, in the nineteenth century considered the stuff of gadgetry, as well as assemblage, collage, mobile sculpture, designer furniture, and patchwork quilts similar to the ones my grandmother pieced together from scraps of material left over from making dresses and aprons. Jazz, once considered lowbrow, cheap, and vulgar, has been appropriated by major "classical" composers.

"Found art" raises ordinary objects of ordinary significance to the level of art. In 1917 French-born Marcel Duchamp submitted a ready made urinal, with the title *Fountain* and signed "R. Mutt," to the New York Exhibition of Independent Artists. The society's board of directors rejected the piece.

In 1952 the American composer and iconoclast John Cage bewildered the musical world with the premiere of "4′ 33″", which was, in Cage's words, a "Solo to be performed in any way by anyone." At the performance, a tuxedo-clad musician walked onto the stage, took his place at the piano, arranged the score on the music stand, used a stopwatch to clock exactly four minutes, thirty-three seconds, stood up, picked up the score, and left the stage.

The Metropolitan Museum of Art in New York City is home to a 1965 work by Ohio-born Joseph Kosuth, *One and Three Chairs,* which consists of a wooden folding chair, a photograph of a chair, and a dictionary definition of a chair.

Duchamp defended R. Mutt's urinal-as-art by arguing that whether Mr. Mutt himself had molded the piece was of no significance; he had found it, had noted that it clearly was of well-modulated design, and had placed it so that its ordinary significance was transformed under a new point of view.[1] Cage's ostensible point with "4′ 33″" is that the experience of listening to music not only involves hearing the reproduction of the notes that the composer writes on the staff, but also ambient sounds and, perhaps especially, silence—such as that interspersed between the composer's notes. Have you noticed how dramatic that pause is between "*The land of the free,*" (brief silence) and "*and the home of the brave!*" when we sing our National Anthem? And intentionally or not, Kosuth's *One and Three Chairs* (can you believe Kosuth was only twenty years old when he created it?) presents a nice puzzle for Plato's theory of art: what is the object and what is the representation?

But is R. Mutt's urinal *art?* Is 4 minutes and 33 seconds of ambient noise *music?* Is a folding chair, with accompanying photograph and dictionary definition, *sculpture?* These works seem totally outside the ken of Plato and Aristotle, although they do seem to represent a rebellion against the established order of aesthetic canons that is central to Marcuse's theory of the negative function of art, as do, for example, Andres Serrano's 1987 *Piss Christ,* a photograph of a crucifix submerged in urine, and the homoerotic photographs of Robert Mapplethorpe. Ironically, however, the works of Serrano and Mapplethorpe drive home Plato's warning that art has seductive power, as evidenced by the 1989 challenge to the National Endowment for Arts (see "Contemporary Application," this chapter): critics saw Serrano's work as an attack on religious values, and Mapplethorpe's work as a threat to the American family. Notice, however, that the objections were not that the works in question were not art, or that they were bad art, but that they were dangerous.

Questions of the form "What is X" provided the themes for many of Plato's dialogues: for example, the question "What is justice?" provided the central theme of the *Republic,* "What is piety?" the theme of *Euthyphro,* and "What is love?" the theme of the *Symposium.* But significantly, Plato devoted none of his dialogues to the question "What is art?" In his paper "The Artworld" Arthur C. Danto speaks directly to this question as it relates to twentieth century transformations of the conception of art: while Danto rejects Plato's theory of art, he adopts a distinctively Platonic approach in his enquiry. Although Danto draws his examples almost exclusively from the visual arts, his observations also are applicable to other arts such as music and dance.

Arthur C. Danto is Johnsonian Professor Emeritus of Philosophy at Columbia University, an art critic for *The Nation,* and one of the most distinguished American contributors to recent literature on the philosophy of art.

"The Artworld" appeared in *The Journal of Philosophy.*[2] The theory that Danto advances in the paper was very influential in the late 1960s and the 1970s with the so-called "conceptual art" movement.

Danto begins his paper with the argument that although Plato's theory of art as imitation ("mimesis"), what Danto calls the "Imitation Theory of Art," is inadequate as a theory of art for the twentieth century, some kind of artistic theory is necessary if we are to identify a piece of art *as art;* and he suggests that we replace the imitation theory with one in which we recognize that the modern artist aims "not at illusion but reality"—a "Reality Theory of Art." The "theory" Danto has in mind may not be as fully articulated as Darwin's Theory of Evolution or as Einstein's General Theory of Relativity, although a philosopher might try for that; rather, it is a rough idea that *could be* so articulated. Indeed, at one point Danto explicitly compares certain episodes in the history of art with certain episodes in the history of science, episodes that Kuhn probably would call revolutions; and you may see a further parallel between what Danto calls theories and what Kuhn called paradigms. (Danto's paper appeared just two years after the publication of Kuhn's *The Structure of Scientific Revolutions.*) Kuhn argued that with a paradigm shift there is a corresponding shift in what counts as a scientific fact; Danto argues that with a shift in theory there is a corresponding shift in what counts as art: and ". . . part of the reason for this lies in the fact that terrain is constituted artistic in virtue of artistic theories, so that one use of theories, in addition to helping us discriminate art from the rest, consists in making art possible."

You may find that some of the artists Danto mentions are unfamiliar to you. Please don't try to identify all of them as you read, but concentrate on the examples Danto is using to make his case. A note: Danto uses the abbreviations "IT" and "RT" for the "Imitation Theory of Art" and the "Reality Theory of Art" respectively. Also, Testadura is a fictional character ("Testadura" is Italian for "hard head"), a plain speaker not schooled in art history or theory.

Arthur C. Danto's "The Artworld"

| HAMLET: | Do you see nothing there? |
| THE QUEEN: | Nothing at all; yet all that is I see. |

Shakespeare, Hamlet, iii.iv

ARTHUR C. DANTO, "The Artworld"

Hamlet and Socrates, though in praise and deprecation respectively, spoke of art as a mirror held up to nature. As with many disagreements in attitude, this one has a factual basis. Socrates saw mirrors as but reflecting what we can already see; so art, insofar as mirrorlike, yields idle accurate duplications of the appearances of things, and is of no cognitive benefit whatever. Hamlet, more acutely, recognized a remarkable feature of reflecting surfaces, namely that they show us what we could not otherwise perceive—our own face and form—and so art, insofar as it is mirrorlike, reveals us to ourselves, and is, even by socratic criteria, of some cognitive utility after all. As a philosopher, however, I find Socrates' discussion defective on other, perhaps less profound grounds than these. If a mirror-image of *a* is indeed an imitation of *a,* then, if art is imitation, mirror-images are art. But in fact mirroring objects no more is art than returning weapons to a madman is justice; and reference to mirrorings would be just the sly sort of counterinstance we would expect Socrates to bring forward in rebuttal of the theory he instead uses them to illustrate. If that theory requires us to class *these* as art, it thereby shows its inadequacy: "Is an imitation" will not do as a sufficient condition for "is art." Yet, perhaps because artists *were* engaged in imitation, in Socrates' time and after, the insufficiency of the theory was not noticed until the invention of photography. Once rejected as a sufficient condition, mimesis was quickly discarded as even a necessary one. . . .

It is, of course, indispensable in socratic discussion that all participants be masters of the concept up for analysis, since the aim is to match a real defining expression to a term in active use, and the test for adequacy presumably consists in showing that the former analyzes and applies to all and only those things of which the latter is true. The popular disclaimer notwithstanding, then, Socrates' auditors purportedly knew what art was as well what they liked; and a theory of art, regarded here as a real definition of 'Art', is accordingly not to be of great use in helping men to recognize instances of its application. Their antecedent ability to do this is precisely what the adequacy of the theory is to be tested against, the problem being only to make explicit what they already know. . . . Theories, on this account, are somewhat like mirror-images on Socrates' account, showing forth what we already know, wordy reflections of the actual linguistic practice we are masters in.

But telling artworks from other things is not so simple a matter, even for native speakers, and these days one might not be aware he was on artistic terrain without an artistic theory to tell him so. . . .

. . . Suppose one thinks of the discovery of a whole new class of artworks as something analogous to the discovery of a whole new class of facts anywhere, viz., as something for theoreticians to explain. In science, as elsewhere, we often accommodate new facts to old theories via auxiliary hypotheses. . . . Now the Imitation Theory of Art (IT) is, if one but thinks it through, an exceedingly powerful theory, explaining a great many phenomena connected with the causation and evaluation of artworks, bringing a surprising unity into a complex domain. Moreover, it is a simple matter to shore it up against many purported counterinstances by such auxiliary hypotheses as that the artist who deviates from mimeticity is perverse, inept, or mad. . . . Suppose, then, tests reveal that these hypotheses fail to hold, that the theory, now beyond repair, must be replaced. And a new theory is worked out, capturing what it can of the old theory's competence, together with the heretofore recalcitrant facts. One might, thinking along these lines, represent certain episodes in the history of art as not dissimilar to certain episodes in the history of science, where a conceptual revolution is being effected and where refusal to countenance certain facts, while in part due to prejudice, inertia, and self-interest, is due also to the fact that a well-established, or at least widely credited theory is being threatened in such a way that all coherence goes.

Some such episode transpired with the advent of post-impressionist paintings [during the last years of the nineteenth century]. In terms of the prevailing artistic theory (IT), it was impossible to accept these as art unless inept art: otherwise they could be discounted as hoaxes, self-advertisements, or the visual counterparts of madmen's raving. So to get them accepted *as* art . . . required not so much a revolution in taste as a theoretical revision of rather considerable proportions, involving not only the artistic enfranchisement of these objects, but an emphasis upon newly significant features of accepted artworks, so that quite different accounts of their status as artworks would now have to be given. . . .

To be sure, I distort by speaking of a theory: historically, there were several, all, interestingly enough, more or less defined in terms of the IT. . . . [but] I shall speak as though there were one replacing theory, partially compensating for historical falsity by choosing one which was actually enunciated. According to it, the artists in question were to be understood not as unsuccessfully imitating real forms but as successfully creating new ones, . . . and the post-impressionists were to be explained as genuinely creative, aiming. . . "not at illusion but reality." This theory (RT) furnished a whole new mode of looking at painting, old and new. Indeed, one might almost interpret the crude drawing in Van Gogh and Cézanne. . . as so many ways of drawing attention to the fact that these were *non-imitations,* specifically intended not to deceive. Logically, this would be roughly like printing "Not Legal Tender" across a brilliantly counterfeited dollar bill, the resulting object (counterfeit *cum* inscription) rendered incapable of deceiving anyone. It is not an illusory dollar bill, but then, just because it is non-illusory it does not automatically become a real dollar bill either. It rather occupies a freshly opened area between real objects and real facsimiles of real objects: it is a non-facsimile, if one requires a word, and a new contribution to the world. . . . By means of this theory (RT), artworks re-entered the thick of things from which socratic theory (IT) had sought to evict them: if no *more* real than what carpenters wrought, they were at least no *less* real. . . .

It is in terms of RT that we must understand the artworks around us today. Thus Roy Lichtenstein paints comic-strip panels, though ten or twelve feet high. These are reasonably faithful projections onto a gigantesque scale of the homely frames from the daily tabloid, but it is precisely the scale that counts. . . . A *photograph* of a Lichtenstein is indiscernible from a photograph of a counterpart panel from *Steve Canyon;* but the photograph fails to capture the scale, and hence is . . . inaccurate [as] a reproduction. . . . Lichtensteins, then, are not imitations but *new entities.* . . . [And] in what I hope are not unwitting footnotes to Plato, two of our pioneers—Robert Rauschenberg and Claes Oldenburg—have made genuine beds.

Rauschenberg's bed hangs on a wall, and is streaked with some desultory housepaint. Oldenburg's bed is a rhomboid, narrower at one end than the other. . . . As beds, these sell at singularly inflated prices, but one *could* sleep in either of them. . . . Imagine, now, a certain Testadura—a plain speaker and noted philistine—who is not aware that these are art, and who takes them to be reality simple and pure. He attributes the paintstreaks on Rauschenberg's bed to the slovenliness of the owner, and the bias on the Oldenburg bed to the ineptitude of the builder or the whimsy, perhaps, of whoever had it "custommade." These would be mistakes, but mistakes of rather an odd kind, and not terribly different from that made by the stunned birds who pecked at the sham grapes of [the painter of ancient Greece] Zeuxis. They mistook art for reality, and so has Testadura. But it was meant to *be* reality, according to RT. Can one have mistaken reality for reality? What, after all, prevents Oldenburg's creation from being a misshapen bed? This is equivalent to asking what makes it art, and with this query we enter a domain of conceptual inquiry where native speakers are poor guides: *they* are lost themselves.

Danto continues, advancing his argument with the help of two related concepts— "Artworld" and the " 'Is' of Artistic Identification." An artworld is a frame of reference, including a knowledge of art history and theory, within which we grasp the significance of an artifact: "To see something as art requires something the eye cannot descry—an atmosphere of artistic theory, a knowledge of the history of art: an artworld." The 'is' of artistic identification is to be distinguished from the 'is' of identity ("Boise is the capital of Idaho") and the 'is' of predication ("Janet Jackson is beautiful"), but ". . . is the sense of *is* in accordance with which a child, shown a circle and a triangle and asked which is him and which his sister, will point to the triangle saying 'That is me;' . . . or in the gallery I point, for my companion's benefit, to a spot in the painting before us and say 'That white daub is Icarus'." The 'is' of artistic identification identifies an object as a work of art, is what *makes* an object a work of art.

Danto asks us to imagine two artists' canvases of equal rectangular dimensions, each painted white with a horizontal black line across the middle, virtually indistinguishable from each other. The artists have named their canvases *Newton's First Law* and *Newton's Third Law,* respectively. The first artist explains, "a mass, pressing downward, is met by a mass pressing upward: the lower mass reacts equally and oppositely to the upper one." The second artist explains, "the line through the space is the path of an isolated particle. The path goes from edge to edge, to give the sense of its *going beyond.*" Or we, not having heard the artists' explanations, might identify "the upper area with a clear and cloudless sky, reflected in the still surface of the water below, whiteness kept from whiteness only by the unreal boundary of the horizon." In accepting one identification rather than another, we in effect "exchange one *world for another.*" But then there is poor Testadura, who

> protests that *all he sees is paint:* a white painted oblong with a black line painted across it. And how right he is: that is all he sees or anybody can, we aesthetes included. So, if he asks us to show him what there is further to see, to demonstrate through pointing that this is an artwork (*Sea and Sky*), we cannot comply, for he has overlooked nothing (and it would be absurd to suppose he had, that there was something tiny we could point to and he, peering closely, say "So it is! A work of art after all!"). We cannot help him until he has mastered the *is of artistic identification* and so *constitutes* it a work of art.

I want to call special attention to this last sentence, because it is crucial to Danto's Theory of Artistic Identification. What it implies is this—that we do not find an object, a broken piece of marble, for example, and *discover* that it is a work of art, or even *interpret* it as a work of art. Rather, through the 'is' of artistic identification, we *constitute* it a work of art, we *make it into* a work of art.

Danto uses as an example the work of Pop artist Andy Warhol, who displays stacks of Brillo carton facsimiles as they might be placed in a supermarket stockroom. They are made out of plywood, not cardboard, but why not? Michelangelo made facsimiles of human beings out of marble. Anyway, the Brillo people might make their boxes out of plywood without making them into artworks, and Warhol his out of cardboard without their ceasing to be art.

> Never mind that [Warhol's] Brillo box may not be good, much less great art. The impressive thing is that it is art at all. But if it is, why are not the indiscernible Brillo boxes that are in the stockroom? Or *has* the whole distinction between art and reality broken down?
>
> . . . What in the end makes the difference between a Brillo box and a work of art consisting of a Brillo box is a certain theory of art. It

Philosophy and Popular Culture

The Simpsons: Questions About the Philosophy of Art

It's summer, and the living is good, especially with freshly-shaven shoulders. But wouldn't life be better with a backyard barbeque pit? Homer Simpson thinks so, and he buys a barbeque pit kit at the local Megalomart. However, Homer's barbecue pit doesn't look like the one on the box, and so he flies into a rage and smashes the barbeque pit, turning a mess into even more of a mess. Fortunately for Homer, Mr. Burns, Homer's boss, thinks that the mess is modern art and buys it! Homer is now an artist, respected by art critics and adored by art dilettantes and Eurotrash.

Pretend you are Homer's neighbor. You are a little jealous of all the attention that Homer is receiving, and you wish that he could be brought down. That is exactly what happens. After getting a solo art exhibit that is advertised in *Art in America,* Homer is criticized because all of his art works are too similar. Homer is not growing as an artist. Fortunately for Homer, Lisa comes to the rescue, advising Homer to do something *really* radical. That night, Homer and Bart stop up the sewer drains with doormats, put snorkels on the animals at the zoo and release them, then open the fire hydrants and flood the town of Springfield. Bart asks, "Are you sure this is art and not vandalism?" Homer replies, "That's for the courts to decide, son."

Homer's conceptual art piece, "The Grand Canals of Springfield," seems to be successful. The patients in the burn unit at the hospital feel relief from the pain as the flood waters soak them. Milhouse's flood pants work just fine. Homer and Marge are kissing on the rooftop. Even Jasper Johns seems happy—but that may be because he just stole Marge's latest painting. As for you, if you can't beat Homer, why not go boating?

Questions to Consider

Can a work of art be created by accident, without the conscious intention of an artist? Is conceptual art really art? What is the value—other than financial value—of art? Must art be a physical object, or can it be a feeling? And what role should government play in determining what counts as art?

is the theory that takes it up into the world of art, and keeps it from collapsing into the real object which it is (in a sense of *is* other than that of artistic identification). Of course, without the theory, one is unlikely to see it as art, and in order to see it as part of the Artworld, one must have mastered a good deal of artistic theory as well as a considerable amount of the history of recent New York painting. It could not have been art fifty years ago. But then there could not have been, everything being equal, flight insurance in the Middle Ages, or Etruscan typewriter erasers. The world has to be ready for certain things, the Artworld no less than the real one. It is the role of theories, these days as always, to make the Artworld, and art, possible. . . . It is but a matter of choice: and the Brillo box of the Artworld may be just the Brillo box of the real one, separated and united by the *is* of artistic identification. . . . Nor would these things be artworks without the theories and histories of the Artworld.

And, to return to the views of Hamlet with which we began this discussion, Brillo boxes may reveal us to ourselves as well as anything might: as a mirror held up to nature, they might serve to catch the conscience of our kings.

Notes

1. *The Blind Man No. 2* (May, 1917).
2. Arthur C. Danto, "The Artworld," *The Journal of Philosophy* 61 (1964), pp. 571–84.

The Main Points in Chapter Seven

1. Plato criticized the poets of classical Greece on the ground that they presented mere imitations or copies of reality that took their listeners farther away from the truth. He thus raised a question—about the value or purpose of art—that has been debated ever since.

2. Plato's great disciple and pupil, Aristotle, defended the poets, saying that through their tragedies we are able to experience powerful emotions of anger and pity, and purge our souls of them.

3. The most unusual defense of art in the history of the debate comes from twentieth-century social theorists like Herbert Marcuse who defend art as an expression of the *negative,* and *oppositional,* in human personality and society. Art, Marcuse claims, is thus a medium of social revolution.

4. Addressing twentieth-century transformations of conceptions regarding what counts as art, American philosopher Arthur C. Danto claims that an artifact becomes art through our identification of it as a work of art.

Questions for Discussion and Review

1. There is overwhelming evidence that art, in some form or another, occurs in every human society, however technologically primitive or advanced. In short, art is *natural* to human beings. Does that, by itself, prove that art is a good thing? Might something that is natural and universal nevertheless be a bad thing, something to be repressed or stamped out?

2. It is easy enough to see in what sense a realistic painting is a representation, image, or mere appearance of the object it pictures. But what representational relation, if any, does music bear to the world? We are accustomed to separating out some artistic activities as belonging to what are called the *fine* arts. That distinction, however, only dates back to the fifteenth and sixteenth centuries. Is there any important difference between ballet, opera, classical music, poetry, sculpture, and painting on the one hand, and fairy tales, folk songs, rock music, macramé, basket weaving, and leather work on the other?

3. One of the principal charges against pornography is that its sole purpose is to arouse prurient desires in its readers or viewers. In defense of the civil rights of pornographers, some people respond that pornography has a political or social purpose. But what is wrong with arousing prurient desires?

4. Most pornography in American society portrays women in a degrading fashion, and that fact has led many feminists to argue that pornography violates the rights of women and should be banned. Now, pornography, almost without exception, is bad art, whatever else it is. But suppose we are confronted with a great work of art that is also morally objectionable, because of its representation of women, or Jews, or the Irish, or working people, or because of its attack on religion, or on democracy. Should our *moral* objections take precedence over our *aesthetic* judgments?

5. If Marcuse is correct, art performs a valuable social function precisely by being negative, offensive, a reproach to decent people. If that is true, then do we not destroy art's positive function by *tolerating* it?

The Primary Source: Philosophical Readings and Commentary

Aristotle, *Poetics*

Plato, *Republic*

ABCNEWS

CONTEMPORARY APPLICATION

Pornography, Art, and Censorship

Twenty-four hundred years ago, Plato began the debate over the role of the arts in a good society, and the argument has raged without stop ever since. In recent decades, the focus of the debate in the United States has been pornography and obscenity, with complicated legal questions of constitutional rights getting tangled up with the more traditional disagreements about the good and bad effects of art. A great deal of attention, of course, has been concentrated on the impact of explicit sexuality and violence on the young. For every psychologist who testifies that boys and girls are made more violent or more sexually promiscuous by what they see on television, in movies, and on the newsstands, there is another one ready to prove that such vicarious sexual or violent experience actually drains away destructive passions and leaves children less prone to commit antisocial acts. It all sounds very much like a modern-dress replay of the dispute between Plato and Aristotle!

Frequently, the psychological and legal arguments dominate the discussion so completely that we lose sight entirely of the original issue, which is the proper role or function of art. But sometimes, even today, the debate rises to an impressive level of philosophical generality.

Our first readings deal with a question that unites politics and art: Should Congress continue to fund the National Endowment for the Arts (NEA)? Conservative critics of the NEA have for years attacked it on the grounds that it has chosen to fund what the critics claim is pornography, not art. On one side are those who argue that public funds should only be used to support artistic activity of which the general public would approve. After all, the money comes from our taxes, so our values should be the standard for what gets funded. On the other side are those who argue that great art cannot be hobbled by "community standards" that all too often embody the lowest common denominator of aesthetic taste. Great art, these defenders of the NEA say, has always been offensive to the powers that be. Great art is *meant* to be offensive. We see, in this contemporary debate, the same disagreements that separate Plato from Marcuse.

DON'T CAVE IN TO THE NEA
Jeff Jacoby

After years of turmoil at the National Endowment for the Arts, Congress adopted a significant reform: It curtailed the agency's power to bestow grants on individuals. For decades such grants had been used to subsidize some of the crudest stuff ever to masquerade as art.

Examples abound. Here are three:

The NEA repeatedly lavished money on the photographer Joel-Peter Witkin, whose images no one will ever confuse with Ansel Adams's. One of his exhibited photos shows amputated genitalia perched atop two skulls. Another depicts a scene titled "Testicle stretch with the possibility of a crushed face." Still others are too proctologically nasty to describe in a family newspaper.

An early NEA favorite was Judy Chicago, who was generously rewarded for her sculpture "The Dinner Party." It purported to illustrate the role of women in history by means of a triangular table set for 39. The place settings consisted of vaginas on dinner plates, each commemorating a famous woman.

Peter Orlovsky scored a $10,000 grant from the NEA for his poetry. Even the *titles* of some of Orlovsky's work are unprintable. The poems themselves explore such uplifting themes as ejaculating on the family cat and a mother performing oral sex on her infant son.

The elimination of most grants to individuals didn't correct the NEA's fundamental flaw, which is that government shouldn't be meddling in the arts in the first place. But it was certainly a step forward.

Now comes William Ivey, the chairman of the arts endowment, with a call to step back.

"The individual artist is at the center of what art is," Ivey told an audience at Chicago's Museum of Contemporary Art last month. "We want to get back to the business of supporting individual artists."

Do we? Subsidizing individual artists with tax dollars cuts deeply against the grain of a society in which all citizens are presumed equal. Hundreds of thousands of Americans call themselves artists; how can any government bureaucracy presume to choose the dozen or so who deserve a check from the Treasury? And how can any thoughtful taxpayer be confident that the bureaucrats will make the right choice?

The NEA's history of grant-making to individuals was rife with favoritism, nepotism, and logrolling.

"The writer Geoffrey Wolff, who would go on to win a $20,000 NEA fellowship in 1987," journalist Mark Lasswell reported in 1990, "served on the literature panel that awarded his brother, writer Tobias Wolff, a $20,000 grant in 1985....A young artist named Amanda Farber won a $5,000 award based on the recommendation of a panel that included her stepmother, Patricia Patterson....The peer panel that recommended Karen Finley and Holly Hughes for their disputed grants included Jerry Hunt, a musician who has frequently collaborated with Finley, and Ellen Sebastian, a director who has worked with Hughes. But wait, it gets better: The panel also recommended awards to Hunt and Sebastian!"

A system in which arts insiders get to distribute government money to their friends and allies is a system begging to be corrupted. If Congress lets the NEA resume dispensing money to individuals, all the old abuses will resume as well.

Serious artists do not need government grants. The notion that artists must be protected from struggle and poverty is belied by the countless tales of painters, musicians, and writers whose talent and passion were sharpened for years against a whetstone of financial trouble.

Willem de Kooning, who immigrated to America as a stowaway on a cattle boat, labored long as a sign painter and carpenter before achieving renown for his abstract expressionist paintings. James Baldwin grew up in the poverty of a Harlem slum and wouldn't have been James Baldwin if he hadn't. The fiction and poetry of Edgar Allan Poe came from the pen of a man who had been forced out of college and disowned by his family and who suffered in a private hell of debt and alcoholism. Irving Berlin, poor son of poor parents, supported himself as a singing waiter in New York's Bowery.

It ill serves artists to liberate them from the risks and pressures of real life. No true artist was ever silenced for lack of a $10,000 handout from the NEA. By contrast, NEA handouts have encouraged scabrous pseudo-artists to keep churning out "art" that the public doesn't like and would never willingly support.

Endless young men work and work at honing their basketball skills, enduring countless hours of unrewarded practice in the hope of one day playing in the NBA. Unknown rock bands beyond number devote every spare minute to perfecting their sound and playing hole-in-the-wall gigs, driven by a love of music and the dream of a big recording contract. Who imagines that a National Endowment for Basketball is required to sustain the quality of hoops in this country? Who believes that without a National Endowment for Rock 'n' Roll, struggling rockers would give up in despair?

Artists—real artists—are no different. It isn't the government for whom they write and paint and dance. The state is not the mainstay of their art. The public is—their public, the patrons and donors and audiences who are drawn to their work and support it willingly. We wouldn't dream of letting the government pass judgment on rock and roll or basketball. Is art any less sacred?

From "Don't Cave in to the NEA" by Jeff Jacoby, *The Boston Globe*, March 4, 1999.
Jeff Jacoby is a Globe columnist. This story ran on page A19 of the Boston *Globe* on March 4, 1999. © Copyright 1999 Globe Newspaper Company.

ATTACK ON NEA IS AN OBSCENITY
Afi-Odelia E. Scruggs

Pssst, come here. I've got something to tell you.

Come closer. I can't talk much louder. I'm on the run.

I'm living underground. I'm a purveyor of obscene art.

There are lots of us here in the Cleveland metropolitan area. We're in the Ohio Chamber Orchestra Society, the Canton Symphony Orchestra Association, and DANCECleveland. There are free-lance artists as well, people just trying to make a living off our music or dance or sculpture or books.

It's a tough life, with lots of casualties. Artists and arts organizations are becoming an endangered species, under the gun of the conservative politicians.

What happened? How did orchestras and writers become such a threat to the moral fiber of this society?

We all got money from the National Endowment for the Arts.

The organizations received direct grants from the endowment. Individuals like myself received awards from the Ohio Arts Council. The arts council was founded in 1965—the same year as the NEA—and is funded by the endowment and the state legislature.

My crime was leading a youth choir at an inner-city church in Cleveland. The Ohio Arts Council gave me $875 to run a nine-month apprenticeship program. The money bought gospel CDs and materials for drums, and took the children to at least two concerts.

I'm sure if NEA opponents had known, they would have stormed the sanctuary.

This fiscal year, Congress has only given the endowment $10 million. That's just enough to shut the endowment down.

In fiscal years 1996 and 1997, the agency got $99 million—and that was a 40 percent funding cut from previous years.

For years, the endowment chugged along without raising the eyes or ire of anyone on Capitol Hill.

Then came some controversial NEA-funded exhibits, including 175 photographs by Robert Mapplethorpe.

The exhibit, at the Contemporary Arts Center in Cincinnati, included five photographs of men in sexually explicit poses and two that critics said constituted child *pornography*. Within hours of the show's opening on April 7, 1990, police had cleared out the gallery and videotaped the pictures for evidence.

Arts Center Director Dennis Barrie, who later worked for the Rock and Roll Hall of Fame and Museum, and the gallery were indicted for pandering *pornography*. A jury acquitted them both. The jurors decided that seven pictures, while offensive, were still artistic.

But that was before Jesse Helms proclaimed that the endowment was financing obscene art at taxpayers' expense.

That was before conservatives decided any government support for the arts was a waste of money.

Two years ago, Republicans agreed to cut the endowment's budget in fiscal years 1996 and 1997, and to kill it this fiscal year.

Despite that, the endowment still gave out $67 million in national grants last year. More than $1 million went to Ohio organizations and individuals.

That's a lot of art—or a lot of obscenity, depending on your point of view.

I don't think that teaching children to sing "Go Tell It on the Mountain" will harm them for life. And I have to agree with the Cincinnati jurors. A work of art cannot be condemned because we find the subject matter distasteful. As far as using tax money, I would prefer to support a Mapplethorpe photo over a B-52, but I don't withhold the portion of my taxes that go for defense.

As far as endowment opponents are concerned, I'm an enemy soldier.

I can hear the battle cries. It seems the Philistines are at the gates.

So enjoy events such as the Ohio Chamber Orchestra Society's concerts at Cain Park.

Your federal taxes may not be supporting such filth much longer.

DECENCY A VALID CONCERN FOR NEA
Editorial

One of our favorite cartoons shows an artist demanding that a bureaucrat give him another government grant so he can finish a painting—which, we can see, is a picture of the same bureaucrat with a label that assaults him with an obscene name.

The cartoon captures two essential parts of the argument, pending before the U.S. Supreme Court, over whether the government can impose decency standards on the arts projects it funds with taxpayers' money: one, that many in the arts community have come to consider such grants as entitlements, and two, that some think art is only about sneering condescendingly and insultingly at the values that a majority in society hold.

The issue arises out of a 1990 law that required the National Endowment for the Arts to consider more than "artistic excellence and merit" when passing out funding. Henceforth,

Congress said, the agency must also "take into consideration general standards of decency and respect for the diverse beliefs and values of the American public." Some artists sued, claiming the law denied them the freedom of expression guaranteed by the First Amendment.

Despite a 2-1 ruling by the 9th Circuit Court of Appeals in San Francisco in the plaintiffs' favor, it's obvious to any fair-minded person that no freedom is being denied in this case. No one has told them or any other artists what they can or cannot paint, sculpt, or perform. They are welcome to produce any work they believe is important to them, and to try their best to persuade others to display or purchase it.

The issue is what criteria the NEA will use in deciding which few artists out of hundreds of thousands will receive taxpayers' money to help them in their pursuit of the muse. What of the huge number of artists whose grant applications fail for reasons unrelated to "decency and respect"? Have they been denied constitutional protections as well?

If arts grants were entitlements, given automatically to everyone who "qualified," like welfare or food stamps, then the artistic specialists in shock, sex, religious bigotry, child pornography, and the grotesque might have a case. But in fact the NEA has always used—can only use—subjective judgments in choosing who should receive the taxpayers' support for their work.

Given that reality, it is hardly wrong to add the factors of decency to the others that go into those judgments. In fact, it is eminently right to do so, because the bureaucrats are acting, in effect, as the agents of the citizens whose money is being spent.

Some artists may love to insult that citizenry, and in this country they are wholly entitled to do so. But unlike the one in the cartoon, they ought to have to find their own funds to buy the paint to do it.

From "Decency a Valid Concern for NEA," Editorial Section, December 1, 1997. Copyright © 1997, *The Atlanta Constitution*, Editorial, The Atlanta Journal and Constitution, December 1, 1997.

Now let us turn to two thinkers who take up the debate over pornography in a deliberately philosophical manner. We begin with an attack on censorship by the late poet, novelist, social critic, and philosopher Paul Goodman. Goodman was trained at the University of Chicago in the philosophy of Plato and Aristotle, a fact that shows in everything he subsequently wrote. Goodman faces the issue of pornography head on by challenging the usually unexamined assumption that it is harmful to arouse powerful sexual passions. He also points out, quite rightly, that there is something absurd and insulting in saying both that Joyce was a great writer and that he did not intend to arouse the feelings that his novel so obviously and successfully arouses. Such a defense is a little like defending a great magician by saying that he did not mean to fool us.

PORNOGRAPHY, ART, AND CENSORSHIP
Paul Goodman

Present thinking about obscenity and pornography is wrongheaded and damaging. In order to protect vital liberties, the higher, more intellectual courts often stand out against the police, the postmasters, and popular prejudice; yet since they don't give the right reasons, the issues are never settled. And worse, the courts lend themselves to the sexual attitude which, at this moment in our history, creates the very "hard-core" pornography that is objected to. That is, the court corrupts, it helps the censors corrupt. It ought to give light and provide leadership, and instead it stands in the way of progress. And worst of all, finally, by misunderstanding the nature of art and speech, the court emasculates them and prevents them from playing their indispensable social role. . . .

Judge Woolsey's method in clearing *Ulysses* is as follows: he defines the obscene as the pornographic, as "tending to stir the sex impulses or to lead to sexually impure and lustful thoughts," and he proceeds to show that the book does neither but "is a sincere and serious attempt to devise a new literary method for the observation and description of mankind." Let us postpone the literary criticism till the next section, but here stop short at the definition of obscenity.

The notion that sexual impulse or stirring sexual impulse is a bad thing comes from an emotional climate in which it was generally agreed that it would be better if sexuality did not overtly exist, when people bathed and slept fully clothed, and a bull was called a hecow. Then anything which was sexual in public, as by publication of "detailed representation in words or pictures," violated society's self-image and was certainly obscene. In our times such a notion cannot define obscenity. The pornographic is not *ipso facto* the obscene. As Judge Jerome Frank pointed out in 1949, "No sane man thinks that the arousing of normal sexual desires is socially dangerous." We live in a culture where all High Thought insists on the beauty and indeed hygienic indispensability of sexual desires, and where a vast part of commerce is busy in their stimulation.

Let me proceed to a philosophical question raised by these decisions, which is, in my opinion, even more important for our society than the sexual matter: what is the nature of speech and art? To protect their "serious" books, the courts attempt to distinguish speech as communication of an idea or even as talking *about* a subject, from speech as an action doing something to its speaker, subject, and hearer. This is the tactic of Woolsey when he devotes most of his opinion to Joyce's "new method for the observation and description of mankind."

Woolsey's doctrine is insulting to the artist. He says that the book did "not tend to excite lustful thoughts, *but* the net effect was a tragic and powerful commentary" (italics mine). Surely the author wants to say, "It is lustful among other things, and *therefore* its net effect is tragic."

In our culture an artist is expected to move the reader; he is supposed to move him to tears, to laughter, to indignation, to compassion, even to hatred; but he may not move him to have an erection or to mockery of public figures making a spectacle of themselves. Why not? By these restrictions we doom ourselves to a passionless and conformist community. Instead of bracketing off the "classics," as especially the British courts do—indeed, the legal definition of a classic seems to be a "nonactionable obscenity"— let us pay attention to the classical pornography and we shall see that it is not the case, as the court feels obliged to prove, that a work has a "net" social use despite its sexual effect, but rather that the pornography, in a great context and spoken by a great soul, *is* the social use. Aristophanic comedy was still close to a seasonal ritual to encourage rebelliousness and lead to procreation. Rabelais is disgraceful like a giant baby, and this *is* the Renaissance. Catullus teaches us the callous innocence of highborn youth, free of timidity and pettiness; and Tom Jones is a similar type, with a dash of English sentimentality. If we may believe their preludes, both the *Arabian Nights* and the *Decameron* are cries of life in the face of death; and in our times Jean Genet, one of our few fine writers, is pornographic and psychopathic because only so, he tells us, can he feel that he exists in our inhuman world. But apart from these lofty uses, there are also famous pornographic books made just for fun, since sex is a jolly subject.

For a while, the anti-censorship side of the debate had the good publicity. Very few people want to defend censorship of political, religious, or moral opinions, and it is difficult to say exactly when a novel, a play, or a movie ceases to be "political" and becomes simply a commercial exploitation of sex and violence. In our next selection, however, we encounter a serious, thoughtful defense of censorship from a thinker who, like Plato, takes the moral health of the body politic as the highest good. The key to Walter Berns's defense of censorship is his provocative question, "What if, contrary to what is now so generally assumed, shame is natural to man?" In other words, what if it is natural to be aroused by sex and violence, *and equally natural to feel the moral emotion of shame for being aroused?* What if the primary role of society is not to release our natural impulses but to restrain them, not to make us shameless but to strengthen, direct, and use our shame for humanly good purposes. In that case, it will be no defense of pornographic books that we all have a "natural" desire to read them. Quite to the contrary, that fact will simply make it all the clearer that society must help us control that ugly side of our souls.

I have deliberately given the pro-censorship side of the debate the lion's share of space here because I suspect that your sympathies will lie with Paul Goodman. As John Stuart Mill pointed out, there is much to be gained from forcing ourselves to face arguments that contradict our own opinions.

PORNOGRAPHY VS. DEMOCRACY: THE CASE FOR CENSORSHIP
Walter Berns

The case against censorship is very old and very familiar. Almost anyone can formulate it without difficulty. One has merely to set the venerable Milton's *Areopagitica* in modern prose, using modern spelling, punctuation, and examples. This is essentially what the civil libertarians did in their successful struggle, during the past century, with the censors. The unenlightened holder of the bishop's imprimatur, Milton's "unleasur'd licencer" who has never known "the labour of book-writing," became the ignorant policeman or the bigoted school board member who is offended by "Mrs. Warren's Profession," or the benighted librarian who refuses to shelf *The Scarlet Letter,* or the insensitive customs official who seizes *Ulysses* in the name of an outrageous law, or the Comstockian vigilante who glues together the pages of every copy of *A Farewell to Arms* she can find in the bookstore. The industrious learned Milton, insulted by being asked to "appear in Print like a punie with his guardian and his censors hand on the back of his title to be his bayle and surety," was replaced by Shaw, Hawthorne, Joyce, or Hemingway, and those who followed in their wake, all victims of the mean-spirited and narrow minded officials who were appointed, or in some cases took it upon themselves, to judge what others should read, or at least not read. The presumed advantage of truth when it grapples with falsehood became the inevitable victory of "enduring ideas" in the free competition of the market. With these updated versions of old and familiar arguments, the civil libertarians have prevailed.

They prevailed partly because of the absurdity of some of their opposition, and also because of a difficulty inherent in the task their opponents set for themselves. The censors would proscribe the obscene, and even assuming, as our law did, that obscene speech is no part of the speech protected by the First Amendment to the Constitution, it is not easy to formulate a rule of law that distinguishes the nonobscene from the obscene. Is it the presence of four-letter words? But many a literary masterpiece contains four-letter words. Detailed descriptions of sexual acts? James Joyce provides these. Words tending to corrupt those into whose hands they are likely to fall? But who is to say what corrupts or, for that matter, whether anything corrupts or, again, what is meant by corruption? Is it an appeal to a "prurient interest" or is it a work that is "patently offensive"? If that is what is meant by the obscene, many a "socially important work," many a book, play, or film with "redeeming social value" would be lost to us. The college professors said so, and if college professors do not know the socially important, who does? Be that as it may, they succeeded in convincing the Supreme Court, and the result was the complete rout of the "forces of reaction." To the college professors, therefore, as well as to the "courageous" publishers and the "public-spirited" attorneys who had selflessly fought the cases through the courts, a debt of gratitude is owed by the lovers of Shaw, Hawthorne, Joyce, and Hemingway—and others too numerous to detail here. In the same spirit one might say that never has there been such a flourishing of the arts in this country.

Just as it is no simple task to formulate a rule of law that distinguishes the nonobscene from the obscene, it is still more difficult to distinguish the obscene from the work of genuine literary merit. In fact, it is impossible—and our failure to understand this may be said to be a condition, if not a cause, of our present situation. Our laws proscribe obscenity as such and by name, and we are unwilling to admit that great literary and dramatic works can be, and frequently are, obscene. In combination these two facts explain how it came about that we now have, with the sanction of the law, what is

probably the most vulgar theatre and literature in history. The paradox is readily explained. The various statutes making up the law have made obscenity a criminal thing, and our judges assume that if a work of art is really a work of art, and not vulgar rubbish, it cannot be obscene. Thus, Judge Woolsey, in his celebrated opinion in the *Ulysses* case, recounts how he had asked two literary friends whether the book was obscene within the legal definition, which he had explained to them, and how they had both agreed with him that it was not. But of course *Ulysses* is obscene. Not so obscene as an undoubted masterpiece, Aristophanes' "Assembly of Women," for example, which would not be a masterpiece—which would not be anything—were its obscenity removed, but obscene nevertheless.

The trouble stems from the fact that the Tariff Act of 1930 would exclude "obscene" books from the country, and Judge Woolsey, being a sensible man, did not want this to happen to *Ulysses*. So he fashioned a rule to protect it. But the same rule of law protects *The Tropic of Cancer*, because according to the rule's necessarily clumsy categories, the latter is no more obscene than the former, however it compares on another scale and whatever the aesthetic distances separating its author, Henry Miller, and James Joyce as writers. Eventually, and for the same reason, the protection of the law was extended to *Trim, MANual,* and *Grecian Guild Pictorial,* the homosexual magazines involved in a case before the Supreme Court in 1962, and then to *Fanny Hill.*

Underlying this unfortunate development is the familiar liberal idea of progress. Rather than attempt to inhibit artists and scientists, the good polity will grant them complete freedom of expression and of inquiry, and will benefit collectively by so doing. What is good for the arts and sciences is good for the polity: this proposition has gone largely unquestioned among us for 200 years now. The case for censorship rests on its denial, and can be made only by separately examining its parts. What is good for the arts and sciences? What is good for the polity? The case for censorship arises initially out of a consideration of the second question.

The case for censorship is at least as old as the case against it, and, contrary to what is usually thought today, has been made under decent and even democratic auspices by intelligent men. To the extent to which it is known today, however, it is thought to be pernicious or, at best, irrelevant to the enlightened conditions of the twentieth century. It begins from the premise that the laws cannot remain indifferent to the manner in which men amuse themselves, or to the kinds of amusement offered them.

We turn to the arts—to literature, films, and the theatre, as well as to the graphic arts . . . for the pleasure to be derived from them, and pleasure has the capacity to form our tastes and thereby to affect our lives. It helps determine the kind of men we become, and helps shape the lives of those with whom and among whom we live. So one can properly ask: Is it politically uninteresting whether men derive pleasure from performing their duties as citizens, fathers, and husbands or, on the other hand, from watching their laws and customs and institutions being ridiculed on the stage? Whether the passions are excited by, and the affections drawn to, what is noble or what is base? Whether the relations between men and women are depicted in terms of an eroticism wholly divorced from love and calculated to destroy the capacity for love and the institutions, such as the family, that depend on love? Whether a dramatist uses pleasure to attach men to what is beautiful or to what is ugly? We may not be accustomed to thinking of these things in this manner, but it is not strange that so much of the obscenity from which so many of us derive our pleasure today has an avowed political purpose. It would seem that the pornographers know intuitively what liberals have forgotten, namely, that there is indeed a "causal relationship . . . between word or pictures and human behavior." At least they are not waiting for behavioral science to discover this fact.

The purpose is sometimes directly political and sometimes political in the sense that it will have political consequences intended or not. This latter purpose is to make us shameless, and it seems to be succeeding with astonishing speed. Activities that were once confined to the private scene—to the "ob-scene," to make an etymological assumption—are now presented for our delectation and emulation in center stage. Nothing that is appropriate to one place is inappropriate to any other place. No act, we are to infer, no human possibility, no possible physical combination or connection, is shameful. . . . Nothing prevents a dog from enjoying sexual intercourse in the marketplace, and it is unnatural to deprive men of the same pleasure, either actively or as voyeurs in the theatre. Shame itself is unnatural, a convention devised by hypocrites to inhibit the pleasures of the body. We must get rid of our "hang-ups."

The Importance of Shame

But what if, contrary to what is now so generally assumed, shame is natural to man, in the sense of being an original feature of human existence? What if it is shamelessness that is unnatural, in the sense of having to be acquired? What if the beauty that men are capable of knowing and achieving in their living with each other derives from the fact that man is naturally a "blushing creature," the only creature capable of blushing?

To speak in a manner that is more obviously political, there is a connection between self-restraint and shame, and therefore a connection between shame and self-government or democracy. There is, therefore, a political danger in promoting shamelessness and the fullest self-expression or indulgence. To live together requires rules and a governing of the passions, and those who are without shame will be unruly and unrulable; having lost the ability to restrain themselves by observing the rules they collectively give themselves, they will have to be ruled by others. Tyranny is the natural and inevitable mode of government for the shameless and self-indulgent who have carried liberty beyond any restraint, natural and conventional.

Such, indeed, was the argument made by political philosophers prior to the twentieth century, when it was generally understood that democracy, more than any other form of government, required self-restraint, which it would inculcate through moral education and impose on itself through laws, including laws governing the manner of public amusements. It was the tyrant who could usually allow the people to indulge themselves. Indulgence of the sort we are now witnessing did not threaten his rule, because his rule did not depend on a citizenry of good character. Anyone can be ruled by a tyrant, and the more debased his subjects the safer his rule. A case can be made for complete freedom of the arts among such people, whose pleasures are derived from activities divorced from their labors and any duties associated with citizenship.

One who undertakes to defend censorship in the name of the arts is obliged to acknowledge that he has not exhausted his subject when he has completed that defense. What is missing is a defense of obscenity. What is missing is a defense of the obscenity employed by the greatest of our poets—Aristophanes and Chaucer, Shakespeare and Swift—because it is impossible to believe, it is unreasonable to believe, that what they did is indefensible; and what they did, among other things, was to write a good deal of obscenity. Unfortunately, it would require a talent I do not possess to give a sufficient account of it.

They employed it mainly in comedy, but their purpose was not simply to make us laugh. Comedy, according to Aristotle, makes us laugh at what is ludicrous in ugliness, and its purpose is to teach, just as tragedy teaches by making us cry before what is destructive in nobility. The latter imitates what is higher, the former what is lower, but they are equally serious; Aristotle discussed both, and Shakespeare, for example, was a comic as well as a tragic poet.

Those aspects of his soul that make man truly human and distinguish him from all other beings—higher or lower in the natural order of things—require political life. And no great poet ever denied this. Man's very virtues, as well as their counterparts, his vices, require him to be governed and to govern; they initiate demands that can be met only in political life—but the poet knows with Rousseau that the demands of human virtue cannot be fully met in political life because they transcend political life. The poet knows the beauty of that order beyond the polity; he reminds us that there is an order outside the conventional and that we are part of that natural order, as well as of the conventional. Shakespeare knows with Rousseau that there is a tension between this natural order and the conventional or legal order, and his purpose is to resolve it, at least for some men, at the highest possible level. These men must first be shown that this world of convention is not the only world, and here is where obscenity may play a part—that beyond Venice there is Portia's Belmont, the utopia where the problems that plague Venice do not exist. Obscenity can be used to ridicule the conventional. But it is used in the name of the natural, that order outside the conventional according to which the conventional may be criticized and perhaps, if only to an extent, reformed. Obscenity in the hands of such a poet can serve to *elevate* men, elevate them, the few of them, above the conventional order in which all of us are forced to live our mundane lives. Its purpose is to teach what is truly beautiful—not what convention holds to be beautiful—and to do so by means of pleasure, for obscenity can be pleasurable.

How to express in a rule of law this distinction between the justified and the unjustified employment of obscenity is no simple task. That I have admitted and willingly concede. I have also argued that it cannot be done at all on the premise from which our law has proceeded. I have, finally, tried to indicate the consequences of a failure to maintain the distinction in the law: not only will we no longer be able to teach the distinction between the proper and the improper, but we will no longer be able to teach—and will therefore come to forget—the distinction between art and trash. Stated otherwise, censorship, because it inhibits self-indulgence and supports the ideal of propriety and impropriety, protects political democracy; paradoxically, when it faces the problem of the justified and unjustified use of obscenity, censorship also serves to maintain the distinction between art and trash and, therefore, to protect art and, thereby, to enhance the quality of this democracy. We forgot this. We began with a proper distrust of the capacities of juries and judges to make sound judgments in an area that lies outside their professional competence; but led by the Supreme Court we went on improperly to conclude that the judgments should not be made because they cannot be made, that there is nothing for anyone to judge. No doubt the law used to err on occasion; but democracy can live without "Mrs. Warren's Profession," if it must, as well as without *Fanny Hill*—or to speak more precisely, it can live with the error that consigns "Mrs. Warren's Profession" to under-the-counter custom along with *Fanny Hill*. It remains to be seen whether the true friend of democracy will want to live in the world without under-the-counter custom, the world that does not know the difference between "Mrs. Warren's Profession" and *Fanny Hill*.

Source: "Pornography vs. Democracy: The Case for Censorship" by Walter Berns. *The Public Interest* (Winter 1971). Reprinted by permission of the author and the Public Affairs Conference Center, Kenyon College.

Finally, here are two brief comments on the Mapplethorpe debate: one by Meg Greenfield, writing on the "liberal" side for *Newsweek,* and the other by William F. Buckley, writing on the "conservative" side in the magazine he founded, *The National Review.* You might be interested to learn that the director of a Cincinnati art gallery in which the exhibit appeared was acquitted of all charges at a trial held after these two comments were published.

SUMMER STORM
Meg Greenfield

The summer's much debated exhibit of Robert Mapplethorpe's photographs—some beautiful, some revolting—drew huge crowds at a private gallery in Washington, having earlier been expelled from the august Corcoran Gallery. This predictable surge of interest and popularity showed that *all* the parts in the classic drama among artist, patron, and public were in good working order. As is mandated by tradition, the artists were raising hell about repression, the patron—government in this case—was raising hell about the artists, and the public was thronging in unprecedented numbers to avail itself of the denounced works of art.

What may be distinctive to our time and culture is the earnestness of the argument over whether the Mapplethorpe photographs and other current offending works are in fact art. Sometimes, in our age of scienceism gone mad, it seems as if people believe that a panel of experts, such as those who decide on government grants to painters and so forth, have some pure scientific method of determining whether the object before them qualifies as art. These panels' deliberations are made to sound like laboratory findings soon to be disclosed in the *New England Journal of Medicine*. In this they are as close as we get to those European "academies" once so famous for their ruthlessness as arbiters of suitable artistic expression.

In our day the need for certification of this kind is probably made more acute by the anarchy of our total artistic product and the consequent inability of socially ambitious would-be collectors to know whether or not they should buy the blob before them and, equally important, whether or not for future tax purposes it will be considered the real thing. But it is not the distinctiveness of our time that interests me. Rather it is the traditional, familiar, commonplace nature of the tensions now being argued over as if they had never existed before. At the heart of the controversy is the relationship of artist and patron, especially if the patron is the state.

We are supersensitive, as we should be, to the perils of state intrusion into the artist's choice of subject, style, message. And we are very suspicious of artists overtly engaged in the glorification of the state or the promotion of its political interests. There is good reason for this too. In the centuries before art became so generally detached from public sponsorship and public purposes, the state was more likely to inspire transcendent works—I will enter the Aeneid, a hymn to the Emperor Augustus and a fancied-up propaganda-type history of Rome as Exhibit A. But as often as not in our time, when art has long since gone its private way, the result of state intervention is something foolish or hideous or oppressive—or, in rare cases, all three, like the infamous architecture of the Italian Fascists and the "socialist realism" of the Soviet state.

It is a curious fact that although the American government ultimately does much more to influence art in this country through its educational, tax, and construction policies than through its direct-grant endowment programs, it is the latter programs that draw the fire. This is surely because the transaction of artist and official is so much more clearly delineated here. And though these transactions between artist and of-ficial proceed smoothly for the most part, as we have seen this summer, the calm on both sides is about a quarter of an inch deep and conceals—barely—a latent, at-the-ready mutual hysteria.

Thus some in the art world seem to be making wild demands for license to do whatever they want on taxpayer subsidy and characterizing all resistance to this as police-state brutality. And some in Congress, notably Sen. Jesse Helms, are proposing a truly absurd and repressive denial of funds from federal art programs to anything much more controversial than Little Bo-peep. It seems obvious to me that the Helms effort should be resoundingly defeated. And my guess is that if it is, everyone will retract his horns a little and stop going out of his way to challenge the other side. But the socially defiant nature of our contemporary art will not change, and neither will the socially conservative nature of most of the people who go into government, and, above all, neither will the inherently unhappy relationship between artist and patron.

Patron and Genius

In the famous 1775 preface to his Dictionary, Samuel Johnson let his ungenerous patron, the Earl of Chesterfield, have it: "Seven years, my Lord, have now passed, since I waited in your outward rooms, or was repulsed from your door; during which time I have been pushing on my work through difficulties . . . and have brought it at last to the verge of publication, without one act of assistance, one word of encouragement, or one smile of favor." It's all there: the resentment, the contempt, the humiliation of one who knows himself to be the intellectual superior of a patron from whom he has to beg favors and who has a more exalted place in the society than he.

Sometimes there is a sickly exchange of obsequiousness—the patron buttering up a genius whose work he doesn't really understand, the genius buttering up the moneybags for whom he has disdain. The romantic painter and poet William Blake spent several years in the pay of a dilettante named William Hayley, who himself wrote horrible poems with names like "The Grateful Snake," and who, when he wasn't flattering Blake, was trying to bend him away from his vast, unconventional talent. "I am determin'd to be no longer Pester'd with his Genteel Ignorance & Polite Disapprobation," Blake wrote to a friend. But soon enough we find Blake addressing the abominated Hayley this way: "You, Dear Sir, are one who has my Particular Gratitude, having conducted me thro' Three that would have been the Darkest Years that ever Mortal Suffer'd . . ."

Who can be happy or even rational in these circumstances? You are trapped in dependence on one you think a fool, if you are the artist; you are condescended to and defied by one who only feigns gratitude to you for gifts given, if you are the patron, and unceremoniously told to butt out. Why *should* the course of this untrue love run smooth? I think we should all get together and work to defeat Senator Helms's awful legislation—and then sit back and relax until, as it surely will, it happens again.

Source: Meg Greenfield, "Summer Storm," *Newsweek,* September 4, 1989.

SHUTTERBUGGERY
William F. Buckley

The Mapplethorpe uproar roars on, even though the controversial photo exhibit, which includes plenty of explicit perversity, has been removed from its scheduled site to a small gallery under purely private auspices. The predictable cries of censorship are ringing off the Capitol walls, and everyone from George Will to *The Village Voice* has been sneering at the philistinism of Jesse Helms for introducing a measure to deny federal funding to filthy art.

The funny thing is, Helms is right. The monster from North Carolina seems to be the only public figure who truly appreciates Robert Mapplethorpe's art. It has fallen to him to point out not only that the Emperor is wearing no clothes but that he is performing unnatural acts. To say this is not to disparage Mapplethorpe's art but to specify it.

That Mapplethorpe (who died of *AIDS* in March) was wondrously gifted is undeniable. His arresting portraits of clothed people and his subtly gorgeous still-lifes would have made his reputation, if not as many headlines, without benefit of sodomy.

But it was intrinsic to Mapplethorpe's art to try to aestheticize the obscene. He deliberately chose subjects that shock the normal sense of decency and displayed them for the sake of their abstract form. He counted on and exploited the dual reaction to create tension in the viewer: what is indecent and immoral becomes stunningly beautiful. And, thus, especially disturbing.

But to pretend the obscenity isn't *there*—that it exists only in the dirty mind of Jesse Helms—is as false to the pictures as to deny their beauty. Some of the acts Mapplethorpe photographs would cause comment at a hairdressers' convention. Which is simply to say, we have a right to be shocked when someone tries to shock us.

But is it art? Yes, yes, it's art, maybe great art—and so what? Great artistry may be used immorally, just as a saintly artist may produce banality. There is no strict correlation between the moral and the aesthetic, and there is no need for morality to grovel before the claims of Art. Anyone who wants to subsidize a Mapplethorpe is free to do so. The public should be free not to.

Source: "Shutterbuggery" by the editors of National Review, National Review, September 1, 1989. © 1989 by National Review, Inc., 215 Lexington Ave., New York, NY 10016. Reprinted by permission.

Søren Kierkegaard

Søren Kierkegaard (1813–1855) was the founder and most brilliant spokesman of the style of philosophizing known as "existentialism." His life was devoted to an unending inward reflection on human existence and the terror and uncertainty that each of us experiences in the face of his or her own death. Kierkegaard was deeply religious, though he rejected what he felt to be the superficial, self-satisfied Lutheranism of his native Denmark. In a series of books, some on philosophical topics, others more directly religious in their focus, he redefined the nature of faith, making it radically subjective and totally alien to the processes of ordinary systematic reason.

Kierkegaard was a witty, brilliantly provocative writer. His works abound in complex ironies that are challenges to the reader. He seems always to seek to unsettle his readers, to put us off balance and thereby force us to examine our lives as Kierkegaard had examined his own. One of his many literary devices to achieve this was the practice of publishing his books under pseudonyms. The *Philosophical Fragments,* for example, was published with its author listed as "Johannes Climacus." Farther down on the page there appeared the statement, "Responsible for publication: S. Kierkegaard." By this and other devices, Kierkegaard hoped to block any attempt by his readers to classify his position and pigeonhole him, for Kierkegaard was convinced that such techniques of systematic professional philosophy were merely ways of defusing a book and making it safe.

As he himself pessimistically predicted, Kierkegaard has fallen into the hands of professors and systematizers, and even his challenge to established philosophy has itself come to be treated merely as one more philosophy, namely, existentialism. Kierkegaard would have laughed, or perhaps he would have wept, to see his struggle with death and eternity reduced to an "ism."

Philosophy of Religion

405

Kierkegaard's Encounter with Faith

Søren Kierkegaard was born in 1813 to a father fifty-six and a mother forty-four. His early life and education were very closely supervised by his father, who demanded both a scholarly mastery of classical languages and a highly charged imaginative appreciation of the literature his young son read. The young Søren had laid upon him the full weight of the guilt that extreme Pietist Protestantism so often inflicted upon its communicants. Although Kant and Kierkegaard thus had roughly the same sort of religious upbringing, Kierkegaard completely lacked Kant's quiet inner confidence and peace. He reacted first against the torment of his religious training by plunging himself into a life of physical self-indulgence, eating, drinking, and dressing the dandy. But these distractions could not free him from the black gloom that hung over him, and he decided finally to return to his studies and become a pastor.

The dramatic turning point in Kierkegaard's private life was his engagement, and then the breaking of it, to seventeen-year-old Regine Olson. Kierkegaard wrote endlessly of his feelings for Regine, of the philosophical significance of marriage, love, and the problems of such a life commitment, but one cannot help thinking that she was more important to him as a subject for meditation than as a real, live woman. After pouring out a series of essays and books on aesthetic, moral, and religious topics, Kierkegaard died at the relatively early age of forty-two.

Kierkegaard's inner emotional life, his lifelong struggle with religious faith, and his reaction to the dominant Hegelian philosophy of his day are all so intimately intertwined that it is very difficult to speak of any one without immediately bringing in all three. There is hardly space in an introductory text of this sort to explore the subject fully, but a few systematic remarks may be helpful to you. I especially want you to develop an interest in Kierkegaard because, in my opinion, he is, after the immortal Plato, the most gifted artist among all of the important philosophers who have come down to us in the Western tradition. If you pick up one of his books, many of which are easily available in paperback editions, you will find him profound, troubling, witty, touching, and, in the end, deeply rewarding.

The passionate center of Kierkegaard's thought and life is his confrontation with the ever-present terror of existential dread—the obsessive, unavoidable fact of my own impending death, the infinity of the universe, and the meaninglessness of my own brief life in comparison. Every man, woman, and child faces these terrible, fundamental facts of the human condition. We may deny them, flee from them, repress them, distract ourselves to escape from them, but always they are there, at the edge of consciousness, waiting to return in the darkness of night. The first lesson Kierkegaard teaches us, both in his books and by his life, is that this dread of death and meaninglessness must be faced, confronted, not shoved aside again and again. If I may speak personally—and the greatest honor we can pay to Kierkegaard is precisely to be honest, each one of us, about our own encounter with the fear of death—I first came face to face with this dread as a teenager. I was obsessed with fears of death, and the more I thrust them from my mind, the more intensely they returned. In my case, the fear was not of pain, or age, or sickness, but simply of nonbeing. The more I turned the thought over in my mind, the closer my own eventual death seemed to come, until finally I would seize any distraction to divert my attention from what was, and of course still is, an unavoidable fate.

For Kierkegaard, the dread of death was both heightened and complicated by the hope of eternal life that the religion of his fathers held out to him. All of you have heard the expression "Trust in the Lord." But how many of you have actually asked yourselves what it means to "trust in the Lord"? What does it mean to "believe in" God, to have **faith** in Him?

Well, what it does *not* mean is believing *that* God exists. In our increasingly nonreligious society, when a person says that she "believes in God," we automatically assume that she means that she believes there is such a thing as God. But in the Judeo-Christian religious tradition, particularly in the extremely individualistic Protestant sort of Christianity that was Kierkegaard's heritage, the phrase "belief in God" has quite a different meaning. To believe in God, to trust in Him, to have faith in Him, means to believe that He will keep His promise to humanity; it is to have faith that He will keep the pact, or covenant, that He made with the beings He created. That pact is testified to first in what we call the Old Testament, and then again in a renewed form in the New Testament.

The promise, of course, is the promise of salvation, of a life after death, of true happiness, of fruitfulness, of a union of the soul with God. (Needless to say, long books could be written on the various interpretations that Jews, Christians, and Muslims have placed upon this notion of a covenant with God. The version I am summarizing here is something like what Kierkegaard would have learned and brooded upon.) According to the Old Testament, God made a promise to Noah, and He repeated it to Abraham. He renewed it again and again, despite the failure of the Hebrews to keep His Law and follow His commands. Finally, God embodied that Law (or Word or Logos) in the Person of Jesus Christ, so that His offer of salvation might be made once

Faith   In Christianity, trust that God will keep the promise He made to the Israelites in the Old Testament and renewed to all mankind in the New Testament (hence, "trust in the Lord"). Originally, the promise was to make the Israelites fruitful and populous. In the New Testament, the promise is of life eternal in heaven. According to some Christians, men and women are unable to have and sustain this trust without the miraculous help of God.

more. With the birth, suffering, and death of Jesus, God sealed His free gift of eternal life. As the price of that blessedness, He asked only faith, an unstinting, unconditioned, unqualified belief by us that He would keep His promise of this free gift.

Other Christian traditions had emphasized the role of right behavior, or "good works," either as part of the price of salvation or as worldly evidence of one's true belief. But the Pietist strain of Protestantism placed a very heavy emphasis upon the pure possession of that unconditioned faith in God. So it was that for Kierkegaard, the central religious problem quite naturally became the problem of faith.

Abraham and Isaac, with the Angel. A drawing of Abraham by the great seventeenth-century Dutch artist Rembrandt, preparing to sacrifice his only son, Isaac, at God's command. In one of his most powerful books, *Fear and Trembling*, Kierkegaard interpreted the story of Abraham and Isaac as evidence of Abraham's perfect faith in the Lord. *(Undated engraving) (Source: Corbis/ Bettmann.)*

You might think, on first reflection, that the Christian message would be a very welcome message indeed. After all, life is short, bedeviled by suffering, terminated by the absolute finality of unavoidable death. It was good enough news to be told, in the Old Testament, that God would grant life everlasting to those who kept His commandments. But we are weak, imperfect creatures, and it soon became clear that doing God's bidding was a task too hard for us, even with the promise of salvation to lead us on. He took upon Himself, in the Person of His Son, the atonement for *our* sins, and offered to us the priceless pearl of salvation for the merest asking. All we needed to do was believe that we would receive it. What could possibly be better news than that? Small wonder that this message was called the Gospel, which means "good news." Small wonder too that those who spread the message were called evangelists, which means "bringers of good news."

But strange to tell, the glad tidings of God's free gift have brought fear, dread, doubt, torment, and tortured self-examination to countless hearers, among them Søren Kierkegaard. The gift is so great, the price so small—and yet, the price of faith must be paid freely, unhesitatingly, without doubts or second thoughts. Therein lie the seeds of terror. Do I truly believe? Is my faith pure? Can I trust in the Lord, or is there lurking deep within my heart a doubt that so great a gift will be conferred on so undeserving a creature as myself? Out of this inner hell Kierkegaard tore the writings by which we remember him. His doubts and fears concerned his very *existence* as an individual, mortal creature longing to believe in God's promise, not the abstract, impersonal logical relationships among disembodied forms, or "essences." Hence, Kierkegaard's way of thinking has come to be called **existentialism.** Indeed, Kierkegaard is universally acknowledged to be the first true existentialist philosopher. Whether he would have appreciated such a categorization and sterilization of his inner torment is of course not so clear.

In his lifelong struggle with the problem of faith, Kierkegaard did battle with three enemies, against whom he turned not only his considerable philosophical and theological gifts but also a brilliant, convoluted, ironic wit. The first of his enemies was the established Christianity of his own day, the solid, comfortable, Sunday-sermon Lutheranism of nineteenth-century Denmark. Like so many passionate prophets before him, Kierkegaard accused the established church of mouthing empty formulae that were neither lived nor understood. Sin, redemption, damnation, salvation—all were the subjects of elegant

Existentialism   The philosophical doctrine, associated originally with Søren Kierkegaard, according to which our being as subjective individuals (our *existence*) is more important than what we have in common objectively with all other human beings (our *essence*). Of primary concern for Kierkegaard was his relationship to God. Later existentialists emphasized the individual's creation of himself or herself through free individual choices.

sermons and pious attitudes that did not for a moment interfere with the secular, weekday activities of this world. Kierkegaard once observed that just as it is hard to jump up in the air and land exactly on the spot from which one began, so too it is hard to become a Christian when one has been born a Christian. He meant that those who were born into Christianity, who were baptized, confirmed, and raised in the official emptiness of its dogmas and rituals, might actually find it more difficult to take the message of Christianity seriously than would a pagan to whom the divine promise came as wonderful, terrible, astonishing news. Kierkegaard devoted many of his books to a sustained effort to breathe new existential significance into the familiar phrases and concepts of Christian theology.

His second enemy was the complacent middle-class culture of his society, the "bourgeois" culture of solid tradesmen and lawyers—sound, self-confident people who disdained anyone so odd, so passionate, so disruptive as Kierkegaard. The word "bourgeois" has drifted into our vocabulary these days as a catchall term for what we in America call "middle-class" life, but in nineteenth-century Europe, it had a much richer, more resonant set of associations. Historically, a "bourgeois," or a "burgher," was simply a resident of a "bourg" or "burg," which in the late Middle Ages was a walled city. By extension, the word came to mean a member of the urban merchant class and also a "freeman" or citizen of one of the cities whose charter came from the king rather than from the feudal aristocracy. The burghers of the European cities were men of substance, solid citizens, true to their word in business deals, extremely conservative in their family relationships, jealous of their rights as city leaders, forward looking in commerce, and quite often supporters of a strong monarchy against the ancient and dispersed powers of the landed aristocracy. For the burghers of Copenhagen, religion was first of all a matter of propriety, of respectability, and only then a matter of conscience or salvation. One dressed in one's finest clothes on Sunday and went with one's family to church; one sat in a front pew, purchased at great expense, where one was seen by one's neighbors. One listened piously to the sermon, which, though heavy on damnation, was conveniently light on social responsibility, and then one returned to one's substantial townhouse for a good Sunday dinner.

As you can imagine, the unthinking religiosity, the self-satisfied complacency of the solid citizens of Denmark made Kierkegaard furious. Many of his most spectacular literary tricks and devices, and particularly his extremely heavy irony, are aimed at puncturing that complacency and somehow reaching the real human beings behind those masks.

The final enemy was the official philosophy of Kierkegaard's day, the vast, pompous, elaborate philosophical systems constructed by the disciples and followers of the great German philosopher Georg Hegel. The Hegelian philosophy, as it was expounded by the professors of Europe, put itself forward as the objective, impersonal, purely rational, totally systematic, absolutely final truth about just about everything. It was turgid, jargon filled, and completely self-confident. It claimed to wrap up space, time, eternity, being, history, man, the state, and God in one vast metaphysical synthesis that simultaneously answered all of our questions about the universe and also—rather conveniently—demonstrated the superiority of precisely the social and religious system then dominant in European society.

In short, Kierkegaard's three enemies were really one and the same enemy in different disguises. The Christianity of his day was bourgeois Christianity, buttressed and justified by the official philosophical system. The burghers were Establishment Christians, who—though they knew precious little philosophy—were justified and rationalized by that same philosophy. And the philosophy, though it claimed to be the purest product of reason, was a thoroughgoing justification of the reign of the burghers and the ascendency of their religion.

A nineteenth-century bourgeois gentleman and lady friend as the painter Toulouse-Lautrec saw them. *The Englishmen at the Moulin Rouge,* Painting by Henri Raymound de Toulouse-Lautrec, French, 1864–1901. Oil on cardboard. H. 33¾ W. 26 in. Signed (lower left): T-Lautrec. *(Source:* The Metropolitan Museum of Art.*)*

Karl Marx, facing this very same union of religion, philosophy, and the ascendent bourgeoisie, turned his attack on the social and economic consequences, for Marx was a secular man, concerned with this-worldly issues of justice, poverty, and work. Kierkegaard, before all else a man of God, attacked the same union of forces on its religious front. He cared nothing at all for worldly happiness or misery. Rather, he brushed all secular considerations aside and instead demanded that the good Christians of Denmark begin to pay to eternal life as much attention as they regularly gave to a daily profit.

Kierkegaard's onslaught was complex and subtle and, hence, is impossible to summarize in a few paragraphs. Two ideas lie at the heart of his religiophilosophical message, and we can at least take a first step toward understanding them. These notions are the inwardness, or subjectivity, of truth, and the irrational, unarguable "leap of faith." Now that sounds more like a Hegelian mouthful than a bit of biting wit, so let us take a look at each.

The Hegelian philosophers put their doctrines forward as *rational* and *objective*. They were, in a way, like today's scientists. All of you have noticed, I imagine, that there is a very big difference in the teaching style and approach of science professors as compared to professors of literature or philosophy. In a literature class, you are encouraged to express your own "interpretation" of Dickens or Mailer or Shakespeare. In a philosophy class—I hope!—you are prompted to think out your own position, to develop your own arguments, and to defend whatever point of view you think closest to the truth. But nobody teaches calculus or physics that way. Can you imagine a physics quiz with questions like, "Write a ten-minute essay on your impressions of Boyle's law," or "Take a position for or against relativity and defend it—in your answer, make reference to the text." Hardly! Scientists quite confidently assume that their knowledge is objective, and that what they teach is a matter neither of "opinion" nor of personality. In the same way, the Hegelian philosophers represented themselves as objective, rational discoverers of the truth. Their private fears, hopes, terrors, and joys were no more a part of their philosophy, they thought, than would a modern biochemist's neuroses be a part of her theory of DNA. To be sure, readers might be curious, in a gossipy way, about the personal lives of the great philosophers, just as we today like to read stories about Albert Einstein. But no one would suppose for a moment that there was any important scientific connection between those delightful or depressing glimpses into the scientist's private life and the scientific truth of his theories.

In a total reversal of the received philosophical-scientific opinion of his day, Kierkegaard argued that Truth is Subjectivity. In other words, he denied the objective impersonality of truth and insisted, instead, that all truth must be inward, dependent upon the subject, particular rather than universal, personal rather than interpersonal or impersonal.

When Kierkegaard says that Truth is Subjectivity, he is denying the ancient philosophical doctrine that the truth of an idea or a statement consists

"You seem troubled, Brother Timothy. Is anything worrying you? I mean, besides the sins of the world, the vanities of mankind, and that sort of thing." *(Source:* The Cartoon Bank.)

in its conformity to an independent object. When I say, "That is a very good picture of Jim," I mean that the picture looks like Jim, that it resembles, or copies, or conforms to the objective nature of Jim's body. When I say, "It is true that Sacramento is the capital of California," I mean that the real world—California, in this case—actually has the characteristics that my statement says it has. In other words, truth is conformity to the objective state of things in the world. Or, Truth is Objectivity. If this familiar conception of truth is correct, then the truth of a statement or belief depends only on the relationship between the statement or belief and the world, *not* on the relationship between the statement or belief and the person who thinks it. If Truth is Objectivity, then it does not matter, so far as truth is concerned, whether I believe Sacramento to be the capital of California passionately, calmly, tentatively, with all my heart, or simply because a friend told me so.

Kierkegaard does not care about the capitals of states or nations, of course. He cares about salvation, the Christian message. And when it comes to salvation, *how* you believe is as important as *what* you believe, he thought. The Hegelian system builders wanted to treat the Christian message as though it were merely one subpart of their grand structure of objective knowledge. So "Jesus died for my sins" would be treated by them as more or less on a par with "Space is three-dimensional and homogeneous." Each statement would be true if it corresponded correctly to the objective state of things, false otherwise. But that treatment of the promise of salvation as "objective" is precisely wrong, Kierkegaard insisted. Truth does not consist in the proper relationship between the belief and the *object;* rather, it consists in the proper relationship between the belief and the *subject,* the individual human being who holds that belief. *How* he or she holds it is the criterion of its truth. In order for the belief to be true, it must be held passionately, unconditionally, absolutely without inner reservation or doubt.

But—and here we come to the second of Kierkegaard's great ideas, the "leap of faith"—that belief in God's promise of eternal life can have no rational justification, no evidence, no proof. Theologians since the time of Aristotle have sought to *prove* the existence of God, to prove the truth of this or that religious doctrine. Sometimes they used evidence of their senses—what they could see, hear, and touch. At other times they erected abstract arguments of pure logic, deducing the absolute, objective truth of Christianity (or Islam, or Judaism). But Kierkegaard believed that all such attempts at rational justification are doomed to total failure. The absolute gap between finite man and infinite God makes any rational bridge building between the two on man's part futile. God may reach down to man, though how He can manage that is beyond our comprehension. But man can no more reason his way into the presence of God than a mathematician, by doggedly adding unit to unit, can calculate his way to infinity.

Because reason is inadequate to the task of supporting our belief in God's promise, Kierkegaard said, our only hope is an absolutely unconditional leap of faith. I must take the plunge and say, with all of my heart, *Credo*—I believe.

Can we not perhaps look for a little bit of support from reason? Might not reason at least show that God's promise is probable? That the weight of the evidence inclines us toward God's promise? That a reasonable person could tend to believe God's promise?

Not a bit of it! That is just what a solid, smug merchant or a pompous, self-important professor would say. Can't you just imagine the two of them sitting in front of the fire, the burgher after a long day at the counting house, the professor after a day of serious, important lectures. The burgher leans back in his comfortable chair, puffs a bit on his pipe (one would not want to speak too quickly on such matters—it might show a lack of seriousness), and then asks, "Is it your opinion that the weight of the evidence, objectively and impartially considered, inclines us to the view that God has promised us eternal life rather than eternal death?" The professor takes a sip of beer, strokes his beard thoughtfully, and answers, "Well, on the one hand, Hegel, in the *Phenomenology of Mind,* seems to suggest that God does make such a promise; but on the other hand, Kant, in the *Critique of Pure Reason,* argues that we cannot know with certainty that such a promise has been made. In the light of recent research which I understand has been reported in the latest issue of the Berlin *Journal of Metaphysics,* I would judge professionally that the answer is a qualified yes."

Both the subjectivity of truth and the leap of faith are central to the writings of Kierkegaard. The *Concluding Unscientific Postscript to the Philosophical Fragments* is Kierkegaard's major systematic exposition of his philosophical theology. The title, in typical Kierkegaardian fashion, is an elaborate joke. The *Philosophical Fragments* is short—not quite 100 pages. The *Postscript,* on the other hand, runs more than 500 pages. By calling his most important work a mere "postscript" to the *Fragments,* a lengthy p.s. to a short letter, so to speak, Kierkegaard was laughing at the self-important philosophers of his day. The word "unscientific," of course, is another dig at the Hegelian systematizers, who called everything they did "scientific."

The *Philosophical Fragments* deals with the contrast between secular truth and religious truth, between the objective and the subjective, between reason and faith, between wisdom and salvation. Kierkegaard imagines all these contrasts as gathered together into the person of Socrates, who is the greatest of all teachers, and Jesus, who is not a teacher in the rational sense, but the Saviour. Kierkegaard's argument goes like this (yes indeed, Kierkegaard uses arguments to show us that arguments cannot be used in matters of faith. I leave it to you to determine whether there is a contradiction in his mode of procedure): Secular knowledge of morality is something that can be learned through rational self-reflection. Teachers like Socrates help us to bring our moral knowledge to consciousness by probing questions that force us to justify our beliefs. But since in some sense this moral knowledge already lies within each of us, a teacher—even so great a teacher as Socrates—is merely helpful; if we had to, we could get along without one. As philosophers say, a teacher is "accidental" rather than "essential." But salvation is a matter of the fate of my soul. It is a matter of my *existence,* not merely of my state of knowledge. And salvation is not something I can acquire on my own if I am forced to do so. Salvation requires that God reach down and lift me up to His Kingdom. Somehow, the gulf between myself and God must be crossed. Thus salvation is totally different from the acquisition of wisdom, for there is no gulf to be crossed on the road to wisdom. I need only to look carefully and critically enough inside myself.

Jesus is God's instrument for bridging the gulf between Himself and myself. Jesus is the Saviour. And since salvation concerns my *existence,* the actual, historical reality of Jesus is all-important. You see, it does not really matter to me whether Socrates ever actually lived. Once I have learned from Plato's Dialogues how to engage in Socratic questioning, it would make no difference if I were to discover that the Dialogues were a hoax and that there never had been any Socrates. But if God never actually became Man in the form of Jesus Christ, if Christ never died for my sins, then I am damned rather than saved. The mere Idea of the Saviour is not enough. I need to be absolutely certain that God did actually become Man, that He really died for my sins, that God did renew His free gift to me through His only begotten Son.

But just because I need so desperately to know that Jesus really lived, I am hopelessly at a loss for evidence or argument sufficient to my need. Can I rest comfortably in the belief that I have been promised eternal life when the evidence for my belief is merely probable, merely the sort of evidence that a historian or philosopher can produce? No, too much is at stake: Salvation is everything; it is eternity of life rather than death. I am reduced by my terror and my need to infinite concern for something that defies rational grounding. In short, I am reduced to an absolute *leap of faith.*

When Kierkegaard tells me that I must make a *leap of faith,* he is not at all suggesting that such a leap is frivolous, or random, or something that just pops into my head. Quite to the contrary, Kierkegaard believes that I must prepare for this leap, as a ballet dancer might prepare during half a lifetime for an exquisite leap on stage. I must turn my back on all the solid, substantial, everyday pleasures and concerns that tie most men and women, leaden, to the ground and make it impossible for them to take the leap of faith. I must cultivate a special relationship to life, to the universe, and to God in order even to attempt the leap. Thus, the leap is not *irrational* in the sense of being silly or mindless, but it *is* an act that cannot be grounded in argument, proof, or step-by-step justification. There is no such thing, Kierkegaard thinks, as having a little bit of faith.

In the following passage from the *Concluding Unscientific Postscript,* Kierkegaard tries to help us understand what is involved in *faith.* The text, which comes from a section entitled "The Subjective Thinker," focuses on the contrast between the sort of relationship I could have to some other human being, such as Socrates, and my unique relationship to the divine Saviour, Jesus.

SØREN KIERKEGAARD,
Concluding Unscientific Postscript to the Philosophical Fragments

Faith and One's Relationship to Others and to God

The mode of apprehension of the truth is precisely the truth. It is therefore untrue to answer a question in a medium in which the question cannot arise. So for example, to explain reality within the medium of the possible, or to distinguish between possibility and reality within possibility. By refraining from raising the question of reality from the aesthetic or intellectual point of view, but asking this question only ethically, and here again only in the interest of one's own reality, each individual will be isolated and compelled to exist for himself. Irony and hypocrisy as opposite forms, but both expressing the contradiction that the internal is not the external, irony by seeming to be bad, hypocrisy by seeming to be good, emphasize the principle anent the contemplative inquiry concerning ethical inwardness, that reality and deceit are equally possible, and that deceit can clothe itself in the same appearance as reality. It is unethical even to ask at all about another person's ethical inwardness, insofar as such inquiry constitutes a diversion of attention. But if the question is asked nevertheless, the difficulty remains that I can lay hold of the other's reality only by conceiving it, and hence by translating it into a possibility; and in this sphere the possibility of a deception is equally conceivable. This is profitable preliminary training for an ethical mode of existence: to learn that the individual stands alone.

It is a misunderstanding to be concerned about reality from the aesthetic or intellectual point of view. And to be concerned ethically about another's reality is also a misunderstanding, since the only question of reality that is ethically pertinent is the question of one's own reality. Here we may clearly note the difference that exists between faith *sensu strictissimo* on the one hand (referring as it does to the historical, and the realms of the aesthetic, the intellectual) and the ethical on the other. To ask with infinite interest about a reality which is not one's own is faith, and this constitutes a paradoxical relationship to the paradoxical. Aesthetically it is impossible to raise such a question except in thoughtlessness, since possibility is aesthetically higher than reality. Nor is it possible to raise such a question ethically, since the sole ethical interest is the interest in one's own reality. The analogy between faith and the ethical is found in the infinite interest, which suffices to distinguish the believer absolutely from an aesthetician or a thinker. But the believer differs from the ethicist in being infinitely interested in the reality of another (in the fact, for example, that God has existed in time).

Precisely in the degree to which I understand a thinker I become indifferent to his reality; that is, to his existence as a particular individual, to his having really understood this or that so and so, to his actually having realized his teaching, and so forth. Aesthetic and speculative thought is quite justified in insisting on this point, and it is important not to lose sight of it. But this does not suffice for a defense of pure thought as a medium of communication between man and man. Because the reality of the teacher is properly indifferent to me as his pupil, and my reality conversely to him, it does not by any means follow that the teacher is justified in being indifferent to his own reality. His communication should bear the stamp of this consciousness, but not directly, since the ethical reality of an individual is not directly communicable (such a direct relationship is exemplified in the paradoxical relation of a believer to the object of his faith), and cannot be understood immediately, but must be understood indirectly through indirect signs.

When the different spheres are not decisively distinguished from one another, confusion reigns everywhere. When people are curious about a thinker's reality and find it interesting to know something about it, and so forth, this interest is intellectually reprehensible. The maximum of attainment in the sphere of the intellectual is to become altogether indifferent to the thinker's reality. But by being thus muddle-headed in the intellectual sphere, one acquires a certain resemblance to a believer. A believer is one who is infinitely interested in another's reality. This is a decisive criterion for faith, and the interest in question is not just a little curiosity, but an absolute dependence upon faith's object.

The object of faith is the reality of another, and the relationship is one of infinite interest. The object of faith is not a doctrine, for then the relationship would be intellectual, and it would be of importance not to botch it, but to realize the maximum intellectual relationship. The object of faith is not a teacher with a doctrine; for when a teacher has a doctrine, the doctrine is *eo ipso* more important than the teacher, and the relationship is again intellectual, and it again becomes important not to botch it, but to realize the maximum intellectual relationship. The object of faith is the reality of the teacher, that the teacher really exists. The answer of faith is therefore unconditionally yes or no. For it does not concern a doctrine, as to whether the doctrine is true or not; it is the answer to a question concerning a fact: "Do you or do you not suppose that he has really existed?" And the answer, it must be noted, is with infinite passion. In the case of a human being, it is thoughtlessness to lay so great and infinite a stress on the question whether he has existed or not. If the object of faith is a human being, therefore, the whole proposal is the vagary of a stupid person, who had not even understood the spirit of the intellectual and the aesthetic. The object of faith is hence the reality of the God-man in the sense of his existence. But existence involves first and foremost particularity, and this is why thought must abstract from existence, because the particular cannot be thought, but only the universal. The object of faith is thus God's reality in existence as a particular individual, the fact that God has existed as an individual human being.

Christianity is no doctrine concerning the unity of the divine and the human, or concerning the identity of subject and object; nor is it any other of the logical transcriptions of Christianity. If Christianity were a doctrine, the relationship to it would not be one of faith, for only an intellectual type of relationship can correspond to a doctrine. Christianity is therefore not a doctrine, but the fact that God has existed.

The realm of faith is thus not a class for numskulls in the sphere of the intellectual, or an asylum for the feeble-minded. Faith constitutes a sphere all by itself, and every misunderstanding of Christianity may at once be recognized by its transforming it into a doctrine, transferring it to the sphere of the intellectual. The maximum of attainment within the sphere of the intellectual, namely, to realize an entire indifference as to the reality of the teacher, is in the sphere of faith at the opposite end of the scale. The maximum of attainment

Søren Kierkegaard, *Concluding Unscientific Postscript to the Philosophical Fragments*

within the sphere of faith is to become infinitely interested in the reality of the teacher.

Can We Prove that God Exists?

When students are introduced to the study of philosophy, one of the standard moves is to go through what are usually referred to as the "proofs of the existence of God." This is a set of arguments, developed over the past 2,400 years by many different philosophers, which purport to demonstrate that there is, or exists, an infinite, omnipotent, omniscient, benevolent creator of the universe who goes by the name of God. When I teach an introduction to philosophy course, I try to slip in the proofs for the existence of God just before Christmas in the fall semester, and just before Easter in the spring semester. It seems fitting somehow.

Is anyone ever convinced by the proofs? Well you may ask. I have, from time to time, started off my presentation of them by asking how many members of the class believe in God. I mean by that, of course, how many believe that there is a God, not how many believe that He will keep His promise of eternal life. Anyway, I count the hands, and then I present one of the proofs. Usually I try out what is called the Cosmological Argument, and sometimes I go right into the real number-one proof, which is called the Ontological Argument. (We will get to these in a minute, do not despair.) After running through the proof, I ask whether there are any objections or criticisms. Usually there aren't any (how many students are going to tell their professor that they think he is crazy?). Then I ask for another show of hands on those who believe in God. Now it is the most peculiar thing, but even though no one ever objects to my proofs or raises any doubts, not a single person is ever converted to the faith by them. I do not think I have convinced a single, solitary nonbeliever in all the years I have been proving the existence of God. Next I run through the standard refutations for the proofs. (In philosophy, there is an argument against just about everything that there is an argument for.) Same result. I never make agnostics out of the believers, any more than I have made believers out of the agnostics.

When you stop and think about it, there is really something wonderful and mad about a finite, mortal man or woman undertaking to *prove* that God exists. It is as though the philosopher rears up on her hind legs and says, "God! You may be out there, You may exist, but unless You fit into my syllogisms, unless You follow from premises, unless You are a theorem in my system, I won't acknowledge Your existence!" When it comes to sheer effrontery, to what the Greeks called *hubris* and the Jews call *chutzpah,* there just isn't anything to match it.

Philosophers have never been known for their humility, and a fair number of great ones have had a shot at proving the existence of God. Aristotle tried it, and so did St. Thomas Aquinas. Occam had a proof, Descartes had several, Spinoza came up with some, and even William James, the American pragmatist, offered his own rather odd version of reasons for believing in the existence of God. In this section, we are going to take a close look at the three most famous proofs. These aren't all the proofs, by any means, but they will give you a good idea of some of the different tactics that philosophers have used over the ages. The three proofs are called the *Argument from Design,* the *Cosmological Proof,* and the *Ontological Proof.* We will examine the version of the Argument from Design offered by the eighteenth-century English philosopher William Paley; the Cosmological Argument as it was set forth by the great medieval theologian St. Thomas Aquinas; and the Ontological Argument in its original version, as stated by the man who thought it up, the eleventh-century logician St. Anselm. Since David Hume and Immanuel Kant are the two best proof-for-existence-of-God-refuters who have ever lived, we will look at their refutations together with the proofs. Here we go. Do not be surprised if you hear Kierkegaard laughing at us along the way.

William Paley: The Argument from Design

Our first proof for the existence of God is at once the most obvious, the most natural, the most ancient, the most persuasive, the easiest to understand, and—alas—the philosophically weakest. The **Argument from Design** is quite simple. We observe that certain man-made objects exhibit an internal purposive organization, a fitting of parts to the function of the whole. In a watch, to take the example that Paley himself uses, the various springs and pins and hands are all made precisely to serve the purpose of keeping and telling time. This rational, purposive order in the watch is the direct result of the conscious, rational, purposive activity of its creator, the watchmaker. From the character of the watch, we naturally infer the existence of a watchmaker, whether we actually know him or not. If you show me a watch (or a chair or a painting or even a simple stone axe) and say, "It is so old that no one can remember who made it," I would never dream of saying, "Perhaps no one made it." The intelligence of its creation inheres in its internal organization. The watch is, if you will permit a bad pun, intelligently produced on the face of it. Well, Paley argues (and so have countless other theologians and philosophers over the ages), nature is more wonderfully organized than the most subtle human contrivance. The human eye far exceeds a camera in sensitivity

> **Argument from Design**   The attempt to prove the existence of God by demonstrating the high degree of organization and purposive order in the universe, and arguing that such design must be the product of an intelligent, powerful, purposeful creator. The argument is very old but was very popular in the eighteenth century.

and fidelity of reproduction; the human brain cannot be duplicated by the most sophisticated computer; the merest one-celled microscopic organism exhibits a biochemical complexity and adaptation that taxes the analytic powers of all science. Who can doubt for a moment that nature has its Creator, an intelligent, purposeful, all-powerful Maker, who in His infinite wisdom has adjusted means to end, part to whole, organ to organism, throughout the whole of space and time?

The technical name for this is an *argument from analogy.* You have probably encountered ratios or proportions in high school math—problems like: "Eight is to four as six is to x. Solve for x." When I was in school, the way to state that mathematically was either like this: $8:4::6:x$, or else like this: $8/4 = 6/x$. The solution, of course is $x = 3$. The same sort of "analogy" turns up in aptitude tests. "Fire engine is to fire department as _____ is to police department." The answer is "police car." The point is that if we already know the relationship between one pair of things (such as the numbers 8 and 4, or a fire engine and the fire department), then when we are presented with only one member of another pair, we may be able to figure out what the other member of the pair is (3 in the math example, or a police car in the other case). Now all this may seem like baby talk to you, but philosophers frequently build powerful arguments from what look like very simple pieces.

WILLIAM PALEY

William Paley (1743–1805) was an English churchman whose writings in defense of Christianity were widely read and much admired in the eighteenth and nineteenth centuries. Paley was a defender of utilitarianism in moral philosophy and of the truths of revelation in theology (a position known as *theism*). His book *Natural Theology* was a systematic presentation of the so-called Argument from Design for the existence of God, an argument that David Hume had vigorously attacked in his *Dialogues Concerning Natural Religion.*

Paley and the other arguers from design draw up two sorts of analogies. The first is between an artificially constructed object and its human maker, on the one hand, and a particular organism or bit of natural organization and its divine Creator, on the other. So we get:

| Watch is to watchmaker as the human eye is to x. x = God.

The other analogy is between an artificially constructed object and its human maker, on the one hand, and the whole universe and its divine Creator, on the other. So this time we get:

| Watch is to watchmaker as the universe is to x. x = God.

Here is Paley's own statement of the argument. Because he tends to be rather wordy, I have edited it down to the bare bones.

WILLIAM PALEY,
Natural Theology

In crossing a heath, suppose I pitched my foot against a *stone,* and were asked how the stone came to be there, I might possibly answer, that for any thing I knew to the contrary it had lain there for ever, nor would it, perhaps, be very easy to show the absurdity of this answer. But suppose I had found a *watch* upon the ground, and it should be inquired how the watch happened to be in that place, I should hardly think of the answer which I had before given, that for any thing I knew the watch might have always been there. Yet why should not this answer serve for the watch as well as for the stone; why is it not as admissible in the second case as in the first? For this reason, and for no other, namely, that when we come to inspect the watch, we perceive—what we could not discover in the stone—that its several parts are framed and put together for a purpose, e.g. that they are so formed and adjusted as to produce motion, and that motion so regulated as to point out the hour of the day; that if the different parts had been differently shaped from what they are, or placed after any other manner or in any other order than that in which they are placed, either no motion at all would have been carried on in the machine, or none which would have answered the use that is now served by it.

This mechanism being observed—it requires indeed an examination of the instrument, and perhaps some previous knowledge of the subject, to perceive and understand it; but being once, as we have said, observed and understood, the inference we think is inevitable, that the watch must have had a maker—that there must have existed, at some time and at some place or other, an artificer or artificers who formed it for the purpose which, we find it actually to answer, who comprehended its construction and designed its use.

Were there no example in the world of contrivance except that of the eye, it would be alone sufficient to support the conclusion which we draw from it, as to the necessity of an intelligent Creator. It could never be got rid of, because it could not be accounted for by any other supposition which did not contradict all the principles we possess of knowledge—the principles according to which things do, as often as they can be brought to the test of experience, turn out to be true or false.

If other parts of nature were inaccessible to our inquiries, or even if other parts of nature presented nothing to our examination but disorder and confusion, the validity of this example would remain the same. If there were but one watch in the world, it would not be less certain that it had a maker. If we had never in our lives seen any but one single kind of hydraulic machine, yet if of that one kind we understood the mechanism and use, we should be as perfectly assured that it proceeded from the hand and thought and skill of a workman, as if we visited a museum of the arts, and saw collected there twenty different kinds of machines for drawing water, or a thousand different kinds for other purposes. Of this point each machine is a proof independently of all the rest. So it is with the evidences of a divine agency. The proof is not a conclusion which lies at the end of a chain of reasoning, of which chain each instance of contrivance is only a link, and of which, if one link fail, the whole falls; but it is an argument separately supplied by every separate example. An error in stating an example affects only that example. The argument is cumulative, in the fullest sense of that term. The eye proves it without the ear, the ear without the eye. The proof in each example is complete, for when the design of the part, and the conduciveness of its structure to that design is shown, the mind may set itself at rest; no future consideration can detract any thing from the force of the example.

William Paley,
Natural Theology

This argument has an antique sound, of course. It was written almost 200 years ago, after all. But the principle underlying it is one we use today in interplanetary exploration. When astronauts first walked on the moon, they looked for evidences of intelligent life, though they did not really expect to find such evidences on an atmosphereless body. Now how on earth (or elsewhere) could they possibly tell what would be evidence of intelligent life? Having no advance knowledge of the sorts of creatures that might inhabit other parts of the universe, by what signs could the astronauts infer their existence and presence? The answer is obvious. Any sort of device, or instrument, or machine that exhibited some purposive internal organization, and that seemed not to grow naturally in that environment, would permit them to infer by analogy the existence of some (presumably) nonhuman intelligent maker.

Anyone who has been enraptured, bemused, or awestruck by the wonder of nature will appreciate the psychological force of the Argument from Design. Can the order of planets, stars, and galaxies, the underlying simplicity and regularity of natural forces, the exquisitely delicate adjustment of part to part in living things really just be? Must there not be some intelligence directing, organizing, creating this vast interconnected universe?

FIG. 48.—VERTICAL SECTION OF THE EYE.   (Enlarged.)

C, The Cornea.	Ch. The Choroid.
A, The Aqueous Humor.	R, The Retina.
I, The Iris.	N. The Optic Nerve.
P, The Pupil.	DD. The Eyelids.
L, The Crystalline Lens.	X, The Levator Muscle of the Upper
H, The Ligament of the Lens.	Lid.
B, The Ciliary Process.	Y, The Upper Straight Muscle of the
V, The Cavity containing the Vit-	Eye.
reous Humor.	Z, The Lower Straight Muscle.
S, The Sclerotic.	

Vertical cross-section of the eye. The complexity of the human eye, the exact fitting of its structure to the purpose of sight, was viewed by many scientifically minded theologians as evidence of the existence and benevolence of God. (Undated illustration.) *(Source: Corbis/Bettmann.)*

Well, maybe so, but the Argument from Design will not prove it. There are basically two things wrong with the Argument from Design. First, even if it is correct, it does not prove what Paley and most other Christian, Jewish, or Muslim theologians want it to prove. And, second, it does not really prove much of anything at all. The first point is liable to slip by us because we are so mesmerized by the word "God." In the great Western religions, God is conceived as an infinite, eternal, omnipotent (infinitely powerful), omniscient (all-knowing) creator of the universe. But the most that the Argument from Design can prove, even if it is sound, is that there is a *very* long-lived (not eternal), very powerful (not omnipotent), very wise (not omniscient) world organizer who has worked up the raw materials of space, time, and matter into a reasonably well-integrated machinelike universe. After all, the watchmaker does not create his materials; he merely fashions them to his purposes. And the human eye is not infinitely complex, it is just a good deal more complex than a camera. So if the analogy is taken strictly, we can at best demonstrate the existence of a conscious, purposeful, powerful, very knowledgeable, very old world-maker. But if we label that world-maker "God," then we may mistakenly slip into identifying him or her or it with the God of the Old and New Testaments, the God of the great Western religions, the God who lays down com-

Proofs for the Existence of God

Argument from Design

Premise: The purposive organization of man-made objects is evidence of the intelligence and purpose of the maker.

Premise: The world contains many natural objects (animals, plants, the human eye, and so on) whose organization is clearly purposive and the world itself is purposively organized.

Conclusion: By analogy, there must exist a maker of the universe who has made it according to a plan. That world-maker, or Creator, is God.

Cosmological Argument

Premise: We know, by the evidence of our senses, that in the world some things are moved.

Premise: Everything that is moved must be caused to move by something else.

Argument: If each thing that moves is in turn moved by something that itself moves, which in its turn requires a cause of motion that itself moves, then there will nowhere be a first mover, and hence no motion at all. But there is motion.

Conclusion: Hence, there must be a first mover that is not itself moved. That first mover is what we call God.

Ontological Argument

Premise: I possess the idea of a being than which no greater can be conceived. That idea includes within it everything that belongs essentially to such a being.

Premise: To exist in actuality is greater than merely to be possible.

Argument: The idea of that, than which nothing greater can be conceived, includes the idea of its existence, which thus belongs to it necessarily.

Conclusion: Hence, that, than which nothing greater can be conceived, exists, and it is this that we call God.

mandments, punishes the wicked, offers the free gift of eternal life, and so forth. And absolutely nothing in the analogy justifies any of those conclusions.

But the argument is not very sound, as David Hume pointed out in one of his most brilliant works, the *Dialogues Concerning Natural Religion.* Hume actually wrote the *Dialogues* in the 1750s, twenty years before his death in 1776, but he was prevailed upon by his friends (including the economist and philosopher Adam Smith) to withhold them from publication because the forcefulness of their attack on received religious opinions would open Hume to condemnation. Eventually, they were brought out posthumously in 1779 by his nephew. The work is a three-person discussion of all the principal arguments for the existence of God, in which first one character and then another comes to the fore. In the subtlety of their development and pacing, the *Dialogues* have something of the quality of a Baroque trio, and I think it may fairly be said that Hume is the only great philosopher after Plato to use the dialogue form to its full literary effect. The work is in twelve parts, and this selection comes from Part Two. The speaker is the skeptic, Philo:

DAVID HUME,
*Dialogues Concerning
Natural Religion*

In reality, Cleanthes, continued he, there is no need of having recourse to that affected skepticism, so displeasing to you, in order to come at this determination. Our ideas reach no farther than our experience: We have no experience of divine attributes and operations: I need not conclude my syllogism: You can draw the inference yourself. And it is a pleasure to me (and I hope to you too) that just reasoning and sound piety here concur in the same conclusion, and both of them establish the adorably mysterious and incomprehensible nature of the supreme Being.

What I chiefly scruple in this subject, said Philo, is not so much, that all religious arguments are by Cleanthes reduced to experience, as that they appear not to be even the most certain and irrefragable of that inferior kind. That a stone will fall, that fire will burn, that the earth has solidity, we have observed a thousand and a thousand times; and when any new instance of this nature is presented, we draw without hesitation the accustomed inference. The exact similarity of the cases gives us a perfect assurance of a similar event; and a stronger evidence is never desired nor sought after. But wherever you depart, in the least, from the similarity of the cases, you diminish proportionably the evidence; and may at last bring it to a very weak *analogy,* which is confessedly liable to error and uncertainty. After having experienced the circulation of the blood in human creatures, we make no doubt that it takes place in Titius and Maevius: But from its circulation in frogs and fishes, it is only a presumption, though a strong one, from analogy, that it takes place in men and other animals. The analogical reasoning is much weaker, when we infer the circulation of the sap in vegetables from our experience that the blood circulates in animals; and those, who hastily followed that imperfect analogy, are found, by more accurate experiments, to have been mistaken.

If we see a house, Cleanthes, we conclude, with the greatest certainty, that it had an architect or builder, because this is precisely that species of *effect,* which we have experienced to proceed from that species of cause. But surely you will not affirm, that the universe bears such a resemblance to a house, that we can with the same certainty infer a similar cause, or that the analogy is here entire and perfect. The dissimilitude is so striking, that the utmost you can here pretend to is a guess, a conjecture, a presumption concerning a similar cause; and how that pretension will be received in the world, I leave you to consider.

Were a man to abstract from every thing which he knows or has seen, he would be altogether incapable, merely from his own ideas, to determine what kind of scene the universe must be, or to give the preference to one state or situation of things above another. For as nothing, which he clearly conceives, could be esteemed impossible or implying a contradiction, every chimera of his fancy would be upon an equal footing; nor could he assign any just reason, why he adheres to one idea or system, and rejects the others, which are equally possible.

Again; after he opens his eyes, and contemplates the world, as it really is, it would be impossible for him, at first, to assign the cause of any one event, much less, of the whole of things or of the universe. He might set his fancy a rambling; and she might bring him in an infinite variety of reports and representations. These would all be possible; but being all equally possible, he would never, of himself, give a satisfactory account for his preferring one of them to the rest. Experience alone can point out to him the true cause of any phenomenon.

David Hume, *Dialogues Concerning Natural Religion*

Although Hume's refutation stands pretty well on its own feet, it also draws upon the more fundamental criticisms which Hume developed of causal reasoning of all sorts.

Thomas Aquinas: The Cosmological Argument

Christian theologians derive their beliefs about God from two sources. The first is *revelation,* consisting of those truths which God has revealed to us through the holy writings of the Old and New Testaments or through His miraculous appearance to particular individuals. Revelation must of course be interpreted, and therein lies the origin of many learned disputes and bloody wars. But everyone agrees that the *fact* of revelation is simply a miracle, to be taken on faith. The second source is *reason,* our natural human power of analysis, argument, observation, and inference. We must wait for revelation. We cannot make it happen, and we cannot predict when or where God will reveal Himself. But reason is our own instrument, and we can deploy it at will to seek out the origins of the universe and the existence and nature of a Creator. The greatest of all the rational theologians, by universal agreement, is the thirteenth-century Christian philosopher St. Thomas Aquinas. His elaboration and codification of the rational metaphysical basis for Christian theology remains to this day the dominant intellectual influence in the Roman Catholic Church. The philosophy known as Thomism is an enduring monument of medieval intellectual architecture, as impressive in its way as the great Cathedral of Notre Dame in Paris.

Aquinas actually offers five separate *proofs* for the existence of God in his most important work, the *Summa Theologica.* The first three of these are variations of the same argument, and we shall examine them all together. In each case, Aquinas begins with some fact about the world: the first argument takes off from the fact that things *move* in the world around us; the second from the fact that every event that is observed to take place is made to happen, or is caused, by something else that precedes it; the third from the fact that there are at least some things in the world whose existence is not necessary, which are, in metaphysical language, "possible."

Aquinas then reasons that the observed motion, or event, or possible thing, is the last in a chain of motions or causes or possible things, and he asserts that such a chain cannot reach back endlessly to prior motions, to earlier causes, to other possible things on which this thing depends for its existence. Somewhere, the chain must end, with a mover that is not itself also moved by something else, with a cause that is not itself caused by yet another cause, with a being whose existence is not merely possible but necessary. That first mover, first cause, or necessary being is God.

If the task of proving the existence of God were not such a serious business, we might say that the **Cosmological Argument** is a very sophisticated answer to the four-year-old's question, "Where did I come from, Mommy?" Now a straight answer would be, "You came from inside Mommy's womb." And after a few more details have been added, that answer usually satisfies a four-year-old. Eventually, the obvious follow-up question will occur to a six- or seven-year-old, namely, "Where did you come from, Mommy?" A somewhat longer story about Grandma and Grandpa should handle that one. But sooner or later, a bright child is going to start brooding on the *real* problem. Maybe I came from Mom and Dad, each of whom came in turn from a mother and father; maybe the earliest human mothers and fathers evolved through a combination and mutation and selection from prehuman mammals, who in turn evolved from reptiles, or what have you; and maybe life itself sprang up spontaneously through chance rearrangements of amino acid-like compounds, which in turn emerged from the stuff of which the earth was formed, but *damn it,* somewhere the buck has got to stop! If there is not anything that was *first,* then how can there be anything at all? If the existence of each particular thing is to be explained by saying that it came from some preceding thing, then we have no explanation at all. We just have a chain that leads so far back into the misty past that finally we get tired of asking and mistake our fatigue for an answer. In short, an "infinite regress" is no answer at all. We might just as well have answered the very first question by saying, "Shut up and don't ask silly questions!"

So we might summarize Aquinas' proofs by saying that if the universe makes any sense at all, if it is through and through rational, then there must be a necessary being, a first mover, a first cause. Here are the three proofs as Aquinas stated them. Notice that he does not waste any words. He proves the existence of God three times in the space it takes Plato to introduce one of the characters in a Dialogue.

Cosmological Argument   The attempt to prove the existence of God by starting with the mere fact of motion, or change, or the existence of things in the universe, and then arguing that these must have their origin in a being that does not move, or does not change, or does not merely happen to exist. The earliest form of the argument is to be found in the writings of Aristotle.

La Creazione dell'uomo. God's creation of Adam, as rendered by the great Italian painter Michelangelo. (*Source:* Art Resource N.Y.)

The existence of God can be proved in five ways.

The first and more manifest way is the argument from motion. It is certain and evident to our senses that in the world some things are in motion. Now whatever is moved is moved by another, for nothing can be moved except it is in potentiality to that towards which it is moved; whereas a thing moves inasmuch as it is in act. For motion is nothing else than the reduction of something from potentiality to actuality. But nothing can be reduced from potentiality to actuality, except by something in a state of actuality. Thus that which is actually hot, as fire, makes wood, which is potentially hot, to be actually hot, and thereby moves and changes it. Now it is not possible that the same thing should be at once in actuality and potentiality in the same respect but only in different respects. For what is actually hot cannot simultaneously be potentially hot; but it is simultaneously potentially cold. It is therefore impossible that in the same respect and in the same way a thing should be both mover and moved, i.e., that it should move itself. Therefore, whatever is moved must be moved by another. If that by which it is moved be itself moved, then this also must needs be moved by another, and that by another again. But this

ST. THOMAS AQUINAS, *Summa Theologica*

cannot go on to infinity, because then there would be no first mover, and consequently, no other mover, seeing that subsequent movers move only inasmuch as they are moved by the first mover, as the staff moves only because it is moved by the hand. Therefore it is necessary to arrive at a first mover, moved by no other, and this everyone understands to be God.

The second way is from the nature of efficient cause. In the world of sensible things we find there is an order of efficient causes. There is no case known (neither is it, indeed, possible) in which a thing is found to be the efficient cause of itself; for so it would be prior to itself, which is impossible. Now in efficient causes it is not possible to go on to infinity, because in all efficient causes following in order, the first is the cause of the intermediate cause, and the intermediate is the cause of the ultimate cause, whether the intermediate cause be several, or one only. Now to take away the cause is to take away the effect. Therefore, if there be no first cause among efficient causes, there will be no ultimate, not any intermediate, cause. But if in efficient causes it is possible to go on to infinity, there will be no first efficient cause, neither will there be an ultimate effect, nor any intermediate efficient causes; all of which is plainly false. Therefore it is necessary to admit a first efficient cause, to which everyone gives the name of God.

ST. THOMAS AQUINAS

St. Thomas Aquinas (1225–1274) is the greatest intellectual figure of the high medieval culture that flourished in Europe during the thirteenth century. Aquinas was an Italian theologian and philosopher who spent his life in the Dominican Order teaching and writing. His writings, which run to many volumes, set forth in extremely systematic form a full-scale theory of God, man, and the universe. The official dogma of the Church, as established by revelation and interpretation of holy scriptures, was combined by Aquinas with the secular metaphysical doctrines of Aristotle and the post-Aristotelian Greek and Roman philosophers.

Aquinas' philosophical synthesis of philosophy and theology became the accepted teaching of the Roman Catholic Church. It is known today as Thomism, and in various forms it continues to exercise a profound intellectual influence both on Church doctrine and on the philosophical work of Catholic and non-Catholic thinkers.

The third way is taken from possibility and necessity, and runs thus. We find in nature things that are possible to be and not to be, since they are found to be generated, and to be corrupted, and consequently, it is possible for them to be and not to be. But it is impossible for these always to exist, for that which can not-be at some time is not. Therefore, if everything can not-be, then at one time there was nothing in existence. Now if this were true, even now there would be nothing in existence, because that which does not exist begins to exist only through something already existing. Therefore, if at one time nothing was in existence, it would have been impossible for anything to have begun to exist; and thus even now nothing would be in existence—which is absurd. Therefore, not all beings are merely possible, but there must exist something the existence of which is necessary. But every necessary thing either has its necessity caused by another, or not. Now it is impossible to go on to infinity in necessary things which have their necessity caused by another, as has been already proved in regard to efficient causes. Therefore we cannot but admit the existence of some being having of itself its own necessity, and not receiving it from another, but rather causing in others their necessity. This all men speak of as God.

St. Thomas Aquinas, *Summa Theologica*

Hume has an answer to these arguments as well as to the argument from design. In Part IX of his *Dialogues,* he considers a version that reasons from cause and effect to the existence of a first cause, whose existence must therefore be necessary. It is thus a combination of the second and third of Aquinas' proofs. Hume's refutation, put this time into the mouth of the character named Cleanthes, begins with a paragraph that also is a refutation of the third great proof, the ontological argument. More of that a little later.

DAVID HUME,
Dialogues Concerning Natural Religion

I shall begin with observing, that there is an evident absurdity in pretending to demonstrate a matter of fact, or to prove it by any arguments *a priori*. Nothing is demonstrable, unless the contrary implies a contradiction. Nothing, that is distinctly conceivable, implies a contradiction. Whatever we conceive as existent, we can also conceive as non-existent. There is no Being, therefore, whose non-existence implies a contradiction. Consequently there is no Being, whose existence is demonstrable. I propose this argument as entirely decisive, and am willing to rest the whole controversy upon it.

It is pretended that the Deity is a necessarily existent Being; and this necessity of his existence is attempted to be explained by asserting that, if we knew his whole essence or nature, we should perceive it to be as impossible for him not to exist as for twice two not to be four. But it is evident, that this can never happen, while our faculties remain the same as at present. It will still be possible for us, at any time, to conceive the non-existence of what we formerly conceived to exist; nor can the mind ever lie under a necessity of supposing any object to remain always in being: in the same manner as we lie under a necessity of always conceiving twice two to be four. The words, therefore, *necessary existence,* have no meaning; or, which is the same thing, none that is consistent.

But farther, why may not the material universe be the necessarily existent Being, according to this pretended explication of necessity? We dare not affirm that we know all the qualities of matter, and for aught we can determine, it may contain some qualities, which, were they known, would make its non-existence appear as great a contradiction as that twice two is five. I find only one argument employed to prove, that the material world is not the necessarily existent Being; and this argument is derived from the contingency both of the matter and the form of the world. "Any particle of matter," it is said, "may be *conceived* to be annihilated; and any form may be *conceived* to be altered. Such an annihilation or alteration, therefore, is not impossible." But it seems a great partiality not to perceive, that the same argument extends equally to the Deity, so far as we have any conception of him; and that the mind can at least imagine him to be non-existent, or his attributes to be altered. It must be some unknown, inconceivable qualities, which can make non-existence appear impossible, or his attributes unalterable. And no reason can be assigned, why these qualities may not belong to matter. As they are altogether unknown and inconceivable, they can never be proved incompatible with it.

Add to this, that in tracing an eternal succession of objects, it seems absurd to inquire for a general cause or first Author. How can any thing, that exists from eternity, have a cause, since that relation implies a priority in time and a beginning of existence?

In such a chain too, or succession of objects, each part is caused by that which preceded it, and causes that which succeeds it. Where then is the difficulty? But the *whole,* you say, wants a cause. I answer, that the uniting of these parts into a whole, like the uniting of several distinct counties into one kingdom, or several distinct members into one body, is performed merely by an arbitrary act of the mind, and has no influence on the nature of things. Did I show you the particular causes of each individual in a collection of twenty particles of matter, I should think it very unreasonable, should you afterwards ask me, what was the cause of the whole twenty. This is sufficiently explained in explaining the cause of the parts.

 David Hume,
*Dialogues Concerning
Natural Religion*

St. Anselm: The Ontological Argument

Here it is, the most famous, the most mystifying, the most outrageous and irritating philosophical argument of all time! Read it carefully and see what you think.

And so, Lord, do thou, who dost give understanding to faith, give me, so far as thou knowest it to be profitable, to understand that thou art as we believe; and that thou art that which we believe. And, indeed, we believe that thou art a being than which nothing greater can be conceived. Or is there no such nature, since the fool hath said in his heart, there is no God? (Psalms XIV. 1). But, at any rate, this very fool, when he hears of this being of which I speak—a being than which nothing greater can be conceived—understands what he hears, and what he understands is in his understanding; although he does not understand it to exist.

For, it is one thing for an object to be in the understanding, and another to understand that the object exists. When a painter first conceives of what he will afterwards perform, he has it in his understanding, but he does not yet understand it to be, because he has not yet performed it. But after he has made the painting, he both has it in his understanding, and he understands that it exists, because he has made it.

Hence, even the fool is convinced that something exists in the understanding, at least, than which nothing greater can be conceived. For, when he hears of this, he understands it. And whatever is understood, exists in the understanding. And, assuredly that, than

ST. ANSELM,
Proslogion

S T .   A N S E L M

Saint Anselm (1033–1109) was born in Italy and was trained there for the priesthood. In 1093, he was appointed Archbishop of Canterbury in England by the Norman king William Rufus. His most important philosophical work is the *Proslogion,* in which he set forth a startling and radically new proof for the existence of God. The proof, known now as the Ontological Argument, has been defended over the past nine centuries by Descartes, Spinoza, and others. St. Thomas Aquinas, on the other hand, claimed it was not a valid proof, and he rejected it.

This drawing shows the ceremony in which Anselm (standing, with hand raised) was appointed Archbishop of Canterbury by the king.

which nothing greater can be conceived, cannot exist in the understanding alone. For, suppose it exists in the understanding alone: then it can be conceived to exist in reality; which is greater.

Therefore, if that, than which nothing greater can be conceived, exists in the understanding alone, the very being, than which nothing greater can be conceived, is one, than which a greater can be conceived. But obviously this is impossible. Hence, there is no doubt that there exists a being, than which nothing greater can be conceived, and it exists both in the understanding and in reality.

And it assuredly exists so truly, that it cannot be conceived not to exist. For, it is possible to conceive of a being which cannot be conceived not to exist; and this is greater than one which can be conceived not to exist. Hence, if that, than which nothing greater can be conceived, can be conceived not to exist, it is not that, than which nothing greater can be conceived. But this is an irreconcilable contradiction. There is, then, so truly a being than which nothing greater can be conceived to exist, that it cannot even be conceived not to exist; and this being thou art, O Lord, our God.

So truly, therefore, dost thou exist, O Lord, my God, that thou canst not be conceived not to exist; and rightly. For, if a mind could conceive of a being better than thee, the creature would rise above the Creator, and this is most absurd. And, indeed, whatever else there is, except thee alone, can be conceived not to exist. To thee alone, therefore, it belongs to exist more truly than all other beings, and hence in a higher degree than all others. For, whatever else exists does not exist so truly, and hence in a less degree it belongs to it to exist. Why, then, has the fool said in his heart, there is no God (Psalms XIV. 1), since it is so evident, to a rational mind, that thou does exist in the highest degree of all? Why, except that he is dull and a fool?

St. Anselm,
Proslogion

Whenever I read the *Ontological Argument,* I have the same feeling that comes over me when I watch a really good magician. Nothing up this sleeve; nothing up the other sleeve; nothing in the hat; presto! A big, fat rabbit. How can Anselm pull God out of an idea? At least the Argument from Design and the Cosmological Argument start from some actual fact about the world, whether it is the apparently purposeful organization of living things, or the motion of bodies in space, or whatever. But the Ontological Argument starts from a mere idea in the mind of the philosopher and undertakes to prove, from that idea alone, that there must actually be something corresponding to the idea. The argument makes no use at all of facts that might be gathered by observation or analysis of the world. Philosophers call an argument of this sort an *a priori* argument. Propositions that can be known to be true without consideration of factual support, merely from an analysis of the concepts involved in the judgments, are called propositions *knowable a priori,* or simply, "*a priori* propositions."

Now philosophers have for a long time held that there are *a priori* propositions, or propositions whose truth can be known merely from a consideration of their meaning. For example, consider the proposition, "If an aardvark is a mammal, then it bears its young live." Is that true? Well, your first reaction might be to ask yourself whether you know what an aardvark is, or maybe to look it up in the encyclopedia. But stop and think about it for a moment. A mammal is an animal that bears its young live rather than laying eggs. That is what we *mean* when we call something a mammal. This is part of the definition of the word "mammal." So if anything is to be classified as a mammal, it will have to be the sort of thing that bears its young live, otherwise we would not call it a mammal, we would call it something else, or even just say that we do not have a word for it. If you think about it, you will realize that you can decide about the truth of my proposition without knowing anything about aardvarks, indeed without ever having heard the word "aardvark" before. Whatever aardvarks are, "If an aardvark is a mammal, then it bears its young live." In short, you can know the truth of the proposition *a priori,* or even more briefly, it is an *a priori* proposition.

But are there any aardvarks? Ah well, that is quite another question. My *a priori* proposition only tells me that if there are any, and if they are mammals, then they bear their young live. It does not tell me whether there are any. Indeed, it does not even tell me whether aardvarks are mammals. It just says, *if* there are aardvarks and they are mammals, then they bear their young live. Propositions that can be known to be true merely on the basis of the meanings of the words used in them are called tautologies, and you can make up tautologies all day long, with no more material to work with than the English language.

The **Ontological Argument** seems to depend on a tautology too. First, Anselm *defines* the word "God" as meaning "a being than which nothing greater can be conceived." Then he argues that this concept of a greatest being must include the notion that the being cannot be conceived not to exist. In other words, he argues that when we spell out the definition of "God" as "a being than which nothing greater can be conceived," we will find that the definition includes the characteristic "necessarily existing," just as when we spell out the definition of "mammal" we find that it includes the notion "bearing its young live."

Ontological Argument   The attempt to prove the existence of God by starting with nothing more than the mere concept of the most perfect being. The argument is extremely controversial and has been rejected as invalid by many religious philosophers, including the leading medieval proponent of the Cosmological Argument, St. Thomas Aquinas.

Well, "Mammals bear their young live" is a tautology; it is true by definition; we can know it to be true merely by understanding the words used in
the statement. It follows from the definition. So too, Anselm claims, "God necessarily exists" is a tautology; it too is true by definition; it too can be known
merely through an understanding of the words used in the statement. But
there is one enormous difference. The statement about mammals, and all of
the other ordinary tautologies that have ever been thought up, say nothing
about whether something *exists*. Ordinary tautologies just tell us that *if* there
are any things fitting a certain definition, *then* they have the following characteristics. If there are mammals, then they bear their young live; if there are
any bachelors, then they are unmarried (because "bachelor" means "unmarried man"); if there are any triangles, then they have three angles; and so
forth. The Ontological Argument is the only case in which a tautology is used
to prove that something—namely, God—exists.

Now of course philosophers who use the Ontological Argument are perfectly well aware that this is a very special and peculiar sort of tautology. If
they can prove the existence of God this way, why can't I use the same trick
to prove the existence of a perfect horse, or a necessarily existent ox, or a
mosquito than which none greater can be conceived? Their answer is that
God is different from all of the other beings in or out of the universe, and that
God's existence is a different sort of existence from the existence of every
created thing. God is infinite, all other things are finite; God's existence is necessary, the existence of every other thing is merely contingent; God is perfect,
all else is imperfect; and God's existence follows *a priori* from His definition,
whereas the existence of every other thing, since it depends ultimately on
God and not on itself alone, follows *not* from its own definition but only from
God's act of creation.

The Ontological Argument remains to this day one of the most controversial arguments in all of philosophy. Some very devout theologians, including St. Thomas Aquinas, have believed that it was wrong, invalid, a confusion.
Several of the greatest philosophers of the seventeenth century, including
Descartes and Spinoza, thought it was valid and developed their own versions
of it. In his great *Critique of Pure Reason,* Immanuel Kant offered an elaborate
refutation of the argument that for more than 100 years was thought to have
permanently laid it to rest. In this century, however, there has been a revival
of philosophical interest in the Ontological Argument, and philosophers like
myself, who grew up thinking that Kant had once and for all finished it off,
now find the technical journals full of new versions of the Ontological Argument, in which the latest tools of formal logic are used to give the old
warhorse some new life.

Let us wind up this discussion of proofs for the existence of God with
Kant's refutation of the Ontological Argument. This is a difficult passage,
harder even than the argument itself, which was no breeze. Please do not expect to understand everything Kant is saying. I have been studying Kant for

forty-five years, and I am not sure what he means sometimes. But read through this selection two or three times, with the aid of your professor. Kant always repays hard work, and his treatment of the Ontological Argument is one of his most brilliant efforts.

One bit of explanation before you begin. Kant asks whether the proposition "God exists" is an *analytic* or a *synthetic* proposition. An analytic proposition, according to Kant, is a statement that merely spells out, or *analyzes,* what is already contained in the subject of the statement. For example, the proposition "Triangles have three angles" tells us nothing new about triangles. All it does is repeat what is already contained in the idea of a triangle. Synthetic propositions, on the other hand, add something to what is contained in the idea of the subject of the proposition. "Bachelors are unhappy" is synthetic (whether or not it is true!), because being unhappy is *not* part of what we mean by being a bachelor. "Bachelors are unmarried" is analytic, however, for being unmarried *is* part of what we mean by being a bachelor. Kant argues, as you will see, that any proposition that asserts the existence of something must be a synthetic proposition. He thinks that this claim successfully undermines the Ontological Argument.

Kant's Critique of the Ontological Argument

Notwithstanding all these general considerations, in which every one must concur, we may be challenged with a case which is brought forward as proof that in actual fact the contrary holds, namely, that there is one concept, and indeed only one, in reference to which the not-being or rejection of its object is in itself contradictory, namely, the concept of the *ens realissimum*. It is declared that it possesses all reality, and that we are justified in assuming that such a being is possible (the fact that a concept does not contradict itself by no means proves the possibility of its object: but the contrary assertion I am for the moment willing to allow). Now "all reality" includes existence; existence is therefore contained in the concept of a thing that is possible. If, then, this thing is rejected, the internal possibility of the thing is rejected—which is self-contradictory.

My answer is as follows. There is already a contradiction in introducing the concept of existence—no matter under what title it may be disguised—into the concept of a thing which we profess to be thinking solely in reference to its possibility. If that be allowed as legitimate, a seeming victory has been won: but in actual fact nothing at all is said: the assertion is a mere tautology. We must ask: Is the proposition that *this* or *that thing* (which, whatever it may be, is allowed as possible) *exists,* an analytic or a synthetic proposition? If it is analytic, the assertion of the existence of the thing adds nothing to the thought of the thing; but in that case either the thought, which is in us, is the thing itself, or we have pre-supposed an existence as

IMMANUEL KANT,
Critique of Pure Reason

belonging to the realm of the possible, and have then, on that pretext, inferred its existence from its internal possibility—which is nothing but a miserable tautology. The word "reality," which in the concept of the thing sounds other than the word "existence" in the concept of the predicate, is of no avail in meeting this objection. For if all positing (no matter what it may be that is posited) is entitled reality, the thing with all its predicates is already posited in the concept of the subject, and is assumed as actual; and in the predicate this is merely repeated. But if, on the other hand, we admit, as every reasonable person must, that all existential propositions are synthetic, how can we profess to maintain that the predicate of existence cannot be rejected without contradiction? This is a feature which is found only in analytic propositions, and is indeed precisely what constitutes their analytic character.

I should have hoped to put an end to these idle and fruitless disputations in a direct manner, by an accurate determination of the concept of existence, had I not found that the illusion which is caused by the confusion of a logical with a real predicate (that is, with a predicate which determines a thing) is almost beyond correction. Anything we please can be made to serve as a logical predicate; the subject can even be predicated of itself; for logic abstracts from all content. But a *determining* predicate is a predicate which is added to the concept of the subject and enlarges it. Consequently, it must not be already contained in the concept.

"*Being*" is obviously not a real predicate; that is, it is not a concept of something which could be added to the concept of a thing. It is merely the positing of a thing, or of certain determinations, as existing in themselves. Logically, it is merely the copula of a judgment. The proposition, "God is omnipotent," contains two concepts, each of which has its object—God and omnipotence. The small word "is" adds no new predicate, but only serves to posit the predicate *in its relation* to the subject. If, now, we take the subject (God) with all its predicates (among which is omnipotence), and say "God is," or "There is a God," we attach no new predicate to the concept of God, but only posit the subject in itself with all its predicates, and indeed posit it as being an *object* that stands in relation to my *concept*. The content of both must be one and the same; nothing can have been added to the concept, which expresses merely what is possible, by my thinking its object (through the expression "it is") as given absolutely. Otherwise stated, the real contains no more than the merely possible. A hundred real thalers do not contain the least coin more than a hundred possible thalers. For as the latter signify the concept, and the former the object and the positing of the object, should the former contain more than the latter, my concept would not, in that case, express the whole object, and would not therefore be an adequate concept of it. My financial position is, however, affected very differently by a hundred real thalers than it is by the mere concept of them (that is, of their possibility). For the object, as it actually exists, is not analytically contained in my concept, but is added to my concept (which is a determination of my state) synthetically; and yet the conceived hundred thalers are not themselves in the least increased through thus acquiring existence outside my concept.

 Immanuel Kant, *Critique of Pure Reason*

The Problem of Evil

The two approaches to religion that we have been looking at in this chapter—the subjective, faith-based approach, and the objective, rational approach—meet their greatest challenge in the problem of evil, or perhaps I should say the "problems" of evil, because we can distinguish three different, although related, problems that confront us when we contemplate the existence of evil in the world: the existential problem, the logical problem, and the evidential problem. All three problems arise out of fundamental beliefs about the nature of God.

According to Judeo-Christian and Islamic teachings, God is omnipotent (all-powerful), omniscient (all-knowing), and all-good (righteous, loving, benevolent): God can do anything, knows everything, and is the very essence of goodness. But the world is full of suffering, natural disaster, human depravity, and death. Thousands of people die every day from starvation. Earthquakes destroy entire communities, killing hundreds, or even thousands, of people in their wake. Adult men kidnap, molest, and cruelly murder little children. In the wards of almost every large hospital are children dying from incurable cancer or other diseases. How can God, who is all-powerful, all-knowing, and infinitely good, cause—or even permit—such evil? Couldn't an omnipotent God have arranged things differently?

It isn't as if we expect a loving, benevolent God to protect us from each and every risk. Often God is portrayed as a loving father, and our own fathers didn't keep us from trying to do things that might lead us to harm. They understood that in order for us to learn to cope with the world around us, and to prepare for productive lives, we would have to learn to deal with risk. They didn't stop us from climbing trees because we might fall and break an arm—and some of us did just that.

We also can understand that sometimes people bring misfortune upon themselves. For example, a man consumes too much alcohol and gets himself into a fatal automobile accident. A tourist who knows better carelessly drinks unpurified water and contracts cholera. An adventurer steps too close to the edge of a precipice or the rim of an active volcano, and falls to his death.

And sometimes misfortune seems deserved, as when we are punished for being mean to a younger sibling, or for lying to a parent, or for cheating on an exam.

But what do we say to a young mother whose baby is dying of cancer? Surely the baby didn't bring the disease on herself, or take some foolish risk. Or what about the parents of a young girl kidnaped from her own bedroom, raped, tortured and brutally murdered? What important life lesson did the girl learn from the experience, that would help her prepare for a happy, productive life? And what about the Holocaust, the WWII extermination of millions of Jews and other people that the Nazis thought were undesirable? Some observers of the Holocaust are reported to have asked, "Where was God?" (We probably shouldn't take the question literally, since God also is said to be omnipresent [everywhere]). "Why didn't God do anything about the slaughter of millions?" "What possible justification could there be for God to allow such evil?"

Many true believers, when faced with such hard questions, simply submit to what they think must be the will of God: "We shouldn't ask such questions," they say. "These things are simply beyond our understanding. 'God moves in mysterious ways, His wonders to perform.'" This is their way of dealing with the problem of evil.

Other people, however, of a more critical bent, would like to *understand* how an omnipotent, omniscient, all-good God can allow little children to suffer from incurable diseases, or idly stand by while millions of Jews are incinerated in extermination ovens, or do nothing about the devastation of floods, earthquakes, and tornados.

How do we come to terms, at a deeply personal level, with the evil that we see in the world? How does it affect our belief in God, or our thinking about the meaning of life? How can we help others cope with terrible loss? This is the existential problem of evil, and the classic statement of the problem is in the Old Testament Book of Job.

Job was a prosperous, righteous man who befell hardship after hardship and yet retained his belief and trust in God. According to the story, enemy tribes stole Job's livestock and killed some of his servants. Fire from heaven consumed his sheep and more servants. Other enemies stole his camels and killed still more servants. Some of his children were killed when a mighty wind blew down the house in which they were eating and drinking. And then Job was afflicted with painful boils from his head down to the soles of his feet. His wife even counseled him to "Curse God, and die!" Throughout all these ordeals Job's faith remained steadfast. Although his faith was tested, Job did not come to the conclusion that God does not exist. He somehow found a way to deal with the existential problem of evil.

The Book of Job has a happy ending: the Lord rewarded Job in his latter days with more sheep, camels, oxen, and children than he had before. Of course not all of us suffer such horrible hardships as Job did, but neither do some of our stories have such happy endings.

By now you probably have noticed that the existential problem of evil is a problem for atheists as well as believers. Nonbelievers and believers alike, each in their own way, must find a way to deal with the evil in the world around them, although believers may experience the problem more acutely since they must reconcile evil with their conception of God.

The *logical* and *evidential* problems of evil provide the bases for the most important arguments against the existence of God, the arguments from evil. (In what follows, I shall use 'the problem of evil' and 'the argument from evil' interchangeably.) These arguments are different, in an important way, from the arguments we have considered so far. We have seen that Aquinas, Anselm, Paley, and others, advanced arguments to prove that God exists. And Kant, Hume, and others pointed out what they saw as weaknesses in such arguments: they argued in effect that the arguments do not prove that God exists. But of course showing that an argument doesn't prove that a proposition is true isn't the same thing as proving that the proposition is false. The difference is similar to one we learned in high school geometry: our failure to prove that a theorem is true—for example, that the square of the hypotenuse is equal to the sum of the squares of the other two sides—isn't the same as proving that the Pythagorean theorem is false, which, of course, it isn't.

The aim of the arguments from evil is to prove that God does not exist—or at least to prove that belief in God is irrational—because God's existence is incompatible with the presence of evil in the world. The argument arising from the logical problem of evil revolves around apparent logical inconsistencies between certain claims about the nature of God, on the one hand, and claims about evil, on the other. Here is the way David Hume posed the problem in the *Dialogues Concerning Natural Religion* you have already met in this chapter. Cleanthes and Philo have been talking about the variety of miseries and afflictions faced by human beings. Philo then poses the problem. This passage is taken from the Tenth Dialogue:

> [God's] power we allow is infinite. Whatever he wills is executed: But neither man nor any other animal is happy: Therefore he does not will their happiness. His wisdom is infinite: He is never mistaken in choosing the means to any end: But the course of nature tends not to human or animal felicity: There it is not established for that purpose. Through the whole compass of human knowledge, there are no inferences more certain and infallible than these. . .
>
> *Epicurus's* old questions are yet unanswered. Is he willing to prevent evil, but not able? Then is he impotent. Is he able, but not willing: then he is malevolent. Is he both able and willing? Whence then is evil?

There it is. As Epicurus says, if God is willing to prevent evil (benevolent) but not able, then he is not omnipotent. If he is able (omnipotent) but not willing, then he is not benevolent. [And, though Epicurus does not add this, if God is able to prevent evil, and willing to prevent evil, then he must not know about it, in which case he is not omniscient.]

Here is the way the Oxford philosopher J. L. Mackie stated the problem in his paper, "Evil and Omnipotence:"

> In its simplest form the problem is this: God is omnipotent; God is wholly good; and yet evil exists. There seems to be some contradiction between these three propositions, so that if any two of them were true, the third would be false. But at the same time all three are essential parts of most theological positions: the theologian, it seems, at once *must* adhere and *cannot consistently* adhere to all three.[1]

Please notice that the logical argument from evil does not prove atheism, the view that no supernatural deity ('god' with a small 'g') exists. (It leaves open the possibility that there might be a god with any two of the traditional attributes, for example.) But it does set out to prove that God, at least as God is portrayed in Judeo-Christian and Islamic teachings, does not exist. Moreover, it attempts to prove that God so portrayed cannot exist—there are logical inconsistencies between claims about God as portrayed, on the one hand, and claims about evil, on the other.

Other thinkers come to believe that although claims about the nature of God, and claims about the evil in the world, are not logically inconsistent, the presence of evil in the world nevertheless provides overwhelming evidence that an omnipotent, omniscient, all-good God simply does not exist.

For some people, the problem of evil leads, not to the conviction that God does not exist, but to agnosticism, the "I just don't know" position. In his *Autobiography,* John Stuart Mill, whom you met in Chapter 6, wrote eloquently about the crisis of faith that his father, James Mill, experienced when he was faced with the challenge of the problem of evil:

> My father, educated in the creed of Scotch presbyterianism, had by his own studies and reflexions been early led to reject not only the belief in revelation, but the foundations of what is commonly called Natural Religion. . . . [D]oubtless after many struggles, he yielded to the conviction, that concerning the origin of things nothing whatever can be known. This is the only correct statement of his opinion; for dogmatic atheism he looked upon as absurd . . . [but h]e found it impossible to believe that a world so full of evil was the work of an Author combining infinite power with perfect goodness and righteousness (John Stuart Mill, *Autobiography,* 25-26).[2]

Some thinkers have responded to the problem of evil by suggesting that evil is illusory, or that it is merely the privation of good, or even that it does not exist at all! Given the enormity of the Holocaust, or the suffering caused by smallpox epidemics in the past, this seems wildly implausible to me, and I have found that many of my students have felt the same way. Others have suggested that perhaps God is not omnipotent, so that the inconsistency apparent in the problem of evil as we have stated it does not arise; and according to the religious teachings of Manichaeism, the universe is divided into two contending realms, one good, governed by God, and the other evil, governed by Satan. But most believing Christians, Jews, and Muslims find these suggestions unsatisfactory, if not downright heretical.

So what can a faithful Christian, Jew, or Muslim possibly say in response to the challenge posed by the problem of evil? *Theodicy* is the attempt to defend the goodness and omnipotence of God in the face of evil in the world—in the words of John Milton, "[To] justify the ways of God to men" (*Paradise Lost,* I.26),[3] or, in the words of Alexander Pope, "[To] vindicate the ways of God to man" (*An Essay on Man,* I.16).[4]

One line of defense, the "free will defense," relies on the distinction between moral evils and natural evils. Moral evils are those that inhere in or are caused by the wicked actions of human beings, such as the Holocaust, rape, murder, and torturing the innocent. Moral evils are said to be compatible with God's infinite goodness because they flow, not directly from God, but from the free will which God has granted human beings. As we saw in Chapter 3, the notion of free will is itself problematic, but here is the way it is used as a defense against the problem of evil: God, being omnipotent, could have created human beings in any way he saw fit. One way would have been to create human beings incapable of choosing to rape or murder or torture the innocent, or even to think impure thoughts—in short, without free will. Such creatures would never choose evil because they could not choose evil. But they would be mere automata, not moral agents, not fully human beings. And, it is argued, a world with fully human beings in it, even those who commit moral evils, is better than a world of automata.

In contrast, natural evils are those caused by natural forces, such as the eruption of Mt. Vesuvius in 71 A.D. that destroyed Pompeii and Herculaneum, the Bubonic Plague that decimated the population of Western Europe in the 14th century A.D., and the Lisbon Earthquake that killed 60,000 in 1755. What defense is available to the believer here?

Perhaps the most promising tack is the one taken by the brilliant German seventeenth-century logician, mathematician, and philosopher Gottfried Leibniz, who agreed that there is evil in the world, but went on to argue that the world nevertheless is the best of all the possible worlds that God could have created. Yes, God is omnipotent, omniscient, and all good, and, yes there is evil in the world. Sound paradoxical? Here's the way Leibniz built his case.

Leibniz began with the premise that this world, since it was created by an infinite and benevolent God, must be the very best world that it was possible to create. In effect, he imagined God before the Creation turning over in his Divine Mind all of the possible worlds that he might bring into existence. Clearly, if he thought it would be better to create no world at all, he would have simply refrained from creating one. And among all the logically possible worlds he could create, obviously he would choose the best one, since he is infinitely good.

What is more, since he is infinitely wise, whatever he thinks must be true. So this is the best of all possible worlds, despite the evil that is in it:

> [I]t must be confessed that there is evil in this world which God has made, and that it was possible to make a world without evil, or even not to create a world at all, for its creation has depended on the free will of God; but I deny [that] . . . Whoever makes things in which there is evil, which could have been made without any evil, or the making of which could have been omitted, does not choose the best . . . [T]he best plan is not always that which seeks to avoid evil, since it may happen that the *evil is accompanied by a greater good*. For example, a general of an army will prefer a great victory with a slight wound to a condition without wound and without victory (*Theodicy, Abridgment of the Argument*).[5]

Other, more homely, examples come to mind. When does a drink of cool, clear water taste best? When we are thirsty! When does hearing someone say, "I love you," thrill us the most? When we have been hurting, hoping to hear that someone say it. In these cases, pleasure and joy (good) are actually intensified by the pains (evil) that preceded them.

But, again, what of the Holocaust? What of the young mother whose baby is dying of cancer? What good could possibly offset these evils? Leibniz claims that, from our limited perspective, we just can't see the way that evil fits into the whole picture:

> The infinite wisdom of the Almighty allied with his boundless goodness has brought it about that nothing better could have been created, everything taken into account, than what God has created. As a consequence all things are in perfect harmony and conspire in the most beautiful way . . . Whenever, therefore, some detail of the work of God appears to us reprehensible, we should judge that we do not know enough about it and that according to the wise who would understand it, nothing better could even be desired (*ibid.*).

Imagine a great painting cut up into a jigsaw puzzle. Each individual piece may appear to be nothing more than an ugly splotch; but once the puzzle is complete, and we can see the painting as a whole, we see that it is beautiful and that each piece fits into harmonious unity. In the words of Alexander Pope,

> All Discord, Harmony, not understood;
> All partial Evil, universal Good (*ibid*, I.291–292).

In short, despite the presence of evil, "This is the best of all possible worlds." The fallacy in the argument from evil lies in the fact that the existence of God *is* compatible with the presence of evil in the world—when it is properly understood.

Voltaire viciously lampooned the doctrine that this is the best of possible worlds in *Candide,* and many others have not been convinced by the arguments of Leibniz and Pope. The debate continues. But it may be just about the best that the rationalist tradition in religious thought can manage with regard to the problem of evil. Still, as Nelson Pike observed,

> Within most theological positions, the existence of God is taken as an item of faith or embraced on the basis of an a priori argument. Under these circumstances, where there is nothing to qualify as a "hypothesis" capable of having either negative or positive "evidence," the fact of evil in the world presents no special problem for theology . . . [W]hen the existence of God is accepted prior to any rational consideration of the status of evil in the world, the traditional problem of evil reduces to a noncrucial perplexity of relatively minor importance ("Hume on Evil").[6]

So maybe we are back to where we started, with Kierkegaard, who believed that God's promises can have no rational justification, no evidence, no proof, and that our only hope is to take that "leap of faith."

Approaches to the problem of evil clearly reflect the two approaches to religion that we have been looking at in this chapter—the subjective, faith-based approach, and the objective, rational approach. For those who are drawn to the objective, rational approach, the problem continues to be a thorny one. For those drawn to the subjective, faith-based approach, the problem may come down to nothing more than "a noncrucial perplexity of relatively minor importance."

Notes

1. J. L. Mackie, "Evil and Omnipotence," *Mind* LXIV, No. 254. Copyright 1955 by Oxford University Press.
2. John Stuart Mill, *Autobiography,* Jack Stillinger, ed., Riverside Editions, Houghton Mifflin Company, Boston, Copyright 1969 by Jack Stillinger, pp. 25–26.
3. John Milton, *Paradise Lost,* Modern Library College Editions, New York, Distributed by McGraw-Hill, Inc., Copyright 1969 by Random House, Inc. Originally published in 1667.
4. Alexander Pope, *An Essay on Man,* The Library of Liberal Arts, published by the Bobbs-Merrill Company, Inc., Indianapolis, New York, Kansas City, Copyright 1965, The Bobbs-Merrill Company, Inc. Originally published in 1733–1734.
5. Gottfried Wilhelm Leibniz, *Leibniz: Selections,* Philip P. Wiener, ed., Scribner, New York, Copyright 1951 by Charles Scribner's Sons.
6. Nelson Pike, "Hume on Evil," *Philosophical Review* LXXII, No. 2. Copyright 1963 by Cornell University.

The Main Points in Chapter Eight

1. The nineteenth-century Danish philosopher Søren Kierkegaard struggled throughout his life to come to terms with the Protestant Christianity of northern Europe, focusing in complex ways on such religious concepts as *faith, the Saviour, sin,* and *dread.* His many writings were at one and the same time an exploration of the experience of religious faith and a critique of the middle-class society in which he lived.

2. Rejecting the teachings of Hegel, who was the leading philosophical influence of that time, Kierkegaard asserted that truth lies in what is *subjective, inward,* and *immediate,* not *objective* and *universal.* Kierkegaard's approach to these central questions of human existence has come to be called existentialism.

3. For several thousand years, philosophers have argued about whether it is possible to actually prove the existence of a divine and infinite being—God. The arguments designed to prove that God exists traditionally have been grouped under three headings:

   a. The *Argument from Design* seeks to prove that there is a God by pointing to the evidences in nature of purpose or design and then reasoning that they must be the result of an intelligent, purposive designer, namely God. William Paley, in the late eighteenth century, gave the most elaborate version of this argument, although in one form or another it goes all the way back to ancient times.

   b. St. Thomas Aquinas' *Cosmological Argument* starts from the fact that there is motion in the world, or from the fact that things in the world come into being and pass away, and then reasons that there must be a first cause of motion, or a first unalterable cause of existence, which itself has no higher cause and neither comes to be nor passes away.

   c. St. Anselm's *Ontological Argument* begins with the mere *concept* of an infinite being and argues that from a logical analysis of the concept, we can conclude that something corresponding to the concept—an infinite being, or God—*must* exist. The Ontological Argument, which dates from the Middle Ages, has been the subject of a very vigorous debate in philosophy for the past seven centuries.

4. The problem of evil poses the question; how can a God who is all-powerful, all-wise, and all-good permit so much pain, suffering, and evil in the world?

Pleasantville: Questions About Religion and Ethics

You settle down for an evening of television viewing, but something seems to be wrong with that remote control that the weird television repairman—the one who looks like an older version of Barney Fife on *The Andy Griffith Show*—gave you. Suddenly, you and your sibling have been zapped into the 1950s black-and-white film, *Pleasantville.*

Almost as suddenly, things begin to change in Pleasantville. A girl gives a boy an apple, and he takes a bite. Teenagers begin to enthusiastically experiment with sex. Mr. Johnson, owner of the local soda shop, begins to create art. The basketball team loses. Most shocking of all, color appears, first in flowers, then in people. People turn from black and white to flesh-colored as they themselves change, whether by experiencing art or literature or by revealing a caring nature. Pleasantville changes, and it changes forever. There is no going back to the days of black and white.

Questions to Consider

Is the change from the stereotypical black-and-white 1950s to the frightening but colorful freedoms of today good or bad? Is it possible that some people are good simply because they have never been challenged by change? Should we reevaluate the Garden of Eden myth? Should we seek to achieve knowledge of good and evil? Is the fact that we have developed from animals that don't know the difference between good and evil to human beings who can acquire knowledge of the difference something to be deplored or something to be celebrated?

Questions for Discussion and Review

1. Have you ever had an experience that you could properly describe as religious? I have in mind not only dramatic experiences like visions and conversions, but also more commonplace, socially embedded experiences such as receiving communion, becoming *bar mitzvah,* serving as a godparent for a young relative, or even simply attending religious services. Think about that experience, and ask yourself: Did it put you in touch, do you think, with a realm outside of, or different from, the everyday world? What significance did the experience have for you? Did it change your life? Why? Why not? What would change your life?

2. Read through the proofs for the existence of God carefully. Think about them. Do any of them convince you? If the answer is no (and it usually is), then what purpose do you think those proofs serve? Would it make a difference to you if the proofs were beefed up, made better? How would Jesus have responded to attempts to prove the existence of God?

3. Let us suppose that you reject the proofs for the existence of God, and even reject the claim that there is a God. How then do you explain the fact that there is a universe? Do we need an explanation for the fact that we exist? Why is there in general something, and not nothing?

4. Suppose we make contact with an alien race on a distant planet and discover that they, like us, worship a divine being who has revealed himself to them in a set of holy writings. Suppose that when we finally learn how to translate their language into ours, it turns out that their holy writings and the New and Old Testaments say roughly the same things. Would that prove that there is a God? Suppose, on the other hand, that they have no cultural practice that looks even remotely like religion. Would that undermine the claims of our religion? Why?

The Primary Source: Philosophical Readings and Commentary

Anselm, St.: *Proslogion*

Aquinas, Thomas: *Summa Theologica*

Augustine: *Confessions; City of God*

Aurelius, Marcus: *Meditations*

Bhagavad Gita: *Path of Yoga*

Boethius: *The Consolation of Philosophy*

Buddha: *The Fire Sermon; The Dhammapadda; The Vagrakkhedika, Heart Sutra*

Confucius: *Analects*

Hick, John: *The Philosophy of Religion*

Hume, David: *Dialogues Concerning Natural Religion*

James, William: *The Varieties of Religious Experience*

Jaspers, Karl: *The Axial Period*

Kant, Immanuel: *Critique of Practical Reason; Critique of Pure Reason*

Kierkegaard, Soren: *Philosophical Fragments; Concluding Unscientific Postscript to the Philosophical Fragments*

Lao Tzu: *Tao Te Ching*

Paley, William: *Natural Theology*

Plotinus: *Enneads*

Russell, Bertrand: *Why I am Not a Christian*

St. Anselm, *ProslogionUpanishads*

Upanishads

CONTEMPORARY APPLICATION

Cults: Religion or Fanaticism?

Thus far in this chapter we have been looking at religion from a number of different points of view, but whatever our viewpoint, we have been assuming that we know well enough what religion is. Or perhaps we should say, we have been assuming that we know what religions are. Christianity, Judaism, Islam, Buddhism—these are all religions, surely. Roman Catholicism, Episcopalianism, Methodism, Orthodox, Reform, Conservative Judaism, Shi'ite and Sunni Islam—these are religious "denominations," as we like to say.

But what about the Moonies (followers of the Reverend Sun Myung Moon)? Scientology (or Dianetics, as it was originally known)? The Branch Davidians? The followers of Jim Jones? Are these religions, or denominations of a religion? Or are they *cults?* Are these groups, movements, churches, gatherings somehow not real religion? Do they deserve the respect that we automatically give to established or recognized religions?

At first it seems easy enough to draw a distinction between *real* religions and mere *cults.* But the closer we look into the matter, the harder it becomes to identify the traits or characteristics that clearly distinguish what we are inclined to consider genuine religions from what we want to dismiss as cults. The size of the group surely cannot be, by itself, the determining factor, for every one of the major religions to which we give respect and recognition started life as a small band of believers. One need only think, for example, of Jesus and his twelve disciples.

Thomas Hobbes, in *Leviathan,* offers an extraordinary pair of definitions of *religion* and *superstition* that dramatically highlight the difficulty in distinguishing religions from cults. *"Fear* of power invisible, feigned by the mind, or imagined from tales publicly allowed [is] *religion;* not allowed [is] *superstition."*

Hobbes is saying that the only difference between religion and superstition is that religion is a set of beliefs that is socially allowed or acceptable, whereas superstition is a set of beliefs that is not socially allowed or acceptable. Now, since what is socially acceptable at one time may become socially unacceptable at another, and vice versa, it follows, according to Hobbes, that what we now call a religion might at a later time be considered a cult or superstition, and what we now consider a cult or superstition might at a later time be considered a religion.

In these selections, we find the same uncertainty about how to classify the Branch Davidians, Moonies, Scientologists, and others who are so often referred to as cultists. If you think that a willingness, or even an eagerness, to die for one's beliefs is the true mark of a *cult,* you might recall the fact that the early Christians marched willingly into the Roman Coliseum, there to be torn apart by wild beasts for the amusement of the crowd.

THE END TO INNOCENT ACCEPTANCE OF SECTS: SHARPER SCRUTINY IS JONESTOWN LEGACY
Don Lattin

When 50 members of a doomsday *cult* vanished last month in Colorado, Hal Mansfield knew exactly how to get the world's attention.

"This is Jonestown waiting to happen," said Mansfield, director of the Religious Movement Resource Center in Fort Collins, Colo.

Twenty years after the murder-suicide in Jonestown, Guyana, of 914 members of the Peoples Temple, the Rev. Jim Jones remains the personification of cultic evil.

Two words are all it takes to demonize a *new religious movement*—whether it deserves the label or not:

"Another Jonestown."

Those who study cults, sects, and new religious movements are bitterly divided into two camps—factions of experts branding their adversaries as "apologists" or "alarmists."

J. Gordon Melton, founder of the Institute for the Study of American Religion in Santa Barbara, said "professional cult hunters" like Mansfield are too quick to see the potential for mass suicide in the latest Christian sect or new religious movement.

"They believe that all these groups are bad and brainwash their members," he said.

In Melton's view, "brainwashing doesn't exist."

"Jonestown became the stereotype of a cult," Melton said. "But Jones was actually a member of a mainline Protestant denomination, the Disciples of Christ, and was very involved in the ecumenical movement in California. It's the story of a mainline church gone bad, not a new religion.

"Around 2,500 people kill themselves every year in California," Melton added. "It's not beyond reason to see that people in religion can find something to die for. You don't need a brainwashing model to explain that."

"Jim Jones and the members of Peoples Temple performed an act of revolutionary suicide."

Those in the Melton camp point out that most religions start off in an intense "cultic" manner, clashing with the values of mainstream culture.

Attacking Cult Apologists

Anti-cult leaders such as Margaret Singer, adjunct professor emerita of psychology at the University of California at Berkeley, said "cult apologists" like Melton "blindly defend" dangerous sect leaders like Jones.

"Anything that calls itself a religion is, by definition, good," she said. "People like Melton are not really scholars of group pressure or group process. We really study these groups and analyze how influence is put upon people by clever and conniving people who want power."

According to Singer and others on her side of the cult wars, a destructive sect is easily distinguished from a legitimate religion.

They say cults are marked by charismatic leaders who claim special powers, promote an "us vs. them" philosophy, practice brainwashing and use deceptive recruitment and fund-raising techniques. Followers undergo dramatic changes in diet, sleep patterns, and privacy; become alienated from friends and family; and are exploited financially, physically, and sexually.

"Venal people see how easy it is to pick up the lonely and the depressed and sell them a bill of goods," Singer said. "There are so many people out there looking for easy answers to life's complicated problems."

Those who know Monte Kim Miller, the Colorado doomsday prophet, say the Jonestown comparisons are no exaggeration.

Colorado Group on the Run

Last month, Miller and about 50 members of his Concerned Christians sect disappeared from their homes in the Denver area, leaving behind hundreds of worried relatives.

They vanished in the days leading up to October 10, when Miller prophesied that an apocalyptic disaster would wipe Denver off the map.

Those who have watched the group think it may eventually resurface in Israel. Miller, the self-proclaimed last prophet on earth, predicts he will die in the streets of Jerusalem in December 1999 and reappear three days later.

Bill Honsberger, a Colorado evangelical missionary who has monitored the group, notes that both Miller and Jones began their ministries as respected religious leaders.

Miller even began as a speaker on the anticult circuit. "Twelve or 13 years ago, he was appearing in some of the biggest churches in Denver, speaking out against the New Age movement," Honsberger said.

In recent years, however, Miller said he could channel the voice of God and began comparing himself to the two witnesses in the apocalyptic pages of the Book of Revelation, the last chapter of the Bible.

"We sat at his house with him for two hours," Honsberger recalled. "We started out talking about how he became a Christian, and pretty soon he showed how he could speak for God. He'd shift his position, contort his face, and say things like, 'God will kill you for opposing his true prophet.' "

According to Honsberger, Miller preaches that his followers "must take up the cross and be willing to die for God. But you stand up for God by being loyal to him. It's the same mentality as Jones, but the manipulation is even more glaring. He has incredible control."

Mansfield said some of Miller's followers have called their families since they disappeared last month to say they are all right. But they would not reveal their location.

Mansfield also concurs with Honsberger about the Jim Jones similarities.

"What's going on inside this guy's head now is anybody's guess," he said, "but I think some sort of suicide is possible."

Rash of Apocalyptic Sects

Singer noted that there has been no shortage of violent religious sects in the 1990s, many of them with apocalyptic overtones.

Seventy-two members of the Branch Davidian Christian sect died when a hellish inferno engulfed their compound in Waco, Texas. In Japan, the Aum Shrini Kyo cult unleashed a nerve-gas attack on subway riders. In Canada and Europe, 75 members of the Order of the Solar Temple killed themselves in search of new life in a place called Sirius.

And in the spring of 1997, 39 members of Heaven's Gate, a Southern California cult blending Bible prophesy, spiritualism, and UFO lore, killed themselves in the belief that they would rendezvous with a spaceship trailing the Hale-Bopp comet.

Janja Lolich, who runs the Cult Recovery and Information Center in Alameda, said Jonestown remains the landmark event of the anti-cult movement.

Lolich said he hoped the 20th anniversary of Jonestown will serve as a warning for "young people who don't have Jonestown in their memory bank."

"Often the public comes away with the idea that only wacky people get involved in these groups," she said. "But they are often wonderful people with a real sense of idealism."

New Light on the Temple

Focusing on the members of Peoples Temple—and not just on Jim Jones—is the central concern of Mary McCormick Maaga in her new book *Hearing the Voices of Jonestown*.

"Passion for social justice blinded them to their own cause," Maaga said. "They increasingly focused on their detractors and defectors and concerned relatives. They were importing food and losing the battle against jungle diseases. Jones was addicted to drugs.

"Their Christian communal socialist experiment wasn't working, and they were very concerned about proving their enemies wrong."

Reducing the complexity of Jonestown to a madman brainwashing his vulnerable flock, Maaga said, is too simple an explanation.

"There were other people in leadership, and if they hadn't agreed to the suicide, it couldn't have gone off," she said. "But we like to just focus on Jim Jones because it's easier to pinpoint evil in a single human being."

From: *The San Francisco Chronicle,* News Section. November 13, 1998. ©San Francisco Chronicle. Reprinted by permission.

Don Lattin is a *Chronicle* religion writer.

GATED RELIGIONS; HEAVEN'S GATE AND OTHER FRINGE RELIGIONS

The suicide of 39 members of Heaven's Gate, a quasi-religious group that mixed elements of apocalyptic Christianity with sci-fi space travel, has once again focused attention on what scholars call *new religious movements* and critics refer to as *cults*. Despite its unique theology, which included the belief that a UFO trailing the Hale-Bopp comet would transport members to a "Level Above Human," Heaven's Gate was not unusual in one regard. It is just one of many new religious movements that have been spawned over time by America's open, pluralistic approach to faith. And while Heaven's Gate met a tragic end, other new religious movements have flourished. Some have even achieved mainstream status.

Scholars say the separatist notions of groups such as Heaven's Gate may be responsible for their doom. Groups like the Church of Jesus Christ of Latter-day Saints and Sun Myung Moon's Unification Church—both of which have, at times, been vilified as dangerous cults—have found success by negotiating more positive relations with the surrounding social environment rather than attempting to live in a state of relative isolation.

Lonnie Kliever, chairman of religious studies at Southern Methodist University in Dallas, noted that new religions have had a "remarkable history" in this country over the past 150 years: "We've been a bit of a greenhouse for innovative and original new religious movements, and that's allowed by our pluralistic approach to religions in our society and the constitutional guarantees." Many new groups disappear after a few years without the sort of deadly exit orchestrated by Heaven's Gate simply because they fail to sustain themselves. But others become "fully integrated into the mainstream of religious life," Kliever said.

The Unification Church is one such example. Its control of the *Washington Times,* a prominent, conservative newspaper in the nation's capital, has gained the church a large measure of acceptance. Unification-sponsored "family values" conferences held around the globe attract world leaders and such well-known figures as Ralph Reed of the Christian Coalition. In the mid-19th century the Church of Jesus Christ of Latter-day Saints, more commonly known as the Mormon Church, was considered by most established U.S. Christian churches as a dangerous cult that practiced polygamy. Today 14 Mormons are members of Congress. Once-ridiculed Hare Krishnas, members of a Hindu sect transplanted to the U.S. during the spiritually turbulent '60s, today are members of mainstream interfaith organizations and are taken seriously by religion scholars.

Heaven's Gate, on the other hand, remained a small group, isolated and mobile. Its core members ended their time on Earth at a rental property in an exclusive San Diego County community. "There's all the difference in the world in a group that says the world is so evil that our only hope is to escape this world," said Kliever, "and a religion which says this Earth is God's creation, and although it has erred and strayed from God's will, . . . through his church in the latter days God will re-establish a kingdom of heaven on Earth."

On Heaven's Gate's Web site, an introduction to the group's beliefs affirmed what it called "separation from the world." Distinguishing Heaven's Gate from other religious groups, the introduction said: "Unless you are currently an active student or are attempting to become a student of the present Representative from the Kingdom of Heaven—you ARE STILL 'of the world,' having done no significant separation from worldliness, and you are still serving the opposition to the Kingdom of Heaven." The introduction was signed by Do, "The Present Representative"—one of the names reportedly used by Marshall Herff Apple-white, the former opera singer who went on to lead and die with the Heaven's Gate group.

According to H. Newton Malony, a psychology professor at Fuller Theological Seminary in Pasadena, California, while society may become more accepting of unusual beliefs, it is less likely to welcome unorthodox practices. Mormons at one time practiced polygamy, but their church renounced that marriage form in 1890. Unification Church members, who believe Jesus failed in his messianic mission when he was crucified, have toned down their aggressive evangelistic tactics, which once included inviting lone young people arriving at bus stations to dinner and weeklong retreats. "We don't have freedom of absolute practice," Malony said. "Either homicide or suicide are anathema in our society."

CULT WARS GIVE NEW RELIGIONS A BAD NAME: DON'T SAY CULT OR 'SECT'. THE APPROVED TERM IS THE LESS THREATENING 'NEW RELIGIOUS MOVEMENT'
Harvey Shepherd

AIDS. Race. Child abuse. Survivalism. The place of women. The apocalypse.

Montreal scholar Susan J. Palmer's academic specialty brings her into contact with many of the issues modern society finds particularly threatening. It has also brought her court appearances, police interrogations, and other nervous moments.

Palmer's speciality is itself pretty threatening to some people.

She and a small network of scholars across North America and Europe who share her interest sometimes jokingly refer to it as "the cult wars."

Actually, in Palmer's solemn moments, which tend to be few, she does not approve of terms like "sect" or "cult" although those words have been known to cross her lips. The approved term seems to be "new religious movements."

"Little is known about them," she said. "There are a lot of strong opinions about 'cults,' but most of them are uninformed."

Few if any generalizations about new religious movements are true of all or even most of them, she said in an interview. But she does think they are a good place to study social trends affecting society as a whole.

"They are like fragments of mirror that sort of magnify social change," she said.

"Today's society is pluralistic and undergoing rapid change, and new religious movements, taken together, tend to reflect and exaggerate much of what is going on in the larger society," she said.

Some groups mirror and exaggerate the neoconservative trends in today's society. Others, like the Raelians, flying-saucer enthusiasts, seem anxious to rush into the future as quickly as possible.

In her view, a society's responses to "cults" are also a significant measure of its health in general, and how open that society is to change and to the impact of other cultures.

Lately, she said, "les sectes" have been having a particularly hard time in France, which has seen a range of crackdowns of various kinds on groups ranging from the Jehovah's Witnesses and Scientologists to the Aumists, a hyper-syncretic group whose "holy city" in the Alps in the south of France has had no end of difficulty with various civil authorities.

(The Aumists also have a group in Quebec, with a centre in the Laurentians.)

Palmer suspects that "les sectes" in France are, to a large extent, serving as whipping boys for authorities, media, and a large part of the population that are having trouble getting used to the growing Muslim minority in France.

"This threatens their worldview and they take it out on 'les sectes.' They can bash minorities that are labeled as not real religions," Palmer said.

The latest of several books that Palmer has written or edited, alone or with others, and that treat the interaction of social trends and new religious movements, is a forthcoming collection of essays on children in new religions, due for publication (by Rutgers University Press) in the spring. She is co-editor with a British scholar, Charlotte Hardman.

It is no coincidence, she said, that child abuse is a currently topical theme in Western society generally and has also become a favourite accusation for members and groups in the anticult movement to level against "sects" and "cults" in general.

At the same time, the issue of children in new religious movements has taken on new importance for several of them. Since a number of new religious movements began and grew rapidly in the 1960s and 1970s, with a membership made up largely of teenagers, in relatively recent years they have seen a second generation, sons and daughters of the first, grow into teenage years and early adulthood.

Accusations of child abuse have given the anti-cult movement something of a new lease on life now that theories about "brainwashing" by cults have lost a good deal of credibility and some parts of the anti-cult movement have been discredited through association with the dubious tactics of some "deprogrammers."

To a considerable extent, Palmer said, the anti-cult movement has moved away from working with parents to try to remove and "deprogram" members of new religious movements. But there's a new tactic instead: furnishing ammunition to parents involved in court battles over child custody with their former partners, members of "sects" and "cults."

Palmer has served as an expert witness, in court cases over custody or similar issues, in Halifax, Vermont, and England, and is advising a lawyer in another case in France. She worked with lawyers for the "cultist" spouse in three cases and the non-cult spouse in the other.

Palmer checked out a convention in Philadelphia last May organized by a body called the American Freedom Foundation to discuss "Children in Cults."

"The message they were putting out was that all cults separate kids from their parents and all cult leaders are pederasts," she said.

"I found it incredible. I had just co-edited a book on the subject."

In fact, she said, the attitudes of adults in new religious movements toward their children run pretty well the imaginable gamut.

At one extreme, there has been child abuse in some groups, extending to murder in, for example, the bloody Solar Temple murder-suicides in Switzerland and Quebec in 1994.

Palmer collaborated a few years ago in the production of a documentary movie on The Family, an evangelical and communal group active in many countries that was once known as the Children of God and that still takes an open attitude to sex between consenting adult members.

At one time, it countenanced sexual activity between adult and child members, but it has cleaned up its act in that regard.

However, the movement continues to pay for its past sins as its communes continue to be raided by civil authorities from time to time in different countries.

At the other extreme, there are groups like the Raelians and the Raj-neeshees, which tend to have an open attitude toward sex but discourage their followers from having children, much less abusing them. Raelians are also particularly scrupulous about insisting that Raelians' children who want to join the movement make their own informed choice.

To take another example, there is the group that Palmer and her daughter Sylvia, 15, visited in Italy last fall: the Nazione di Damanhur. This group attracted a good deal of attention in the Italian media about four years ago when it became known that it had had a large and secret underground temple in the Italian Alps for the previous 25 years or so.

Palmer said this group also regards religion as a matter for informed adult consent. There is a rite of passage for teenagers inclined to stay in the group, but there is little pressure on anyone to go through it.

Indeed, while members of the Nazione stress a wholesome style of life for themselves, a good many of their adolescent children seem to go through a phase of cigarettes, body-piercing, and the like without provoking undue strain on the home front.

Palmer said that new religious movements face something of a bind these days as they wrestle with the issue of handing their traditions on to a second generation.

She said anthropological research shows that the way societies have passed on traditions through the ages has been through some sort of coming-of-age ritual, generally preceded by some sort of ordeal. If new religious movements neglect this, she said, they are likely to lose their children.

But when they seek to adopt such rituals, they are denounced by anti-cultists as child abusers, she said. If somebody today were trying to start up modern Judaism as a new religious movement, there is a good chance that anti-cultists would attack the Hebrew studies and other preparations for the teenage rites of passage—the bar mitzvah and bat mitzvah—as brainwashing, and circumcision as child abuse.

Palmer acknowledges that her family background may be partly responsible for her interest in new religious movements. Her great-grandparents, members of a polygamist group of Mormons, moved to Canada rather than obey a U.S. law against polygamy.

When not visiting or studying new religious movements, Palmer is often to be found playing ancient instrumental music or singing in a choir specializing in Bulgarian folk songs. Latterly, she has also been devoting much of her time to martial arts—in particular, a hybird form called kajukenbo—and reports that the internal politics of martial-arts groups, with their ortho-doxies, charismatic leaders, and rifts, seem a lot like those of many new religious movements.

Palmer lives in central Montreal with her daughter, Sylvia, and son, Sandor, 18.

"We are a utopian commune," she told her note-taking interviewer. "Put that in."

From: *The Gazette* (Montreal), Religion Section, p. 67, January 2, 1999.

Harvey Shepherd, The *Gazette* (Montreal).

HOW TO WRITE A PHILOSOPHY PAPER

Introduction

Most of you will be called on to submit one or more papers as part of the written work for your course in philosophy, and this requirement may well have you stumped. Even though you have, by now, read at least a few chapters of this book and participated in a number of classes, you may have no idea at all about how to write a paper in philosophy. No doubt, you wrote papers in high school for English courses, perhaps also for social studies courses, even for science courses. But philosophy is something quite different. Where do you start? What sort of library research should you do, if any? Should you put down your own ideas, those of your professor, ideas you have found in your course reading? Are you expected to come up with your *own* philosophy?

This appendix is designed to answer these questions. I will give you a simple, clear, almost foolproof way of writing a satisfactory philosophy paper; I will give you some tips and hints and warnings that may help you to avoid the most common problems in writing philosophy papers; I will take you through a careful critique and analysis of a real course paper written by one of my students at the University of Massachusetts (who shall remain anonymous, of course); and I will then rewrite the student paper so that you can see how the author could have improved it.

If you read this appendix carefully and follow its guidelines when writing papers for your philosophy course, I am absolutely certain that you will write good papers, from which you will learn a great deal *About Philosophy*.

A Simple, Foolproof Method for Writing Philosophy Papers

A philosophy paper is a defense of a *thesis,* in which the thesis is *explained* and *analyzed, arguments* are given in support of the thesis, possible *objections* to the thesis are stated and examined, and *responses* are given to the objections. A philosophy paper thus has five parts:

1. The statement of the thesis
2. The analysis and explanation of the thesis
3. The arguments in support of the thesis

4. The examination of objections to the thesis

5. The response to the objections

The simplest, most foolproof way to write a philosophy paper is to organize it in precisely this order: Thesis, Analysis of Thesis, Arguments for Thesis, Objections to Thesis, and Response to Objections. It is not necessary to stick to this order, of course, and after you become better at writing philosophy papers, you may want to experiment with other systems of organization. But if you have never written a philosophy paper before, and you are not really quite sure what you are doing, it might be a good idea to stick to this structure. It can't lose!

Let's take a close look at each of these five elements in turn.

1. The Thesis

A philosophy paper is a defense of a thesis, so the first step is to get clear what a thesis is. A *thesis* is a statement that makes some clear, definite assertion about the subject under discussion. For example, if the topic of your paper, the subject under discussion, is *the morality of abortion,* here are some of the many *theses* you might choose to defend:

▋ Abortion is morally wrong under all circumstances.
▋ A woman has an absolute right to decide whether to have an abortion.
▋ Abortion is morally right only to save the life of the mother.

Each of these is a clear, definite statement that takes a position on the morality of abortion, a position that the rest of the paper will attempt to defend.

Let's try another example. Suppose the subject under discussion is *the existence of a Supreme Being.* Among the theses you might choose to defend are:

▋ There is no God but Allah.
▋ It is logically impossible for there to be a Supreme Being.
▋ Human beings are incapable of determining whether there is a Supreme Being.

Now let's look at some examples of things that look like theses, but aren't:

▋ The scientific status of astrology
▋ Abortion, pro and con
▋ Why I believe in God

These aren't *theses* because they don't *assert* anything. All three of these are what we might call *topics.* You can certainly write a philosophy paper about one of these topics, but you must first choose a *thesis* about the topic, a thesis that you will defend in the paper. By the way, watch out especially for fake theses like the third one ("Why I believe in God"). A philosophy paper is not a personal report of how you feel or what you believe. It is an *argument* for a thesis.

Those of you who took part in formal debate team competitions in high school may think that all of this looks very much like a debate. You are absolutely right. Philosophy *is* very much like debating.

One more word about the thesis of your paper. Learning to do philosophy is a lot like learning to play basketball or tennis. You can't learn if you just stand on the sidelines and watch other people. So writing a philosophy paper is a way of getting in some philosophy practice. When you pick the thesis of your paper, don't think that you must pick something you deeply believe, something you would be willing to die for. Just choose a clear, simple, straightforward thesis that you think you can do a good job of defending. No one will be mad at you if you defend the other side of the question a week later.

But whatever you do, don't pick a wishy-washy thesis that hedges your bets, like "There is much to be said on both sides of the abortion question," or "There are good arguments for and against the existence of God." Take a stand, plant your feet squarely on the ground, and argue for your thesis as well as you can.

Since we have already used the example of the morality of abortion, let's continue to use it. For the remainder of this appendix, our thesis will be:

❙ Abortion is morally wrong under all circumstances whatsoever.

2. The Analysis and Explanation of the Thesis

The first step in the defense of a thesis is to explain what you mean by it. Since we are using as an example the thesis "Abortion is morally wrong under all circumstances whatsoever," we must state exactly what we mean by the term *abortion,* by the phrase "morally wrong," and by the qualifying clause "in all circumstances whatsoever." This may seem like a trivial exercise to you, but watch out—in philosophy, a lot can get loaded into an innocent-looking definition.

For example, we will want to make it clear that by "morally wrong" we mean something quite different from "against the law" or "legally wrong." It is one thing to argue that abortion, suitably defined, violates some state or federal law in the United States or elsewhere. It is quite another thing to argue that abortion is morally wrong, that it violates some principle that all persons ought to abide by. If we are arguing about the law, we shall have to cite the criminal codes, judicial decisions, Supreme Court opinions, or law books. But if we are arguing about what is right and wrong, then we shall have to appeal to some other sorts of considerations—*unless we want to claim that "morally wrong" and "legally wrong" are one and the same, which would itself be a very powerful, highly debatable claim.*

How shall we understand "in any circumstances"? Are we claiming that abortion is wrong, even in cases in which the pregnancy resulted from incest or rape? Do we mean that abortion is wrong, even if the fetus cannot possibly survive and the mother will die without the abortion? Are we claiming that abortion is wrong, even if prenatal testing reveals that the fetus has a fatal congenital disease and cannot survive for more than a few hours after birth?

Notice, at this stage we are not *arguing*, we are just explaining what we mean by the thesis. And since it is our thesis, we can interpret it any way we wish. But how we interpret the thesis will shape the rest of the paper, for it will determine what sorts of arguments we give and what sorts of objections we must consider. For example, if we interpret "in any circumstances" to mean "even if the pregnancy resulted from rape," then we will have to consider the objection that a woman should not be required against her will to risk her life. But if we exclude pregnancies resulting from rape, then that isn't an objection against our position, so we don't have to consider it in this paper.

You can begin to see how the paper will be shaped and determined by how we interpret our thesis. That is why explaining and analyzing the thesis is such an important step, one we must take before moving on to the arguments.

For purposes of our discussion, let us agree to interpret our thesis in the following way (remember, this is just one of countless possible interpretations—not in any sense the *right* interpretation, just the interpretation we have chosen in order to write this paper):

> "Abortion is morally wrong under all circumstances whatsoever" means "Terminating a human pregnancy at any stage before birth, so long as the fetus is alive, violates the objective and universal principles of Judeo-Christian morality, and is therefore wrong without exception for rape, incest, danger to the life of the mother, or any other circumstance, including even a circumstance in which the abortion might save the lives of many other innocent people."

Notice that I have interpreted "morally wrong" to mean "contrary to the objective and universal principles of Judeo-Christian morality." Needless to say, that is not the only way "morally wrong" can be interpreted. We might also have interpreted it to mean "in conflict with the Principle of Utilitarianism," or "incompatible with the Categorical Imperative." Let me repeat: *You can choose any thesis you wish, and interpret it in any plausible manner you wish, so long as you make it clear to your reader what you are doing.*

Before moving on to the main body of your paper, which is the Argument for the Thesis, review what you have written. Make sure that you have stated a genuine thesis (not just a topic), and that you have explained clearly what that thesis means. Here, as always, you must try very hard to put yourself into the mind of your reader and ask whether he or she will understand exactly what your thesis means. Reading what you have written as your reader will read it is actually the hardest part of all writing. *You* may think you know what you have in mind, but unless you put it down on paper clearly, precisely, and accurately, your reader won't have a clue. One way to check on yourself is to give what you have written to a friend and ask him or her to tell you what he or she thinks you have said. Don't give any hints, and don't argue. If your friend doesn't understand what you have written in the same way you understand it, then there is probably something wrong with what you have written. (Choose an intelligent friend!)

3. The Arguments in Support of the Thesis

We have come to the heart of the paper—the arguments for the thesis. This is where you show your stuff. You have to come up with arguments that are designed to persuade your reader that your thesis is true. What is an argument? To put it as simply as possible, an argument for a thesis is a reason for believing that the thesis is true. There are many different sorts of reasons you can give in support of a thesis. In the next few paragraphs, we will take a brief look at some of the most important. Just remember: When you are putting forward an argument in support of your thesis, ask yourself, "If I didn't already believe my thesis, would this reason convince me that thesis is true? Would it at least make me more inclined to believe that it is true? Would it tend to convince a reasonable reader who is open-minded enough so that he or she is willing to listen to reasons?" If the answer is yes, then you have your hands on a genuine argument. If the answer is no, then leave it out of the paper and look for a better argument.

Let's take a look at some very simple examples. Philosophy may strike you as pretty difficult, but like many difficult things, it is made up of simple parts. Don't try to be too fancy. Just look for straightforward arguments that tend to support your thesis.

If you are trying to show that abortion is morally wrong, you might begin by arguing that abortion is the taking of an innocent life, and the taking of an innocent life is morally wrong. This is an example of what is perhaps the most widely used form of argument—what we can call *instantiation*. "Instantiation" means "giving an instance of." In this case, we have appealed to the general rule:

I Taking an innocent life is morally wrong.

Then we have argued that abortion is an *instance* of this general rule—it is the taking of an innocent life. If we spell out our argument completely, it looks like this:

I Taking an innocent life is morally wrong.
I Abortion is the taking of an innocent life.
I Therefore, abortion is morally wrong.

This argument, in turn, is an instance of a very general form of argument that looks like this:

▌ All *A*'s are *B*'s (where *A* = acts of taking an innocent life, and *B* = morally wrong acts)
▌ *C* is *A* (where *C* = abortion, and *A* again = acts of taking an innocent life)
   Therefore *C* is *B* (i.e., abortion is a morally wrong act)

The point is that *if C is an A, and if* all *A*'s are *B*'s, then *C must be a B*. Arguments of this sort are sometimes called *syllogisms*. In the Middle Ages, philosophers spent a great deal of time analyzing such arguments in order to figure out which kinds were good arguments and which were not.

Instantiation, or showing that the matter under discussion is an instance of a general rule, is a technique of argument that can be used in a very wide variety of circumstances. Notice that if it is to be convincing to your reader, then your reader must already be persuaded that the taking of an innocent life is morally wrong. Otherwise, even though your reader agrees that abortion is the taking of an innocent life, he or she won't be led to the conclusion that it is morally wrong.

A second form of argument, which in a sense is the reverse of instantiation, is *generalization*. Suppose you are trying to persuade your reader that the taking of an innocent life is morally wrong, as a first step toward springing the above argument, and thereby proving that abortion is morally wrong. You might proceed like this (imagine yourself actually talking to your reader):

▌ Will you agree that shooting down someone walking along the street is morally wrong? Yes.
▌ Will you agree that bombing civilians who happen to live near a war zone is morally wrong? Yes.
▌ Will you agree that smothering a baby in its crib is morally wrong? Yes.
▌ Can you see that what all these cases have in common, *what makes them all morally wrong,* is the fact that they are cases of taking an innocent life (crucial step here—you must get your reader to agree to this)?
▌ Well (now your trap snaps shut on your reader), if what makes these three acts morally wrong is the fact that they are cases of taking an innocent life, if that is *why* they are wrong, then it follows by simple parity of reasoning that *any* act that is the taking of an innocent life must also be wrong. In other words, taking an innocent life is morally wrong.

The trick here is figuring out just what it is that all three cases have in common, in virtue of which they are morally wrong. If you fix on some other characteristic, which isn't, so to speak, the *wrong-making* characteristic, then you won't come up with a defensible generalization. For example, the person gunned down in the street, the civilians near the war zone, and the baby in the crib might all be Americans, or male, or Caucasian, or rich, or they might all have the same astrological sign. But none of those things is what makes the killing of them morally wrong. What makes the killing of them morally wrong is the fact that they are innocent—that is, they haven't done anything to warrant being killed, they just happened to be there. If the person gunned down in the street *isn't* innocent, if she is a serial murderer on her way to commit yet another heinous crime, then maybe it wouldn't be wrong to kill her, for killing her would not be the taking of an innocent life.

So we now have two kinds of arguments you can use singly or together in your attempt to convince your reader that your thesis is true: instantiation and generalization.

A third form of argument, especially useful in replying to an opponent's objections, is the *counterexample*. A counterexample is a particular case—an instantiation—designed to show that an opponent's generalization is wrong. Suppose, for example, that your opponent, trying to show that abortion is morally right, argues that a pregnant woman has a right to have an abortion because having an abortion is choosing to do something with your own body, and (here comes the generalization), *persons have an absolute right to do with their own bodies whatever they choose.* You can try to come up with a *counterexample* to this generalization that will show that it is not in fact a true universal principle.

For example, you might point out that using your hands to strangle someone you don't like is an example of doing with your body (your hands) whatever you choose, and yet your opponent surely will not agree that you have an absolute right to strangle someone you don't like. Now your opponent may, of course, just reply with an absolutely straight face, "Of course you have a right to strangle someone you don't like," but that is not likely.

More probably, your opponent will point out that this is an example (strangling someone) that involves inflicting injury on someone else in addition to doing what you choose with your own body, and that makes it different from abortion. In this case, your opponent is appealing to a slightly different principle, namely, *Persons have an absolute right to do with their own bodies whatever they choose, so long as they do not injure others.*

Now you can respond by pointing out that abortion *does* involve injury to another person, namely to the fetus. This is an example of yet a fourth technique of argument, which we can call *counter-instantiation*—showing that a case is not an instance of the generalization your opponent has cited, but is in fact an instance of a different generalization. Your opponent can now respond that a fetus is not a person, and hence that abortion doesn't fall under the generalization you have just invoked.

Notice that this last move—arguing that the fetus is not a person—involves two more kinds of arguments that play a role in philosophical debates: *citing facts* and *drawing conceptual distinctions.* When your opponent says the fetus is not a person, he or she may be calling attention to facts (the fetus is not biologically fully developed, it cannot live independently of the mother's body, etc.) that tend to show that it is in fact different from the things we usually call persons. This is an example of citing facts. In addition, your opponent may be pointing out that the concept *person,* which plays a central role in the generalization you have invoked, cannot properly be applied to a fetus. This is an example of drawing a conceptual distinction.

Well, you are beginning to get the idea. In this central part of your paper, your job is to produce arguments in support of your thesis, using instantiation, generalization, counterexample, counter-instantiation, citing of facts, drawing conceptual distinctions, and any of the other forms of argument you can find. The success of your paper, to a very considerable extent, will depend on how well you can think up arguments in support of your thesis.

There is no set of rules that will produce good arguments. This is a skill you have to learn through practice. Just keep one idea clearly in mind: What makes an argument a good one is its ability to persuade an intelligent, reasonable reader or listener who doesn't already agree with your thesis. If you test arguments against that standard, you will be able to judge whether they are good.

4. The Examination of Objections to the Thesis

This is the part of your paper in which you put yourself into an imaginary opponent's shoes and try to figure out what objections he or she might raise to your thesis. The techniques you use in this exercise are precisely the ones we have just been looking at in the previous section: instantiation, generalization, counterexample, counter-instantiation, and so forth. The trick—and it is a very difficult trick—is to think up the *strongest* objections you can to your thesis. Don't just put up some cream-puff objections that anyone can knock over.

This is hard to do because by the time you have written the third part of the paper—the arguments for the thesis—you will probably have convinced yourself that you are right. Try to think of this part of the paper as damage control, or setting up a defense perimeter, or taking out insurance. If you can come up with some really strong objections to your thesis and *still* succeed in defending the thesis, then you will probably persuade your reader, because you will have thought of the objections that the reader has in mind as he or she reads your paper. There is nothing that wins a reader over more completely than to have the author say, "Now you may be thinking to yourself, but what about this, and this, and this" when that is just what the reader is thinking, and then having the author come up with really plausible replies.

So, play devil's advocate for a bit and think up the best objections you can to your own thesis.

5. The Response to the Objections

And finally, having thought up some dandy objections, answer them. Once again, you are going to use the techniques of argument we discussed above (notice that most of your paper—Parts 3, 4, and 5—consists of arguments; that is what philosophy is all about).

And then you are done! You have stated a thesis, analyzed and explained it, argued for it, considered objections to it, and responded to objections. That is a philosophy paper. Not so hard after all, is it?

Notice, by the way, that this method tells you what to put into the paper, what to leave out, what to do next, and when you are done. Should you cite a fact? Yes—if it serves to strengthen your thesis or weaken your opponent's objection; otherwise, no. Should your paper have footnotes? Well, if you cite a fact, put in a footnote stating the source of your knowledge of that fact (unless it is so well-known a fact that any reader can be expected to know it. If you refer to Washington, D.C., as the nation's capital, don't put in a footnote to the encyclopedia).

How do you know how long to make your paper? The simple answer is, just long enough to state a thesis, explain it, defend it, and respond to objections to it. If your instructor assigns a paper of, say, three pages in length, then you must choose a thesis that can be adequately explained and defended in three pages. If the assignment is for a ten-page paper, then choose a thesis that calls for that much explanation and defense. Don't pad! Don't add paragraphs or pages just to bulk up the paper so that it feels weighty. As Abraham Lincoln said when someone asked him how long his legs were, "Just long enough to reach the ground."

But what about an assignment to discuss or criticize someone else's views? For example, suppose your assignment is to write a paper critically analyzing some view of the relation between mind and matter, or to write a paper about Kant's Categorical Imperative. These topics may look very different from the topics we have been talking about. Can the method I have just laid out be used for these assignments as well?

Absolutely. Suppose the assignment is to write a paper on Kant's Categorical Imperative. The first thing you must do is decide what you are going to try to show about the Categorical Imperative. In other words, you must *choose your thesis*. For example (and this is, I ought to warn you, a pretty wacky example), you might decide to defend the thesis that

> Kant's Categorical Imperative is identical to the Principle of Utilitarianism.

(I don't think anybody in the world thinks that this thesis is true—I warned you it was pretty wacky.) Now that you have your thesis, the next step is to analyze and explain it. That means explaining how you understand the Categorical Imperative, stating what you take to be the Principle of Utilitarianism, and then explaining what you mean when you say that the two are "identical."

Now you are going to have to produce some arguments in support of your thesis. Some of your arguments will be textual citations from Kant's writings (citations of fact) to show that your interpretation of his Categorical Imperative is the correct one. Some of your arguments will be conceptual analyses designed to clarify the relationship between these two apparently different principles. And so forth.

When it comes to considering objections, your number one objection will of course be that Kant himself believed his Categorical Imperative to be absolutely opposed to the Principle of Utilitarianism. So you will, in effect, have to argue against Kant in your reply to objections.

But you get the point. Even when you are writing a paper in which you are supposed to discuss or analyze or criticize some philosopher's position, you can still use the five-step method set out above.

I can't guarantee that you will get an A if you follow this method. That depends on how *well* you do at following it. But I am willing to bet that if you study this appendix carefully and follow the five-step method intelligently, you won't fail. And I guarantee it will help you to clarify your ideas, sharpen your arguments, and thereby improve your philosophizing.

A Few Tips, Hints, and Warnings

The basic instructions for writing a good philosophy paper are now in your hands, but it might be helpful for me to give you a few tips, hints, and warnings designed to help you avoid some of the most common mistakes and problems.

1. Let me start with a piece of advice that is not so much a tip or hint as it is the Prime Directive (as they say on *Star Trek*).

   Write clear, grammatical, correctly spelled, proper English prose (unless you are writing Spanish, Hebrew, Cambodian, German, or some other natural language, in which case write *that* language clearly, grammatically, correctly spelled, and properly).

   There are two reasons why it is important for you to make sure that you use language in a grammatically correct fashion. First of all, writing correctly is like playing in tune on a musical instrument, or learning the rules of a sport. You can't interpret a piece of music if you can't even play the notes properly, and you can't play baseball if you don't even know that a batter gets three strikes. Written language has rules just like music or baseball, and learning them is the first step in writing well.

   The second reason why writing correct prose is so important in a philosophy paper is that until you can write in a grammatically precise and correct fashion, you will not be able to state a thesis for defense, or put together an argument in support of a thesis. As we will see when we analyze an actual student paper in the next section, incorrect grammar obscures an author's meaning. Indeed, if you aren't careful to write clearly, you may fool yourself as well as your readers. You may not know what you yourself mean by your thesis or your arguments, in which case you won't be able to tell whether you have made a case for your thesis at all.

2. Don't wander from the basic outline when writing your paper, and don't mix together materials that belong in different parts of the paper.

Once you have stated your thesis, start to explain and analyze it. Leave out anything that doesn't help to explain or analyze your thesis. You may be eager to get to your argument because you may have a really good idea you want to try out. Wait for it! Once you get to the argument stage, don't drift off into expressing opinions or telling stories that don't advance the argument. Make sure both you and the reader know, at every stage, what you are doing, where you are going, and how what you are saying connects up with your central task of defending your thesis.

3. Try to use language as precisely as possible.

Vague words like "stuff" or "thing" are evidence of a sloppy mind. Your prose should be proper to the subject—not forced or stilted, not full of words you wouldn't ever use except in a philosophy paper, but nevertheless carefully chosen. Think how inappropriate it would be for Dan Rather or Tom Brokaw to start the evening news by saying, "Hey, like the guys in Washington did, like, a lot of weird stuff today, ya know?"

4. Asking a question without answering it is *not* an appropriate way to present an argument.

For example, "What would happen if every woman who wanted an abortion got one?" is not an argument. "If every woman who wanted an abortion got one, millions of innocent lives would be lost" *is* an argument, or rather it is part of an argument. The whole argument might look like this:

▌ It is wrong to cause the loss of millions of innocent lives.
▌ If every woman who wanted an abortion got one, millions of innocent lives would be lost.
▌ Therefore, it would be wrong for every woman who wants one to get an abortion.

Similarly, "What right does the state have to tell a woman she can't have an abortion?" isn't an argument. But "The state has no right to tell a woman she cannot get an abortion" *is* an argument. And so forth.

5. It is perfectly all right to use an argument from a lecture you have heard or a book you have read.

Arguments are a little like arithmetical formulas. I don't know who first said "Two plus two equals four," but it is there for anyone to use. However, when you adopt an argument as your own, you take responsibility for it. By including it in your paper, you are saying that you believe it is a good argument. Even if you footnote it, indicating where you first encountered it, it is still on your neck! So use any arguments you like, so long as you are ready to stand behind them. And remember: An argument either stands on its own feet, or it doesn't stand at all. You don't make a bad argument better by pointing out in a footnote that a famous philosopher used it.

A Student Paper

The time has come to give a real example of a paper, submitted by a student in my Introduction to Philosophy course in the fall of 1990. I have chosen this paper because it has a great many serious problems, and yet it has some interesting ideas in it that deserve to be stated clearly and forcefully.

We are going to look at this paper in three stages. First, I will simply reproduce the paper exactly as the student submitted it, complete with misspellings, grammatical errors, and typographical errors. I am going to italicize every misspelled word or typo, and you ought to check each word to make sure you know how it is spelled or why it is a typographical error.

Then I will take a few sample sentences or paragraphs that are ungrammatically written or poorly constructed, and analyze them, showing you what is wrong and how it might be fixed up. Please don't imagine that everything that is left alone is all right! After reading my analyses and reconstructions of the sample passages, you ought to see whether you can do the same thing with other problem passages.

Finally, I will offer a rewritten version of the entire paper, along the lines laid out above. It is not my aim to turn this into a perfect paper. I want to show you how this student, following the guidelines in this Appendix, could have turned the actual paper into a much better paper, one that made the thesis clearer, the argument more persuasive, and the exposition clearer.

The paper we are going to look at was written by a student who had read the chapter "The Philosophy of Art" and had viewed a Ted Koppel *Nightline* show devoted to the dispute surrounding the exhibit of Robert Mapplethorpe's photographs. The specific paper topic to which the student was responding was this:

The debate over whether the Mapplethorpe photographs should be exhibited in publicly funded museums has been long on hysterics and short on reasoned arguments. Choose one side of the controversy and defend it *by explicit appeal to some theory of the nature and social value of art*. Do not simply say whether you approve or disapprove of the exhibit. Defend your position by talking about what art is and what role art should play in our society.

Student Paper

Displaying explicit nude photographs in a public art gallery will hurt the *credability* of our society because of the fact that the artist has created these photos to capture attention by controversy not his own merit.

We as *americans* have established our own religion. Most of us say that we never go to church, but we do. These churches do not bear the characteristics of traditional houses of worship. These new churches have tellers, drive-up windows, and twenty-four hour express machines. All these now serve as modern day clergy and aid us in our worship to our new god, MONEY.

When did everything become about money? Why as a mature society have we let this get so out of hand? We sell everything for money, our bodies, our country and natural resources, and most of all our values. What's to stop us from selling our children like slaves, if the price is right?

we have to stop prostituting our morals for money. We have to preserve things with value and authentic beauty.

If you look at a dictionary the definition of art will read as follows: The activity of creating *beautiful* things, the authentic value of an artist expressed by his values. If we let the purpose of art be compromised, for *many,* we are therefore selling beauty. If we allow someone in our society to mock art, we are guilty of the destruction of a tradition that has existed since the beginning of time.

The Mapplethorpe photographs are a black mark on the history of art. They *deface* the idea of beauty that is associated with art. These photos are not art, they are not beauty, they are merely pornography in disguise. We are allowing this artist to destroy the ideal of art. This man is using us and our social values to gain publicity, not by his own merit, but instead by controversy. By drawing attention to the photographs we have fallen into his premeditated trap and are all therefore guilty of destroying a tradition. Art in its true form, gains monetary value due to the beauty it *pocesses* to the purchaser, not because someone set out to seek publicity.

This exhibit hangs in a museum with legitimate art. *we* can not be expected *expected* to make the distinction between the two to our children? We can not expect our *chindren,* after being brought up with the ideals that this is art, to respect significant pieces of art. If you go into a store you are *accostomed* to the fact that *item of comparative* value are placed next to each other. How would you explain the fact that two pieces of art placed side-by-side do not have the same *"value"*? (By value I do not mean money, but instead social value.)

We have to teach our children the difference between real art and pornography. If we don't we can not expect them to tell the difference between photographs taken by a genius like *Anstel* Adams and the centerfold of Penthouse magazine, they are both just pictures, right?

If we try to justify these photographs by saying that this type of behavior is now *excepted* by our society, we are *beong* selfish. There is no justification in saying that what is good for society now will also be good for societies to come. These future societies should be entitled to view past art works in the same way that we did, for beauty *no* controversy.

Historians say that art reflects the society as well as the time in which it was created. This would give a message to the world that we have given up our morals.

Selfishness is what is going to bring the world as we now know it to an end. We have already allowed it to destroy our faith in the church (thanks to T. V. evangelists), police department, etc . . . We can not allow it to interfere with the only faith we have left.

Even after the misspellings and typographical errors are corrected, this is not a good paper, but it does have some interesting ideas in it which, with a good deal of clarification and reorganization, might form the core of a good, solid philosophical argument. Let us try to identify some of the principal shortcomings of the paper as it now is, after which we will have a shot at improving it.

The very first problem with the paper is that a reader will have a great deal of trouble figuring out what its *thesis* is. The assignment was to choose one side of the debate over whether the Mapplethorpe photographs should be exhibited in publicly funded museums, and the author of this paper pretty clearly is opposed to showing the exhibit, so we might naturally suppose that the thesis of the paper is:

❚ The Mapplethorpe photographs should not be exhibited in publicly funded museums.

But if you read the paper carefully, you will find that there is not a single argument in it that has anything to do with the *public funding* of the museum (in Cincinnati) where the show caused such a fuss. The arguments in this paper would apply with equal force to the exhibiting of the photographs in a privately funded museum. Thus, the paper's author never engages with one of the central issues in the debate, which is whether tax money, collected by law from *all* citizens, should be used to fund an exhibit that offends the moral, aesthetic, or religious sensibilities of some of them.

The second problem is that the paper has no very clear organization or focus. In all, there are ten paragraphs in the paper, including one ("We have to stop prostituting our morals etc.") that has not been indented properly. A close reading suggests that only six of the paragraphs—numbers 1, 5, 6, 7, 8, and 9—are about art and the Mapplethorpe exhibit. The other four—numbers 2, 3, 4, and 10—are about something quite different, namely the establishment in the United States of a new religion in which we worship money. Now the author clearly thinks that there is a connection between these two themes. To put it simply, the connection seems to be that in exhibiting the Mapplethorpe photographs in public art galleries, the curators of those galleries are contributing to the ongoing corruption of American values, a corruption that is manifested by the elevating of money above art or beauty. The last paragraph appears to claim that faith in art is the only faith we have left now that selfishness has destroyed religion, so we ought not to allow the exhibiting of the Mapplethorpe photographs, since in showing them and looking at them we are falling into a trap selfishly laid by the artist.

The third problem with the paper is that the individual arguments are not clearly, coherently, or forcefully stated, nor are they assembled in a way that will lead a reader to the conclusion the author is trying to establish. Take a look, for example, at the rather interesting and imaginative argument in paragraph 7. The background premise of the argument in this paragraph is that the Mapplethorpe photographs are not true art. Incidentally, it isn't quite clear whether the author thinks this premise has been established in the previous paragraph, or is simply assuming it. At any rate, given that starting point, the argument of paragraph 7 proceeds like this:

❚ It is important to bring up our children to appreciate and respect the beauty of true art, to be able to recognize genuine artistic value when they encounter it.

❚ Just as our children learn, when they go shopping, that items of roughly equivalent monetary value will be exhibited in the same store (they wouldn't expect to find an expensive necklace in a K-Mart, or a cheap reproduction of a painting in a fine art gallery), so they should be able to expect that objects of roughly equivalent aesthetic value will be found together in a museum. If the Mapplethorpe photographs, which have no aesthetic value at all, are exhibited next to paintings or photographs of genuine artistic merit, our children will become confused, and our attempts to teach them the correct aesthetic standards of value will be undermined.

❚ Therefore, the Mapplethorpe photographs ought not to be exhibited in a public art gallery.

Whether you think this argument is persuasive or not, I think you will grant that it is interesting and imaginative, and it forces the reader to think more deeply about the issue. But in the original language of paragraph 7, it is very unclearly and diffusely stated.

There are even more serious difficulties with the longest paragraph in the paper, paragraph 6. Let us first clear up one factual matter. The exhibit under discussion was actually a *posthumous* exhibit. Robert Mapplethorpe had died before it was assembled and exhibited, so the author is wrong to claim that Mapplethorpe is "using us" to gain publicity. However, it is at least possible that the people who organized the exhibit were doing so, although nothing in the materials presented to the class contained any evidence of such a plot.

The central difficulty with the paragraph is the unclarity of its line of argument. The author starts out by saying that the photographs are destroying the ideal of art because they are pseudo-art, pornography. Then he/she goes on to a quite different claim, that Mapplethorpe has set a trap for us by creating a controversy that draws audiences into the museum and further destroys the authentic tradition of great art (presumably by leading us to confuse pornography with art). Finally, in the last sentence, which in a properly constructed paragraph would sum up the argument of the paragraph, the author makes an entirely new point, namely that true art becomes monetarily valuable because of its aesthetic appeal to the person who purchases it (and thereby confers monetary value on it).

This is a mess! At least three different arguments are jumbled together, with no indication of the connections among them. Clearly, the only way for the author to salvage this paragraph is first to decide exactly what argument it is supposed to present, second to remove from the paragraph anything that doesn't serve to advance that argument, and finally to rewrite what remains so that it lays out a single argument clearly and logically.

How could the author reorganize and rewrite this paper so as to make it a clear, forceful, persuasive argument? The first step is to decide what the thesis of the paper is going to be. Since the author never really addresses the question, whether *public* financing should be used to support the exhibition of the Mapplethorpe photographs, let us set that matter to one side and instead formulate a thesis that can draw under it as many of the lines of argument in the paper as possible. Pretty clearly, the natural thesis for this paper is something like this:

> Robert Mapplethorpe's photographs ought not to be exhibited in art museums.

Now let us construct a defense of that thesis out of the materials in this paper. As I go along, I will indicate which paragraphs I am drawing on in reconstructing the argument. Remember, the aim of this exercise is *not* to write a completely new paper. Rather, it is to reshape the materials already in the actual student paper so that they are clearer, more orderly and coherent, and thereby more persuasive. The result won't be a perfect paper. It may not even be a paper that deserves an A grade. But if we are successful, it will be the best paper that can be created from the ideas about this subject that the author seems to have had in mind. Here goes.

Reconstructed Student Paper

In this paper I am going to defend the thesis that Robert Mapplethorpe's photographs ought not to be exhibited in art museums. [*You don't actually have to begin a paper this way, officially announcing your thesis, but it can't hurt, and it may help to keep you focused on your thesis, so that you don't drift off into side issues that fail to advance the argument for the thesis.*]

When I speak of art, I mean either the activity of creating beautiful things, an activity engaged in by the artist, or else the beautiful and aesthetically valuable works resulting from that activity. [*This is Step 2, the explanation and analysis of the thesis. See paragraph 5 of the original paper.*] There is a long tradition in our society of cherishing and preserving true works of art. [*This seems to be one of the unstated premises of the paper—see paragraph 5, for example.*] Exhibiting the Mapplethorpe photographs mocks that tradition, and undermines it.

The Mapplethorpe photographs are a black mark in the history of art exhibits. Their appearance in an art gallery defaces the true works of art exhibited there. [*Paragraph 6. The image of defacing is a good one, given the subject of the paper, but strictly speaking, it isn't used properly here. Nevertheless, we are trying to rewrite this paper, not write a new one. Notice that we must change "history of art" to "history of art exhibits" since the author doesn't think the photographs are art.*] These photos are not art, they are not beautiful, they are merely pornography in disguise. By exhibiting the photographs in an art museum as though they were art, we are allowing Mapplethorpe and the people putting on the exhibit to destroy the ideal of art. They are using us and our respect for art to gain publicity for the photographs, not on the basis of their merit but merely as a consequence of the controversy surrounding them. We have fallen into a trap laid for us by the people promoting the exhibit, and we are thereby as guilty as they of destroying the tradition of true art in our society.

We have a duty to keep the tradition alive by teaching our children the difference between real art and pornography. If we don't, we cannot expect them to tell the difference between truly artistic photographs, such as those taken by the great photographer Ansel Adams, and cheap pornography like the centerfold of Penthouse magazine. Our children are likely to think that they are both art, since they are both pictures. [*Paragraph 8. Notice the way I have altered the language of the paragraph to bring out the connection of its argument with the premise laid down at the end of our first paragraph.*]

The Mapplethorpe exhibit hangs in a museum together with legitimate art. How then can we hope to make the distinction between the two to our children? After all, our children are accustomed to finding, when they go into a store, that items of comparable monetary value will be placed side by side on the shelves. They would not expect to find a costly bracelet exhibited next to a cheap imitation. How can we possibly explain to them the fact that cheap pornography is hanging side by side with aesthetically valuable art? If our children are brought up to suppose that such photographs are art, we cannot expect them to respect significant pieces of art. [*Paragraph 7. This is probably the most interesting and original argument in the paper. It deserves to be spelled out clearly so that the reader can appreciate its force.*]

Why then are the Mapplethorpe photographs allowed to be exhibited in a museum supposedly dedicated to preserving the tradition of aesthetic value? I suggest that the answer is the corrupting influence of money. [*The paper needs something like this as an introduction to the paragraphs on money and art. Otherwise, it is difficult to see their connection to the materials on educating children.*] We Americans have established our own religion. Most of us say that we never go to church, but we do. These churches do not bear the characteristics of traditional houses of worship. These new churches have tellers, drive-up windows, and twenty-four-hour express machines. All these now serve as modern-day clergy and aid us in our worship to our new god, MONEY. [*Paragraph 3.*]

When did everything become about money? Why as a mature society have we let this get so out of hand? We sell everything for money, our bodies, our country and natural resources, and most of our values. We would even sell our children like slaves if the price were right. Now it appears that we are allowing our selfishness to lead us to sell the last things of value we have left, our art. [*Paragraphs 3 and 10. I have left in the rather lurid bit about selling our children. It is too dramatic to be rhetorically effective, but as I have already noted, I am trying to rewrite this paper, not write a new one. Notice that the last sentence spells out something that seems to be implicit in several of the paragraphs of the original paper, and yet is never actually stated clearly by the author.*] True art gains monetary value as a result of the beauty it possesses for the purchaser, not because of any publicity that may be associated with it. [*Paragraph 6, last sentence. This isn't true, of course. What the author really means, I suspect, is that art shouldn't acquire monetary value merely as the result of publicity, but of course it does. In a paper like this, it is very important to keep clear the distinction between what is and what ought to be.*]

Some people might try to justify the Mapplethorpe photographs by saying that the behavior represented in them is accepted by our society, and therefore that it is all right to show them. [*Paragraph 9. This is the one place in the paper where the author attempts to state and rebut possible objections to the thesis. I am not at all sure that my interpretation of the first sentence of Paragraph 9 is correct. The language of the original is unclear, and I have been forced to choose an interpretation that may differ from the author's intention. This is one of those places where it is especially important to ask yourself whether a reader will be able to figure out exactly what you had in mind.*] But I believe that if we were to adopt that attitude, we would be acting selfishly, ignoring the interests of generations yet to come. Past generations have handed on to us museums in which true works of art are exhibited solely for their beauty, not because they caused controversy. [*This seems to be what the author has in mind. It is, of course, quite false! Past generations have been swayed as much by controversy as our generation is. However, let us continue.*] Future generations have a right to expect that we will hand on to them museums governed by the same concern for aesthetic value. Historians say that art reflects the society as well as the time in which it was created. If we allow the Mapplethorpe exhibit to appear in our museums, we will send a message to the world that we have given up our aesthetic principles. [*The rest of Paragraph 9. I have changed the end of the last sentence from "morals" to "aesthetic principles" because the author hasn't actually said anything thus far about moral principles, only about aesthetic or artistic principles.*]

To sum up, the exhibitors of the Mapplethorpe photographs are prostituting their principles for money. We have to preserve things with aesthetic value and authentic beauty, and keep them separate from things that have no aesthetic merit, such as the Mapplethorpe photographs. [*Paragraph 4, with alterations.*]

Well, there it is. If you examine the rewritten paper and the original version carefully, you will see that the rewritten version incorporates almost all of the original paper, together with some clarifications and additions. The big difference is that the new version is better organized and more coherently stated, so that a reader can follow the argument. It begins with a *thesis;* briefly *analyzes* and *explains* the thesis; spends most of its time *arguing* for the thesis; *states possible objections* (or at least states one possible objection— this is the weakest part of the paper); *replies to the objections;* and ends with a brief summation.

If you will subject your own first drafts to the same sort of close analysis and criticism, following the procedures set forth in this Appendix, you will very quickly find yourself writing good, solid philosophy papers. Good luck!

Glossary

Alienation   According to Marx, it is the condition of being at war with one's own nature, the products of one's labor, and one's fellow workers. Marx argued that capitalism undermines the human capacity for creative and productive work, making men and women unhappy in their work, dissatisfied in their leisure, and unable to fulfill their human potential. Marx derived the concept of alienation from German philosophers of the early nineteenth century.

Analytic Proposition   A statement that merely spells out what is already contained in the subject of the statement.

Anarchist   One who believes that no state has any right to rule and that governmental authority is illegitimate and undesirable.

a posteriori   As a consequence of experience of objects—an adverb used to modify verbs of cognition, as "to know *a posteriori*" or "to apprehend *a posteriori*." Propositions are said to be knowable *a posteriori* when they are knowable only as a consequence of an experience of the objects they make assertions about.

a priori   Prior to, or independently of, experience—an adverb used to modify verbs of cognition, as "to know *a priori*." Propositions are said to be knowable *a priori* when they are knowable prior to, or independently of, any experience of the objects they make assertions about.

Argument from Design   The attempt to prove the existence of God by demonstrating the high degree of organization and purposive order in the universe, and arguing that such design must be the product of an intelligent, powerful, purposeful creator. The argument is very old but was very popular in the eighteenth century.

Bourgeoisie   See Proletariat

Capitalism   An economic system based on concentration of private ownership of the means of production in relatively few hands, a large class of propertyless workers who work for wages, and production for sale and profit rather than for use. The money invested by the property owners for the purpose of making a profit is called *capital,* hence the system is called capitalism.

Categorical Imperative   A term invented by Immanuel Kant to refer to a command that orders us to do something unconditionally—that is, regardless of what we want or what our aims and purposes are. According to Kant, we experience the principles of morality as Categorical Imperatives. The term also is used, by Kant and those following him, to refer to one particular moral principle, which Kant calls the Highest Moral Law.

Catharsis   Literally, a cleansing or purging. Aristotle uses the term to describe the effect on us of powerful dramatic performances. By watching a play whose events arouse fear and pity within us, he thought, we are purged of those emotions, so that we leave the theater liberated or cleansed. The opposing view is that such plays (and, by extension, movies and television programs) arouse in us feelings we otherwise would not have, and should not have, such as certain aggressive and sexual feelings.

Cogito, Ergo Sum   "I think, therefore I am"—the phrase used by Descartes to prove his own existence.

Copy Theory of Ideas The theory that all of our ideas are either copies of sense impressions or combinations and rearrangements of copies of sense impressions.

Cosmological Argument The attempt to prove the existence of God by starting with the mere fact of motion, or change, or the existence of things in the universe, and then arguing that these must have their origin in a being that does not move, or does not change, or does not merely happen to exist. The earliest form of the argument is to be found in the writings of Aristotle.

Cosmology Literally, the study of the order of the world. Now used to refer to the branch of astronomy that investigates the organization and structure of the entire physical universe, including its origins. In philosophy, cosmology is a part of the subfield called metaphysics, or the study of first principles.

Determinism The most extreme form is sometimes called fatalism, a view much encountered in fictional literature but rarely held either by philosophers or by people in general. It says that the future is always immutably fixed in such a way that there is nothing anyone could ever do to alter the course of events. Determinists, however, generally prefer to say that human actions and choices are links in a causal chain. Every event is caused, but the cause may be extremely complex.

Dialogue A process of question and answer between two people.

Double Consciousness W. E. B. Du Bois identifies this as the way of understanding oneself experienced by African Americans. Because of the constant repetition of negative judgments by white people, the Negro develops a doubled sense of self—seeing himself or herself both as white people do, and as he or she sees himself

or herself. Du Bois believed this was both a great burden and a source of special insight into the nature of American society.

Dualism The Mind-Body Theory that there are two fundamentally different kinds of things in the universe—bodies and minds—neither of which can be reduced to, or analyzed into, the other.

Empiricism/Rationalism Empiricism and rationalism are the two leading epistemological theories of the past four centuries. *Empiricism* is the theory that all human knowledge comes from the evidence of our five senses, and therefore we can never know more, or know with greater certainty, than our senses will allow. *Rationalism* is the theory that at least some human knowledge comes from reason, unaided by the senses, and therefore we can know about things that the senses do not reveal to us, and can know with greater certainty than the senses alone will allow.

Epistemological Skepticism The doctrine that no adequate justification can be given for any of our beliefs about the world, not even for apparently rock-solid beliefs that there is a physical world, that I have a body, that the sun will rise tomorrow, or that fire causes heat. The aim of epistemological skepticism is to focus our attention on the relationship between our beliefs and their justification, not actually to get us to stop believing.

Epistemological Turn A shift in philosophy from an emphasis on metaphysics to an emphasis on epistemology.

Epistemology Literally, the study of knowledge. Epistemology is the study of how we come to know things, what the limits are of our knowledge, and what sort of certainty or uncertainty attaches to our knowledge. Psychology also studies how we come to know, but epistemology is concerned less with the mechanics of knowing than with the possibility of defending, proving, or justifying what we think we know. Since the early seventeenth century, epistemology has been the most important branch of philosophy.

Ethical Relativism　The theory that whether an act is right or wrong depends on—is relative to—the society in which one lives. Sometimes ethical relativists merely claim that we must take social contexts and rules into account, but sometimes they assert that one and the same act is right for men and women in one society and wrong for men and women in another. Frequently confused with *Ethical Skepticism,* which doubts that any acts are right or wrong, and *Ethical Nihilism,* which denies that any acts are either right or wrong.

Ethics　In philosophy, the systematic study of how we ought to act, both toward ourselves and to others; and also the study of what things, character traits, or types of persons are good, estimable, admirable, and what kinds are bad, reprehensible, worthy of being condemned. Ethics deals both with general rules or principles, and also with particular cases.

Existentialism　The philosophical doctrine, associated originally with Søren Kierkegaard, according to which our being as subjective individuals (our *existence*) is more important than what we have in common objectively with all other human beings (our *essence*). Of primary concern for Kierkegaard was his relationship to God. Later existentialists emphasized the individual's creation of himself or herself through free individual choices.

Experiment　A controlled interaction with nature designed to yield observations that will help confirm or disconfirm some hypothesis about the way the world is. Experiments are usually carried out with the aid of specialized equipment, referred to as "instruments," although some experiments use nothing more than ordinary, available items.

Faith　In Christianity, trust that God will keep the promise He made to the Israelites in the Old Testament and renewed to all mankind in the New Testament (hence, "trust in the Lord"). Originally, the promise was to make the Israelites fruitful and populous. In the New Testament, the promise is of life eternal in heaven. According to some Christians, men and women are unable to have and sustain this trust without the miraculous help of God.

Free Will　The freedom of human beings is assumed in the sense that we are not entirely circumscribed by an ineluctable and predetermined destiny. We can, within limits, make our own destiny.

The General Will　A term invented by Jean-Jacques Rousseau to describe the decision by the citizens of a republic to set aside their private and partisan concerns and instead collectively aim at the general good. According to Rousseau, to say that a society "has a general will" is to say that all of the members of the society are public-spiritedly aiming at the general good in their political actions and deliberations. Rousseau was very pessimistic about the possibility of ever achieving a general will.

Historical Materialism　The Marxist theory that ideas and social institutions develop only as a reflection of a material economic base.

Idealism　The Mind-Body theory that everything in the universe is either minds, or ideas in minds (hence, *idealism*). Bodies, according to the idealist, are simply particular collections of ideas. Thus, a table is simply the interconnected set of all of the ideas—concepts, images, feels, sights, sounds, and so on—that I think of as ideas of a table.

Identity Crisis   A term invented by psychoanalyst Erik Erikson to refer to the period of instability, uncertainty, and personality formation through which teenagers pass in societies like ours. Erikson intended to suggest, by the term, that the period is one of genuine flux and indeterminacy, with the outcome—a healthy, coherent adult personality—hanging in the balance.

Intrinsic Value/Instrumental Value   To say that something has *intrinsic value* is to say that it is valuable, good, worthwhile, purely for itself alone, regardless of what it may produce or lead to. Some people say that pleasure has intrinsic value, others that beauty does, still others that moral goodness does. *Instrumental value* is the value something has as a means, or an instrument, for producing or getting something else. A tool or instrument for some purpose is said to be instrumentally valuable.

Irony   A mode of discourse by which the speaker communicates, to the real audience, a meaning opposite from that conveyed to the superficial, or apparent, audience.

Laissez-Faire   Literally, allow to do. Laissez-faire is the system of free market exchanges, with an absolute minimum of government control, which nineteenth-century liberals believed would result in the most efficient use of resources and the greatest material well-being for a society. *Laissez-faire capitalism* refers to the early stage in the development of capitalism, when firms were small, owner-run, and controlled both in their purchases and in their sales by market pressures.

Law of Contradiction/Law of the Excluded Middle   The two basic laws of formal logic. The *Law of Contradiction* states that

a statement and its contradictory cannot both be true. For example, the statement, "Fire is hot" may be true, and it may be false. Its contradictory, "It is not the case that fire is hot" may be true, and it may be false. But it cannot be that *both* the statement *and* its contradictory are true. The *Law of the Excluded Middle* says that for any statement, either it is true *or* its contradictory is true. Thus, either fire is hot, or it is not the case that fire is hot.

Legitimate Authority   The right to give commands that others have a moral obligation to obey. States claim legitimate authority when they say that they have a right to pass laws that citizens or subjects *ought* to obey, regardless of whether they are in danger of being caught for not obeying. Democratic states base their claim to legitimate authority on the fact that they are elected by the people whom they rule and, therefore, speak with the voice of the people.

Logic   The discipline that investigates the correct principles of formal reasoning—sometimes characterized as the science of the laws of thought.

Marxism   The economic, political, and philosophical doctrines first set forth by Karl Marx and then developed by his disciples and followers. Although Marx himself considered his theories scientific, his followers have often treated them as a form of secular religion. The principal doctrines are: first, that capitalism is internally unstable and prone to fall into economic crises; second, that the profits of capitalist enterprises derive from the exploitation of the workers, who receive in wages less than they produce; third, that as capitalism develops, workers will tend to become more self-aware of their situation—and hence more likely to overthrow capitalism by force; and fourth, that the society that comes into existence after capitalism is destroyed will be socialist and democratic in its economic and political organization.

Materialism   The Mind-Body theory that everything in the universe is matter (hence, *materialism*). Minds, according to the materialist, are simply collections of very small bodies or structures and organizations of bodies (such as nerve cells in the brain). Perceptions, to the materialist, are particular sorts of interactions between bodies, and so are thoughts, emotions, and feelings of pleasure and pain.

Metaphysics   In modern philosophy, the study of the most fundamental principles of the nature of things. The term derives from an early description of the set of essays by Aristotle, called by him "First Philosophy," which came after the Physics in an edition of Aristotle's works (*ta meta ta physika,* or "after the Physics").

Method of Doubt   The suspension of judgment in regard to knowledge claims until they have been demonstrated to be either true or false.

Mind-Body Problem   The *Mind-Body Problem* is the problem of explaining exactly what the relationship is between our minds and physical bodies in space. There are really *three* problems lumped together under this heading: First, do minds and bodies causally interact with one another, and if so, how? Second, how, if at all, can I (i.e., my mind) gain knowledge about bodies—indeed, can minds really know anything at all about bodies, or do minds only know about themselves? And third, what is the special relationship between *my* mind and *my* body? In the twentieth century, the Mind-Body Problem led philosophers to a related problem, the *Problem of Other Minds:* How, if at all, can I know of the existence and contents of minds other than my own? Is there anyone out there, or am I alone in a world of mere bodies?

Monad   A simple substance without parts—the fundamental element in the metaphysical theories of Leibniz.

Natural Law   A rational principle of order or a norm in accordance with which the universe has been created or organized. Both the physical universe and the moral order of human society are thought, by one major philosophical tradition, to be guided by natural law.

Ontological Argument   The attempt to prove the existence of God by starting with nothing more than the more concept of the most perfect being. The argument is extremely controversial and has been rejected as invalid by many religious philosophers, including the leading medieval proponent of the Cosmological Argument, St. Thomas Aquinas.

Philosophy   Literally, love of wisdom, philosophy is the systematic, critical examination of the way in which we judge, evaluate, and act, with the aim of making ourselves wiser, more self-reflective, and therefore better men and women.

Popular Sovereignty   The doctrine that ultimate political authority (sovereignty) belongs to the people who are governed.

Pre-established Harmony   Leibniz's claim that God prearranges things in such a way that the ideas in our minds correctly correspond to the objects in the world, even though there is no actual interaction between the world and our minds. Leibniz needed this implausible hypothesis because, according to his metaphysical theories, substances cannot really have an effect on one another.

Principle of Sufficient Reason   A principle, stated by Leibniz, according to which no fact can be real and no statement true unless it has a sufficient reason why it should be thus.

Proletariat/Bourgeoisie   The *bourgeoisie* is the middle class consisting of factory owners, shopkeepers, bankers, financiers, and their associates. "Bourgeoisie" comes from the medieval term *bourg,* meaning "walled city." Burghers, or bourgeois, were the inhabitants of a walled city—by extension, the merchants and master craftsmen who formed the economic elite of the city as opposed to the aristocracy, whose wealth and power were based on landholdings. In Marx's writings, the *proletariat* is the urban population of wage-earning workers. "Proletariat" comes from the old Latin word for the lowest class of people in Rome.

Psycho-Physical Dualism   The Mind-Body theory that minds are one kind of substance and bodies are another. The defining characteristic of mind, according to the dualist, is consciousness or thought. The defining characteristic of body is spatial extension (and sometimes also force or impenetrability). For the dualist, the major problem is to explain how mind and matter interact and affect one another.

Rationalism   See Empiricism

Repression/Sublimation   Two terms from the psychological theories of Sigmund Freud, referring to the primitive operations of the human mind. *Repression* is the forcible pushing out of consciousness of desires, wishes, thoughts, or feelings that the mind considers bad, dangerous, or otherwise unacceptable. According to Freud, what is repressed does not go away, but remains, with all of its emotional power, in the unconscious portion of the mind. *Sublimation* is the redirecting of sexual or aggressive energies into socially or morally acceptable channels—for example, aggressive energies directed away from

physical violence and into philosophical arguments, or sexual energies diverted from immediate sexual activity into flirting.

Second Sight   As W. E. B. Du Bois states, this is a result of growing up with a double consciousness; possibly penetrating the "veil" and seeing the world as it truly is.

Social Contract   A voluntary, unanimous agreement among all the people of a society to form themselves into a united political community and to obey the laws laid down by the government they collectively select. In seventeenth- and eighteenth-century political theory, the legitimacy claims of the state are said to rest on an actual or a hypothetical social contract.

Social Relationships of Production   The system of relationships into which people enter by virtue of the role they play in the material production of goods and services in society.

Socialism   An economic and a social system based on collective social ownership of the means of production, rational planning of economic investment and growth, roughly equal distribution of goods and services, and production for the satisfaction of human need rather than for private profit. Modern socialism dates from the teachings of the French socialists of the early nineteenth century, but the leading socialist philosopher is the German, Karl Marx.

Socratic Method   A technique of using probing questions, developed by Socrates, for the purpose of prodding, pushing, and provoking unreflective persons into realizing their lack of rational understanding of their own principles of thought and action, so that they can set out on the path to philosophical wisdom. As used by Socrates, this method was a powerful weapon for deflating inflated egos.

Solipsism Literally, the belief that I am the only person in the universe. Somewhat more generally, solipsism is an extreme form of epistemological skepticism that refuses to acknowledge the existence of anything other than my own mind. Some philosophers have even argued that I cannot be sure of anything but my own mind *right now,* since my memories might also be mistaken.

Sovereignty Supreme political authority. A right to rule that takes precedence over all else.

State, the The group of people who rule, give orders, run things, and enforce the rules of social groups within defined territorial limits or borders.

Sublimation See Repression

Tabula Rasa Literally, blank tablet. The term was used by John Locke to summarize his claim that the mind comes into life blank, or empty, and is written on by experience as though it were a clay or wax tablet waiting to be marked by a writing stylus. Locke was arguing against the widely held view that the mind comes to experience with ideas that are built into it (or "hardwired," as computer types like to say).

Teleology A study of the purposes, or ends, of natural things—also, the belief that nature has a purpose or goal toward which it tends.

Theory Neutral To say that scientific data or observations are *theory neutral* is to say that the description of them does not presuppose the truth of one scientific theory as opposed to another. If scientific observations, or descriptions of scientific data, do involve or presuppose some theory, then they are said to be *theory laden.*

Transcendence A going beyond the given natural or social reality—in Marcuse, the imaginative leap beyond the given social world, with its repressions, oppressions, and its reality-oriented sacrifices, to the conception of possible future social orders in which some of the repressed-libidinal energy has been liberated.

Truth of Fact Truth that can be certified only by appeal to empirical evidence.

Unity of Consciousness A phrase invented by Immanuel Kant to describe the fact that the thoughts and perceptions of any given mind are bound together in a unity by being all contained in one consciousness. Kant claimed that this fact—the *unity* of individual consciousness—could only be explained by postulating a fundamental mental activity of holding together, or "synthesizing," those thoughts and perceptions.

Utilitarianism The moral theory that holds that everyone—private individuals or law-making governments—should always seek to produce the greatest happiness for the greatest number of people. *Act Utilitarianism* asserts that each of us should use this rule in choosing every single act that we perform, regardless of whether we are private citizens or legislators making general laws for a whole society. *Rule Utilitarianism* says that governments should use this rule in choosing the general laws they enact, but then should simply treat individuals fairly according to the existing rules, with like cases handled in a like manner.

Suggestions for Further Reading

Chapter 1: What Is Philosophy?

John Austin, *Sense and Sensibilia*

Alfred J. Ayer, *Language, Truth, and Logic*

René Descartes, *Discourse on Method*

Ernest Gellner, *Words and Things*

G. W. F. Hegel, Introduction, *The Philosophy of History*

Martin Heidegger, *What Is Metaphysics?*

David Hume, "The Epicurean," "The Stoic," "The Platonist," and "The Sceptic," in *Collected Essays*

Richard Rorty, *Philosophy and the Mirror of Nature*

Jean-Paul Sartre, *Existentialism as a Humanism*

Wilfred Sellars, "Philosophy and the Scientific Image of Man," in *Frontiers of Science and Philosophy,* ed. R. Colodny

Chapter 2: Theory of Knowledge

J. L. Austin, *Sense and Sensibilia*

A. J. Ayer, *The Foundations of Empirical Knowledge*

George Berkeley, *Three Dialogues Between Hylas and Philonus*

V. C. Chappell, ed., *Hume: A Collection of Critical Essays*

R. M. Chisholm, *Perceiving—A Philosophical Study*

Daniel Dennett, *Brainstorms*

H. G. Frankfurt, *Demons, Dreamers, and Madmen*

C. A. Fritz, *Bertrand Russell's Construction of the External World*

Douglas Hostadter, *Gödel, Escher, Bach*

A. Kenny, *Descartes: A Study of His Philosophy*

C. I. Lewis, *An Analysis of Knowledge and Valuation*

G. E. Moore, "The Refutation of Idealism," in A. C. Ewing, ed., *The Idealist Tradition from Berkeley to Blanshard*

H. H. Price, *Perception*

Bertrand Russell, *Human Knowledge*

Peter Strawson, *The Bounds of Sense*

R. J. Swartz, ed., *Perceiving, Sensing, and Knowing*

Robert Paul Wolff, *Kant's Theory of Mental Activity*

Chapter 3: Metaphysics and Philosophy of Mind

Bruce Aune, *Metaphysics: The Elements*

Lynn Ruder Baker, *Saving Belief*

Thomas Hobbes, *Leviathan*

C. I. Lewis, *Mind and the World Order*

Gilbert Ryle, *The Concept of Mind*

Sidney Shoemaker, *Self-Knowledge and Self-Identity*

Peter Strawson, *Individuals*

Chapter 4: Philosophy of Science

Robert Ackermann, *Data, Instruments, and Theory*

Herbert Feigl and May Brodbeck, *Readings in The Philosophy of Science*

Norwood Hanson, *Patterns of Discovery*

Thomas Kuhn, *The Structure of Scientific Revolutions*

Bruno Latour, *Science in Action*

Karl Popper, *The Logic of Scientific Discovery*

Jerome Ravetz, *Scientific Knowledge and Its Social Problems*

Chapter 5: Ethical Theory

Aristotle, *Nicomachean Ethics*

Kurt Baier, *The Moral Point of View*

Michael D. Bayles, ed., *Contemporary Utilitarianism*

John Dewey, *Human Nature and Conduct*

Erik H. Erikson, *Childhood and Society*

W. K. Frankena, *Ethics*

C. Gilligan, *In a Different Voice*

S. Hoaglund, *Lesbian Ethics*

Rosalind Hursthouse, *On Virtue Ethics*

Immanuel Kant, *Groundwork of the Metaphysic of Morals*

——, "On a Supposed Right to Lie from Altruistic Motives"

C. I. Lewis, *Values and Imperatives*

John Stuart Mill, *Utilitarianism*

G. E. Moore, *Principia Ethica*

W. D. Ross, *The Right and the Good*

Bertrand Russell, "What I Believe," in *Why I Am Not a Christian and Other Essays*

M. G. Singer, *Generalization in Ethics*

S. F. Toulmin, *The Place of Reason in Ethics*

Edward Westermarck, *Ethical Relativity*

Chapter 6: Social and Political Philosophy

Carl Cohen, ed., *Communism, Fascism, and Democracy*

Milton Friedman, *Capitalism and Freedom*

John Kenneth Galbraith, *Economics and the Public Purpose*

G. W. F. Hegel, *The Philosophy of Right*

Thomas Hobbes, *Leviathan*

L. T. Hobhouse, *The Metaphysical Theory of the State*

V. I. Lenin, *State and Revolution*

Walter Lippman, *The Public Philosophy*

Herbert Marcuse, *An Essay on Liberation*

——, *Eros and Civilization*

Karl Marx, *Capital*, Volume I

—— and Friederich Engels, *The Communist Manifesto*

——, *A Contribution to the Critique of Hegel's Philosophy of Right*

C. B. McPherson, *The Political Theory of Possessive Individualism*

John Stuart Mill, *On Liberty*

——, *Utilitarianism*

——, *On Representative Government*

Kenneth Minogue, *The Liberal Mind*

Richard E. Neustadt, *Presidential Power*

Robert Nozick, *Anarchy, State, and Utopia*

Michael Oakeshott, *Rationalism in Politics*

J. Roland Pennock and John Chapman, eds., *Anarchism* (NOMOS, Vol. XIX)

Plato, *Crito*

John Rawls, *A Theory of Justice*

George F. Reedy, *The Twilight of the Presidency*

Eugene V. Rostow, ed., *Is Law Dead?*

George Bernard Shaw, *The Intelligent Woman's Guide to Socialism and Capitalism*

Henry David Thoreau, *On Civil Disobedience*

Friedrich Von Hayek, *The Road to Serfdom*

Robert Paul Wolff, *In Defense of Anarchism*

Chapter 7: Philosophy of Art

Monroe Beardsley, *Aesthetics*

Clive Bell, *Art*

Harry M. Clor, *Obscenity and Public Morality*

R. G. Collingwood, *The Principles of Art*

Patrick Devlin, *The Enforcement of Morals*

John Dewey, *Art as Experience*

G. W. F. Hegel, Introduction, *Philosophy of Fine Art*

John Hospers, *Meaning and Truth in the Arts*

Immanuel Kant, *Critique of Judgment*

Susanne Langer, *Philosophy in a New Key*

Karl Marx, *Economic-Philosophic Manuscripts of 1844*

Plato, *Symposium*

G. Plekhanov, *Art and Social Life*

I. A. Richards, *The Principles of Literary Criticism*

Morris Weitz, *Philosophy of the Arts*

Richard Wollheim, *Art and Its Objects*

Chapter 8: Philosophy of Religion

A. J. Ayer, *Language, Truth, and Logic*, Chapter VI

J. Baillie, *The Essence of the Presence of God*

Ludwig Feuerbach, *The Essence of Christianity*

H. M. Garelick, *The Anti-Christianity of Kierkegaard*

Charles Hartshorne, *The Logic of Perfection*

J. Hick, ed., *The Existence of God*

William James, *The Will to Believe*

A. Kenny, *Aquinas: A Collection of Critical Essays*

Søren Kierkegaard, *Fear and Trembling*

A. C. Macintyre, *Difficulties in Christian Belief*

Ashley Montagu, ed., *Science and Creationism*

A. Plantinga, ed., *The Ontological Argument*

——, *God and Other Minds*

Bertrand Russell, *Why I Am Not a Christian and Other Essays*

Photo Credits

Chapter 1

Page 2: Courtesy of the Library of Congress. Page 26: Corbis/Bettmann. Page 28: Library of Congress. Page 42: Photofest.

Chapter 2

Page 46: Corbis/Bettmann. Page 72: Library of Congress. Page 87: Everett Collection.

Chapter 3

Page 98: Library of Congress. Page 118: B.C. (6/12/74) By permission of Johnny Hart and Creators Syndicate, Inc. Page 127: Photofest.

Chapter 4

Page 140: Courtesy of the Library of Congress. Page 150: Brown Brothers. Page 158: Courtesy MIT Museum. Page 173: Getty Images, Inc - Liaison.

Chapter 5

Page 190: Courtesy of the Library of Congress. Page 210: Corbis/Bettmann. Page 242: photolibrary.com. Page 276: ©2000 Warner Bros. International Television Distribution. A Time Warner Entertainment Company. All Rights Reserved./Globe Photos, Inc.

Chapter 6

Page 288: Courtesy of the Library of Congress. Page 291: The Granger Collection. Page 295: Corbis/Bettmann. Page 308: The Granger Collection. Page 296: The Metropolitan Museum of Art, Harris Brisbane Dick Fund, 1932. [32.35(124)]. Page 314: ©The New Yorker Collection 1969 Warren Miller from cartoonbank.com. All Rights Reserved. Page 319: Library of Congress. Page 329: Corbis/Bettmann. Page 338: Getty Images, Inc.

Chapter 7

Page 356: Art Resource, N.Y. Page 362: "Oarsmen at Chatou," Auguste Renoir, French (1841-1919). "Oarsmen at Chatou." Canvas 32 × 39 1/2 (0.813 × 1.003). ©Board of Trustees, National Gallery of Art, Washington, D.C.; Gift of Sam A. Lewisohn, 1951. 1951.5.2 (1062). "Echo (Number 25, 1951)," Jackson Pollock, "Echo (Number 25, 1951)." 1951. Enamel on unprimed canvas, 7 ft. 7 7/8 in. × 7 ft. 2 in. (233.4 × 218.4 cm.). The Museum of Modern Art/Licensed by Scala-Art Resource, NY. Acquired through the Lillie P. Bliss Bequest and the Mr. And Mrs. David Rockerfeller Fund. "The Three Musicians," Pablo Picasso, Spanish, 1881-1973. "The Three Musicians," summer 1921. Oil on canvas, 6 ft. 7 in. × 7 ft. 3 3/4 in. (200.7 × 222.9). The Museum of Modern Art/Licensed by Scala-Art Resource, NY. ©2000 Estate of Pablo Picasso/Artists Rights Society (ARS), New York. Page 370: Corbis/Bettmann. Page 374: Corbis/Bettmann. Page 388: TM and ©Twentieth Century Fox Film Corp./Photofest.

Chapter 8

Page 404: Corbis/Bettmann. Page 411: Henri Raymound de Toulouse-Lautrec, French (1864-1901), "The Englishmen at the Moulin Rouge." Oil and gouache on cardboard. H. 33-3/4, W. 26 in. Signed (lower left): T-Lautrec. The Metropolitan Museum of Art, Bequest of Miss Adelaide Milton de Groot (1876–1967), The Metropolitan Museum of Art. [67.187.108]. Page 413: ©The New Yorker Collection 1960 James Stevenson from cartoonbank.com. All Rights Reserved. Page 421: Library of Congress. Page 430: Corbis/Bettmann. Page 433: Corbis/Bettmann. Page 447: ©1998 New Line Cinema/Getty Images, Inc.

Index

INTERNAL DOCUMENT: PEARSON EDUCATION
HIGHER EDUCATION & PROFESSIONAL

SINGLE PC LICENSE AGREEMENT AND LIMITED WARRANTY

READ THIS LICENSE CAREFULLY BEFORE OPENING THIS PACKAGE. BY OPENING THIS PACKAGE, YOU ARE AGREEING TO THE TERMS AND CONDITIONS OF THIS LICENSE. IF YOU DO NOT AGREE, DO NOT OPEN THE PACKAGE. PROMPTLY RETURN THE UNOPENED PACKAGE AND ALL ACCOMPANYING ITEMS TO THE PLACE YOU OBTAINED THEM.

1.   GRANT OF LICENSE and OWNERSHIP: The enclosed computer programs <<and data>> ("Software") are licensed, not sold, to you by Pearson Education, Inc. publishing as Pearson Prentice Hall ("We" or the "Company") and in consideration of your purchase or adoption of the accompanying Company textbooks and/or other materials, and your agreement to these terms. We reserve any rights not granted to you. You own only the disk(s) but we and/or our licensors own the Software itself. This license allows you to use and display your copy of the Software on a single computer (i.e., with a single CPU) at a single location for <u>academic</u> use only, so long as you comply with the terms of this Agreement. You may make one copy for back up, or transfer your copy to another CPU, provided that the Software is usable on only one computer.

2.   RESTRICTIONS: You may <u>not</u> transfer or distribute the Software or documentation to anyone else. Except for backup, you may <u>not</u> copy the documentation or the Software. You may <u>not</u> network the Software or otherwise use it on more than one computer or computer terminal at the same time. You may <u>not</u> reverse engineer, disassemble, decompile, modify, adapt, translate, or create derivative works based on the Software or the Documentation. You may be held legally responsible for any copying or copyright infringement that is caused by your failure to abide by the terms of these restrictions.

3.   TERMINATION: This license is effective until terminated. This license will terminate automatically without notice from the Company if you fail to comply with any provisions or limitations of this license. Upon termination, you shall destroy the Documentation and all copies of the Software. All provisions of this Agreement as to limitation and disclaimer of warranties, limitation of liability, remedies or damages, and our ownership rights shall survive termination.

4.   **LIMITED WARRANTY AND DISCLAIMER OF WARRANTY:** Company warrants that for a period of 60 days from the date you purchase this SOFTWARE (or purchase or adopt the accompanying textbook), the Software, when properly installed and used in accordance with the Documentation, will operate in substantial conformity with the description of the Software set forth in the Documentation, and that for a period of 30 days the disk(s) on which the Software is delivered shall be free from defects in materials and workmanship under normal use. The Company does <u>not</u> warrant that the Software will meet your requirements or that the operation of the Software will be uninterrupted or error-free. Your only remedy and the Company's only obligation under these limited warranties is, at the Company's option, return of the disk for a refund of any amounts paid for it by you or replacement of the disk. THIS LIMITED WARRANTY IS THE ONLY WARRANTY PROVIDED BY THE COMPANY AND ITS LICENSORS, AND THE COMPANY AND ITS LICENSORS DISCLAIM ALL OTHER WARRANTIES, EXPRESS OR IMPLIED, INCLUDING WITHOUT LIMITATION, THE IMPLIED WARRANTIES OF MERCHANTABILITY AND FITNESS FOR A PARTICULAR PURPOSE. THE COMPANY DOES NOT WARRANT, GUARANTEE OR MAKE ANY REPRESENTATION REGARDING THE ACCURACY, RELIABILITY, CURRENTNESS, USE, OR RESULTS OF USE, OF THE SOFTWARE.

5.   **LIMITATION OF REMEDIES AND DAMAGES:** IN NO EVENT, SHALL THE COMPANY OR ITS EMPLOYEES, AGENTS, LICENSORS, OR CONTRACTORS BE LIABLE FOR ANY INCIDENTAL, INDIRECT, SPECIAL, OR CONSEQUENTIAL DAMAGES ARISING OUT OF OR IN CONNECTION WITH THIS LICENSE OR THE SOFTWARE, INCLUDING FOR LOSS OF USE, LOSS OF DATA, LOSS OF INCOME OR PROFIT, OR OTHER LOSSES, SUSTAINED AS A RESULT OF INJURY TO ANY PERSON, OR LOSS OF OR DAMAGE TO PROPERTY, OR CLAIMS OF THIRD PARTIES, EVEN IF THE COMPANY OR AN AUTHORIZED REPRESENTATIVE OF THE COMPANY HAS BEEN ADVISED OF THE POSSIBILITY OF SUCH DAMAGES. IN NO EVENT SHALL THE LIABILITY OF THE COMPANY FOR DAMAGES WITH RESPECT TO THE SOFTWARE EXCEED THE AMOUNTS ACTUALLY PAID BY YOU, IF ANY, FOR THE SOFTWARE OR THE ACCOMPANYING TEXTBOOK. BECAUSE SOME JURISDICTIONS DO NOT

ALLOW THE LIMITATION OF LIABILITY IN CERTAIN CIRCUMSTANCES, THE ABOVE LIMITATIONS MAY NOT ALWAYS APPLY TO YOU.

6.   GENERAL: THIS AGREEMENT SHALL BE CONSTRUED IN ACCORDANCE WITH THE LAWS OF THE UNITED STATES OF AMERICA AND THE STATE OF NEW YORK, APPLICABLE TO CONTRACTS MADE IN NEW YORK, EXCLUDING THE STATE'S LAWS AND POLICIES ON CONFLICTS OF LAW, AND SHALL BENEFIT THE COMPANY, ITS AFFILIATES AND ASSIGNEES. THIS AGREEMENT IS THE COMPLETE AND EXCLUSIVE STATEMENT OF THE AGREEMENT BETWEEN YOU AND THE COMPANY AND SUPERSEDES ALL PROPOSALS OR PRIOR AGREEMENTS, ORAL, OR WRITTEN, AND ANY OTHER COMMUNICATIONS BETWEEN YOU AND THE COMPANY OR ANY REPRESENTATIVE OF THE COMPANY RELATING TO THE SUBJECT MATTER OF THIS AGREEMENT. If you are a U.S. Government user, this Software is licensed with "restricted rights" as set forth in subparagraphs (a)-(d) of the Commercial Computer-Restricted Rights clause at FAR 52.227-19 or in subparagraphs (c)(1)(ii) of the Rights in Technical Data and Computer Software clause at DFARS 252.227-7013, and similar clauses, as applicable.

Should you have any questions concerning this agreement or if you wish to contact the Company for any reason, please contact in writing: Legal Department, Prentice Hall, 1 Lake Street, Upper Saddle River, NJ 07450 or call Pearson Education Product Support at 1-800-677-6337.